MARTHA STEWART'S
LEGAL TROUBLES

MARTHA STEWART'S LEGAL TROUBLES

EDITED BY

Joan MacLeod Heminway

THE UNIVERSITY OF TENNESSEE
COLLEGE OF LAW

CAROLINA ACADEMIC PRESS
Durham, North Carolina

Library of Congress Cataloging in Publication Data

Martha Stewart's legal troubles / edited by Joan MacLeod Heminway.
   p. cm.
  Includes bibliographical references and index.
  10-digit ISBN 1-59460-236-0 (alk. paper)
  13-digit ISBN 978-59460-236-8 (alk. paper)
  1. Stewart, Martha--Trials, litigation, etc. 2. Trials (Fraud)-- United
States. 3. Securities fraud--United States. 4. Insider trading in securities--
Law and legislation--United States--Criminal provisions. I. Heminway,
Joan MacLeod. II. Title.

KF225.S74 2006
345.73'0268--dc22   2006020307

Carolina Academic Press
700 Kent Street
Durham, NC 27701
Telephone (919) 489-7486
Fax (919) 493-5668
www.cap-press.com

Printed in the United States of America

CONTENTS

PART I
PRETRIAL ENFORCEMENT ISSUES RELEVANT TO
THE CRIMINAL ACTION

PART II

**SUBSTANTIVE LEGAL ISSUES RELEVANT TO
THE CRIMINAL ACTION**

PART III

LEGAL MATTERS OUTSIDE THE CRIMINAL ACTION

ACKNOWLEDGMENTS

It has been my privilege to work with an outstanding group of legal scholars in composing this volume. I read their related work before asking them to participate, and I read and edited their completed chapter manuscripts—and I still respect and like them after all that! If that doesn't say something about the quality of these authors, I don't know what does....

Of course, behind each of us is a cast of characters serving in various supporting roles. Many of us worked with research assistants to assist us in completing original works that appear in edited form in this book or to compose our chapters for inclusion in this book. Special thanks go to Miranda Christy, Mara Davis, Kimberly Ford, Tamara Lindsay, and David Patterson in that regard. All, or nearly all, of the authors would acknowledge that errors in reprinted works were caught by the editors and staff of the various law reviews and journals in which we originally published those works. Accordingly, we should acknowledge the editors and staff of the *American Criminal Law Review*, *Buffalo Criminal Law Review*, *Cardozo Law Review*, *Lewis & Clark Law Review*, *Maryland Law Review*, *Ohio Northern University Law Review*, *Penn State Law Review*, *Texas Journal of Women and the Law*, and *Washburn Law Journal*. Reprint permissions, where required, were granted by these law reviews and journals, for which we also thank the editors.

Most of us vetted our included work with colleagues in and outside our home institutions in formal or informal ways. A number of us relied on faculty research stipends or other funding from our Deans (or other sources) to support our work on this book. To all of these colleagues and funding sources, we offer our thanks. I must especially call out for mention here my former Dean, Thomas Galligan, who has provided inspiration and support to me in this and so many other projects. I am already missing him as he now has moved into his new role as President of Colby-Sawyer College in New Hampshire.

My secretarial and administrative assistant, Sean Cary von Gunter, did yeoman's work on this manuscript and the related Teacher's Manual. He faithfully entered edits, caught and fixed formatting glitches and coding errors, and identified a few typos of his own. The poor dear even is starting to recognize and be able to accurately correct errors in legal citation format, although his graduate studies are in a totally different field.

We also must thank the folks at Carolina Academic Press for their belief in what we want to accomplish with this volume. They are a terrific group, and I look forward to continued work with them in the future.

Finally, no set of acknowledgments is complete without the mention of personal challenges and family. One of our authors lost a precious godchild during the drafting process. Another suffered through the perilous Gulf Coast hurricane season of 2005 while the proposal for this book was being assembled. No doubt others dealt with challenges unknown to me above and beyond my requests relating to this book. At times like these, family is so important. And so I must give a special "shout out" here to my loving and patient husband of 21+ years, Merrit, who is accepting of both my endless ideas for new projects and the accompanying odd and lengthy work hours. I also must thank my two children, Scott and Kate, who (in addition to being exceptionally patient with me during the process of producing this book) scheduled a special, in-home showing of *Napoleon Dynamite* for me as a reward for completing the manuscript for this volume. What more could a mother ask for?

JMH
October 2006

INTRODUCTION

Martha Stewart is a modern media icon. She has sought out and achieved public notoriety in her life and work. As such, she requires no personal or professional introduction in these pages.

Yet, Stewart's legal troubles have put her in a new kind of limelight. Since 2002, lawyers and legal scholars—some of whom knew next-to-nothing about Stewart at the turn of the century—have become interested in Stewart's sale of 3,928 shares of common stock in a company called ImClone Systems Incorporated and its legal aftermath. A veritable academic "cottage industry" has grown up around Stewart's related interactions with law and the legal system. Stewart's investigation, prosecution, and criminal trial have become case studies for those interested in identifying and exploring the strengths and weaknesses of federal criminal law and procedure in the white collar crime context. Moreover, securities law experts have fixated not only on the U.S. Securities and Exchange Commission's cutting-edge application of federal insider trading regulation under Rule 10b-5 to the Stewart stock trade, but also on the unusual criminal charge brought against Stewart for securities fraud under that same federal securities regulation, Rule 10b-5. And corporate law folks have become interested in legal issues emanating from related stockholder derivative litigation brought in Delaware for asserted breaches of fiduciary duty.

It is this growing body of work that compelled the creation of this volume. The contributing authors are law professors and legal scholars specializing in criminal, corporate, or securities law. Although the book is intended principally as a supplemental resource for academic courses involving white collar crime and business law both in and outside the law school context, its contents also are likely to be of interest to practicing lawyers in these fields and to heartier (!) elements of the general public who desire to understand more about Stewart's interactions with law and the legal system than the public news media typically can convey. It is for all of these audiences that we write this book.

The Basic Format of this Volume

The chapters in this volume are organized into three main parts. Each chapter tells a discrete legal story and can be read either on its own or together with other chapters of the volume. All of the chapters, however, are united in their use of Martha Stewart's legal troubles as a jumping-off point or case study. The text of each chapter is followed by several questions relating to the chapter that can be used by students and other readers as a means of confirming and extending their understanding of the text. Each chapter then concludes with full legal scholarship endnotes.

Part I

Part I includes Chapters 1 through 5. This part addresses pretrial enforcement issues (principally—although not exclusively—questions relating to prosecutorial discretion, including the discretion to charge criminal conduct).

Along those lines, Chapter 1 focuses on the legal claim for which Stewart originally was investigated—a possible insider trading violation in connection with Stewart's December 2001 sale of ImClone Systems Incorporated common stock. In this chapter, Professor Joan MacLeod Heminway identifies various ways in which Rule 10b-5, the U.S. Securities and Exchange Commission's key rule governing insider trading, can be selectively enforced in insider trading cases. Building on these ideas, Professor Heminway suggests ways in which the investigation of Martha Stewart may have been biased.

In Chapter 2, Professor Ellen S. Podgor asserts that, for various reasons, increasing types of objectionable conduct are being criminalized. The chapter describes various aspects of this "overcriminalization," which Professor Podgor ultimately contends is responsible for the criminal prosecution of Stewart.

The remainder of Part I is devoted to various perspectives on the prosecutorial discretion to charge criminal conduct and the relationship of those perspectives to the criminal charges for which Stewart was indicted. In Chapter 3, Professors Michael L. Seigel and Christopher Slobogin identify the Stewart prosecution as an example of "redundant charging"—the pursuit of a criminal defendant on multiple related charges for the same conduct. Professors Seigel and Slobogin critique this practice and suggest that courts adopt a "law of counts" to better manage the prosecutorial process.

Chapter 4 explains how the breadth and depth of U.S. federal criminal law impacted Stewart's indictment and contemporaneous criminal actions involving Arthur Andersen and Enron. In this chapter, Professor Geraldine Szott Moohr expresses concern about the power vested in federal prosecutors in this broad, deep, legal construct (an adversarial system in name only), which she contrasts with the European inquisitorial system. Ultimately, she concludes that a "[c]lose examination of inquisitorial processes is likely to provide insights for dealing with the imbalance between prosecutor and defendant that now characterizes the federal system."

Finally, Chapter 5 hones in on the Rule 10b-5 securities fraud charge brought against Stewart in her criminal indictment. Here, Professor Heminway assesses the validity of that unusual charge in light of both the elements of a Rule 10b-5 claim and the elements of prosecutorial discretion. Although she finds a basis for the Rule 10b-5 action against Stewart in both sets of elements, her analysis raises questions as to whether Rule 10b-5 should be used by prosecutors in this manner.

Part II

Part II consists of Chapters 6 through 10. This part of the book directly addresses the substance of the criminal charges brought against Stewart in June 2003. In Chapter 6, provocatively entitled "Martha, Scooter, and Slick Willy: Uncovering the Cover-up Crimes," Professor Stuart P. Green looks at the types of criminal prosecutions brought against Stewart, I. Lewis ("Scooter") Libby, and former President Bill ("Slick Willy") Clinton, among others—prosecutions for crimes committed in covering up other possible wrongful conduct. Noting that public reactions to these types of charges vary, Professor Green constructs an analytical framework for use in determining when cover-ups are blameworthy and applies that framework in analyzing the cover-up charges brought against Stewart.

Chapter 7 focuses specifically on the obstruction of justice charge leveled against Stewart. In that chapter, Professor Podgor uses the *Stewart* case as a catalyst for suggesting that obstructive conduct should not be criminally actionable unless it is material. Among other things, Professor Podgor argues that materiality should be a required element of proof for obstruction of justice because of the inclusion of materiality in other, similar criminal statutes.

The last three chapters of Part II of this volume concentrate on the securities fraud charge brought against Stewart in Count Nine of her criminal indictment. In Chapter 8, Professor Heminway critiques the judicial decision to acquit Stewart of that charge. Her reflections relate to matters of criminal procedure, substantive law, and legal reasoning. Ultimately, Professor Heminway concludes that the evidence of scienter in the *Stewart* case was sufficient to present to the jury for decision. However, she also notes that an opinion granting a judgment of acquittal could have been constructed on alternative grounds that were left undecided by the *Stewart* court.

Professor Donald C. Langevoort also is critical of the court's determination to grant a judgment of acquittal to Stewart on the securities fraud charge. To that end, Chapter 9 represents Professor Langevoort's analysis of the state of mind—or "scienter"—element of the Rule 10b-5 charge against Stewart. In this chapter, Professor Langevoort outlines the somewhat amorphous (and often misunderstood) nature of the scienter component of a Rule 10b-5 action and uses research in behavioral law and economics to clarify these murky scienter waters. He then applies his analysis to the Stewart judgment of acquittal on the securities fraud charge. He concludes both that the court misconstrued the scienter requirement in rendering its decision and that Stewart seemingly had the required state of mind based on a behavioral science analysis. He then reflects on the scienter component of the SEC's settled civil insider trading claim against Stewart, concluding that scienter may have provided viable bases for a defense in that civil action.

Focusing on another element of the securities fraud charge against Stewart, Chapter 10 examines whether Stewart's alleged misstatements are "material" under prevailing Rule 10b-5 standards and case law. In this chapter, Professor Heminway outlines the Supreme Court's key pronouncements on materiality and applies them to the facts of the *Stewart* case, concluding that Stewart's public statements are not apparently material.

Part III

Part III of this volume turns to legal issues external to the Stewart criminal trial. Each of the three chapters in this part of the book covers a distinct topic. In Chapter 11, Professor Kathleen F. Brickey describes and considers three post-trial matters emanating from the *Stewart* case. Specifically, the chapter focuses on questions relating jury selection and misconduct, the alleged perjured testimony of a government expert witness, and federal sentencing parameters and discretion. Each of these issues is important in its own right as a miniature case study of the penumbra of a large-scale criminal trial. These trials seem to be surrounded by spin-off legal issues that prolong their existence and continue to impact the lives of those involved. Interestingly (at least for Stewart followers), Professor Brickey concludes that these post-trial matters and the continued legal issues involving and invoking Stewart's trading in ImClone's securities may inure to Stewart's long-term benefit.

Chapter 12 turns directly to the insider trading claims brought against Stewart by the U.S. Securities and Exchange Commission in June 2003. These are claims that never were tried. (The Commission and Stewart settled these charges in the summer of 2006.) In this chapter, Professor Jeanne L. Schroeder explains the principal insider trading theories—classic insider trading and misappropriation—in terms of the passions of envy and jealousy as they apply to property. Using literature in theology, psychology, and philosophy, Professor Schroeder defines the concepts of envy and jealousy and their relationship to property rights and relates this construct to the two dominant theories of insider trading. Professor Schroeder ultimately determines that the misappropriation theory, the theory under which Stewart was pursued for insider trading liability, is confused and contradictory because it (unlike classic insider trading) is rooted in trade secret principles and manifests as envy. In the process, Professor Schroeder rationalizes the classic theory of insider trading regulation as a fitting response to jealousy—an appropriate protection of public company property rights conferred upon investors under the federal securities laws. Moreover, she uses her analysis to question the validity of the U.S. Securities and Exchange Commission's insider trading charges against Stewart.

Finally, Chapter 13 concludes the volume with a reflection on the Delaware stockholder derivative suit against Stewart, yet a third cause of action arising out of the same single sale of ImClone common stock that led to the criminal action and civil insider trading proceeding addressed in the preceding 12 chapters. In this chapter, Professor Lisa M. Fairfax describes both the ways in which director independence comes into play in Delaware shareholder derivative litigation and the historic role that social ties have played in the judicial assessment of director independence. She then identifies both the promise and challenges associated with the consideration of social ties in making independence assessments and suggests a way in which courts can resolve the resulting conflict.

Editorial Notes

There are many ways that this book can be read other than "cover to cover." I offer here a few suggestions based on my perspectives on the text and my experience as a law professor. These ideas are in no way intended to be limiting; rather, they are intended to stimulate further thought about how to creatively use the included material in classroom teaching and book discussion groups.

Prosecutorial Process

For those interested in the benefits and detriments of our current federal system of criminal prosecution, I recommend the whole of Part I of the book, Chapters 1-5. Each chapter provides a different view of the decision to prosecute Stewart. Was she targeted because of who she was, in addition to or in lieu of what she did? Was her conduct really the "stuff" of federal criminal law? Was she charged for too many crimes based on the same alleged wrongful conduct? Does our federal system of prosecution afford too much power to prosecutors in a case like Stewart's? Did prosecutors in the *Stewart* case have sufficient discretion and substantive grounds to charge Stewart with each of the crimes of which she was accused? The chapters in Part I address these and other related issues.

White Collar Crime

Stewart's 2004 criminal action raised a number of interesting federal criminal law and procedure issues that are addressed most directly in Chapters 6, 7, and 11. The different, yet overlapping, elements of crimes involving false statements and obstruction of justice are at issue in Chapters 6 and 7, while Chapter 11 focuses on the application of the laws and processes governing jury selection and conduct, perjury, and sentencing to specific circumstances involving the *Stewart* case.

Securities Fraud and Insider Trading

The elements of federal securities fraud under Rule 10b-5 are covered in varying ways in Chapters 5, 8, 9, and 10, with Chapters 5 and 8 offering a general treatment based on the Stewart criminal indictment and acquittal and Chapters 9 and 10 presenting in-depth analyses of scienter and materiality, respectively, as distinct elements of the federal criminal securities law charge against Stewart.

Those interested in Stewart's possible insider trading violations under Rule 10b-5 (the matter for which she originally was pursued by the U.S. government) should find Chapters 1, 9, and 12 most helpful in advancing their understanding. The substantive law of insider trading is summarized in both Chapters 1 and 12, and the scienter element of the insider trading case brought against Stewart is analyzed in Chapter 9. These chapters underscore the complexity of federal insider trading regulation.

Delaware Corporate Law

Chapter 13 explores a single Delaware corporate law issue raised by a stockholder derivative suit brought against Stewart and her fellow directors of Martha Stewart Living Omnimedia, Inc.—whether director social ties may be taken into account in determining director independence and, if so, how those ties should be assessed. This is an important issue under Delaware law on which the courts have not been entirely clear or consistent over time. At the risk of reopening a corporate law Pandora's Box, this chapter tackles both the issue and a solution—and in the process, effectively forces the reader to question the specialized civil procedure rules applicable to stockholder derivative actions under Delaware law.

Comparative Legal Systems

Although American legal scholars often are ethnocentric in their reflections on law and legal policy, theory, and systems, Chapter 4 provides some comparative context on prosecutorial power and discretion in its discussion of differences in the U.S. federal model for criminal prosecutions and the European inquisitorial prosecutorial system. This chapter indicates that we may have something to learn about criminal procedure from our brothers and sisters in France....

Law and Behavioral Finance

Chapter 9 provides insights on the application of cognition research to the important "state of mind" element of a federal securities fraud violation under Rule 10b-5. By describing and applying this research and existing behavioral finance scholarship to the scienter requirement, this chapter contributes to a burgeoning corporate finance literature that has become important to our understanding of the way in which our securities markets operate—and should operate.

Law and Literature

Students (literal or figurative) of literature and others desiring to further their cultural literacy are likely to find Chapter 12 an interesting read. This chapter uses well-known and lesser-known literature in philosophy, psychology, and religion to illuminate and inform the murky law of insider trading.

Sources and Citations

Legal scholarship is, by tradition, heavily footnoted and multi-sourced. In an effort to make the text of this volume more readable, we have used chapter endnotes, rather than footnotes. Citations are presented in *Bluebook* form (conforming as nearly as possible to the Eighteenth Edition of *The Bluebook, A Uniform System of Citation*, published in 2005 and distributed by The Harvard Law Review Association).

PART I

PRETRIAL ENFORCEMENT ISSUES RELEVANT TO THE CRIMINAL ACTION

CHAPTER 1

WAS MARTHA STEWART TARGETED?*

Joan MacLeod Heminway

Martha Stewart has served out her jail time and home confinement for conspiracy, obstruction of justice, and making false statements in connection with the federal investigation of a December 2001 securities trading transaction.[1] Moreover, she was the subject of a civil enforcement action alleging violations of U.S. securities laws and regulations governing insider trading relating to the same transaction.[2] This, in and of itself, is not remarkable. Many rich and powerful people—and many others in less financially and socially advantaged situations—have been pursued and brought to account for crimes and civil violations relating to securities trading transactions. In particular, in these post-Enron times,[3] much of the public has become numb to the pain of new revelations of possible securities fraud, including insider trading. In this landscape, the Martha Stewart insider trading investigation (including the related criminal trial and insider trading proceeding) is just one of many examples.

Yet, the Martha Stewart investigation somehow seems different—out of proportion to its apparent financial magnitude.[4] The human and monetary resources that have been deployed by the U.S. Congress in connection with possible lawmaking, the U.S. Securities and Exchange Commission ("SEC"), and the U.S. Department of Justice ("DOJ")[5] in pursuing Martha Stewart seem vast when compared to the gross profit she made from her December 27, 2001 sale of approximately 4,000 shares of ImClone Systems Incorporated ("ImClone") common stock.[6] The facts, as we now know them,[7] suggest that the

---

* This chapter is an updated version of a law review article entitled *Save Martha Stewart? Observations About Equal Justice in U.S. Insider Trading Regulation*, originally published at 12 TEX. J. OF WOM. & L. 247 (2003) and reprinted here with permission.

3

considerable governmental resources spent pursuing Martha Stewart result from an express decision to single her out for potential criminal prosecution or civil enforcement based on some characteristic or characteristics personal to her or to one or more groups of which she is an actual or perceived member. For example, one may conclude that she has been singled out for investigation because she is (1) a woman, (2) a member and financial supporter of the Democratic party, (3) a public figure, or (4) a combination of some or all of the foregoing—that is, a very visible and controversial female public figure with political interests adverse to those of the Bush administration.[8]

The selective or targeted use of government resources in investigating and bringing civil enforcement proceedings or prosecuting criminal actions is an accepted part of civil and criminal enforcement.[9] Those charged with enforcing our laws must have evidence of a possible violation of those laws before they may begin the inquiry and investigation process. This type of information may be more available for some people or classes of people than for others. Moreover, federal investigators have only limited resources available for use in pursuing possible violators.[10] Accordingly, each prosecutor or enforcement agent must pick and choose those against whom the laws within its jurisdiction will be enforced.[11] This enforcement discretion,[12] while broad, is subject to statutory, regulatory, and constitutional limits in certain cases.[13] Even validly exercised enforcement discretion, however, may tilt the enforcement playing field in directions that do not well serve the intended purpose of and policies underlying the applicable legal or regulatory scheme. Enforcement bias[14] that does not favorably serve the intended purpose of or policies underlying the laws or regulations being enforced should be identified and eradicated.

Since 2002, congressional, SEC, and DOJ emphasis on securities fraud investigations, prosecutions, and civil and administrative enforcement actions (many of which include facts supporting insider trading allegations) has kept U.S. insider trading regulation in the spotlight.[15] In this environment, important questions about selective enforcement[16] of insider trading violations remain unanswered. Among these questions is the extent to which the nature of U.S. insider trading regulation allows for selective enforcement and the introduction of enforcement bias based on the nature and composition of the enforcement body or the personal background or characteristics of the individual enforcement agents.[17] This question can be answered only by reference to the structure of the applicable system of regulation and by analysis of the impact of that structure on the effective enforcement of insider trading prohibitions. The structure of U.S. insider trading regulation consists of two components that create a unique opportunity for selective enforcement: (1) an unclear, imprecise set of substantive legal standards developed principally in decisional law (on the basis of specific facts and circumstances presented in individual cases)[18] and (2) an enforcement process characterized by a mosaic of governmental bodies (and agents within those bodies) that make decisions and take action in a relatively unconstrained procedural environment.[19]

This chapter first describes the basic structure of insider trading regulation in the United States and then identifies potential structural sources of selective enforcement (both substantive and procedural) and certain easily recognizable bases for enforcement bias in the application of that regulation using the Martha Stewart insider trading investigation as an example.[20] Finally, the chapter recommends more rigorous investigation into possible sources of selectivity and bases for bias in the enforcement of alleged insider trading violations and offers preliminary suggestions for ways in which the identified potential for bias may be obviated or overcome in a manner that is consistent with the current federal regulatory and political environment.

The Structure of U.S. Insider Trading Regulation

Basic Statutory and Regulatory Content

Insider trading regulation in the United States involves all three branches of our federal government in multiple roles. Congress has enacted the basic statutory framework in the form of federal securities legislation. These statutes are interpreted by agency regulations promulgated by the presidentially appointed SEC[21] under the authority of those statutes. Significant interpretation and gap-filling is undertaken by administrative law judges and the federal judiciary in connection with individual cases and controversies.

Insider trading typically is prosecuted, litigated, or otherwise enforced under Rule 10b-5,[22] a regulation adopted by the SEC under Section 10(b) of the Securities Exchange Act of 1934, as amended (the "1934 Act").[23] Section 10(b) is a statutory prohibition on the use or employment,

> in connection with the purchase or sale of any security…, [of] any manipulative or deceptive device or contrivance in contravention of such rules and regulations as the Commission may prescribe as necessary or appropriate in the public interest or for the protection of investors.[24]

Promulgated by the SEC under Section 10(b) as one of the expressly authorized "rules and regulations necessary or appropriate in the public interest or for the protection of investors," Rule 10b-5 makes it

Disclose or Abstain

unlawful for any person, … [t]o employ any device, scheme, or artifice to defraud … or … [t]o engage in any act, practice or course of business which operates or would operate as a fraud or deceit upon any person, in connection with the purchase or sale of any security.[25]

Application of the Statute and Rule in the Insider Trading Context

The application of Section 10(b) and Rule 10b-5 to insider trading cases is not intuitive or obvious. The nature of the prohibited conduct (manipulation, deception, and fraud) is not clearly defined in Section 10(b) or Rule 10b-5, and neither "insider trading" nor "insider" is explicitly defined (or even mentioned) in these core operative provisions.[26] The inevitable result of this construction of the existing regulatory system is that neither Section 10(b) nor Rule 10b-5 provides clear interpretive or enforcement guidance. Accordingly, the SEC (through civil enforcement, administrative proceedings and rule making, and interpretive pronouncements) and the federal judiciary (in both civil and criminal adjudication) have stepped into the void to provide some guidance in the interpretation and development of U.S. insider trading regulation under Rule 10b-5. As a result, that body of regulation is largely an invention of the SEC and the federal judiciary. A number of key legal rules have emerged, resulting in three basic types of insider trading that may be actionable under Rule 10b-5: "classic," tipper/tippee, and misappropriation.

Classic Insider Trading Liability

Under decisional law defining classic insider trading under Rule 10b-5, public issuers of securities and their insiders—those with "a relationship of trust and confidence" to the issuer's stockholders—cannot trade in the issuer's securities while in possession of material, nonpublic information.[27] Therefore, when a public issuer or one of its insiders is in possession of undisclosed material information, the issuer or insider must either disclose the information before trading or abstain from trading in the issuer's securities. This directive commonly is referred to as the "disclose or abstain" rule.[28]

The regulation of classic insider trading through the "disclose or abstain" rule leaves much to further interpretation. What facts constitute the requisite "relationship of trust and confidence" necessary to insider status? What does the rule mean by "possession"? What is "material" information? When is information "nonpublic"? To what type of nonpublic information does the duty apply? What measure of culpability or mental state is required for liability in a criminal action? What measure of culpability or mental state is required for liability in a civil action? Some of these questions have been answered, at least to some extent, by intervening SEC rulemaking, SEC interpretive guidance, or decisional law.[29] Much ambiguity and imprecision, however, remains.[30]

Tipper/Tippee Liability

Trading by a tippee—one who obtains information directly or indirectly from a tipping insider for an inappropriate purpose, i.e., a purpose outside the scope of the business and operations of the issuer—also may be regulated as insider trading under Rule 10b-5.[31] A tippee "assumes a fiduciary duty to the shareholders of a corporation not to trade on material nonpublic information only when (1) the insider has breached his fiduciary duty to the shareholders by disclosing the information to the tippee and (2) the tippee knows or should know that there has been a breach."[32]

Because tippee liability derives from an effective transfer (from the insider to the tippee) of the duty imposed by the "disclose or abstain" rule,[33] the uncertainties surrounding application of that rule also exist in tippee liability cases. Tippee cases involve additional uncertainties, however. To find a tippee trader liable for insider trading, the court first must determine a breach by the insider of his or her fiduciary duty to the issuer in disclosing material, nonpublic information to the tippee.[34] The court then must find that the tippee either knew or should have known that the insider has committed that breach.[35] The court must make these determinations and findings in addition to resolving any ambiguities relating to the application of the "disclose or abstain" rule to the tippee's trade after receipt of nonpublic information from the insider.

Misappropriation

The third type of insider trading liability cognizable under Rule 10b-5 is misappropriation.[36] Misappropriation liability arises out of a securities trading transaction conducted by a person in possession of material, nonpublic information obtained not from an insider, but from another source to which the trader owes a fiduciary duty—a duty that is breached by the trader's use of the nonpublic information in her securities trading transaction.[37] The insider trading liability in this context is based on the "fiduciary-turned-trader's deception of those who entrusted him with access to confidential information."[38]

Misappropriation liability is an insider trading theory of relatively recent vintage, only having been endorsed by the U.S. Supreme Court in 1997.[39] Accordingly, there is much room for interpretation of its various facets.[40] Of special importance in defining the misappropriation theory is the nature of the fiduciary duty to the information source that, if breached, results in potential insider trading liability.[41] Moreover, misappropriation liability (like the classic and tippee theories) is premised on the notion that a putative trader should abstain from market transactions unless and until all material information in possession of the trader has been disclosed.[42] Therefore, misappropriation liability is subject to the same criticisms, with regard to a lack of clarity and precision, to which the "disclose or abstain" rule is subject. While the U.S. Supreme Court finds the misappropriation theory definite enough to support findings of criminal liability,[43] the law governing misappropriation liability is far from clear.[44]

Ambiguities

In all, the ambiguities surrounding application of Rule 10b-5 in the insider trading context are significant to the extent that they do not permit insiders and those receiving information from insiders and others to conduct their securities trading transactions with any degree of certainty that they will avoid insider trading liability. If a person is in possession of undisclosed information about an issuer of securities that is or may be material, the only clear choice for that person, should she want to avoid liability, is to abstain from trading in the issuer's securities.

Moreover, ambiguities in the substance of U.S. insider trading regulation present enforcement issues for the SEC and the DOJ and adjudicatory issues for the federal courts. Enforcement agents and judges alike must struggle with uncertainties similar to those that plague insiders and others who may be subject to insider trading restrictions. The complexities of the substance of U.S. insider trading regulation are matched only by the complexities of the related enforcement process.

The Enforcement Process

The various forms of actionable insider trading may be investigated and judicially enforced both civilly and criminally.[45] The SEC also has the statutory authority to bring administrative actions against violators of the federal securities laws.[46] In addition, the U.S. Supreme Court has accepted the existence of implied private rights of action (including class actions) under Rule 10b-5 for insider trading and other forms of securities fraud.[47] Even with effective interagency coordination, this patchwork of available legal actions may result in parallel—and potentially inconsistent—investigation and enforcement of the same potential violation by the SEC, the DOJ, and private litigants.[48]

Insider trading enforcement activities begin with information about a possible violation. This information may be obtained from a variety of sources in a number of different contexts. These sources include: surveillance activities conducted by the SEC, the Federal Bureau of Investigation ("FBI"), or other governmental agencies; trading data gathered by the securities markets and other players within the securities industry; publicly available news reports; and independent informant reports.[49]

Based on information about a possible violation, the SEC or the DOJ (through the FBI) then may commence an investigation to gather additional facts related to the matter to determine the existence of an actual violation and to develop its case.[50] Although there are some basic parameters for both preliminary inquiries and informal investigations, the manner in which the investigation proceeds is highly dependent upon the facts of each case and may vary between the two principal enforcement bodies and within each respective organization.[51] At this stage, the agencies typically will review available documentary evidence and interview cooperative witnesses while also pursuing and obtaining subpoenas to compel production of additional documents and testimony.[52]

If the enforcement body assembles information it believes to be sufficient to support a proceeding against an alleged violator, an appropriate proceeding may, but need not, be brought.[53] If the SEC determines to bring an insider trading proceeding, it also must decide what kind of proceeding—judicial or administrative—to bring. The SEC also may refer a matter that has been investigated internally to the DOJ for possible criminal enforcement.[54] The DOJ then may, but need not, prosecute the matter.[55]

Potential Sources of Enforcement Selectivity and Bias

Opportunities for Enforcement Selectivity and Bias

The relatively complex system of insider trading regulation in the United States provides many opportunities for selective—or targeted— enforcement.[56] These opportunities exist throughout the enforcement process. Specifically, possibilities for selective enforcement exist at the following critical junctures (among others) in the process of investigating and enforcing a potential insider trading violation:

- when information is received by the SEC, the DOJ, or a self-regulatory organization, like the NYSE (an "SRO"), indicating a potential insider trading transaction;
- when a decision is made to pursue an investigation based on that information;
- during the investigation;
- when the decision is made to pursue enforcement through civil or criminal proceedings; and
- during the enforcement proceeding.

At each juncture, sources of selective enforcement may exist. These opportunities for selective enforcement relate to both the substance of U.S. insider trading regulation and the nature of the insider trading enforcement process. Opportunities for selectivity based on substance are created by gaps, ambiguities, and imprecision in the substantive regulatory framework. Opportunities for the exercise of selectivity in the enforcement process are created by many factors, notably (1) a lack of objective, institutionalized enforcement guidelines for use in decision making at various stages in the enforcement process and (2) the nature and composition of the enforcement body (or the personal background or characteristics of the individual enforcement agent) making decisions at these various stages of the enforcement process.

Receipt of Information Indicating a Possible Violation

The source or sources of information received by the SEC, the DOJ, or an SRO concerning a possible insider trading violation may be the first opportunity for the exercise of selectivity in the enforcement process. Certain information sources, especially the news media (which may tend to focus on specific types of transactions, corporations, and individuals) and private informants (who may have a narrow informational base or a personal vendetta or other agenda unrelated to enforcing insider trading prohibitions) may result in the selective reporting of information regarding possible insider trading violations.[57]

The surveillance criteria used by the SEC and the FBI to identify potential insider trading transactions also may narrow the scope of information available to enforcement officials. In this regard, it is important to ask and answer a number of questions about the surveillance process. For example, what market and transaction data is routinely collected or reviewed by the SEC? Why? How broad-based are the data collected? If all available data are not reviewed, what is the basis for selecting data for review? Are criteria for data retrieval and review strictly followed? It is possible that the SEC or the DOJ may, through data collection or review criteria, screen out or include information that either forecloses or instigates the investigation of potential violators on a selective basis.

Decision to Pursue an Investigation

The criteria used by representatives of the SEC and the DOJ in determining whether to pursue an investigation of a possible insider trading violation may also introduce an element of selectivity into the investigation process.[58] Both the nature of these criteria and the extent to which these criteria are consistently and uniformly applied could affect whether a particular alleged violator is investigated based on the information then available to enforcement authorities. It would be important to identify, for instance, whether (and if so, to what extent) information received by the relevant enforcement body is discounted as unreliable, otherwise unworthy of further investment of resources, or required to be corroborated by other available information before the SEC or the DOJ makes a determination to proceed with the investigation process.[59]

The decision making methodology used by individual decision makers at the SEC and the DOJ (in closing an informal inquiry or in recommending or granting a formal investigative order) and other characteristics personal to those decision makers also may be a source of selectivity at this stage of the enforcement effort. Even if decisions as to further investigation are based on criteria that are uniformly applied on a consistent, institutionalized basis, an inquiry into the actual decision making process is appropriate. It is important to understand, in this context, whether there is a particular type of potential violator that enforcement decision makers are more likely to pursue or ignore at this stage in the enforcement process based on the manner in which individual decision makers consider and use the information at their disposal. This inquiry may reveal potential sources of bias.

Conduct of the Investigation

The manner in which the investigation is conducted also presents an opportunity for selectivity.[60] Specifically, inquiries into both the guidelines for conducting insider trading investigations at the SEC and the DOJ and the ways in which investigators comply with these guidelines are appropriate. For example, the content of any existing investigatory guidelines at the SEC and the DOJ may not be neutral. The applicable guidelines may place certain alleged violators in different positions in the enforcement hierarchy, making it more or less likely that the SEC or the DOJ will recommend enforcement proceedings for those individuals.

Moreover, as in the pre-investigation stage, a lack of—or failure to consistently and uniformly apply—institutionalized guidelines for insider trading investigations allows the introduction of selectivity based on the nature of the investigative process employed by, and other personal characteristics of, the investigator. Characteristics unique to the investigator may impact the nature and extent of an investigation, resulting in the assembly of a higher volume or quality of information about some alleged violators and their transactions than is assembled about others.

Decision to Pursue Enforcement Proceedings

The process of determining whether to pursue legal proceedings against an insider presents another opportunity for selective enforcement. To seek enforcement through legal proceedings, the enforcement agent must first determine that she has sufficient information to present a case to the administrative law judge or to a federal court.[61] This determination is made by applying substantive U.S. insider trading regulations to the facts gathered during the investigation process. The process does not always result in a clear legal theory of the case. Incomplete or inconsistent facts, as well as the lack of clarity and precision in the substantive regulation of insider trading, allow enforcement agents to construe the law in novel ways to arrive at a legal theory that supports the initiation of enforcement proceedings against a specific alleged violator.

Assuming that the enforcement agents are able to construct a case supporting an insider trading violation based on the available facts, the relevant decision makers at the SEC or the DOJ then must determine whether to exercise their discretion to pursue enforcement in appropriate legal proceedings.[62] At the SEC, the exercise of enforcement discretion at this juncture may be impacted by many factors, including the nature and magnitude of the alleged violation, the desired remedy, and agency-based or externally focused strategic considerations.[63] These factors allow for the exercise of broad discretion, especially regarding the extent to which the SEC's own strategic considerations may be determinative of the decision to pursue enforcement.

At the DOJ, the U.S. Attorneys are bound to follow the Principles of Federal Prosecution, a statement of sound prosecutorial policies and practices."[64] These Principles

> have been designed to assist in structuring the decision-making process of attorneys for the government. For the most part, they have been cast in general terms with a view to providing guidance rather than to mandating results. The intent is to assure regularity without

regimentation—to prevent unwarranted disparity without sacrificing necessary flexibility.[65]

Specifically, the principles call for each U.S. Attorney to prosecute or recommend prosecution when there is sufficient evidence of a federal crime, unless: (1) the prosecution would serve no substantial federal interest; (2) the matter is being effectively prosecuted in another jurisdiction; or (3) an alternative to criminal proceedings exists.[66] There are numerous definitional questions involved in interpreting the rule and its three exceptions.[67] These definitional questions are so numerous, in fact, that the principles arguably provide little meaningful guidance to federal prosecutors and, therefore, little protection against selective enforcement.[68]

Again, in the absence of effective, institutionalized statutory or regulatory guidelines regarding the exercise of enforcement discretion that are consistently and uniformly applied, few constitutional or other constraints on enforcement discretion exist.[69] Accordingly, the nature of the decision making process, together with other characteristics of the applicable decision makers, presents the opportunity for selective enforcement. As a general matter, the decision whether to pursue enforcement proceedings against an alleged violator is made at a high level in the hierarchy of an enforcement organization. At the SEC, the decision is made by the Commissioners—the members of the SEC—whereas decision making earlier in the process typically is made by SEC staff members in the Division of Enforcement.[70] At the DOJ, the U.S. Attorney with jurisdiction over the alleged violator generally decides whether to prosecute, whereas FBI personnel, in consultation with Assistant U.S. Attorneys on staff, may make investigative decisions earlier in the enforcement process, to the extent that the investigation is being conducted at the DOJ.[71]

Conduct of Enforcement Proceedings

Another significant opportunity for selective enforcement exists in the substantive case actually presented by the SEC or the DOJ in the chosen enforcement proceeding. As earlier noted, enforcement authorities may selectively use the ambiguity in U.S. insider trading regulation in constructing their case against an alleged insider trader. More specifically, having determined to pursue enforcement proceedings against a potential violator under factual circumstances not clearly tested in earlier decisional law (or otherwise settled by SEC regulation or interpretation), the SEC or the DOJ may argue for an expansion of the law to cover these untested factual circumstances.[72] The unclear and imprecise legal standards in U.S. insider trading regulation provide the basis for this argument.[73]

The success or failure of an SEC or DOJ argument to increase the scope of insider trading protections is determined by an administrative law judge (in an administrative enforcement proceeding) or the federal judiciary (in a civil or criminal enforcement proceeding brought in federal court). Accordingly, once the SEC or the DOJ has presented its case, the opportunity for selective enforcement rests substantially on the shoulders of the judiciary. As with other aspects of the decision making process involved in investigating and enforcing alleged insider trading violations, the nature of the adjudicatory process used by, and characteristics personal to, individual members of the federal judiciary (including administrative law judges) may influence the judiciary to either accept or reject the law-expanding arguments of the SEC or the DOJ.[74]

Bases of Potential Enforcement Bias in the Martha Stewart Investigation

Thankfully, not every opportunity for selective application of the law or possibility of bias results in the exercise of actual bias against an alleged insider trader. Actual selective application of the law, when combined with a biased process or decision maker, however, may result in biased decision making. The actual experience of bias, in individual cases or in aggregated groupings of cases, may not best serve the purposes and underlying policies of insider trading regulation in the United States.

Selective application of U.S. insider trading regulation by biased decision makers may result in enforcement bias on the basis of any number of suspect classifications, too numerous to list in this chapter, and an infinite number of factual scenarios. Accordingly, the possibility of enforcement bias in U.S. insider trading regulation is best explored by analysis of a specific set of facts. The Martha Stewart insider trading matter, about which much has been written in the press, provides an accessible example.[75]

There are a number of easily identifiable bases for the exercise of bias in the Martha Stewart insider trading investigation. In the case of each basis, the ambiguities of substantive U.S. insider trading regulation and the lack of objective, institutionalized enforcement guidelines that are consistently and uniformly applied together create the opportunity for selectivity. The random, individualized nature of the enforcement process, as well as attributes or characteristics personal to the enforcement agent, create the opportunity for enforcement bias.[76] This section focuses on three potential bases for enforcement bias that may have been, or may be, important or determinative in the conduct of the Martha Stewart insider trading investigation and sets forth certain publicly available information that may be relevant to each basis for bias.

lations.

Martha Stewart Is a Woman

Like Leona Helmsley before her, Martha Stewart may have endured a grueling and detailed investigation and may be facing the prospect of protracted legal proceedings simply because she is a woman.[77] Martha Stewart is, of course, not the first woman to be subject to investigation for possible insider trading violations.[78] However, the Martha Stewart investigation represents a highly publicized attempt to enforce U.S. insider trading regulation against a woman.[79] Accordingly, the SEC may be pursuing its insider trading enforcement action against Martha Stewart to hold her out as an example to other women (presumably as a deterrent) that alleged violations of U.S. insider trading regulation committed by women will be vigorously pursued. As earlier noted, strategic enforcement action is common and is an accepted part of overall enforcement discretion.[80]

Other possible sources of gender bias in the Martha Stewart investigation include the nature, motivation, and agenda of the organizations and individuals that have offered information to the SEC and the DOJ, as well as the enforcement decision makers at the SEC and the DOJ. As a general matter, women not only lack majority status in many federal government bodies, but are also underrepresented in the "permanent Federal workforce" as compared to the civilian labor force.[81] The House Energy and Commerce Committee that investigated Martha Stewart and tendered evidence to the DOJ on her case (as part of its general investigation of trading activity involving ImClone's common stock) was comprised of eight women and forty-nine men.[82] Moreover, women are underrepresented at the SEC and the DOJ, as compared to the "Relevant Civilian Labor Force."[83] The numerical underrepresentation of women in these key enforcement structures, while lacking in formal equality, may not be, without more, a source of actual enforcement bias.[84] However, this underrepresentation, together with a lack of (1) feminine values and norms in enforcement and (2) decision making power and influence of women in constructing and implementing the enforcement process, represent potential sources of enforcement bias that may favor or disfavor Martha Stewart and other women.[85] Yet, without empirical evidence in the U.S. insider trading regulation context, it is impossible to determine the probability of enforcement bias resulting from the gender or gender bias of the participants in the enforcement process.

Martha Stewart Is a Democrat

Some commentators have wondered why relatively early on in her investigation Martha Stewart received a Wells Call[86] regarding alleged insider trading and a congressional "go ahead," as well as a trial in the public media, on related claims of perjury and obstruction of justice stemming from her testimony before the House Committee on Energy and Commerce. By contrast Kenneth Lay, the former Chief Executive Officer of Enron Corp. (who reportedly cashed out in excess of $70,000,000 of Enron Corp. stock before its market price fell following the public dissemination of facts regarding previously unreported off-balance sheet financing transactions[87]), did not receive a Wells Call or become subject to legal proceedings of any kind until well after the events that resulted in his 2006 criminal trial.[88] Many also have asked why President Bush's trading transactions in the common stock of Harken Energy Corp. did not receive more investigative or enforcement attention.[89] Some of these commentators focus on political party affiliation and contributions as a principal distinguishing factor between Martha Stewart, on the one hand, and Ken Lay and President Bush, on the other.[90] Martha Stewart is a Democrat and a financial contributor to the Democratic Party; Kenneth Lay is a Republican and a financial contributor to the Republican Party, and President Bush is also a Republican.[91]

Although information about enforcement bias based on political party affiliation and support may be limited and inconclusive, there is factual support for the premise that political party affiliation and support is a source of enforcement bias in the Martha Stewart investigation. The SEC or the DOJ may be using Martha Stewart's political party affiliation strategically. On one hand, Stewart's affiliation with and contributions to the Democratic Party, while public, are not key identifying factors. However, many are aware of her party affiliation, and this awareness provides a basis for the strategic use of enforcement discretion. By investigating Martha Stewart, the SEC and the DOJ can send a strong message that Democrats are not immune from insider trading enforcement.[92]

Another basis for this source of potential enforcement bias is a lack of majority status or other power and influence on the part of Democrats in key parts of the enforcement structure in existence during the Stewart investigation, including the organizations and individuals that offered information to the SEC and the DOJ (e.g., the House Energy and Commerce Committee), as well as the enforcement decision makers at the SEC and the DOJ. For example, the House Energy and Commerce Committee that investigated Martha Stewart consisted of twenty-six Democrats and thirty-one Republicans.[93] In the SEC, at least at the important level of the Commissioners themselves, the basis for bias is less clear, however. Under statutory law, not more than three of the five Commissioners of the SEC may be members of the same political party, and the statute directs the President of the United States to appoint, "by and with the advice and consent of the Senate," members of different political parties to the SEC "alternately as nearly as may be practicable."[94] This statutory provision both creates and forecloses opportunities for the exercise of enforcement bias on the basis of political party affiliation.[95]

Martha Stewart Is a Public Figure

Martha Stewart is an easily identifiable and visible social, cultural, and media force in the United States. She leads a highly public life and has a well known personal and professional dossier. The visibility of Martha Stewart's life and work also provides a basis for enforcement bias, even if the precise nature of the bias may be hard to gauge.[96] The SEC and the DOJ may be using the Martha Stewart investigation to send a message to the investing public that public figures are not immune from insider trading enforcement.[97]

The potential for bias based on Martha Stewart's status as a public figure derives not just from the extensive use of her name, image, and voice in the public media, but also (and perhaps more significantly) from the polarizing reactions to her highly public life and work.[98] Martha Stewart can be seen as thoroughly modern and yet also as a traditionalist. She is both feminist and antifeminist—a substantial and powerful public company founder and director (having formerly worked, ironically enough, as a stock broker)[99] and a domestic diva,[100] touting conventional female roles in society and the family by purveying recipes, dispensing home decorating hints, and popularizing legions of craft projects.[101] Informants and decision makers involved at various junctures in the insider trading enforcement structure may come from either the "Save Martha" or "Surrender Martha" side of public opinion, and we do not know which.[102] If enforcement bias emanates from this source, it is hard to prove with reliable, objective data.

Moreover, if the media is a source of information used by enforcement agents at any stage of the insider trading enforcement process, there is another potential basis for enforcement bias in the Martha Stewart insider trading investigation. The press tends to focus its attention on large transactions, well-capitalized issuers, and public figures.[103] Martha Stewart's status as a public figure and director of a NYSE-traded public company may have put her at an advantage or disadvantage in the enforcement process. Information about Martha Stewart is widely available, and there were many investigative journalists in the field to assist the U.S. Congress, the SEC, and the DOJ in assembling information during the investigatory stages of the process.

Finally, because of Martha Stewart's status as a public figure, the SEC or the DOJ may have felt some pressure to investigate her stock trade and to initiate or refrain from commencing enforcement proceedings against her.[104] The media has covered the investigation of Martha Stewart's ImClone stock trade in great detail from the start. This extensive media coverage may have created a public expectation that Martha Stewart would be held accountable for her actions, regardless of whether those actions violate U.S. insider trading rules. Enforcement officials at the SEC or the DOJ may have perceived that this expectation exists and may not have wanted to frustrate it (and, in so doing, give the impression that public figures can violate or evade the law with impunity). Alternatively, the media attention paid to the Martha Stewart investigation may have created some public sympathy for Stewart, making it less likely that the SEC or the DOJ would pursue enforcement of certain claims against her. These and other related phenomena may create an actual insider trading enforcement bias against or for Stewart and other public figures.

Preliminary Recommendations and Suggestions for Further Inquiry and Change

Further Investigate Potential Sources of Enforcement Selectivity and Bias

The bases for bias in the Martha Stewart investigation described above are just that—bases for bias. One could argue whether—and, if so, how—these sources of potential bias have resulted in the exercise of actual bias in her case or in any similarly situated case.[105]

Rather than argue the point, it seems prudent to suggest more rigorous investigation of these and other identified bases for the exercise of actual bias in U.S. insider trading regulation.[106] With empirical evidence supporting or contradicting the existence of actual bias in U.S. insider trading regulation, those advocating change will be armed not only with better evidence of the need for reform but also with information that enables them to target reform efforts in a more meaningful way.[107] For example, evidence of the exercise of actual gender bias at any stage in the insider trading enforcement process may lead to reform efforts targeted to limiting or eradicating gender bias at that stage in the process, as opposed to broader reform initiatives.

Data regarding actual bias can be obtained from studies and anecdotal evidence.[108] Some studies can be conducted using publicly available information; some will require access to personnel and internal records at the SEC and the

DOJ (which may or may not be forthcoming).[109] The details of any comprehensive study of bias in insider trading enforcement should be determined by a combined team of social scientists and legal scholars. However, any study ideally should have certain basic parameters. The researchers should gather data from investigations and enforcement decision making at both the SEC and the DOJ and from both administrative and court proceedings (civil and criminal). Independent data should be gathered at each stage of the enforcement process for each source of bias identified for study. In this way, data can be reported both individually and on various collective bases and can easily be compared, contrasted, and read with other data, both public and non-public, regarding the nature of the applicable enforcement agencies and their officials. The purpose of this suggested data retrieval structure is two-fold—to allow for highly informed decision making and to permit the use of the data in as many ways as possible.

Anecdotal evidence of actual bias may be obtained in interviews of officials and staff or found in internal SEC or DOJ meeting notes, memoranda, or electronic mail messages, some of which may be subject to disclosure under the Freedom of Information Act ("FOIA").[110] For the same reasons identified above with respect to study data, researchers seeking anecdotal data should seek information regarding both the SEC and the DOJ, all possible enforcement proceedings, and each stage in the enforcement process. Anecdotal data, together with available data from studies of the enforcement process, will best enable scholars, courts, legislators, and regulators to identify sources of actual bias and suggest or implement corrective substantive or procedural changes to the structure of insider trading regulation.

Identify Ways in Which the Potential for Bias May Be Obviated or Limited

Even without empirical evidence of existing, actual bias in U.S. insider trading enforcement, reform may be desirable. The potential for selectivity and bias is both significant and pervasive, raising questions as to the efficacy of U.S. insider trading regulation. These questions are serious ones, in light of the purpose of U.S. insider trading regulation and the low level of public confidence in the U.S. public securities markets that results from ineffective enforcement.[111] United States insider trading regulation is intended to promote the integrity of U.S. securities trading markets by prohibiting the use of confidential information in trading transactions when that use constitutes or arises from a breach of fiduciary duty or another duty of trust or confidence.[112] Enforcement of the law against specific people or classes of people may or may not serve that policy objective. The exercise of actual or perceived enforcement bias may, in fact, give the investing public the impression that certain alleged violators are immune from enforcement, thereby undercutting the integrity of the market at a time when public confidence in the U.S. securities markets is at a low point.

Accordingly, means of obviating or limiting the potential for enforcement bias seem appropriate. These reforms may be instituted at any level in the regulatory structure, from the operative statutory law to related SEC rules and regulations to internal agency guidelines applicable to investigations and the initiation and conduct of enforcement proceedings.[113] Substantive insider trading reform could, for example, add precision to the duty to "disclose or abstain" by more clearly identifying the classes of people who may violate U.S. insider trading principles. This reform may be accomplished by better defining, in law or regulation, both insiders and others whose use of material, nonpublic information triggers the imposition of insider trading liability.[114] Better clarity as to the definition of insider trading or the scope of information governed by U.S. insider trading information also could be beneficial.[115] For example, one might inquire whether it is enough (to trigger liability) that an insider has conveyed to someone outside the issuer the fact that she plans to sell some securities and, if that type of information is to be considered material, nonpublic information, under what circumstances liability should be imposed.[116] These and other substantive reforms should focus on clarifying the legal basis for U.S. insider trading regulation in an manner and with an effect that is consistent with established underlying legislative and regulatory policy objectives.

U.S. insider trading regulation also may benefit from procedural reform. Reform proposals of a procedural nature may be adopted in addition to or in lieu of any substantive reform and could include changes in the information retrieval and analysis systems used by the SEC and the FBI (as well as the SROs) in the decision to initiate and (as applicable) conduct, inquiries and investigations. In this area, both sources and types of information could be regulated to limit or avoid selective enforcement or enforcement bias. Procedural reforms also could incorporate specific, institutionalized enforcement guidelines, consistently and uniformly applied.[117] Examples of this type of reform could consist of parallel and meaningful investigatory guidelines for the SEC and the FBI or more specific, detailed criteria for use by the SEC and the U.S. Attorney in determining whether to initiate enforcement proceedings against an alleged insider trader. The specific nature of any procedural reforms should be based on a detailed review of current procedures and should be designed to serve the legislative and regulatory policies underlying U.S. insider trading regulation.

Conclusion

The system and enforcement of insider trading regulation in the United States present significant opportunities for selective enforcement and the exercise of enforcement bias. These prospects for selectivity and bias arise out of both the unclear and imprecise substance of U.S. insider trading regulation and the relatively unrestricted nature of the related multiple and overlapping enforcement processes. Although the opportunity for selectivity and bias may or may not result in the exercise of actual bias in any individual case or group of cases, the threat to the integrity of our securities markets is a clear and present danger.[118] U.S. insider trading regulation can best deter unlawful activity and support and promote the integrity of the securities markets if it more clearly and precisely identifies and punishes those who undermine or challenge that market integrity by engaging in transactions based on their privileged access to significant, undisclosed information.[119] Otherwise, the potential for a veritable witch hunt exists, in which U.S. insider trading regulation could be used as a tool in a goal-oriented process to root out and punish market participants in accordance with a social, political, or economic agenda other than that for which U.S. insider trading regulation was intended.

Especially (but not exclusively) if evidence of actual insider trading enforcement bias can be shown, some reform in U.S. insider trading regulation is desirable, if not necessary, and can be achieved in a variety of ways. It makes sense both to assemble additional information regarding selectivity and bias in insider trading enforcement and to institute reform in the near term to restore market integrity.[120]

Questions

1. Was Martha Stewart targeted for investigation and prosecution because she is a woman, democrat, public figure, or anything else? What is the basis for your answer?
2. Assuming that Stewart was investigated or sued by the SEC on some basis unrelated to the policies underlying insider trading law under Rule 10b-5, is that investigation or enforcement an abuse of governmental resources? Why, or why not? Under what circumstances, if any, may selective enforcement of laws be desirable?

3. Is it realistic to assume that research and reform efforts can eradicate or significantly restrict the existence or application of enforcement bias? Why, or why not? How should we go about identifying and implementing possible reforms?

Notes

1. Although for many readers she may need no introduction, Martha Stewart is a director and the former Chief Executive Officer of Martha Stewart Living Omnimedia, Inc., a public company built around Stewart's ideas for home decorating, cooking, gardening, crafts, and other domestic pursuits. Termed "domestic diva" and the like by the media (*see* sources cited *infra* note 77), Stewart's company has become a major media and merchandising company. *See* Martha Stewart Living Omnimedia, Inc., Annual Report on Form 10-K (filed March 7, 2006), *available at* http://www.sec.gov/Archives/edgar/data/1091801/000095012306002702/y18218e10vk.htm (last visited March 12, 2006). The author is a subscriber to *Martha Stewart Living* magazine, has purchased *Martha by Mail* and Martha Stewart Everyday retail items, and owns several *Martha Stewart Living* books.

2. *See* SEC v. Martha Stewart, No. 03 CV 4070 (NRB) (S.D.N.Y. filed June 4, 2003), *available at* http://www.sec.gov/litigation/complaints/comp18169.htm [hereinafter SEC Complaint]. In a separate action brought the same day as this enforcement action, the United States Attorney for the Southern District of New York obtained a criminal indictment against Stewart regarding alleged false statements in connection with the same securities trading transactions. *See* U.S. v. Martha Stewart, No. 03 Cr. (S.D.N.Y. filed June 4, 2003), *available at* http:// news.findlaw.com/nytimes/docs/mstewart/usmspb60403ind.pdf. The indictment did not charge Stewart with criminal insider trading violations. *See also* Alex Beam, *Brand Names That Stand the Test of Time*, BOSTON GLOBE, June 12, 2003, at D1 ("She wasn't indicted on insider-trading charges, after all, but on several lesser counts."); Michael P. Malloy, *The Spin She's In*, L.A. TIMES, June 11, 2003, Part 2, at 13 ("The criminal indictment doesn't charge her with insider trading."); *Martha Stewart Reacts to Charges*, CORP. OFFICERS AND DIR. LIABILITY LITIG. REP., June 30, 2003, at 13 ("Although the indictment does not specifically accuse Stewart of insider trading, it says she violated the antifraud provisions of federal securities law by issuing false statements regarding her stock sale to prevent the stock price of her company, Martha Stewart Living Omnimedia, from dropping."); Tom Petruno, *Insider Trading, Tough to Prove, Isn't Part of Stewart Criminal Case*, L.A. TIMES, June 5, 2003, Part 3, at 1; William Safire, *Fight It, Martha*, N.Y. TIMES, June 12, 2003, at A35 ("The U.S. Attorney has not accused her of the crime of insider trading."); *Some Surprised by Martha Stewart Charges*, *at* http://asia.news.yahoo.com/030606/ap/d7rgclto2.html (June 7, 2003) ("Still, prosecutors did not actually indict Stewart on the charge of insider trading, an extremely difficult charge to prove in a criminal case."). Stewart also has been the subject of a number of class actions and other private civil suits asserting (among other things) trading on nonpublic information, a number of which expressly allege violations of U.S. insider trading laws and regulations. *See, e.g., Cauley Geller Bowman & Coates, LLP Announces Martha Stewart Living Omnimedia, Inc. Investors Have Until October 7 to File Lead Plaintif Motion –MSO*, Sept. 26, 2002, *at* http://biz.yahoo.com/pz/020926/32125.html (last visited Sept. 8, 2003); *Martha Stewart Class Action Filed*, CNN

MONEY, *at* http://money.cnn.com/2003/02/04/news/ companies/stewart_lawsuit/ (Feb. 4, 2003); *Martha Stewart Sued Over Big Stock Sale*, ST. PETERSBURG TIMES ONLINE, Aug. 23, 2002, *available at* http://www.sptimes.com/2002/08/23/Business/Martha_Stewart_sued_ o.shtml; Greg B. Smith, *Martha Hit with Suit*, N.Y. DAILY NEWS, Aug. 21, 2002, *available at* http://www.nydailynews. com/news/story/12783p-12099c.html. For ease of reference, these laws and regulations, together with applicable decisional law, are collectively referred to as "U.S. insider trading regulation" or "insider trading regulation in the United States."

3. The reference to "post-Enron times" may conjure images and emotions of many kinds and may mean different things to different readers. In this context, the term is intended merely to create a temporal setting for the reader and refers to the corporate and financial environment in the United States following the revelation by Enron Corp. and federal regulators of possible significant misstatements and omissions in Enron's financial disclosures to the public. This revelation and the related investigation proved to be the first of a number of highly publicized allegations of corporate fraud in connection with the public disclosure of material information by high profile corporations with publicly traded securities.

4. The *New York Post* reported that Martha Stewart's profit from the sale of her Im-Clone shares totaled $42,000. Lauren Barack et al., *Experts: Fraud Case Could Cost*, N.Y. POST, Oct. 23, 2002, at 33. The *Chicago Tribune* published an article asserting that Stewart avoided a trading loss of $36,500. *See* David Greising, *Out of Spotlight Maybe, But Still in Hot Water*, CHI. TRIB., Sept. 15, 2002, at C1. The complaint filed by the U.S. Securities and Exchange Commission asserts that Stewart avoided losses of $45,673. *See* SEC Complaint, *supra* note 2, at ¶ 19; *see also* Melana Zyla Vickers, *Small-Time Enforcement Costs Taxpayers Big Time*, USA TODAY, June 10, 2003, at 13A (noting that "Stewart is accused of pocketing $45,673 in insider-trading profits—small change compared with as much as $11 billion in inflated earnings that telecom giant WorldCom hoodwinked its investors into believing it had").

The apparent intensity and magnitude of the Martha Stewart insider trading investigation is, in part, a creation of the highly public nature of the investigative process in her case and the resulting media attention. *See* Rachel Beck, *Is Martha Stewart Case All That? Stock-Sale Scandal Involving the Domestic Doyenne Makes Headlines, But Is She Really Corporate Culprit No. 1?*, Oct. 29, 2002, *available at* http://ww.sunspot.net/business/bal-martha1029,0, 5788812.story?coll=bal-business-indepth; *Crossfire: Is Martha Stewart a Scapegoat?* (CNN television broadcast, Sept. 9, 2002), *transcript available at* http://www.cnn.com/2002/ ALLPOLITICS/09/09/cf.crossfire/ ("[A]ll of us in the media are just going to go wild with this and cover it, cover every moment of it....") [hereinafter Crossfire-Scapegoat]; Larry Kudlow, *Martha's a Good Thing*, NAT'L REV. ONLINE, June 20, 2002, *at* http://www.nationalreview.com/kudlow/kudlow062002.asp; Jeffrey Toobin, *Fact: Annals of Law: Lunch at Martha's, Problems with the Perfect Life*, NEW YORKER, Feb. 3, 2003, at 38 ("As unpleasant as the insider-trading investigation has been, the coverage by the press—a cascade of ridicule and abuse—may have been harder to take."). This aspect of the Martha Stewart investigation may invoke, for some readers, memories of the highly publicized tax evasion case against Leona Helmsley in the late 1980s. *See* Ann Mumford, *Leona Helmsley: The Construction of a Woman Tax Evader*, in FEMINIST LEGAL STUDIES (1997); Christopher Byron, *Imagine No Martha*, N.Y. POST, July 8, 2002, at 31. Tellingly, the entertainment industry also jumped on the Martha Stewart bandwagon with a made-for-television piece, starring Cybill Shepherd as Stewart, that aired on NBC on May 19, 2003. *See* Terry Kelleher & Amy Bonawitz, *Cybill Shepherd Sounds Off*, PEOPLE, May 26, 2003, at 26; Dalton Ross, et al.,

What to Watch, ENT. WEEKLY, May 23, 2003, at 67; Tom Shales, Martha Stewart, *Done to Perfection*, WASH. POST, May 19, 2003, at C01; Jon W. Sparks, *Cybill's Crits Assess Her Martha*, COM. APPEAL (Memphis, TN), May 20, 2003, at C1.

5. *See* Alison Beard & Julie Earle, *Celebrities May Be Tip of Insider Trading Iceberg: Experts Say Illegal Activity Is Rampant But Limited Resources Mean That Prosecutions Remain Rare*, FIN. TIMES (London), June 20, 2002, at 25; Andrew Pollack, *Martha Stewart Questions Widen, Punishing the Stock*, N.Y. TIMES, June 27, 2002 (late ed.), at C2.

6. *See* SEC Complaint, *supra* note 2, at ¶ 19; Barack et al., *supra* note 4; Beck, *supra* note 4; Bradley W. Skolnik, *Is Justice Served by Martha Stewart Circus?*, INDIANAPOLIS STAR, June 8, 2003, at 3E ("Stewart does the 'perp walk' for a relatively modest $229,000 insider-trading case while the likes of Enron's Ken Lay, WorldCom's Bernard Ebbers, and the whole gang of corrupt stock analysts and investment bankers and centimillionaire Wall Street CEOs seems to be getting off largely with fines and civil penalties.").

7. Certain publicized facts regarding Martha Stewart's sale of ImClone common stock in December 2001 are important to an analysis of the bases of potential insider trading enforcement bias. A brief restatement of those facts, summarized from media accounts, is here in order.

On December 27, 2001, Martha Stewart sold 3,928 shares of ImClone common stock for approximately $227,824, or an average price of over $58.00 per share. *See* SEC Complaint, *supra* note 2, at ¶ 19; Kudlow, *supra* note 4; Dan Harris, *Good Morning America: "Trading Downward": E-mails and Phone Calls May Shed Light on Stewart's Dumping of ImClone Shares* (ABC television broadcast, Aug. 9, 2002) *transcript at* http://abcnews.go.com/sections/GMA/GoodMorningAmerica/GMA020809Stewart_Emails.html; David Wilson, *The Whys of Martha Stewart Selling*, BLOOMBERG NEWS, June 21, 2002, *at* http://www.bloomberg.com/feature/feature1024667880.html. Stewart had desired to dispose of these shares in a tender offer made by Bristol-Myers Squib Co. in November 2001, but that tender offer was oversubscribed, and her tender was prorated to exclude these 3,928 shares from the offer. *See* Kudlow, *supra* note 4; Wilson, *supra*. In a June 2002 letter to the House Energy and Commerce Committee and in government interviews, Stewart explained that the stock transaction had been prompted by a prior arrangement with her stock broker that he would sell her stock when the market price fell below $60 per share. *See* SEC Complaint, *supra* note 2, at ¶ 23. There are also allegations, however, that Stewart had a telephone conversation with her broker on that day. *See* SEC Complaint, *supra* note 2, at ¶¶ 18–19; Harris, *supra*. After the close of the market on December 28, 2001, an ImClone press release announced that the FDA had denied regulatory approval of Erbitux, a key ImClone cancer drug under testing. *Id.* According to the SEC, at the close of trading on December 31, 2001, ImClone's common stock was trading at $46.00 per share. *See* SEC Complaint, *supra* note 2, at ¶ 14. By January 3, 2002, the closing price of ImClone's common stock had fallen to $41.27, and by January 10, 2002, the closing price of ImClone's common stock had fallen to $34.22. *See* historical stock prices for ImClone (symbol IMCL) *at* http://www.finance.yahoo.com (last visited Jan. 25, 2003).

8. *See* Beard & Earle, *supra* note 5 (characterizing the Martha Stewart investigation as "celebrity scandal"); Paul Begala & Tucker Carlson, *Crossfire: McAulife Slams Bush; Should UNC Teach Koran to Freshmen?* (CNN television broadcast, Aug. 12, 2002), *available at* LEXIS, News & Business Library, News Group File (referencing Martha Stewart's status as a celebrity and a member of the Democratic party) [hereinafter *Crossfire-McAuliffe*]; Gloria Borger, *Why Hate Martha?*, U.S. NEWS & WORLD REP., July 8, 2002, at 17 (contending

that Martha Stewart is being pursued because she is a "high-profile woman"); Pat Buchanan et al., *Buchanan & Press: Is GOP Exploiting 9/11?* (MSNBC Aug. 12, 2002), *available at* LEXIS, News & Business Library, News Group File; Byron, *supra* note 4 (noting that defenders of Martha Stewart argue she is being "scapegoated by people who want to drive women out of business and back into the kitchen"); Patrice Hill, *Stewart a Top Donor to Democratic Coffers; Mogul Focus of Republican Probe*, WASH. TIMES, Aug. 21, 2002, at A01; *Crossfire-Scapegoat*, *supra* note 4 (referencing Martha Stewart's status as a celebrity and a member of the Democratic party); Holman W. Jenkins Jr., *An Autumnal Resolution: Give Martha a Break*, THE WALL ST. J., Sept. 4, 2002, at A23 (asserting that Congress pursued Martha Stewart "solely because she's a celebrity"); Kudlow, *supra* note 4 (referencing Martha Stewart's status as a member of the Democratic party); *Martha Stewart Case Reveals Double Standard, Libertarians Say*, *at* http://www.lp.org/press/archive.php?function=view&record=628 [hereinafter *Martha Stewart Case Reveals Double Standard*] (referencing political and celebrity status as possible differentiators) (last viewed on Aug. 26, 2003) (on file with TEX. J. WOMEN & L.); Alexandra Stanley & Constance L. Hays, *Martha Stewart's To-Do List May Include Image Polishing*, N.Y. TIMES, June 23, 2002 (highlighting Martha Stewart's status as a "rich, powerful, and fair-haired business woman"); Greta Van Susteren, *Fox on the Record with Greta Van Susteren: Interview with Geoffrey Fieger, Michael Musto, Mike Norman* (Fox News Network television broadcast, Aug. 22, 2002), *available at* LEXIS, News & Business Library, News Group File (referencing Martha Stewart as a "powerful, aggressive woman" and her status as a member of the Democratic party).

9. *See* CHARLES H. WHITEBREAD & CHRISTOPHER SLOBOGIN, CRIMINAL PROCEDURE, AN ANALYSIS OF CASES AND CONCEPTS 545 (4th ed. 2000); Jeffrey J. Pokorak, *Probing the Capital Prosecutor's Perspective: Race of the Discretionary Actors*, 83 CORNELL L. REV. 1811, 1813 (1998) (describing the breadth of criminal prosecutorial discretion).

10. *See* WHITEBREAD & SLOBOGIN, *supra* note 9, at 547 (referencing a lack of attorney time and investigative and other resources as factors in the exercise of prosecutorial discretion); Richard M. Phillips, et al., *SEC Investigations: The Heart of SEC Enforcement Practice*, *in* THE SECURITIES ENFORCEMENT MANUAL, TACTICS AND STRATEGIES 35 (Richard M. Phillips ed., 1997); Beard & Earle, *supra* note 5 (quoting Professor Stephen Bainbridge as saying that the SEC and the DOJ "devote their limited resources to areas that are high profile"); William Hicks, *Securities Regulation: Challenges in the Decades Ahead*, 68 IND. L.J. 791, 807 (1993) ("Limited resources prevent the government from detecting and prosecuting all violations of the federal securities laws."); Harvey L. Pitt & Karen L. Shapiro, *Securities Regulation By Enforcement: A Look Ahead At the Next Decade*, 7 YALE J. ON REG. 149, 171 (1990) (identifying the SEC's limited resources as a reason for the careful targeting of enforcement activities); Skolnik, *supra* note 6 (noting that "federal resources to fight white-collar crime are stretched ... thin, due in part to the need to divert resources to the war on terrorism").

11. *See* Pokorak, *supra* note 9, at 1813 (noting that "[l]imited resources and crowded criminal dockets force prosecutors to make quasi-judicial decisions ...").

12. The term "enforcement discretion" is used in this chapter to refer broadly to the judgment permitted to be exercised by enforcement officials to determine whether to initiate criminal or civil investigations or proceedings against suspected violators of U.S. insider trading regulation. The more commonly used term, "prosecutorial discretion," while often used to convey the same meaning, may be more narrowly interpreted to apply only to criminal enforcement. *See, e.g.*, WHITEBREAD & SLOBOGIN, *supra* note 9, at 545 (assuming an application of the term in the criminal enforcement context only).

13. As a general matter, constitutional limits on enforcement discretion are few and narrowly interpreted. *See id.* at 550–62; Richard Bloom, *Twenty-Eighth Annual Review of Criminal Procedure: II. Preliminary Proceedings: Prosecutorial Discretion,* 87 Geo. L.J. 1267 (1999) (summarizing constitutional and other constraints on criminal prosecutorial discretion); P.S. Kane, Comment, *Why Have You Singled Me Out? The Use of Prosecutorial Discretion for Selective Prosecution,* 67 Tul. L. Rev. 2293, 2303–05 (1993) (describing Equal Protection Clause limits placed on criminal prosecutorial discretion). Scholars and litigants have argued, however, that the criminal enforcement of U.S. insider trading regulation raises due process concerns. *See* SEC v. Willis, 777 F. Supp. 1165, 1173–74 (S.D.N.Y. 1991); Daniel J. Bacastow, *Due Process and Criminal Penalties Under Rule 10b-5: The Unconstitutionality and Inefficiency of Criminal Prosecutions for Insider Trading,* 73 J. Crim. L. & Criminology 96 (1982); Jill E. Fisch, *Start Making Sense: An Analysis and Proposal for Insider Trading Regulation,* 26 Ga. L. Rev. 179, 181 (1991).

14. As used in this chapter, the term "enforcement bias" refers to the conscious or unconscious discriminatory use of enforcement discretion to the detriment or benefit of a particular person or group based on identifying characteristics that are not related to insider trading regulation or to its underlying policies. *See generally* Todd Lochner & Bruce E. Cain, *Equity and Efficacy in the Enforcement of Campaign Finance Laws,* 77 Tex. L. Rev. 1891, 1929–30 (1999) (using the term similarly to describe the relationship between comparative economic and other campaign resource deficiencies and Federal Election Commission audits); William J. Stuntz, *Race, Class, and Drugs,* 98 Colum. L. Rev. 1795, 1801, 1829 (1998) (using the term in a substantially similar manner with respect to the relationship between class and race, on the one hand, and drug enforcement); J. Hoult Verkerke, Note, *Compensating Victims of Preferential Employment Discrimination Remedies,* 98 Yale L.J. 1479, 1494 (1989) (using the term to describe disproportionate judicial enforcement of Title VII favoring unskilled and low-skilled workers).

15. *See, e.g.,* Ken Belson, *U.S. Tries Simpler Tack Against Ex-Chief of Qwest,* N.Y. Times, Jan. 20, 2006, at C3 (describing proceedings against Joseph P. Nacchio for insider trading in Qwest Communications securities); Kevin Cahillane, *The Smartest Guy in Summit?,* N.Y. Times, March 5, 2006, at 14NJ (noting, with respect to Enron's former executives, "Mr. Fastow has pleaded guilty to two counts of wire and securities fraud and is serving a 10-year prison sentence, and Mr. Lay and Mr. Skilling are on trial in Federal District Court in Houston on fraud and conspiracy charges, with an additional count of insider trading for Mr. Skilling."); Andrew Pollack, *ImClone Considers Selling Itself as It Replaces Its Chief Again,* N.Y. Times, Jan. 25, 2006, at C3 (noting Samuel Waksal's insider trading in ImClone securities).

16. The term "selective enforcement" describes the exercise of enforcement discretion to pursue certain enforcement inquiries, investigations, or proceedings and to not pursue others. In the area of criminal law, this selectivity is frequently referred to as "selective prosecution," "discriminatory prosecution," or "arbitrary prosecution." *See* Whitebread & Slobogin, *supra* note 9, at 551–52; Bloom, *supra* note 13, at 1271–75; Kane, *supra* note 13, at 2301–05 (discussing claims of selective prosecution on racial grounds); Beard & Earle, *supra* note 5; *Martha Stewart Case Reveals Double Standard, supra* note 8. Prosecutors may, for instance, selectively enforce the law against one or more alleged violators to hold them out as public examples with the objective of deterring further violations of that law. *See* Whitebread & Slobogin, *supra* note 9, at 552–53; Byron, *supra* note 4. The SEC has not been free from judicial scrutiny on the grounds of selective enforcement. *See, e.g.,* Arthur

Lipper Corp. v. SEC, 547 F.2d 171, 182 (2d Cir. 1976), *cert. denied*, 434 U.S. 1009 (1978); Winkler v. SEC, 377 F.2d 517, 518 (2d Cir. 1967) (asserting bias in the relief awarded).

17. Specifically, enforcement bias in the insider trading context may allow for a discriminatory application of the law through which some classes of "insiders" and their "tippees" may escape investigation, trial or other proceedings, criminal guilt, or civil or administrative liability for insider trading. At the same time, other classes may be investigated, pursued in the media, administrative proceedings, or the courts; or jailed, fined, censured, or found liable for monetary damages.

18. See Bacastow, *supra* note 13; William S. Feinstein, *Securities Fraud: Pleading Securities Fraud with Particularity—Federal Rule of Civil Procedure 9(b) in the Rule 10b-5 Context: Kowal v. MCI Communications*, 63 GEO. WASH. L. REV. 851, 854 (1996) (describing the provisions of both the statute and rule governing insider trading as "vague and open-ended"); Fisch, *supra* note 13; Kevin R. Johnson, *Liability for Reckless Misrepresentations and Omissions under Section 10(b) of the Securities Exchange Act of 1934*, 59 U. CIN. L. REV. 667, 674 (1991) (noting that "the courts have been less than precise in defining what exactly constitutes a reckless misrepresentation" under this insider trading regulation); Donald C. Langevoort, *Rule 10b-5 as an Adaptive Organism*, 61 FORDHAM L. REV. 7 (1993) (describing the applicable legal rule as having "a fluid character" and as "being sufficiently open ended," with contours that are "sufficiently indistinct"); Painter et al., *Don't Ask, Just Tell: Insider Trading After* United States v. O'Hagan, 84 VA. L. REV. 153, 188–91 (1998) (highlighting ambiguities in the misappropriation theory of insider trading); Lynda M. Ruiz, *European Community Directive on Insider Dealing: A Model for Effective Enforcement of Prohibitions on Insider Trading in International Securities Markets*, 33 COLUM. J. TRANSNAT'L L. 217, 229 (1995) ("A review of legislative, executive and judicial initiatives reveals ambiguity regarding the parameters of the U.S. prohibition on insider trading...."). The observation that imprecise or vague laws raise the specter of selective and biased enforcement is not a new one. A number of scholars and courts, including the U.S. Supreme Court, have noted this relationship. *See, e.g.*, Grayned v. City of Rockford, 408 U.S. 104, 108–09 (1972) (noting the dangers of arbitrary and discriminatory enforcement in support of the "void for vagueness" doctrine); Brian C. Harms, *Redefining "Crimes of Moral Turpitude": A Proposal to Congress*, 15 GEO. IMMIGR. L.J. 259, 272–73 (2001) (mentioned in connection with a constitutional "void for vagueness" analysis); John F. Manning, *Textualism and the Equity of the Statute*, 101 COLUM. L. REV. 1, 66 n.263 (2001); Gregory L. Maxim, Comment, *The EPA's Title Bout—Remedying One Injustice with Another*, 30 MCGEORGE L. REV. 1091, 1125–26 (1999) (mentioned in connection with a constitutional "void for vagueness" analysis).

19. *See* Bacastow, *supra* note 13, at 132–33; Pitt & Shapiro, *supra* note 10, at 175–78 (describing the complex interactions between the SEC and the DOJ with respect to alleged insider trading violations).

20. In choosing this example (and in entitling this chapter), the author is not asking the reader to sympathize with Martha Stewart or to exonerate her from responsibility or liability for any violations of law she may have committed. Nor is the author asserting that actual bias existed in the Martha Stewart insider trading investigation. *See* Mumford, *supra* note 4, at 181–82. Rather, the Martha Stewart example represents both the genesis of the author's consideration of the issues discussed in this chapter and a vehicle intended to draw the uninitiated into the baroque and motivationally complex world of U.S. insider trading regulation. The author is aware that the choice of this example may be uncomfortable for some, including certain feminist legal scholars, because the chapter may be perceived as pro-

moting the heroism of Martha Stewart—a biological woman who succeeded in a male-dominated corporate world and is alleged to have "engaged in abuses which were once the prerogative of the male." *Id.* at 192. Nevertheless, the example is, in the author's view, instructive.

21. *See infra* notes 94–95.

22. 17 C.F.R. § 240.10b-5 (2003).

23. 15 U.S.C. § 78j(b) (2003).

24. *Id.*

25. 17 C.F.R. § 240.10b-5.

26. Numerous commentators have noted this deficiency. *See, e.g,.* Ronald E. Bornstein & N. Elaine Dugger, *The Global Securities Market: International Regulation of Insider Trading,* 1987 COLUM. BUS. L. REV. 375, 385 (1987); Paula J. Dalley, From *Horse Trading To Insider Trading: The Historical Antecedents Of The Insider Trading Debate,* 39 WM. & MARY L. REV. 1289, 1351 (1998); Michael P. Dooley, *Insider Trading: Comment from an Enforcement Perspective,* 50 CASE W. RES. L. REV. 319, 320 (1999); Fisch, *supra* note 13, at 185–86; Dennis S. Karjala, *Federalism, Full Disclosure, and the National Markets in the Interpretation of Federal Securities Law,* 80 NW. U. L. REV. 1473, 1523 (1986); Roberta S. Karmel, *Outsider Trading on Confidential Information—A Breach in Search of a Duty,* 20 CARDOZO L. REV. 83, 86 (1998); Ronald F. Kidd, *Insider Trading: The Misappropriation Theory Versus An "Access To Information" Perspective,* 18 DEL. J. CORP. L. 101, 131–32 (1993); Fred D'Amato, Comment, *Equitable Claims To Disgorged Insider Trading Profits,* 1989 WIS. L. REV. 1433, 1435 (1989); Elyse Diamond, Note, *Outside Investors: A New Breed Of Insider Traders?,* 60 FORDHAM L. REV. 319, 320 (1993); John I. McMahon, Jr., Note, *A Statutory Definition Of Insider Trading: The Need To Codify The Misappropriation Theory,* 13 DEL. J. CORP. L. 985, 985–87 (1988); Karen Schoen, Comment, *Insider Trading: The "Possession Versus Use" Debate,* 148 U. PA. L. REV. 239, 249 (1999).

27. *See* Chiarella v. United States, 445 U.S. 222, 228 (1980).

28. *Id.* at 226–27.

29. For an example, see the recently enacted Rule 10b5-1 under the 1934 Act (clarifying when a purchase or sale of securities "constitutes trading 'on the basis of' material, non-public information"). 17 C.F.R. § 240.10b5-1 (2006). Also, in *Ernst & Ernst v. Hochfelder,* 425 U.S. 185, 193 n.12 (1976), the Supreme Court found that scienter is a required element of a Rule 10b-5 action and indicated that the scienter requirement may be met by evidence of reckless conduct.

30. *See supra* note 18.

31. *See* Dirks v. SEC, 463 U.S. 646 (1983). Initially, many observers thought Martha Stewart was likely being pursued as a tippee of a classic insider under the rule of law established in the *Dirks* case. *See* Michael Freedman & Emily Lambert, *Will She Walk?,* FORBES, July 7, 2003, at 46, 47 ("Prosecutors first pursued an ironclad case: that Waksal tipped off Stewart, before the news broke, that the Food and Drug Administration had dealt a setback to an ImClone cancer drug, prompting her to dump 3,938 shares and avoid a $45,000 loss."); Greising, *supra* note 4, at C1 ("Stewart is in the same heap of trouble as anyone else who made a perfectly timed trade, after frequent phone communications with a close pal at the top of a company that was about to release some startlingly bad news."); Dan Haar, *Fair's Fair: Maybe It's Time for a Ranking of Rascals,* HARTFORD COURANT (Conn.), Oct. 1, 2002, at E1 (describing Stewart "as one who, if the accusations are true, profited from an insider tip"); *Hardball* (MSNBC television broadcast, June 3, 2003, *available at* LEXIS, News & Business library, News file) (comments of Adrian Michaels, indi-

cating that Stewart may have received material nonpublic information directly from Im-Clone insider Waksal); *ImClone's Ex-CEO to Pay $800, 000 for Insider Trading*, ANDREWS SEC. LITIG. & REG. REP., Mar. 26, 2003 (indicating Stewart allegedly was tipped by ImClone insider Waksal). *But see* Sean J. Griffith, *Being Martha Stewart: Will Her Celebrity Status End Up Doing Her In?*, CHI. TRIB., Nov. 19, 2002, at N25 (correctly analyzing the publicized facts regarding the asserted tip by Stewart's broker to Stewart).

According to publicized facts, the material, nonpublic information that Stewart had was information about ImClone stock trades being made by Waksal and his family. *See* SEC Complaint, *supra* note 2, at ¶¶ 18 & 19. This information apparently came to Stewart through her stockbroker. *See id.* Stewart allegedly telephoned Waksal after requesting that her ImClone stock be sold. *See* Diane Brady et al., *Sorting Out the Martha Mess*, BUS. WK., July 1, 2002, at 44; Jenkins, *supra* note 8; Alex Kuczynski & Andrew Ross Sorkin, *For Well-Heeled, Stock Tips Are Served With the Canapés*, N.Y. TIMES, July 1, 2002 (Late Ed.), at A1; Pollack, *supra* note 5; Stanley & Hays, *supra* note 8. Interestingly, the SEC's insider trading action against Stewart did not assert that Stewart received material, nonpublic information from Waksal in breach of his well known fiduciary duty to ImClone and its stockholders. Rather, the SEC's complaint against Stewart asserted (among other things) that Stewart received material, nonpublic information about Waksal family ImClone stock trading from her broker; that her broker breached his duty of client confidentiality (owed to his employer, Merrill Lynch); that Stewart knew or acted in reckless disregard of the broker's duty and of his breach of that duty; and that her sale of ImClone stock while in possession of the stock trading information about the Waksal family violates Rule 10b-5's insider trading "disclose or abstain" rule. *See* SEC Complaint, *supra* note 2, at ¶¶ 27–33. These allegations appear to suggest that the SEC desired to extend tippee liability to tippees of third-party brokers who misappropriate personal trading information from insiders. *See* Andrew Countryman, *Civil Suit Against Stewart May Break New Ground*, CHI. TRIB., June 10, 2003, at C1 (asserting that "[t]he underpinnings of the Stewart case lie in what's known as the 'misappropriation' theory"); Freedman & Lambert, *supra* note 31, at 47 (stating that, in the Stewart case, the SEC "must resort to the more tenuous theory of 'misappropriation'"). For information about misappropriation liability in U.S. insider trading regulation, see *infra* notes 36–44 and accompanying text.

The SEC's argument is not without a basis in the policies underlying the federal securities laws. Professors Strudler and Orts likely would term the broker's behavior a form of "frontrunning" (even though Stewart's broker tips, rather than trades on, nonpublic client information) and find that both the broker's conversion of the nonpublic information and the tippee's trade violate the policies underlying U.S. insider trading regulation. *See* Alan Strudler & Eric W. Orts, *Moral Principle in the Law of Insider Trading*, 78 TEX. L. REV. 375, 429–34 (1999).

32. *See Dirks*, 463 U.S. at 660.

33. *Id.* at 659 ("the tippee's duty to disclose or abstain is derivative from that of the insider's duty").

34. *See id.* at 661–67; SEC v. Adler, 137 F.3d 1325, 1333 (11th Cir. 1998).

35. *See Dirks*, 463 U.S. at 660; SEC v. Lambert, 38 F. Supp. 2d 1348, 1351 (S.D. Fla. 1999). These ambiguities arise out of the same regulatory context as those applicable to classic insider trading. *See* authorities cited *supra* note 18.

36. *See* United States v. O'Hagan, 521 U.S. 642 (1997).

37. *See id.* at 652–53.

38. *Id.* at 652.

39. *See id.* at 642.

40. On this basis and on other grounds, there has been significant criticism of the misappropriation theory of insider trading as endorsed by the Supreme Court in the *O'Hagan* case. *See, e.g.,* Karmel, *supra* note 26, at 109; Donna M. Nagy, *Reframing the Misappropriation Theory of Insider Trading Liability: A Post-O'Hagan Suggestion,* 59 Ohio St. L.J. 1223 (1998); Richard W. Painter, *Insider Trading and the Stock Market Thirty Years Later,* 50 Case W. Res. L. Rev. 305, 306–07, 310 (1999); Painter et al., *supra* note 18, at 188–91. To the extent that scholars and other observers construe the SEC's enforcement action against Stewart as an extension of the misappropriation theory, *see supra* note 31, additional criticism is likely to follow.

41. As a partial answer to the question, the SEC adopted Rule 10b5-2 in 2000. 17 C.F.R. §240.10b5-2 (2006). By its terms, the Rule "provides a non-exclusive definition of circumstances in which a person has a duty of trust or confidence for purposes of the 'misappropriation' theory of insider trading under Section 10(b) of the Act and Rule 10b-5."

42. In fact, misappropriation could have been a possible alternate theory for imposing liability in the *Chiarella* case—the case in which the Supreme Court first blessed the "disclose or abstain" rule—if that matter had been put to the jury at trial. *See* Chiarella v. United States, 445 U.S. 222, 235–37 (1980).

43. *See* United States v. O'Hagan, 521 U.S. 642, 665–66 (1997).

44. *See* Judith G. Greenberg, *Insider Trading and Family Values,* 4 Wm. & Mary J. Women & L. 303, 305–06 (1998); Karmel, *supra* note 26, at 84; Painter et al., *supra* note 18, at 188–91.

45. The SEC is authorized to enforce the federal securities laws, including the 1934 Act. 15 U.S.C. §§78d, 78u, 78u-1, 78u-2, and 78u-3 (2003). This enforcement authority, however, does not extend to criminal prosecutions; criminal enforcement authority rests with the DOJ. 15 U.S.C. §78u(d); 17 C.F.R. §202.5(f) (2003). All actions to enforce Rule 10b-5's insider trading prohibitions must be brought in a federal court. 15 U.S.C. §78aa (2003); *see* Donna M. Nagy et al., Securities Litigation and Enforcement Cases and Materials 833 (2003). For an excellent discussion of Section 10(b) and other hybrid statutes, together with issues involved in and suggestions for interpreting the same, see Margaret V. Sachs, *Harmonizing Civil and Criminal Enforcement of Federal Regulatory Statutes: The Case of the Securities Exchange Act of 1934,* 2001 Ill. L. Rev. 1025 (2001).

46. 15 U.S.C. §78u-3.

47. *See* Superintendent of Ins. v. Bankers Life & Cas. Co., 404 U.S. 6, 13 n.9 (1971). *See also* Thomas Lee Hazen, The Law of Securities Regulation 571–73 (4th ed. 2002); Sachs, *supra* note 45, at 1040.

48. *See* Hazen, *supra* note 47, at 879–81; Nagy et al., *supra* note 45, at 14. The U. S. Congress also has investigative powers in connection with its legislative function. *See* McGrain v. Daugherty, 273 U.S. 135, 174 (1927); Townsend v. United States, 95 F.2d 352, 355 (D.C. Cir. 1938), *cert. denied,* 303 U.S. 664 (1938); United States v. Seymour, 50 F.2d 930, 933–34 (D. Neb. 1931); Richard B. Zabel & James J. Benjamin Jr., *Congress' Role in Investigating Fraud: Are Legislators' Aggressive Approach in Hearings Helping or Hindering the Process?,* N.Y. L.J., Dec. 16, 2002, at 9. Congress has exercised these powers in connection with a number of recent insider trading allegations, including those involving Martha Stewart. *See* Kudlow, *supra* note 4; Jayne O'Donnell, *ImClone CEO denies tipping off brother,* USA Today, June 14, 2002, at 1B; Pollack, *supra* note 5; Edmund Sanders, *Senate Committee Chides Enron Board; Energy: Directors' failure to heed warnings about accounting practices underscored during hearing on the firm's collapse,* L.A.

TIMES, May 8, 2002, Part 3, at 6; Byron York, *Joe's Fishing Trip*, NAT'L REV. ONLINE, May 24, 2002, *at* http://www.national review.com/york/york052402.asp; Zabel & Benjamin Jr., *supra*.

49. *See* Phillips et al., *supra* note 10, at 34–35. The National Association of Securities Dealers, Inc. (NASD) or a stock exchange may conduct its own inquiry based on data available to it and also may supply information to the SEC. *See id.*; NAGY ET AL., *supra* note 45, at 723.

> Often, an investigation will be triggered when the SEC, NASD or NYSE identifies market activity that is suspicious in light of subsequent events (e.g., the price of a company's stock increases dramatically in advance of a positive announcement). The investigators (sometimes at the SEC, sometimes at the NASD or NYSE) will then ask each relevant company for a chronology of events leading to the announcement and a list of individuals (both company personnel and others) who knew the critical information before it was announced. The investigators will also ask broker dealers to identify the customers who made timely trades in the securities. Often, the investigators will ask if anyone with advance knowledge of the critical information knows any of the individuals who made timely trades. The SEC will then proceed by questioning witness [sic] (sometimes through telephone interviews, sometimes by taking testimony) and obtaining documents (including telephone and bank records). The SEC looks for circumstances that indicate that the timely trade was suspicious, evidence linking the trader to persons with advance knowledge, and evidence linking an individual who made timely trades to other individuals who made timely trades.

Kenneth B. Winer et al., *SEC Enforcement*, *at* http://www.realcorporatelawyer.com/ faqs/enforcement.html (last visited Mar. 21, 2006).

50. *See* SEC v. Dresser Indus., Inc., 628 F.2d 1368 (D.C. Cir. 1980) (en banc). Although the DOJ can and does exercise independent investigative powers over insider trading matters (through the FBI), the SEC generally exercises primary investigative authority in potential insider trading cases. *See* 15 U.S.C. §78u(d); 17 C.F.R. §202.5(b) (2003); ALDEMAN, ET. AL., *Criminal Enforcement of the Securities Laws; A Primer for the Securities Practitioner*, in THE SECURITIES ENFORCEMENT MANUAL, TACTICS AND STRATEGIES, *supra* note 10, at 308; U.S. ATT'Y MANUAL 9-4.126, *available at* http://www.usdoj.gov/usao/eousa/foia_reading_room/usam (last visited Mar. 21, 2006); *The Investor's Advocate: How the SEC Protects Investors and Maintains Market Integrity*, *at* http://www.sec.gov/about/whatwedo.shtml#org (last visited Mar. 21, 2006); *About the Economic Crimes Unit: Securities/Commodities Fraud*, *at* http://www.fbi.gov/hq/cid/fc/ec/about/about_scf.htm (last visited Oct. 7, 2003) [hereinafter *The Investor's Advocate*]. This chapter assumes initiation of an investigation by the SEC, unless otherwise noted. At the SEC, the preliminary investigative phases are referred to as preliminary or informal inquiries or investigations. 17 C.F.R. §202.5(a) (2003); NAGY ET. AL., *supra* note 45, at 624–25; Ralph C. Ferrara & Philip S. Khinda, *SEC Enforcement Proceedings: Strategic Considerations When the Agency Comes Calling*, 51 ADMIN. L. REV. 1143, 1148–50 (1999); Phillips et al, *supra* note 10, at 35–40; *The Investor's Advocate*, *supra*; Winer et al., *supra* note 49. A formal SEC investigation order may ensue. *See* HAZEN, *supra* note 47, at 878; Ferrara & Khinda, *supra*, at 1150; Phillips et al., *supra* note 10, at 40–43. The term "investigation," as used in this chapter with respect to the SEC, refers to either phase or both phases, and also may include the commencement of proceedings, as the context may require.

51. *See* 17 C.F.R. §202.5(a); NAGY ET AL., *supra* note 45, at 623–24; Phillips et al., *supra* note 10, at 36–40; Winer et al., *supra* note 49.

52. *See* 17 C.F.R. §202.5(a); HAZEN, *supra* note 47, at 878–79; Ferrara & Khinda, *supra* note 50, at 1155–61; Phillips et al., *supra* note 10, at 34–43, 55–59.

53. *See* NAGY ET AL., *supra* note 45, at 641–42; William R. McLucas et al., *A Practitioner's Guide to the SEC's Investigative and Enforcement Process*, 70 TEMPLE L. REV. 53, 111 (1997) ("At the conclusion of an investigation, the staff may determine to take no action or to recommend that the Commission bring enforcement proceedings.").

54. 15 U.S.C. §78u(d).

55. The DOJ has authority to either decline or pursue prosecution after an SEC referral. *See* U.S. ATT'Y MANUAL, *supra* note 50, at 9-2.020 ("The United States Attorney is authorized to decline prosecution in any case referred directly to him/her by an agency unless a statute provides otherwise."); *id.* at 9-2.030 ("The United States Attorney is authorized to initiate prosecution by filing a complaint, requesting an indictment from the grand jury, and when permitted by law, by filing an information in any case which, in his or her judgment, warrants such action.").

56. A number of commentators have noted the existence of some form of selective enforcement of U.S. insider trading regulation under Rule 10b-5. *See* Dooley, *supra* note 26, at 323; Karmel, *supra* note 26, at 84; James H. Lorie & Victor Niederhoffer, *Predictive and Statistical Properties of Insider Trading*, 11 J.L. & ECON. 35, 37 (1968); Henry G. Manne, *Insider Trading and the Law Professors*, 23 VAND. L. REV. 547, 554 (1970); Pitt & Shapiro, *supra* note 10, at 171–72.

57. *See* NAGY ET AL., *supra* note 45, at 624 (listing "disgruntled customers and whistleblowing employees" as likely sources of information leading to SEC inquiries); Phillips et al., *supra* note 10, at 35 (noting that informants may include "disappointed investors" and "disgruntled former employees"); *accord* Winer et al., *supra* note 49. Informants may be motivated to come forward with information about possible insider trading violations by bounty provisions added to the 1934 Act by the Insider Trading and Securities Fraud Enforcement Act of 1988. 15 U.S.C. §78u-1 (2003).

58. Factors considered at the SEC may include "the priorities of the Commission at the time the information is received, the workload of the office receiving the information, the complexity of the issues, the magnitude of the investor harm resulting from the possible violation and whether the matter is appropriate for referral to an SRO, a state securities regulator, or another government agency." Phillips et al., *supra* note 10, at 35.

59. *See* Ferrara & Khinda, *supra* note 50, at 1153 (noting that the SEC Division of Enforcement need not prove to the Commissioners that a violation has occurred in order to obtain authorization for a formal investigation).

60. The SEC's authority to conduct investigations is quite broad, allowing the SEC significant discretion. *See* 17 C.F.R. §202.5(a); Phillips et al., *supra* note 10, at 32–33.

61. The procedure at the SEC at this stage is characterized by a somewhat complex set of chess moves. First, it is important to note that

[t]he Staff does not have authority to institute an enforcement proceeding. If the Staff tentatively decides to recommend that the Commissioners authorize the institution of an enforcement proceeding, the Staff usually will notify counsel to the perspective [sic] defendant. This notification is referred to as a "Wells Call." Upon receiving a Wells Call, counsel should meet with the Staff to learn the basis

for the Staff's tentative decision. Counsel can then prepare a document, referred to as a "Wells Submission," to persuade the Staff not to recommend the action or to recommend a less severe action. In addition, counsel can meet with the Staff and attempt to dissuade the Staff from proceeding with the proposed recommendation. If the Staff decides to proceed with the recommendation, the Staff submits to the Commission a memorandum setting forth its recommendation and the basis for its recommendation. Defense counsel does not have an opportunity to see this recommendation memorandum. At a meeting that is open to the Staff but closed to the public (including the proposed defendants and their counsel), the Commission decides whether to authorize the institution of the enforcement action based on the recommendation of the enforcement Staff, the Wells Submissions filed by proposed defendants, and input from other interested Divisions (e.g., the Office of the Chief Accountant, the Division of Corporation Finance, and the Office of General Counsel)."

Winer et al., *supra* note 49. *See* McLucas et al., *supra* note 53, at 111; Phillips et al., *supra* note 10, at 97–108. Of course, the SEC may decide not to recommend enforcement action after conclusion of an investigation. *See* 17 C.F.R. §202.5(d); McLucas et al., *supra* note 53, at 111; Phillips et al., *supra* note 10, at 96–97. At the DOJ, the U. S. Attorney has broad discretion to prosecute "any case which, in his or her judgment, warrants such action," subject to certain constitutional, statutory, and other limits. U.S. ATT'Y MANUAL, *supra* note 50, at 9-2.030; *see also infra* notes 64–67 and accompanying text.

62. *See* 17 C.F.R. §202.5(b); U.S. ATT'Y MANUAL, *supra* note 50, at 9-2.030.

63. *See The Investor's Advocate, supra* note 50.

64. U.S. ATT'Y MANUAL, *supra* note 50, at 9-27.001.

65. *Id.*

66. U.S. ATT'Y MANUAL, *supra* note 50, at 9-27.230, 9-27.240, 9-27.250.

67. *See* Michael A. Simons, *Prosecutorial Discretion and Prosecution Guidelines: A Case Study In Controlling Federalization,* 75 N.Y.U. L. REV. 893, 934–35 (2000).

68. "While the creation and publication of the Principles was an important step in bringing prosecutorial charging decisions into the sunshine, at bottom the Principles of Federal Prosecution are so vague as to be meaningless." Simons, *supra* note 67, at 934 (footnotes omitted).

69. *See supra* note 13 and accompanying text. In this connection, the Principles of Federal Prosecution note that

> [u]nder the Federal criminal justice system, the prosecutor has wide latitude in determining when, whom, how, and even whether to prosecute for apparent violations of Federal criminal law. The prosecutor's broad discretion in such areas as initiating or forgoing prosecutions, selecting or recommending specific charges, and terminating prosecutions by accepting guilty pleas has been recognized on numerous occasions by the courts. *See, e.g.,* Oyler v. Boles, 368 U.S. 448 (1962); Newman v. United States, 382 F.2d 479 (D.C. Cir. 1967); Powell v. Ratzenbach, 359 F.2d 234 (D.C. Cir. 1965), *cert. denied,* 384 U.S. 906 (1966). This discretion exists by virtue of his/her status as a member of the Executive Branch, which is charged under the Constitution with ensuring that the laws of the United States be 'faithfully executed.' U.S. Const. Art. §3. *See* Nader v. Saxbe, 497 F.2d 676, 679 n. 18 (D.C. Cir. 1974).

U.S. ATT'Y MANUAL, *supra* note 50, at 9-27.110. There are also statutory and policy-oriented constraints on criminal enforcement discretion. *See id.* at 9-2.110–9-2.120.

70. *See The Investor's Advocate, supra* note 50; Winer et al., *supra* note 49.

71. U.S. ATT'Y MANUAL, *supra* note 50, at 9-2.001, 9-2.030.

72. This decision making process is the tradition in the development of insider trading regulation under Rule 10b-5. The *O'Hagan* misappropriation theory represents an extension of the duty-based decisional law regarding tippee liability evidenced in the *Dirks* case; the decisional law regarding tippee liability represents an extension of *Chiarella's* duty-based "disclose or abstain" rule; and the "disclose or abstain" rule represents an expansive interpretation of the language in Rule 10b-5, founded on an earlier SEC administrative proceeding, *In re Cady, Roberts & Co.*, 40 S.E.C. 907 (1961). *See* Symposium, *Insider Trading: Law, Policy, and Theory After O'Hagan: Transcript of the Roundtable on Insider Trading: Law, Policy, and Theory After O'Hagan*, 20 CARDOZO L. REV. 7, 13, 16 (1998) (comments of Daniel J. Kramer and Roberta S. Karmel, respectively); Benjamin D. Briggs, Notes & Comments: *United States v. O'Hagan: The Supreme Court Validates the Misappropriation Theory of Insider Trading and Rule 14e-3(a), but Does the Court's Decision Help or Hinder the Quest for Guiding Principles?*, 15 GA. ST. U. L. REV. 459, 464–67 (1998). Had it not been settled by the SEC in August 2006, the Martha Stewart civil insider trading case could have provided another example. *See supra* note 31; Mark J. Astarita, *The Story of Martha and the Telephone Call*, at http://www.seclaw.com/docs/marthastewartindictmentseccivil0603 (last visited Mar. 21, 2006) (asserting that the SEC's insider trading enforcement action against Stewart "is an attempt by the SEC to expand its powers and authority beyond all permissible bounds"); Countryman, *supra* note 31; Freedman & Lambert, *supra* note 31, at 46 (noting the views of securities lawyers that the Stewart civil and criminal cases "would extend securities laws further than ever before, in terms of who is an insider and what is insider information"); Raymond J. Keating, *Martha May Stand, and That's "A Good Thing,"* NEWSDAY, June 10, 2003, at A32 ("[M]any experts have commented in recent days that the SEC's insider trading charge pushes the bounds of case law."); Malloy, *supra* note 2 (intimating that the SEC insider trading case against Stewart is "at the edges of the law").

73. *See supra* Parts II.A and II.B.

74. For example, a judge's ideas about gender, party politics, or other matters may impact his or her interpretation of one or more of the various elements of a successful insider trading case. *See* Greenberg, *supra* note 44, at 306 (contending that "the lines the courts have drawn, defining which types of relationships violate the insider trading rules, are influenced by the court's conception of gender roles, and the closely related realms of market and family"). *See generally* Theresa M. Beiner, *What Will Diversity on the Bench Mean for Justice?*, 6 MICH. J. GENDER & L. 113 (1999); Cynthia Grant Bowman, *Women and the Legal Profession*, 7 AM. U. J. GENDER SOC. POL'Y & L. 149 (1998/1999); Jeffrey M. Shaman, *The Impartial Judge: Detachment or Passion?*, 45 DEPAUL L. REV. 605, 626 (1996) ("The case law is ... replete with instances where judges have expressed racial, ethnic, or gender bias....").

75. *See supra* notes 4–8.

76. The importance of the enforcement agent or body to the achievement of equal justice is expressly acknowledged in the *U.S. Attorney Manual's* Principles of Prosecution. "Important though these principles are to the proper operation of our Federal prosecutorial system, the success of that system must rely ultimately on the character, integrity, sensitivity, and competence of those men and women who are selected to represent the public interest in the Federal criminal justice process. It is with their help that these principles

have been prepared, and it is with their efforts that the purposes of these principles will be achieved." U.S. ATT'Y MANUAL, *supra* note 50, at 9-27.001.

77. *See* Borger, *supra* note 8; Mumford, *supra* note 4, at 171–74. In 1991, Leona Helmsley was convicted of federal tax evasion (among other related charges) based on the fact that she signed a joint tax return prepared by accountants. *See* U.S. v. Helmsley, 985 F.2d 1202, 1204 (2d Cir. 1993); U.S. v. Helmsley, 941 F.2d 71 (2d Cir. 1991), *cert. denied*, 502 U.S. 1091 [hereinafter *Helmsley I*]. Harry Helmsley, her husband, was too ill to prosecute, and the DOJ therefore focused its enforcement efforts on Leona Helmsley. *See Helmsley I, supra*, at 78. The press has fueled the gender fire in the Martha Stewart case by referring to her using a series of feminine monikers. *See, e.g.*, Barack et al., *supra* note 4 ("Domestic Diva"); Beck, *supra* note 4 ("domestic doyenne"); *Love and Martha*, FIN. TIMES (London), Feb. 5, 2003, at 14 ("dowager of domesticity"); Stanley & Hays, *supra* note 8 (using and defining the term "blondenfreude" and applying it to the Martha Stewart insider trading investigation); Paula Zahn, et al., *CNN People in the News: Profiles of Martha Stewart, Will Smith* (CNN television broadcast, July 6, 2002) *available at* LEXIS, News & Business Library, News Group File ("queen of domesticity"). These labels, among other media aspects of the Martha Stewart investigation, are reminiscent of the media's portrayal of Leona Helmsley. *See* Mumford, *supra* note 4, at 169–70 (noting the use by the media and commercial enterprises of Helmsley's self-constructed public persona as the "queen" of a hotel chain).

78. *See, e.g.*, Barry Flynn, *Deadline Looms in Insider Trading Case for Woman*, ORLANDO SENTINEL, Feb. 14, 2002, at B1; David Glovin, *Girlfriend Faces Charge of Insider Trading*, TORONTO STAR, Mar. 28, 2000, *available at* LEXIS, News Library, News Group File; *Insider-Trading Defendant Settles with SEC*, L. A. TIMES, Apr. 11, 2000, at C2; Timothy L. O'Brien, *He Said, She Said: When Insiders Share a Pillow*, N. Y. TIMES, Jan.19, 2003, at § 9, at 1; *SEC files trading charges*, DENV. POST, June 5, 1998, at C-02.

79. *See, e.g.*, *supra* notes 4–8.

80. *See supra* note 16.

81. 2001 FEORP ANN. REP. 31, *available at* http://www.opm.gov/feorp01/ (last visited Mar. 21, 2006) [hereinafter ANNUAL REPORT]. In racial terms, Hispanic women and non-minority women are underrepresented in the permanent Federal workforce, as compared with the civilian labor force. *Id.* at 13.

82. *See* http://energycommerce.house.gov/107/members/members.htm (last visited Oct. 24, 2003) (on file with author). At the time Martha Stewart was investigated, there were 61 women and 374 men in the House overall. *See Women in the U.S. Congress*, at http://us-govinfo.about.com/library/weekly/aa121198.htm. Congress is a key legal structure, and the underrepresentation of women in important components of the Congress may be a cause for concern in legislation as well as enforcement. *See* Robin West, *The Aspirational Constitution*, 88 NW. U. L. REV. 241, 250 (1993) ("[W]e have good reason to believe that a Congress with a significant number of women will be more responsive to the needs of women ... and hence will be a better Congress and enact better laws because of that fact....").

83. ANNUAL REPORT, *supra* note 81, at 34, 35. Only one of the five SEC commissioners was a woman at the time the research was completed for the law review article forming the basis of this chapter. *See Current SEC Commissioners*, at http://www.sec.gov/about/commissioner.shtml (last visited Mar. 17, 2003). Currently, two female commissioners serve on the SEC. *Id.* (last visited Mar. 21, 2006). Prior to the current SEC, there has never been more than one female commissioner at any given time during the history of the SEC. *Concise Directory, Historical Summary*, at http://www.sec.gov/about/concise.shtml#history (last visited Mar. 21, 2006).

84. Neither the gender nor any other characteristic of an enforcement agent necessarily has bearing on the agent's ability to carry out her legal duties, especially in the context of a facially gender-neutral regulatory scheme. One does not need to accept the notion that enforcement is gendered, however, to acknowledge that gender hostility or affinity may exist in the enforcement context. Women's interests may, in fact, be underrepresented and underserved in U.S. insider trading regulation enforcement because of a lack of representation of women in the enforcement process. *See infra* note 85. For example, the possibility that enforcement authorities desire to make an example of women in the U.S. insider trading regulation context may cause one to question whether the exercise of enforcement discretion against women may be easier if women are not involved in the enforcement process. *See* sources cited *supra* note 16.

However, merely increasing the number of women in various enforcement bodies may not necessarily benefit women. The enforcement structure in U.S. insider trading regulation, as part of our entrenched governmental order, may be seen as inherently patriarchal. *See* Mary Becker, *Patriarchy and Inequality: Towards a Substantive Feminism*, 1999 U. CHI. LEGAL F. 21, 23–26 (1999). The effects of a patriarchal system are not necessarily countered by formal equality. For example, women in enforcement who have male-typical values may participate as coequals to men in proliferating an enforcement bias against women. As Professor Becker cogently summarizes:

> If all that happens in the next ten years is that more male-identified and male-centered women get more power in patriarchal institutions, most women are likely to be no better off than they are today.
>
> If we could jump into an ideal world without any transition, jump into a world in which women had as much power as men (for example, a world in which 50 percent of those in the Senate, the House of Representatives, the Supreme Court, and the Cabinet were suddenly women), [Catharine] MacKinnon's solution might work. All those women with power would then be able to reward qualities other than those associated with masculinity, and might well do so. But MacKinnon's approach is not a blueprint for getting to such a world because, in the short term, giving more power only to a few women—those who rise within patriarchal institutions—will not challenge patriarchy.

Id. at 39 (footnote omitted). *But see* Susan J. Carroll, *The Politics of Difference: Women Public Officials as Agents of Change*, 5 STAN. L. & POL'Y REV. 11 (1994) (arguing that women elected public officials may behave differently than men).

85. *See* Becker, *supra* note 84, at 39. Other scholars also have called for law enforcement reform focused on the nature and composition of the enforcement agents, frequently calling for greater numbers of women in enforcement roles. Professor Jenny Rivera notes:

> There is also the issue of patriarchy and the attitudes of those in the position of enforcing the laws, whether they be prosecutors, judges or court officers.... There is a need for extensive change in attitudes. Indeed, women and people of color must be brought into legislative and law enforcement positions in significant numbers to help facilitate such change.

Jenny Rivera, Symposium, *The Civil Rights Remedy of the Violence Against Women Act: Legislative History Policy Implications & Litigation Strategy, A Panel Discussion Sponsored by the Association of the Bar of the City of New York*, September 14, 1995, 4 J.L. & POL'Y 409,

417–18 (1994). Similarly, Mary Jo White observes, after noting the significant number of female U.S. Attorneys:

> What we are seeking, of course, is the day that it is no longer news that a woman has been appointed or elected to any high position. The focus should be on the person and his or her qualifications, not on gender. This business of numbers and women firsts can be—and is—overblown sometimes. But we should also not kid ourselves—some numbers do matter.... The numbers and percentages do matter to how much clout and comfort we have in any given professional setting.

The 2002 Sandra Day O'Connor Medal of Honor Recipient—Mary Jo White, 26 SETON HALL LEGIS. J. 263, 266–68 (2002).

86. For an explanation of the Wells Call, see *supra* note 61. Martha Stewart is reported to have received a Wells Call in or about October 2002. *See* John Crudele, *ImClone-SAC Link—Hedge Fund Called Waksal Same Day as Martha*, N.Y. POST, Jan. 23, 2003, at 031; Greg Farrell, *SEC Close to Filing Charges on Stewart*, USA TODAY, Oct. 22, 2002, at 1A; Randi F. Marshall, *Stewart Case Lull Sparks Speculation*, NEWSDAY (New York), Nov. 26, 2002, at A58; Thomas S. Mulligan & Walter Hamilton, *SEC Likely to Charge Martha Stewart; The Staff Recommends Civil Action in the ImClone Insider Trading Case, a Source Says*, L.A. TIMES, Oct. 22, 2002, Pt. 1, at 1; Greg B. Smith, *Heat's on Martha Again; Feds To File Civil Suit, Criminal Probe Still On*, DAILY NEWS (New York), Jan. 18, 2003, at 7; Paul Tharp & John Lehmann, *Martha Scandal Heating Up*, N.Y. POST, Jan. 18, 2003, at 014.

87. *See* Mary Flood & Tom Fowler, *Grand Jurors Eye Lay; $70 Million in Stock Sales Focus of Probe*, HOUS. CHRON., Oct. 24, 2002; *Lay May Face Insider Trading Charges*, Aug. 29, 2002, *at* http://www.nysscpa.org/home/2002/802/4week/article40.htm (last visited Mar. 21, 2006).

88. Many of these commentators fail to note that the facts regarding Lay's numerous securities transactions are significantly different from those regarding the single ImClone stock sale engaged in by Martha Stewart. For example, Lay's sales were made over time, starting in December 2000. *See* Flood & Fowler, *supra* note 87. Some of the sales were made to pay off loans. Some of Lay's sales were made on a programmed basis under a plan meeting the requirements of Rule 10b5-1(c), 17 C.F.R. §240.10b5-1. *Id.* Lay sold his stock back to Enron Corp. (which presumably had at least the same amount of information that Lay individually had at the time of the sale), not to uninformed investors in the open market. *See* Kurt Eichenwald, *Enron Inquiry Is Now Examining Whether Company Inflated Assets*, N.Y. TIMES, Dec. 26, 2002, at A1. Also, Lay sold shares of a corporation of which he then was an insider, not publicly held shares of a third-party corporation. *Id.* Accordingly, he likely would be pursued for enforcement purposes under the classic insider trading theory, while Stewart, who traded in shares of a corporation as to which she is not apparently an insider, is being pursued under a variant of the tippee liability theory. *See supra* note 31. It should be noted here, however, that Stewart also is being pursued in private actions for insider trading in connection with certain sales by her of stock of Martha Stewart Omnimedia, Inc. at times when she allegedly knew that she would be investigated for insider trading violations in connection with her December 2001 sale of ImClone's stock. *See Martha Stewart Sued by Investor*, *at* http://news.bbc.co.uk/1/hi/business/2210598.stm (last visited Mar. 21, 2006) ("The lawsuit alleges that Ms Stewart sold shares in her own company, Martha Stewart Living Omnimedia, because she knew she could be investigated on suspicion of insider trading in the ImClone case."); Smith, *supra* note 2 ("Stewart dumped 3 million shares of Martha Stewart Living Omnimedia stock Jan. 8, the same day ImClone first learned it was

the subject of an insider trading probe, according to the suit."). Accordingly, it may be misleading to directly compare possible claims against the two alleged insider traders.

89. *See* Buchanan et al., *supra* note 8; *Cooking with Martha: What's Good for the Goose*, *at* http://www.thedailyenron.com/documents/20020703081640-38022.asp (July 3, 2002); Paula Dwyer, *The Ghosts That Won't Go Away*, Bus. Week, July 22, 2002, at 34; Hill, *supra* note 8; *Martha Stewart Case Reveals Double Standard, supra* note 8; Paul Krugman, *Everyone Is Outraged*, N.Y. Times, July 2, 2002, at A21; Van Susteren, *supra* note 8. *But see* Byron York, *The Democrats' Latest Hit Job*, Nat'l Rev. Online, July 3, 2002, *at* http://www.nationalreview.com/york/york070302.asp (last visited Mar. 21, 2006) (expressing the view that President Bush is being inappropriately targeted). Vice President Dick Cheney's trading transactions in the stock of Halliburton Co. raise similar questions. *See Martha Stewart Case Reveals Double Standard, supra* note 8.

90. *See* Hill, *supra* note 8; *Martha Stewart Case Reveals Double Standard, supra* note 8; Van Susteren, *supra* note 8.

91. *See* Jim Lehrer, *The NewsHour with Jim Lehrer: Building Walls; 401 (Chaos); Language Skills; Political Wrap* (television broadcast, Jan. 18, 2002), *available at* LEXIS, News & Business Library, News Group File; Van Susteren, *supra* note 8

92. *See* sources cited *supra* note 16.

93. *See* http://www.polisci.com/almanac/legis/comm/01060.htm (last visited Jan. 25, 2003) (list of members of the House Committee on Energy and Commerce). As a whole, the House of Representatives for the 107th Congress (during which time Martha Stewart's investigative hearings were conducted) consisted of 221 Republicans, 212 Democrats, and two others. *See* http://clerk.house.gov/histHigh/Congressional_History/partyDiv.php (last visited Oct. 3, 2003).

94. 15 U.S.C. §78(d)(a) (2003).

95. *See* Pitt & Shapiro, *supra* note 10, at 169–70. Among other things, the President's political party affiliation and the political party composition of Congress may impact the extent to which politics influences SEC enforcement.

96. *See* Beard & Earle, *supra* note 5; Begala & Carlson, *supra* note 8; Borger, *supra* note 8; *Crossfire-McAuliffe, supra* note 8; *Crossfire-Scapegoat, supra* note 8; Jenkins, *supra* note 8. *But see* Greising, *supra* note 4 (discounting the impact of Stewart's "big name" on her possible liability for violation of insider trading prohibitions). The specter of public figure bias, which can benefit or detriment a putative defendant, has been noted by a number of commentators. *See* Dooley, *supra* note 26, at 323 ("publicity and other considerations that appear likely to advance the agency's interests often determine its choice of an enforcement target"); Beth A. Wilkinson & Steven H. Schulman, *When Talk is not Cheap: Communications with the Media, the Government and Other Parties in High Profile White Collar Criminal Cases*, 39 Am. Crim. L. Rev. 203, 210 (2002) ("In a close case, where the question of whether to indict is one of clear prosecutorial discretion, the prosecutor knows he is unlikely to be second-guessed for failing to indict a media darling."). Former SEC Chairman Harvey Pitt once wrote (referring to the SEC) that "[w]hen required to choose between proceeding against a relatively nondescript target and a highly visible one … an enforcement agency generally is apt to choose the highly visible target if it wants to achieve the greatest deterrent effect for its enforcement efforts.… A case of smaller dimensions (in terms of the magnitude or complexity of the illegal conduct alleged) with a more visible target may be deemed to be more appropriate than a larger case with a less visible target." Pitt & Shapiro, *supra* note 10, at 184.

97. *See* Jenkins, *supra* note 8. The choice to prosecute female public figures is also a common use of enforcement discretion. *See* sources cited *supra* note 16. In addition to the Leona Helmsley case earlier referenced, there have been many notable female celebrity prosecutions for alleged or actual criminal violations of various kinds. Among the more memorable modern female celebrity prosecutions are those of Zsa Zsa Gabor (driving without a license and related charges) and, more recently, Winona Ryder (shoplifting). *See* Nick Madigan, *Actress Sentenced to Probation for Shoplifting*, N.Y. TIMES, Dec. 7, 2002, at A12; *Meeting Again*, N.Y. TIMES, Mar. 4, 1990, Sec. 4, at 7. The notoriety of celebrity defendants in these and other cases effectively turns each defendant into a media-sponsored "poster child" for a public service campaign against the crime allegedly committed.

98. *See* Matthew Arnold, *Celebrity Clients—Shielding Your Client From Overexposure*, PR WEEK (US), Sept. 30, 2002, at 20; Borger, *supra* note 8; Kudlow, *supra* note 4; Stanley & Hays, *supra* note 8. A serious question exists as to whether the media may advantage or disadvantage a public figure criminal defendant at and prior to trial. *See* Mumford, *supra* note 4, at 171 n.12 (and accompanying text). More specifically, the question should be asked as to whether both Helmsley and Stewart have been prejudged in the media to such an extent that bias is the logical result. *Id.* at 175. Media coverage of the Martha Stewart investigation has been extraordinary and wide-ranging. *See* Toobin, *supra* note 4. Even cartoonists have gotten into the act, many of whom have featured Stewart in jail-related cartoons that mock her public identity as a style maven. *See* Martha Stewart Jokes, *at* http://politicalhumor.about.com/cs/marthastewart/index.htm (last visited Mar. 21, 2006). Moreover, since the filing of the criminal indictment and civil enforcement action against her, Stewart has fought back in the news media. On June 5, 2003, Stewart purchased a full-page advertisement in *USA Today* stating her innocence and inviting the public to her "special Website," http://www.marthatalks.com. *See An Open Letter From Martha Stewart*, USA TODAY, June 5, 2003, at 7A. In its first 17 hours, the website received 1.7 million hits. *See* Bruce Horowitz, *Stewart uploads her cause to Web site*, USA TODAY, June 6, 2003, at 1B. This Web site no longer is active.

99. *See* Zahn, *supra* note 77.

100. *See supra* note 77.

101. In this area of inquiry, Martha Stewart's gender and public figure status fuse to form a unified, if somewhat contradictory, analytical whole. If Leona Helmsley is "the apotheosis of the punishment of the 1980s stereotype career woman," Mumford, *supra* note 4, at 176–79, then Martha Stewart is her parallel in the early 21st century. There exist in the public those who are delighted to see Stewart fall from grace. *See* Stanley & Hays, *supra* note 8. One journalist aptly notes:

> Let's face it: Martha can't catch a break. Not only is she a high-profile woman; she's also an easy target as an insider who broke into the boys club of finance. Now she's getting punished for her temerity. "How many men who have been accused of insider trading have been treated this way?" asks Betty Spence, President of the National Association for Female Executives. "The coverage is this big because she's a woman." Was Ken Lay ever accused, as Stewart was, of "clawing" his way to the top?
>
> Then again, it's not only the men who are making fun of Martha; we women are having at it, too. Some of us just don't like her, which is allowed. But why cheer for her failure? Maybe it's because there's a certain elite comfort that Martha's success comes from the celebration of the very kitchen that we baby

boom women pledged to escape. Or maybe it's because there's no missing the obvious irony of perfect Martha Stewart making a mess. We love irony, not ironing.

Borger, *supra* note 8.

102. *See* http://www.savemartha.com (last visited Mar. 21, 2006) (a website apparently created and supported by Martha Stewart sympathizers that features and links to information regarding the Martha Stewart investigation and purveys related products); http://www.surrendermartha.com (last visited Mar. 21, 2006) (a website formerly featuring products unsympathetic to Martha Stewart that now purveys unrelated merchandise).

103. *See* MARSHALL MCLUHAN, UNDERSTANDING MEDIA 215 (Seventh Printing 1998) ("[I]n its selection of the newsworthy, the press prefers those persons who have already been accorded some notoriety existence in movies, radio, TV, and drama."). Moreover, because the press views bad news as the only real news, *see id.* at 205, it desires to unmask and document deemed falls from grace. *See* Arnold, *supra* note 98; Borger, *supra* note 8; Stanley & Hays, *supra* note 8.

104. *See* Byron, *supra* note 4; Phillips et al., *supra* note 10, at 35 ("[I]nvestigations sometimes are undertaken into seemingly minor violations because they relate to activities that have received significant press coverage....").

105. Interestingly, however, many members of the November 2002 audience for delivery of an early draft of the law review article that formed the basis for this chapter, were quick to comment that one or more of the identified bases for bias in the Martha Stewart matter, taken in the context of U.S. insider trading regulation and the then publicized facts regarding Stewart's December 2001 sale of ImClone stock, indicate actual bias, at least circumstantially. Although this chapter acknowledges the potential validity of that viewpoint, the author recommends a more conservative approach to the determination of actual bias in the Martha Stewart matter, preferring instead to use the chapter both as a vehicle for identification of the potential for the existence of actual bias in and outside the Martha Stewart case and as an impetus for further, more thorough, analysis.

106. Although this appears to be a safe and conservative approach, the retrieval and analysis of empirical data on actual bias has some risks. For one thing, the research design or implementation may be faulty. For another, results of the research, regardless of the integrity and accuracy of that research, erroneously may be considered conclusive for all purposes, for all time, thereby affecting legislative, regulatory, enforcement, and societal behavior in ways that ultimately prove to be inconsistent with the policy underpinnings of U.S. insider trading regulation or otherwise undesirable. *See* Theresa A Gabaldon, *Assumptions About Relationships Reflected in the Federal Securities Laws*, 17 WIS. WOMEN'S L.J. 215, 248–49 (2002).

107. *See* Kane, *supra* note 13, at 2306 (discussing reforms that would allow the use of statistical evidence of racial discrimination in making a case for discriminatory prosecution); Mumford, *supra* note 4, at 184 ("[U]ntil the experience of women at the hands of the tax collection authorities in both the UK and the U.S. is addressed, the foundations for understanding will remain incomplete.").

108. Research of varying kinds already has been conducted to identify bias in a number of contexts. *See, e.g.,* Bowman, *supra* note 74, at 165–68 (gender bias in the courts); Kane, *supra* note 13, at 2295–300 (racial bias in criminal investigations and prosecutions).

109. The SEC has a web site (http://www.sec.gov) with significant amounts of information on charges and settlements, among other things. Regrettably, however, the site has only limited search capabilities. Accordingly, even if relevant information about the

defendant (e.g., gender, political party affiliation, public-figure status, etc.) were available through the site, the site would not permit ready access to that information. The web site for the U.S. Department of Justice (http://www.usdoj.gov), while also a fine source of public information, is similarly unhelpful in regard to obtaining evidence of actual bias.

110. 5 U.S.C. §552 (2003). Certain memoranda circulated internally within the executive branch may, however, be privileged and not subject to mandatory disclosure under the FOIA. *See* Kane, *supra* note 13, at 2308.

111. Dave Barry, *Crack Accounting*, Wash. Post, Aug. 4, 2002, at W32; Chris Bury & Dave Marash, *Nightline: A Matter of Trust: Has Main Street Lost Faith in Wall Street?* (ABC News television broadcast, June 13, 2002), *available at* LEXIS, News & Business Library, News Group File; Chris Reidy, *Seeking Calm for Roiled Markets*, B. Globe, July 12, 2002, at C1.

112. As one scholar cogently summarizes:

> Why is the insider's use of nonpublic information unfair? The answer can be explained, in part, by the importance of the capital markets to the large publicly held corporation. Absent a system in which corporations have ready access to capital markets, access which is facilitated by the availability of safe, liquid, regulated markets for secondary trading, the public corporation would be unlikely to attain the same size and dominance. This growth, in turn, provides management with unparalleled opportunities for wealth and status. Thus, in a sense, the corporate insider's superior access, due to his position, may be partially attributed to government and public participation in the markets. It is the fact that an insider has obtained his informational advantage because of his position, *and* the fact that this position is attributable to the presence of other less-privileged transactors in the market, that makes the insider's use of nonpublic information unfair.

Fisch, *supra* note 13, at 227–28. *See also* Nagy, *supra* note 40, at 1271–72 (referring to general insider trading policy underlying the misappropriation theory of liability). Said another way, U.S. insider trading regulation is designed to prevent insiders from benefiting personally from any information advantage they may have over other traders in the secondary markets.

113. It should be noted that the implementation of substantive or procedural changes in U.S. insider trading regulation might not correct observed decision making biases. The corrective capacity of law and regulation in addressing biases is unclear, at best. *See* Stephen M. Bainbridge, *Mandatory Disclosure: A Behavioral Analysis*, 68 U. Cin. L. Rev. 1023, 1056–58 (2000).

114. For an intriguing set of proposals along these lines, see Gabaldon, *supra* note 106, at 248 (2002) (suggesting, among other things, mandatory reporting by those with whom insiders have privately discussed the issuer's business and the imposition of liability on any of those people if he, she, or it trades in the issuer's securities before the information becomes public).

115. Reform of this nature often has been suggested. *See generally*, Fisch, *supra* note 13. The SEC's promulgation of Rules 10b5-1, 17 C.F.R. §240.10b5-1, and 10b5-2, 17 C.F.R. §240.10b5-2, and its issuance of *Staff Accounting Bulletin No. 99*, at http://www.sec.gov/interps/account/sab99.htm (last modified Aug. 18, 1999), represent steps in the direction of enhanced clarity.

116. Based on the SEC Complaint and news accounts, it is possible that this is the only information that Martha Stewart had when she made her December 2001 trade in ImClone shares. *See supra* notes 2, 7.

117. *See* Susan E. Spangler, *Snatching Legislative Power: the Justice Department's Refusal to Enforce the Parental Kidnapping Prevention Act*, Comment, 73 J. CRIM. L. & CRIMINOL-OGY 1176, 1200 n.113 (1982) ("Professor Davis ... has argued that 'the assumptions on which prosecutors' uncontrolled discretion is founded are in need of reexamination ... that a full study of the prosecuting power is likely to produce a movement in the direction of greater control of discretion, through more confinement, more structuring, more checks, and more procedural protections.'"). The benefits of clear, written, enforcement guidelines may extend beyond the alleged insider traders to the government agencies and the public at large. *See* Kane, *supra* note 13, at 2307.

118. This phrase is borrowed from the 1994 Paramount Pictures film of the same name, based on a novel by Tom Clancy and starring Harrison Ford, but also was earlier used by Justice Oliver Wendell Holmes in *Schenck v. United States*, 249 U.S. 47 (1919).

119. *See* Fisch, *supra* note 13.

120. It should be noted that substantive or procedural reform in U.S. insider trading regulation also may ensure more efficient and effective resource utilization in the pursuit of alleged insider traders, although that matter is beyond the scope of this chapter.

CHAPTER 2

DID OVERCRIMINALIZATION ALLOW FOR THE PROSECUTION OF MARTHA STEWART?[*]

Ellen S. Podgor

Prosecutorial discretion plays an important role in deciding who will be charged with criminal conduct and what, if any, charges will be pursued.[1] As a result of numerous factors, prosecutorial power has expanded in recent years. For one, there is an increased number of federal criminal statutes. Further, broad interpretations of these statutes play a key role in offering new options for prosecutors as they exercise their discretion. Prosecutors also have the liberty to charge "cover-up" crimes,[2] such as making false statements or obstructing justice, as opposed to proceeding against the underlying conduct. Additionally, prosecutors have significant leeway in pursuing extraterritorial conduct, and they may now proceed against conduct that at one time may have been left to civil actions. Finally, the administration's decision to proceed outside the criminal justice process through use of the "enemy combatant" status has offered prosecutors an additional option.

In examining new dimensions to prosecutorial discretion, this chapter looks at the exercise of discretion in the charging of Martha Stewart with criminal conduct. The question asked here is whether prosecutors had too much discretion in deciding whether Martha Stewart should have been charged with a crime.

---

[*] This chapter is derived from *Jose Padilla and Martha Stewart: Who Should Be Charged With Criminal Conduct?*, originally published at 109 PENN ST. L. REV. 1059 (2005), Ellen S. Podgor © 2005.

Expanded Prosecutorial Discretion

Increased Federal Legislation

On May 11, 1998, in an address to the 75th Annual American Law Institute Meeting, Chief Justice William H. Rehnquist described the burden on the federal system of justice caused by over-federalization.[3] He repeated earlier criticisms of "Congress and the President for their propensity to enact more and more legislation, which brings more and more cases into the federal court system."[4]

The impact of federalization on the criminal justice process received heightened consideration when the American Bar Association appointed a task force to examine this issue in 1998. The ABA Report on the "Federalization of Criminal Law," a report from a committee chaired by Edwin Meese, III and William W. Taylor, III, stressed the "dramatic increase in the number and variety of federal crimes."[5] A startling statistic from this Report was that "of all federal crimes enacted since 1865, over forty percent [were] created since 1970."[6] The Report told of how new crimes are added to the role of federal criminality "not because federal prosecution of these crimes is necessary but because federal crime legislation in general is thought to be politically popular."[7]

The dismay with increased federalization is not unique to one political party. It is a problem seen by groups espousing a wide array of political and ideological views. For example, the Heritage Foundation has a special group that regularly meets to discuss overcriminalization concerns.[8] Likewise, the National Association of Criminal Defense Lawyers ("NACDL") notes overfederalization as one of its missions, "urg[ing] Congress to reject its tendency to federalize crime and repeal legislation that is contrary to our system of federalism and sound crime control policy."[9] In a 1998 article, then NACDL President Gerald B. Lefcourt, National District Attorneys Association President William L. Murphy, and ABA Criminal Justice Section Chair Ronald Goldstock stated that,

> [c]riminal and social problems are increasingly being addressed by the Congress with what many have come to regard as a purely political response—calls to federalize more criminal activity and to lengthen already unwieldy prison terms.... There can be little doubt that increased federal prosecutive authority has adversely affected the Department of Justice's ability to fulfill its role of enforcing traditional federal offenses.... [10]

Overbroad Federal Statutes

The increase in new legislation, permitting increased federal prosecution, is not the only cause of overfederalization and overcriminalization. There is also legislation that lacks sufficient specificity, allowing prosecutors to use federal statutes to bring into the federal system conduct that is normally handled by state and local bodies.[11]

Generic statutes allow federal prosecutors discretion to proceed criminally against conduct that might normally be considered state or local criminal activity. For example, the mail fraud statute,[12] an 1872 federal statute that was focused on re-codifying the Postal Act and criminalizing lottery schemes that used the postal system, allows for federal prosecution of a wide array of conduct.[13] Jed Rakoff, now a federal district court judge, has called the mail fraud statute the prosecutor's "Stradivarius" or "Colt 45."[14] Schemes to defraud, whether they involve diet drug fraud,[15] "divorce mill" fraud,[16] or securities fraud,[17] may lead to charges of mail fraud when there is some mailing, no matter how "routine" or "innocent" the mailing might be.[18] The Supreme Court has stated that the mailing does not have to be an essential part of the scheme to defraud.[19]

Equally permissive is the wire fraud statute, a law that was modeled after the mail fraud statute, although enacted in 1952.[20] Even when the wire used as the basis for the prosecution passes from one place within a state to another place within the same state, wire fraud may be charged if the wire happened to have passed, unbeknownst to the sender, outside the state.[21]

Prosecutors also have enormous discretion to bring criminal charges for conspiracy to defraud, which Justice Learned Hand referred to as the "darling of the modern prosecutor's nursery."[22] Under the generic conspiracy statute, prosecutors can bring charges of conspiracy to commit a specific offense or a conspiracy to defraud the government. When conspiracy to defraud is alleged, there are few restraints on the government's ability to prosecute.[23] As noted by Professor Abraham Goldstein, "[t]he phrase [conspiracy to defraud] has had no fixed meaning."[24]

Congress sometimes increases the possibility of new conduct being covered by existing statutes through statutory amendments that are tacked onto legislation with no relationship to the amendment. For example, Congress increased the scope of the mail fraud statute in an amendment included in the Anti-Drug Abuse Act of 1988, where Congress defined a scheme or artifice to defraud to include "a scheme or artifice to deprive another of the 'intangible right of honest services.'"[25] Congress went even further when it added in 1994, as part of the Violent Crime Control and Law Enforcement Act of 1994, that mail fraud would no longer require a mailing.[26] Mail fraud charges may now be brought if the accused deposits or causes to be deposited "any matter or thing whatever to be sent or delivered by any private or commercial interstate carrier."[27]

Courts have imposed some limits when executive discretion appears to stretch a statute beyond its intent. For example, in the case of *United States v. Brown*,[28] the Eleventh Circuit Court of Appeals, in reversing a mail fraud conviction, stated that "the fraud statutes do not cover all behavior which strays from the ideal; Congress has not yet criminalized all sharp conduct, manipulative acts, or unethical transactions."[29] Court-imposed limits, such as those imposed on the mail fraud statute, however, are not a commonplace occurrence.

Statutes Charging Extraneous Conduct

In addition to an increased number of federal criminal statutes, and the enormous breadth of many statutes that allow for a wide range of conduct to be prosecuted, prosecutors have a further tool: crimes that do not explicitly relate to the conduct under investigation, but arise as a result of the investigation itself. These crimes, sometimes termed "cover-up" crimes,[30] include offenses such as making false statements,[31] obstructing justice,[32] and committing perjury.[33]

Prosecutors need tools to protect witnesses providing information during an investigation. They also need tools to protect the evidence that is the subject of the investigation, as receiving truthful information before a grand jury is important in criminal prosecutions.

An individual who lies to a government investigator is subject to a charge of making a false statement under the false statement statute.[34] Likewise, committing perjury and making a false declaration are charges used when someone does not testify truthfully in a court or provides conflicting statements.[35] Finally, obstruction of justice is a charge used when someone destroys documents, intimidates witnesses, or impedes the government's investigation of a matter. [36]

Often, these statutes are easier to satisfy than statutes addressing the actual criminal conduct.[37] Thus, there is a strong advantage if the prosecution can proceed under one of these statutes, as opposed to proceeding directly against the criminal conduct that was the subject of the initial investigation.

Extraterritorial Prosecutions

As a result of globalization, there is a wider range of conduct that can be prosecuted in the federal system.[38] Prosecutors may prosecute extraterritorial conduct when the company or activity involved in the alleged criminality is entirely outside the United States.[39] In some instances, the statutes focus specifically on the extraterritorial conduct, as with the Foreign Corrupt Practices Act.[40] In other instances, however, the statute may fail to specify whether extraterritorial conduct may be prosecuted, and prosecutors may proceed premised on a theory of objective territoriality, a theory that permits prosecution of conduct that "effects" the United States.[41] In a globalized world, conduct that might previously have had little influence on the United States may now easily rise to the level of having an "effect" on the country.[42]

Civil v. Criminal Prosecution

Prosecutorial discretion, thus, is in part a function of the increased number of statutes available for prosecuting conduct, the existence of overbroad statutes that allow for a wide range of conduct to be subject to federal prosecution, and extraterritorial application that allows not only for state and local conduct, but also international conduct, to be the subject of a criminal prosecution in the United States. Another factor is whether an individual is charged with criminal conduct or whether the activity might fall outside the criminal justice system.

Prosecutors often have the discretion to proceed with either criminal or civil actions, and in many instances, they have the option to proceed with both. This is particularly true with tax cases,[43] securities matters,[44] and antitrust actions.[45] All of the statutes covering these areas of law not only provide for civil remedies, but also permit criminal actions. Some statutes place a higher burden on the government in criminal matters, such as requiring an explicit *mens rea* of willfulness.[46] When proceeding criminally, a prosecutor also has the added burden of proving his or her case beyond a reasonable doubt.

Professors John Coffee[47] and Kenneth Mann[48] have written about activity that falls within both the criminal and civil spheres. As stated by Professor Coffee, "the criminal sanction has been applied broadly, and sometimes thoughtlessly, to a broad range of essentially civil obligations, some of which were intended as aspirational standards and others which are inherently open-ended and evolving in character."[49]

Proceeding Outside the Criminal Justice Process

A relatively unused avenue, until recently, was for the government to proceed outside the criminal justice process by not bringing criminal charges, but by holding an individual as an "enemy combatant." In the recent Supreme Court decision of *Hamdi v. Rumsfeld*, the Court considered, *inter alia*, whether the government had the authority to hold a United States citizen as an enemy combatant.[50] Hamdi, who was detained and interrogated in Afghanistan, was transferred to the United States naval base in Guantanamo in January 2002. Upon finding that he was an American citizen, the government transferred him to a naval brig in Norfolk, Virginia, where he remained until sent to a brig in Charleston, South Carolina.[51] The government maintained that Hamdi could be held indefinitely as an enemy combatant.[52]

As a result of a Petition for Writ of Habeas Corpus, filed by Hamdi's father, the Supreme Court reviewed this custodial arrangement. The Court cited a post-September 11 Congressional action authorizing the use of military force as the basis for holding Hamdi as an enemy combatant. It ruled that the government could, in fact, hold as enemy combatants "individual[s] who, it alleges, [were] 'part of or supporting forces hostile to the United States or coalition partners' in Afghanistan and who 'engaged in an armed conflict against the United States' there."[53] Although the Court held that there is "no bar to this Nation's holding one of its own citizens as an enemy combatant," it is necessary to determine that the individual is, in fact, an enemy combatant.[54] The Court stated that "due process demands that a citizen held in the United States as an enemy combatant be given a meaningful opportunity to contest the factual basis for that detention before a neutral decision maker."[55] "[A] citizen-detainee seeking to challenge his classification as an enemy combatant must receive notice of the factual basis for his classification, and a fair opportunity to rebut the Government's factual assertions before a neutral decision maker."[56]

Hamdi's case is another example of the government's enormous discretion in deciding whether to proceed outside the criminal process. Originally held as an enemy combatant, he was eventually released by the government and sent to Saudi Arabia upon forfeiture of his U.S. citizenship.[57]

In the case of John Walker Lindh, prosecutors elected not to go outside of the criminal justice process.[58] Lindh eventually pled guilty in the Eastern District of Virginia District Court for the crimes of supplying services to the Taliban and of "carrying an explosive during the commission of a felony."[59] He received a sentence, pursuant to a plea agreement, of twenty years.[60] Concern about the possibility of the government proceeding outside the criminal justice process is noted in the Lindh plea agreement, which explicitly states that "the United States agrees to forego any right it has to treat the defendant as an unlawful enemy combatant" unless the defendant engages in future terrorist conduct.[61]

Martha Stewart

Martha Stewart was prosecuted within our judicial process. She was charged with extraneous or "cover-up"[62] conduct. As opposed to charging her with insider trading, the conduct being investigated, prosecutors presented evidence that eventually led to Stewart's conviction of an alleged scheme to obstruct justice, making false statements, and obstruction of an agency proceeding.[63] Less known and discussed by the press is the civil suit filed by the Securities and Exchange Commission against Martha Stewart and Peter Bacanovic.[64] This civil action, which was settled in August 2006, asked for remedies, such as disgorgement of the profits from the sale of ImClone stock, a stock that eventually went up in value.[65]

In the criminal action, Stewart received a jury conviction, a five-month jail sentence, followed by a five-month house arrest and two year's probation, and a $30,000 fine.[66] Some claim that this sentence is too lenient, while others are horrified by its harshness. As noted in a headline in the Christian Science Monitor, "Stewart's Sentence Leaves Few Satisfied."[67]

U.S. Attorney David Kelley claimed that Stewart was prosecuted in order to protect "the integrity of this system."[68] The bottom line, however, is that Martha Stewart was never prosecuted for the criminal acts which were initially under investigation. Accordingly, the Stewart case is also an example of the government proceeding both civilly and criminally against the same defendant. Prosecutorial discretion permitted this to happen.

Conclusion

The Martha Stewart prosecution revolves around the government's desire to obtain information. In the case of Martha Stewart, the government wanted information and called on her to speak before the Securities and Exchange Commission. She went, and she talked, but they did not like what was said. Therefore, they proceeded to charge her with crimes related to lying instead of proceeding exclusively in the civil sphere or charging substantive crimes. Although the government aim may have been to send a message that it is improper to lie before an administrative agency, one has to wonder if the message received will be to tell individuals not to voluntarily speak with the government.

Broad prosecutorial discretion warrants oversight. In the Martha Stewart case prosecutors had too many choices, little guidance in making the choices, and no real oversight of the decisions made. The legislature's overcriminalization and overfederalization provided much of this discretion, discretion that seriously impedes uniformity in the federal criminal justice system.

Questions

1. What choices did prosecutors have in deciding whether to proceed against Martha Stewart?
2. What is the effect of the choice taken by prosecutors to proceed against Martha Stewart with charges of obstruction of justice and will this prosecution have a deterrent effect on future criminality?
3. Is there a problem in the criminal justice system when prosecutors can proceed against Martha Stewart with criminal charges and yet hold others outside the criminal justice system as enemy combatants?

Notes

1. *See* Richard Bloom, *Prosecutorial Discretion*, 87 GEO L.J. 1267 (1999); Ellen S. Podgor, *Department of Justice Guidelines: Balancing "Discretionary Justice,"* 13 CORNELL J.L. & PUB. POL'Y 167 (2004); Ellen S. Podgor, *The Ethics and Professionalism of Prosecutors in Discretionary Decisions*, 68 FORDHAM L. REV. 1511 (2000).

2. *See generally* Kathleen F. Brickey, *From Enron to WorldCom and Beyond: Life and Crime After Sarbanes-Oxley*, 81 WASH. U. L.Q. 357 (2003) (explaining how the Sarbanes-Oxley Act provided prosecutors with new mechanisms for prosecuting fraud); Kathleen F. Brickey, *Andersen's Fall from Grace*, 81 WASH. U. L.Q. 917 (2003) (explaining how a recently enacted witness tampering statute allowed the government to charge Andersen with obstruction of justice despite the fact that no legal proceedings were pending at the time that documents were destroyed); Stuart P. Green, *Uncovering the Cover-up Crime*, 42 AM. CRIM. L. REV. 9 (2005); Geraldine Szott Moohr, *An Enron Lesson: The Modest Role of Criminal Law in Preventing Corporate Crime*, 55 FLA. L. REV. 937 (2003).

3. Chief Justice William H. Rehnquist, Remarks at the 75th Annual American Law Institute Meeting (May 11, 1998) (on file with author), also excerpted in *Chief Justice Raises Concerns on Federalization*, 30 THE THIRD BRANCH (Administrative Office of the United States Courts, Washington D.C.), June, 1998, at 1, *available at* http://www.uscourts.gov/ttb/jun98ttb/index.html (last visited Feb. 18, 2005).

4. *Id.*

5. James A. Strazzella, *The Federalization of Criminal Law*, 1998 A.B.A. CRIM. JUST. SEC. 2.

6. *Id.*

7. *Id. See also* James Strazzella, *The Federal Role in Criminal Law*, 543 ANNALS AM. ACAD. POL. & SOC. SCI. 9 (1996) (providing a broad overview of the influence that federal legislation and federal courts have on criminal law and introducing articles on the topic by other commentators).

8. *See* Paul Rosenzweig, *The Over-Criminalization of Social and Economic Conduct*, HERITAGE FOUND. POL'Y RES. & ANALYSIS (April 17, 2003), *at* http:// www.heritage.org/Research/LegalIssues/lm7.cfm (last visited Feb. 15, 2005); *see also* http://www.overcriminalized.com/ (last visited Feb. 15, 2005).

9. National Association of Criminal Defense, *Legislation: Overfederalization*, at http://www.nacdl.org/public.nsf/legislation/overcriminalization (last visited Feb. 15, 2005).

10. Ronald Goldstock, Gerald Lefcourt & William Murphy, *Justice That Makes Sense*, 21 CHAMPION 6, 7–8 (1997).

11. In some cases, these statutes are subject to challenges for being vague. *See generally* Anthony G. Amsterdam, Note, *The Void-for-Vagueness Doctrine in the Supreme Court*, 109 U. PA. L. REV. 67 (1960); Robert Batey, *Vagueness and the Construction of Criminal Statutes—Balancing Acts*, 5 VA. J. SOC. POL'Y & L. 1 (1997).

12. 18 U.S.C. § 1341 (2005).

13. *See* Ellen S. Podgor, *Mail Fraud: Opening Letters*, 43 S. C. L. REV. 223 (1992); Ellen S. Podgor, *Do We Need a "Beanie Baby" Fraud Statute?*, 49 AM. U. L. REV. 1031 (2000).

14. Jed S. Rakoff, *The Federal Mail Fraud Statute*, 18 DUQ. L. REV. 771, 771 (1980).

15. *See* United States v. Andreadis, 366 F.2d 423 (2d Cir. 1966).

16. *See* United States v. Edwards, 458 F.2d 875, 878 (5th Cir. 1972).

17. *See* Carpenter v. United States, 484 U.S. 19 (1987).

18. *See* Schmuck v. United States, 489 U.S. 705, 715 (1989) (stating that the Court's precedents do not preclude routine and innocent mailings from fulfilling the mailing element of the mail fraud statute and citing Carpenter, 484 U.S. at 28, in support); *see also* Pereira v. United States, 347 U.S. 1, 8–9 (1954) (explaining that the mailing does not need to be contemplated as an essential element of the fraud and that one can be found to have caused a mailing even if he did not intend to do so, but knew or could foresee that the mails would be used in the ordinary course of business).

19. *See Schmuck*, 489 U.S. at 711.

20. *See* 18 U.S.C. § 1343 (2005).

21. *See* United States v. Bryant, 766 F.2d 370, 375 (8th Cir. 1985).

22. Harrison v. United States, 7 F.2d 259, 263 (2d Cir. 1925).

23. See 18 U.S.C.A. § 371 (2005). There is detailed information related to the scope of acceptable prosecutorial conduct in the Notes and Decisions, Section VII.

24. Abraham S. Goldstein, *Conspiracy to Defraud the United States*, 68 YALE L.J. 405, 417 (1959). *See also* Ellen S. Podgor, *Criminal Fraud*, 48 AM. U. L. REV. 729, 730–31 (1999).

25. 18 U.S.C. § 1346 (2005).

26. Violent Crime Control and Law Enforcement Act of 1994, Pub. L. No. 103-322, § 250006, 108 Stat. 1796, 2087 (1994).

27. *Id.*

28. United States v. Brown, 79 F.3d 1550 (11th Cir. 1996).

29. *Id.* at 1562.

30. *See generally* Brickey, *From Enron to WorldCom and Beyond*, *supra* note 2; Brickey, *Andersen's Fall from Grace*, *supra* note 2; Green, *supra* note 2; Moohr, *supra* note 2.

31. *See* 18 U.S.C. § 1001 (2000).

32. *See id.* §§ 1501–1520.

33. *See id.* § 1621.

34. *Id.* § 1001(a).

35. *See id.* §§ 1621, 1623.

36. *See* 18 U.S.C. § 1503 (2004).

37. *See* Brogan v. United States, 522 U.S. 398, 416 (1998) (Ginsburg, J., concurring) ("The prospect remains that an overzealous prosecutor or investigator—aware that a person has committed some suspicious acts, but unable to make a criminal case—will create a crime by

surprising the suspect, asking about those acts, and receiving a false denial."); *Martha Stewart Misgivings*, WALL ST. J., Mar. 8, 2004, at A16.

38. *See generally* Ellen S. Podgor, *"Defensive Territoriality": A New Paradigm for the Prosecution of Extraterritorial Business Crimes*, 31 GA. J. INT'L & COMP. L. 1 (2002).

39. *See* United States v. Nippon Paper Indus. Co., 109 F.3d 1, 4 (1st Cir. 1997).

40. *See* 15 U.S.C. § 78dd-1 (2000).

41. *See, e.g.*, United States v. Larsen, 952 F.2d 1099, 1100–01 (9th Cir. 1991); Chua Han Mow v. United States, 730 F.2d 1308, 1311–12 (9th Cir. 1984).

42. The Supreme Court heard oral arguments on November 9, 2004 regarding "whether application of the common law revenue rule puts beyond the reach of the federal wire fraud statute, 18 U.S.C. § 1343, the use of interstate wires for the purpose of executing a scheme to defraud a foreign sovereign of its property rights in accrued tax revenue." United States v. Pasquantino, 336 F.3d 321 (4th Cir. 2003), *cert. granted*, 124 S. Ct. 1875 (2004).

43. *See, e.g.*, United States v. LaSalle Nat'l Bank, 437 U.S. 298, 311 (1978).

44. *See* 17 C.F.R. § 240.10b-5 (2006).

45. *See* 15 U.S.C. § 1 (2004).

46. *See, e.g.*, Sansone v. United States, 380 U.S. 343, 344 (1965) (examining § 7201 of the Internal Revenue Code of 1954).

47. *See, e.g.*, John C. Coffee, Jr., *Paradigms Lost: The Blurring of the Criminal and Civil Law Models - And What Can Be Done About It*, 101 YALE L.J. 1875 (1992).

48. *See, e.g.*, Kenneth Mann, Punitive Civil Sanctions: *The Middleground Between Criminal and Civil Law*, 101 YALE L.J. 1795 (1992).

49. John C. Coffee, Jr., *Does "Unlawful" Mean "Criminal"?: Reflections on the Disappearing Tort/Crime Distinction in American Law*, 71 B.U. L. REV. 193, 201 (1991).

50. Hamdi v. Rumsfeld, 124 S. Ct. 2633, 2635 (2004) (plurality opinion).

51. *Id.* at 2636.

52. *Id.*

53. *Id.* at 2639.

54. *Id.* at 2640.

55. *Id.* at 2625.

56. Hamdi v. Rumsfeld, 124 S. Ct. 2633, 2648 (2004) (plurality opinion).

57. *See* Joel Brinkley, *From Afghanistan to Saudi Arabia, via Guantanamo*, N.Y. TIMES, Oct. 16, 2004, at A4.

58. *See* Guy Taylor, *Top Court Hears 'Enemy Combatant' Case; Lawyers Urge Criminal Trial for U.S. Citizens*, WASH. TIMES, April 29, 2004, at A04.

59. Plea Agreement at 1, U.S. v. Lindh, No. 02-37A (E.D. Va.), *available at* http://news.findlaw.com/hdocs/docs/lindh/uslindh71502pleaag.pdf (last visited Feb. 19, 2005).

60. *Id.* at 2.

61. *Id.* at 9. The plea agreement in the Lindh case came under scrutiny when the government decided that Hamdi could be released. *See John Walker Lindh is Asking President Bush to Reduce His 20-Year Prison Sentence After Being Convicted of Helping the Taliban* (NPR radio broadcast, Sept. 29, 2004).

62. *See supra* note 2. *See also* Ellen S. Podgor, Arthur Andersen, *LLP, and Martha Stewart: Should Materiality be an Element of Obstruction of Justice?*, 44 WASHBURN L.J. 583 (2005).

63. United States v. Stewart, No. S1 03 Cr. 717 (S.D.N.Y.), superseding indictment, *available at* http://news.findlaw.com/hdocs/docs/mstewart/usmspb 10504sind.pdf (last vis-

ited Mar. 19, 2005). *See also* Michael L. Seigel & Christopher Slobogin, *Prosecuting Martha: Federal Prosecutorial Power and the Need for a Law of Counts*, 109 Penn St. L. Rev. 1107 (2005).

64. Complaint, SEC v. Stewart, No. 03 CV 4070 (S.D.N.Y.), *available at* http://news.findlaw.com/hdocs/docs/mstewart/secmspb60403cmp.html (last visited Feb. 19, 2005); *see also* Joan MacLeod Heminway, *Save Martha Stewart? Observations About Equal Justice in U.S. Insider Trading Regulation*, 12 Tex. J. Women & L. 247 (2003).

65. *See* Reuters, *ImClone Swings to a Profit*, CNN Money, July 21, 2004, *at* http://money.cnn.com/2004/07/21/news/midcaps/imclone.reut/index.htm (last visited Feb. 19, 2005).

66. *See* Constance L. Hays, *5 Months in Jail, and Stewart Vows, "I'll Be Back,"* N.Y. Times, July 17, 2004, at A1. On March 18, 2005, the Second Circuit sent the sentencing issue in her case to the district court for review. *See* Kristen Crawford, *Martha Could Get Resentenced*, *available at* http://money.cnn.com/2005/ 03/18/news/newsmakers/martha_sentencing/index.htm (last visited Mar. 18, 2005). The conviction was affirmed by the Second Circuit. *See* United States v. Stewart, 433 F.3d 273 (2d Cir. 2006).

67. Ron Scherer, *Stewart's Sentence Leaves Few Satisfied*, Christian Sci. Monitor, July 19, 2004, *available at* http://www.csmonitor.com/2004/0719/p03s02-usju.html (last visited Feb. 19, 2005).

68. *See Martha Stewart Misgivings*, *supra* note 37.

CHAPTER 3

FEDERAL PROSECUTORIAL POWER AND THE NEED FOR A LAW OF COUNTS[*]

Michael L. Seigel & Christopher Slobogin

Martha Stewart's case has spawned a cottage industry of commentary. Many have pointed out that the well-known queen of domestic perfection was not prosecuted for insider trading—which was the original focus of the government's investigation and the offense that most casual observers think sent her to jail—but rather for *lying* about why she traded, charges that have been characterized as both "trivial" and "extraneous."[1] It has also been argued that, even looking at only those facts most favorable to the government, the insider trading case against Stewart was extremely tenuous (although the SEC brought a civil petition against Stewart on that ground that was eventually settled).[2] On these assumptions, some have suggested that the Stewart prosecution was motivated by sexism or politics, and others view it as proof positive that federal prosecutors have become godlike in their ability to convict anyone they want.[3]

The ills purportedly manifested by Stewart's trial and tribulations range from a paucity of controls over prosecutorial decision-making to the "pathological" proliferation of vague statutes that criminalize innocuous or marginally immoral behavior.[4] Proposed solutions to the types of problems evidenced in the *Stewart* case include more stringent self-regulation of prosecutors based on "proportionality" or "neutrality" principles,[5] adoption of continental practices that better train and monitor prosecutors,[6] and giv-

* This chapter is derived from *Prosecuting Martha: Federal Prosecutorial Power and the Need for a Law of Counts*, 109 PENN ST. L. REV. 1107–1131 (2005), Michael L. Seigel & Christopher Slobogin © 2005.

ing judges the power to "nullify" overbearing prosecutorial charging decisions.[7] The consistent concern underlying these proposals is that prosecutors have too much discretion.

This chapter uses the *Stewart* case to take a closer look at the various types of discretion prosecutors wield. Unlike many other commentators, including some in this volume, we are not persuaded that the case against Stewart was brought in bad faith or that it was unwarranted at its core. As we discuss in the first part of this chapter, prosecutors had ample reason for investigating her conduct and charging her with a crime. At the same time, for reasons advanced in the second section of this chapter, other prosecutorial decisions in her case give us greater pause.

In particular, we critique an aspect of the Stewart prosecution that has yet to be the subject of sustained analysis, having to do with a phenomenon that we call "redundant charging." That phrase refers to prosecutors' nearly unrestricted ability to manufacture closely related charges based on the same course of conduct. After describing the problem, we propose that courts develop a "law of counts" to remedy it.

The Decision to Investigate and Charge Stewart

Far more white collar crime takes place in the United States than federal prosecutors have the resources to pursue.[8] As a result, only a small percentage of this alleged criminal conduct is targeted for federal prosecution. A close look at the winnowing process reveals that prosecutors—and even criminal investigators—play a smaller role in selecting cases for criminal treatment than is commonly believed. Most of the time, white collar investigations are initiated, not by members of the Department of Justice, but by employees of regulatory agencies such as the SEC, IRS, or EPA. Often, the administrative investigation is triggered by a flag raised during a routine screening process. In other cases, the conduct would have escaped official notice (as most white collar crime probably does) but for a citizen's tip—for example, from an estranged spouse, nosy neighbor, or a disgruntled shareholder or employee.

Most white collar crime detected by the government is fully disposed of at the regulatory level.[9] On occasion, however, agency personnel decide, for one reason or another,[10] that the behavior of the putative defendant warrants a criminal investigation. When lower level bureaucrats make such a determination, some form of supervisory review takes place to confirm that a referral for criminal treatment is appropriate. Thus, only a small percentage of white collar cases ever make it to the U.S. Attorney's doorstep.[11]

Even fewer cases get in the door. Due to their relative lack of resources, U.S. Attorney's Offices usually employ a set of intake guidelines to screen out potential cases that are too insignificant to warrant a federal prosecutor's attention. These guidelines vary from office to office, administration to administration, and crime to crime.[12] They depend to some degree on priorities set by the Department of Justice as well as on local conditions. If an agency refers a matter that does not meet the guidelines, it is promptly declined. If the matter meets the guidelines, it is assigned to an Assistant United States Attorney for evaluation and further development.

Something akin to the process just described took place in Martha Stewart's case. On December 31, 2001, the first trading day after the Food and Drug Administration announced publicly that ImClone's key cancer-fighting drug Erbitux had not been approved for further study, the value of ImClone stock dropped a precipitous eighteen percent. Prompted by this development, the internal compliance department of Merrill Lynch reviewed ImClone trading immediately preceding the announcement. It discovered sales by various members of the Waksal family as well as the sale by Martha Stewart. After some further internal investigation, Merrill Lynch referred the matter to the Securities and Exchange Commission ("SEC").[13]

One can only imagine the SEC's reaction to seeing such a famous name appear in the referral. It presumably figured out fairly quickly that Waksal and Stewart were close friends. This raised the specter—wrong as it turned out—that Stewart had traded after receiving an inside tip from the company's CEO.[14] In any event, given these facts, the SEC would have been remiss not to pursue the lead from Merrill Lynch. On January 7, 2002, SEC staff attorneys interviewed Peter Bacanovic, Waksal's former employee as well as his and Stewart's broker at Merrill Lynch.[15] On January 8, the SEC issued a voluntary request for production of documents to ImClone.

It was only at this point, sometime between January 8th and January 25th, that the Federal Bureau of Investigation ("FBI") and the U.S. Attorney's Office actively joined the investigation.[16] Thus the U.S. Attorney's Office's determination to participate in the Stewart case came only after the SEC had been tipped about her potentially illicit trading and its initiation of an official inquiry. From the public record, it is difficult to discern whether the prosecutors were asked aboard by agency investigators or instead learned about the case from another source and joined the investigation on their own. Either way, at the time they became involved, there was significant circumstantial evidence suggesting that Stewart had committed insider trading as a classic tippee—evidence that could not be ignored.

Of course, the possibility exists that prosecutors decided to pursue Stewart's case for suspect reasons, based on sexism, a political agenda, or a desire to bask in the media limelight. But in a high profile case like Stewart's, the conscientious prosecutor is strongly motivated to take a leading role early in the investigation to ensure that no embarrassing missteps take place. Further, it is perfectly legitimate to target conspicuous violators so that the deterrent effect of criminal enforcement is maximized.[17] Perhaps most important, if a high profile case identified by the SEC were *not* aggressively investigated under his or her watch, the U.S. Attorney would undoubtedly be accused of favoring the rich and famous.[18] All of these considerations likely influenced the U.S. Attorney's decision to join and pursue the securities investigation.

But what about the prosecutors' ultimate decision to charge Stewart for lying, rather than insider trading? Once again, we can only speculate as to why the latter charge was not brought. The original theory of the case—that Stewart had traded on a tip from the company's CEO—did not pan out; the tip came solely from inside the brokerage house. Although courts deciding the issue thus far have agreed that this conduct constitutes a violation of insider trading law,[19] the Supreme Court has yet to rule on a case in which a putative inside trader received her tip from a misappropriator. There are several reasons why the U.S. Attorney's Office might not have wanted Stewart's case to be the one to test that proposition in the latter forum (where Stewart surely would have taken it). First, Stewart had the resources to mount the most vigorous, expert defense. Second, the mere fact of Stewart's notoriety might give her a tactical advantage; subconsciously, judges and justices are more likely to have sympathy for someone with fame and fortune. Third, losing to a celebrity at the Supreme Court level would be a conspicuous black eye for the Department of Justice. Better, then, to place this issue on the civil side—which the SEC did—where the government's burden of proof is lower (critical to success on the *mens rea* issue) and where a loss would not be so harmful to the government's prestige.[20]

But then why not leave Stewart alone? Others in this volume express concern over what have been aptly named "sideshow" charges, especially when those charges are primarily based on denials of other, more substantive (alleged) criminal conduct.[21] That concern is appropriate in some cases.[22] But Stewart's cover-up went beyond a simple denial;[23] as we detail in the next section, the prosecution also had solid reason to believe that Stewart had made *numerous* false statements, altered evidence (if only momentarily), and suborned perjury by her broker.

In short, at the time of charging, the prosecution reasonably could have believed that Stewart had done something plainly wrong, separate and apart from trading on inside information. She not only gave into the understandable but regrettable human instinct to dissemble when confronted with a hand in the cookie jar, but she also tried to muddy the evidentiary trail and lasso a colleague into covering up the swindle.[24] Stewart's conduct may have been near the threshold where prosecutors should avoid filing an indictment, but her conduct was not "trivial." And the charges were not "extraneous" to the criminal justice system's legitimate goals of punishing blameworthy actions and ensuring the efficient prosecution of criminal acts.[25]

The Decision to Charge Stewart with Five Counts

Although we think the decision to investigate Martha Stewart and to prosecute her for her cover-up was justifiable, we are more troubled by the *number* and *type* of charges filed against her. The indictment in the *Stewart* case is an illustration of the tremendous power prosecutors have to shape the contours of a crime, and to split it up—perhaps arbitrarily—into many different but overlapping counts. In order to explore these issues further, we begin with a description of that document.

The Indictment

The indictment against Stewart begins with a conspiracy count, and alleges that Stewart and Bacanovic conspired to obstruct justice, make false statements, and commit perjury. The forty-one numbered paragraphs that comprise this count also provide virtually all the allegations supporting the subsequent false statement and obstruction of justice charges. Thus, this part of the indictment must be described not only to understand the conspiracy count but also to grasp the government's entire case against Stewart.

The first twenty-one paragraphs of the conspiracy count provide the government's version of why Stewart sold her shares in ImClone. The indictment details how Bacanovic, Stewart's broker at Merrill Lynch, discovered that Waksal, the president and chief executive officer of ImClone, called in an urgent order to Merrill Lynch to sell all his ImClone stock on the morning of December 27, 2001.[26] It also notes the probable reason Waksal was so persistent about selling at that time: the Food and Drug Administration was about to deny approval for his company's vaunted anti-cancer agent, Erbitux. In fact, the public announcement of the denial was made the next day.[27]

On the morning of December 27, the indictment alleges Bacanovic called Stewart to tell her about the Waksal transaction. He was unable to reach her, however, and simply left a message that he thought ImClone "is going to start trading downward." Since he was on vacation, he directed Douglas Fanueil, his assistant, to tell Stewart about the Waksal order if and when she called back. When Stewart did return Bacanovic's call, Fanueil told her that Waksal was trying to sell all of his ImClone stock, at which point she directed Fanueil to sell all of her ImClone stock as well.[28] That sale provided her with $45,673 more than she would have received had she waited to sell until the next business day when the news became public, after which ImClone's stock value declined approximately 18%.[29]

At no point prior to the sale was Stewart told why Waksal was selling his stock or the source of information about his sale. The indictment alleges, however, that Waksal and Stewart were personal friends, implying that she knew the reason for Waksal's action. The indictment also points out that Stewart had been a licensed security broker from 1968 through 1975, that she had served on the board of directors of the New York Stock Exchange for about four months in 2002, and that Merrill Lynch policy specifically prohibited its brokers from revealing information about one client's transactions to another unless there was a "need to know" about such matters.[30] These allegations insinuate that both Stewart and Bacanovic engaged in a knowing violation of Rule 10b-5, the insider trading law,[31] he as the "tipper" (who misappropriated confidential information) and she as the "tippee" (who knew the information was misappropriated). As noted above, however, Stewart was never formally charged with that offense.

The next twenty paragraphs of the indictment, still within the conspiracy count, describe the various schemes that Stewart and Bacanovic allegedly devised to hide the real reason Stewart sold her ImClone stock. Although there were several such schemes, it is important to recognize that they all centered around one decision. As the indictment put it, Stewart and Bacanovic "agreed that rather than tell the truth about the communications with Stewart on December 27, 2001, they would instead fabricate and attempt to deceive investigators with a fictitious explanation for her sale—that Stewart sold her ImClone stock on December 27, 2001, because she and Bacanovic had a pre-existing agreement to sell the stock if and when the price dropped to $60 per share."[32] All of the remaining actions the indictment attributes to Stewart and Bacanovic were directed at maintaining this "sale-at-sixty" story.

Focusing solely on the allegations as they pertain to Stewart, the indictment next alleges that, once Stewart learned federal investigators were seeking an interview with her, she changed the phone message from Bacanovic that had read "Peter Bacanovic thinks ImClone is going to start trading downward" to "Peter Bacanovic re imclone" (although she almost immediately told her assistant to change the message back to the original wording).[33] It also alleges that she made several false statements during the ensuing interview, an interview that was conducted by members of the SEC, the FBI, and the U.S. Attorney's office on February 4, 2002, with Stewart's lawyers present. Specifically, the indictment avers, Stewart made the following false statements during the interview: she had an agreement with Bacanovic that he would sell her ImClone shares when ImClone's price reached $60 per share; she did not know whether Bacanovic's phone message of December 27 was recorded on her phone message log; she talked to Bacanovic (rather than Fanueil) on December 27 and much of that conversation was about *her* company's stock; and Bacanovic had not yet informed her that he had been questioned by the federal government.[34]

Federal agents also interviewed Stewart by phone on April 10, 2002. The indictment alleges that, on this occasion, Stewart made several other false statements, to wit: she did not recall discussing Waksal or his sale of ImClone stock on December 27 with anyone from Merrill Lynch; she and Bacanovic had agreed to sell her ImClone stock when it reached $60 a share; and Bacanovic had told her on December 27 that ImClone was selling below that amount.[35] The conspiracy count ends by alleging that all of these statements, as well as those made during the February 4 interview and the manipulation of the phone log, were in furtherance of the conspiracy to make false statements and obstruct justice.[36] The conspiracy to commit perjury allegation is less clearly delineated, but is based on a combination of Bacanovic's false testimony under oath to an SEC officer repeating the "sell-at-sixty" story and the fact that Stewart made several calls to Bacanovic both the day before and the day of this testimony.[37]

The remainder of the indictment, as it pertains to Stewart, is relatively brief. The two false statements counts, based on 18 U.S.C. § 1001(a), incorporate the paragraphs already described and are based on the same allegations. The indictment includes two counts of false statements because there were two meetings between Stewart and federal investigators, the February 4 office interview and April 10 phone interview.[38] The obstruction of justice count, under 18 U.S.C. § 1505, references the same paragraphs in the conspiracy count that the false statements counts reference and is based on precisely the same conduct as those counts.[39]

The final count against Stewart is the most innovative. It alleges that she committed securities fraud under Rule 10b-5 when she repeated the "sale-at-sixty" story and various sub-components of it to *The Wall Street Journal*, the public at large, and a securities analysts' conference, all in an effort to mislead investors and bolster the value of her own company's stock.[40] As noted above, the trial judge, Miriam Cederbaum, acquitted Stewart on this count. The judge reasoned that the prosecution did not prove that Stewart made these statements with the intent to defraud. While Stewart may have known the statements were false and that they would be widely disseminated, there was no evidence that she or her lawyer "reached out to," "chose," "organized," or decided to "take advantage of" the fora for these statements and thus, Judge Cederbaum reasoned, there was no evidence of the necessary intent.[41]

The judge allowed, however, the other four counts to go the jury. Stewart was convicted on all four. Judge Cederbaum ordered that Stewart be imprisoned for five months and serve five months under house arrest, the lowest possible sentence she could receive under the Federal Sentencing Guidelines, and that she pay a fine of $30,000, the highest possible fine she could be forced to pay under the Guidelines.[42] Although Stewart appealed all four convictions, she eventually decided to waive bail pending the outcome of the appeal (which she lost a few months after her home confinement ended).

The Problem: Charge Redundancy

The foregoing description of Stewart's indictment reveals our concern about charge redundancy. As we concluded earlier, Stewart clearly took enough steps in her efforts to hide her malfeasance from investigators that she deserved to be charged with some type of crime. But that single cover-up resulted in five separate charges. Telling the "sale-at-sixty" story and related fibs to federal agents on February 4 gave rise to *two* crimes: making false statements and obstruction of justice. When the story was repeated during a separate interview, a *third* crime of making false statements occurred (and presumably another obstruction charge could have been added). Had she been found to possess an intent to deceive, a *fourth* crime would have occurred when she told the story to the public. And when she consulted with Bacanovic to make sure the story would stick, she committed a *fifth* crime.

In fact, prosecutors in Stewart's case were conservative in their approach. In each of the false statement counts, they identified as "specifications" particular statements made by Stewart that were allegedly untrue: eight in count three and three in count four. Under existing case law, prosecutors could have charged each of these lies as a discreet false statement, resulting in *eleven* § 1001 counts instead of just two.[43] Moreover, nothing prevented prosecutors from seeking out Stewart for further discussions, presumably resulting in more false statements, or even asking her to testify under oath before the SEC, resulting in the possibility of multiple perjury counts.[44] In addition, the longer the investigation lingered, the more often Stewart could be counted on to declare her innocence in public fora. Each of these occasions would, in theory, be a new "execution" of securities fraud—and another potential count.[45] As long as Stewart stuck to her story, and as long as her lawyer let her talk, the counts would pile up.

How is this possible? And what are the consequences? We explore the answer to these questions by looking at three possible sources of limitation on redundant charging: the federal criminal code, the Constitution, and the Federal Sentencing Guidelines.

The So-Called Criminal Code

One might assume that the substantive criminal law would impose meaningful limitations on redundant charging. A rational legislature should seek to avoid promulgating numerous overlapping and vague criminal provisions. Unfortunately, this assumption is incorrect, at least in connection with federal criminal law. There is, of course, a body of law that deals with crime on the federal level, most of which can be found at Title 18 of the United States Code. Indeed, Title 18 is often referred to as the United States' "criminal code," but this moniker is misleading. The name implies that a committee of lawmakers and scholars met at a historic place and time to organize the common law of crimes into a coherent body of law setting forth criminal conduct and the penalties faced for engaging in it. The name further implies that this committee, or a second group of experts, periodically reviews the operation of the code and suggests additions and modifications to it. This scenario does describe, more or less, the creation and maintenance of some areas of American procedural law, such as the Federal Rules of Civil Procedure, the Federal Rules of Criminal Procedure, and the Federal Rules of Evidence.[46] But it does not represent the manner in which the federal "criminal code" has evolved.

Unlike its procedural cousins, the substantive federal criminal law consists of statutes passed on an ad hoc basis. As a political body, Congress addresses criminal issues from a political standpoint and passes criminal laws to satisfy the outrage of the day. It pays scant attention to how the new statutes fit with the old ones. Congress pays equally little attention to how the penalties for one crime can be squared with the penalties imposed for another. Many new criminal statutes tend to (1) duplicate or at least significantly overlap with ones in place; (2) incorporate existing crimes into a new, overarching scheme; or (3) plug a hole discovered in existing law, but with little effort to make the law a rational whole. Although the statutes are subjected to an internal bureaucratic process that places them alphabetically by topic in Title 18 (or occasionally, somewhere else in the federal titles), the resulting "code" is a mess in every sense of the word, as many commentators have recognized.[47]

Given the breadth and variety of the federal criminal code, it is likely that a defendant's behavior will potentially violate a multitude of overlapping criminal statutes, especially where white collar crime is involved. The same course of fraudulent conduct, for example, might constitute mail fraud (if the mails have been used to carry part of it out);[48] wire fraud (if a telephone or the internet was used as part of the execution of the scheme);[49] securities fraud under Title 18 (if the subject of the fraud related to securities);[50] securities fraud under Title 15 (if the subject of the fraud related to the purchase or sale of securities);[51] false statements to an agency of the government (if an agency, including the SEC, was one of the "victims" of the fraud) under Title 18;[52] and false statements to the SEC under Title 15.[53] If two defendants are involved, a conspiracy charge can likely be added. And if, as with Martha Stewart and Peter Bacanovic, the defendants attempt to cover up their fraud once an investigation begins, they will probably be liable for a second conspiracy charge and the additional substantive crimes of false statements, obstruction of justice,[54] and perjury.[55]

Nothing in the code tells a prosecutor how to sort through these options. Thus, she can bring every one of these charges as long as she believes each element can be proven beyond a reasonable doubt. And a prosecutor's choices do not end there, because she must also decide how many times the defendant committed each crime. For example, the crime of mail fraud is not measured by the overall scheme; it is defined as the use of the mails to execute that scheme. Thus, courts have held that every time a defendant mails a letter in connection with his fraud, the defendant has engaged in a discrete violation of the statute.[56] A similar approach is taken with false statements under § 1001 and false claims under 18 U.S.C. § 287; courts have held that each false statement or claim is a separate violation of the respective statutes.[57] Therefore, during one ongoing course of conduct, the same substantive criminal law can and often is violated multiple times.[58]

In short, the federal criminal code places virtually no restraints on redundant charging. Instead, through its design and application, it creates and exacerbates the problem.

The Constitution: Double Jeopardy Doctrine

One inclined to reduce redundant charging of the sort just described might naturally think of the Fifth Amendment's double jeopardy clause as a source of restriction. After all, that clause prohibits multiple prosecutions or punishments for the "same offense."[59] To the extent that a multi-charge, multi-count indictment smacks of piling on, this prohibition might reasonably be thought to apply. But it doesn't, at least under the Supreme Court's interpretation of the double jeopardy prohibition.

There are numerous ways "same offense" could be defined for double jeopardy purposes. The most rigid, of course, would be to take it literally. But no court has done so in modern times. At the least, courts have considered an offense and its lesser included offenses as the same offense for double jeopardy purposes, a test which has been called the "same elements" test. At the other end of the spectrum, some courts have adopted a "same trans-action" test, which holds that the double jeopardy clause requires the prosecution to join at one trial and punish as the same crime "all the charges against a defendant that grow out of a single criminal act, occurrence, episode, or transaction."[60] Somewhere in between is the "same conduct" test, which looks at the extent to which the conduct underlying two charges is the same.[61]

The Supreme Court's vacillations on the same offense issue are too nuanced to be described in detail here. Suffice it to say that the Court now subscribes to the same elements test, after flirting with the same conduct test. In *Blockburger v. United States*,[62] the Court held that, in the absence of clear legislative intent, two offenses are normally different for double jeopardy purposes when "each provision requires proof of an additional fact which the other does not."[63] A few subsequent cases suggested that the Court was willing to broaden this test under certain circumstances,[64] and, in *Grady v. Corbin*,[65] the Court formally adopted a version of the same conduct test. But three years later, in *United States v. Dixon*,[66] five members of the Court reversed *Grady* because it had no "constitutional roots," conflicted with longstanding precedent, and was confusing to apply.[67] *Dixon* reinstated the *Blockburger* test as the default rule for defining "same offense" when determining whether multiple prosecutions are permitted.

Under the *Blockburger* test, a false statement charge and an obstruction of justice charge are separate offenses, because the former statute requires proof of a false statement while the latter does not, and the latter statute requires proof of intent to impede an impending proceeding while the former does not.[68] Conspiracy to engage in these actions is yet another separate offense because it requires proof of an agreement.[69] Thus, in the Stewart case, the prosecution could have subjected Stewart to several different trials without violating the double jeopardy clause.

Most prosecutors would not want multiple trials, of course, if not from a sense that they would be oppressive, then simply because of efficiency concerns. More important as a practical matter is whether, when the charges are tried in one trial and all lead to conviction (as occurred in Stewart's case), the sentences can be stacked. Although the history described above demonstrates that the Supreme Court has been somewhat opaque regarding the definition of same offense in *re-prosecution* cases, it has been very clear as to that term's meaning in connection with *multiple punishments*. In *Missouri v. Hunter*,[70] the Court held that legislative intent alone determines the scope of the "same offense" analysis for determining when cumulative punishments may be imposed,[71] and that when legislative intent is not ascertainable, the *Blockburger* test applies.[72]

Since Congress has not made clear whether consecutive sentences are permissible for the false statement and obstruction of justice laws, or for conspiracy to commit those crimes, the apposite same-offense rule in Stewart's case is the *Blockburger* test. Because, as explained above, that test treats all of these crimes as separate offenses, Judge Cederbaum could have imposed consecutive sentences for the two false statement charges, the obstruction charge and the conspiracy charge without violating the double jeopardy prohibition.

The outcome is the same for a whole host of similarly worded white collar crimes, because each technically requires proof of a fact the others do not. Mail fraud, false statements, false claims, and obstruction of justice are all separate offenses for double jeopardy purposes.[73] One case has even held that the crime of making false statements (which requires lying about a "material" fact) and the crime of making false statements to secure a passport (which only requires making "any false statement") are different crimes under the Double Jeopardy Clause.[74]

Note further that even if the Court were to reverse *Hunter* and adopt the same transaction test or something similar for multiple punishment analysis, prosecutors could still engage in redundant charging. As long as they joined all crimes that are considered the "same offense" in the same indictment, they could avoid violating the Double Jeopardy Clause. Although they would also know that the punishments for these crimes could not be imposed consecutively, that might not provide much of a deterrent to redundant charging, for reasons developed below.

The Federal Sentencing Guidelines

At this point, some knowledgeable readers might be asking: so what if prosecutors engage in redundant charging? Any resulting unfairness can be corrected after conviction by collapsing similar counts at sentencing. Because that is what happens under the Federal Sentencing Guidelines, complaints about redundant charging in federal cases might be discounted as much ado about nothing.

There can be no dispute that the Guidelines are designed to minimize the effects of multiple charging.[75] Part D of Chapter 3 of the Guidelines deals with multiple counts. The preamble to this section specifically states that its purpose is "to limit the significance of the formal charging decision and to prevent multiple punishments for substantially identical offense conduct."[76] It accomplishes this objective by grouping offenses together for sentencing purposes.

The grouping of counts depends on the type of conduct. For example, most relevant to Martha Stewart's case, Section 3D1.2(b) provides that "[w]hen the counts involve ... two or more acts or transactions connected by a common criminal objective or constituting part of a common scheme or plan" they should be grouped together. The base offense level for conduct of this sort is that of the crime with the highest offense level in the group. In contrast, the guideline most applicable to fraud cases, Section 3D1.2(d), instructs that counts should be combined when "the offense level is determined largely on the basis of the total amount of harm or loss, the quantity of a substance involved, or some other measure of aggregate harm." In these instances, the base offense level corresponds to the magnitude of the aggregated harm.[77]

Given this scheme, multiple charging is not likely to affect the time served by a defendant as long as the prosecution has included a sufficient number of charges in the indictment to cover the maximum guideline sentence. It is for this reason that, despite multiple charges, Stewart received a sentence of only five months in prison and five months of house arrest. It is also for this reason that redundant charging might seem like a benign phenomenon. But it is not. That is because the Sentencing Guidelines only work their count-collapsing magic after conviction, when much of the damage from redundant charging has already occurred.

The Harms of Redundant Charging

Most prosecutors are smart people, skilled lawyers, and rational actors. If redundant charging were innocuous, prosecutors wouldn't waste their time doing it. In fact, prosecutors know or intuit that bringing multiple, duplicative, and overlapping charges provides several tactical advantages.

First and foremost, prosecutors bring multiple charges for similar conduct because it maximizes the probability of conviction at trial on at least one of the charged counts. Put bluntly, more charges lead to more convictions, perhaps even when some jurors entertain a reasonable doubt. Understanding how this might happen requires an appreciation of the dynamics of jury deliberation.

The most obvious way multiple counts can lead to more convictions is that jurors will figure "Where there's smoke there's fire." One reason defendants fight joinder of charges that clearly *are* separate from one another is the fear that jurors will assume that anyone charged with so many crimes must have done something wrong.[78] That fear is even more justified when the charges are very similar to one another.

The effects of multiple charging can be much more insidious than this blunt prejudicing effect, however. Consider first a case in which differences between jurors persist despite deliberation. If only one count is charged, one of three outcomes can result from the jury's split: conviction (if some arms are twisted), acquittal (if other arms are twisted), or a hung jury (if the arm twisting is unsuccessful). The latter two outcomes are anathema to the pros-

Jury

ecution. But if the prosecutor places two or more counts in the indictment, the split among the jurors results in a fourth possibility: a compromise verdict of guilty on some charges and not guilty on the others. Unless the maximum sentence for the charges that lead to conviction is significantly lower than the sentence for the rejected charges, this split verdict is a complete victory for the prosecution, because the judge does not take the acquittal into account at sentencing.[79] Yet the jury is likely to think otherwise; it will generally be unaware that its compromise had no impact on the ultimate outcome in the case.

A slightly different way in which multiple counts might cause a conviction despite a lack of jury unanimity occurs when, as Stewart's attorney suggested in his closing argument,[80] jurors horse-trade counts after discovering they can't agree on any particular one. In essence, they might say to one another, "I'll give you count 1 if you give me count 2." That type of pact can only occur, of course, if there is more than one count.

In both of these compromise verdict scenarios, "the jury dishonors the reasonable doubt standard, because each faction on the jury surrenders its honestly held beliefs on the question of proof beyond a reasonable doubt."[81] That alone is cause for concern. But redundant charging can also have other, more subtle, unfortunate effects. For instance, some jurors simply bristle at the prospect of rubber stamping the prosecution; multiple counts enable these jurors to demonstrate their independence by rejecting some charges without acquitting the defendant altogether. Splitting the verdict also allows jurors to feel they have demonstrated a capacity to obey instructions to consider each count separately and facilitates their ability to look a likable defendant in the eye and say, in effect, "I did what I could for you." In all likelihood, these influences seldom produce erroneous decisions. On the margin, however, the effect of making conviction psychologically more palatable for jurors increases the probability of conviction in each case, and thus, over time, it increases the overall number of convictions obtained by prosecutors.

Redundant charging can skew plea bargaining as well. Most obviously, multiple charges intimidate defendants. On its face, a multi-count indictment can make the potential sentence look devastatingly long. In the case of Stewart, for example, the sentences on the five counts added up to some twenty years in jail.[82] True, given the existence of the Guidelines, the long sentence is normally an illusion, something that the defense attorney presumably explains to the terrified defendant. At best, however, that explanation only lessens the intimidation, since the Guidelines permit a judge to depart upward from a Guideline sentence if certain factors are met.[83]

Further, in a situation analogous to the jury dynamic described above, defendants may be more willing to give up on a valid defense when they can trade, and trading is more likely when there are multiple counts. As Stephanos Bibas explains, "[o]vercharging ... provides high anchors for defendants. If the initial charge and sentence serve as anchors and baselines, any prosecutorial concessions look like discounts or savings—wins for defendants instead of reduced losses."[84]

Multiple charges may also have an effect on defense attorneys engaged in plea bargaining. Defense attorneys like to "win" their cases as much as any litigator. At the same time, there is considerable pressure on defense attorneys to resolve cases efficiently, through pleading their clients guilty in the bargaining process. One way to resolve the tension between these two forces is to define a "win" as a reduction in counts. Even if this reduction will not amount to a shorter sentence, defense attorneys can tell their clients that their superior negotiating skills forced the prosecutor to "drop some charges," a claim that many clients are likely to think is more than cosmetic. This ruse is not just a way defense attorneys can make themselves feel better about representing clients who are convicted. The danger is that it also makes it easier to represent those clients inadequately.[85] Prosecutors are surely aware of this dynamic, and may use redundant charging to take advantage of it.

Redundant charges might be rationalized at sentencing, but that does not explain why the practice takes place in the first instance. It persists for a reason, actually for several reasons. And many of those reasons should not be sanctioned if we want convictions based on a unanimous jury finding of guilt beyond a reasonable doubt and plea agreements that reflect the actual culpability of the defendant.

Proposal

We believe that the power of the prosecution to charge multiple, overlapping, and redundant crimes ought to be curtailed. In a perfect world, the problem would be fixed by Congress, as part of a larger project of building a truly comprehensive and coherent criminal code. Such a code could, akin to Chapter D of the Federal Sentencing Guidelines, contain rules limiting duplicative charging. Nudging the definition of "same offense" for purposes of double jeopardy analysis toward the same conduct or same transaction test would provide further incentive to avoid double charging. But the chances of either occurring soon are infinitesimal.[86] Therefore, we advance a proposal

infinitesimal

that is not quite as bold but is more attainable: we suggest that the courts use their common law power to create a "law of counts."

Under the law of counts, a court would conduct a pre-trial review of an indictment to determine if the charges in it were overlapping in a manner jeopardizing the defendant's right to a fair trial.[87] In so doing, the court could be guided by the same conduct analysis of Supreme Court double jeopardy doctrine[88] and the grouping rules found in the Federal Sentencing Guidelines. The idea would be for the court to merge, for purposes of plea bargaining as well as the jury's deliberation and verdict, all counts that deal with the same conduct or transaction. We are not claiming that this analysis would be an easy task; we do believe, however, that the gradual process of the common law would be the perfect vehicle for the development of a counts doctrine.

A law of counts would not empower courts to ignore legislative mandates. The federal courts would still have to follow clear congressional intent concerning specific crimes and the harms they are designed to deter and punish. So, for example, the practice of charging a conspiracy to commit a crime and the related complete crime would not be altered. However, congressional intent is not always clear in terms of the harm meant to be punished. If a prosecutor were to bring, for instance, separate mail and wire fraud charges for the same essential conduct, or a dozen separate mail fraud counts for each mailing furthering the same scheme, the court, given the ambiguity in those statutes, could exercise its common law power to merge all of the charges into a single count.

Courts have long engaged in a similar analysis in a line of cases assessing whether indictments are defective due to "multiplicity"—a word meant to connote the charging of the same offense in multiple counts.[89] To date, however, multiplicity analysis has been applied in only very limited circumstances, usually involving conspiracy and similar offenses, and usually only when the counts charge the same offense as defined in *Blockburger*.[90] Furthermore, while courts are willing to recognize that multiplicity in an indictment may affect the jury's deliberations, they routinely consider it harmless error if sentences are imposed concurrently;[91] thus, the trial judge operating under the Federal Sentencing Guidelines does not have much incentive to dismiss counts even when they are multiplicitous under the current narrow definition.[92]

For reasons we have discussed, we are not convinced that the effect of redundant charging *is* harmless. Trial judges should take the law of counts seriously and routinely apply it prior to trial, at least when raised by the defense in a timely manner. The authority to do so could come from the Due Process Clause, separation of powers doctrine, or administrative law.[93] Under the

Fourteenth Amendment, courts are obligated to ensure that the adjudication process is fair.[94] Under the separation of powers doctrine, courts have the authority to monitor prosecutorial decisions that affect sentencing, a traditionally judicial function.[95] Under principles developed in the administrative law arena, courts routinely review the rationality of decisions made in the executive branch.[96] As Ronald Wright has shown, New Jersey courts have for some time relied on these types of rationales, in particular the latter two, when regulating various types of prosecutorial charging decisions.[97]

We noted above that the law of counts would be most effective if applied at a preliminary hearing, before serious bargaining takes place. Alternatively, it could be reflected in the judge's instructions to the jury. Either way, the judge's decision on the counts issue would be appealable, to permit fashioning a uniform approach. Over time, the law of counts would exert pressure on prosecutors to modify their charging practices, resulting in fewer multi-count indictments.[98] In this way, charging would become less redundant and more accurately reflect the alleged culpability of the defendant.

Conclusion

Martha Stewart's case illustrates a wide variety of prosecutorial decision-making. We have defended the U.S. Attorney's decision to investigate and prosecute Stewart, but called into question the further decision to charge her with five counts. As a way of curtailing the redundant charging phenomenon, which is widespread, we have suggested that the courts develop a law of counts to cabin prosecutorial charging discretion.

Ideally, perhaps, prosecutors could be relied on to self-regulate in this area. But we think it is unrealistic to expect prosecutors to limit their investigative tactics and charging practices in substantial ways when the courts and legislatures feel no need to do so. Public and official pressure to get tough on crime is immense, as illustrated by the Department of Justice's recent directive that federal prosecutors pursue the maximum charge supported by the evidence.[99] It doesn't help that most state prosecutors are elected and that federal prosecutors also care deeply about their public reputations. With respect to the white collar criminal, which Stewart may not epitomize but certainly exemplifies, the pressure to prosecute aggressively has become particularly intense since Enron and related corporate scams.[100] Further, obtaining convictions under complex fraud statutes is often very difficult, especially when the defendant possesses significant resources, as many white collar defendants do. Prosecutors understandably want to cover all their bases by piling on as many charges as possible.[101]

Thus, our proposal to create a law of counts would not require prosecutors to act against their short-term or long-term interests. Rather, it would be implemented by judges using the interpretive method, without going so far as to confer on them an undefined "nullification" authority. If instituted wisely, it could have a significant impact on prosecutorial discretion without unreasonably curbing it or preventing government from bringing bad people to justice.

Questions

1. Should Stewart have been charged at all? Seigel and Slobogin argue that Stewart's charges were not extraneous or trivial. Leaving aside the possibility of insider trading (which the prosecution decided not to charge), what did she do wrong? In addition to the text of the article, make sure to look at the material in notes 23, 24, 32 and 33. Compare the Seigel and Slobogin analysis to the analyses of other authors in this volume. Who is the most convincing?
2. Why doesn't the United States have a coherent Criminal Code? How would the creation of such a code differ from the creation of the procedural codes referenced by Seigel and Slobogin? Would a comprehensive Criminal Code be likely to solve the multiplicity problem without directly addressing the issue?
3. Are the reasons Seigel and Slobogin give for requiring count-collapsing *before* trial persuasive? Unfortunately, there are no empirical data relating to their claim that jurors are affected by multiple counts in the ways they suggest. Should an attempt to gather such data be undertaken?

Notes

1. Ellen S. Podgor, *Jose Padilla and Martha Stewart: Who Should Be Charged with Criminal Conduct?*, 109 Penn. St. L. Rev. 1059, 1068 (2005) (referring to the "extraneous crimes in the Martha Stewart case"); John Buell, *Is Martha Being Used as a Scapegoat?*, Bangor Daily News (Maine), Aug. 25, 2004 ("[Stewart's] act is trivial in comparison with an economic and political climate that encourages paper profits, short time horizons, and exploitation of customers and workers.").

2. Christopher Westley, *Martha Stewart's Surreal Ordeal*, Feb. 23, 2004, http://www.mises.org/story/1453 (calling the insider trading claim "a truly ridiculous charge when made against someone without any fiduciary responsibility to the firm."). *But see infra* note 19.

3. *See, e.g.,* Joan MacLeod Heminway, *Save Martha Stewart? Observations About Equal Justice In U.S. Insider Trading Regulation*, 12 Tex. J. Women & L. 247, 247 (2003) (claiming that the Stewart prosecution was infected with sexism at many stages). *See also* Buell,

supra note 1 ("Putting Stewart in her place is a strategy designed to appeal to insecure working class males whose votes Bush needs but whose interest he serves only through symbolic politics."); Harry Browne, *What the Martha Stewart Case Means to You*, March 5, 2004, http://www.harrybrowne.org/articles/MarthaStewart2.htm (using the Stewart case to bolster the claim that "modern America [is] a place where anyone can be charged with anything.").

4. Geraldine Szott Moohr, *Prosecutorial Power in an Adversarial System: Lessons from Current White Collar Cases*, 7 BUFF. CRIM. L. REV. 165, 194 (2004) ("Federal prosecutors are subject to minimal supervision and are authorized to make independent decisions that, with few exceptions, are not subject to approval or direction."); William J. Stuntz, *The Pathological Politics of the Criminal Law*, MICH. L. REV. 505, 517 (2001) ("Federal criminal law probably covers more conduct—and a good deal more innocuous conduct—than any state criminal code.").

5. *See* Bruce A. Green & Fred C. Zacharias, *Prosecutorial Neutrality*, 2004 WISC. L. REV. 837 (2004); Rory K. Little, *Proportionality as an Ethical Precept for Prosecutors in Their Investigative Role*, 68 FORDHAM L. REV. 723 (1999).

6. Richard S. Frase, *Comparative Criminal Justice as a Guide to American Law Reform: How Do the French Do It, How Can We Find Out, and Why Should We Care?*, 78 CAL. L. REV. 539, 617 (1990) (advocating adoption of the continental charge screening process); Moohr, *supra* note 4, at 218 (suggesting that the "imbalance produced by prosecutorial power" could be addressed by adopting "the safeguards that constrain prosecutorial power in inquisitorial systems").

7. Stuntz, *supra* note 4, at 569.

8. *See* Heminway, *supra* note 3, at 252 ("[F]ederal investigators have only limited resources available for use in pursuing possible violators. Accordingly, each prosecutor or enforcement agent must pick and choose those against whom the laws within its jurisdiction will be enforced.").

9. *See* CYNTHIA BARNETT, FBI CRIMINAL JUSTICE INFORMATION SERVICES DIVISION, THE MEASUREMENT OF WHITE-COLLAR CRIME USING UNIFORM CRIME REPORTING (UCR) DATA 6, http://www.fbi.gov/ucr/whitecollarforweb.pdf (last visited Feb. 1, 2006).

10. Statutory formulations, which typically distinguish civil versus criminal liability based upon whether the defendant's conduct was "willful," *see, e.g.*, 15 U.S.C. §78ff (2005), are not very helpful in separating out cases for potential criminal treatment because just about all white collar malfeasance can be characterized as willful, given the many meanings this term carries. *See* Ratzlaf v. United States, 510 U.S. 135, 141 (1994). Thus, agencies often rely on other factors, such as the magnitude of the harm or fraud, the criminal history of the subject, and the reaction of the subject to the investigation, in deciding whether to make a criminal referral.

11. *See* Heminway, *supra* note 3, at 261–65.

12. Generally speaking, DOJ's prosecutorial guidelines, found in the *United States Attorney's Manual*, are open to the public, but office-by-office intake guidelines are not. *See* Green & Zacharias, *supra* note 5, at 843 n.23 (referring to individual prosecutorial offices having non-public intake guidelines). In the experience of one of the authors (Seigel), who served as a prosecutor for nearly a decade, internal guidelines are written to be flexible enough to take special situations into account. These might include pursuing a prosecution that does not otherwise meet the guidelines because it is believed that it will lead to other, bigger cases; pursuing a case that manifests a special federal interest; and pursuing a case that will have a greater deterrent impact than its size objec-

tively indicates. Obviously, this creates a huge pocket of discretion in which prosecutors can and do operate.

13. *See* United States v. Stewart, 433 F.3d 273, 283–84 (2d Cir. 2006).

14. If Stewart had traded on a tip from Waksal, she would have been a classic tippee and liable under well settled insider trading law. *See* Dirks v. SEC, 463 U.S. 646, 655–56 (1983).

15. *See* United States v. Stewart, 323 F. Supp. 2d 606 app. A at ¶ 24 (S.D.N.Y. 2004) [hereinafter *Stewart Indictment*].

16. The appellate opinion makes it sound like the SEC, FBI, and U.S. Attorney's Office investigations all started at the moment Merrill Lynch originally referred the matter to the SEC. *See Stewart*, 433 F.3d at 284. We believe that this is most likely a benign simplification of the facts. If the FBI and U.S. Attorney's Office for the Southern District of New York had been involved in the investigation at its inception, no doubt that they would have participated in the January 7th interview.

17. Apparently the SEC routinely targets high-profile defendants. *See* Vikram David Amar, *The Many Ways to Prove Discrimination*, 14 HASTINGS WOMEN'S L.J. 171, 178 n.13 (2004). But courts have refused to find that this type of practice constitutes a violation of the equal protection clause or some other discrimination principle. *See* Falls v. Town of Dyer, Ind., 875 F.2d 146, 148 (7th Cir. 1989) ("A government legitimately could enforce its law against a few persons (even just one) to establish a precedent, ultimately leading to widespread compliance."); United States v. Catlett, 584 F.2d 864, 864 (8th Cir. 1978) (upholding an IRS policy targeting notorious tax protesters); People v. Utica Daw's Drug Co., 16 A.D.2d 12, 21 (N.Y. App. Div. 1962) ("Selective enforcement may ... be justified when a striking example or a few examples are sought in order to deter other violators....").

18. Imagine, for instance, if the prosecutors investigating the Kobe Bryant case had not charged him with rape, even though their case was weak.

19. Criminal cases holding that there is liability in this situation include United States v. Mylett, 97 F.3d 663 (2d Cir. 1996), *cert. denied* 521 U.S. 1119 (1997); United States v. Libera, 989 F.2d 596 (2d Cir. 1993), *cert. denied*, 510 U.S. 976 (1993); United States v. Falcone, 97 F. Supp. 297 (E.D.N.Y. 2000) (reluctantly following the holding in *Libera*). Regulatory cases imposing such liability, which are precedent for criminal cases, include SEC v. Maio, 51 F.3d 623 (7th Cir. 1995); SEC v. Grossman, 887 F. Supp. 649 (S.D.N.Y. 1995); SEC v. Musella, 748 F. Supp. 1028 (S.D.N.Y. 1989).

20. *See* Carrie Johnson, *Stewart Resolves Last of Charges: $195,000 Settles Civil Complaint*, http://www.washingtonpost.com/wp-dyn/content/article/2006/08/07/AR2006080700430.html? nav=rss_email/components (last visited Aug. 16, 2006).

21. Dale A. Oesterle, *Early Observations on the Prosecutions of the Business Scandals of 2002–03: On Sideshow Prosecutions, Spitzer's Clash with Donaldson over Turf, the Choice of Civil or Criminal Actions, and the Tough Tactic of Coerced Cooperation*, 1 OHIO ST. J. CRIM. L. 443, 456–57 (2004) (noting that prosecutions on cover-up charges prevent a public trial on the core charges and that such charges are "an end-run around the more difficult to prove, yet suspected (and hyped), actual offense").

22. Stuart Green has written an article that explores this issue in some detail. Stuart P. Green, *Uncovering the Cover-Up Crimes*, 42 AM. CRIM. L. REV. 9 (2005).

23. It was in such cases that the "exculpatory no" doctrine, which required dismissal of false statement charges based solely on a denial of wrongdoing, was most likely to apply before it was rejected by the U.S. Supreme Court in *Brogan v. United States*, 522 U.S. 398 (1998). While we are uncomfortable with *Brogan*, given the extent to which it permits pros-

ecutors to trap unwary defendants, it would not likely have applied in Stewart's case, given the elaborate nature of her coverup story. *See generally* Scott Pomfret, *A Tempered "Yes" to the "Exculpatory No,"* 96 Mich. L. Rev. 754 (1997).

24. *See* Green, *supra* note 22, at 30 ("Destroying evidence or perjuring oneself in response to a governmental investigation involves more than just the usual breach of the supposed duty to obey the law."). That the conduct Stewart covered up may not have been *clearly* illegal arguably only makes her cover-up more culpable. *Id.* at 33 ("[I]t is ironic that the more serious the crime being covered-up, and the more severe the penal consequences, the stronger is the defendant's claim of self-preservation, and arguably the less wrongful is his act of covering up.").

25. The jury agreed. Specifically it found that, in addition to making nine separate false statements to government authorities, she conspired to make false statements, commit perjury (by Bacanovic), and obstruct an agency proceeding. United States v. Stewart, 323 F. Supp. 2d 606, 609–10 (S.D.N.Y. 2004).

26. *Stewart Indictment, supra* note 15, ¶ 13. This paragraph also alleges that a member of Waksal's family had put in an order to sell stock.

27. *Id.* ¶¶ 12, 19.

28. *Id.* ¶¶ 15–17.

29. *Id.* ¶ 21.

30. *Id.* ¶¶ 2, 6, 12.

31. Insider trading is not expressly forbidden by statute. Rather, the Securities Exchange Act of 1934 proscribes fraud in connection with trading of securities, and the SEC has promulgated a rule ("Rule 10b-5") that criminalizes, in connection with the trading of securities, schemes to defraud, the making of statements that are untrue or misleading or the omission of statements necessary to make a statement not misleading, and a transaction that operates as a fraud or deceit. 17 C.F.R. § 240.10b-5 (2006).

32. *Stewart Indictment, supra* note 15, ¶ 23. Interestingly, the jury acquitted both Stewart and Bacanovic on the charge that they lied about their agreement to sell ImClone when it went below $60.00 (the only two false statement specifications on which they were acquitted). *See* United States v. Stewart, 323 F. Supp. 2d 606, 610–11 (S.D.N.Y. 2004). However, the jury also clearly found that the "sale-at-sixty" agreement was not the reason the ImClone stock was sold. *See id.*

33. *Stewart Indictment, supra* note 15, ¶ 26. Although the latter act could mean she had a change of heart with respect to altering evidence, it more likely evidenced her realization that her assistant had witnessed the change and thus would be able to expose the alteration. The defense made no effort to defend this behavior during trial.

34. *Id.* ¶ 27.

35. *Id.* ¶ 36.

36. *Id.* ¶ 37.

37. *Id.* ¶ 40–41.

38. *Id.* ¶ 44–47.

39. *Id.* ¶ 54–55.

40. *Id.* ¶ 56–67.

41. United States v. Stewart, 305 F. Supp. 2d 368 (S.D.N.Y. 2004). We think the judge's reasoning is suspect. A person can have many motivations for doing something and can be found criminally guilty even if only one of these motivations furnishes the necessary intent to commit the crime. Here, Stewart appeared to be trying to accomplish many things by

falsely proclaiming her innocence; the jury surely could have found that one of them was to reassure nervous investors, the *mens rea* necessary to commit the crime. So, if the issue was intent, the charge should have gone to the jury. The better route, in our opinion, would have been for the judge to declare that the theory of criminal liability set forth in this count of the indictment violated Stewart's First Amendment right to make a simple public declaration of her innocence. Note, however, that by construing it as a factual issue and entering a judgment of acquittal instead of considering it a legal decision and dismissing the count, the judge insulated the matter from government appeal.

42. Constance L. Hays, *Martha Stewart's Sentence: The Overview*, N.Y. Times, July 17, 2004, at A1.

43. *See* United States v. Guzman, 781 F.2d 428, 432 (5th Cir. 1986) (per curiam) ("Where false statements are made in distinct and separate documents requiring different proof as to each statement, the filing of each false document constitutes a crime, and each filing may be alleged in a separate count of the indictment.").

44. *See, e.g.*, 18 U.S.C. § 1505 (2004).

45. *See, e.g.*, United States v. Harris, 79 F.3d 223, 232 (2d Cir. 1996) (explaining that when an act is "chronologically and substantively independent" from the other acts charged as the scheme, it constitutes an execution); United States v. Sirang, 70 F.3d 588, 595 (11th Cir. 1995) (explaining that a single scheme can be executed a number of times, and a defendant may be charged in separate counts for each "execution" of the scheme to defraud); United States v. Molinaro, 11 F.3d 853, 861 n.16 (9th Cir. 1993) ("[T]wo transactions may have a common purpose but constitute separate executions of a scheme where each involves a new and independent obligation to be truthful.").

46. *See* The Rulemaking Process: Judicial Conference Procedures, http://www. uscourts.gov/rules/procedurejc.htm (last visited Feb. 1, 2006).

47. The following description of the federal code is representative:

> The current federal criminal code, title 18 of the United States Code, makes "the federal criminal law almost incomprehensible." It is hard to understand, hard to apply, and hard to explain. Title 18 is a compilation, rather than a code, and it is duplicative, ambiguous, incomplete, and organizationally nonsensical. It has aptly been described as "an odd collection of two hundred years of ad hoc statutes, rather than a unified, interrelated, comprehensive criminal code."

Robert H. Joost, *Federal Criminal Code Reform: Is It Possible?*, 1 Buff. Crim. L. Rev. 195, 195 (1997). *See also* Frank O. Bowman, III, *The Curious History and Distressing Implications of the Criminal Provisions of the Sarbanes-Oxley Act and the Sentencing Guideline Amendments That Followed*, 1 Ohio St. J. Crim. L. 373, 382–83 (2004) (noting "the general confusion created by the absence of meaningful congressional classifications" of economic crimes).

48. 18 U.S.C. § 1341 (2005).

49. *Id.* § 1343.

50. 18 U.S.C. § 1348 (2002).

51. 15 U.S.C. § 78j(b) (2000); 17 C.F.R. § 240.10b-5 (2005).

52. 18 U.S.C. § 1001 (2004).

53. 15 U.S.C. § 78ff (2002); *see* Securities Exchange Act of 1934, § 32, 15 U.S.C. § 78ee(a)(2002) (prohibiting the making of false statements to the Securities and Exchange Commission).

54. 18 U.S.C. § 1505 (1994).

55. 18 U.S.C. §1621 (1994) (relating to perjury generally) or §1623 (relating to perjury before the grand jury or court).

56. *See* Badders v. United States, 240 U.S. 391 (1916) (upholding charging each mailing sent in execution of a scheme as a separate count); United States v. Vaughn, 797 F.2d 1485 (9th Cir. 1986) (upholding defendant's conviction on four counts of mail fraud, each relating to a separate use of the mails); *cf.* United States v. Poliak, 823 F.2d 371 (9th Cir. 1987) (upholding defendant's conviction for ten counts of bank fraud based on ten kited checks).

57. With respect to false statements, see *supra* notes 44 and 46; *see also* Fain v. United States, 265 F. 473 (9th Cir. 1920) (holding that in a prosecution against an agent of the General Land Office for making and presenting false claims against the United States by means of an itemized statement of expenses, several items of which were alleged to be false, each item could be regarded as a separate violation of §287 and constitute a separate count of the indictment).

58. The most egregious example of this phenomenon that we have been able to find at the state level is *Krueger v. Coplan*, 238 F. Supp. 2d 391 (D.N.H. 2002), where state prosecutors charged ninety separate counts of sexual assault based on one twenty-five minute sex act caught on video. While critical of the prosecution's charging decision, the court held it was technically correct, given the way the statute defined the crime.

59. U.S. Const. amend. V.

60. *See* Ashe v. Swenson, 397 U.S. 436, 453–54 (1970) (Brennan, J., concurring) (describing the "same transaction" test).

61. *See generally* Charles Whitebread & Christopher Slobogin, Criminal Procedure: An Analysis of Cases and Concepts 871–73 (4th ed. 2000).

62. 284 U.S. 199 (1932).

63. *Id.* at 304.

64. *See, e.g.,* Illinois v. Vitale, 447 U.S. 410 (1980) (dictum stating that if the prosecution had to prove a failure to slow his car in order to prove homicide, conviction on the former charge would bar a separate trial on the latter); Harris v. Oklahoma, 433 U.S. 682 (1977) (holding that conviction of felony murder for participation in a death caused during a robbery barred a later robbery prosecution, even though robbery and felony murder each require proof of an element the other does not).

65. 495 U.S. 508 (1990).

66. 509 U.S. 688 (1993).

67. *Id.* at 704–11.

68. United States v. Wood, 958 F.2d 963, 973 (10th Cir. 1992).

69. *Cf.* United States v. Felix, 503 U.S. 378 (1992) (ruling that conspiring to sell drugs and attempting to sell drugs are not the same offense for double jeopardy purposes).

70. 459 U.S. 359 (1983).

71. *Id.* at 368 ("Where … a legislature specifically authorizes cumulative punishment under two statutes, regardless of whether those two statutes proscribe the 'same' conduct under *Blockburger*, a court's task of statutory construction is at an end and the prosecutor may seek and the trial court or jury may impose cumulative punishment under such statutes in a single trial.").

72. *Id.*

73. *Cf.* United States v. Green, 964 F.2d 365, 375 (5th Cir. 1992) (ruling that a sentence for mail fraud may be enhanced on obstruction of justice grounds even though conduct for the latter was the basis of conviction for mail fraud).

74. United States v. Ramos, 725 F.2d 1322, 1323–24 (11th Cir. 1984). *See also* United States v. Diogo, 320 F.2d 898, 902 (2d Cir. 1963) (ruling that false statements to immigration authorities under 18 U.S.C. §1546 is a different offense than false statements under 18 U.S.C. §1001).

75. *See* Moohr, *supra* note 4, at 20 n.68 ("The Sentencing Guidelines require that similar charges be grouped, thus mitigating somewhat the effect of multiple charges....").

76. U.S. Sentencing Guidelines Manual, ch. 3, pt. D, introductory comt. (2004).

77. *Id.* at §3D1.3. This discussion assumes, of course, that the Guidelines will survive Blakely v. Washington, 124 S.Ct. 2531 (2004), in one fashion or another. *See* United States v. Booker, 125 S.Ct. 738 (2005) (striking down, as in violation of *Blakely's* requirement that sentence enhancements be found by a jury, the provision in the Guidelines that makes them mandatory).

78. Drew v. United States, 331 F.2d 85 (D.C. Cir. 1964) ("[C]ourts presume prejudice and exclude evidence of other crimes unless that evidence can be admitted for some substantial, legitimate purpose.").

79. *See* U.S. Sentencing Guidelines Manual §1B1 & 1B3 (setting forth "relevant conduct" to be considered at sentencing).

80. *See* Closing Argument of Robert Morvillo, March 2, 2004, at p. 10, *available at* http://www.marthatalks.com/trial_update/closing_argument.html ("The one thing you cannot do is compromise. You can't say, I'll give you Count 2 if you give me Count 3. I'll give you Count 3 if you give me Count 4. Because one count of conviction, it's over for us. It doesn't make any difference which count it is. If you convict on one count, we feel the consequences of that conviction as if you convicted on all counts, so please don't compromise.").

81. Eric L. Muller, *The Hobgoblin of Little Minds? Our Foolish Law of Inconsistent Verdicts*, 111 Harv. L. Rev., 784 (1998). Muller continues, "To be sure, compromise verdicts are undoubtedly quite common, and they help to resolve cases, avoid retrials, and clear crowded dockets. But useful as they may be, compromise verdicts are lawless verdicts." *Id.*

82. Hays, *supra* note 42.

83. *See generally* U.S. Sentencing Guidelines Manual §5K1.1–2.18 (1987).

84. Stephanos Bibas, *Plea Bargaining Outside the Shadow of Trial*, 117 Harv. L. Rev. 2463, 2519 (2004).

85. *Cf.* Michael McConville & Chester L. Mirsky, *The Skeleton of Plea Bargaining*, New L.J. 1373, 1374 (1992) (explaining that under the current plea bargaining system, the defense attorney's "concern is no longer with the sufficiency of the State's evidence but with admonishing the defendant not to be foolhardy and insist upon a trial.... By becoming the 'left hand' of the court while the prosecutor is the 'right hand' the defense lawyer accepts and adopts the system of discounts and penalties which the prosecution relies upon to obtain pleas").

86. With respect to congressional action, one has only to recall the nineteen-year long attempt to reform the federal criminal code, spanning 1968 to 1984, that ended in complete failure. *See* Joost, *supra* note 48, at 202. Expansion of the same offense definition is even less likely, given the Court's decision in *Dixon*. See *supra* text accompanying notes 63–68.

87. In applying the "law of counts," a court would need to ensure that it did not run afoul of the doctrine of "duplicity." As explained by the Sixth Circuit, "a duplicitous indictment is one that charges separate offenses in a single count." United States v. Duncan,

850 F.2d 1104, 1108 n.4 (6th Cir. 1988). The Stewart indictment was duplicitous in the sense that it contained several specifications of false statements in one count. In such situations, the trial court must be careful to instruct the jury that it must unanimously agree that at least one of the specified events occurred in order to convict on that count. *See* U.S. v. Blandford, 33 F.3d. 685, 699 (6th Cir. 1994). The duplicity doctrine should be distinguished from the multiplicity doctrine, which deals with charging the same offense in several different counts. *See infra* text accompanying notes 90–92.

88. Another well thought-out stab at the "same offense" doctrine that might be particularly helpful in developing a law of counts is found in George C. Thomas, *A Blameworthy Act Approach to the Double Jeopardy Same Offense Problem*, 83 Cal. L. Rev. 1027, 1069–70 (1995) (arguing that when legislative intent is unclear, as is usually the case, all "blameworthy act-types"—repetitive acts that "manifest the statutory harm in the same way" and are not "individuated by intent"—should constitute the same offense). Under Thomas's definition, all of the counts in Stewart's case should have been collapsed into two (conspiracy to commit perjury and making false statements).

89. *See* 1A Charles Alan Wright et al., Federal Practice & Procedure §§ 142, 145, at 7–8, 86 (3d ed. 1999).

90. *See, e.g.,* United States v. Graham, 305 F.3d 1094, 1100 (10th Cir. 2002); United States v. Anderson, 872 F.2d 1508 (11th Cir. 1989); United States v. Carter, 576 F.2d 1061, 1064 (2d Cir. 1978); United States v. Mackay, 491 F.2d 616, 619 (10th Cir. 1974); *see generally* United States v. Ashdown, 509 F.2d 793, 800 (5th Cir. 1975) ("[I]t will avail a defendant nothing that the same scheme is incorporated in each count of the indictment.").

91. *United States v. Langford*, 946 F.2d 798 (11th Cir. 1991), is one of the most far-reaching cases on the multiplicity issue. There, the court held that "[t]o avoid the vices of multiplicity in securities fraud cases, each count of the indictment must be based on a separate purchase or sale of securities and each count must specify a false statement of material fact—not a full-blown scheme to defraud—in connection with that purchase or sale." *Id.* at 804. If this reasoning were applied to the *Stewart* case, it might have required dismissal of one of the false statement counts (although not the obstruction count based on the same conduct). Yet *Langford* also held the multiplicity error in that case harmless because sentences on the counts were imposed concurrently, ignoring the defendant's concern about prejudicing the jury and stating that "the principal danger in a multiplicitous indictment is ... that the defendant may receive multiple sentences for a single offense." *Id.* *See also* United States v. Reed, 639 F.2d 896, 905 n.6 (2d Cir. 1981). And, as stated in the Wright et al. treatise, *supra* note 89, "[i]t remains permissible to charge a single offense in several counts" (citing United States v. University C.I.T. Credit Corp, 344 U.S. 218, 221 (1952)).

92. It might also come from an interpretation of the relevant pleading rules. Federal Rule of Criminal Procedure 7(c) provides *inter alia* that "a count may allege that the means by which the defendant committed the offense are unknown or that the defendant committed it by one or more specified means." Although this language is opaque on the redundant charging issue, the Advisory Committee Notes state that it "is intended to eliminate the use of multiple counts for the purpose of alleging the commission of the offense by different means or in different ways." *See* Wright et al., *supra* note 89, at §142. If so, Rule 7(c) might be a useful springboard for creating a law of counts.

93. *Cf.* United States v. Weathers, 186 F.3d 948 (D.C. Cir. 1999) (ruling that failure to raise a multiplicity objection prior to trial waives the claim).

94. In the charging context, the Supreme Court has only been willing to recognize a due process violation when the charging decision is "vindictive," Blackledge v. Perry, 417 U.S. 21, 27 (1974), and has very narrowly construed the equal protection clause. *See* Wayte v. United States, 470 U.S. 598 (1985). But state courts have been willing to think more expansively. For instance, in *People v. Marcy*, the Colorado Supreme Court stated that "separate statutes proscribing with different penalties what ostensibly might be different acts, but offering no intelligent standard for distinguishing the proscribed conduct, run afoul of equal protection under state constitutional doctrine." 628 P.2d 69, 75 (Colo. 1981).

95. *See* State v. Leonardis, 375 A.2d 607, 611 n.5 (N.J. 1977) (noting that "sentencing is a judicial function" and holding that to the extent prosecutorial charging decisions trench on that function, separation of powers might be violated).

96. *Id.* at 615 (noting that even if a prosecutor's decisions are viewed as purely executive in nature, "[t]he judiciary is commonly called upon to review the rationality of decisions by other branches of government or agencies with special expertise").

97. Ronald F. Wright, *Prosecutorial Guidelines and the New Terrain in New Jersey*, 109 PENN. ST. L. REV. 1087 *passim* (2005) (describing the *Leonardis* decision, as well as subsequent New Jersey cases).

98. Again, the New Jersey experience provides a model for this approach. *See* Wright, *supra* note 97 (describing judicial monitoring of charging decisions in New Jersey through appealable decisions regarding the prosecutor's adherence to statewide charging guidelines, developed after judicial pressure to do so).

99. *See* United States Attorneys' Manual 9-27.300 (directing prosecutors to file the most serious readily provable offense).

100. *See, e.g.,* Janet Whitman, *Stock Options Face Scrutiny in Wake of Enron*, WALL ST. J., Apr. 3, 2002, at B7B (commenting that the collapse of Enron created a public outcry for greater accountability of corporate boards of directors and executives).

101. *See* Oesterle, *supra* note 21, at 446–47 (noting that given the complexity of white collar cases, the resources that must be expended to prosecute them, and the wealth of most white collar defendants, prosecutors' "natural response is to favor cases in which investigations are completed quickly and without trial.").

CHAPTER 4

NAVIGATING THE CURRENTS OF FEDERAL CRIMINAL LAW*

Geraldine Szott Moohr

Martha Stewart, the founder and chief executive of Martha Stewart Living Omnimedia, is a nationally recognized author and business woman, a celebrity who is at once credited with and ridiculed for reviving the public's interest in aesthetic domestic arts. Yet, like any ordinary person accused of a crime, she found it difficult to navigate the broad and deep currents of federal criminal law.

The Martha Stewart Case

Stewart attracted the attention of government regulators when she sold 3,928 shares of ImClone stock.[1] Their initial inquiry focused on whether she had engaged in insider trading, that is, buying or selling company stock based on non-public information gained through connections to the firm. Her friend, Sam Waksal, ImClone's founder and major shareholder, had unlawfully traded on the non-public information that the Food and Drug Administration had declined to approve the company's cancer drug,[2] and prosecutors suspected that Stewart also had traded on that information. In an effort to avoid that charge, she explained the reasons for her sale to investigators from the FBI, the SEC, and the U.S. Attorney's office in two inter-

---

* This chapter is derived from *Prosecutorial Power in an Adversarial System: Lessons from Current White Collar Cases and the Inquisitorial Model*, originally published at 8 BUFF. CRIM. L. REV. 165 (2005). Reprinted with permission of the publisher Buffalo Criminal Law Review © 2005.

views.[3] Stewart stated that she sold the shares on the news that the share price had fallen below $60 per share, as previously agreed with her broker and co-defendant, Peter Bocanovic.[4] On three occasions in June of 2002, Stewart assured shareholders of her company that she was innocent of any wrongdoing.[5]

Ultimately, Stewart was not charged with criminal insider trading. She was, however, charged with two counts of making false statements during interviews with government investigators, one count of obstructing an agency proceeding by making false statements before SEC investigators, and conspiring with her Merrill Lynch broker, Peter Bocanovic, to commit those offenses and in the commission of his perjured testimony.[6] The jury found Stewart guilty of all of these counts.[7] Stewart was also charged with one count of securities fraud, based on her statements to shareholders in which she denied criminal conduct.[8] The jury did not consider that charge because the district court found that the government had failed to provide sufficient evidence to support it.[9]

The Breadth and Depth of Federal Criminal Law

Federal prosecutors have a two-fold authority at the indictment stage; the authority to indict or not and the authority to decide what offenses to charge. The government's decision to indict Stewart on criminal charges generated considerable debate, especially given the relatively low value of the trade.[10] Her celebrity status also raised questions: Was she targeted because of who she was? Would it have been unwise not to indict her because of who she was?[11] Although the decision was made easier when her broker's former assistant, Douglas Faneuil, pleaded guilty to a misdemeanor and agreed to cooperate with prosecutors,[12] the prosecutor has virtually unchecked authority to charge or not.

Prosecutors also have great discretion in deciding what specific offenses to charge. This discretion emanates from and is enhanced by the federal criminal code. At once broad and deep,[13] the code provides prosecutors a wide range of broadly written offenses from which to choose. Its breadth is a function of the expansive and open-ended language used in the statutes because such language allows prosecutors to apply seemingly specific statutes to a wide and unspecified range of conduct. The code is also deep in the sense that several offenses often apply to the same substantive conduct. The charges against Stewart reflect both the breadth and depth of the federal criminal code.

Federal Criminal Laws Are Broad

The securities statute under which Stewart was charged is typical of federal fraud statutes, which are broadly written to encompass a wide range of conduct. The mail and wire fraud statutes prohibit schemes to defraud another of property in which the defendant could foresee the occurrence of a mailing or a wire.[14] The term, "a scheme to defraud" prohibits schemes involving money, property, and the honest services of another person, and includes deceptions by affirmative misrepresentation and by a failure to disclose.[15]

The securities statutes are similarly written in open-ended terms, whether by accident or design, to capture a wide range of conduct. The securities provision makes it unlawful to "use or employ, in connection with the purchase or sale of any security ... any manipulative or deceptive device or contrivance" in contravention of rules established by the SEC.[16] The relevant rule, Rule 10b-5, is hardly more specific; it makes unlawful "any untrue statement of a material fact or engaging in any act which operates as a fraud or deceit ... in connection with the purchase or sale of any security."[17] This unspecified conduct establishes a cause of action for civil liability and becomes criminal when the violation is "willful."[18] Over the years, judicial decisions broadly interpreted these terms and gradually expanded the reach of the securities statutes so they applied to several different forms of fraud.[19] The securities laws now broadly include both general misrepresentations and several types of insider trading, such as trading by temporary outsiders and tippees, as well as trading based on the misappropriation of confidential information.[20] Ironically, prosecutors declined to indict Stewart on an insider trading charge, presumably because her conduct did not fit an established category of the offense.[21] This point illustrates both the charging authority of federal prosecutors and the evolving nature of insider trading law.

In drafting such broad provisions and failing to define statutory terms, Congress may have intended to delegate the tasks of defining terms to the judiciary.[22] Courts inevitably define statutory terms, such as "deceptive device," "willfully," "materially," and "in connection with," in the securities statute as they adjudicate cases. Although it is easy to fault the judiciary's propensity to define the elements of white collar crimes, Congress often has left courts little choice but to do so.[23] When courts apply statutory terms to the specific conduct at issue, the decisions establish new benchmarks and determine the future scope and reach of the law.

Congress may not have reckoned, however, with the role that prosecutors have come to play in this process of judicial interpretation. In the first instance the authority delegated to the judiciary devolves to the prosecutor; it is the prosecutor who initially determines whether the conduct at issue is covered by the statute.[24] Having determined that the statute encompasses the defendant's conduct, the government presses for that interpretation before the court. In deference to the executive branch, judges often accede to the government view, resulting in an incremental, but inexorable, expansion of the laws.

This dynamic allowed prosecutors to charge Stewart with a novel and untested form of securities fraud. As noted, the securities fraud statute prohibits deceptions about material facts in connection with the purchase or sale of a security. The government theory was that Stewart committed securities fraud when she publicly asserted her innocence and stated that she had not engaged in insider trading. Stewart made three statements in June 2002 after a Wall Street Journal article broke the news that she was likely to be indicted. The announcements stated that she had sold her ImClone holdings because of a prearranged decision and included a denial that she had possessed information about the firm.[25] According to the government, these statements were materially false and made with the intent to defraud investors by slowing or stopping the erosion of the company's share value.

Scholars and commentators expressed grave concerns about the novelty of the charge and the rights of defendants, and suggested that the government had overreached.[26] Stewart's lawyers moved for dismissal of the securities fraud charge, arguing that it was unwarranted under existing law, violated due process, and infringed First Amendment rights.[27] The trial court rejected the arguments, denied Stewart's dismissal motion, and allowed the government to attempt to prove the allegation. By reaching this decision, the court conferred tacit approval on the government's theory that a denial of personal wrongdoing that was unrelated to a firm could constitute a scheme to defraud the firm's investors. Ultimately, the court acquitted Stewart of securities fraud after finding that, on the evidence presented, no reasonable juror could find beyond a reasonable doubt that Stewart had lied for the purpose of influencing the price of her company's stock.[28] Nevertheless, a precedent of sorts has been established—general statements to investors about personal wrongdoing that is not directly linked to the company may constitute securities fraud.[29]

The ambiguity of the criminal statutes is compounded in white collar cases because the conduct at issue is often ambiguous. As here, unethical conduct may or may not give rise to civil liability, and may or may not be the basis for a criminal charge. It is often unclear whether the charged offense actually prohibits the charged conduct, and there are many examples of instances in which prosecutors and trial courts were mistaken about whether the specific statute applied to the conduct at issue in the case.[30] Whether conduct is criminal can depend on the actor's state of mind[31] or the egregiousness of the conduct and resulting harm[32] and is sometimes a matter of degree.[33] The combination of ambiguous conduct and broad, vague statutes invites the government to classify risky or unethical behavior as criminal.

The Federal Criminal Code Is Deep

Federal criminal law is deep in that it is composed of duplicative statutes that apply to similar conduct. For instance, there are at least 100 federal false statement statutes and 325 offenses involving fraud.[34] This depth gives prosecutors a plethora of offenses from which to choose. Moreover, as in Stewart's case, the same conduct can lead to accusations of multiple crimes.

The crimes that Stewart was convicted of, false statement, obstruction, and conspiracy,[35] were each based on the statements she made to investigators about the reasons for her sale.[36] Stewart told them that she sold her shares because of a pre-arranged decision to sell when the share price declined to $60. In misrepresenting her reasons to government officers, perhaps to "cover up" the sale that provoked investigation, she committed the false statement offense. Because SEC investigators were present when she made the false statement, she obstructed a pending agency proceeding. Moreover, she was charged with conspiring with her broker to violate the law by making false statements and obstructing an agency proceeding. The breadth of conspiracy law gave rise to an additional charge, that Stewart had conspired with her broker in the commission of his perjury.[37]

Contrary to popular perceptions, the authority to charge multiple offenses for the same underlying conduct is not always limited by the Double Jeopardy Clause of the Constitution, which bars multiple punishment for the same offense.[38] The standard for determining when double jeopardy is triggered is rigorous[39] and does little to limit or constrain the practice of basing multiple charges on a single course of conduct.[40] The Sentencing Guidelines mitigate the ultimate effect of multiple charges somewhat by requiring that similar charges be grouped for purposes of sentencing. The Guidelines thus reduce the likelihood that a defendant would receive separate sentences for each offense.[41] Grouping offenses does not, however, lighten the task of defending those accused of multiple crimes for the same basic conduct in the first place. When considering multiple charges, the jury is more likely to conclude that the accused must have engaged in some criminal act.

The cover-up charges brought against Martha Stewart were not particularly exceptional. In this and in other ways, the *Stewart* case is similar to the *Arthur Andersen* and *Enron* cases, which also illustrate the breadth and depth of the federal criminal code.

Considering *Stewart, Andersen,* and *Enron*

Arthur Andersen, LLP, one of five major accounting firms and Enron's chief auditor, was certain to be involved in the SEC inquiry into various Enron-related matters.[42] While preparing for the inquiry, Andersen's lawyers discovered that thousands of emails and documents were missing or destroyed.[43] In January 2002, the firm reported that David Duncan, the Andersen partner in charge of the Enron account, had instructed employees to destroy documents relating to Andersen's work at Enron.[44] In short order, Andersen and Duncan were each charged with one count of obstructing justice.[45] A month after indictment, Duncan pleaded guilty and agreed to cooperate with the government in its case against Andersen.[46] In June, when a jury found the firm guilty,[47] market forces had already stripped the firm of its value and future earnings, and Andersen was formally sentenced to a $500,000 fine.[48]

The obstruction statute with which Andersen was charged is directed toward influencing or "tampering" with potential witnesses.[49] The government alleged that Duncan and Arthur Andersen, by directing Andersen employees to shred documents, had knowingly and corruptly persuaded the employees to withhold or alter documents for use in an official proceeding.[50] The charge illustrates again the depth of the federal criminal code. In addition to the separate provisions that protect agency proceedings and witnesses, at issue in the *Stewart* and *Andersen* cases, several other obstruction provisions prohibit similar conduct.[51] Section 1503 is known for its powerful omnibus clause, a catch-all provision that applies broadly to a wide range of non-coercive but corrupt endeavors to influence the due administration of justice.[52] The Sarbanes-Oxley Act, passed in July 2002, added two provisions that deal specifically with destroying documents.[53] Congress also amended section 1512, with which Andersen and Duncan were charged, and it now also applies to the individuals who actually withhold or alter documents.[54] There is significant overlap between these provisions, and their relationship to one another has yet to be clarified.[55]

As in Stewart's case, the Andersen prosecution also illustrates the interplay between prosecutors and courts that incrementally broadens the scope of white collar offenses. In the *Andersen* case, however, the Supreme Court rejected the interpretation of statutory language that had been urged by the prosecutor and accepted by the district court. The obstruction provision at issue includes two culpability elements, "knowingly" and "corruptly persuades."[56] The government, urging an expansive application, obtained a jury instruction based on an interpretation of the term "corruptly persuades" that ignored the term "knowingly." The instruction effectively removed Andersen's culpability from consideration, and the jury convicted the firm. Although the

Fifth Circuit upheld the jury instruction, the Supreme Court reversed, commenting that "[I]t is striking how little culpability the instructions required."[57] The ultimate safeguard of a Supreme Court ruling is small comfort, however, given how few cases reach the Court. Moreover, all expansive interpretations are not appealed; Stewart had no incentive to appeal and argue against the prosecutors' interpretation of the securities fraud statute after she was acquitted of that charge.

The *Stewart* and *Andersen* cases demonstrate the consequences that follow the announcement of a criminal investigation. These effects or collateral consequences occur outside of and apart from state-imposed consequences, the stigma of conviction, and punishment. Collateral consequences that affect business firms generally include financial losses, class-action civil suits, enforcement actions by regulatory agencies, and being barred from receiving government contracts.

Individuals also suffer collateral consequences; they are barred from practice before the SEC and can be sued by investors and government agencies.[58] Following disclosure of the government inquiry, Martha Stewart and her company were sued by corporate shareholders.[59] Upon indictment, she resigned as chief executive and chairwoman of her company, taking the title of "founding editorial director."[60] This interim title took a permanent cast following settlement of the SEC suit, under which Stewart may not serve as a chief executive or director of any public company for at least five years.[61]

The reaction of the marketplace, which independently responds in ways that can impose severe financial costs on the firm, is a collateral consequence of a different order. The *Andersen* case illustrates this dynamic. If the firm was indicted or found guilty, demand for Andersen's services was sure to diminish; there is no market for an accounting firm with a tarnished reputation. The market responded quickly and decisively, and even before the trial began, the ultimate survival of the $9 billion company with offices throughout the world, hundreds of partners, and 28,000 employees was in question.

Although courts may reprimand or punish business firms after trial by dissolving them, in this case, Andersen essentially dissolved at the indictment stage, well in advance of adjudication and sentencing. For this reason, indicting a firm like Andersen is often controversial.[62] It is also exceedingly rare.[63] Even so, the mere threat of a criminal charge motivates firms to conduct in-house investigations, cooperate fully with prosecutors, distance themselves from the conduct of their agent, and jettison employees involved in the transaction.[64]

Because Duncan had pleaded guilty, only the Andersen partnership was tried for the crime of obstructing justice. Yet, like the *Stewart* case, the Andersen indictment illustrates the most basic authority of prosecutors–to charge or not. Indictments of a business entity are based on the doctrine of respondeat superior, which makes firms criminally liable for crimes committed by their agents. The standard for liability under this doctrine is similar to the standard used to establish tort liability.[65] Its rationale, to encourage firms to monitor their employees, is the same rationale that underlies the civil counterpart.[66] If an agent, such as David Duncan, commits a crime while acting within the scope of his authority and has acted for the benefit of the corporation, the firm may be found guilty of the agent's offense.[67] Thus, once the agent's guilt is established it is relatively easy, barring exceptional circumstances, to convict the firm.

A decision to charge a corporation or other entity is governed by guidelines formulated by the Department of Justice ("DOJ"), which direct prosecutors to consider nine factors when deciding whether to indict a business entity.[68] The factors include the pervasiveness of wrongdoing within the corporation, the corporation's history of similar conduct, timely and voluntary disclosure, existence and adequacy of a compliance program, remedial efforts, collateral consequences, and the adequacy of prosecuting individuals and civil or regulatory enforcement actions.[69] These guidelines do not overly constrain the discretion to charge corporations.

Several factors argued against Andersen's indictment; the firm had reported the document destruction, was cooperating with investigators, and was negotiating compensation of investors harmed by Enron's collapse. In deciding to indict, prosecutors reportedly were swayed by Andersen's involvement in frauds at Sunbeam and Waste Management and its perceived failure to appreciate the seriousness of its past conduct.[70] Andersen sought to avoid indictment and, when that failed, tried to seek some other means of resolving the matter with prosecutors. Andersen's efforts included firing Duncan, proposing a merger with another firm, and considering a reform plan put forward by Paul Volcker, former chair of the Federal Reserve Board.[71] Comparisons with other firms[72] reveal the obvious, that decisions to charge remain opaque. The absence of transparency serves to enhance prosecutorial authority.

In the first instance, Stewart and Andersen were undone by their own conduct; in the second, by the testimony of cooperating witnesses at trial. Stewart's conviction hinged on the testimony of her broker's assistant,[73] who had pled guilty to a misdemeanor charge and testified against Stewart at trial.[74] At the sentencing hearing, the federal prosecutor asked for "extra leniency" because of the substantial assistance he had provided the government.[75] Similarly, the government's evidence in the *Andersen* case included testimony by David Duncan, who had ordered employees to destroy records.[76] Neither case is exceptional in this regard. They are, in this sense, similar to cases against the Enron defendants, even though the *Enron* cases involve multiple and complex accounting frauds and many defendants.

The indictment of Stewart, Andersen, and the Enron defendants followed what has become a routine progression, as prosecutors charged lower level employees and officers and obtained plea and cooperation agreements from them. In the Enron matter, four top executives, Andrew Fastow, former Chief Financial Officer, Jeffrey Skilling, former Chief Executive, Richard Causey, former Chief Accounting Officer, and Ken Lay, former Chief Executive, were indicted on various counts of securities fraud, wire fraud, insider trading, conspiracy, and money laundering.[77] Twenty other Enron officers have been indicted.[78] As of January 2006, eighteen of the twenty-four former Enron employees now indicted, including Andrew Fastow and Richard Causey, have agreed to cooperate with prosecutors.[79] The trial of Ken Lay and Jeffrey Skilling had just begun as this chapter was in the final stages of production and, although the outcome of the trial is uncertain, many of the cooperating witnesses are certain to testify for the government.

The indictment, plea, and cooperation agreement of Andrew Fastow illustrate how the authority bestowed by broad statutes reinforces the ability of the government to negotiate plea and cooperation agreements. First, prosecutors used information provided by two mid-level executives[80] to indict Fastow on ninety-eight counts that include charges of wire fraud, money laundering, obstruction of justice, and conspiring to commit wire fraud, securities fraud, and other offenses.[81] Second, Lea Fastow, wife of Andrew Fastow and a former assistant treasurer at Enron, was indicted on tax charges, conspiracy, and money laundering.[82] She was charged with hiding taxable income that had been derived from the frauds at Enron and for filing false tax returns for four years. The false returns had reportedly not decreased the couple's tax liability, and Lea Fastow was charged with tax perjury, which carries a maximum sentence of three years, rather than tax evasion, which carries a maximum penalty of five years.[83]

After an unusually public negotiation,[84] Andrew Fastow ultimately pleaded guilty to two counts of conspiracy and began to cooperate with the government. He is likely to serve ten years in prison, the maximum sentence for the conspiracy counts to which he pled.[85] Under an agreement in which she pled guilty to one count of tax perjury, Lea Fastow ultimately received a one-year sentence.[86] Just as the plea of Lea Fastow and the cooperation agreements of other executives hastened Fastow's agreement, his cooperation enabled the government to indict Skilling and Lay.[87]

The *Stewart, Andersen,* and *Enron* cases indicate that much of the success of the current criminal investigations into corporate fraud is a result of the prosecutor's ability to use the breadth and depth of substantive criminal law to negotiate plea and cooperation agreements. The authority granted by the breadth and depth of white collar statutes is strengthened by the discretionary authority to charge business entities and the collateral consequences that flow from indictment and conviction. In addition, high statutory penalties, inflexible Guideline sentencing, and the influence that prosecutors exercise under the Guidelines further strengthen the authority of prosecutors.[88] But in the first instance, the power to charge and to tailor the charges, which is based on a broad and deep criminal code, enables prosecutors to negotiate pleas and cooperation agreements that aid in pursuing other defendants.

Prosecutorial Power in an Adversary System

The significant resources devoted to the *Stewart, Andersen,* and *Enron* cases underline the importance of prosecuting corporate executives who engage in frauds that harm the public, investors, and employees. Such prosecutions serve both retributive and utilitarian goals. These cases demonstrate that prosecutors have sufficient tools and authority to investigate and to convict corporate defendants. Finally, the cases demonstrate the inextricable link between the federal prosecutors' charging authority and the breadth and depth of substantive criminal laws. The vesting of so much authority in individuals in one branch of government creates a certain unease. Could errors in judgment or process be corrected before grave injury is imposed? Are there sufficient safeguards against abuse? In a robust adversary system, one can confidently respond to these concerns in the affirmative. A strong adversarial system, in which prosecutor and defendant have equal standing to make their cases to a neutral, objective judge, ensures the absence of error and abuse. Yet, one consequence of the enhanced authority of federal prosecutors is that it diminishes the adversarial nature of the federal criminal justice system.

This effect may seem counterintuitive in white collar crime cases. After all, those accused of federal white collar crimes are likely to be represented by counsel even before charges are filed, during the investigation and grand jury proceedings.[89] Internal investigations by firms and grand jury subpoenas alert corporate executives, and they prudently hire lawyers. The fact that potential defendants are represented by legal counsel at an early stage leads to the perception that these stages are adversarial in nature, but they are not. The decision to charge and the choice of offenses are made by the prosecutor, not by an independent third party. Nor are these decisions subject to review. Although defense counsel may seek an interview with the prosecutor or the prosecutor's supervising attorney to argue against indictment or about charges, neither official is obliged to grant the interview, much less consider the request.[90]

The European inquisitorial system presents a perspective from which we can assess the charging authority of federal prosecutors. I have compared the roles and authorities of federal and inquisitorial prosecutors in detail elsewhere,[91] and focus here on the comparison of just one variable, the power of prosecutors in the charging stage of a criminal matter.

In both the federal and the European systems, a criminal investigation culminates in the decision to bring charges against the accused. Not surprisingly, prosecutors in both systems have broad authority over initial charging decisions. For instance, prosecutors in both systems may charge the accused with less serious crimes.[92] There are, however, important distinctions between the systems at the charging stage of a criminal matter.

Unlike the federal prosecutor, the French prosecutor relinquishes control over serious cases when, as required, he or she refers the case to an examining magistrate. If the magistrate approves the prosecutor's decision to press charges, he or she must open another independent judicial investigation. This second-level investigation is no mere formality. In 1980, examining magistrates dismissed twenty per cent of referred cases for insufficient evidence.[93] In that event, the prosecutor may continue the investigation. If the examining magistrate agrees that the charges are justified, the matter is referred to the indicting chamber,[94] where the case is again reviewed, this time by three judges who may dismiss or order trial on lesser charges.[95] The prosecutor's work is thus subject to two evaluations, by the examining magistrate and by the indicting chamber. This screening process is more likely to result in the filing of consistent, accurate, and readily provable charges.

In the federal system, the prosecutor's decision to charge is made with the help of a grand jury. In theory, the decision to charge in federal white collar cases belongs to the grand jury, as authorized by the Fifth Amendment.[96] The role of the grand jury is somewhat analogous to that of the inquisitorial system's examining magistrate, that is, to investigate further and to decide whether to charge. The grand jury's mandate is to determine whether there is probable cause to believe that the accused committed a federal offense.[97] Thus, the grand jury is theoretically positioned, as is the examining magistrate in the inquisitorial system, to constrain the enthusiasm of a prosecutor for formally charging the accused.

The enthusiasm is understandable; the federal prosecutor's investigatory task in white collar cases is significant and complex. The secrecy with which white collar crimes are committed and the complexity of fraud often require long and arduous investigation. In such circumstances, the investigation may become less independent and less balanced, and the final conclusions of the prosecutor may reflect biases that result from being closely affiliated with the investigation. Those biases may cause even well-intentioned prosecutors to make mistakes, to conform their findings to earlier hypotheses, to fail to examine issues thoroughly, or fail to make the effort to understand a perspective that is not their own.

Moreover, prosecutors will use the evidence they have collected at the trial in their role as advocates to convince the fact finder of the defendant's guilt. Thus, it would not be surprising if, in presenting evidence to the grand jury, the prosecutor was vested in the outcome of the investigation.[98] Given these considerations, the role of the grand jury to serve as "a protective bulwark standing solidly between the ordinary citizen and an overzealous prosecutor" is significant.[99] In theory, the grand jury may refuse to indict the accused, providing a counterweight to the power of the state and the prosecutor. The reality, however, is far different, and it is widely acknowledged that the typical grand jury is dependent on and heavily influenced by the federal prosecutor.[100]

In most cases, the grand jury depends on the prosecutor for information, acts on evidence provided by the prosecutor, and does not conduct an independent investigation like that undertaken by the French examining magistrate.[101] In the European system, the prosecutor prepares a catalogue of evidence, a dossier of the case. The dossier, which is used by reviewing officers and by the presiding judge at trial, is thus a legally sound basis for prosecution and conviction. Reflecting its use and status, the dossier includes all the evidence in the case, including exculpatory evidence.

In contrast, the evidence that the grand jury considers does not necessarily include exculpatory evidence because federal prosecutors are not required to present even "substantial" exculpatory evidence to the grand jury.[102] Judicial supervision of the government's management of the grand jury is limited, and the prosecutor's responsibility to explain applicable law to the grand jury is generally not subject to review.[103] Moreover, DOJ guidelines generally defer to prosecutors, advising them to provide exculpatory evidence to the grand jury only when they are "personally aware of substantial evidence which directly negates the guilt of a subject of the investigation."[104] Even this deferential standard is not enforceable against the government. Although a prosecutor may find it useful to present exculpatory evidence to the grand jury in order to test the strength of a case before trial,[105] there is no formal requirement that ensures that the grand jury make its decision with full information. Thus, the inquisitorial examining magistrate possesses all available information, including exculpatory evidence, while the federal grand jury may not even be aware that exculpatory evidence exists.

The inquisitorial prosecutor's power is constrained in a second way that implicates the basic choice to charge or not. The authority of the French prosecutor to decline to charge is limited because the victim of a crime, or indeed any French citizen, may file criminal charges directly with the court.[106] This practice encourages prosecutors to file charges[107] and is significant because, unlike the federal prosecutor, the French prosecutor may not drop or reduce the severity of charges once they have been filed.[108] From that point, the magistrate and ultimately the trial court have sole discretion to decide whether the charges fit the facts alleged. In contrast, the federal prosecutor retains discretion to adjust the number and severity of the charges.

In sum, the discretion and authority of federal prosecutors in performing the charging function far exceeds that of French prosecutors. The inquisitorial system is organized to provide checks on prosecutors' power to charge defendants, through supervisory review and the inability of prosecutors to drop or reduce the charges. In addition, continental prosecutors' power to charge or not is constrained by the possibility that a citizen will file charges if they do not.

As the case of Martha Stewart and other high-profile cases reveal, the power of the federal prosecutor rests on a web of interrelated factors that include broad and deep substantive laws, judicial deference in interpreting statutes, authority to negotiate plea bargains, and influence over the final sentence. When combined with the unreviewed charging power, the breadth and depth of substantive criminal laws is perhaps the prime source of prosecutorial authority.

Judge Gerard Lynch has noted that current prosecutorial practices in the federal system depart significantly from an adversarial model and move the federal system closer to the inquisitorial system used in Western Europe.[109] I would add that our system not only resembles the continental model, but that it operates without the benefit of institutional arrangements that curtail the power of the inquisitorial prosecutor. The enhanced authority of federal prosecutors makes the federal system less than adversarial. Broad applications of an ambiguously written and duplicative criminal law permit prosecutors to exercise virtually unlimited discretion in deciding whether the conduct at issue merits criminal penalties.[110] Broadly written laws that are subject to continuous reinterpretation may inject too much "free play" into the system,[111] leading to the misuse of government power and an over reliance on illegitimate criteria for selection.[112] Yet in the absence of a strong adversary institution, there is no counterweight that would operate as a check on prosecutorial authority.

In considering how to redress this imbalance, one might begin with a reform of the federal criminal law. This endeavor is an obvious place to start, though it is a long-term effort fraught with obstacles. In the short run, decision makers might look to the inquisitorial system as a model for incremental change. Close examination of inquisitorial processes is likely to provide insights for dealing with the imbalance between prosecutor and defendant that now characterizes the federal system.

Conclusion

The treacherous currents of federal criminal law are both broad and deep. Although this review has been limited to white collar cases, the substantive federal criminal law also presents significant concerns when applied to those who cannot afford competent counsel. Even the Martha Stewarts of the world, who generally have financial resources, are well-represented, and have benefit of counsel well in advance of indictment, are subject to substantial challenges in defending themselves before the full force of executive branch authority. The implications of the power that federal prosecutors exercise in white collar cases have even greater force when that power is applied to defendants who are less able to navigate the currents of federal criminal law.

Questions

1. Why might a legislator reasonably prefer open-ended language in a criminal statute? In writing such statutes, does Congress delegate too much authority to the executive and judicial branches? Broadly written statutes are said to encourage selective prosecutions. Why would this be the case? Was the indictment of Stewart a selective prosecution? What role may her celebrity have played in the decision to indict?
2. What are the advantages and disadvantages of indicting defendants for several different crimes that are all based on a single course of conduct? Should the practice be discouraged?
3. In what ways are the enforcement decisions in the *Stewart* case similar to the prosecutions of Arthur Andersen and the Enron defendants? How do the cases differ? Taken as a whole, how do the cases inform our understanding of the federal criminal justice system?
4. Given the complexity of many white collar investigations, is it realistic to expect a grand jury to act independently of prosecutors? Should the federal system incorporate the inquisitorial system's supervisory review of charg-

ing decisions? Are there other methods of monitoring the discretionary authority of federal prosecutors?

Notes

1. United States v. Stewart, 03 Cr. 717 (MGC), (S.D. N.Y. June 4, 2003) [hereinafter Indictment].

2. Waksal pleaded guilty to charges of insider trading and is currently serving a seven-year sentence. *See* Kathleen F. Brickey, *From Enron to WorldCom and Beyond: Life and Crime after Sarbanes-Oxley*, 81 Wash. U. L. Q. 357, 392, Appendix A, *Major Corporate Fraud Prosecutions: March 2002–August 2003* (2003).

3. *See* Indictment, *supra* note 1.

4. *See id.*

5. *See id.*

6. *See id.*

7. United States v. Stewart, 433 F.3d 173 (2d Cir. 2006)

8. *See* Indictment, *supra* note 1.

9. United States v. Stewart, 305 F. Supp. 2d 368 (S.D. N.Y. 2004).

10. *See* Joan MacLeod Heminway, *Save Martha Stewart? Observations About Equal Justice in U.S. Insider Trading Regulation*, 12 Tex. J. of Women & L. 247, 249–51 (2003).

11. *See* Jonathan D. Glater, *Stewart's Celebrity Created Magnet for Scrutiny*, N.Y. Times, March 7, 2004, at A11; Kurt Eichenwald, *Prosecutors Have Reasons for Stalking Celebrities*, N.Y. Times, June 5, 2003, at C4.

12. *See* United States v. Faneuil, 02-CR-1287 (S.D. N.Y. Oct. 2, 2002) (Misdemeanor Information).

13. Or, in the words of Professor Julie O'Sullivan, "sprawling and redundant." *See* Julie R. O'Sullivan, Federal White Collar Crime: Cases and Materials 18 (2d ed. 2004).

14. 18 U.S.C. §§ 1341, 1342, 1346 (2000). *See* Schmuck v. United States, 489 U.S. 705 (1989).

15. *See* John C. Coffee, *The Metastasis of Mail Fraud: The Continuing Story of the Evolution of a White-Collar Crime*, 21 Am. Crim. L. Rev. 1, 19 (1983); Geraldine Szott Moohr, *Mail Fraud Meets Criminal Theory*, 67 U. Cin. L. Rev. 1 (1998).

16. 15 U.S.C. § 78j(b) (2001).

17. 17 C.F.R. § 240.10b-5 (2006).

18. 15 U.S.C. § 77ff(a) (2001).

19. *See* Lawrence M. Solan, *Statutory Inflation and Institutional Choice*, 44 Wm. & Mary L. Rev. 2209, 2238–46 (2003) (analyzing development of insider trading law and suggesting that expansive judicial interpretations are more likely when a government agency is charged with civil, remedial enforcement). For a critique of the agency's role, see *United States v. O'Hagan*, 521 U.S. 642, 691 (1997) (Thomas, J., dissenting, with Chief Justice Rehnquist).

20. *See* United States v. O'Hagan, 521 U.S. 642 (1997).

21. The SEC was not so restrained and filed a civil enforcement action against Stewart for insider trading. The suit was ultimately settled. *See infra* text accompanying note 62.

22. *See* Daniel C. Richman, *Federal Criminal Law, Congressional Delegation, and Enforcement Discretion*, 46 U.C.L.A. L. Rev. 757 (1999) (discussing the institutional forces that motivate Congress to enact ambiguous and broad statutes).

23. *See* H. J. Inc. v. Northwestern Bell Tel. Co., 492 U.S. 229 (1989) ("Congress has done nothing in the interim further to illuminate RICO's key requirement of a pattern of racketeering.... It is, nevertheless a task we must undertake in order to decide this case."); United States v. Brumley, 116 F.3d 728 (5th Cir. 1997) (en banc) *cert. denied*, 522 U.S. 1028 ("We must next find the meaning of honest services as used in this federal statute.").

24. Chuck Ruff discussed the responsibility of federal prosecutors in interpreting criminal statutes almost 30 years ago. *See* Charles F.C. Ruff, *Federal Prosecution of Local Corruption: A Case Study in the Making of Law Enforcement*, 655 Geo. L.J. 1171 (1977). Yet, the dynamic continues to occupy commentators. *See* Dan M. Kahan, *Is Chevron Relevant to Federal Criminal Law?*, 110 Harv. L. Rev. 469 (1996); Geraldine Szott Moohr, *Mail Fraud and the Intangible Rights Doctrine: Someone to Watch over Us*, 31 Harv. J. On Leg. 153 (1994); William J. Stuntz, *The Pathological Politics of Criminal Law*, 100 Mich. L. Rev. 505 (2001).

25. *See* Indictment, *supra* note 1.

26. *See, e.g.*, David Mills & Robert Weisberg, *Flunking the Martha Test*, Wall St. J., Jan. 16, 2004, at A10 (Stanford Law School professors Mills and Weisberg concluded that a statement of innocence about an offense unrelated to the firm does not defraud shareholders); Brooke A. Masters, *Securities Charge Could Be Biggest Threat to Stewart*, Wash. Post, June 19, 2003, at E2 (quoting David E. Marder, former SEC enforcement lawyer "[the government] has alleged you manipulated stock prices simply by protesting your innocence"); William Safire, *Fight It, Martha*, N.Y. Times, June 12, 2003, at A35; Alex Berenson, *Defining Martha Stewart's Alleged Crime*, N.Y. Times, June 8, 2003, at Wk p. 5.

27. *See* United States v. Stewart, 03 Cr. 717 (MGC) (S.D.N.Y. Oct. 6, 2003) (Memorandum of Law in Support of Martha Stewart's Omnibus Pre-Trial Motions).

28. *See* United States v. Stewart, 305 F. Supp. 2d 368 (S.D.N.Y. 2004).

29. For commentary on the district court's opinion in this regard, see Chapter 8 in this volume.

30. *See, e.g.*, Securities and Exchange Comm'n v. Zandford, 535 U.S. 813 (2002); United States v. Handakas, 286 F.3d 92 (2d Cir. 2002); United States v. Brown, 79 F.3d 1550 (11th Cir. 1996); United States v. Jain, 93 F.3d 436 (8th Cir. 1996).

31. *See* United States v. Cueto, 151 F.3d 620 (7th Cir. 1998), *cert. denied*, 526 U.S. 1016 (1999) (holding that otherwise lawful conduct obstructed justice because it was motivated by an improper purpose).

32. *See* United States v. Regent Office Supply Co., 421 F.2d 1174 (2d Cir. 1970); *Brown*, 79 F.3d 1550 (distinguishing lawful statements about a product from unlawful statements that would defraud investors).

33. In the words of Justice Holmes, "[T]he law is full of instances where a man's fate depends on his estimating rightly, that is, as the jury subsequently estimates it, some matter of degree." Nash v. United States, 229 U.S. 373, 377 (1913) (discussing Sherman Act antitrust charges).

34. *See* United States v. Wells, 519 U.S. 482, 505–09 & nn.8–10 (Stevens, J., dissenting) (noting the number of federal false statement statutes); Jeffrey Standen, *An Economic Perspective On Federal Criminal Law Reform*, 2 Buff. Crim. L. Rev. 249, 290 (1998) (reporting his count of fraud offenses).

35. 18 U.S.C. §1001 (prohibiting "knowingly and willfully" making a false statement to a federal official acting within the jurisdiction of the executive, legislative, or judicial branches); 18 U.S.C. §1505 (prohibiting obstructing the due and proper administration of the law authorizing an agency proceeding); 18 U.S.C. §371 (conspiring to commit an offense against the United States).

36. These offenses provide breadth, as well as depth. *See, e.g.,* Brogan v. United States, 522 U.S. 398, 408 (1998) (Ginsburg, J., concurring) (calling attention to the extraordinary authority the false statement statute confers on prosecutors).

37. *See* United States v. Stewart, 433 F.3d 273 (2d Cir. 2006).

38. U.S. Const. amend. V.

39. *See* Blockburger v. United States, 284 U.S. 299 (1932) (no double jeopardy where provisions of a criminal statute require proof of a fact that another other statute does not); United States v. Holmes, 44 F.3d 1150, 1153–54 (2d Cir. 1995) (stating test for double jeopardy is "whether congress intended to authorize separate punishments for the conduct in question").

40. *See* United States Woodward, 469 U.S. 105 (1985) (charging defendant with false statements, 18 U.S.C. §1001, and failing to report transportation of currency, 31 U.S.C. §1058, did not violate the Double Jeopardy Clause).

41. *See* United States Sentencing Guidelines Manual [hereinafter USSG] (2003), Part D, §§3D1.1 to 3D1.5 (grouping of charges depends on several factors, such as the amount of the victim's loss).

42. For commentary on the Arthur Andersen case, see Kathleen F. Brickey, *Andersen's Fall From Grace,* 81 Wash. U. L. Q. 917 (2003); Stephan Landsman, *Death of an Accountant: The Jury Convicts Arthur Andersen of Obstruction of Justice,* 78 Chicago-Kent L. Rev. 1203 (2003).

43. *See* Richard A. Oppel, Jr., *Andersen Says Lawyer Let Its Staff Destroy Files,* N.Y. Times, Jan. 14, 2004, at A13.

44. *See* Kurt Eichenwald, *Enron's Many Strands: The Accountants; Miscues, Missteps and the Fall of Andersen,* N.Y. Times, May 8, 2002, at C1.

45. *See* Arthur Andersen LLP v. United States, 125 S.Ct. 2129 (2005).

46. *See* United States v. Duncan, CRH-02-209 (S.D. Tex. April 7, 2002) (Guilty Plea and Cooperation Agreement).

47. *See Andersen,* 125 S.Ct. 2129.

48. *See* Mary Flood & Tom Fowler, *Enron's Auditor Is Given the Max,* Houston Chron., Oct. 17, 2002, at A1.

49. 18 U.S.C. §1512(b)(2)(A) and (B).

50. *See Andersen,* 125 S.Ct. 2129.

51. *See, e.g.,* 18 U.S.C. §1503 (influencing an officer or juror), 18 U.S.C. §1510 (obstructing a criminal investigation), and 18 U.S.C. §1513 (retaliating against witnesses).

52. *See* United States v. Thomas, 916 F.2d 647, 650 n.3 (11th Cir. 1990).

53. *See* 18 U.S.C. §1519 (pertaining to federal investigations and bankruptcy); 18 U.S.C. §1520 (pertaining to corporate audit records); Sarbanes-Oxley Act of 2002, Pub. L. No. 107-204, 116 Stat. 745 (2002) at §802.

54. *See* 18 U.S.C. §1512(c).

55. For further discussion of the obstruction statutes, see Chapter 7 of this volume.

56. 18 U.S.C. §1512(b)(1).

57. *See Andersen,* 125 S.Ct. at 2136. David Duncan, without objection from the government, has withdrawn his guilty plea. *See The Fall of Enron: Charge Against Duncan Dropped,* Houston Chron., Dec. 15, 2005, at 3.

58. *See* Kathleen F. Brickey, *Enron's Legacy*, 8 BUFF. CRIM. L. REV. 221, 252 & Table 3 (2004) (presenting summary indicating that 28 individuals or firms involved in Enron criminal actions are also the subject of parallel SEC proceedings).

59. *See* Constance L. Hays, *Amended Lawsuit Accuses Some Stewart Executives*, N.Y. TIMES, Feb. 5, 2003, at C2.

60. *See* Sara Kugler, *Martha Stewart to Go Back to Work After Five-Month Prison Sentence*, AP WIRE, March 7, 2005.

61. *See* Landon Thomas, Jr., *Stewart Deal Resolves Stock Case*, N.Y. TIMES, Aug. 8, 2006 at C1. The securities laws authorize courts to prohibit any person whose "conduct demonstrates unfitness" from serving as an officer or director of publicly held companies. *See* 15 U.S.C. 78t(e) (criminal matter); 15 U.S.C. 78u(d)(2) (civil matter). The Sarbanes-Oxley Act amended those specific provisions to change the standard from "substantially unfit" to "unfit." *See* Sarbanes-Oxley Act of 2002, *supra* note 54, at §305; *see also id.* at §1105 (applying to Section 10(b) enforcement actions).

62. *Compare* Lou Dobbs, *There's More to Journalism Than 'Just the Facts'*, WALL ST. J., April 9, 2002, at A26 (criticizing the Justice Department for indicting Andersen because of its effect on employees, retirees, and Enron plaintiffs) *with* James O'Toole, *Spreading the Blame at Andersen*, N.Y. TIMES, Mar. 26, 2002, at A27 (arguing that the all partners was responsible for either managerial incompetence or ethical turpitude).

63. *See* Benjamin M. Greenblum, *What Happens to a Prosecution Deferred? Judicial Oversight of Corporate Deferred Prosecution Agreements*, 105 COLUM. L. REV. 1863, 1864 n.1 (2005) (providing data showing that organizations comprised less than one percent of federal convictions in 2002).

64. *See* Ellen S. Podgor, *White Collar Cooperators: The Government in Employer-Employee Relationships*, 23 CARDOZO L. REV. 795, 808 (2002).

65. *See* New York Central & Hudson River R.R. Co. v. United States, 212 U.S. 481 (1909) (analogizing criminal guilt with tort liability).

66. *See* United States v. Sun-Diamond Growers of California, 138 F.3d 961 (D.C. Cir. 1998), *aff'd on other grounds*, 526 U.S. 398 (1999).

67. *See New York Central*, 212 U.S. 481.

68. *See Memorandum from Deputy Attorney General Larry D. Thompson to United States Attorneys of Jan. 20, 2003 re Principles of Federal Prosecutions of Business Organizations*, *available at* http://www.usdoj.gov/eousa/foia_reading_room/ usam/title9.

69. *Id.*

70. *See* Eichenwald, *supra* note 45.

71. *Id.*

72. KPMG, one of the top four accounting firms, has accepted a deferred prosecution agreement in an action involving the fraudulent marketing of tax shelters. *See* Kathryn Kennealy, *The KPMG Deferred Prosecution: Warning Flags for Defense Rights*, 29 Nov. CHAMPION 44 (2005); J. Gregory Sidak, *The Failure of Good Intentions: Fraud and the Collapse of American Telecommunications After Deregulation*, 20 YALE J. ON REG. 207 (2003) (discussing damage to the industry caused by WorldCom and the anticompetitive purpose of its fraud and recommending that the FCC revoke its licenses and liquidate the firm).

73. *See* Brooke A. Masters, *Witness in Stewart Trial Is Spared Prison Time*, N.Y. TIMES, July 24, 2004, at E1.

74. Faneuil pled guilty to violating 18 U.S.C. §837 for withholding information from authorities and was sentenced to a $2000 fine. *Id.*

75. *Id.*

76. *See* Kurt Eichenwald, *Andersen May Find Its Fate in Hands of the Man it Fired*, N.Y. Times, March 25, 2003, at A1; Kurt Eichenwald, *Andersen Team Tries to Pick Apart Main Witness*, N.Y. Times, May 18, 2002, at B1.

77. United States v. Skilling, No. H-04-25 (S-2) (S.D. Tex. July 7, 2004) (Indictment of Skilling, Causey, and Lay); United States v. Fastow, No. H-2-02-0665 (S.D. Tex. Oct. 31, 2002) (Indictment).

Lay is also accused of bank fraud and making false statements to banks regarding pledges made to secure bank loans; he will be tried separately on these charges. *See* Alberto Cuadra & Robert Dibrell, *A Look at the Trial*, Houston Chron., Jan. 29, 2006, at A23.

78. *See* Kathleen F. Brickey, *Enron-Related Prosecutions: March 2002–January 2006* (unpublished) (on file with author). In addition, Enron-related defendants include Arthur Andersen and David Duncan, three NatWest bankers, and six Merrill Lynch analysts. *Id; see also* Brickey, *supra* note 2, at 382–401, Appendix A, *Major Corporate Fraud Prosecutions: March 2002–August 2003*.

79. *See* Brickey, *Enron-Related Prosecutions: March 2002–January 2006*, *supra* note 80.

80. *See* Mary Flood, *Ex-Enron Accountant Surrenders*, Houston Chron. Jan. 23, 2004 at A1 (reporting that David Delainey and Wesley Colwell provided information about Fastow's role in the fraud).

81. *See* United States v. Fastow, No. H-2-02-0665 (S.D. Tex. Oct. 31, 2002) (Indictment).

82. *See* John A. Townsend, *An Analysis of the Fastow Plea Agreements*, 2004 Tax Notes Today 44–46 (2004) (on file with author).

83. *See id.* at 4 (noting that DOJ tax prosecutors do not usually pursue bare tax perjury and suggesting that prosecutors may have had "other axes to grind").

84. *See* Geraldine Szott Moohr, *Prosecutorial Power in an Adversarial System: Lessons from Current White Collar Cases*, 8 Buff. Crim. L. Rev. 165, 184 & n.18 (2004).

85. *See* United States v. Andrew Fastow, CRH-02-0665 (S.D. Tex. Jan. 15, 2004) (Plea Agreement).

86. *See* Mary Flood, *Lea Fastow Leaves Prison*, Houston Chron., June 7, 2005. The judge rejected the five-month term suggested by prosecutors. Nor did Lea Fastow receive preferential treatment. She served nearly eleven months in Houston's Federal Detention Center, which is more restrictive than a federal minimum security prison camp, and the remaining five weeks of her sentence in a halfway house rather than in home detention. She is also subject to a year of supervised release. *Id.*

87. *See* Mary Flood, *Ex-Enron Accountant Surrenders*, Houston Chron., Jan. 23, 2004, at A1 (reporting that Fastow had explained the fraudulent nature of one of Enron's special purpose entities that resulted in overstatement of Enron's earnings); Brooke A. Masters, *Focus Kept Narrow in Indictment of Lay*, Wash. Post, July 10, 2004, at E1 (reporting that prosecutors used information from five cooperating witnesses); United States v. Skilling, No. H-04-25 (S-2) (S.D. Tex. July 7, 2004) (Indictment).

88. The Sentencing Guidelines allow prosecutors, but not defendants or judges, to request a downward departure from the guideline sentence if the defendant has provided substantial assistance to authorities. *See* U.S. Sentencing Guidelines Manual § 5K1.1 (2005).

The operation of the Guidelines and section 5K1.1 has been altered by *United States v. Booker*, 125 S.Ct. 738 (2005). In *Booker*, the Supreme Court held that application of the Sentencing Guidelines violated the Sixth Amendment right to a jury trial. *Id.* The Court also held, however, that discretionary use of the Guidelines did not implicate the Sixth Amendment and severed the mandatory provisions from the statute, making judicial use of the Guidelines discretionary. *Id.* Given the absence of a certain sentence after *Booker* and the alteration of the authority between prosecutors and judges, in the future white collar defendants may decline to plead or reach less harsh agreements with prosecutors.

89. For commentary on the defense function during the pre-indictment stage, see KENNETH MANN, DEFENDING WHITE-COLLAR CRIME: A PORTRAIT OF ATTORNEYS AT WORK 192–201 (1985).

90. *See* Gerard Lynch, *The Expanding Prosecutorial Role from Trial Counsel to Investigator and Administrator,* 26 FORDHAM URB. L.J. 679, 696–97 (1999).

91. *See* Moohr, *supra* note 86.

92. The following discussion relies heavily on the scholarship of Professor Richard Frase, among others. *See* Richard S. Frase, *Comparative Criminal Justice As a Guide to American Law Reform: How Do the French Do It, How Can We Find Out, and Why Should We Care?* [hereinafter *Comparative Criminal Justice*], 78 CAL. L. REV. 539 (1990); Richard S. Frase, *France* in CRAIG M. BRADLEY, CRIMINAL PROCEDURE: A WORLDWIDE STUDY 143 (1999); Richard S. Frase, *The Search for the Whole Truth About American and European Criminal Justice,* 3 BUFF. CRIM. L. REV. 785 (2000); *see also* PHILIP L. REICHEL, COMPARATIVE CRIMINAL JUSTICE SYSTEMS (3d ed. 2002); COMPARATIVE CRIMINAL PROCEDURE (John Hatchard et al. eds., 1996); Thomas Weigend, *Criminal Procedure: Comparative Aspects* in 1 ENCYCLOPEDIA OF CRIME AND JUSTICE 444 (Joshua Dressler ed., 2d ed. 2002).

93. *See* Frase, *Comparative Criminal Justice, supra* note 94, at 625 n.461.

94. *See id.* (noting that the prosecutor may appeal the magistrate's refusal to refer the matter to the indicting chamber).

95. *See id.* at 625 n.462.

96. U.S. CONST., amend V.

97. *See* United States v. Calandra, 414 U.S. 338, 343 (1974).

98. *See* Gerard E. Lynch, *Our Administrative System of Justice,* 66 FORDHAM L. REV. 2117, 2132 (1998) (noting that a prosecutor may become "the jury in her own case").

99. United States v. Dionisio, 410 U.S. 1, 17 (1983). Every federal defendant is not indicted by a grand jury; those charged with misdemeanors and those who plead guilty may be indicted through the filing of an information document.

100. As one court has remarked, a prosecutor could convince a grand jury to indict a ham sandwich. United States v. Reyes, 167 F. Supp. 2d 579, 592 (S.D.N.Y. 2001); R. Michael Cassidy, *Toward a More Independent Grand Jury: Recasting and Enforcing the Prosecutor's Duty to Disclose Exculpatory Evidence,* 18 GEO. J. LEGAL ETHICS 361, 361 (2000).

101. *See* Daniel C. Richman, *Grand Jury Secrecy: Plugging the Leaks in an Empty Bucket,* 36 AM. CRIM. L. REV. 339, 342–45 (1999).

102. *See* United States v. Williams, 504 U.S. 36 (1992). The government is required, however, to give the defendant exculpatory evidence. *See* Brady v. Maryland, 373 U.S. 83, 86 (1963).

103. *See* Bank of Nova Scotia v. United States, 487 U.S. 250 (1988) (reversing dismissal of the indictment granted because of prosecutorial errors in the grand jury proceedings where errors did not prejudice defendant); Vasquez v. Hillery, 474 U.S. 254, 260–64 (1986) (dismissal is appropriate when error, such as racial discrimination in selection of grand jurors, is fundamentally unfair); In re Grand Jury 79-01, 489 F. Supp. 844 (N.D. Ga. 1980).

104. *See* U.S. Dep't of Justice, U.S. Attorney's Manual § 9-11.233, *available at* http://www.usdoj.gov/usao/eousa/foia_reading_room/usam.

105. *See* Ellen S. Podgor, *The Ethics and Professionalism of Prosecutors in Discretionary Decisions*, 68 FORDHAM L. REV. 1511, 1516 (2000). The prosecutor who "seeks justice" would clearly want to present full information to the grand jury. *Id.*

106. *See* Weigend, *supra* note 94.

107. *See id.* (noting that this privilege may go too far in subjecting the magistrate's discretion to the judgment of an individual victim).

108. *See* Frase, *Comparative Criminal Justice, supra* note 94, at 613, 617–25.

109. *See* Lynch, *supra* note 100; *see also* Kahan, *supra* note 24.

110. *See* John C. Coffee, *The Metastasis of Mail Fraud: The Continuing Story of the Evolution of a White-Collar Crime*, 21 AM. CRIM. L. REV. 1 (1983).

111. Anthony G. Amsterdam, Note, *The Void for Vagueness Doctrine in the Supreme Court*, 109 U. PA. L. REV. 67 (1960).

112. John C. Jeffries, Jr., *Legality, Vagueness, and the Construction of Penal Statutes*, 71 VA. L. REV. 189, 212 (1985).

CHAPTER 5

A "NOVEL" SECURITIES FRAUD
CHARGE*

Joan MacLeod Heminway

On February 27, 2004, a federal trial court judge sitting in New York acquitted Martha Stewart of securities fraud.[1] The charge on which the court acquitted Stewart was based on the claim that Stewart had willfully misrepresented a material fact in connection with the purchase or sale of a security.[2]
The material fact allegedly misrepresented was Stewart's publicly articulated
reason for the sale of 3,928 shares of common stock of ImClone Systems Incorporated ("ImClone") on December 27, 2001.[3] According to the government's case, this alleged misstatement regarding Stewart's sale of ImClone's
stock—a personal transaction—was made by her in an effort to maintain an
artificially high market price for the publicly traded common stock of Martha
Stewart Living Omnimedia, Inc., the corporation founded by Stewart and
built around her domestic and marketing talents ("MSLO").[4]

Commentators, including legal scholars, have asked whether bringing the securities fraud charge was an appropriate use of prosecutorial discretion.[5] This
chapter further explores that question in light of the elements of a criminal action for securities fraud and applicable legal standards governing prosecutorial
conduct. Specifically, the chapter begins by presenting a general overview of the
elements of and burdens of proof for criminal securities fraud actions under
Section 10(b) of the Securities Exchange Act of 1934, as amended (the "1934
Act"),[6] and Rule 10b-5 adopted by the Securities and Exchange Commission
(the "SEC") under Section 10(b) of the 1934 Act ("Rule 10b-5").[7] Then, it briefly

---

* This chapter is derived from *Martha Stewart Saved! Insider Violations of Rule 10b-5
for Misrepresented or Undisclosed Personal Facts or Transactions*, originally published at 65
MD. L. REV. 380 (2006), and is included here with the permission of the publisher, Maryland Law Review.

recounts the facts relevant to the securities fraud charge brought against Stewart. Next, the chapter considers whether the prosecution's Rule 10b-5 charge against Stewart comports with law, reflecting on both prosecutorial standards relevant to charging decisions and the application of the elements of securities fraud to the facts of Stewart's case, as those facts were known at the time the indictment in the *Stewart* case (the "Indictment") was filed. The chapter concludes by making some general observations about the Stewart securities fraud charge.

Securities Fraud under Rule 10b-5

Martha Stewart was prosecuted by the U.S. government under Section 10(b) of the 1934 Act ("Section 10(b)") and Rule 10b-5. Although securities fraud actions brought under Rule 10b-5 have roots in common law actions for misrepresentation and deceit, the Supreme Court has long been clear that actions under Rule 10b-5 have their own elements.[8] The elements of a securities fraud charge or claim under Rule 10b-5 differ depending on whether public (criminal or civil) or private enforcement is sought; but three principle components are at the core of all Rule 10b-5 actions:

- manipulation or deception (including by the misrepresentation of, or omission to state, a material fact);[9]
- in connection with the purchase or sale of a security;[10]
- with scienter.[11]

Successful private actions under Rule 10b-5 also require pleading and proof of: standing (based on an actual purchase or sale of securities);[12] reliance by the plaintiff purchaser or seller on the defendant's conduct;[13] causation of the plaintiff's loss;[14] and damages.[15] Private actions are subject to a specific statute of limitations,[16] and class actions have certain specialized procedural and substantive requirements.[17] Criminal prosecutions under Rule 10b-5 are subject to constraints not applicable to civil claims, including requirements imposed by the 1934 Act and federal criminal procedure.[18]

Core Elements

Manipulation or Deception

The requirement that a Section 10(b) claim involve manipulation or deception raises a question as to exactly what constitutes manipulation or deception. There is no definition of either term in the 1934 Act or the rules and regulations promulgated by the SEC under Section 10(b). Rule 10b-5 itself does not adequately serve this definitional purpose.

> Rule 10b-5 did not describe any particular practice that it deemed manipulative or deceptive, as the statutory scheme had anticipated. Instead, the SEC promulgated a regulation that spoke with the same generality as the statute, making it unlawful "[t]o employ any device, scheme, or artifice to defraud, [t]o make any untrue statement of material fact or ... [t]o engage in any act, practice, or course of business which operates or would operate as a fraud or deceit." ... The rule as promulgated drew upon no specific expertise of the SEC. Its generality meant, moreover, that either the Commission or the courts would have to give it substance through case-by-case adjudication.[19]

To a significant degree, federal courts have determined the meaning of the relevant language in Section 10(b) and Rule 10b-5; the manipulation or deception element has been the subject of numerous decisions over the years since Rule 10b-5 was adopted.[20] As a general matter, the Supreme Court has stated that it views "manipulation" as more of a "term of art" relating to exploitative conduct involving market transactions in securities.[21] Deception, on the other hand, involves dishonest conduct that has meaning in a broader context.[22] Legal scholars also have contributed to the debate over the meaning of these terms.[23] Yet, clarity has not been achieved.

Moreover, Rule 10b-5 (read, as it must be, in light of Section 10(b)), has three separate component parts, each of which addresses a different type of wrongful conduct. "Significantly, this rule covers not only misrepresentations, but devices, schemes, or artifices to defraud; and acts, practices, and courses of business which could operate as a fraud."[24] Said another way, "market manipulation carries with it liability under Rule 10b-5(a) and (c), separate from ... omissions liability" under Rule 10b-5(b).[25] These three bases for liability under Rule 10b-5 must be individually alleged and proven.[26] Again, many of the important terms are undefined in the 1934 Act and beg for interpretation.[27] One thing can be said with some certainty, however. A mere breach of fiduciary duty does not satisfy this element.[28]

Where allegations of manipulation or deception involve misstatements of, or omissions to state, material facts, litigants must contend with the meaning of the word "material." The judicially constructed definition of "material" under Rule 10b-5 consists of two alternative standards. A misstatement or omission is material if there is "... a substantial likelihood that a reasonable shareholder would consider it important" in making an investment decision.[29] Alternatively, an omission is material if there is "... a substantial likelihood that the disclosure of the omitted fact would have been viewed by reasonable investor as having significantly altered the 'total mix' of information made available."[30] Subsequent decisional law has construed these alternative standards in various contexts.[31]

"In Connection With" the Purchase or Sale of a Security

Federal courts have advanced a number of legal standards defining the Rule 10b-5 requirement that the subject manipulation or deception occur "in connection with" the purchase or sale of a security.[32] The requirement is intended to be read broadly,[33] but not so broadly that it is devoid of content.[34] The U.S. Supreme Court most recently addressed this element in 2002, finding that "a fraudulent scheme in which the securities transactions and the breaches of fiduciary duty coincide" satisfies the "in connection with" requirement.[35] More than 30 years earlier, the U.S. Supreme had construed the "in connection with" element by stating that the identified manipulation or deception must at least "touch" the acquisition or disposition of a security.[36] Yet earlier, the Second Circuit had interpreted the "in connection with" requirement to encompass manipulative or deceptive conduct on which a reasonable investor would rely.[37] Other courts have embellished the definitional standards adopted in these cases.[38] For example, some courts are willing to find the requisite connection to a securities transaction if a proven misstatement of a material fact occurs in a medium calculated to reach investors.[39] Moreover, although there must be some relationship between the asserted manipulation or deception and a securities transaction, alleged misrepresentations need not relate to the investment value of a particular security to satisfy the "in connection with" element.[40]

> The fraud in question must relate to the nature of the securities, the risks associated with their purchase or sale, or some other factor with similar connection to the securities themselves. While the fraud in question need not relate to the investment value of the securities themselves, it must have more than some tangential relation to the securities transaction.[41]

Scienter

As a third core element of Rule 10b-5 claims, the federal government, the SEC, and private plaintiffs must allege and prove that the defendant had scienter—a prescribed state of mind.[42] Mere negligence on the part of a defendant is not enough.[43] Moreover, allegations and proof of intentional misconduct, while sufficient to satisfy the scienter requirement, may not be necessary.[44] Although the U.S. Supreme Court has not yet ruled expressly on the specific required level of culpability, federal courts generally acknowledge that recklessness is sufficient to meet the scienter requirement under Rule 10b-5.[45] The claimant must establish that the defendant was aware of the "true state of affairs and appreciated the propensity of the misstatement or omission to mislead"[46] or acted with reckless disregard for the truth.[47] Essentially, scienter is the intent to manipulate or deceive.[48] This element of a Rule 10b-5 claim is difficult to allege and prove; evidence of scienter often is circumstantial.[49]

Criminal enforcement under Rule 10b-5 adds an important requirement that impacts these core elements.[50] To be the subject of successful criminal prosecution under the 1934 Act, a violation must be willful.[51] Although the definition of the word "willful" in this context is uncertain,[52] recent decisional law under the 1934 Act and other federal statutes generally indicates that the government must at least show that the defendant acted with knowledge of the wrongfulness of his conduct under the law that he is accused of violating.[53]

> A defendant acts willfully when he acts intentionally and deliberately and his actions are not the result of an innocent mistake, negligence, or inadvertence. While proof of specific intent is not needed, the government must establish that the defendant had some evil purpose and intended to commit the prohibited act.[54]

Elements and Other Special Rules Applicable to Private Enforcement Actions

Although the 1934 Act does not provide an express private right of action for violations of Rule 10b-5, private actions under Rule 10b-5 long have been implied.[55] In addition to the core elements described above, private plaintiffs claiming violations of Rule 10b-5 must have standing, prove three additional elements (reliance, loss causation, and damages), and, in the class action setting, meet certain additional requirements. These elements are not applicable to the criminal action against Stewart, but they do provide important background to and context for the three core elements. Over the years, the Supreme Court has established and tinkered with these elements in an effort to regulate the volume and nature of private litigation under Rule 10b-5.[56]

Courts have imposed a standing requirement for private actions under Rule 10b-5, mandating that a plaintiff be an actual seller or purchaser of a security.[57] Forbearance—expressly deciding *not* to engage in a securities transaction as a result of conduct otherwise proscribed under Rule 10b-5, does not satisfy this element of proof.[58] However, a defendant in a Rule 10b-5 action need not be a seller or purchaser.[59]

A private action plaintiff also must prove reliance on the alleged manipulative or deceptive conduct of the defendant.[60] Reliance often is equated with or described as "transaction causation"—but for the conduct of the defendant, the plaintiff would not have engaged in the subject purchase or sale of a security.[61] Certain common facts and circumstances give rise to a presumption of reliance, allowing the plaintiff to avoid affirmative proof of reliance as an initial burden.[62] These presumptions of reliance may be rebutted by a defendant, however, by a showing that refutes the rationale underlying the presumption.[63]

Loss causation is a further important element in private actions under Rule 10b-5. To satisfy this element, the plaintiff must prove that, but for the defendant's conduct, the plaintiff would not have suffered the claimed loss.[64] As recently construed by the U.S. Supreme Court, proof of this element requires proof by the plaintiff that an actual economic loss has been suffered by him.[65] It is not sufficient, for example, that the plaintiff alleges that securities purchased and held by her had an inflated price at the time they were purchased.[66]

Another important element in private actions under Rule 10b-5 is damages.[67] A plaintiff's recovery cannot exceed her actual damages.[68] A more refined damages cap has been applicable in certain private actions under Rule 10b-5 since 1995.[69] There is no uniform means of calculating damages for Rule 10b-5 claims.[70] Based on the facts and circumstances of his case, a plaintiff may seek (among other measures of damages) out-of-pocket damages,[71] contract damages,[72] or rescissory damages.[73] Rescission also may be an available remedy.[74]

Moreover, cases brought as securities class actions under federal law have their own set of applicable rules. More than ten years ago, class actions brought under Rule 10b-5 became subject to significant additional requirements as a result of the enactment of the Private Securities Litigation Reform Act of 1995 (the "PSLRA").[75] Among these additional requirements are certain more stringent pleading standards that Congress made applicable to all private actions brought under Rule 10b-5. As a result of the PSLRA, for example, a private action plaintiff alleging one or more material misstatements or materially misleading omissions in violation of Rule 10b-5 must specifically set forth, among other things, each statement or omission and explain why any omission is misleading.[76] Moreover, a private action plaintiff bringing Rule 10b-5 claims now must allege facts "with particularity" that give rise to a "strong inference" that the defendant acted with the requisite scienter.[77]

Applicable Burdens of Proof

As a final general matter, it is significant to note that the burden of proof in criminal and civil actions under Rule 10b-5 is different. Criminal allegations in Rule 10b-5 actions, like those in other criminal prosecutions, must be proven by the government beyond a reasonable doubt.[78] Although no single, simple definition exists,[79] "[t]he standard of proof beyond a reasonable doubt means proof to a virtual certainty."[80] Civil actions under Rule 10b-5, whether public or private, need only be proven by the SEC or a private plaintiff by a preponderance of the evidence.[81] Although numerous definitions of this standard also exist,[82] in essence, "[t]he standard of preponderance of the evidence translates into more-likely-than-not."[83] Like the substantive elements, the burden of proof in a Rule 10b-5 action may impact the exercise of enforcement discretion, the determination of motions, and the final outcome of the case.

The Evidence: *U.S. v. Martha Stewart*

This part of the chapter briefly reviews the evidence that led to the indictment of Martha Stewart for securities fraud under Rule 10b-5. The synopsis presented here is based solely on the Indictment. The summary is organized on the basis of the three core Rule 10b-5 elements, as set forth in the preceding part of this chapter.

Manipulation or Deception

The government's case as to manipulation or deception, as expressed in its contentions in the Indictment, is built around four public statements made by or on behalf of Stewart in June 2002.[84] In each case, the Indictment asserts that the statement made constitutes a misrepresentation of material fact and that material facts omitted from each statement render the statement misleading.[85]

Statement Released on June 7, 2002 in the Wall Street Journal

First, Stewart's legal counsel made a statement to the *Wall Street Journal* on Stewart's behalf on June 6, 2002 that was published by the *Wall Street Journal* on June 7, 2002.[86] The Indictment avers that this statement includes misrepresentations and conceals the material fact that Stewart had traded her ImClone shares after having been informed that ImClone president and chief executive officer Samuel Waksal and members of his family were selling or attempting to sell their ImClone shares.[87] The statement offers that Stewart sold her ImClone shares because of a "stop loss" order that authorized and directed the sale of her shares "if the stock ever went below $60."[88] The Indictment asserts that the materiality of the alleged false and omitted facts derives from the fact that "STEWART's reputation, as well as the likelihood of any criminal or regulatory action against STEWART, were material to MSLO's shareholders because of the negative impact that any such action or damage to her reputation could have on the company which [sic] bears her name...."[89] In support of this materiality theory, the Indictment quotes a statement from the MSLO initial public offering prospectus (filed with the SEC in 1999)[90] and also notes an initial MSLO stock price drop after the public announcement of Stewart's sale of her ImClone shares.[91]

June 12, 2002 Press Release

The second statement referenced in the Indictment is a June 12, 2002 public announcement that Stewart prepared and caused to be issued.[92] Again, the Indictment alleges that this statement contains false information and conceals the material fact that Stewart had traded her ImClone shares after having been told that Samuel Waksal and members of his family were selling or attempting to sell their ImClone shares.[93] This statement includes: more detailed facts about the alleged $60 "stop loss" order relating to Stewart's ImClone shares and related communications between Stewart and her stockbroker; and a representation by Stewart that she did not have nonpublic information about ImClone when she sold her ImClone shares.[94] The materiality of the misrepresented and omitted facts in this June 12, 2002 statement is supported by the same allegations in the Indictment that support the materiality of the facts included in and omitted from the June 7, 2002 statement.[95]

June 18, 2002 Press Release Read by Stewart at a June 19, 2002 Conference

The third statement referenced in the Indictment was prepared, approved, and caused to be issued by Stewart on June 18, 2002, on the eve of a speech scheduled to be given by Stewart on June 19th.[96] The occasion of the speaking engagement was a conference for securities analysts and investors.[97] According to the Indictment, Stewart's June 18, 2002 statement asserted that her June 12, 2002 statement explained the facts relating to the sale of her ImClone shares and that the sale of her ImClone shares was based on publicly available information.[98] The Indictment also avers that, in the June 18, 2002 statement, Stewart repeats her assertion that she sold her ImClone shares in accordance with a prior agreement with her broker that the shares be sold once the per share price of ImClone's common stock fell below $60 and states that she cooperated completely with the SEC and the U.S. Attorney's office.[99] Stewart read the June 18, 2002 statement at the June 19, 2002 conference.[100] According to the Indictment, the June 18, 2002 statement includes misrepresentations and conceals the same information that the June 7, 2002 and June 12, 2002 statements conceal.[101] The government alleges that the facts included in and omitted from these statements are material on the same bases as those included in and omitted from the June 7, 2002.[102]

"In Connection With" the Purchase or Sale of a Security

The representations and allegations in the Indictment supporting the claim that any manipulative or deceptive conduct by Stewart was in connection with the purchase or sale of a security are somewhat skimpy and conclusory. The government's case emanates from the status of MSLO as a public company. The Indictment represents that "MSLO's common stock was listed and traded on the New York Stock Exchange ... under the symbol MSO."[103] The Indictment further alleges that Stewart made or caused someone to make the three allegedly false and misleading statements relating to the sale of her ImClone shares "to defraud and deceive purchasers and sellers of MLSO common stock and to maintain the value of her own MSLO stock by preventing a decline in the market price of MSLO's stock,"[104] tying Stewart's asserted misrepresentations to purchase and sale transactions occurring in the public market for MSLO common stock.

Scienter

The evidence of scienter set forth in the Indictment is circumstantial. The essential story that the Indictment tells begins with the fact that Stewart, based on her knowledge and experience as a public company chairman and chief executive officer, licensed stock broker, and New York Stock Exchange director, knew of the effects that public statements have on a public company's stock price.[105] In addition, according to the Indictment, Stewart owns or has the option of acquiring a substantial percentage of MSLO's publicly traded common stock.[106] Based on that knowledge, experience, and stock position, the story continues, Stewart made false and misleading statements to the public about the reasons for the sale of her ImClone shares "in an effort to stop or at least slow the steady erosion of MSLO's stock price caused by investor concerns."[107] Moreover, Stewart allegedly made these statements "with the intent to defraud and deceive purchasers and sellers of MSLO common stock and to maintain the value of her own MSLO stock by preventing a decline in the market price of MSLO's stock."[108] The Indictment provides no additional, specific factual support for these allegations of purpose and intent.

Charging Martha Stewart with Securities Fraud: A Good Thing?[109]

Should Martha Stewart have been charged with securities fraud? The answer to this question requires a review of the facts underlying Stewart's case in light of prosecutorial discretion (as informed by standards and guidance applicable to federal criminal prosecutions), the elements of a Rule 10b-5 charge (as described in the first part of this chapter), and (to a limited extent) the burden of proof in a criminal action. This analysis assumes that Stewart misrepresented the reason for selling her ImClone shares on December 22, 2001.

Factors in the Prosecutorial Decision to Charge

Prosecutors have the power and discretion to determine both whether and with what a possible criminal defendant will be charged.[110] Federal prosecutorial decisions to charge are subject to professional responsibility standards and U.S. Department of Justice ("DOJ") and office guidelines.[111] From an ethical standpoint, Rule 3.8 of the American Bar Association's Model Rule of Professional Conduct (the "Model Rules") provides that "[t]he prosecutor in a criminal case shall: (a) refrain from prosecuting a charge that the prosecutor knows is not supported by probable cause."[112] Similarly, DR 7-103(A) of the American Bar Association's Model Code of Professional Responsibility (the "Model Code") states that "[a] public prosecutor or other government lawyer shall not institute or cause to be instituted criminal charges when he knows or it is obvious that the charges are not supported by probable cause."[113] Each of these professional conduct rules relies heavily on the elusive definition of "probable cause."[114] All of the states and the District of Columbia have adopted a version of one of these rules.[115] Federal prosecutors are subject to the rules of the state or territory in which they practice.[116]

Supplemental to these professional responsibility and conduct rules, the DOJ has adopted Principles of Federal Prosecution ("Principles") applicable to U.S. Attorneys that are set forth in the *United States Attorneys' Manual*.[117] The Principles include a number of rules applicable to prosecution and charging decisions. For example, under the Principles, a federal prosecutor is required to have "probable cause to believe that a person has committed a Federal offense within his/her jurisdiction" before he or she can "commence or recommend prosecution."[118] This rule reinforces the ethical mandates of the Model Rules and the Model Code by using a "probable cause" standard. Moreover,

[t]he attorney for the government should commence or recommend Federal prosecution if he/she believes that the person's conduct constitutes a Federal offense and that the admissible evidence will probably be sufficient to obtain and sustain a conviction, unless, in his/her judgment, prosecution should be declined because:

1. No substantial Federal interest would be served by prosecution;
2. The person is subject to effective prosecution in another jurisdiction; or
3. There exists an adequate non-criminal alternative to prosecution.[119]

The Principles also specify certain matters that a federal prosecutor should not consider in commencing or recommending prosecution.[120] Finally, "once the decision to prosecute has been made, the attorney for the government should charge, or should recommend that the grand jury charge, the most serious offense that is consistent with the nature of the defendant's conduct, and that is likely to result in a sustainable conviction."[121] Additional charges only should be filed when, in the government attorney's judgment, the additional charges:

1. Are necessary to ensure that the information or indictment:
    A. Adequately reflects the nature and extent of the criminal conduct involved; and
    B. Provides the basis for an appropriate sentence under all the circumstances of the case; or
2. Will significantly enhance the strength of the government's case against the defendant or a codefendant.[122]

The Principles are supplemented from time to time by clarifying pronouncements, including internal memoranda from the U.S. Attorney General.[123] Also, individual offices of the U.S. Attorneys may have their own guidelines.[124]

These ethical standards and elements of professional guidance do not, however, provide dispositive advice and are subject to significant interpretation.[125] Within the contours of these ethical and professional mandates, determinations of whether and what to charge are made based on the elements of applicable crimes and the then available facts,[126] in the context of broad, but not open-ended, prosecutorial discretion.[127] The constraints may be, among other things, constitutional, practical, and moral.[128] However, judicial challenges to charging decisions are rarely successful.[129] Claims of bias or selective prosecution are particularly difficult to prove and are judicially disfavored.[130]

Moreover, compliance with the applicable ethical standards and professional guidance may not be actively monitored or enforced in practice. Both policing and enforcement, to the extent that either exists, are handled by the DOJ's Office of Professional Responsibility.[131] Significantly, defendants may not have a cause of action based on a prosecutor's violation of these applicable standards and guidelines.[132] In fact, the Principles themselves ordain this status.[133]

The Validity of the Stewart Securities Fraud Charge

Given the standards, guidance, and discretion applicable to prosecutorial charging decisions, the contours of applicable law, and the allegations of the Indictment, the decision to charge Stewart with securities fraud under Rule 10b-5 is apparently legally valid, although the analyses giving rise to this conclusion do raise some significant unanswered questions regarding prosecutorial discretion and important interpretive questions under each of the Rule 10b-5 elements that would need to be resolved at trial (and, perhaps, on appeal).[134] The nature of the conduct proscribed by Rule 10b-5 is broad and amorphous (and, in fact, is constantly evolving to include new undesired behaviors).[135] In this expansive and changing environment, the government has set forth allegations in the Indictment that could, if proven true, satisfy each of the three key elements of its case, and these allegations collectively are sufficient to constitute probable cause. Moreover, there is no evidence of any actual abuse of discretion in the charging decision.[136]

Manipulation or Deception

For example, the Indictment addresses whether Stewart's alleged misrepresentations as to the reason for the sale of her ImClone stock are actionable under Rule 10b-5 by detailing the four public statements made by Stewart and asserting that they are manipulative and deceptive because of their falsity.[137] Yet, it is not clear that Stewart's alleged misstatements about her personal stock sale are fraudulent devices, schemes, artifices, acts, practices, or courses of business or deceitful acts, practices, or courses of business that are proscribed by Rule 10b-5.[138] This author has not found any reported case with facts substantially similar to those alleged in the Indictment. However, it is conceivable, based on the facts set forth in the Indictment, that Stewart's public statements "artificially" affected the market for MSLO's stock, raising the possibility that her conduct was manipulative under Rule 10b-5.[139] Moreover, the allegations describe conduct (i.e., misrepresenting Stewart's reason for the ImClone stock sale) that could be deemed deceptive under existing decisional law, since the definition of "deception" is fact-specific.[140]

Further, to the extent the government's allegations of manipulation or deception rely on Stewart's misstatement of a material fact, the Indictment adequately alleges materiality.[141] Based on the facts alleged in the Indictment, it is possible that a court or jury could find it substantially likely that a reasonable investor would find Stewart's alleged misrepresentation important in buying or selling MSLO securities. In the alternative, a court or jury may determine that it is substantially likely that Stewart's omissions of facts would be viewed by MSLO investors as significantly altering the total mix of information made available to them.

It is not clear, however, that a court would or should find Stewart's alleged misstatements to be material under Rule 10b-5, even assuming the accuracy and completeness of the government's allegations in the Indictment. [142] The Stewart case involves the dissemination of noncorporate information—facts about an insider's personal trading transaction involving the securities of another corporation, rather than facts about the issuer's financial condition, results of operations, business plans, or securities. The misrepresentation of personal facts by an insider is less likely to be material than the misstatement of corporate facts by an insider; it may not be *substantially* likely that a *reasonable* investor would find personal facts about an insider—specifically, assertions of the insider's innocence of a crime unrelated to the corporation—important in making an investment decision in the corporation's securities.[143] It is only because of Stewart's key executive status and strong identification with MSLO[144] that we even entertain an argument as to materiality, and those facts, taken alone, may not be sufficient to make out a case for materiality.[145] However, this materiality argument has not been tested, and in any event, the personal-rather-than-corporate angle may better be addressed through the "in connection with" element.

"In Connection With" the Purchase or Sale of a Security

The Indictment raises even more interesting issues with respect to satisfaction of the "in connection with" requirement in Stewart's case. Do any alleged manipulative or deceptive activities conducted by Stewart have the requisite connection with a purchase or sale of securities under Rule 10b-5?

It is important to note at the outset that the *Stewart* criminal action is not based on manipulation or deception conducted by Stewart in her capacity as a corporate officer of MSLO acting on its behalf to communicate matters to securityholders. Nor is the case about manipulation or deception committed against a party in privity with Stewart during the course of a securities transaction between Stewart and that other party. In those types of cases, the connection between the defendant's conduct and the purchase or sale of a security is clear.[146]

Rather, the claims in the *Stewart* case, as alleged, involve a corporate insider's misrepresentations of facts relating to a personal transaction made by Stewart in her individual capacity—the public sale of securities in another,

unaffiliated corporation, one in which she was *not* an insider. The Indictment alleges that this misrepresentation constituted fraud, manipulation,
and deception *not* as to the purchasers of Stewart's ImClone stock, but instead as to those trading in securities of MSLO in the public market. In a
case like this, the appropriate test to be used in applying the "in connection
with" requirement is less clear.[147] Fundamentally, many of the approaches
used by courts are grounded in the courts' understanding and application
of the policies underlying the 1934 Act in general and Rule 10b-5 specifically.[148] The U.S. Supreme Court recently used these policies to explain its
application of the "'coincidence' test" applied by it in interpreting the "in
connection with" element.[149]

Yet, there is a connection between Stewart's statements about the reason
for the sale of her ImClone shares and any market purchase or sale of MSLO
securities made between the time of those statements and the times that they
may have been corrected in the market. Any misstatements of a material fact
by Stewart are connected to market purchases and sales of MSLO securities
by a possible, but thin, thread: the thread consisting of Stewart's strong identification with MSLO.[150] Under existing decisional law, it is possible that a
court would find that this thin thread constitutes a sufficient connection. For
example, Stewart consciously could leverage her identification with MSLO
by making public statements to affect the public market for MSLO's stock
and deceive its investors such that her conduct coincides with securities transactions.[151] Moreover, publicly disseminated misstatements about a corporate
executive whose personal identity, like that of Stewart, is effectively synonymous with the corporation's identity may necessarily "touch" on transactions
in the corporation's securities.[152] In addition, a court or jury could find that
Stewart's alleged misrepresentations constitute fraudulent, deceptive, or manipulative conduct on which a reasonable investor would rely in making an
investment decision.[153] Under these circumstances, it appears that the alleged
facts on the "in connection with" element support a Rule 10b-5 charge.

Scienter

Assuming Stewart misrepresented a material fact in connection with the
purchase or sale of a security, it is essential that a prosecutor also assess
whether her manipulation or deception was carried out with the requisite state
of mind. Were her misstatements intentional, willful, or knowing? Were they
merely reckless? Did she appreciate the likely effect that her statements would
have on the market for MSLO securities? How does the scienter analysis impact the decision to pursue Stewart's alleged misrepresentations in a criminal,
rather than civil, action?

In the Indictment, the government essentially alleges that Stewart knew that public statements affect public company stock prices, that her ownership of a controlling interest in MSLO gave her a motive to positively affect MSLO's stock price, that Stewart intentionally misrepresented the reason for the sale of her Im-Clone shares to sustain the market price of MSLO's publicly traded common stock, and that Stewart intended to deceive MSLO investors in making those misstatements.[154] In making these allegations, the prosecution has set out its case in a manner, akin to motive and opportunity pleading in the civil litigation arena,[155] that satisfies the scienter element of Rule 10b-5.[156] At the same time, the allegations in the Indictment, by mentioning Stewart's intent to manipulate or deceive MSLO investors in connection with their purchases and sales of securities in the market, apparently satisfy the willfulness requirement necessary to a lawful criminal prosecution.[157] Specifically, the Indictment alleges facts that, if proven true, may be deemed to establish that Stewart voluntarily acted with knowledge of the consequences of her actions and knew that her conduct was unlawful.[158]

Probable Cause and Other Prosecutorial Standards and Guidance

The preceding analysis of the Indictment's allegations in relation to the elements of a criminal violation of Rule 10b-5 supports a conclusion that the government had probable cause to charge Stewart with securities fraud. Said another way, based on the broad-based standards underlying the elements of a Rule 10b-5 violation and the somewhat unique facts alleged in the Indictment, the prosecution had a reasonable belief that Stewart committed securities fraud.[159] The federal grand jury that indicted Stewart found probable cause, resulting in the issuance of the Indictment.[160] Moreover, it is not obvious from the face of the Indictment that there is an absence of probable cause, nor is there any indication that the government otherwise possessed information negating the existence of probable cause, to charge Stewart with securities fraud.

In addition, although getting into the head of a prosecutor is as difficult as getting into the head of a criminal defendant, the Indictment indicates that the government believed that Stewart's conduct constitutes a criminal violation of Rule 10b-5,[161] and it is fair to assume that the government found it probable that the admissible evidence would be sufficient to obtain and sustain a conviction. Moreover, in this post-Enron era, it is axiomatic that a prosecutor would find that a substantial federal interest would be served by charging a public figure chief executive officer with securities fraud.[162] Further, it is not clear that Stewart would have been subject to effective prosecution in another jurisdiction.[163] On these issues, the government appears to be compliant with the Principles.

However, a non-criminal alternative to prosecution did exist in the Stewart case. An SEC enforcement action or administrative proceeding could have been brought against Stewart for violation of Rule 10b-5, subject to the scienter requirement and lower burden of proof applicable in civil proceedings.[164] Although the availability and adequacy of this alternative deserves careful scrutiny in the Stewart case, the prosecutor may well have decided that these alternatives were not "adequate," such that criminal prosecution was warranted.[165]

There also is a possibility, although it would be difficult to prove, that bias or improper influences played a role in the decision to bring the securities fraud charge against Stewart. For example, prosecutors may have been influenced by her sex, her political affiliation, her publicized professional or personal activities, or her beliefs.[166] Further, as always is possible, individuals involved in the prosecution of Stewart could have been influenced by their own personal feelings concerning Stewart[167] or by the possible effect of the charging decision on their own professional or personal circumstances.[168] Admittedly, these motivations would be difficult to substantiate.[169]

Finally, the Stewart securities fraud charge apparently was the most serious offense that is consistent with the nature of Stewart's conduct,[170] and the prosecution likely found that the charge would result in a sustainable conviction.[171] The prosecutorial decisions to bring additional charges in the Indictment are similarly subject to prosecutorial standards, guidance, and discretion but are not the subject of this chapter.[172]

Observations on the Martha Stewart Securities Fraud Indictment

The foregoing analysis of the securities fraud charge brought against Martha Stewart highlights a number of interesting and potentially important aspects of a Rule 10b-5 case brought against a corporate insider on the basis of misrepresentations made by the insider about personal facts. Although the *Stewart* case was a criminal action, it nevertheless sends messages about both criminal and civil claims under Rule 10b-5, including class actions. This part of the chapter consolidates important points from the foregoing analysis of the Stewart securities fraud charge and sets forth key observations regarding that analysis.[173]

Rule 10b-5 Allegations Based on Misrepresented Personal Facts

A legally valid criminal charge or civil claim under Rule 10b-5 for misrepresentations relating to an insider's personal facts is possible, even if unusual.[174]

Facts satisfying each of the key elements of a Rule 10b-5 claim—activities, including misrepresentations of material fact, constituting manipulation or deceit, conducted in connection with the purchase or sale of a security, with scienter—may be alleged with respect to misstatements about personal matters or transactions.[175] However, the lack of a perfect fit between the elements of a Rule 10b-5 claim (as defined under existing decisional law) and misrepresentations of wholly noncorporate facts complicates both the construction of adequate allegations in an indictment or complaint and the determination of probable cause in a criminal action. Principal questions relate to: whether the misstated personal information about the insider is "material;"[176] whether the insider's statements about private, individual facts are made "in connection with" a purchase or sale of securities;[177] and whether the insider made the subject misrepresentations with the requisite scienter under Rule 10b-5[178] and, if applicable, criminal intent under Section 32(a) of the 1934 Act.[179] Moreover, in private actions, there likely would be difficult questions as to reliance (or transaction causation)[180] and loss causation,[181] as well as the adequate pleading of scienter.[182] At the heart of these questions is the corporate insider's ability to manipulate the market for the corporation's securities or deceive the investors in those securities with misstated or undisclosed personal information. A narrow set of facts seemingly supports this type of claim. The investing public must strongly identify the insider with the corporation in order for the insider to have this ability.[183] Absent a strong insider-corporate identity (which is relatively rare, but not unique[184]), a Rule 10b-5 claim alleging that the insider manipulated the market for the corporation's securities or deceived the corporation's investors by misrepresenting personal information will fail to satisfy the requisite elements. No doubt, future courts contending with this type of Rule 10b-5 claim will wrestle with factual issues relating to the strength of insider-corporate identity.

Prosecutorial Conduct in the Context of Rule 10b-5

Although a number of noted scholars and other commentators already have written about the charging decisions in the *Stewart* case,[185] a few generalized observations are warranted in light of the analysis included in this chapter. Specifically, it is important to note several points about the interaction between prosecutorial discretion and the substantive aspects of Rule 10b-5. While these observations are not new, the Stewart prosecution sheds additional light on these subjects and reinforces existing scholarship. Each of these observations bears further thought and analysis in the context of a Rule 10b-5 charge against an insider based on misrepresentations of personal facts.

Attacks on prosecutorial discretion are common. In large part, this results from the fact that the exercise of prosecutorial discretion is regulated by standards that are so broad as to run the risk of being meaningless.[186] The potential for exploitation is apparent and is a source of concern regardless of whether actual abuse occurs with any significant frequency.[187] In particular, the application of this wide-ranging discretion in the field by individual U.S. Attorneys in different offices in the context of broad criminal prohibitions that are substantially shaped by standards-based decisional law (as is the case for criminal prosecutions under Rule 10b-5) can have far-reaching effects on the substantive content of the law.[188]

As a result, these potential effects should be considered in a more formalized way in the prosecutorial decisionmaking process. Attempts to push the somewhat nebulous judicially constructed boundaries of Rule 10b-5 should be considered carefully and viewed by the judiciary with suspicion. Prosecutors and the SEC, as governmental actors, should be required to justify their decisions to enforce Rule 10b-5 in these marginal cases by reference not simply to applicable professional guidelines and statutory, regulatory, and decisional substantive law rules, but also to the policy justifications for those rules. What should be required in these rare circumstances is not merely a superficial, check-the-box kind of review, but rather a thoughtful consideration and discussion as to the probable impact of the rule of the case on the rule of law and the relationship of that impact to underlying policy. Although this level of consideration may appear unduly burdensome, it only would apply to a small number of cases; the vast majority of Rule 10b-5 actions involve factual circumstances that are well within the accepted contours of Rule 10b-5. The *Stewart* case is not; it presents challenges under each of the three core elements of a Rule 10b-5 cause of action and raises those issues in the context of a criminal prosecution, where the burden of proof is higher. There appears to be little wisdom in raising a case of this kind in a criminal context.

Conclusion

"Section 10(b) is aptly described as a catchall provision, but what it catches must be fraud."[189] Yet, the nature of securities fraud under Section 10(b) and Rule 10b-5 continues to evolve to include new types of conduct and potential enforcement targets. The Martha Stewart Rule 10b-5 prosecution begins to explore the current outer limits of securities fraud under Rule 10b-5 in a post-Enron world. For key corporate executives—in particular, those who are strongly identified with the corporations they manage—the calculus as to the conduct and disclosure of their personal affairs now has changed.[190] They now should know that they may be subject to legal action based on a misrepresentation of (or a failure to disclose) personal fact. Those that desire these actions to succeed may argue for more specific guidance on the interplay between this kind of misstatement and the various applicable elements of Rule 10b-5 claims.

However, if this is not what Congress, the SEC, or corporate America desires, it is now time to speak up and take action. Moderate action could include lawmaking, rulemaking, or interpretive guidance on the meaning of the elements under Rule 10b-5 in cases involving misrepresentations of personal facts. Possible solutions lie in establishing rebuttable presumptions, shifting burdens of proof, and clarifying the substantive nature of inquiries under each element. Adding precision to the application of Rule 10b-5 in this context certainly would give key executives better guidance regarding disclosure of their personal affairs.

On the other hand, a more radical solution may be suggested. Perhaps, no cause of action should exist based on an executive's misstatement of personal information; perhaps, investors should be made responsible for their own investment decision making—at least to some extent—when it is based on information of a noncorporate nature.[191] Adoption of this solution requires that lawmakers revisit the key policy underpinnings of the 1934 Act, investor protection and market integrity promotion. This inquiry may well lead one to conclude that, in protecting investors who trade based on personal information about public company executives, we are not promoting market integrity. That conclusion could serve as a catalyst for far-reaching legal change.

Questions

1. Assume a civil action could be brought against Martha Stewart by the U.S. Securities and Exchange Commission or private plaintiffs based on the same evidence that led to Stewart's indictment. Why would prosecutors want to bring criminal charges against Stewart rather than leaving the matter to public or private civil enforcement?

2. Assume the government can prove at trial all of the facts presented in the Indictment. As a juror, would you vote to convict? Why, or why not?

3. If Stewart had remained silent about the facts surrounding her December 2001 sale of ImClone stock, should that be actionable? Is the voluntary dis-

closure of false information different from the withholding of information? Why, or why not?

Notes

1. *See generally* United States v. Stewart, 305 F. Supp. 2d 368 (S.D.N.Y. 2004) (granting Martha Stewart's motion for a judgment of acquittal on the securities fraud charge).

2. Superseding Indictment, United States v. Martha Stewart and Peter Bacanovic, S1 03 Cr. 717 (MGC) (S.D.N.Y. filed Jan. 7, 2004) *available at* http://news.findlaw.com/hdocs/ docs/mstewart/usmspb10504sind.pdf [hereinafter Indictment], ¶¶ 56–66; 305 F. Supp. at 370 ("Count Nine of the Indictment charges that defendant Stewart made materially false statements of fact regarding her sale of ImClone securities with the intention of defrauding and deceiving investors by slowing or stopping the erosion of the value of the securities issued by her own company, Martha Stewart Living Omnimedia"). The Indictment also suggests that the statements made by Stewart were misleading in that they omitted certain material facts necessary to make them not misleading. Indictment, *supra*, at ¶¶ 60, 61, 63 & 64. For ease of reference (and because the essence of the claim against Stewart lies in alleged misrepresentations), this chapter generally will reference the basis of the claims as misrepresentations or misstatements.

3. Specifically, the Indictment alleges that "STEWART made or caused to be made a series of false and misleading public statements during June 2002 regarding her sale of ImClone stock on December 27, 2001 that concealed and omitted that STEWART had been provided information regarding the sale and attempted sale of the Waksal Shares and that STEWART had sold her ImClone stock while in possession of that information." Indictment, *supra* note 2, at ¶ 60.

4. *Id.* ("STEWART made these false and misleading statements with the intent to defraud and deceive purchasers and sellers of MSLO common stock and to maintain the value of her own MSLO stock by preventing a decline in the market price of MSLO's stock."); Geraldine Szott Moohr, *Prosecutorial Power in an Adversarial System: Lessons from Current White Collar Cases*, 7 BUFF. CRIM. L. REV. 165, 179 (2004) ("The government's theory was that Stewart committed securities fraud when she publicly asserted her innocence. According to the prosecution, her denials of wrongdoing were materially false statements, made with the intent to defraud investors by slowing or stopping the erosion of the company's share value.").

5. *See, e.g.*, Lawrence S. Goldman, *Martha and Lynne: The Stewart Sisters and the Expansion of White Collar Criminal Prosecution*, 27 CHAMPION 8 (2003) (criticizing the use of criminal prosecution for fraud in the *Stewart* case); Stuart P. Green, *Uncovering the Cover-Up Crimes*, 42 AM. CRIM. L. REV. 9 (2005) (critiquing the lack of a rigorous method for prosecutors and others to analyze charges for so-called cover-up crimes); Moohr, *supra* note 4 (critiquing the prosecution's power to decide what to charge, using the *Stewart* case as an example); Dale A. Oesterle, *Early Observations on the Prosecutions of the Business Scandals of 2002–03: On Sideshow Prosecutions, Spitzer's Clash With Donaldson Over Turf, the Choice of Civil or Criminal Actions, and the Tough Tactic of Coerced Cooperation*, 1 OHIO ST. J. CRIM. L. 443 (2004) (questioning the Stewart prosecution as an example of a "sideshow" prosecution); Ellen S. Podgor, *Jose Padilla and Martha Stewart: Who Should Be Charged with Criminal Con-*

duct?, 109 PENN ST. L. REV. 1059 (2005) (commenting on "extraneous" charging in the *Stewart* case); Michael L. Seigel & Christopher Slobogin, *Prosecuting Martha: Federal Prosecutorial Power and the Need for a Law of Counts*, 109 PENN. ST. L. REV. 1107 (2005) (questioning "redundant charging" in the *Stewart* case); *Martha Stewart Is No Ken Lay*, L.A. TIMES, June 8, 2003, at M4 (reader opinions regarding the Indictment); Harvey A. Silverglate & Andrew Good, *Stop Creative Prosecutions*, NAT. L.J., August 30, 2004, at 26 (asserting that the Martha Stewart securities fraud charge is an example of the use of a "creative prosecution" theory).

6. 15 U.S.C. §78j(b) (2000). Section 10(b) of the 1934 Act broadly prohibits manipulation and deception in connection with the purchase or sale of securities and authorizes the SEC to adopt rules and regulations "necessary or appropriate in the public interest or for the protection of investors." *Id.*

7. 17 C.F.R. §240.10b-5 (2005). Rule 10b-5 proscribes the following in connection with the purchase or sale of a security: fraudulent devices, schemes, and artifices; material misrepresentations; misleading omissions of material fact with respect to statements made; and acts, practices, and courses of business that operate or would operate as a fraud or deceit.

8. *See* Blue Chip Stamps v. Manor Drug Stores, 421 U.S. 723, 744–745 (1975) (noting that "the typical fact situation in which the classic tort of misrepresentation and deceit evolved was light years away from the world of commercial transactions to which Rule 10b-5 is applicable.")

9. *See* Santa Fe Industries, Inc. v. Green, 430 U.S. 462 (1977) ("Only conduct involving manipulation or deception is reached by §10(b) or Rule 10b-5."); THOMAS LEE HAZEN, THE LAW OF SECURITIES REGULATION 570 (4th ed. 2002); MARC I. STEINBERG, SECURITIES REGULATION 524 (4th ed. 2004).

10. *See* S.E.C. v. Zandford, 535 U.S. 813 (2002); Sup't of Ins. v. Banker's Life and Cas. Co., 404 U.S. 6 (1971); ALAN R. PALMITER, SECURITIES REGULATION 277 (2d ed. 2002); STEINBERG, *supra* note 9, at 524.

11. *See* Aaron v. S.E.C., 446 U.S. 680, 701–02 (1980); Ernst & Ernst v. Hochfelder, 425 U.S. 185, 212 (1976); HAZEN, *supra* note 9, at 578; STEINBERG, *supra* note 9, at 524.

12. *See Blue Chip Stamps*, 421 U.S. 723; Birnbaum v. Newport Steel Corp., 193 F.2d 461 (2d Cir. 1952); STEINBERG, *supra* note 9, at 523.

13. *See* Central Bank, N.A. v. First Interstate Bank, N.A., 511 U.S. 164, 180 (1994) ("A plaintiff must show reliance on the defendant's misstatement or omission to recover under 10b-5."); Basic Inc. v. Levinson, 485 U.S. 224, 243 (1988) ("reliance is an element of a Rule 10b-5 cause of action."); STEINBERG, *supra* note 9, at 524.

14. *See* Huddleston v. Herman & MacLean, 640 F.2d 534, 549 n.24 (5th Cir. 1981), *aff'd in part, rev'd in part on other grounds*, 459 U.S. 375 (1983); STEINBERG, *supra* note 9, at 524.

15. *See* Dura Pharm's, Inc. v. Broudo, 544 U.S. 336, 338 (2005) ("A private plaintiff who claims securities fraud must prove that the defendant's fraud caused an economic loss."); STEINBERG, *supra* note 9, at 524.

16. *See* 28 U.S.C. §1658(b) (2002) (providing that a private right of action for, among other things, manipulation or deceit "may be brought not later than the earlier of—(1) 2 years after the discovery of the facts constituting the violation; or (2) 5 years after such violation."); STEINBERG, *supra* note 9, at 524. There is no specific statute of limitations for criminal prosecutions under the 1934 Act. Decisional law therefore assumes that the general five-year period for federal crimes applies to criminal actions under Rule 10b-5. *See* NAGY ET AL., SECURITIES LITIGATION AND ENFORCEMENT: CASES AND MATERIALS 845 (2003). Although one federal circuit court has found that no statute of limitations applies to SEC enforcement

actions, S.E.C. v. Rind, 991 F.2d 1486, 1492 (9th Cir. 1993), it is possible that the general five-year statute of limitations provided in 28 U.S.C. §2462 applies to enforcement actions under Rule 10b-5 (to the extent they do not seek equitable relief). *See, e.g.,* Catherine E. Maxson, Note, *The Applicability of Section 2462's Statute of Limitations to SEC Enforcement Suits in Light of the Remedies Act of 1990,* 94 MICH. L. REV. 512 (1995).

17. *See* 15 U.S.C. §78u-4 (2000) (providing specialized pleading requirements for private securities class actions); STEINBERG, *supra* note 9, at 524.

18. *See infra* notes 50–54 & 78–80 and accompanying text.

19. Edmund W. Kitch, *Federal Vision of the Securities Laws,* 70 VA. L. REV. 857, 860–61 (1984) (footnotes omitted). *See also* Norman S. Poser, *Misuse of Confidential Information Concerning a Tender Offer as a Securities Fraud,* 49 BROOKLYN L. REV. 1265, 1278 (1983) ("Rule 10b-5—the only rule under section 10(b) that is used to prohibit misuse of non-public information—does not, however, define any specific practices."); Charles M. Yablon, *Fundamental Corporate Changes: Causes, Effects, and Legal Responses: Poison Pills and Litigation Uncertainty,* 1989 DUKE L.J. 54, 73 n.67 (1989) ("Rule 10b-5's prohibition of all 'fraudulent and deceptive' practices may not very clearly define the conduct being prohibited").

20. *See, e.g.,* Santa Fe Industries, Inc. v. Green, 430 U.S. 462, 477 (1977) (equating "manipulation" in the Section 10(b) context with "artificially affecting market activity in order to mislead investors"); Ernst & Ernst v. Hochfelder, 425 U.S. 185, 199 (1976) ("Use of the word 'manipulative' is especially significant.... It connotes intentional or willful conduct designed to deceive or defraud investors by controlling or artificially affecting the price of securities."); United States v. Mulheren, 938 F.2d 364, 368 (2d Cir. 1991) (in which the court assumes, without deciding the matter, that manipulation may exist "where the purpose of his transaction is solely to affect the price of a security."); Pappas v. Moss, 393 F.2d 865, 869 (3d Cir. 1968) (stating that "the definition of 'deception' may vary with the circumstances" and finding deception in a board of directors' adoption of resolutions containing two material misrepresentations).

21. *Santa Fe,* 430 U.S. 462 at 476–77. *See also Ernst,* 425 U.S. at 199 (stating that the word "is and was a term of art when used in connection with securities markets."); NAGY ET AL., *supra* note 16, at 23 ("The term 'manipulative' has a specialized meaning"); STEINBERG, *supra* note 9, at 558 ("the Supreme Court has construed that word as a term of art encompassing market operations.").

22. *See Pappas,* 393 F.2d at 869. *See also* NAGY ET AL., *supra* note 16, at 23 ("Deception includes outright misrepresentations as well as statements that mislead by omission, even if such statements are literally true (so-called half-truths).").

23. *See* James D. Cox, Ernst & Ernst v. Hochfelder: *A Critique and an Evaluation of its Impact upon the Scheme of the Federal Securities Laws,* 28 HASTINGS L.J. 569, 574–75 (1977); Elizabeth A. Nowicki, *10(b) or not 10(b)?: Yanking the Security Blanket for Attorneys in Securities Litigation,* 2004 COLUM. BUS. L. REV. 637, 678, 682–88 (2004); Steven R. Salbu, *Tipper Credibility, Noninformational Tippee Trading, and Abstention from Trading: An Analysis of Gaps in the Insider Trading Laws,* 68 WASH. L. REV. 307, 345–46 (1993).

24. United States v. Drobny, 955 F.2d 990, 997 (5th Cir. 1992).

25. Corsair Capital Partners, L.P. v. Wedbush Morgan Secs., Inc., 24 Fed. Appx. 795, 797 (9th Cir. 2001). *See also* Harris v. Union Electric Co., 787 F.2d 355, 361 (8th Cir. 1986) (in which the plaintiffs describe the two types of claims under Rule 10b-5 as "disclosure fraud" and "transaction fraud.").

26. "[W]here the sole basis ... is alleged misrepresentations or omissions, plaintiffs have not made out a market manipulation claim under Rule 10b-5(a) and (c)." Lentell v. Mer-

rill Lynch & Co., Inc., 396 F.3d 161, 177 (2d Cir. 2005) (citing Schnell v. Conseco, Inc., 43 F. Supp. 2d 438, 447–48 (S.D. N.Y. 1999)).

27. *See* Ernst & Ernst v. Hochfelder, 425 U.S. 185, 199 n.20 (1976) (noting dictionary definitions for "device" and "contrivance").

28. *See* Santa Fe Industries, Inc. v. Green, 430 U.S. 462, 474–80 (1977).

29. Basic Inc. v. Levinson, 485 U.S. 224, 231 (1988) (citing to *TSC Industries, Inc. v. Northway, Inc.*, 426 U. S. 438, 449 (1976)).

30. *Id.* at 231–32 (citing to *TSC Industries*, 426 U.S. at 449).

31. *See, e.g.,* Semerenko v. Cendant Corp., 223 F.3d 165, 178 (3d Cir. 2000) (citing to *In re Burlington Coat Factory Sec. Litig.*, 114 F.3d at 1425, in noting "that, in the context of an efficient market, 'the concept of materiality translates into information that alters the price of the firm's stock.'"); United States v. Bingham, 992 F.2d 975, 976 (9th Cir. 1993) ("The government would have us adopt two per se rules, the first saying that falsification of the identity of a buyer or seller of securities is always material, and the second that officer or director status is always material. We decline the government's invitation to adopt such per se rules."); Garcia v. Cordova, 930 F.2d 826, 827 (10th Cir. 1991) ("[W]e find the asset appraisal information here to be immaterial as a matter of law due to its speculative and unreliable nature"). *See generally* Joan MacLeod Heminway, *Materiality Guidance in the Context of Insider Trading: A Call for Action*, 52 Am. U.L. Rev. 1131 (2003) (analyzing two examples in an insider trading context and citing numerous cases on materiality).

32. *See* Jennifer O'Hare, *Preemption under the Securities Litigation Uniform Standards Act: If it Looks Like a Securities Fraud Claim and Acts Like a Securities Fraud Claim, is it a Securities Fraud Claim?*, 56 Ala. L. Rev. 325, 329 (2004) (stating that "the courts have struggled with the meaning of the 'in connection with' element" and citing to scholars who have commented on this issue).

33. Sup't of Ins. v. Bankers Life and Cas. Co., 404 U.S. 6, 12 (1971) ("Section 10(b) must be read flexibly, not technically and restrictively."); SEC v. Softpoint, Inc., 958 F. Supp. 846, 862 (S.D.N.Y. 1997) ("courts have liberally construed the requirement that violative conduct must occur 'in connection with' the purchase or sale of a security.").

34. SEC v. Zandford, 535 U.S. 813, 820 (2002) ("[T]he statute must not be construed so broadly as to convert every common-law fraud that happens to involve securities into a violation of §10(b)"); Angelastro v. Prudential-Bache Secur., 764 F.2d 939, 945 (3d Cir. 1985) ("[T]here is a danger in construing the 'in connection with' requirement so broadly that virtually any type of misconduct related to a securities transaction even in the most tenuous or tangential way might be claimed to give rise to a federal securities law violation."); French v. First Union Sec., Inc., 209 F. Supp. 2d 818, 827 (D. Tenn. 2002) ("Although Zandford espoused an expansive reading of the 'in connection with' language, there still must be a connection between the action and some sort of securities transaction.").

35. *Zandford*, 535 U.S. 813 at 825.

36. *Sup't of Ins.*, 404 U.S. at 12–13 ("The crux of the present case is that Manhattan suffered an injury as a result of deceptive practices touching its sale of securities as an investor."). This formulation has been criticized by some as being too broad a statement of the "in connection with" element. *See* Chemical Bank v. Arthur Anderson & Co., 726 F.2d 930, 942–43 (2d Cir.), *cert. denied*, 469 U.S. 884 (1984); IIT v. Vencap, Ltd., 519 F.2d 1001, 1014 n.26 (2d Cir. 1975).

37. S.E.C. v. Texas Gulf Sulphur Co., 401 F.2d 833, 860–61 (2d Cir. 1968) (en banc), *cert. denied*, 394 U.S. 976 (1969).

38. *See, e.g.*, Rowinski v. Salomon Smith Barney Inc., 398 F.3d 294, 301 (3d Cir. 2005) (citing standards under the cases cited *supra* notes 33–37 and others); McGann v. Ernst & Young, 102 F.3d 390, 392–96 (9th Cir. 1996) (discussing the compatibility of the *Texas Gulf* standard with later cases); Pelletier v. Stuart-Jones Co., 863 F.2d 1550 (11th Cir. 1989) (using the "touch" test); *Softpoint*, 958 F. Supp. at 862 (citing and discussing numerous cases on the "in connection with" requirement); O'Hare, *supra* note 32, at 329–34 (citing and commenting on various cases).

39. *See, e.g.*, Semerenko v. Cendant Corp., 223 F.3d 165, 176 (3d Cir. 2000) (holding that class action plaintiffs "may establish the 'in connection with' element simply by showing that the misrepresentations in question were disseminated to the public in a medium upon which a reasonable investor would rely, and that they were material when disseminated."); In re Ames Dep't Stores Inc. Stock Litig., 991 F.2d 953, 965 (2d Cir. 1993); S.E.C. v. Rana Research, Inc., 8 F.3d 1358, 1362 (9th Cir. 1993); In re Leslie Fay Cos. Sec. Litig., 871 F. Supp. 686, 697 (S.D.N.Y. 1995).

40. *Zandford*, 535 U.S. at 820 ("neither the SEC nor this Court has ever held that there must be a misrepresentation about the value of a particular security in order to run afoul of the Act."); Angelastro v. Prudential-Bache Securities, Inc., 764 F.2d 939, 942–44, *cert. denied*, 474 U.S. 935 (1985); A.T. Brod & Co. v. Perlow, 375 F.2d 393, 396 (2d Cir. 1967).

41. Ambassador Hotel Co. v. Wei-Chuan Inv., 189 F.3d 1017, 1026 (9th Cir. 1999).

42. Ernst & Ernst v. Hochfelder, 425 U.S. 185, 193 (1976).

43. *Id.*

44. Warren v. Reserve Fund, Inc., 728 F.2d 741, 745 (5th Cir. 1984). Some courts do reference intentionality or "purpose" in articulating the scienter requirement. *See, e.g.*, In re Merrill Lynch & Co. Research Reports Sec. Litig., 289 F. Supp. 2d 416, 427 (S.D.N.Y. 2003) ("The requisite state of mind, or scienter, in an action under Section 10(b) and Rule 10b-5, that the plaintiff must allege is a purpose to harm by intentionally deceiving, manipulating or defrauding.").

45. *See, e.g.*, Nathenson v. Zonagen Inc., 267 F.3d 400, 408 (5th Cir. 2001); Hollinger v. Titan Capital Corp., 914 F.2d 1564, 1568 n.6 (9th Cir. 1990); Keirnan v. Homeland, Inc., 611 F.2d 785, 788 (9th Cir. 1980); Sunstrand Corp. v. Sun Chem. Corp., 553 F.2d 1033, 1045 (7th Cir. 1977); NAGY ET AL., *supra* note 16, at 110 ("[E]very federal court of appeals to confront the question has held recklessness sufficient for these purposes").

46. PALMITER, *supra* note 10, at 283. *See also* AUSA Life Ins. Co. v. Ernst & Young, 206 F.3d 202, 221 (2d Cir. 2000) (criticizing the district court's opinion on the basis that it "inappropriately makes the scienter issue one of 'what did the defendant want to happen' as opposed to 'what could the defendant reasonably foresee as a potential result of his action.'"); SEC v. Falstaff Brewing Corp., 629 F.2d 62, 77 (D.C. Cir. 1980) (scienter exists when a defendant knows "the nature and consequences of his actions").

47. Advanta Corp. Sec. Litig., 180 F.3d 525, 535 (3d Cir. 1999); HAZEN, *supra* note 9, at 575, 592.

48. Ernst & Ernst v. Hochfelder, 425 U.S. 185, 193 n.12 (1976); In re *Merrill Lynch & Co.*, 289 F. Supp. 2d at 427 ("[T]he requisite state of mind for actionable securities fraud under Rule 10b-5 is the intent to deceive, manipulate or defraud, not merely the intent to utter an untruth."); PALMITER, *supra* note 10, at 282.

49. *See* Herman & MacLean v. Huddleston, 459 U.S. 375, 390 n.30 (1983) (noting that proof of the requisite state of mind in a Rule 10b-5 action "is often a matter of inference from circumstantial evidence.").

50. There is some debate over whether the scienter requirement, earlier described as an element of a Rule 10b-5 claim, collapses into or is synonymous with the willfulness requirement imposed in criminal prosecutions under Rule 10b-5, as described in this paragraph of the text.

> While civil actions require scienter and criminal actions require willfulness, it is unclear whether there is a meaningful distinction between the terms. In other words, it is debatable whether willfulness in criminal cases requires something above the ordinary scienter required in civil cases. At least one commentator has argued that "courts have interpreted the term willfully, as used in [section] 32, to mean that only ordinary scienter is necessary to support a criminal conviction." This may be because "[section] 32 was drafted before [section] 10(b) was interpreted to require a showing of scienter." Until a court interpreting section 32(a) addresses the meaning of "willfully" in that provision, this question remains unresolved.

Xueming Jimmy Cheng et al., *Securities Fraud*, 41 AM. CRIM. L. REV. 1079, 1088 (2004) (footnotes omitted). *See also* Michael H. Dessent, *Joe Six-Pack, United States v. O'Hagan, and Private Securities Litigation Reform: A Line Must Be Drawn*, 40 ARIZ. L. REV. 1137, 1189 (1998). Professor Margaret Sachs answers the question simply, logically, and definitively. "The differentiated intent rule applies only if Congress expected courts to define these civil intent requirements less stringently than the willfulness requirement for criminal actions." Margaret V. Sachs, *Harmonizing Civil and Criminal Enforcement of Federal Regulatory Statutes: The Case of the Securities Exchange Act of 1934*, 2001 U. ILL. L. REV. 1025, 1054 (2001). Her compelling argument references Congress's assumed knowledge, in enacting Section 32(a), of a 1933 Supreme Court case construing willfulness under the federal tax laws. *Id.* at 1054–55. In the interests of clarity, the willfulness requirement is set out separately from the scienter element in this chapter.

51. 15 U.S.C. § 78ff(a) (2000).

52. *See, e.g.,* Spies v. United States, 317 U.S. 492, 487 (1943) ("[W]illful, as we have said, is a word of many meanings, its construction often being influenced by its context."); Kelly Koenig Levi, *Figure This: Judging or Federal Fraud? A Proposal To Criminalize Fraudulent Judging and Officiating in the International Figure Skating Arena*, 25 HASTINGS COMM. & ENT. L.J. 97, 114 (2002) ("Courts ... are not uniform in their determination of the level of conduct that satisfies 'willful.' Some conclude that specific intent is necessary, while others hold that recklessness is sufficient.").

53. *See, e.g.,* Ratzlaf v. United States, 510 U.S. 135, 149 (1994) ("[T]he jury had to find he knew the ... [conduct] in which he was engaged was unlawful."); Cheek v. United States, 498 U.S. 192, 201 (1991) ("Willfulness ... requires the Government to prove that the law imposed a duty on the defendant, that the defendant knew of this duty, and that he voluntarily and intentionally violated that duty."); United States v. Gross, 961 F.2d 1097, 1102 (3d Cir. 1992) ("conviction on the false statements charges required the government to show that Gross acted with knowledge of the wrongfulness of his actions."); United States v. Peltz, 433 F.2d 48, 55 (2d Cir. 1970) (defining willfulness under Section 32 of the 1934 Act as the defendant's realization that his actions were wrong under the securities laws "and that the knowingly wrongful act involve a significant risk of effecting the violation that has occurred"). *See also infra* note 54 and accompanying text.

54. Cheng et al., *supra* note 50, at 1088 (footnotes omitted). Under the rule in certain cases, however, "[p]roof of a specific intent to violate the law is not necessary to uphold a conviction under § 32(a) of the Act, provided that satisfactory proof is established that the

defendant intended to commit the act prohibited." United States v. Schwartz, 464 F.2d 499, 509 (2d Cir.), *cert. denied*, 409 U.S. 1009 (1972). *See also Peltz*, 433 F.2d at 54 ("A person can willfully violate an SEC rule even if he does not know of its existence."); James P. Hemmer, *Resignation of Corporate Counsel: Fulfillment or Abdication of Duty*, 39 HASTINGS L.J. 641, 644 (1988) ("Although the term 'willful' has not been construed uniformly by the courts in criminal cases, generally that element will be satisfied if the defendant acted voluntarily and intentionally."); William B. Herlands, *Criminal Aspects of the Securities Exchange Act of 1934*, 21 VA. L. REV. 139, 148–49 (1934); Levi, *supra* note 52, at 114 ("At minimum, most courts conclude that the defendant must have intended to do a wrongful act, but need not have intended to violate the law."). Some courts indicate that recklessness may be sufficient to support the willfulness requirement for criminal prosecutions under the federal securities laws. *See* NAGY ET AL., *supra* note 16, at 839–40; Levi, *supra* note 52, at 114; Sachs, *supra* note 50, at 1053 & 1055.

55. Merrill Lynch, Pierce, Fenner & Smith, Inc. v. Dabit, 2006 U.S. LEXIS 2497, *14 (2006).

56. *Id.* at *17–18; Frederick Mark Gedicks, *Suitability Claims and Purchases of Unrecommended Securities: An Agency Theory of Broker-Dealer Liability*, 37 ARIZ. ST. L.J. 535, 563 (2005) ("Beginning in the late 1970s, the Supreme Court began to impose new limits on … private actions under Rule 10b-5.… Especially significant in this regard were the Court's determinations that 10b-5 liability requires pleading and proof of scienter, or an intention to defraud, as well as reasonable reliance on a defendant's false or misleading statement, as part of the plaintiff's prima facie case."); Richard G. Himelrick, *Pleading Securities Fraud*, 43 MD. L. REV. 342, 343 (1984) ("In securities litigation, insistence upon detailed pleading coincides with substantive efforts, including conspicuous examples in the Supreme Court, to control the expansion of rule 10b-5."); Sachs, *supra* note 50, at 1046–47.

57. Merrill Lynch, 2006 U.S. LEXIS 2497 at *15–18; Blue Chip Stamps v. Manor Drug Stores, 421 U.S. 723 (1975) (affirming the rule in *Birnbaum v. Newport Steel Corp.*, 193 F.2d 461 (2d Cir. 1952), and holding that a failure to purchase stock does not confer standing to sue under Rule 10b-5); HAZEN, *supra* note 9, at 584; PALMITER, *supra* note 10, at 273.

58. *Blue Chip Stamps*, 421 U.S. at 725.

59. Baretge v. Barnett, 553 F.2d 290, 291 (2d Cir. 1977) ("the rule does not require that defendant be the seller of the stock or that plaintiff have purchased the stock from defendant."); S.E.C. v. Texas Gulf Sulphur Co., 401 F.2d 833, 860 (2d Cir. 1968) ("The mere fact that an insider did not engage in securities transactions does not negate the possibility of wrongful purpose"); HAZEN, *supra* note 9, at 575.

60. *See* sources cited *supra* note 13.

61. *See* Newton v. Merrill Lynch, Pierce, Fenner & Smith, Inc., 259 F.3d 154, 172 (3d Cir. 2001) ("Reliance, or transaction causation, establishes that but for the fraudulent misrepresentation, the investor would not have purchased or sold the security.").

62. *See* Basic Inc. v. Levinson, 485 U.S. 224, 241–49 (1988); Affiliated Ute Citizens v. United States, 406 U.S. 128, 153–154 (1972).

63. *See Basic*, 485 U.S. at 248–49.

64. *See Newton*, 259 F.3d at 173 ("Loss causation demonstrates that the fraudulent misrepresentation actually caused the loss suffered.").

65. Dura Pharm's, Inc. v. Broudo, 544 U.S. 336, 338, 342–44 (2005).

66. *Id.*

67. *Id.* at 1631.

68. 15 U.S.C. §78bb(a) ("no person permitted to maintain a suit for damages under the provisions of this title shall recover, through satisfaction of judgment in one or more actions, a total amount in excess of his actual damages on account of the act complained of."); PALMITER, *supra* note 10, at 287.

69. 15 U.S.C. §78u-4(e); PALMITER, *supra* note 10, at 287.

70. HAZEN, *supra* note 9, at 624; Lewis D. Lowenfels & Alan R. Bromberg, *Compensatory Damages in Rule 10b-5 Actions: Pragmatic Justice or Chaos?*, 30 SETON HALL L. REV. 1083, 1084 (2000) ("there is no clear rule guiding the measure of damages under Rule 10b-5 and hence little predictability for counsel or the client.").

71. PALMITER, *supra* note 10, at 288. Out-of-pocket losses (damages actually and proximately caused by the defendant's violative conduct) are the most common measure of damages in Rule 10b-5 cases and typically are equal to the difference between the fair value of what the plaintiff received and the fair value of what the plaintiff would have received had there been no violative conduct. Affiliated Ute Citizens v. United States, 406 U.S. 128, 155 (1972); Huddleston v. Herman & MacLean, 640 F.2d 534, 555 (5th Cir. 1981), *aff'd in part and rev'd in part on other grounds*, 459 U.S. 375 (1983); Ross v. Bank South, N.A., 885 F.2d 723, 742–743 (11th Cir. 1989).

72. PALMITER, *supra* note 10, at 288. Contract damages, also known as "benefit-of-the-bargain" damages or referenced as damages calculated under a "'loss of the bargain' rule," allow the plaintiff to recover his or her loss of the benefit of the bargain in contractual transactions. McMahan & Co. v. Wherehouse Entertainment, 65 F.3d 1044, 1049 (2d Cir. 1995); Hackbart v. Holmes, 675 F.2d 1114, 1121–22 (10th Cir. 1982); Norte & Co. v. Huffines, 288 F. Supp. 855, 864 (S.D.N.Y. 1968), *modified*, 416 F.2d 1189 (2d Cir. 1969), *cert. denied*, 397 U.S. 989 (1970).

73. PALMITER, *supra* note 10, at 288. Rescissory damages attempt to put the plaintiff in the same financial position the plaintiff would be in if the transaction were rescinded by, for example, allowing a plaintiff-seller to recover the purchaser's profits (profit disgorgement) or a plaintiff-purchaser to recover the difference between her purchase and resale price. Janigan v. Taylor, 344 F.2d 781, 786 (1st Cir.), *cert. denied*, 382 U.S. 879 (1965) (profit disgorgement); Speed v. Transamerica Corp., 135 F. Supp. 176, 186–94 (D. Del.1955), *modified on another point and aff'd*, 235 F.2d 369 (3d Cir. 1956). Generally, rescissory damages only are appropriate when rescission has been made impossible (because, for example, stock bought or sold by the plaintiff has been resold). Glick v. Campagna, 613 F.2d 31, 37 (3d Cir. 1979) ("If the defendant no longer owns the stock or it is otherwise unavailable because of a merger or other intervening event, then the court may award rescissory damages to place the plaintiff in the same financial position he would have been were it possible to return the stock.").

74. Flaks v. Koegel, 504 F.2d 702, 707 (2d Cir. 1974) ("The plaintiffs are ... requesting ... rescission and are simply seeking the recovery of the amounts paid for their stock. This is an appropriate remedy under sections 10(b) and 17"); PALMITER, *supra* note 10, at 287; Robert B. Thompson, *The Measure of Recovery under Rule 10b-5: A Restitution Alternative to Tort Damages*, 37 VAND. L. REV. 349, 367 (1984) ("When courts recognized the existence of private causes of action under rule 10b-5, most courts also acknowledged that a rule 10b-5 plaintiff could seek rescission instead of pursuing an action for damages."). Rescission is an equitable remedy that restores the parties to a transaction to their respective positions before the transaction. The remedy consists of unwinding the purchase and sale transaction between the parties, resulting in (a) a plaintiff-seller getting her

stock back in exchange for the purchase price or (b) a plaintiff-purchaser returning the stock she purchased in exchange for the purchase price she paid. Huddleston, 640 F.2d at 554 ("Rescission is the avoidance or undoing of the transaction. Its purpose is to return the defrauded purchaser to the status quo ante; it contemplates the return of the injured party to the position he occupied before he was wrongfully induced to enter the transaction."). Generally, rescission only is appropriate when the parties to the transaction are litigants and when their positions have not changed significantly since the transaction took place. *Id.* at 554–55.

75. Pub. L. No. 104-67, 109 Stat. 737 (codified in scattered sections of Title 15 of the United States Code).

76. 15 U.S.C. §78u-4(b)(1); Chen v. Navarre Corp., 299 F.3d 735, 742 (8th Cir. 2002).

77. 15 U.S.C. §78u-4(b)(2); *Chen,* 299 F.3d at 745.

78. Apprendi v. N.J., 530 U.S. 466, 476–477 (2000) (tracing the requirement to roots in constitutional due process and rights of the accused); United States v. Gaudin, 515 U.S. 506, 510 (1995) (same).

79. *See, e.g.,* United States v. Hernandez, 176 F.3d 719, 728 (3d Cir. 1999) ("Reasonable doubt is not an easy concept to understand, and it is all the more difficult to explain."); Jessica N. Cohen, *The Reasonable Doubt Jury Instruction: Giving Meaning to a Critical Concept,* 22 Am. J. Crim. L. 677 (1995) (arguing that trial judges should define the standard for jurors); James Joseph Duane, *What Message Are We Sending to Criminal Jurors When We Ask Them to "Send a Message" With Their Verdict?,* 22 Am. J. Crim. L. 565, 665 (1995) ("The words 'beyond a reasonable doubt' are notoriously obscure and are 'not self-defining for jurors.'"); Thomas V. Mulrine, *Reasonable Doubt: How in the World is it Defined?,* 12 Am. U.J. Int'l L. & Pol'y 195 (1997) (recommending approaches to better defining the standard).

80. Kevin M. Clermont & Emily Sherwin, *A Comparative View of Standards of Proof,* 50 Am. J. Comp. L. 243, 251 (2002). *See also* Jackson v. Virginia, 443 U.S. 307, 315 (1979) ("by impressing upon the factfinder the need to reach a subjective state of near certitude of the guilt of the accused, the standard symbolizes the significance that our society attaches to the criminal sanction and thus to liberty itself."); Black's Law Dictionary 1272 (7th ed. 1999) (defining "reasonable doubt" as "the doubt that prevents one from being firmly convinced of a defendant's guilt, or the belief that there is a real possibility that a defendant is not guilty"); Kimberly A. Pace, *Recalibrating the Scales of Justice Through National Punitive Damage Reform,* 46 Am. U.L. Rev. 1573, 1618 (1997) ("The purpose of criminal law is to punish and deter (retributive), using a 'beyond a reasonable doubt' burden of proof, which means that the prosecutor must prove that there is no reasonable question that the defendant committed the act."); Lawrence M. Solan, *Convicting the Innocent Beyond a Reasonable Doubt: Some Lessons about Jury Instructions from the* Sheppard *Case,* 49 Clev. St. L. Rev. 465, 473 (2001) ("The expression 'proof beyond a reasonable doubt' is means for accomplishing an end—the requirement that a person should not be convicted unless the government proves its case to 'near certitude.'").

81. Herman & MacLean v. Huddleston, 459 U.S. 375, 387–90 (1983).

82. *See* Matthew Stohl, *False Light Invasion of Privacy in Docudramas: The Oxymoron Which Must be Solved,* 35 Akron L. Rev. 251, 282 n.13 (2002) ("'preponderance of the evidence' is ... subject to numerous definitions.").

83. Clermont & Sherwin, *supra* note 80, at 251. *See also* 5 C.F.R. 1201.56(c)(2) (2005) (defining the standard to mean "[t]he degree of relevant evidence that a reasonable person, considering the record as a whole, would accept as sufficient to find that a contested

fact is more likely to be true than untrue."); Cohen, *supra* note 79, at 693 (defining the standard as "more likely than not"); Vern R. Walker, *Restoring the Individual Plaintiff to Tort Law by Rejecting "Junk Logic" About Specific Causation*, 56 ALA. L. REV. 381, 460 (2004) ("Courts have interpreted this phrase as meaning 'more likely than not,' 'probably true,' or 'more probably true than false.' The 'weight' or 'convincing force' or 'probative value' of the evidence supporting the finding must be 'greater than' the weight of evidence against the finding.").

84. Indictment, *supra* note 2, at ¶ 60. Both the Indictment and the court's opinion on Stewart's motion for acquittal reference three statements, but information was publicly disseminated by Stewart four times. *See id.*

85. *Id.*

86. *Id.* at ¶ 61.

87. *Id.* The government's allegations regarding the concealed facts are included in the Indictment at ¶¶ 15–17.

88. *Id.* (quoting from *Martha Stewart Sold ImClone Stock*, WALL ST. J., June 7, 2002).

89. *Id.* at ¶ 57.

90. *Id.*

91. *Id.* at ¶ 58.

92. *Id.* at ¶ 63.

93. *Id.*

94. *Id.*

95. *See supra* notes 89–91 and accompanying text.

96. Indictment, *supra* note 2, at ¶ 64.

97. *Id.*

98. *Id.*

99. *Id.*

100. *Id.* at ¶ 65.

101. *Id.*; *see supra* notes 87 & 93 and accompanying text.

102. *See supra* notes 89–91 and accompanying text.

103. Indictment, *supra* note 2, at ¶ 1.

104. *Id.* at ¶ 60. The Indictment also allows that Stewart's public misrepresentations were made "in an effort to stop or at least slow the steady erosion of MSLO's stock price caused by investor concerns." *Id.*

105. *Id.* at ¶¶ 1 & 2.

106. *Id.* ¶ 59.

107. *Id.* at ¶ 60.

108. *Id.*

109. The trademark for "Good Things" is registered in the name of MSLO. U.S. Patent & Trademark Office, Reg. No. 2947861, *available at* http://tess2.uspto.gov/bin/show-field?f=doc&state=4nhf87.4.10. MSLO also has applied for a service mark for "Good Things." U.S. Patent & Trademark Office, Serial No. 78386149, *available at* http://tess2.uspto.gov/bin/showfield?f=doc&state=4nhf87.5.20. The trademark for "A Good Thing" was filed by another applicant and abandoned. U.S. Patent & Trademark Office, Serial No. 78080819, *available at* http://tess2.uspto.gov/bin/showfield?f=doc&state=4nhf87.2.33.

110. R. MICHAEL CASSIDY, PROSECUTORIAL ETHICS 13–14 (2005); Moohr, *supra* note 4, at 177 ("The power of the prosecutor to charge is two-fold; the power to indict or not ... and the power to decide what offenses to charge."). The charges in the Indictment

are the result of a grand jury process. Use of the terms "prosecution" and "government" in this chapter in reference to the charging in the *Stewart* case therefore generally includes both the grand jury and the U.S. Attorneys.

111. CASSIDY, *supra* note 110, at 14–24; Bennett L. Gershman, *Moral Standard For The Prosecutor's Exercise Of The Charging Discretion*, 20 FORDHAM URB. L.J. 513, 513 (1993) ("Various legal, political, experiential, and ethical considerations inform and guide the charging decision."); Peter Krug, *Prosecutorial Discretion and Its Limits*, 50 AM. J. COMP. L. 643, 650 & 652 (2002) (outlining these and other sources of prosecutorial guidance). Prosecutors generally also are guided in their charging decisions by the American Bar Association Standards of Criminal Justice. Standard 3-3.9, *Discretion in the Charging Decision*, American Bar Association Standards for Criminal Justice (3d ed. 1993). *See also* Krug, *supra*, at 651; Ellen S. Podgor, *The Ethics and Professionalism of Prosecutors in Discretionary Decisions*, 68 FORDHAM L. REV. 1511, 1517–18 (2000).

112. Rule 3.8, *Special Responsibilities of a Prosecutor*, American Bar Association Model Rules of Professional Conduct, *available at* http://www.abanet.org/cpr/ mrpc/rule_3_8.html (last visited June 25, 2005).

113. DR 7-103(A), *Performing the Duty of Public Prosecutor or Other Government Lawyer*, American Bar Asociation Model Code of Professional Responsibility, *available at* http://www.abanet.org/cpr/mrpc/mrpc_home.html through the "Lawyer Ethics and Professionalism" button on the toolbar (last visited June 25, 2005).

114. Brinegar v. United States, 338 U.S. 160, 175 (1949), *quoting* Carroll v. United States, 267 U.S. 132, 161 (1925) ("'The substance of all the definitions' of probable cause 'is a reasonable ground for belief of guilt.'"); CASSIDY, *supra* note 110, at 15–16; BLACK'S LAW DICTIONARY 1219 (7th ed. 1999) (defining "probable cause" as "[a] reasonable ground to suspect that a person has committed … a crime"); George Fisher, *The Jury's Rise as Lie Detector*, 107 YALE L.J. 575, 579 (1997) ("The sworn testimony of a named witness who is not obviously delusional is all the prosecutor needs to satisfy probable cause.").

115. Krug, *supra* note 111, at 652.

116. 28 U.S.C. §530B (2000).

117. U.S. Dept. of Justice, *Principles of Federal Prosecution*, U.S. ATTORNEYS' MANUAL 9-27.000, *available at* http://www.usdoj.gov/usao/eousa/foia_reading_room/usam/title9/ 27mcrm.htm#9-27.001 (last visited June 25, 2005) [hereinafter ATTORNEYS' MANUAL].

118. ATTORNEYS' MANUAL 9-27.200. *See also* Bordenkircher v. Hayes, 434 U.S. 357, 364 (1978) ("So long as the prosecutor has probable cause to believe that the accused committed an offense defined by statute, the decision whether or not to prosecute, and what charge to file or bring before a grand jury, generally rests entirely in his discretion.").

119. ATTORNEYS' MANUAL 9-27.220. The Principles go on to define each of the three reasons for declining to bring charges against a prospective criminal defendant. ATTORNEYS' MANUAL 9-27.230, 9-27.240 & 9-27.250.

120. The relevant Principle states that,

> [i]n determining whether to commence or recommend prosecution or take other action against a person, the attorney for the government should not be influenced by:
>   1. The person's race, religion, sex, national origin, or political association, activities or beliefs;

2. The attorney's own personal feelings concerning the person, the person's associates, or the victim; or

3. The possible affect of the decision on the attorney's own professional or personal circumstances.

ATTORNEYS' MANUAL 9-27.260. *See* Robert H. Jackson, *The Federal Prosecutor,* 31 J. AM. INST. L. & CRIMINOLOGY 3, 5 (1940) (published April 1, 1940 address at the Second Annual Conference of United States Attorneys).

121. ATTORNEYS' MANUAL 9-27.300.

122. ATTORNEYS' MANUAL 9-27.320.

123. *See, e.g., Memorandum from Attorney General John Ashcroft to All Federal Prosecutors, Department Policy Concerning Charging Criminal Offenses, Disposition of Charges, and Sentencing* (Sept. 22, 2003), *available at* http://news.findlaw.com/hdocs/docs/doj/ashcroft 92203chrgmem.pdf (last visited June 25, 2005) (subject to a number of important exceptions, "[i]t is the policy of the Department of Justice that, in all federal criminal cases, federal prosecutors must charge and pursue the most serious, readily provable offense or offenses that are supported by the facts of the case").

124. *See* Thomas E. Baker, *A View to the Future of Judicial Federalism: "Neither Out Far Nor In Deep,"* 45 CASE W. RES. L. REV. 705, 749 (1995) ("The Department of Justice and the typical U.S. Attorney's Office have written prosecution guidelines, often labelled [sp] 'declination policies,' that describe principles for informed exercise of federal prosecutorial discretion."); Roger Conner et al., *The Office of U.S. Attorney and Public Safety: A Brief History Prepared for the "Changing Role Of U.S. Attorneys' Offices In Public Safety" Symposium,* 28 CAP. U.L. REV. 753, 770 (2000) ("U.S. Attorneys' offices have guidelines for individual prosecutions."); Krug, *supra* note 111, at 650 ("local prosecutorial offices have formally adopted written standards."). This decentralization has been in existence for decades. *See* Jackson, *supra* note 120, at 3 ("Your responsibility in your several districts for law enforcement and for its methods cannot be wholly surrendered to Washington. It is an unusual and rare instance in which the local District Attorney should be superseded in the handling of litigation....").

125. Laurie L. Levenson, *Working Outside the Rules: The Undefined Responsibilities of Federal Prosecutors,* 26 FORDHAM URB. L.J. 553, 558 (1999) ("charging decisions take place in a gap in the rules—a gap intentionally left so that prosecutors can tailor justice. In order to fill the gap, prosecutors must apply both a practical sense of what is right and a moral standard.").

126. The resulting analyses are complex.

> If deciding how to charge a case were as simple as reading a statute and deciding whether its elements might apply to the defendant's behavior, then new prosecutors who have demonstrated their academic acuity should be equipped to handle the task. Experienced prosecutors know, however, that the charging decision is much more complicated. The difficulty comes in evaluating those factors that are not defined by statute, including the severity of the crime, the defendant's role in the crime, the defendant's past and possible future cooperation, injury to the victim, complexity in trying the case and the likelihood of success.

Id. at 559.

127. Wayte v. United States, 470 U.S. 598, 607 (1985) ("In our criminal justice system, the Government retains 'broad discretion' as to whom to prosecute."); Bordenkircher v. Hayes, 434 U.S. 357, 365 (1978) ("There is no doubt that the breadth of discretion that

our country's legal system vests in prosecuting attorneys carries with it the potential for both individual and institutional abuse. And broad though that discretion may be, there are undoubtedly constitutional limits upon its exercise."); Gershman, *supra* note 111, at 513 ("The prosecutor's decision to institute criminal charges is the broadest and least regulated power in American criminal law. The judicial deference shown to prosecutors generally is most noticeable with respect to the charging function."); Krug, *supra* note 111, at 646 ("Prosecutors enjoy something close to a monopoly on the use of prosecutorial authority."); Daniel C. Richman & William J. Stuntz, *Al Capone's Revenge: An Essay On The Political Economy Of Pretextual Prosecution*, 105 COLUM. L. REV. 583, 608–09 (2005) ("Federal criminal law gives U.S. Attorneys and their assistants an enormous range of charging options: The scope of responsibility may be small, but jurisdiction is quite large. The combination means that federal prosecutors have both the time and the authority to do what they want"). Professor Ellen Podgor ably summarizes the state of prosecutorial discretion.

> Prosecutorial discretion is a reality. Its existence has been consistently endorsed by the United States Supreme Court. Although Congress has recently extended the application of ethical rules to federal prosecutors, these rules do not directly supervise a prosecutor's discretionary decisions. Further, discretionary decisions will seldom reach a level of being "vexatious, frivolous, or in bad faith" to warrant a monetary award under the Hyde Amendment.

Podgor, *supra* note 111, at 1511–12 (footnotes omitted).

128. *Wayte*, 470 U.S. at 608 ("[T]he decision to prosecute may not be "'deliberately based upon an unjustifiable standard such as race, religion, or other arbitrary classification,'" including the exercise of protected statutory and constitutional rights. It is appropriate to judge selective prosecution claims according to ordinary equal protection standards.") (citations and footnote omitted); Gershman, *supra* note 111, at 513 n.3 ("Legal considerations include an evaluation of the strength of the case, the credibility of complainants and witnesses, the existence and admissibility of corroborating proof, and the nature and strength of the defense."); *id.* at 513 n.4 ("Political considerations include an assessment of the harm caused by the offense, the availability of investigative and litigation resources, the existence of non-criminal alternatives, and an alertness to relevant social and community concerns."); *id.* at 513 n.5 ("Experiential considerations include the prosecutor's background, training, experience, intuition, judgment, and common sense."); *id.* at 522 ("My objective is ... to provoke inquiry into the degree of moral confidence that a prosecutor should have before bringing criminal charges. My thesis is that the prosecutor should engage in a moral struggle over charging decisions, and should not mechanically initiate charges."); Leslie C. Griffin, *The Prudent Prosecutor*, 14 GEO. J. LEGAL ETHICS 259, 276 (2001) (footnotes omitted) ("Prosecutions cannot be based upon race, religion, the exercise of rights, or other arbitrary classifications. It is difficult, however, for defendants to prove such constitutional violations."); Eric L. Muller, *Constitutional Conscience*, 83 B.U.L. REV. 1017, 1070–71 (2003) ("It is ... well settled that a judge has the power to dismiss a criminal charge on the basis that it was unconstitutionally vindictive or selective.").

129. CASSIDY, *supra* note 110, at 20–24; Gershman, *supra* note 111, at 513 ("Limited constitutional and statutory constraints on charging are manifested in the presumption of prosecutorial good faith, and are reflected in the courts' acknowledgment that they lack the knowledge and expertise to supervise the prosecutor's exercise of discretion.").

130. Oyler v. Boles, 368 U.S. 448, 456 (1962) (" … the conscious exercise of some selectivity in enforcement is not in itself a federal constitutional violation."); CASSIDY, *supra* note 110, at 23 ("[A] presumption of legality attaches to a prosecutor's charging decision."); Muller, *supra* note 128, at 1071 ("Allegations of vindictive and selective prosecution are legion, but successful claims are exceedingly rare. Courts have also drastically limited the ability of criminal defendants to get discovery to support a claim of impermissibly selective prosecution."); Podgor, *supra* note 111, at 1518–19 ("Despite studies tending to show that prosecutors have exhibited bias in some of their charging decisions, courts have been reluctant to scrutinize the prosecutorial decision-making process."). In sum,

> "[t]o obtain discovery on a selective prosecution claim, a defendant must offer 'some evidence' of discriminatory effect and discriminatory intent." In order to prove selective prosecution, a defendant must prove that similarly situated individuals were not prosecuted and that he was singled out for prosecution on arbitrary grounds. The Court has set a high threshold of proof for these cases and gives a "presumption of regularity" to prosecutorial decisions.…

Griffin, *supra* note 128, at 276 (footnotes omitted).

131. Ellen S. Podgor, *Department of Justice Guidelines: Balancing "Discretionary Justice,"* 13 CORNELL J. L. & PUB. POL'Y 167, 186–89 (2004).

132. *Cf.* United States v. Caceres, 440 U.S. 741 (1979) (refusing to allow exclusion of evidence in violation of applicable Internal Revenue Service regulations). For a recent summary of cases on this point, see Podgor, *supra* note 131, at 189–94.

133. ATTORNEYS' MANUAL 9-27.150.

134. The charges based on these allegations have been described by some as unusual or "novel." Memorandum Opinion, United States v. Martha Stewart and Peter Bacanovic, S1 03 Cr. 717 (MGC) (S.D.N.Y. filed [Jan. 26, 2004]) *available at* http://news.findlaw.com/ hdocs/docs/mstewart/usmspb12604opn.pdf (last visited July 6, 2005) [hereinafter Memorandum Opinion], 5–6; Moohr, *supra* note 4, at 179. *See also* Stephen Bainbridge, *Was Martha Stewart's Denial Material? The Problem with Count 9,* Dec. 4, 2003, *at* http://www.professorbainbridge.com/2003/ 12/was_martha_stew.html (last visited July 5, 2005) (noting and endorsing the court's view that the Rule 10b-5 charge is "a bit of a stretch"); Henry Blodget, *The Charges Against Martha,* SLATE, Dec. 3, 2003, *at* http://slate.msn.com/id/ 2091480/entry/2091866/#ContinueArticle (last visited July 6, 2005) (terming the Rule 10b-5 charge "controversial"). However, it is important to note that the court denied Stewart's motion to dismiss the Rule 10b-5 charge. *See* Brief for Defendant-Appellant Martha Stewart, United States v. Martha Stewart and Peter Bacanovic, 04-3953(L)-cr (2d Cir. filed Oct. 20, 2004), at 16–17 *available at* http://lawprofessors.type-pad.com/whitecollarcrime_blog/files/Brief.pdf; Cynthia A. Caillavet, Comment: *From* Nike v. Kasky *To Martha Stewart: First Amendment Protection For Corporate Speakers' Denials Of Public Criminal Allegations,* 94 J. CRIM. L. & CRIMINOLOGY 1033, 1040 (2004).

135. *See* Joan MacLeod Heminway, *Save Martha Stewart?: Observations About Equal Justice In U.S. Insider Trading Regulation,* 12 TEX. J. WOMEN & L. 247, 256–61 (2003) (describing this pattern in insider trading litigation under Rule 10b-5); Donald C. Langevoort, *Rule 10b-5 as an Adaptive Organism,* 61 FORDHAM L. REV. S7 (1993) (a seminal work on Rule 10b-5's flexibility); Moohr, *supra* note 4, at 179 (noting, in the contest of a discussion of criminal litigation under Rule 10b-5, that a pattern of "prosecutors raising new interpretations and courts acceding to them—leads to an incremental, but inexorable, expansion of the laws.").

136. *Cf.* Kathleen F. Brickey, *Enron's Legacy*, 8 Buff. Crim. L. R. 221, 256 (2004) (noting, after a review of corporate fraud cases, including the *Stewart* case, that "there is no evidence of 'scapegoating' for the sake of expediency."). One commentator expressly refutes any allegation that Stewart was prosecuted because of her public-figure status.

> For example, some critical commentary in the wake of the indictment of Martha Stewart extolled the use of federal prosecutorial discretion to target a celebrity—as always assuming, for argument's sake, that the indictment satisfies the Principles of Federal Prosecution—because of the greater deterrent value such a prosecution provides. My view, and the implicit view of the United States Attorney who brought the indictment, is that Stewart's celebrity status is not a relevant difference and that her indictment must be justified without regard to it, notwithstanding the likely gain in general deterrence. (Whether in practice a potential defendant's notoriety exerts a subtle and improper influence is another matter. Certainly on occasion it does.)

Harry Litman, *Pretextual Prosecution*, 92 Geo. L.J. 1135, 1164–1165 (2004) (footnotes omitted).

137. *See supra* notes 19–31 and accompanying text.

138. *Id.*

139. *See* sources cited *supra* notes 20 & 23.

140. *See id.*

141. *See supra* notes 89–91, 95 & 102 and accompanying text.

142. *See* Bainbridge, *supra* note 134. Chapter 10 of this volume addresses the issues raised in this paragraph in greater detail.

143. *Cf. id.*

144. *See* Jeffrey Sagalewicz, Comment: *The Martha Duty: Protecting Shareholders from the Criminal Behavior of Celebrity Corporate Figures*, 83 Or. L. Rev. 331, 334–37 (2004); Krysten Crawford, *Time to cut Martha loose?*, CNN/Money, May 20, 2004, *at* http://money.cnn.com/2004/05/19/news/midcaps/marthastewart/ (last visited June 28, 2005); Susan C. Walker, *Martha Settling Down, Along With Company's Stock Price*, FOXNews.com, March 13, 2005, *at* http://www. foxnews.com/story/0,2933,150206,00.html (last visited June 28, 2005); *When the CEO is the Brand, But Falls from Grace, What's Next?*, Knowledge@Wharton, April 7, 2004, *at* http://knowledge.wharton.upenn.edu/index. cfm?fa=viewArticle&ID=956 (last visited June 28, 2005) [hereinafter *CEO is the Brand*].

145. *Cf. id. But cf.* S.E.C. v. Electronics Warehouse, Inc., 689 F. Supp. 53, 66 (D. Conn. 1988) ("An indictment for mail fraud of the president and founder of the issuing corporation was a fact that any reasonable investor would have considered important in making the decision to invest"); In re. Franchard Corp., 42 S.E.C. 163, 172–73 (1964) (finding information about the wrongful conduct of a founder, key executive, and major stockholder to be material because, among other things, it is "germane to an evaluation of the integrity of his management" and it evidences "the possibility of a change in the control and management of registrant").

146. *See, e.g.,* O'Hare, *supra* note 32, at 329 ("[I]n false corporate publicity cases, the courts have adopted a foreseeability test, asking if the company's 'assertions are made … in a manner reasonably calculated to influence the investing public.'"); *id.* ("in a classic securities fraud case in which a person selling securities lies to the purchaser, there is no question that the fraud was 'in connection with' the purchase or sale of a security because the wrongdoer defrauded the victim into purchasing or selling his securities.").

147. *See id.* at 330–31 (describing various means used by courts to interpret the "in connection with" element in less certain cases).

148. *See id.* at 330.

149. S.E.C. v. Zandford, 535 U.S. 813, 821–24 (2002); *see also* O'Hare, *supra*, note 32, at 331–34.

150. *See* sources cited *supra* note 144.

151. *See supra* note 35 and accompanying text.

152. *See supra* note 36 and accompanying text.

153. *See supra* note 37 and accompanying text.

154. *See supra* notes 105–108.

155. *See* O'Hare, *supra* note 32, at 335 n.64 (noting the acceptance of this pleading method in two circuits under the enhanced pleading requirements of the Private Securities Litigation Reform Act of 1995).

156. The Indictment allegations include facts analogous to some of those listed as evidence of scienter in *Greebel v. FTP Software, Inc.*, 194 F.3d 185, 196–97 (1st Cir. 1999), notably those involving financial self-interest. It is important to note here, however, that the government is not bound by the enhanced pleading requirements for scienter enacted by Congress in the PSLRA. *See supra* note 77 and accompanying text.

157. *See supra* note 51 and accompanying text.

158. *See supra* notes 52–54 and accompanying text.

159. Although the allegations in the Indictment regarding scienter are not directly supported with specific facts, *see supra* notes 105–08 and accompanying text, they readily support a reasonable belief that Stewart committed securities fraud under Rule 10b-5. It does not matter, for purposes of the professional conduct rules governing prosecutorial charging decisions, that the prosecutor may not be able to prove the truth of the allegations at trial. Tracey L. Meares, *Rewards for Good Behavior: Influencing Prosecutorial Discretion and Conduct with Financial Incentives*, 64 FORDHAM L. REV. 851, 864 (1995) ("the ethical rules do not clearly prohibit the prosecutor from deciding to charge an accused with offenses which the prosecutor has probable cause to believe are factually justified but which the prosecutor believes she probably will not be able to prove beyond a reasonable doubt at trial."); Kenneth J. Melilli, *Prosecutorial Discretion in an Adversary System*, 1992 B.Y.U. L. REV. 669, 680–81 ("Probable cause is little more than heightened suspicion, and it is not even remotely sufficient to screen out individuals who are factually not guilty.").

160. Gerstein v. Pugh, 420 U.S. 103, 119 (1975) ("an indictment, 'fair upon its face,' and returned by a 'properly constituted grand jury,' conclusively determines the existence of probable cause"); Rodriguez v. Ritchey, 556 F.2d 1185, 1191 (5th Cir. 1977) ("an indictment by a properly constituted grand jury conclusively determines the existence of probable cause"); Niki Kuckes, *The Useful, Dangerous Fiction of Grand Jury Independence*, 41 AM. CRIM. L. REV. 1, 19 (2004) ("a grand jury indictment is deemed a 'judicial' probable cause determination"); Andrew D. Leipold, *Why Grand Juries Do Not (and Cannot) Protect the Accused*, 80 CORNELL L. REV. 260, 299 (1995) ("Once the indictment is returned, the issue of probable cause is conclusively determined.").

161. *See supra* note 119 and accompanying text. The Indictment is carefully and logically constructed to make out a valid securities fraud claim. *See* Indictment, *supra* note 2.

162. *See supra* note 119 and accompanying text. Among the expressly factors supporting a conclusion that charging is in the federal government's interest are "[f]ederal law enforcement priorities" and "[t]he deterrent effect of prosecution," both of which would seem

to relate to charging Stewart with securities fraud in June 2003. *See* ATTORNEYS' MANUAL 9-27.230.

163. *See supra* note 119 and accompanying text.

164. *See supra* notes 78–80 and accompanying text (regarding applicable burdens of proof). Private actions, both under Rule 10b-5 and under state law theories, also could vindicate some of the policy goals underlying Stewart's criminal prosecution. In this regard, Professor Podgor notes that

> [t]he prosecutor's discretionary power is magnified in the white collar crime context, where the characterization of conduct as criminal instead of tortious may be within the prosecutor's realm of decision-making. Whether a prosecutor should pursue wrongful conduct in an administrative arena or the criminal courts can also be a prosecutorial decision. Internal limits for prosecution used in a particular United States Attorney's Office may be the controlling factor in some of these decisions. Offices might use different threshold levels for proceeding with prosecutions.

Podgor, *supra* note 111, at 1519 (footnote omitted).

165. The *U.S. Attorneys' Manual* encourages prosecutors to consider "all relevant factors" in making the determination of whether a non-criminal alternative is adequate, but lists three factors specifically: [t]he sanctions available under the alternative means of disposition; [t]he likelihood that an effective sanction will be imposed; and "[t]he effect of non-criminal disposition on Federal law enforcement interests." ATTORNEYS' MANUAL 9-27.250. Given the close involvement of the SEC with the U.S. Department of Justice in the investigation and enforcement of possible violations of law relating to Stewart's sale of her ImClone shares, *see*, *e.g.*, *SEC Charges Martha Stewart, Broker Peter Bacanovic with Illegal Insider Trading*, June 4, 2003, *available at* http://www.sec.gov/news/press/2003-69.htm (in which the SEC "acknowledges the assistance of the U.S. Attorney's Office for the Southern District of New York and the Federal Bureau of Investigation in the investigation of this matter."), these and other factors likely were (or at least could have been) assessed.

166. *See supra* note 120 and accompanying text. *See also* Heminway, *supra* note 135 (making similar and additional arguments about the SEC's decision to bring an enforcement action against Stewart for insider trading violations based on the sale of her ImClone shares); Blodget, *supra* note 134 ("it is also plausible that Stewart ... is being prosecuted primarily because she is famous and rich—prosecuting famous, rich executives being a sure-fire way to incite riotous public support, remedy the perceived mistakes of the past (toothless regulation and/or spineless enforcement), and advance careers.").

167. *See supra* note 120 and accompanying text. *See also* Heminway, *supra* note 135, at 277–78 (noting that the public may have mixed feelings about Stewart); Jeanne L. Schroeder, *Envy and Outsider Trading: The Case of Martha Stewart*, 26 CARDOZO L. REV. 2023, 2029 (2005) ("The public has long had a love-hate relationship with Stewart. She is widely admired for her design and business acumen even as she's disparaged for her perfectionist impulses and sheer omnipresence.").

168. *See supra* note 120 and accompanying text.

169. In this regard, one scholar notes:

> The Supreme Court has affirmatively recognized judicial authority to review prosecutorial charging decisions in two situations: when the decision to increase charges was vindictive, and when the government improperly selected the de-

fendant based on an impermissible classification. Whether the prosecutor acted vindictively or selected the defendant based on an unacceptable criterion focuses judicial review of prosecutorial conduct squarely on the motivations of the particular attorneys who made the decision. The Court's approach, however, avoided the hard issue of how to ascertain actual intent by adopting tests that made meaningful inquiry into the prosecutor's state of mind irrelevant for a vindictive prosecution claim, and almost impossible for a selective prosecution claim. Any judicial review of the decisions of whether to charge a particular person and which crime should be charged seems to be an area in which the prosecutor's thought process would be of paramount importance. The Court, however, has made intent essentially irrelevant, most likely because it recognized that asking prosecutors why they acted would be fruitless and perhaps even counter-productive.

Peter J. Henning, *Prosecutorial Misconduct and Constitutional Remedies*, 77 WASH. U. L. Q. 713, 734 (1999). The parallels between the difficulty of proving prosecutorial motivation in this context and the difficulty of proving scienter in the *Stewart* case are apparent.

170. *See supra* note 121 and accompanying text. The seriousness of an offense typically is measured by reference to the severity of the penalties imposed upon violators. ATTORNEYS' MANUAL 9-27.300 ("The 'most serious' offense is generally that which yields the highest range under the sentencing guidelines."). Under current law, the penalties for criminal violations of Rule 10b-5 include fines of up to $5,000,000, imprisoned for up to 20 years, or both. 15 U.S.C. § 78ff(a) (2000). (As an alternative under current law, one might bring a federal criminal action under the securities fraud provision included in the Sarbanes-Oxley Act of 2002, which provides for fines as provided under the federal criminal law, or imprisonment of up to 25 years, or both. 18 U.S.C. § 1348 (2002).) Current penalties for conspiracy include fines as provided under federal criminal law or imprisonment for up to five years, or both. *Id.* at § 371. Obstruction of justice currently carries possible penalties that include fines as provided under the federal criminal law, imprisonment of up to five years, or both. *Id.* at § 1505. The crime of making false statements subjects defendants to penalties that include fines as provided under the federal criminal law, imprisonment of up to five years, or both. *Id.* at § 1001(a). Finally, perjury is punishable by fines as provided under the federal criminal law, imprisonment of up to five years, or both. *Id.* at § 1621. Fines for individuals under Title 18 of the United States Code are provided for in *Id.* at § 3571(b). None apparently would be in excess of the $5,000,000 fine imposed by 15 U.S.C. § 78ff(a) (2000).

171. *See supra* note 121 and accompanying text.

172. It is fair to note, however, that the possibility of overcharging is present in the *Stewart* case. *See* Seigel & Slobogin, *supra* note 5; *supra* note 122 and accompanying text.

> Overcharging is systemic. It flows from the structure of criminal law that facilitates this charging practice because many categories of crime contain lesser-included offenses and because the same criminal conduct is described by different overlapping offenses. The practice of overcharging also flows from the discrepancy between the amount of information the prosecutor has at the outset of the case and what the prosecutor expects to be able to prove at trial. Because the prosecutor may not have as much information as she would like at the charging stage, she may often believe that it is in her best interests to charge the defendant with the most serious and as many crimes at the outset of the case to preserve

options for prosecution at a later time. Overcharging is also due in part to an ab-
horrence of losing that is central to prosecutorial culture.

Meares, *supra* note 159, at 868–69.

173. This part of the chapter focuses on descriptive observations, but the need for normative observations is apparent. Should prosecutors pursue criminal actions under Rule
10b-5 on the basis of public misstatements made by an insider about her personal affairs?
The answer to this question is both provocative and important. Ultimately, a response to
this and other similar inquiries would involve resolution of tensions between the application of Rule 10b-5 in this unusual context and, for example, First Amendment and (in the
event of material nondisclosures) privacy issues. In fact, Stewart attempted to raise First
Amendment issues in her trial, but was prohibited from doing so by the court. *See* Memorandum Opinion, *supra* note 134, at 4. *See also* Caillavet, *supra* note 134.

174. *See, e.g., supra* notes 147–149.

175. *Id.*

176. *See supra* notes 141–145 and accompanying text.

177. *See supra* notes 146–153 and accompanying text.

178. *See supra* notes 154–156 & 158 and accompanying text.

179. *See supra* notes 157 & 158 and accompanying text.

180. *See supra* notes 60–63. For example, absent a valid "fraud on the market" claim,
it may be difficult for a plaintiff to prove that, but for Stewart's public statements regarding the sale of her ImClone shares, he would not have purchased MSLO securities.

181. *See supra* notes 64–66. For example, it may be difficult for a plaintiff to prove that,
but for Stewart's public statements regarding the sale of her ImClone shares, she would not
have suffered a loss (or as large a loss) on the sale of her MSLO securities.

182. *See supra* note 77.

183. *See supra* note 144.

184. *See supra* note 145 and accompanying text. *Cf. CEO is the Brand, supra* note 144.

185. *See* sources cited *supra* note 5.

186. *See* Steven D. Clymer, *Unequal Justice: The Federalization of Criminal Law,* 70 S.
Cal. L. Rev. 643, 697–700 (1997); James Vorenberg, *Decent Restraint of Prosecutorial Dis-
cretion,* 94 Harv. L. Rev. 1521, 1544 (1981). For an interesting, recent critique of the *U.S.
Attorneys' Manual,* see Mark Osler, *This Changes Everything: A Call for a Directive, Goal-
Oriented Principle to Guide the Exercise of Discretion by Federal Prosecutors,* 39 Val. U.L.
Rev. 625, 635–40 (2005).

187. For example, prosecutors, like other decision makers, are subject to cognitive biases that may impact their ability to exercise the broad discretion afforded them. *See* Alafair
S. Burke, *Improving Prosecutorial Decision Making: Some Lessons of Cognitive Science,* 47
Wm. & Mary L. Rev. 1587 (2006) (suggesting that prosecutorial decisionmaking failures
may be the result of cognitive biases).

188. *See* sources cited *supra* note 135.

189. Chiarella v. United States, 445 U.S. 222, 234–235 (1980).

190. *See* Oesterle, *supra* note 5, at 480 ("the threat of the charge undoubtedly substantially increases the potential downside risk of any claim of innocence by a high profile
CEO."). This is true regardless of whether any executive actually would be found guilty of,
or liable for, any Rule 10b-5 violation based on the misstatement of, or omission to state,
personal facts.

191. *Cf. id.* at 480–81 (noting, in reference to the *Stewart* case, that "[p]rosecutors unwittingly were ignorant of a necessary subtlety of securities law long understood by the courts in deciding Rule 10b-5 cases, that not all acts that affect stock price should be actionable.").

PART II

SUBSTANTIVE LEGAL ISSUES RELEVANT TO THE CRIMINAL ACTION

CHAPTER 6 .

MARTHA, SCOOTER, AND SLICK WILLY: UNCOVERING THE COVER-UP CRIMES*

Stuart P. Green

Martha Stewart, though initially subject to scrutiny by the SEC and Department of Justice for alleged insider trading in connection with the sale of
stock she owned in the biotech company, ImClone, was ultimately prosecuted
(and convicted) not for committing that underlying offense, but rather for
covering up her alleged wrongdoing. Specifically, Stewart was alleged to have
made false statements to government agents and obstructed their investigation into the circumstances surrounding her sale of ImClone stock. Among
the grand jury's allegations was that Stewart had agreed with her broker, Peter
Bacanovic, to alter documents that would make it appear that she had sold
her stock pursuant to a pre-existing standing agreement rather than as a result of any inside information.[1]

To the extent that Stewart was prosecuted for covering up her crime rather
than for the underlying crime itself, her case was—at least in a formal sense—
analogous to prosecutions brought against defendants in various other memorable high-profile cases, such as those involving Vice-Presidential aide I.
Lewis Libby (known as "Scooter"),[2] Bill Clinton (often referred to by his de-
tractors as "Slick Willy"),[3] Iran-Contra figures Oliver North and John Poindexter,[4] Watergate figures John Mitchell, H.R. Haldeman, and John Ehrlichman,[5]

* This chapter is derived from *Uncovering the Cover-Up Crimes*, originally published at
42 AM. CRIM. L. REV. 9 (2005). Reprinted with permission of the publisher, American
Criminal Law Review © 2005. Most of the content of this chapter also appears in the author's book, *Lying, Cheating, and Stealing: A Moral Theory of White Collar Crime* (Oxford:
Oxford University Press, 2006).

the Arthur Andersen accounting firm,[6] British politician and novelist Jeffrey Archer,[7] and Credit Suisse First Boston banker Frank P. Quattrone.[8] In each of these cases, a person who had been under investigation for some putative course of illegal conduct allegedly lied to government agents about his involvement in such illegality, destroyed or altered evidence, intimidated a witness, violated a court order, or in some other way hindered the government's case. As a result, the person was prosecuted for obstruction of justice, perjury, false statements, or another similar cover-up crime.[9] In a few of the cases, such charges accompanied charges for the underlying crime; in most, they displaced them.

One of the things that is so intriguing about cases involving cover-up crimes is how dramatically people's moral and legal judgments of these cases vary. For example, many people who view Martha Stewart's acts as relatively innocuous believe that Arthur Andersen deserved substantial punishment for its criminal conduct. Conversely, there are those who believe that while Stewart committed a crime worthy of significant punishment, the Andersen prosecution was somehow unjust. And an even wider range of judgments can be observed in connection with cases of alleged covering up by figures such as Clinton, Libby, North, and Archer.

To some extent, the way one feels about the merits of cases involving cover-up crimes reflects nothing more than one's attitudes towards the polarizing figures who populate them. Those who have a generally favorable impression of Stewart, Libby, Clinton, North, Archer, or Andersen are more likely to minimize the alleged criminality of their actions than those who do not. But such "personality" explanations go only so far.[10] We like to think that we can separate our feelings about a person's overall character—whether empathetic or antipathetic—from judgments about whether such person deserves to be prosecuted, convicted, and sentenced for a specific crime. We believe that we are capable of making rational, impartial, and consistent decisions about matters as important as these. Indeed, we ask no less of prosecutors, judges, and juries.

In fact, as I shall argue, the strikingly broad range of moral judgments that colors cases like these has less to do with the identity of individual defendants than with a deeper form of moral ambivalence that pervades our understanding of the cover-up offenses and of white collar crime more generally. Just as we struggle to distinguish between cases of (illegal) criminal fraud and (legal) "creative accounting," tax evasion and "tax avoidance," extortion and "hard bargaining," and bribery and legal campaign contributions or lobbying,[11] so too do we face difficulties in distinguishing between cases of (illegal) witness tampering and (legal) witness "preparation," criminal contempt and "zealous advocacy," obstruction of justice and non-suspension of "document retention" procedures, and perjury and mere "wiliness" on the witness stand.

As an expression of the kind of intuitive reaction people often have to the prosecution of such crimes, the remarks of securities law scholar and blogger Stephen Bainbridge are typical:

> I find something vaguely Star Chamber-ish about the Quattrone conviction, just as I did with respect to the earlier Martha Stewart conviction. In neither case did the government indict the defendant with respect to the alleged underlying violations. Instead, both were indicted for subsequent acts that allegedly obstructed the investigation. Yet, if that investigation did not result in charges, it seems vindictive to charge obstruction (especially since in neither case was the obstruction very successful in interfering with the investigation).[12]

Other pundits have sounded similar notes of skepticism, suggesting that: (1) in comparison with other offenses, obstruction of justice, contempt, perjury, and false statements just aren't that serious;[13] (2) such behavior often reflects nothing more than legitimate, zealous advocacy,[14] or, at worst, "bad judgment;"[15] and (3) there's something somehow unfair or vindictive or petty about prosecutors pursuing charges for obstruction of justice or perjury rather than, or in addition to, charges relating to the conduct being covered up.[16]

The problem with such judgments, however, is their "ad hoc-ness." They seem to be based on little more than subjective and often inconsistent intuitions about particular cases of note. What we need, and what we lack, is a thoroughgoing analysis of the moral content of the cover-up crimes, a comprehensive framework for thinking about such offenses that could be used across the board in a theoretically consistent manner to evaluate both the statutory treatment of whole categories of criminal behavior and the prosecution and punishment of individual cases. That, in any event, is what I hope to provide here.

———————

This chapter begins with a brief description of those cover-up crimes that are most pertinent to the Martha Stewart case: obstruction of justice and false statements; as well as perjury, contempt, and misprision of felony. As we shall see, there are often real difficulties in determining whether the conduct that underlies such offenses should be treated as a crime (and, if so, which one), a tort, a violation of procedural rules, a professional ethics violation, or as merely aggressive (and perhaps even commendable) business or litigation tactics. This first part also offers several key distinctions that will be helpful in understanding the structure of the obstruction-type crimes, the most important of which is between what I refer to as "wrongful exculpation" and "wrongful inculpation."

In the next part of the chapter, we turn to the the underlying moral concepts that inform the cover-up crimes. We begin by considering the kinds of harms obstructive conduct causes, the kinds of victims it affects, and the kinds of wrongs it entails.[17] As we shall see, obstruction-type offenses involve a complex web of harms to individual litigants, witnesses, jurors, and court officials, as well as to judicial, law enforcement, and legislative processes more generally. The acts underlying these crimes also entail an intricate collection of moral wrongs, including bearing false witness, breach of the duty to take responsibility for one's actions, defiance of governmental authority, coercion, and cheating. At the same time, part of the ambivalence we feel about these acts can be attributed to the influence of various countervailing moral norms, such as that people ought not to be required to assist the government in their own destruction, that informing on others can involve a "breach of trust," and that lawyers ought to defend their clients "zealously."

In the third part of the chapter, we consider the multi-faceted dynamic that determines the extent to which one who engages in conduct constituting a cover-up will be viewed as blameworthy. Here, I suggest, we need to take account of three basic factors. The first is the nature of the conduct being covered up, including whether it was a crime or merely a civil wrong. Second, we need to consider the nature of the government's investigation into the underlying conduct. Of particular concern here are cases in which: (1) a defendant seeks to "obstruct *injustice*," whether because she has been prosecuted under an unjust law, or because she has been prosecuted for illegitimate political reasons or on the basis of speculative information obtained from unreliable informants; or (2) the government has "manufactured" a crime or created a perjury or obstruction "trap" by seeking evidence it knows the subject of its investigation will attempt illegally to cover up. Third, we need to consider the nature of the cover-up itself, including factors such as its scope and means, its effect on the outcome of the investigation or trial, and the social role of the person doing the covering up, including whether she holds a position of public trust.

In the concluding section, I consider how the analytical framework that has been developed might apply in the case of cover-up crimes committed by Martha Stewart.

Legal Framework

This part reviews the law surrounding the cover-up crimes—their elements, where they overlap, and where they do not. In addition, we briefly consider the range of available alternatives to criminal penalties, including procedural, disciplinary, and tort remedies.

Four Preliminary Distinctions

Before we begin our discussion of the elements of the various cover-up crimes, it will be useful to introduce four preliminary distinctions that help define their formal structure.

Wrongful Exculpation and Wrongful Inculpation

The first distinction is between two distinct patterns of deviance that I shall refer to as "wrongful exculpation" and "wrongful inculpation." The pattern of wrongful exculpation (or, more simply, "covering up") is that which was described in the introduction to this chapter: A person who is under investigation for, or has information about, some alleged course of illegal conduct, gives the government false exculpatory evidence (e.g., by falsely denying guilt during an investigation or on the witness stand) or prevents it from obtaining truthful inculpatory evidence (e.g., by intimidating a witness or destroying incriminating evidence). The second pattern, wrongful inculpation, occurs less frequently, or at least is less commonly subject to criminal prosecution. Here, a person who purports to have information about another's conduct gives the government false inculpatory evidence (e.g., by making a false accusation against another) or prevents it from obtaining true exculpatory evidence (e.g., by destroying or withholding true exculpatory evidence). (Of course, a person who makes a false accusation against another so as to throw the government off the trail of the true suspect would have satisfied both patterns.)

A good example of alleged wrongful inculpation can be found in the Martha Stewart case itself.[18] In their interviews with federal agents, Stewart and her stock broker, Peter Bacanovic, had claimed that Stewart's sale of ImClone stock was the result not of inside information, but rather of a "standing order" to sell the stock if it dropped below the price of sixty dollars per share. As support for this contention, Bacanovic produced a stock portfolio worksheet with the notation "@ 60" appearing next to the ImClone listing. The government alleged that the document had been altered and the notation added after the sale had already taken place. In support of this contention, the government introduced as its expert witness Larry Stewart (no relation to Martha), Director of the Secret Service Crime Laboratory, who testified at trial that the ink in which the "@ 60" notation was written was different from the ink in which other notes on the document were written.

Two months after the trial, prosecutors received information suggesting that Larry Stewart had perjured himself during his testimony. In an indictment, prosecutors subsequently alleged that Larry Stewart had been untruthful when he testified: (1) that he had participated fully in the ink-analysis testing of the worksheet and (2) that he was familiar with a proposal for a book about ink-analysis that was to be written by two other Secret Service agents.[19] Larry Stewart was ultimately acquitted of the charges against him, but it is nevertheless instructive to consider the nature of the conduct alleged: namely, an alleged attempt by him to dishonestly burnish his credibility as a witness (and hence unfairly enhance the strength of the prosecution's case).

As we shall see, all but one of the offenses we will be talking about criminalize both wrongful exculpation and wrongful inculpation. The exception is misprision of felony, which criminalizes only the former. To the extent that our system of justice views wrongful conviction as worse than wrongful acquittal (at least ten times so, by some accounts[20]), it seems to follow that, other things being equal, wrongful inculpation should be viewed as morally worse than wrongful exculpation.

Exculpation and Inculpation of Self and Others

We also need to distinguish between inculpation or exculpation that is done on behalf of oneself and that which is done on behalf of some other party. We can identify four variations here: First, a person who is under investigation by government agents and makes a false denial has wrongfully exculpated herself (think again of Martha Stewart). Second, a person who has inculpatory information about another's wrongdoing and lies to government agents about her knowledge of such wrongdoing has wrongfully exculpated someone else. An example is provided by Arthur Andersen, which sought to cover up not only its own crimes, but also those of its client, Enron. Third, a person who makes a false accusation against another party has wrongfully inculpated another. A good example is provided by the 1987 case of Tawana Brawley, the 15-year old girl who falsely claimed that she had been kidnapped and raped by an upstate New York prosecutor named Steven Pagones.[21] Fourth, a person who voluntarily confesses to a crime she did not commit has wrongfully inculpated herself and, theoretically at least, should be subject to prosecution for false statements or perjury.

Cases that fit into this final category are likely to be quite unusual. While the vast majority of false confessions are the result of coercion, trickery, or mental instability, the kind of cases I have in mind here are those in which a person offers a false confession voluntarily. The interesting question is why someone would do that. Three possible scenarios come to mind. A person might falsely confess: (1) in order to protect a child, parent, sibling, spouse, lover, or friend—i.e., by implicitly providing a false exculpation of such person; (2) in order to get attention or sympathy of some sort; (3) because she hopes to receive some reward for doing so (such as money or professional advancement). Obviously, our moral judgment of these self-inculpation cases would vary: we are more likely to look sympathetically on a person who falsely inculpates herself out of altruistic, rather than selfish, motives. In any event, while prosecution for false confession seems to be rare, it is not unprecedented. In one recent Indiana case, prosecutor Stephen S. Pierson was considering bringing charges of false informing against Charles "Chuckie" Hickman, a man who had falsely confessed to murdering 10-year old Katie Collman.[22]

Exculpation and Inculpation through Act and through Omission

A third distinction is between exculpation or inculpation performed through an act, and that which is done through omission. A person who offers false inculpatory or exculpatory testimony, intimidates a witness, or destroys or alters evidence has done an act. A person who fails to produce evidence or appear for testimony has performed an omission. All of the crimes we are considering here require an affirmative act[23] (again, with the possible exception of misprision of felony, which, at least in its common law form, also criminalized omissions[24]). Thus, absent some specific legal obligation to do so, a person who has committed a crime and fails to turn himself in, or knows about another's commission of a crime and fails to turn that person in, will not be held liable for an offense.

Exculpation and Inculpation vis-à-vis the Government and Private Parties

A final preliminary distinction is between wrongful exculpation or inculpation vis-à-vis the government and wrongful exculpation or inculpation vis-à-vis private parties. All of the offenses we will be considering here involve acts that are done toward one or another form of government agency or person acting in an official capacity: a judge, jury, law enforcement official, prosecutor, witness, informant, or legislature. But there is also another category of crimes that involves covering up vis-à-vis private parties, particularly investors. For example, Enron CEO Kenneth Lay was charged not with preventing the *government* from obtaining accurate information about his company's alleged massive fraud, but rather with preventing his company's investors and the public from doing so.[25] Such conduct is usually charged as mail or wire fraud, bank fraud, or securities fraud; it is only when such covering up occurs in connection with an official proceeding that obstruction-type charges can be brought.[26]

The Basic Cover-Up Crimes

This section offers a brief description of five basic cover-up crimes: obstruction of justice, false statements, contempt, perjury, and misprision of felony. This is not to suggest that various other offenses could not also be categorized as such. Money laundering,[27] tax evasion,[28] various immigration offenses,[29] and harboring a criminal[30] all typically involve significant acts of covering-up. Yet for present purposes I will focus on those offenses that seem to have the best claim of being core cover-up crimes, and which incidentally are most relevant to the case of Martha Stewart.

Obstruction of Justice

The basic federal obstruction of justice statutes are contained in twenty sections of Chapter 73 of Title 18 of the U.S. Code.[31] Of particular interest to us here are §§ 1503, 1505, 1510, and 1512. These statutes reach a diverse range of obstructive conduct in a wide array of procedural contexts.

The oldest, broadest, and most commonly used obstruction statute is § 1503, the most important provision of which is the so-called "Omnibus Clause."[32] Under this clause, the prosecution must prove that the defendant (1) corruptly (2) endeavored to interfere (3) with a pending (4) judicial proceeding, and (5) that she knew such proceeding was pending.[33] An investigation is not generally regarded as pending until it has reached the grand jury stage.[34] Like other white collar crimes, such as bribery, fraud, and extortion, obstruction of justice merges inchoate and completed conduct into a single statute.[35] That is, the defendant need not be successful in obstructing justice; it is enough that he "endeavored" to do so. Although our main focus here will be on cases in which the alleged obstructer was a party to the proceedings, there are also numerous obstruction cases involving non-party lawyers, informants, witnesses, judges, and legislators.[36]

In contrast to § 1503, which applies to judicial proceedings, § 1505 applies to administrative and legislative proceedings. Otherwise, the two provisions are closely parallel. In addition to its specific prohibition on obstructing justice in connection with proceedings under the Antitrust Civil Process Act, § 1505 also contains a broad, Omnibus-Clause-like provision.[37] Among the most common means of endeavoring to obstruct justice under the Omnibus Clauses of §§ 1503 and 1505 are: (1) concealing, altering, or destroying documents that pertain to judicial, administrative, or legislative proceedings; (2) giving or encouraging false testimony in such proceedings; (3) making false statements to government agents (provided that there is a direct connection or "nexus" between the defendant's act and a pending proceeding);[38] (4) encouraging a witness to assert his Fifth Amendment privilege (at least when there is no valid reason for doing so);[39] and (5) threatening jurors or court officers.[40] These means of obstruction can involve both wrongful exculpation and wrongful inculpation.

There are also several other obstruction provisions worth mentioning. The main focus of § 1510 is on the obstruction of criminal investigations, such as by means of bribery.[41] Section 1512 was introduced as part of a major expansion of the obstruction of justice statutory scheme effected by the Victim and Witness Protection Act of 1982.[42] Its focus is on tampering with victims, witnesses, and informants, whether by killing, using force, intimidation, or coercion, engaging in misleading conduct, harassment,[43] or retaliation,[44] and applies to proceedings before federal courts and grand juries, Congress, and federal agencies.[45]

As a general matter, the closer to formal adjudication that justice is obstructed, the more likely it is to fall within the letter of the obstruction statutes and to be prosecuted as such.[46] Thus, a person who flushes illegal drugs down the toilet as she is about to be arrested for drug possession is less likely to be prosecuted for obstruction of justice than one who destroys the same evidence in the middle of trial. As we shall see below, although the language of the basic obstruction of justice statutes makes no distinction between obstruction that occurs in criminal cases and that which occurs in civil cases, in practice obstruction charges are almost invariably limited to the former. Obstruction charges can be, and often are, accompanied by charges for the underlying crime allegedly covered up; but of course they need not be, as the Stewart case itself makes clear.

False Statements

In order to gain a conviction under the general federal false statements statutes, 18 U.S.C. § 1001, the government must prove, *inter alia*, that the defendant made a materially false, fictitious, or fraudulent statement or representation within the jurisdiction of the executive, legislative, or judicial branch of the federal government.[47] Unlike perjury, there is no requirement under § 1001 that the statement be made under oath.[48] And, unlike the obstruction of justice statutes, which typically apply only to obstructive acts that occur "downstream," close to formal adjudication, § 1001 applies even to statements made "upstream," at an early stage of an investigation.

Section 1001 can involve wrongful inculpation, wrongful exculpation, or neither. An example of false statements involving the first can be found in *United States v. Rodgers*, in which the Supreme Court affirmed a conviction of a defendant who allegedly lied in telling the FBI that his wife had been kidnapped and in telling the Secret Service that his wife was involved in a plot to kill the President.[49] An example of false statements involving wrongful exculpation is provided by the Martha Stewart case, in which the defendant allegedly lied to government agents in order to cover up an earlier illegality. In such cases, false statements charges can be brought instead of, or in addition to, charges relating to the underlying subject of the investigation.[50]

Contempt

Under 18 U.S.C. §401, a court is given the power to punish by fine or imprisonment "such contempt of its authority" as, *inter alia*, "misbehavior of any person in its presence or so near thereto as to obstruct the administration of justice" or "disobedience or resistance to its lawful writ, process, order, rule, decree, or command." Many of these cases will involve acts that are similar to those that occur in the case of obstruction, such as inducing a prosecution witness to leave the jurisdiction,[51] refusing to answer a question when ordered to do so by a judge,[52] bribing a witness,[53] or persisting in the assertion that one cannot recall a certain event.[54] Other cases look quite unlike obstruction, such as those involving the disruption of proceedings or the abuse of a juror.[55]

Some acts of contempt are treated as civil, others as criminal. If the purpose of the contempt proceeding is to compel obedience to a court order or give substitute relief to the opposing party, then it is regarded as civil. If, on the other hand, the purpose of the contempt proceeding is to vindicate the authority of the court and to punish the contemnor for his conduct, it is regarded as criminal.[56] Both the contempt and obstruction statutes trace their origins to the Judiciary Act of 1831.[57] In the original legislation, contempt was limited to in-court conduct in defiance of the court (such as refusals to answer specific questions while on the stand), while obstruction was limited to out-of-court conduct (such as destruction of evidence).[58] Under modern law, however, contempt sanctions can be imposed for both in-court and out-of-court conduct. Nevertheless, contempt and obstruction are still commonly viewed as complementary rather than as duplicative offenses.

Perjury and False Declarations

In order to gain a conviction under the general federal perjury statute, 18 U.S.C. §1621, the government must show that a defendant (1) under oath before a competent officer (2) knowingly (3) made a false statement (4) that was material to the proceedings.[59] There is also a narrower provision, 18 U.S.C. §1623, which makes it a crime to make a sworn false declaration in a judicial or grand jury proceeding.[60] Both statutes require that the defendant's assertion be not only misleading, but also literally false—a requirement that I have discussed at length elsewhere.[61] Many, though by no means all, cases of perjury and false declarations involve witnesses who have wrongfully exculpated or inculpated. According to the case law, however, neither offense requires that prosecutors prove that a witness' testimony actually had or even was intended to have any obstructive effect on the proceeding in which it was offered. Rather, all that is required is that the statement be material, meaning that it has the capacity to influence the course of the proceeding.[62]

Misprision of Felony

At English common law, misprision of felony was committed by a defendant who, having knowledge of a felony and a reasonable opportunity to disclose it to a responsible official without harm, failed to report such felony.[63] Apparently because no affirmative act was required, however, the offense fell into disfavor, and today it appears to be virtually obsolete in Great Britain.[64] Under U.S. federal law, however, misprision of felony has been continuously criminalized since 1790.[65] The federal statute says that one who "conceals and does not as soon as possible make known" the commission of a felony of which he is aware is guilty of misprision.[66] As interpreted by the courts, passive failure to report a crime does not constitute "concealment;" a defendant must engage in some affirmative act, such as making a false statement to an investigator,[67] seeking to divert the attention of the police,[68] harboring a felon,[69] or retrieving and secreting proceeds of evidence of a crime.[70] Indeed, the affirmative act requirement is so important that one court concluded that a defendant's truthful but incomplete disclosure of what he knew about an alleged counterfeiting operation did not constitute misprision, since it did not result in any greater concealment than would have occurred if the defendant had remained silent.[71]

Unlike all of the other offenses we are considering, misprision of felony criminalizes only wrongful exculpation, not inculpation. Moreover, unlike the other offenses, the government must prove that the principal perpetrator actually committed the offense the defendant is alleged to have covered up.[72] On the other hand, the fact that the government already knows the identity of the principal, and that there was therefore no actual obstruction of the government's investigation, is no defense to charges of misprision.[73] In general, misprision requires that the defendant cover up an offense committed by someone else, rather than by himself. While there are a handful of cases holding that a defendant who takes affirmative steps to conceal his own crime has committed misprision,[74] the usual rule has been that such prosecutions are barred by the Fifth Amendment's prohibition on compelled self-incrimination.[75] Misprision appears to be the least favored of all the criminal offenses being considered here. Despite the addition of an affirmative act requirement, the offense is still only rarely prosecuted,[76] although at least one authority has suggested that federal prosecutors "are currently taking a greater interest" in this crime, in part as a means to avoid otherwise applicable mandatory minimum sentences.[77]

Relationship Between Various Cover-Up Crimes

Given the significant overlap in the kinds of conduct the obstruction of justice, contempt, perjury, false statements, and misprision statutes are meant to prevent and punish, it is not surprising that there are many fact patterns to which more than one statute will apply.[78] For example, there are cases holding that conduct typically associated with obstruction of justice can constitute contempt.[79] At first glance, this is surprising, since the two offenses were once thought to be mutually exclusive, with the line between them coextensive with the courtroom door.[80] In recent years, however, the concept of contempt has evolved, so that it now often does encompass conduct that occurs outside the presence of the court. As a result, more modern cases tend to hold that a defendant's cover-up activity can constitute both obstruction and contempt.[81]

Obstruction of justice also overlaps with perjury and false statements. Perjury requires that a witness lie under oath about a material matter. In order for such conduct to constitute obstruction as well, the prosecution must prove that the defendant's lie in some way obstructed the court in the performance of its duties, as when a witness's sham inability to remember blocked the court's inquiry.[82] In the case of obstruction charges arising out of a non-sworn false statement, the prosecution must prove not only that the defendant lied to a government agent, but also, as the Court indicated in *United States v. Aguilar*, that there was the requisite nexus between the defendant's act and the pending proceeding.[83] As the Court put it, the alleged obstructive act "must have a relationship in time, causation, or logic with the judicial proceedings. In other words, the endeavor must have the 'natural and probable effect' of interfering with the due administration of justice."[84] On the other hand, where a misleading obstructive statement is literally true, and therefore beyond the reach of the perjury or false statements statutes, a witness should at least theoretically be liable for obstruction of justice.[85]

There are also overlaps between misprision of felony and obstruction of justice and between misprision and perjury. For example, in *United States v. Clemons*, a small town sheriff was charged with both misprision and obstruction based on allegations that he had lied to the FBI about his knowledge of his daughter and son-in-law's participation with others in the cultivation and distribution of marijuana.[86] And in *United States v. Salinas*, the defendant was convicted of both misprision and perjury for denying to investigators and a grand jury that he knew anything about a murder when in fact he knew of the murder and the persons who committed it.[87]

Finally, where a witness' false statement under oath violates a court order, the defendant can be prosecuted for both perjury and contempt.[88] This was precisely what happened in *Handler v. Gordon*, involving a judgment debtor who repeatedly defied a court order to answer questions truthfully in a bankruptcy proceeding held to discover his assets.[89] In general, however, the prosecution will be required to present specific evidence demonstrating that such perjury obstructed the court in the performance of its duties.[90]

Alternatives to Criminal Prosecution

As is the case with much white collar crime, conduct that would appear to violate the literal language of the obstruction of justice, contempt, perjury, false statements, or misprision of felony statutes often is not prosecuted as such, and is subject at most to a variety of non-criminal sanctions.[91] In this section, I briefly review the broad range of non-criminal-law means by which wrongful exculpation and wrongful inculpation can be treated.

First, there are various kinds of sanctions that can be imposed under the Federal Rules of Civil and Criminal Procedure. Under Federal Rule of Civil Procedure 37, for example, a party that fails to obey a court order to "provide or permit discovery" can be barred from supporting or opposing designated claims or defenses or introducing certain matters in evidence, have pleadings struck or dismissed, have a judgment rendered by default, or have matters in dispute taken to be established.[92] And, under Federal Rule of Criminal Procedure 16, a defendant who fails to comply with an order to allow the government to inspect and copy various papers, documents, photographs, and the like, or the results of any physical or mental examination or scientific test or experiment, can be prohibited from introducing such undisclosed evidence at trial, or subjected to a continuance.[93]

Second, in at least half a dozen American jurisdictions, a plaintiff can bring a tort action to recover compensatory, and possibly punitive, damages for the loss of a prospective lawsuit caused by an opponent's spoliation of evidence.[94] In some jurisdictions, the spoliation must be intentional; in others, reckless or negligent conduct will do.[95] A typical spoliation case involves a defendant who, having been sued for engaging in some form of wrongdoing (such as causing a serious personal injury to a plaintiff), covers up such wrongdoing by destroying key evidence, thereby making it more difficult for the plaintiff to pursue his case.[96]

Third, there are various ethical rules that apply to cover-up activity as well.[97] Model Rule of Professional Conduct 8.4(d) prohibits conduct that is "prejudicial to the administration of justice."[98] Model Rule 3.4 prohibits a defendant from obstructing another party's access to evidence or unlawfully altering, destroying, concealing, or suppressing evidence.[99] And Model Rule 3.3 essentially prohibits lawyers from committing or suborning perjury when they make representations to the court or put a witness on the stand.[100] Lawyers who violate such rules are subject to a wide range of disciplinary sanctions, including disqualification from a given case, suspension from law practice, revocation of *pro hoc vice* status, preclusion of evidence, striking of pleadings, and dismissal of actions.[101]

Fourth, there is a host of procedural, constitutional, and disciplinary rules that apply specifically to prosecutors and law enforcement officials who wrongfully inculpate by destroying or failing to turn over exculpatory evidence, suborning perjury, or intimidating a witness. The Jencks Act,[102] Federal Rule of Criminal Procedure 16,[103] the rule in *Brady v. Maryland*,[104] and special prosecutorial ethics guidelines[105] all require federal prosecutors to disclose exculpatory evidence of various sorts.

Finally, there is, as we shall see below, a great deal of ostensibly "obstructive" conduct, particularly that engaged in by lawyers, that not only is not subject to criminal sanctions, but is not subject even to civil or disciplinary sanctions. Indeed, as Bruce Green has pointed out, such conduct is often regarded as commendable "zealous advocacy."[106]

Background Moral Norms

Why is there such a broad range of responses to such conduct? One answer may be that we need a finely calibrated system of sanctions to provide an optimal level of deterrence in terms of social costs and benefits.[107] While deterrence is important, however, my interest here is primarily in retribution. I want to ask why certain acts of wrongful exculpation and wrongful inculpation are viewed as more blameworthy than others, and when such blameworthiness justifies the imposition of criminal sanctions.

These questions I propose to answer in two steps. In this part, I consider the basic background moral concepts that inform the law of obstruction, perjury, and the like: the harms they cause; the victims affected; the wrongs entailed; and the rights, if any, involved.[108] In the next part, I look at the particular dynamic that shapes our moral judgment of, and allows us to distinguish among, specific cases of wrongful exculpation and inculpation.

Harms Caused, and Victims Affected

Who, or what, is harmed by crimes such as obstruction of justice and perjury? In some cases, the harm is done to a witness or informant. For example, § 1512(a)(1) prohibits killing or attempting to kill another person with the intent to prevent his attendance or testimony at an official proceeding, production of a document, or communication with law enforcement officials.[109] Section 1512(b) prohibits the use of intimidation, physical force, or threats.[110] And the Omnibus Clause of § 1503 prohibits, among other things, threats and intimidation of jurors and various court officials.[111] These crimes cause harms to victims similar to those entailed by murder, attempted murder, assault, extortion, and battery.

Also significant are the harms caused to opposing litigants. A witness who perjures himself in a criminal case by giving false exculpatory evidence on behalf of the defendant causes obvious harm to the prosecution's case.[112] An informant who files a false police report or perjures himself by giving false inculpatory evidence on behalf of the prosecution causes harm to a defendant's liberty interests.[113] And a defendant in a tort suit who withholds evidence that would have benefited the plaintiff's case causes harm to the plaintiff's property interests.[114]

Perhaps the most significant harms associated with obstruction-of-justice-type offenses, however, are those caused to our system of justice and to society generally. A criminal defendant who destroys evidence that prevents a jury from having sufficient cause to convict has caused a serious harm to the integrity of the criminal justice system. So too has an informant or prosecution witness whose false testimony leads to a wrongful arrest, prosecution, or conviction, or to a wrongful decision to acquit or forgo arrest or prosecution. And even if the jury's verdict or prosecutor's decision turns out to be the correct one, the potential for error has been increased and the integrity of the system seriously undermined.

Wrongs Entailed

Having considered the kinds of harms associated with obstruction-type offenses, we can now turn to the kinds of moral wrongfulness they entail. The first is unique to those cases in which the defendant covers up his own wrongdoing: namely, breach of the supposed duty to take responsibility for one's actions (though exactly to whom such a duty would be owed is a difficult question). We teach our children that one who has done wrong has a moral duty to own up to such wrong. One of our great national myths is that of George Washington and the cherry tree.[115] In contexts as diverse as religion, clinical psychology, and our criminal justice system, we put tremendous weight on the values of repentance, contrition, and remorse. Covering up one's own wrongdoing thus cuts directly against such positive norms. On the other hand, it should be obvious that merely failing to take responsibility for one's actions is not ordinarily the sort of thing that is made a crime. To be sure, it can be a crime, in some special contexts, to fail to submit a tax return[116] or a Clean Water Act monthly hazardous waste discharge monitoring report.[117] But, with the possible exception of the now defunct common law offense of misprision of felony, all of the basic obstruction-type statutes we are considering in this chapter require that the defendant take some affirmative step to cover up his own wrongdoing.

The second form of moral wrongfulness associated with such crimes finds its most familiar expression in the biblical Ninth Commandment, that one shall not bear false witness against one's neighbor. This provision is often interpreted as a general prohibition on lying, or more specifically as a prohibition on lying under oath.[118] But, given the possibility that, as suggested above, wrongful inculpation poses a greater moral risk than wrongful exculpation, perhaps a better interpretation would focus specifically on what it means to bear false witness "against" another.[119]

Third, some unusual cases of obstruction involve a form of coercion. For example, §1512 expressly makes it a crime to "knowingly use[] intimidation or physical force, threaten[] or corruptly persuade[] another person ... with intent to ... influence, delay or prevent" testimony.

Fourth, under §1510(a), it is a crime to use bribery to obstruct, delay, or prevent the communication of information relating to a violation of any criminal statute.[120] Obstruction of this sort reflects much the same moral content as the various bribery statutes, which I have elsewhere analyzed in terms of disloyalty and breach of positional duty.[121]

Fifth, we need to consider the possibility that obstruction-type conduct is wrong because it involves a defiance of governmental authority. Destroying evidence or perjuring oneself in response to a governmental investigation involves more than just the usual breach of the supposed duty to obey the law.[122] As noted above, covering up vis-à-vis the government is treated quite differently from covering up vis-à-vis the public.[123] People who obstruct the operations of justice wrong the government (and perhaps, by extension, the general polity) at two levels: first by violating the law itself, and then by preventing the government from enforcing that law in a proper manner. Such offenses thus reflect a kind of super-*malum prohibitum* quality. Indeed, it is striking that we speak in this context of parties who show "contempt" for a court or legislative body or who, in British usage, "pervert" the course of justice.[124] And we speak as well of "misprision" of felony, the origins of which Blackstone traced to the French *mespris*, which means neglect or contempt.[125]

A final form of moral wrongfulness worth considering in this context is cheating. Cheating involves an intentional violation of a rule for the purpose of gaining an unfair advantage over one's rivals,[126] a phenomenon that would seem inevitable when a litigant destroys evidence, intimidates a witness, or lies on the witness stand.

Focus on the cheating aspect of covering up is also helpful in delineating the often fuzzy distinction between obstruction of justice and mere zealous advocacy. Imagine two cases in which a criminal defense lawyer intentionally engaged in conduct calculated to mislead the jury. In the first case, the lawyer destroys key evidence that would have incriminated his client. Here, there seems to be a clear case of obstruction of justice. In the second case, the lawyer so forcefully and effectively cross-examines a truthful adverse witness that the witness becomes flustered, offers confused and erroneous descriptions of relevant events, and is made to appear mistaken or deceptive in the eyes of the jury. In such a case, virtually every commentator on legal ethics would agree that it would be absurd to bring disciplinary proceedings against the lawyer, let alone a prosecution for obstruction of justice or subornation of perjury, and that in fact she was performing her job admirably.[127]

Given that both cases involve intentional conduct that is in some sense calculated to mislead the jury, the question is why only the first should constitute a crime. One possible answer is simply that the first lawyer has broken the rules, while the second has not. Our system of justice permits, and even encourages, defense lawyers to use clever cross-examination to make truthful prosecution witnesses look like liars, bring motions to suppress otherwise reliable evidence, and advise clients to assert privileges that have the effect of depriving the fact-finder of relevant, inculpatory evidence.[128] But it does not permit lawyers to destroy evidence or put witnesses on the stand whom they know will make literally false statements. In short, it says that certain ways of misleading the jury are permissible, while others are not. Those who comply with the rules play fair; those who do not, cheat.

Unfortunately, this leaves the deeper question of why the line between acceptable and unacceptable conduct has been drawn where it has. Without attempting to develop anything like a comprehensive account, I will simply suggest that the ultimate goal of the prohibitions on obstruction of justice and perjury is to further the interest of truth-finding and to allow the prosecution's case to be put to the test; and it seems likely that the destruction and fabrication of evidence foreclose the truth-finding function in a way that clever cross-examination does not.

Two Countervailing Norms: Self-Preservation and Breach of Trust

In the previous section, I enumerated six moral norms that are potentially violated by one who engages in obstruction of justice, perjury, and the like. In the midst of this discussion, I also described a countervailing norm—namely, that a lawyer who impedes or obstructs the due administration of justice can simultaneously be performing in accordance with the positive norm of "zealous advocacy" upon which our criminal justice system depends. In the present section, I want to mention two additional countervailing norms that may play a role in fostering the ambivalence we feel towards at least some obstruction-like acts: first, the view that people have a right of self-preservation; and second, the view that people ought not to "rat" or "snitch" on others with whom they have a relationship of trust.

The first countervailing norm arises in cases of self-exculpation. While most of us would agree that people ought to take responsibility for their wrongful actions, we also recognize a basic human right not to assist the government in causing one's own destruction.[129] On an earlier occasion, I wrote about the importance of what has been called a right to self-preservation in the narrow context of the recently abandoned "exculpatory no" doctrine of 18 U.S.C. § 1001.[130] I argued there that, despite the obvious lack of textual, legislative, or constitutional support for it, the "exculpatory no" doctrine survived and flourished for as long as it did because it was consistent with deeply held, if mostly tacit, moral intuitions about the right of self-preservation.[131] Acknowledging the significance of the right of self-preservation also helps to explain the often conflicting range of reactions elicited by the cover-up crimes more generally. We recognize that there is something potentially unfair about making it a crime for one suspected of criminal activity to shield himself from government scrutiny. Indeed, it is ironic that the more serious the crime being covered up, and the more severe the penal consequences, the stronger is the defendant's claim of self-preservation and, arguably, the less wrongful is his act of covering up.

The second countervailing norm arises in cases of false exculpation of others. Not only do people have a right not to inform against themselves; they may also have a duty not to reveal secrets about others, at least where there exists a relationship of trust between them.[132] Elsewhere, I have described the antipathy we feel towards the act of taking bribes as being informed by the aversion we feel towards the act of disloyalty that such bribe-taking frequently entails.[133] Here, my argument is that the antipathy we feel towards people who take criminal steps to avoid inculpating others is *mitigated* by our sense that such avoidance is, at least in some cases, based on a legitimate sense of loyalty.[134] More generally, a society in which neighbors rat on neighbors, colleagues on colleagues, and family members on family members is not the sort of society in which most people would want to live.[135]

Assessing the Moral Content of Particular Acts of Obstruction

Having considered the various background concepts that inform our moral understanding of the obstruction-type offenses, we can now take a more detailed look at the complex interplay of factors upon which our judgment of specific cases is based. I group them, loosely, into three broad categories, concerning the nature of: (1) the underlying wrongdoing being covered up; (2) the government investigation into, or adjudication of, such wrongdoing; and (3) the cover-up itself.

Underlying Conduct

In assessing the moral content of the obstruction-type offenses, we will undoubtedly want to consider the moral content of the underlying conduct being wrongfully exculpated or inculpated. For example, other things being equal, covering up (or falsely alleging) a murder should surely be regarded as a more serious crime than covering up (or falsely alleging) a parking violation. Similarly, I would argue, covering up White House leaks regarding the identity of a CIA covert operative in a time of war (as was apparently done in the Scooter Libby case) should be regarded as a more serious crime than covering up an extramarital affair (as in the Clinton case). But the question is why. One possibility might be that acts of false exculpation and inculpation somehow derive whatever wrongfulness they entail from the crime that is being covered up or falsely alleged, just as attempting or conspiring to commit a crime derives its moral content from the crime that is the target of the attempt or conspiracy. Alternatively, it may be simply that the more serious the underlying crime committed, the stronger society's interest in knowing about it, and the more harmful the cover-up.[136] Likewise, the more serious the underlying crime, the more serious the penal consequences for the one wrongly accused, and the more harmful the wrongful inculpation. Under either approach, the natural implication is that, as in the case of jurisdictions that punish attempts or conspiracies in proportion to the seriousness of the target offense,[137] we should punish the cover up (or wrongful accusation) of serious crimes more severely than that of minor ones.

The idea that the moral weight of covering up is related to the moral weight of the underlying crime does in fact spell itself out in important practical contexts. For example, some state statutes impose significantly higher penalties when perjury is committed in a trial in which the defendant is being tried for a crime that could result in sanctions of death or life in prison.[138] Similarly, misprision is a crime only when it involves the covering up of a felony, not a misdemeanor. And though criminal penalties for obstruction of justice are theoretically applicable to obstruction of both civil and criminal proceedings,[139] the offense is far more likely to be prosecuted when the conduct being covered up is the subject of a criminal case than when it is the subject of a civil case. Indeed, cases involving allegations of obstruction of justice and perjury in federal civil proceedings are exceedingly rare; and convictions in that context are virtually nonexistent.[140]

The problem is that the cover-up of criminal proceedings is not necessarily more harmful than the cover-up of civil proceedings. For example, the destruction of key incriminating documents in a large scale, multi-million dollar class action products liability or securities fraud case would surely cause more harm than the destruction of cumulative incriminating evidence in a routine drug possession case. So the question is whether a bright-line rule between criminal and civil proceedings is justified.

One argument, offered by Lawrence Solum and Stephen Marzen, is that the prosecution of obstruction in civil cases would serve little useful purpose. As they put it:

> Even if criminal sanctions are invoked to combat inappropriate evidence destruction in private lawsuits, they are of inherently limited value. Criminal sanctions cannot restore the accuracy of the original factfinding proceeding, nor do they compensate the victim of evidence destruction for its loss in the civil suit. At most, criminal sanctions could deter evidence destruction in civil litigation. The apparent disinterest [sic] of government prosecutors in evidence destruction in civil suits, however, as reflected in the lack of reported prosecutions, renders the obstruction-of-justice statutes rather toothless against such misconduct. Scarce prosecutorial resources simply do not permit prosecution of spoliation in private lawsuits.[141]

But this argument seems flawed. First, it seems to assume that the sole purpose of criminal proceedings is to compensate or deter or restore accuracy, when in fact most commentators would agree that retribution is also an important goal. Second, even if the current lack of prosecutorial interest in prosecuting obstruction in civil cases means that the statutes have been rendered toothless, this hardly means that the statutes could not be enforced more aggressively. Third, it begs the question to assume that scarce prosecutorial resources should be used for prosecuting only that sort of obstruction that arises out of criminal proceedings when this is precisely the question that is being considered.

An alternative argument is that there *is* no moral difference between obstruction of justice in civil and criminal cases and that both should be prosecuted equally. As the Fourth Circuit explained in 1906:

> The contention that a violation of section 5399 [the predecessor to 1503], consisting of obstructing the administration of justice in a civil litigation, between private citizens in a federal court, is not an offense against the United States, need not be discussed at any length. One of the sovereign powers of the United States is to administer justice in its courts between private citizens. Obstructing such administration is an offense against the United States, in that it prevents or tends to prevent the execution of one of the powers of the government.[142]

But this argument seems problematic as well, as it rests on the assumption that the only relevant consideration is that a court proceeding was obstructed, without reference to the proceeding's nature or purpose.

A better view is that criminal proceedings—by definition—implicate the public interest in a way that civil proceedings do not, as is evidenced by their being brought on behalf of "the People" or "the State."[143] Thus, even if the obstruction of civil cases sometimes causes *more* harm than the obstruction of criminal cases, the *kind* of interest vindicated by criminal proceedings is qualitatively different from the kind of interest at stake in civil litigation, and the state's interest in preventing and punishing obstruction of such proceedings is also qualitatively different.

In addition to considering the moral content of the underlying conduct that is being wrongfully exculpated or inculpated, we also need to consider those cases in which the alleged wrongdoing being investigated or adjudicated has not in fact occurred. Consider the following three scenarios: First, suppose a married man is falsely accused of raping a woman he met in a hotel during a business trip and with whom he had a consensual sexual encounter. And imagine that, in order to save his marriage and protect his children, the man falsely denies to investigators that he ever had such an encounter. In that case, the wrongfulness of his covering up obviously could not derive from the wrongfulness of a rape he did not commit; at most, it might derive from the wrongfulness of his marital infidelity. Second, imagine a case in which a man is falsely accused of raping a woman he has in fact never met. Out of fear that he is being framed or railroaded by the authorities, he lies about his whereabouts on the night in question. In such a case, there would be no underlying misconduct at all from which this act of "covering up" could derive moral content. Third, suppose a man who killed in self-defense is accused of murder and, out of fear the authorities will not believe his story, destroys the weapon. Because the defendant's act was justified, there would once again be no underlying act from which the wrongfulness of the cover-up could be drawn. The wrongfulness of his act would seem to relate solely to the reasonableness of his belief that he was being framed or that the authorities would not believe his story.

There are also cases in which the prosecution believes that the underlying conduct did in fact occur, but nevertheless elects to pursue only the lesser charge of covering up. Often, the prosecutor will determine that it is "easier" to prove the lesser charge of obstruction of justice or perjury than the underlying case of insider trading or accounting fraud. Such cover-up cases are typically cheaper to prosecute, more comprehensible to the jury, and less subject to subtle nuances in proof. In some cases, of course, the decision to forgo prosecution for the more serious offense will be necessitated by the very destruction of evidence that forms the basis for the obstruction charge. But in those cases in which there does exist adequate evidence to justify pursuing both the less serious cover-up charge and the more serious underlying charge, the question is whether it is improper for the prosecutor to exercise his discretion to prosecute only the latter. One possible answer is that, given limited prosecutorial resources, prosecutors have something like an ethical duty to pursue more, rather than less, serious charges.[144] But it is unclear how far this principle should extend. Assuming that a prosecutor really does have limited resources at her disposal, perhaps the right thing for her to do is to maximize her utility by pursuing those charges which she stands a better chance of proving, or which would have a greater impact on general deterrence.[145]

We will talk more below about cases in which a defendant seeks to obstruct "injustice." For the moment, it is enough to note that even a person who covers up a crime he did not commit could be said to have done a morally wrongful act. This suggests that while the wrongfulness of the conduct being covered up is a relevant consideration in determining the seriousness of covering up, it is not a necessary one.

Nature of Investigation into Underlying Conduct

In addition to the nature of the underlying wrongdoing, if any, that is being covered up, we need to consider the circumstances that give rise to the cover-up, and particularly the nature of the government's investigation. Here, at least seven possible factors can be identified.

First, there might be cases in which the government is conducting an investigation for the purpose of enforcing an unjust law. For example, imagine that the police in Birmingham, Alabama, in 1963 were investigating a civil rights protester who had violated a local segregated lunch counter ordinance, and that the protester destroyed evidence in order to thwart their investigation. In such cases, we might be tempted to say that what the protester was obstructing was *injustice* rather than justice, and that he was therefore doing nothing wrong.

But this analysis seems to me overly simplistic. The fact that one has a moral right to defy an unjust law does not necessarily give one the right to cover up one's defiance of such law. For a start, it seems unlikely that even a Freedom Rider would be justified in violating § 1512, which makes it a crime to intimidate or harass a witness. More generally, an argument could be made that civil disobedience, by its very nature, requires the defendant to openly accept responsibility for his conduct, and that covering it up would be fundamentally inconsistent with such a device. Moreover, the fact that a particular law or set of laws is unjust does not necessarily mean that all of the other laws in a given legal regime are also unjust. That is, the injustice of the ordinance prohibiting blacks from sitting at the same lunch counters as whites in the Jim Crow South does not necessarily entail that the laws prohibiting the obstruction of justice or perjury in the Jim Crow South were also unjust or immoral. We would have to ask whether such cover-up laws were the product of a thoroughly unjust legal system, whether they were being applied in so discriminatory a manner that they could not be regarded as politically legitimate, and what sorts of punishment, under what conditions, one would suffer if one did not cover up.

Second, there are cases in which a defendant is prosecuted for a crime that is not unjust on its face but is being enforced in an unjust manner. For example, imagine that X is prosecuted for engaging in some criminal act for which she has a perfectly adequate defense, such as that she acted out of necessity or under duress, and that this fact is known to the authorities. Despite the fact that X's conviction for such an offense would once again be unjust, it again does not follow that she would be justified in destroying or fabricating evidence, tampering with the jury, or lying under oath. Even if she is certain that the ultimate just outcome would be her acquittal, X arguably has an obligation to allow the legal system to run its course. The same could be said about otherwise well-founded cases in which a prosecution should properly be barred by a statute of limitations, immunity, or other jurisdictional defect;

or in which the investigation was based on speculative information obtained from unreliable informants with no first-hand knowledge of the facts, or on illegitimate political considerations, or solely to embarrass a potential target. On the other hand, we might at least say that such cover-ups were less wrongful than in cases in which the underlying investigation was legitimate.

Third, even when the underlying investigation is itself legitimate, we would need to consider the relevance of the information sought. For example, even if one believed that Kenneth Starr's investigation into the Whitewater land deal was proper, there would still be a question as to whether it was proper to use that investigation as an occasion to ask President Clinton personal questions about his relationship with Monica Lewinsky. Assuming that the information sought was not reasonably related to the ostensible subject of the investigation, it seems fair to say that Clinton's covering up should be viewed as less wrongful than it otherwise would be.

A fourth consideration is the probability that the investigation will lead to significant probative evidence. In some cases it appears that law enforcement officials and prosecutors have no reasonable expectation that a given witness interview, document request, or line of cross-examination will turn up probative evidence. The sole or principal purpose of such interviews or document requests is to induce the defendant to make a false statement, perjure himself, obstruct justice, or commit contempt. Justice Ginsburg referred in her concurrence in *Brogan v. United States* to the troubling tendency of federal prosecutors to "manufacture" violations of § 1001.[146] In the context of perjury, the phenomenon is known as a "perjury trap." [147] There is also at least one case that has spoken of a "contempt trap."[148] And we might add to this list the equally plausible notion of an "obstruction trap." Thus, if it were the case that government agents conducted their interview of Martha Stewart solely or primarily for the purpose of inducing her to make a false statement or destroy documents, rather than in the belief that such interview was likely to lead to the discovery of probative evidence, then we should consider her false statement to be less culpable than we otherwise would.

Fifth, we would want to know the stage of the proceedings at which the information was being sought. Arguably, the farther "downstream" the obstruction occurs—that is, the closer to formal adjudication—the more blameworthy it is. Certainly, the law of obstruction of justice is structured to reflect such a view.[149] On the other hand, destroying an incriminating document early on in the process, before litigation is pending, and before there has been any opportunity for it to be read or copied, would in some sense be more damaging to the process of truth-finding than destroying it farther downstream, after multiple copies have been made and its contents widely disseminated.

Sixth, regardless of the stage of the proceedings, we might think that the degree to which a cover-up should be regarded as wrongful would vary depending on who was doing the investigating. For example, one might think that it is worse to obstruct a proceeding before a court than an investigation by a bureaucratic federal agency or politically motivated congressional committee. Indeed, the federal scheme of obstruction of justice statutes seem in part to reflect such a distinction. In terms of sentencing, the obstruction of proceedings before departments, agencies, and committees under § 1505 is almost invariably considered a less serious offense than obstruction of court proceedings under § 1503.[150]

Finally, there are cases in which the person covering up is doing so not in response to an investigation initiated by someone else, but rather on his own initiative. For example, imagine a case in which a plaintiff brought a lawsuit alleging that a defendant manufactured a defective product and then destroyed evidence of his own contributory negligence. From a moral perspective, such obstruction would seem to be particularly egregious, since the plaintiff could not even claim that he was exercising a right of self-preservation. Of the cases we have been discussing, the Jeffrey Archer case is most on point. But even Archer might have an argument that his covering up was in some sense defensive: Although it was he who initiated a libel suit against the *Daily Star*, it was the *Daily Star* that arguably first invaded his privacy.

Nature of Covering-Up

Having looked at the significance of the underlying conduct being covered up (or alleged) and the nature of the investigation into such conduct, we can now consider what may well be the most important factor in assessing the moral wrongfulness of obstruction and related offenses—namely, the nature of the cover-up (or the false accusation) itself. Here, we can identify four relevant factors.

For a start, we need to consider the means by which the cover-up was effected. The federal statutes and case law provide a lengthy catalogue: court officials, jurors, and witnesses can be intimidated, bribed, threatened, harassed, and even killed; documents can be destroyed, fabricated, and altered; and judges, juries, and law enforcement officials can be lied to and misled by witnesses and informants. I assume that, other things being equal, it is worse to cover up a crime by killing a witness than by harassing him. But, beyond that, I am reluctant to attempt to rank the seriousness of various methods of obstruction. Thus, for present purposes, questions such as "Which is worse—destroying a (true) inculpatory document or fabricating a (false) exculpatory one?" or "Is there is any moral difference between ordering the destruction of documents and failing to order the suspension of an already-established document destruction program?" will have to remain unanswered.[151]

A second issue to be considered is the scope of the cover-up. Here we would want to know whether the defendant shredded tens of thousands of documents, like Oliver North, or whether instead she conspired to alter a single document, like Martha Stewart. Was a vast corporate enterprise enlisted to assist in the cover-up, as in the Arthur Andersen case, or was it mostly limited to one or two people, as in the case of Jeffrey Archer? Other things being equal, it would seem that the more extensive the cover-up, the more morally wrongful the act.

Third, we will want to ask what effect, if any, the cover-up or false accusation is likely to have on the resolution of the underlying case. For example, how much other evidence did the government have against the defendant, and how probative was it? To what extent, if any, was the government's investigation hindered by the suspect's exculpatory no? Did the informant's false accusation cause investigators to waste limited resources in pursuing a case they otherwise would not have pursued? Did it mean the possibility that a falsely accused might face serious punishment?[152] Did the defendant's covering up cause the prosecution to lose a conviction it otherwise would have obtained? Did it cause the plaintiff to lose a civil suit he otherwise would have won? Did it cause Congress or Parliament to be misled into adopting misguided legislation?

In the Scooter Libby case, it was precisely the effectiveness of the cover-up that explains the need for obstruction and perjury charges. At a press conference announcing the charges, Special Counsel Patrick Fitzgerald was asked why his office had chosen to pursue only the cover-up charges, and not the underlying offenses themselves. In response, he offered an insight that is very much consistent with the approach recommended in this chapter. He began by analogizing the underlying act of leaking classified information to a baseball pitcher's hitting a batter in the head. In such circumstances, he said, the umpire could not properly decide whether and how to penalize the pitcher unless he knew the pitcher's intent when he threw the ball. Analogously, Fitzgerald said, in order to determine whether Libby's acts constituted a crime, one would need to know what his intent was in talking to reporters about Valerie Plame. 'And what we have when someone [commits] obstruction of justice,' Fitzgerald said, is that 'the umpire gets sand thrown in his eyes. He's trying to figure [out] what happened and somebody blocked [his] view.'[153]

The significance of Fitzgerald's analogy should be clear: Libby's alleged act of covering up was harmful because it made it more difficult, perhaps impossible, to know the facts of the underlying leak case. And herein lies a kind of paradox: It is precisely in those cases in which the defendant's act of covering up is most effective that prosecution for cover-up crimes will be most clearly justified. And yet it is in those very same cases—where proof of the underlying offense is wanting—that prosecution for the cover-up alone is most likely to be characterized as unfair or petty or vindictive.

Determining the effect on the government's case of evidence improperly covered up by the defendant is in some sense the converse of the kind of determination that courts make in determining whether perjury by a prosecution witness so affected the jury's deliberations as to justify a new trial. Indeed, this is exactly the inquiry the court was required to make in the Martha Stewart case, after it was alleged that Secret Service Agent and prosecution witness Larry Stewart had lied about his examination of ink samples.[154] Similar is the determination that courts must make in the context of *Brady v. Maryland* as to whether the introduction of exculpatory evidence improperly withheld from the defendant by the prosecution would have affected the outcome of the case.[155] (Indeed, Martha Stewart herself argued, unsuccessfully, that the prosecution had improperly withheld exculpatory evidence regarding ink testing of the Merrill Lynch worksheet.) Just as there are cases in which the improper introduction of incriminating evidence or the improper withholding of exculpatory evidence is held to be harmless error, so perhaps should there be cases in which a defendant's improperly covering up *inculpatory* evidence should be viewed as so inconsequential as to obviate the appropriateness of prosecution for cover-up crimes.[156]

A final factor is the social role played by the person doing the wrongful exculpation or inculpation. As noted at the outset, a surprisingly large number of obstruction and perjury cases seem to involve prominent defendants. Assuming limited prosecutorial resources and two otherwise identical instances of suspected obstruction or perjury, would prosecutors be justified in deciding to prosecute the defendant who is famous, rich, or powerful, rather than the one who is not? From the perspective of general deterrence, prosecutors may well get a bigger "bang for the buck" by prosecuting the celebrity defendant.[157] But, from the perspective of retributive theory, would such selective prosecution be fair? Most commentators agree that perjury and obstruction of justice occur quite commonly in our criminal justice system,[158] though prosecutions for such offenses are comparatively rare.[159] Given equal protection norms, there is undoubtedly something troubling about the fact that a disproportionate number of defendants in such cases seem to be chosen because of their public prominence.

On the other hand, it may be that prominent people who engage in such conduct should be viewed as somehow more blameworthy than people of modest means who do so. At a minimum, an argument could be made that important public officials such as Bill Clinton, Scooter Libby, Jeffrey Archer, John Mitchell, and John Poindexter should be held to a higher standard of law-abidingness and trust than private persons.[160] The same might also be said generally of lawyers, whose obstruction of justice and perjury seem, notwithstanding zealous advocacy norms, particularly noxious crimes.

Conclusion

In the previous pages, I have offered a complex matrix of factors that, I argued, can help us to understand and evaluate the moral content of various acts of obstruction of justice, contempt, perjury, false statements, and misprision of felony. Given the particular focus of this book, it is reasonable to ask how my analytic approach would apply to the case of Martha Stewart.

Recall that Stewart was alleged to have made false statements to government agents about the circumstances surrounding her sale of stock in ImClone and of obstructing the government's investigation by conspiring with Bacanovic to alter documents that would make it appear that she had sold her stock pursuant to a pre-existing standing agreement rather than as a result of any inside information. In applying the framework developed here, let us consider first the seriousness of the underlying conduct Stewart was attempting to cover up: Stewart sold approximately four thousand shares of ImClone stock at an average price of $48.53 per share, yielding proceeds of nearly $200,000.[161] Had she waited and sold her stock after the news that the FDA had rejected Im-Clone's Erbitux application had become public, her shares would have been worth approximately eighteen percent less. In other words, Stewart made approximately $40,000 as a result of her alleged insider trading. Compared to what Bill Clinton and Jeffrey Archer covered up—namely, their personal sexual conduct—this seems significant. However, compared to what Arthur Andersen or Scooter Libby were covering up—one of the largest corporate frauds in American history, and the illegal leaking of the name of a covert CIA operative in a time of war, respectively—Stewart's act seems fairly trivial.

As for the nature of the investigation into such wrongdoing, once again, Stewart's case falls somewhere in the middle of the range. Investigation of suspected violations of the insider trading laws is undoubtedly a more legitimate law enforcement aim than delving into a politician's private sex life, though there is admittedly some debate about whether insider trading ought to be a crime at all.[162]

Perhaps the most important consideration is the nature of Stewart's alleged covering up itself. This is not a case in which the defendant harassed a witness, lied to a jury, or destroyed thousands of documents. Nor is this is a case, presumably like Libby's, in which the defendant's covering-up was so successful that it ultimately made it impossible for the government to go forward with its prosecution for the underlying charges. Indeed, notwithstanding Stewart's best efforts, the government still had enough evidence to sue Stewart for insider trading civilly. On the other hand, to the extent that Stewart sought not only to deny her wrongdoing to investigators but also to alter a key document and conspire with a confederate to do so, her prosecution may well have been justified. At a minimum, given limited prosecutorial resources and the interest the case produced in the public at large, and notwithstanding possible concerns about the unfairness of targeting celebrity defendants, it seems obvious that the prosecution of Martha Stewart gave prosecutors a significant bang for their buck.

Questions

1. Of the various factors suggested for assessing the seriousness of cover-up-type criminality, which should be regarded as the most significant? Which should be regarded as the least significant?
2. How could offenses such as obstruction of justice, perjury, contempt, and false statements be rewritten to avoid redundancies and overlaps?
3. Under what circumstances should cover-up activity be treated by criminal sanctions? When are lesser sanctions sufficient?

Notes

1. In the end, the jury's verdict on the obstruction charge against Stewart included no findings regarding the alleged alteration of the documents. *See* United States v. Stewart, 323 F. Supp. 2d 606, 614 (S.D.N.Y. 2004), *aff'd*, 433 F.3d 273 (2d Cir. 2006). Although her alleged insider trading was never the subject of a criminal prosecution, it did figure in a separate SEC civil suit.

2. In late October 2005, Special Counsel Patrick Fitzgerald announced the indictment of I. Lewis "Scooter" Libby, Vice President Dick Cheney's chief of staff, for obstruction of justice, perjury, and false statements, in connection with a federal grand jury's investigation into allegations that Libby and other high-ranking Bush Administration officials had illegally leaked the name of CIA covert operative Valerie Plame Wilson. *See* David Johnston & Richard W. Stevenson, *The Leak Inquiry: The Overview; Cheney Aide Charged with Lying in Leak Case*, N.Y. TIMES, Oct. 29, 2005, at A1.

3. In late 1998, President Bill Clinton was impeached on charges of perjury and obstruction of justice based on allegations that he had: (1) lied under oath about the nature

of his relationship with White House intern Monica Lewinsky; (2) told Lewinsky to be "eva-sive" in her answers to a federal grand jury; and (3) instructed his personal secretary, Betty Currie, to go to Lewinsky's apartment to reclaim various gifts that he had given her. He was, of course, subsequently acquitted in his trial before the Senate. *See Timeline: Clinton Accused*, WASH. POST, Sept. 13, 1998, *available at* http://www.washingtonpost.com/wp-srv/politics/special/clinton/timeline.htm.

4. In 1990 and 1989, respectively, National Security Advisor Poindexter and his aide Oliver North were convicted of obstructing justice and altering and destroying evidence per-taining to the Iran-Contra Affair, the illegal scheme in which Reagan administration officials sold arms to Iran and diverted the proceeds to right-wing Contra rebels in Nicaragua. Poindexter was also convicted of lying to Congress. Both Poindexter's and North's convic-tions were subsequently overturned on the grounds that they had previously been granted immunity from prosecution. *See* United States v. North, 920 F.2d 940, 948 (D.C. Cir. 1990), *cert. denied*, 500 U.S. 941 (1991).

5. In the mid-1970s, Mitchell, Haldeman, and Ehrlichman—top aides to President Richard Nixon—were found guilty of conspiracy and obstruction of justice (Attorney Gen-eral Mitchell was also found guilty of perjury) in connection with the cover-up of the bur-glary of Democratic Headquarters at the Watergate Apartment Complex in Washington. Along with other White House officials, one or more of the defendants had, among other things, taken steps to prevent the FBI from investigating the scandal, destroyed and altered evidence, and paid off potential witnesses.

6. In June 2002, the Arthur Andersen accounting firm was convicted of obstructing jus-tice in connection with the destruction of tens of thousands of pages of documents related to the federal investigation of its client, Enron. At trial, Andersen argued that, in destroying such documents, it had merely been carrying out its own, pre-existing, so-called document "re-tention" program. Andersen's conviction was ultimately reversed by the Supreme Court, on the grounds that the instruction given to the jury was improper. Arthur Andersen v. United States, 125 S. Ct. 2129 (2005).

7. In July 2001, British thriller writer and life peer Jeffrey Archer was convicted of perjury and perverting the course of justice in connection with a libel case he had initi-ated fourteen years earlier against the tabloid newspaper, the *Daily Star*. The paper had reported that Archer, then deputy chairman of the Conservative Party, had been seeing a prostitute. Archer was alleged to have perverted justice by asking a friend to give him a false alibi and to have committed perjury by lying in an affidavit to the High Court and during testimony in the libel trial. *See Timeline: Stranger than Fiction*, BBC NEWS ON-LINE, Oct. 8, 2002 (providing a chronology of the scandal), http://news.bbc.co.uk/1/hi/uk/1420132.stm.

8. In May 2004, Quattrone was convicted (on retrial) of obstruction of justice for send-ing an email to employees of his firm's technology investment department "strongly advis[ing them] to follow" internal firm document destruction procedures. The email was sent shortly after Quattrone had learned that the firm was being investigated by the FBI and SEC on suspicion that it had engaged in various illegal kickback practices relating to the allocation of initial public offerings among investors. *See* Dan Ackman, *Quattrone 'Very Believable' But Unconvincing*, FORBES.COM, May 3, 2004, http://www.forbes.com/2004/05/03/cx_da_0503 quattrone.html. In March 2006, Quattrone's conviction was reversed on the grounds of "deficient" jury instructions. United States v. Quattrone, 441 F.3d 153 (2nd Cir. 2006).

9. Kathleen F. Brickey is among the various scholars who have used the term "cover-up crime." *See* Kathleen F. Brickey, *Andersen's Fall From Grace*, 81 WASH. U. L.Q. 917, 958 (2003).

10. In addition to the factors identified in the text, there are a host of other special factors that potentially color our perception of these cases. I will cite two here. First, in the case of Arthur Andersen, there are questions about whether it was appropriate to bring a criminal prosecution against the entity itself, thereby causing the demise of the firm and many innocent employees to lose their jobs. Second, in the case of Bill Clinton, there are questions whether his conduct, even if criminal, constituted an adequate constitutional basis for impeachment.

11. Stuart P. Green, *Moral Ambiguity in White Collar Criminal Law*, 18 NOTRE DAME J.L. ETHICS & PUB. POL'Y 501, 501–03 (2004).

12. PROFESSORBAINBRIDGE.COM, http://www.professorbainbridge.com/2004/ 05/quat-trone_convi.html (May 4, 2004).

13. *See, e.g.*, James O. Goldsborough, *We Are a Nation Awash in a Sea of Lies*, SAN DIEGO UNION-TRIB., June 9, 2004, *available at* http://www.signonsandiego.com/ news/op-ed/golds-borough/20030609-9999_mz1e9golds.html (arguing that Stewart's crimes are more akin to minor shoplifting than serious corporate frauds).

14. Stephen Gillers, *The Flaw in the Andersen Verdict*, N.Y. TIMES, June 18, 2002, at A23 (arguing that directive given to Arthur Andersen executives, to the effect that a pre-existing document destruction program should not be suspended despite an impending criminal investigation of Andersen's role in the Enron scandal, was not a crime at all, but rather "the kind of advice lawyers give clients all the time").

15. Doug Henwood, *Free Martha!*, THE NATION, Feb. 9, 2004, *available at* http://www.thenation.com/doc.mhtml?i=20040209&s=henwood (discussing how Martha Stewart's decision to cover up what she believed to be securities fraud by lying to federal investigators reflected "bad judgment" rather than felonious intent).

16. Howard Chapman, *Both Martha and Justice Have Suffered, and Now It Will Get Even Worse*, FORT WAYNE NEWS-SENTINEL, March 12, 2004, *available at* http://www.discovery.org/ scripts/viewDB/index.php?command=view&program=Misc&id=1926.

17. In this, I employ a methodology that is developed more fully in my book, LYING, CHEATING, AND STEALING: A MORAL THEORY OF WHITE COLLAR CRIME (2006).

18. The facts surrounding the charges against Larry Stewart are discussed in Kathleen F. Brickey, *Mostly Martha*, 44 WASHBURN L.J. 517, 527–33 (2005).

19. The allegations against Larry Stewart are described in *United States v. Stewart*, 323 F. Supp. 2d 606, 616–19 (S.D.N.Y. 2004) (holding that Martha was not entitled to a new trial on the basis of Larry's alleged perjury).

20. *See* Alexander Volokh, *On Guilty Men*, 146 U. PA. L. REV. 173 (1997). *See also infra* note 119 and accompanying text.

21. In 1988, a grand jury investigation concluded that Brawley "was not the victim of forcible sexual assault" and that the whole thing was a hoax. *Report of the Grand Jury Concerning the Tawana Brawley Investigation, available at* http://www.courttv.com/legaldocs/ newsmakers/tawana/part1.html. Pagones subsequently won a defamation lawsuit against Brawley and her co-conspirators (including the Reverend, and later presidential candidate, Al Sharpton). However, none of them was ever criminally prosecuted.

22. *See Hickman Released on Bond*, WAVE3TV.COM, undated, *at* http://www.wave3.com/Global/story.asp?S=3377448&nav=0RZFa9v2. In correspondence with the author, Pierson wrote that:

The injury to the Katie Collman murder investigation caused by [Hickman's] false confession was substantial.... [T]he person now charged with molesting and murdering Collman had just been interviewed and was slated for follow-up investigation when Hickman confessed. The investigators switched gears and began investigating the persons named by Hickman as having been involved. Those accusations could not be corroborated and a lot of hours were lost. All in all about nine weeks' delay in solving the case can be attributed to Hickman. In terms of dollars wasted, the probable total is in multiple tens of thousands of dollars.

Letter from Stephen S. Pierson to author (May 31, 2005) (on file with the author). At the time of this writing, it was unclear whether the charges would ever be brought.

23. This is not to suggest that statutes making it an offense to fail to report various forms of criminal activity are unknown in modern law. Indeed, there is reason to think that such statutes are becoming more common. *See, e.g.,* the Anti-Terrorism, Crime and Security Act 2001, c.27 (U.K.) § 117 (a person who "has information which he knows or believes might be of material assistance·... in preventing the commission by another person of an act of terrorism ... commits an offence if he does not disclose the information as soon as reasonably practicable"). *See generally* Sandra Guerra Thompson, *The White-Collar Police Force: "Duty to Report" Statutes in Criminal Law Theory,* 11 Wm. & Mary Bill Rts. J. 3 (2002) (discussing recently enacted laws that require individuals to report suspicions of a wide range of criminal conduct, including hazardous waste discharges, money laundering, and child, elder, and domestic abuse).

24. For a discussion of misprision of felony, see *infra* notes 63–76 and accompanying text.

25. Kurt Eichenwald, *Ex-Chief of Enron Pleads Not Guilty to 11 Felony Counts,* N.Y. Times, July 9, 2004, at C1.

26. There is an interesting parallel here to bribery, which traditionally required that the person taking the bribe be a public official. Today, various statutes also make it a crime for a bribe to be taken by certain kinds of private actors, such as investment advisers, bank employees, labor officials, and radio disc jockeys. Nevertheless, bribery of government officials and commercial bribery are almost always treated under separate statutory provisions. *See generally* Stuart P. Green, *What's Wrong With Bribery, in* Defining Crimes: Essays on the Special Part of the Criminal Law 143, 146 (R.A. Duff & Stuart P. Green eds., 2005).

27. 18 U.S.C. § 1956 (2006) (laundering of monetary instruments); 18 U.S.C. § 1957 (engaging in monetary transactions in property derived from specified unlawful activity).

28. 26 U.S.C. § 7201 (attempting to evade or defeat tax); 18 U.S.C. § 7206 (tax perjury).

29. 8 U.S.C. § 1324 (bringing in and harboring certain aliens).

30. 18 U.S.C. § 1071 (concealing a person from arrest); 18 U.S.C. § 1072 (concealing an escaped prisoner).

31. 18 U.S.C. §§ 1501–20.

32. In addition to the Omnibus Clause, § 1503 also contains a provision making it a crime to endeavor to influence or retaliate against a juror or court officer.

33. Ellen Podgor has offered an argument to the effect that, as in the case of false statements, obstruction of justice should also include an element of "materiality." Ellen S. Podgor, *Arthur Andersen, LLP and Martha Stewart: Should Materiality be an Element of Obstruction of Justice?,* 44 Washburn L.J. 583 (2005).

34. Sarah N. Welling et al., Federal Criminal Law and Related Actions: Crimes, Forfeiture, the False Claims Act and RICO 163 (1998).

35. This aspect of white collar crime is discussed more generally in Green, *supra* note 17, at 36–37.

36. Welling et al., *supra* note 34, at 162.

37. Section 1505 makes it a crime to corruptly influence, obstruct, or impede "the due and proper administration of law under which any pending proceedings is being had before any department or agency of the United States, or the due and proper exercise of the power of inquiry under which any inquiry or investigation is being had by either House, or any committee of either House or any joint committee of the Congress." 18 U.S.C. § 1505.

38. United States v. Aguilar, 515 U.S. 593, 597 (1995). For further discussion, see *infra* text accompanying notes 83–84.

39. United States v. Cintolo, 818 F.2d 980 (1st Cir. 1987), *cert. denied*, 484 U.S. 913 (1987).

40. *E.g.*, United States v. Bashaw, 982 F.2d 168, 171 (6th Cir. 1992). *See generally* J. Kelly Strader, Understanding White Collar Crime 202–05 (2002) (discussing application of omnibus provision).

41. 18 U.S.C. § 1510. This provision was passed in order to close a loophole in earlier law which protected witnesses only during judicial proceedings themselves and not during the prior investigation. United States v. San Martin, 515 F.2d 317, 320 (5th Cir. 1975).

42. Victim and Witness Protection Act of 1982, Pub. L. No. 97-291, 96 Stat. 1248 (1982).

43. 18 U.S.C. § 1512.

44. Retaliation presents a somewhat problematic category, as it will involve covering up only where it is part of a larger process of coercing witnesses and informants through threats of retaliation, and even then the actual retaliation could be seen as part of a cover-up only if it is designed to show others that the threats they face are serious. (Thanks to Antony Duff for his help in formulating this point.)

45. The definition of "official proceeding" as used in § 1512 is found in 18 U.S.C. § 1515(a). Section 1512 has the effect of increasing protection for victims and witnesses beyond what was previously available only under § 1503, by lowering the threshold of what constitutes obstruction inasmuch as it prohibits tampering by intimidation and harassment as well as force and threats. Section 1512 also includes a provision that provides an affirmative defense if the defendant can prove that his conduct consisted solely of lawful conduct and that his sole intention was to "encourage, induce, or cause the other person to testify truthfully." Although the Victim and Witness Protection Act eliminated the prior reference in § 1503 to witnesses, presumably in deference to § 1512's more specialized focus, a majority of courts have held that witness tampering can be prosecuted not only under § 1512 but also under the amended version of the Omnibus Clause of § 1503.

46. *See* Chris Sanchirico, *Evidence Tampering*, 53 Duke L.J. 1215, 1225 (2004) (stating that "the law tends to penalize evidence tampering only when it occurs far downstream in the flow from primary activity through filing, discovery, and trial").

47. 18 U.S.C. § 1001(a)(2).

48. Like perjury, however, § 1001 has usually been held to require literal falsity. Stuart P. Green, *Lying, Misleading, and Falsely Denying: How Moral Concepts Inform the Law of Perjury, Fraud, and False Statements*, 53 Hastings L.J. 157, 196–98 (2001). In addition to § 1001, there are also numerous other "kindred" federal statutes that make it a crime to make a false statement in one or more specific procedural contexts, such as in applications to federal bank loan and credit agencies and in connection with government procurement contracts. *See generally* Kathleen F. Brickey, Corporate Criminal Liability 327–41 (3d ed. 2002).

49. United States v. Rodgers, 466 U.S. 475, 476 (1984).

50. Section 1001 can also be violated when a defendant makes a fraudulent statement to the government either to obtain money or to resist a claim. *See, e.g.,* United States v. Shah, 44 F.3d 285, 288 (5th Cir. 1995) (affirming conviction under § 1001 for making a false statement in a solicitation to the General Services Administration).

51. State v. Jones, 226 P. 433, 434–35 (Or. 1924). Most of the citations in this paragraph are borrowed from Dan B. Dobbs, *Contempt of Court: A Survey,* 56 CORNELL L. REV. 183 (1971).

52. People v. Gilliam, 227 N.E.2d 96, 99 (Ill. 1967).

53. State v. Weinberg, 92 S.E.2d 842, 846 (S.C. 1942).

54. Handler v. Gordon, 140 P.2d 622, 622–23 (Colo. 1943).

55. *In re* Fountain, 108 S.E. 342, 343 (N.C. 1921).

56. As I have described elsewhere, criminal contempt is in many respects indistinguishable from other crimes: (1) it consists of criminal law-like "elements" (namely, the *actus reus* of misbehavior or defiance of a court order and the *mens rea* of intent or willfulness); (2) contemnors have available to them a range of traditional criminal law defenses (including physical impossibility, mistake of law, and mistake of fact); (3) the constitutional rights available to defendants in other kinds of criminal cases have increasingly been made available to contemnors; and (4) such criminal sanctions are imposed primarily for punitive purposes. *See* Stuart P. Green, *Why It's a Crime to Tear the Tag Off a Mattress: Overcriminalization and the Moral Content of Regulatory Offenses,* 46 EMORY L.J. 1533, 1604–05 & nn. 239–45 (1997).

57. 4 Stat. 487 (1831).

58. JAMIE S. GORELICK ET AL., DESTRUCTION OF EVIDENCE § 5.6 (1989).

59. 18 U.S.C. § 1621 (1994).

60. 18 U.S.C. § 1623 (1994).

61. *See* Green, *supra* note 48. The leading case is *Bronston v. United States,* 409 U.S. 352 (1973) (holding that a literally true statement, even if misleading, does not constitute a false statement). Although perjury and false declarations partially overlap, there are some important differences between the two: whereas § 1621 adheres to the traditional "two-witness rule" (meaning that the government's case must rest either on two live witnesses or on one witness plus some corroborative evidence), § 1623 has no such requirement. *See* Hammer v. United States, 271 U.S. 620, 626 (1926) (holding the general rule for perjury prosecution requires corroborated evidence). Instead, § 1623 allows the use of inconsistent statements to prove guilt, without requiring the government to prove which of the statements was false. Also, unlike § 1621, § 1623 contains a limited recantation defense. Obviously, a witness who lies under oath about some criminal activity in which he has engaged can be prosecuted for both perjury (or false declarations) and the underlying crime.

62. WELLING ET AL., *supra* note 34, at 217.

63. *See* Daniel B. Yeager, *A Radical Community of Aid: A Rejoinder to Opponents of Affirmative Duties to Help Strangers,* 71 WASH. U. L.Q. 1, 30 (1993) (noting that prior to the establishment of a professional police force, ordinary citizens present when a felony was committed were expected to assist in the enforcement of the law by apprehending the felon or, if unable to do so, by raising hue and cry). *See also* Steven J. Heyman, *Foundations of the Duty to Rescue,* 47 VANDERBILT L. REV. 673, 685–90 (1994) (discussing the common law principle that every citizen had a duty to prevent a felony as part of a greater duty to assist in preserving the peace).

64. *See* Gerard E. Lynch, *The Lawyer as Informer*, 1986 DUKE L.J. 491, 518 (1986) (arguing that absence of any moral duty to inform contributed to dearth of successful prosecutions in England).

65. 18 U.S.C. §4 (2000). The original statute was part of the Crimes Act of April 30, 1790, ch. 9, §6, 1 Stat. 113 (1790), and related to concealment of a felony "upon the high seas, or within any ... place ... under the sole and exclusive jurisdiction of the United States." The 1909 amendment to the statute extended its reach to anyone who concealed a felony "cognizable by the courts of the United States." Act of March 4, 1909, ch. 321, §146, 35 Stat. 1114 (1909).

66. 18 U.S.C. §4.

67. *See* United States v. Barksdale-Contreras, 972 F.2d 111, 115 (5th Cir. 1992) (deeming as concealment false statements made to police during the course of a kidnapping). The citations in this and the next several notes are borrowed from WELLING ET AL., *supra* note 34, §3.1, at 99.

68. *See* United States v. Stuard, 566 F.2d 1, 1–2 (6th Cir. 1977) (per curiam) (holding intentional concealment of circumstances surrounding theft of whiskey as sufficient grounds for conviction of misprision of felony).

69. *See* Lancey v. United States, 356 F.2d 407, 410–11 (9th Cir. 1966) (ruling that failure to inform police of whereabouts of missing felon while permitting felon to conceal fruits of crime constitutes misprision of felony).

70. *See* United States v. Gravitt, 590 F.2d 123, 126 (5th Cir. 1979) (finding retrieval of duffel bag containing clothing, guns, and money for the purpose of later dividing it among cohorts satisfies affirmative action requirement needed for conviction of misprision of felony).

71. *See* United States v. Ciambrone, 750 F.2d 1416, 1418 (9th Cir. 1984).

72. *See* United States v. Davila, 698 F.2d 715, 717 (5th Cir. 1983). Notably, the court held that the prosecution could still establish guilt in a misprision prosecution even when the principal has been found not guilty of committing the initial felony. *See id.* at 720–21.

73. *Lancey*, 356 F.2d at 409–10.

74. *See, e.g.*, United States v. Daddano, 432 F.2d 1119, 1125 (7th Cir. 1970) (delineating between act of concealment and disclosure of facts that might lead to conviction for a crime, the latter of which would threaten Fifth Amendment guarantees against self-incrimination).

75. *See* United States v. Kuh, 541 F.2d 672, 676–77 (7th Cir. 1976) (distinguishing *Daddano* as an "unusual" case).

76. *Yeager*, *supra* note 63, at 8.

77. WELLING ET AL., *supra* note 34, §3.1, at 101. *See also* Robert E. Meale, Comment, *Misprision of Felony: A Crime Whose Time Has Come, Again*, 28 U. FLA. L. REV. 199 (1975).

78. Whether it ultimately makes sense from a policy perspective to have so many overlapping statutes applicable to the same kinds of conduct is a question that lies beyond the scope of this paper. For a recent discussion, see Michael L. Seigel & Christopher Slobogin, *Prosecuting Martha: Federal Prosecutorial Power and the Need for a Law of Counts*, 109 PENN ST. L. REV. 1007 (2005) (offering a proposed solution to the problem of charge redundancy that might be used even if comprehensive federal criminal code reform is unattainable).

79. *See* Jay M. Zitter, Annotation, *Attorney's Conduct in Delaying or Obstructing Discovery as Basis for Contempt Proceeding*, 8 A.L.R. 4TH 1181, 1183 (1982 & Supp. 2004).

80. *See, e.g.*, Millinocket Theatre v. Kurson, 39 F. Supp. 979, 980 (D. Me. 1941) (holding defendant who destroyed incriminating evidence while in his own office, rather than in the presence of the court, liable for obstruction of justice but not contempt).

81. *E.g.*, United States v. Howard, 569 F.2d 1331, 1336 n.8 (5th Cir. 1978) (holding concurrent violation of Rule 6(e) and § 1503 permit conviction for both contempt and obstruction of justice); United States v. Walasek, 527 F.2d 676, 680 (3d Cir. 1975) (finding that a single act may violate multiple statutes, specifically §§ 401 and 1503, which deal with contempt occurring within and without the court, respectively).

82. United States v. Griffin, 589 F.2d 200, 204 (5th Cir. 1979).

83. United States v. Aguilar, 515 U.S. 593, 597 (1995).

84. *Id.* at 599.

85. *See supra* note 61. Presumably, however, the witness would have to do more than simply offer a misleading statement in order to be guilty of obstruction, since, as *Bronston* recognizes, the witness will invariably be subject to further questioning and cross-examination.

86. No. 97-5719, 1998 WL 833770, at *2–3 (6th Cir. Nov. 19, 1998) (per curiam). A jury found the defendant guilty of misprision but not of obstruction. *Id.* at *2. In upholding the misprision conviction, the Sixth Circuit held that, unlike obstruction, which requires that a false statement be "material," misprision has no such requirement. *Id.* at *3.

87. United States v. Salinas, 956 F.2d 80, 81 (5th Cir. 1992).

88. *See generally* J.A. Bock, Annotation, *Perjury or False Swearing as Contempt*, 89 A.L.R. 2D 1258 (1963).

89. *See* Handler v. Gordon, 140 P.2d 622, 622 (Colo. 1943).

90. *In re* Michael, 326 U.S. 224, 227–28 (1945); *Ex parte* Hudgings, 249 U.S. 378, 383 (1919).

91. *Cf.* Green, *supra* note 11, at 514 (discussing how many white collar crimes can be handled through both criminal prosecution and civil actions); Stuart P. Green, *Plagiarism, Norms, and the Limits of Theft Law: Some Observations on the Use of Criminal Sanctions in Enforcing Intellectual Property Rights*, 54 HASTINGS L.J. 167, 195–240 (2002) (concerning various means, both criminal and civil, by which acts amounting to plagiarism are treated).

92. FED. R. CIV. P. 37(b)(2). For further discussion of remedies available under the Federal Rules of Civil Procedure, see GORELICK ET AL., *supra* note 58, at 65–137; Sanchirico, *supra* note 46, at 1262–69.

93. FED. R. CRIM. P. 16(d)(2). The obligation of the defendant to produce such documents arises only if the defendant first requests similar material from the prosecution and the request is complied with. FED. R. CRIM. P. 16(b)(1). Also, the defendant must intend to use such material in its case-in-chief at trial or, in the case of scientific reports, intend to call the witness who prepared the report. *Id.*

94. *See* MARGARET M. KOESEL ET AL., SPOLIATION OF EVIDENCE: SANCTIONS AND REMEDIES FOR DESTRUCTION OF EVIDENCE IN CIVIL LITIGATION 50–51 (2000) (discussing the existence of an independent tort claim for spoliation in certain jurisdictions).

95. *Id.*

96. On the other hand, it should be noted that plaintiffs who seek to recover damages for false *inculpatory* statements made to the police, in court pleadings, or on the witness stand generally cannot recover for defamation. *See, e.g.*, David W. Eagle, Note, *Civil Remedies for Perjury: A Proposal for a Tort Action*, 19 ARIZ. L. REV. 349, 349 (1977) (stating that no tort claim exists for perjury committed at any step in the judicial process).

97. *See generally* GORELICK ET AL., *supra* note 58, at 249–74; Sanchirico, *supra* note 46, at 1283–85.

98. MODEL RULES OF PROF'L CONDUCT R. 8.4(d) (2003).

99. MODEL RULES OF PROF'L CONDUCT R. 3.4(a) (2003).

100. *See* Model Rules of Prof'l Conduct R. 3.3 (2003).

101. Gorelick et al., *supra* note 58, at 266–70 (discussing sanctions for attorney violation of ethical rules regarding destruction of evidence).

102. 18 U.S.C. § 3500 (2000) (stating government obligations following demands for production of statements and reports of witnesses).

103. Fed. R. Crim. P. 16(a) (stating disclosure obligations of the government).

104. 373 U.S. 83, 87 (1963) ("[S]uppression by the prosecution of evidence favorable to the accused upon request violates due process where the evidence is material.").

105. *See* American Bar Association, Standards for Criminal Justice 61 (2d ed. 1980) (stating the standard for disclosure of evidence by a prosecutor).

106. *See* Bruce A. Green, *The Criminal Regulation of Lawyers*, 67 Fordham L. Rev. 327 (1998); Bruce A. Green, *Zealous Representation Bound: The Intersection of the Ethical Codes and the Criminal Law*, 69 N.C. L. Rev. 687 (1991).

107. For an interesting discussion of the deterrence question in the context of evidence tampering, see Sanchirico, *supra* note 46, at 1291–93. *See also* Chris W. Sanchirico, *Detection Avoidance*, U. Pa. Inst. L. & Econ. Res. Paper Series, No. 05-18 (August 2005), http://papers.ssrn.com/sol3/papers.cfm?abstract_id=782305.

108. As I have discussed in earlier work, "harmfulness" reflects the degree to which criminal acts cause, or risk causing, harm to others or self. "Wrongfulness" reflects the way in which the criminal act involves a violation of a specific moral norm or set of norms, such as deception, cheating, coercion, exploitation, stealing, promise-breaking, disobeying, or disloyalty. *See* Green, *supra* note 17, chapter 3.

109. *See* 18 U.S.C. § 1512(a)(1) (2000 & Supp. II 2004).

110. *See* 18 U.S.C. § 1512(b) (2000 & Supp. II 2004).

111. *See* 18 U.S.C. § 1503(a) (1996).

112. *See* Bennett L. Gershman, *The "Perjury Trap,"* 129 U. Pa. L. Rev. 624, 636 (1981) (discussing various harms or potential harms associated with perjury).

113. *See, e.g.,* United States v. Rodgers, 466 U.S. 475, 481 (1984) ("The knowing filing of a false crime report, leading to an investigation and possible prosecution, can also have grave consequences for the individuals accused of crime.").

114. *See generally* Dale A. Oesterle, *A Private Litigant's Remedies for an Opponent's Inappropriate Destruction of Relevant Documents*, 61 Tex. L. Rev. 1185 (1983) (discussing the ineffectiveness of the current remedies available to a private party in a civil lawsuit where the opposing party has destroyed evidence).

115. Mason L. Weems, The Life of Washington (1962). *See also* Henry J. Friendly, *The Fifth Amendment Tomorrow: The Case for Constitutional Change*, 37 U. Cin. L. Rev. 671, 687 (1968) (making similar point).

116. 26 U.S.C. § 7203 (2000).

117. 33 U.S.C. § 1319(c) (2000).

118. *See, e.g.,* Nachum Ansel, Jewish Encyclopedia of Moral and Ethical Issues 292–93 (1994) (explaining how Jewish law has traditionally looked at the obligation to tell the truth under oath).

119. In fact, the Bible does distinguish between false exculpation and false inculpation. A witness who falsely inculpates is to receive the same punishment as that which would have been given to the falsely accused. *Deuteronomy* 19:18–19. The punishment for false exculpation, on the other hand, does not appear to be stated.

120. *See* 18 U.S.C. § 1510(a) (2000).

121. *See* Green, *What's Wrong With Bribery, supra* note 26, at 3–8.

122. For further discussion of the moral obligation to obey the law, see GREEN, *supra* note 17, chapter 10.

123. *See supra* text accompanying notes 25–26.

124. In Britain, it is a crime to: (1) intimidate an informant, witness, or juror in an investigation or proceedings for an offense, with the intent to obstruct, pervert, or interfere with such investigation or proceedings; or (2) threaten harm to a person who has been an informant, witness, or juror in such proceedings. Criminal Justice and Public Order Act, 1994, ch. 33, §51.

125. *See* WILLIAM BLACKSTONE, 4 COMMENTARIES *121 (detailing the various types of misprisions and contempts in the English law of the time).

126. Green, *Cheating*, 23 LAW & PHIL. 137, 144 (2004).

127. *See, e.g.*, MONROE H. FREEDMAN & ABBE SMITH, UNDERSTANDING LAWYERS' ETHICS 217 (3d ed. 2004) ("Is it ever proper for a lawyer to cross-examine an adverse witness who has testified accurately and truthfully in order to make the witness appear to be mistaken or lying? Our answer is yes—but the same answer is also given by almost every other commentator on lawyers' ethics."); GEOFFREY C. HAZARD & W. WILLIAM HODES, THE LAW OF LAWYERING §40.3 (3d ed. 2001) ("it is often the duty of an advocate to 'burden' or 'embarrass' an adverse witness, if doing so will make the witness less likely to be believed," and this is true even for truthful witnesses).

128. *See* Green, *Criminal Regulation of Lawyers, supra* note 106, at 362. For a similar analysis, see John A. Humbach, *Just Being a Lawyer*, 4 LEGAL ETHICS 155 (2001) (book review).

129. *See* Kent Greenawalt, *Silence as Moral and Constitutional Right*, 23 WM. & MARY L. REV. 15, 29 (1981); William Stuntz, *Self-Incrimination and Excuse*, 88 COLUM. L. REV. 1227, 1252 (1988). The *locus classicus* concerning the right of self-preservation is THOMAS HOBBES, LEVIATHAN, ch. 14 (Michael Oakeshott ed., 1955).

130. Under this doctrine, a statement that would otherwise have violated 18 U.S.C. §1001 was exempt from prosecution if it conveyed false information in a situation in which a truthful reply would have incriminated the interrogee and was limited to simple words of denial (such as "no, I did not," "none," or "never") rather than more elaborate fabrications. The doctrine, which had been adopted by a majority of the lower federal courts, was overruled by the Supreme Court's 1998 opinion in Brogan v. United States, 522 U.S. 398, 408 (1998). *See generally* Green, *supra* note 48, at 198–201.

131. Green, *supra* note 48, at 201.

132. *See* George C. Harris, *Testimony for Sale: The Law and Ethics of Snitches and Experts*, 28 PEPP. L. REV. 1 (2001); Michael A. Simons, *Retribution for Rats: Cooperation, Punishment, and Atonement*, 56 VAND. L. REV. 1 (2003). *See generally* SISSELA BOK, SECRETS: ON THE ETHICS OF CONCEALMENT AND REVELATION 210–29 (1989) (discussing the moral choices facing whistleblowers).

133. *See* Green, *supra* note 26.

134. For a discussion of the conflict between interpersonal loyalties and duties to society at large as it exists in the context of lawyer informants, see Lynch, *supra* note 64, at 527–32.

135. For a vivid account of life under the eyes of the East German Secret Police, see TIMOTHY GARTON ASH, THE FILE (1997). *See also* Alexandra Natapoff, *Snitching: The Institutional and Communal Consequences*, 73 U. CIN. L. REV. 645 (2005).

136. *Cf.* Lynch, *supra* note 64, at 533 (discussing the moral status of informing as being determined by the loyalties involved and the gravity of harm the informer seeks to prevent).

137. *See* MODEL PENAL CODE AND COMMENTARIES, §5.05, commentary at 484–89 (describing departure of Model Penal Code from traditional approach of grading criminal attempts, solicitations, and conspiracies in proportion to target crimes).

138. *E.g.*, LA. REV. STAT. ANN. §14:23(C) (maximum penalty for perjury committed at capital trial is 40 years; for other felonies, maximum penalty is 20 years).

139. *See* United States v. Blohm, 585 F. Supp. 1112, 1114 (S.D.N.Y. 1984); United States v. Meeks, 642 F.2d 733, 742 n.20 (5th Cir. 1981) (Reavley, J., dissenting), *vacated*, 461 U.S. 912 (1983).

140. Several commentators have noted that there are "no reported criminal convictions for evidence destruction in civil litigation." KOESEL ET AL., *supra* note 94, at 69. As a practical matter, when perjury or obstruction occurs in civil litigation between two private parties, it will be extremely difficult to persuade a prosecutor to use his limited resources to bring a criminal prosecution (although this would seem to be less of an obstacle when the complaining party is a government plaintiff or defendant).

141. GORELICK ET AL., *supra* note 58, at 198.

142. Wilder v. United States, 143 F. 433, 440 (4th Cir. 1906), *cert. denied*, 204 U.S. 674 (1907).

143. *See* Stuart P. Green, *Victims' Rights and the Limits of the Criminal Law*, 14 CRIM. L.F. 335, 343 (2004) (book review). *See also* R.A. DUFF, PUNISHMENT, COMMUNICATION AND COMMUNITY 60–64 (2000); JEFFRIE G. MURPHY & JULES L. COLEMAN, THE PHILOSOPHY OF LAW 113–23 (1984); S.E. Marshall & R.A. Duff, *Criminalization and Sharing Wrongs*, 11 *Can. J.L. & Juris.* 7 (1998).

144. For a critical analysis of the related argument that the criminal law should be used only as a "last resort," see Douglas Husak, *The Criminal Law as Last Resort*, 24 OXFORD J. LEGAL STUD. 207 (2004).

145. On the other hand, there is something to be said for the argument of Dale Oesterle to the effect that, by forgoing the more serious prosecution, "we lose the public trial, and with it the revelation and condemnation of the core corrupt business practices that attracted the public ire and the prosecutor's attention." Dale A. Oesterle, *Early Observations on the Prosecutions of the Business Scandals of 2002–03: On Sideshow Prosecutions, Spitzer's Clash With Donaldson Over Turf, the Choice of Civil or Criminal Actions, and the Tough Tactic of Coerced Cooperation*, 1 OHIO ST. J. CRIM. L. 443, 456 (2004). Of course, the obvious rejoinder here is that, in the American criminal justice system, only a very small percentage of cases ever actually go to trial.

146. Brogan v. United States, 522 U.S. 398, 411–12 (1998) (Ginsburg, J., concurring).

147. *See, e.g.*, People v. Tyler, 385 N.E.2d 1224, 1228–29 (N.Y. 1978). *See also* Gershman, *supra* note 112, at 645 ("If, under the guise of an otherwise legitimate investigation, a prosecutor solicits testimony with the premeditated design of indicting the witness for perjury, the grand jury is put to an unintended and inappropriate use.").

148. People v. Fischer, 423 N.E.2d 349, 351 n.1 (N.Y. 1981).

149. *See generally* Sanchirico, *supra* note 46.

150. Under the Omnibus Clause of §1503, the penalty is imprisonment for not more than ten years, a fine, or both. *See* 18 U.S.C. §1503(b)(3). Under the Omnibus Clause of §1505, the penalty is a fine of not more than $5,000 or imprisonment for not more than five years, or both. *See* 18 U.S.C. §1505.

151. There are interesting cases in which documents are destroyed pursuant to a document destruction program (often euphemistically referred to as a document "retention" program) that was established before the defendant was subject to, or knew about, the in-

vestigation. In such cases, the defendant might argue that the existence of such a program is proof that it lacked the *mens rea* necessary to commit obstruction. For example, at trial in the Arthur Andersen case, the defendant argued that its document destruction was mere "routine housekeeping" which failed to satisfy the element of "corrupt persuasion" necessary to violate 18 U.S.C. § 1512(b). In reversing Andersen's conviction, the Supreme Court basically agreed. Arthur Andersen v. United States, 125 S. Ct. 2129 (2005).

152. Recall that the biblical approach explicitly links the punishment of the false accuser with the punishment that the falsely accused would have suffered. *See supra* note 119.

153. Transcript of Fitzgerald News Conference, (Oct. 28, 2005), *available at* http://www.washingtonpost.com/wp-dyn/content/article/2005/10/28/AR2005102801340.html.

154. United States v. Stewart, 323 F. Supp. 2d 606, 614–23 (S.D.N.Y. 2004) (holding that a new trial was not justified).

155. *See* Brady v. Maryland, 373 U.S. 83, 87–88 (1963). *See also* United States v. Agurs, 427 U.S. 97, 112–13 (1976) (in order to obtain reversal, defendant must typically show that prosecutor's failure to overturn exculpatory evidence had a material effect on trial's outcome).

156. For example, the probability that Martha Stewart's alleged lying to the FBI significantly hindered its investigation seems fairly low. On the other hand, it may well be that Arthur Andersen's massive shredding of Enron-related documents did make it significantly more difficult for the government to develop its case against Enron and its top executives, and that Andersen knew that such difficulties would result. *Cf.* Brickey, *supra* note 9, at 928 ("Destruction of a paper trail crucial to understanding Enron's complex and sometimes byzantine financial transactions could have jeopardized the government's probe of a potentially massive fraud.").

157. *See* Anthony M. Dillof, *Unraveling Unlawful Entrapment*, 94 J. CRIM. L. & CRIM-INOLOGY 827, 888 (2004). *See also* Vikram David Amar, *The Many Ways to Prove Discrimination*, 14 HASTINGS WOMEN'S L.J. 171, 178 n.13 (2003) (book review) (noting targeting of high-profile defendants by Securities and Exchange Commission); Michael A. Simons, *Prosecutorial Discretion and Prosecutorial Guidelines: A Case Study in Controlling Federalization*, 75 N.Y.U. L. REV. 893, 964 n.281 (2000) (citing cases against prominent sports figures brought because of deterrence value). *But cf.* Stuart P. Green, Note, *Private Challenges to Prosecutorial Inaction: A Model Declaratory Statute*, 97 YALE L.J. 488, 500 n.70 (1988) (discussing case in which prosecutors decided not to prosecute rape suspects apparently because of their fame and popularity as professional athletes).

158. For a critical review of the data regarding the incidence of evidence tampering, see Sanchirico, *supra* note 46, at 1231–39. On the incidence of perjury, see Myron W. Orfield, Jr., *Deterrence, Perjury, and the Heater Factor: An Exclusionary Rule in the Chicago Criminal Courts*, 63 COLO. L. REV. 75, 95–114 (1992) (discussing police perjury).

159. BUREAU OF JUSTICE STATISTICS, U.S. DEP'T OF JUSTICE, SOURCEBOOK OF CRIMINAL JUSTICE STATISTICS 2002, at 405, 416 (Kathleen Maguire & Ann L. Pastore eds., 2003) (noting that there were only 114 perjury cases filed in district courts in 2002).

160. *See* U.S. SENTENCING COMMISSION, FEDERAL SENTENCING GUIDELINES MANUAL § 3B1.3 (2004) (sentencing enhancement for "abuse of position of trust"). *Cf.* David A. Sklansky, *Starr, Singleton, and the Prosecutor's Role*, 26 FORDHAM URB. L.J. 509, 531–32 (1999) (considering similar issue).

161. *See* United States v. Stewart, 433 F.3d 273 (2d Cir. 2006); Brickey, *supra* note 18.

162. *See* GREEN, *supra* note 17, at 236 (citing HENRY G. MANNE, INSIDER TRADING THE STOCK MARKET (1996)).

CHAPTER 7

MATERIALITY AS AN ELEMENT OF OBSTRUCTION[*]

Ellen S. Podgor

Martha Stewart[1] was charged by indictment[2] with the crimes of conspiracy,[3] false statements,[4] obstruction of justice,[5] and securities fraud.[6] Despite discussion and press regarding possible insider trading, Martha Stewart was not charged with this offense.[7] Stewart and Peter Bacanovic, her stockbroker, proceeded to trial in January of 2004. In February 2004, the court granted Stewart an acquittal on the securities fraud count.[8] The jury convicted Martha Stewart on the remaining counts, and she was sentenced to a five-month jail sentence, five months of house arrest, two years of probation, and a $30,000 fine.[9] This conviction was affirmed on appeal.[10]

Stewart was alleged to have disposed of shares of ImClone stock in December 2001, at a time when the Food and Drug Administration was considering the approval of a cancer drug made by ImClone.[11] It was also at a time that the FDA had notified ImClone that the application for approval of this drug was being rejected.[12] The indictment stems from statements she was alleged to have made to the Securities and Exchange Commission during its investigation of this matter.

Deputy Attorney General James Comey stated that the decision to prosecute Martha Stewart had to do with her "lying."[13] The obstruction charge in the indictment was also premised upon her providing "false and misleading information to the SEC relating to [her] sale of ImClone stock."[14] Martha Stewart was never charged with the underlying conduct that was the basis for

---

* This chapter is derived from *Arthur Andersen, LLP and Martha Stewart: Should Materiality be an Element of Obstruction of Justice?*, originally published at 44 WASHBURN L. J. 583 (2005). Reprinted with permission of the publisher.

the investigation, but rather was charged with conduct that resulted from the investigation. The obstruction of justice charge in this case concerned obstruction to a government agency under 18 U.S.C. §1505.

The Law of Obstruction of Justice

Although obstruction of justice statutes appear throughout the United States Code,[15] the key obstruction of justice statutes are in chapter 73 of title 18. This chapter includes an array of criminal statutes that prohibit different types of obstructive conduct. For example, specific obstruction of justice statutes pertaining to "[i]nfluencing [a] juror by writing,"[16] "[o]bstruction of court orders,"[17] and "[o]bstruction of State or local law enforcement"[18] appear in chapter 73. Obstructive conduct to legislative bodies is commonly the subject of a §1505 prosecution.[19] Congress also provides criminal penalties for specific types of obstructive conduct, such as "[o]bstruction of criminal investigations of health care offenses."[20] Recent additions by Congress, as a part of the Sarbanes-Oxley Act, include obstruction related to "[d]estruction, alteration, or falsification of records in Federal investigations and bankruptcy"[21] and "[d]estruction of corporate audit records."[22]

Clearly, prosecutors have many statutory choices in presenting charges of obstruction of justice, and oftentimes more than one obstruction statute will apply to the conduct. The enormous discretion afforded to prosecutors to choose charges, defendants, and whether to even proceed with a prosecution, is magnified when prosecutors are provided with several obstruction statutes that allow them to proceed with a prosecution for conduct that was not the subject of their initial investigation.

18 U.S.C. §1503

Section 1503[23] serves as the focal point of the obstruction of justice statutes and provides the backdrop for much of the initial law regarding obstruction of justice. Section 1503 finds its roots in an Act of 1831[24] that criminalized contemptuous conduct.[25] The statute was eventually divided, with §401 condemning "obstructive acts in the court's presence, and 18 U.S.C. §1503 contemptuous conduct away from [the] court."[26]

Initially, §1503 concentrated on obstruction of "officers, jurors, and witnesses."[27] The passage of the Victim and Witness Protection Act of 1982 transferred key aspects of the statute to new statutes, §§1512 and 1513, that were specifically designed to offer protection to witnesses. Section 1512 focuses on obstructive conduct occurring to witnesses, victims, and informants prior to a proceeding,[28] and § 1513 criminalizes retaliatory conduct against witnesses, victims, and informants.[29] Both of these statutes provide for extraterritorial jurisdiction.[30]

Section 1503 criminalizes acts of obstruction to jurors or court officers. It also includes an omnibus clause criminalizing acts of obstruction of the "due administration of justice." The key elements that a prosecutor must prove to sustain a conviction under the omnibus clause of § 1503 are: (1) "corruptly or by threats or force"; (2) endeavored; (3) "to influence, obstruct, or impede, the due administration of justice." To obstruct the "due administration of justice," it is necessary that there be a pending proceeding.[31] Additionally, the accused must know or have notice of this pending proceeding and must intend to influence, obstruct, or impede its administration.[32]

Typically, one finds obstruction of justice charges where an individual attempts to interfere with or destroy evidence related to the criminal process.[33] Sometimes, obstruction under the omnibus clause involves "encouraging or rendering false testimony."[34] Criminal defense attorneys often caution clients of the ramifications of conduct that might impede the "due administration of justice." In recent years, however, obstruction of justice has become a personal concern for criminal defense lawyers.[35] Attorneys have been convicted of obstruction of justice charges despite claims that they were advising witnesses[36] or representing their clients.[37]

For prosecutors, the crime of obstruction of justice is an offense that is relatively easy to prove. This is in part because the statute does not require an actual obstruction.[38] Under the omnibus clause of § 1503, obstruction of justice merely requires an "endeavor" to obstruct justice.[39]

Despite the ease with which prosecutors can prove obstruction cases, there are arguments that remain for defense counsel. Defense counsel has been successful in demonstrating that a defendant has not acted corruptly, a necessary element for this charge.[40] When the government fails to provide a sufficient nexus "between the false statements and the obstruction of the administration of justice," it can prove problematic to securing a conviction.[41] Some courts have also refused to allow obstruction of justice convictions to stand when the conduct forming the obstruction is a mere false statement.[42]

18 U.S.C. § 1505

Section 1505[43] of the obstruction statutes, a statute that served as one of the charges against Martha Stewart, requires there to be "a proceeding pending before a department or agency of the United States."[44] This phrase is the

major difference between § 1503 and § 1505. While § 1503 is used for prosecutions related to courts and judicially related entities such as the grand jury,
§ 1505 focuses on legislative and administrative bodies. The remaining elements of § 1503 are also required in § 1505, these being that "the defendant
knew of or had a reasonably founded belief that the proceeding was pending;
and [] the defendant corruptly endeavored to influence, obstruct, or impede
the due and proper administration of the law under which the proceeding was
pending."[45]

There is an additional parallel between § 1503 and § 1505. Like § 1503,
§ 1505 was revised as a result of the Victim and Witness Protection Act. When
the victims of the obstruction are witnesses, crime-victims, or informants,
prosecutors may use § 1512 or § 1513 as the basis for the charges.[46] Section
1505, like § 1503, retains its generic omnibus clause that allows prosecutions
when there has been an obstruction against the "due and proper administration of the law under which any pending proceeding is being had before any
department or agency of the United States."[47]

In 1996, a new subsection was added to the definition statute,[48] a statute
that supplies definitions of terms for many of the obstruction statutes located
within Title 18.[49] This new subsection, § 1515(b), offers a specific definition
of the term "corruptly" as used in § 1505.[50] The need for this new definition
can be attributed to the District of Columbia Circuit's decision in *United States
v. Poindexter*,[51] where the court held the term "corruptly" as used in § 1505 was
"too vague to provide constitutionally adequate notice that it prohibits lying
to the Congress."[52] The new definition clarifies the term "corruptly" for purposes of § 1505 so that prosecutors can continue to proceed with prosecutions
against individuals who make "false or misleading statement[s]."[53]

Materiality

Generally

Although cases do not generally require "materiality" as an element of obstruction of justice, there is a valid argument that it should be required. The
argument is premised in part on the inclusion of materiality in similar statutes.

Considering materiality in the context of a false statement statute, the
Court held that a statement that has "a natural tendency to influence, or [is]
capable of influencing, the decision of" the decision-making body to which it
was addressed" is material.[54] Thus, extraneous statements that are inconsequential to the decision being made by the decision-making body cannot be

the subject of a false statement charge.[55] It is not necessary, however, that the statement or representation actually influence the body.[56] Having the capacity to influence can be sufficient.[57] In the context of mail fraud, courts have interpreted materiality similarly.[58]

When materiality is included as an element of a statute, it serves to narrow the range of conduct that is subject to prosecution. Some statutes very clearly include materiality as an element of the offense. For example, the perjury[59] and false declarations[60] statutes both explicitly recite materiality as a required element of proof, and courts have placed the burden on the government to prove this element beyond a reasonable doubt.[61] Other statutes, however, are less certain and require courts to consider the statute's history and purpose to discern the intent of Congress.

Materiality in False Statement Statutes

In *United States v. Gaudin,*[62] a case involving the false statements statute, [63] the Supreme Court held that materiality was a question for the jury and not the judge to determine.[64] Respondents in this case were charged with violations of 18 U.S.C. § 1001 for statements made on federal loan documents. Although the trial court stated that materiality was an element of the offense, it did not permit the jury to determine whether sufficient evidence of this element had been presented by the prosecution.[65] The court of appeals reversed, finding that materiality was for the jury to decide, and the Supreme Court then affirmed. In *Gaudin* the government conceded that materiality was an element of § 1001.[66]

A case involving another false statement statute, the statute concerning making a false statement to a federally insured bank, did not have a similar resolution. In *United States v. Wells,*[67] the Supreme Court held that materiality was not an element of a crime under 18 U.S.C. § 1014. Despite the fact that most circuit courts of appeal had held that materiality was in fact an element of § 1014,[68] the Court found that "an unqualified reading of § 1014 poses no risk of criminalizing so much conduct as to suggest that Congress meant something short of the straightforward reading."[69]

In *Wells,* the Court examined the history of this statute and found that in enacting § 1014 Congress was consolidating several existing statutes. Some of these statutes contained materiality as an element and others did not include this term. The Court stated that "[t]he most likely inference in these circumstances is that Congress deliberately dropped the term 'materiality' without intending materiality to be an element of § 1014."[70]

Justice Stevens, in his dissent in *Wells,* noted that "at least 100 federal false statement statutes may be found in the United States Code."[71] While "[a]bout

42 of them contain an express materiality requirement; approximately 54 do not."[72] He expressed a view that the two categories of cases, those with the term included and those with it omitted, were indistinguishable. Since the two classes of statutes had no rationale, he believed that they all should require an element of materiality.[73] Justice Stevens stated that Congress probably intended this result, "as the Government did in *Gaudin*—that the materiality requirement would be implied wherever it was not explicit."[74] Thus, he credited the government's concession in not arguing a requirement for materiality in *Gaudin* and merely focusing on whether the question was for the jury or judge, as an admission that materiality was considered by everyone as an essential element in false statement statutes.

Materiality in Fraud Statutes

The Supreme Court was again faced with the issue of whether a statute required materiality in the case of *Neder v. United States.*[75] *Neder* involved the mail,[76] wire,[77] and bank[78] fraud statutes. The defendant, "an attorney and real estate developer," was alleged to be "engaged in a number of real estate transactions financed by fraudulently obtained bank loans" and to also be "engaged in a number of schemes involving land development fraud."[79] Despite the fact that the mail, wire, and bank fraud statutes did not have explicit language on materiality, the Court found that it was an element of these offenses.[80]

Using the "framework set forth in" *Wells*, the Court explained that the first step required examination of the language of the statute.[81] In this case, all parties agreed that materiality was not included in the language of these fraud offenses.[82] The second step, however, allows courts to interpret words using their common law meaning.[83]

In *Neder*, the Court found "that the well-settled meaning of 'fraud' required a misrepresentation or concealment of *material* fact."[84] As such, the Court found "that materiality of falsehood is an element of the federal mail fraud, wire fraud, and bank fraud statutes."[85]

In *Neder*, the Court found that not "*all* the elements of common-law fraud" should be incorporated in these new federal fraud statutes. The Court held that "[t]he common-law requirements of 'justifiable reliance' and 'damages,' for example, plainly have no place in the federal fraud statutes."[86] Materiality, on the other hand, would be required because it was not "incompatible" with the fraud statutes.[87]

Justice Stevens, writing a concurrence in the *Neder* case, referenced his remarks from his dissent in *Wells*.[88] He noted that "[t]he Court's conclusion that materiality is an element of the offenses defined in 18 U.S.C. §§ 1341,

1343, and 1344 is obviously correct."[89] In some respects his statement on materiality being required for fraud statutes was more forceful than that expressed by the majority.

In addition to Justice Stevens, who concurred in the decision, all three dissenters to the majority opinion agreed with the Court on the issue of materiality being required. Their disagreement with the Court's opinion concerned other parts of the decision.[90] As such, the *Neder* Court was unanimous in its finding that mail, wire, and bank fraud required the government to prove materiality as an element of the offense.

Materiality in Obstruction Statutes

Examining the Statutes

Like the fraud statutes, the key obstruction of justice statutes, 18 U.S.C. §§ 1503, 1505, and 1512, do not use the term materiality. In addition, courts faced with this issue have found that materiality is not an element that the government is required to prove for the substantive crime of obstruction of justice.[91] Lower courts have rejected the application of *Gaudin* to the crime of obstruction of justice.[92] Even when the charge in a case explicitly uses a term of "materiality," a district court found that 18 U.S.C. § 1505 does not require proof of materiality.[93] The Supreme Court, however, has not given explicit guidance on whether materiality should be included in obstruction statutes.

Obstruction in the Context of Sentencing

In the context of sentencing, however, a different picture emerges. In deciding whether to enhance a sentence under the federal sentencing guidelines for "Obstructing or Impeding the Administration of Justice,"[94] courts routinely examine whether a statement is material.[95] Sentencing Guideline § 3C1.1 uses language similar to that found in the obstruction statutes.[96] And like obstruction statutes under §§ 1503, 1505, and 1512(b), the guideline itself makes no mention of materiality.[97] The Commentary to the guidelines, however, uses materiality in describing "the types of conduct to which this [enhancement] applies."[98] When the conduct is premised upon a false statement or the giving of false information, it is required that there be a showing of materiality.[99]

In reflecting on this sentencing guideline, the Seventh Circuit in the case of *United States v. Buckley*[100] held that the government had to prove materiality when obstruction takes the form "of perjury or other lying" and the determination is being made as to whether to enhance a sentence because of this obstructive conduct.[101] Judge Posner, authoring this decision, stated that "a lie that is immaterial to the justice process is not a potential interference with it."[102]

Should Materiality Be Read into the Statute?

Since the obstruction statutes do not explicitly provide for materiality, they fail the first test employed by the Court in *Wells*.[103] Mere omission of materiality language in the statute, however, is not determinative of the issue. As noted by the Court in *Neder*, a common law meaning of the statute may authorize reading in a requirement of materiality.[104] Additionally, an unusually broad statute that criminalizes a vast amount of conduct may indicate Congress's desire to limit the statute.[105] Finally, it is necessary to see if a requirement of materiality is "incompatible" with the statute as a whole.

There are ample arguments that can be made for inserting materiality into obstruction statutes. This is particularly true when the obstruction is premised upon a false statement or "lying" as was alleged in the Martha Stewart case.[106]

When the obstruction is presented as a false statement, consideration needs to be given as to whether the conduct fits a mold closer to *Neder* and *Gaudin*, such that materiality should be required, or is more like *Wells*, such that a materiality requirement is not permitted. This could be considered from the perspective of the particular conduct, limiting the materiality requirement to when the obstructive conduct is premised upon a false statement. Alternatively, it could be applied to all conduct to narrow the breadth of the statute. As previously noted, when the conduct is perjury or a false statement, materiality is considered when determining a sentencing enhancement for obstructive conduct.

Some may claim that materiality is implicit in the element "corruptly endeavored to influence." This argument, however, has a serious flaw in that "corruptly endeavored to influence" is premised upon a subjective determination of what the defendant has done, as opposed to materiality, which generally is defined using an objective standard. Where a subjective presentation can be weakened when a defendant does not present personal evidence on the witness stand, an objective argument may still be viable as the jury is considering the evidence from the standpoint of a reasonable person as opposed to looking to at it solely from the perspective of the accused.

Another argument that might be made as to why materiality should not be read into obstruction statutes is that it is incompatible with the statutes because these statutes merely require an "endeavor" to obstruct justice.[107] In this respect, obstruction statutes operate similarly to attempt statutes in that "efforts to impede the processes of legal justice" may be sufficient.[108] It is not necessary that there be an actual obstruction, as success is not required.[109]

This argument, however, approaches the statute in a vacuum and fails to read the endeavor clause as part of the entire phrase, "endeavors to influence, intimidate, or impede" as used in § 1503 and § 1505 and "knowingly uses intimidation, threatens, or corruptly persuades another person, or attempts to do so," as used in § 1512(b).

Materiality can easily be found in those situations where one attempts to kill a witness who might be crucial to the government's case. Likewise, the defendant who attempts to keep a witness from presenting truthful *material* testimony before a grand jury could meet this element. Finally, in instances pertaining to the destruction of evidence, one merely needs to examine whether the destruction, if accomplished, would be material. Thus, if the evidence was not destroyed, because of either law enforcement intervention or other factors, the test of materiality would rest upon whether the evidence, if it had been destroyed, would be material to the case. As such, the term endeavor is not diametrically opposed to materiality and does not preclude prosecutions.

In the *Buckley* case, Judge Posner provides language that could easily be used for adding materiality to the substantive offense of obstruction of justice.[110] Although his language was used in the context of determining obstructive conduct for the purposes of sentencing, he directly considers endeavor or attempt conduct when he states that "because the offense is one of attempting rather than of succeeding in obstructing justice, all that is required for a lie to be material is that it could, to some reasonable probability, affect the outcome of the process."[111]

Factoring in Materiality in Obstruction Cases

Factoring materiality into obstruction of justice cases can be accomplished in one of three ways. Perhaps the most forceful and surest way of achieving this result is through legislative revision. Specifying materiality as an element in the statute will foreclose any argument of ambiguity.

Alternatively, courts could read an element of materiality into the statute. This is in keeping with the *Neder* decision where the Court read an element of materiality into three fraud statutes.[112] It also provides consistency in that obstruction conduct that increases a sentence should be interpreted in a like manner as the substantive offense. Finally, the breadth and power provided to prosecutors requires some oversight. Reading in an element of materiality limits prosecutorial discretion to using obstruction charges in instances when it is material to the investigation, but precluding their use when it would be inconsequential. In these latter instances, the government is forced to proceed with the investigation and pursue the substantive conduct that they originally considered charging.

Perhaps the easiest way to have materiality considered as an element of the crime would be for prosecutors to self impose this factor in their decision-making process. The creation of a Department of Justice ("DOJ") guideline that restricted obstruction prosecutions to those instances when they are truly necessary, as opposed to when they can merely result in a quick conviction, would provide substantial change to a criticized procedural process.[113]

The use of prosecutorial guidelines as a restraint in a prosecution is not a new innovation for the government. For example, guidelines presently exist in the DOJ restricting the bringing of Racketeer Influenced and Corrupt Organization Act ("RICO") charges.[114] Although the guidelines may not be enforceable at law, and may be overlooked by some prosecutors,[115] a policy would provide a step in the direction of using prosecutorial power wisely.

Conclusion

It is difficult to say whether the result in the trial would be the same if the jury in the *Stewart* case had received a materiality instruction for the obstruction counts. It is quite possible that the jury might have found that the statement given by Martha Stewart was in fact material to the Securities and Exchange Commission's investigation.

What is important is that the jury in this case did not have that opportunity. Instead, the prosecutor proceeded with obstruction charges that allowed the government to obtain a conviction without the need to further investigate or prosecute the underlying conduct that was originally being pursued. One has to wonder if the failure to consider materiality sacrifices important judicial values in an attempt to provide an efficient system.

Questions

1. If materiality is considered an element of obstruction of justice, should prosecutors have charged Martha Stewart with this crime?
2. Does the reversal of the conviction against Arthur Andersen, LLP, a case also premised upon an obstruction of justice charge, have any effect on the conviction against Martha Stewart?

3. Could prosecutors have used 18 U.S.C. § 1503 as the basis of the obstruction charge against Martha Stewart?

Notes

1. At the time of the indictment, Martha Stewart was "chairman (sic) of the board of directors and chief executive officer of Martha Stewart Living Omnimedia, Inc." Superseding Indictment at 1, United States v. Stewart (S.D.N.Y. Jan. 7, 2004) (No. S1 03 Cr. 717 (MGC)), http://news.findlaw.com/hdocs/docs/mstewart/usmspb10504sind.pdf [hereinafter Superseding Indictment].

2. *Id.* at 20–36. There was also a civil suit filed by the Securities Exchange Commission against Martha Stewart and Peter Bacanovic. *See* Complaint, SEC v. Stewart (S.D.N.Y. June 4, 2003) (No. 03 CV 4070 (NRB)), http://news.findlaw.com/ hdocs/docs/mstewart/secmspb60403cmp.html; *see also* Joan Macleod Heminway, *Save Martha Stewart? Observations About Equal Justice in U.S. Insider Trading Regulation*, 12 TEX. J. WOMEN & L. 247 (2003).

3. 18 U.S.C. § 371 (2000).

4. 18 U.S.C. § 1001 (2000).

5. 18 U.S.C. § 1505 (2000).

6. 15 U.S.C. § 78j(b), ff (1997); 18 U.S.C. § 2 (2000).

7. A key issue presented in Martha Stewarts appeal to the Second Circuit concerns the "barrage of pretrial leaks and in-court accusations" that "left the indelible impression that she was guilty of that offense." Brief for Defendant-Appellant Martha Stewart at 2, United States v. Stewart, reporter (2d Cir. Oct. 8, 2004) (No. 04-3953(L)-cr), http://lawprofessors.typepad.com/whitecollarcrime_blog/files/ Brief.pdf (last visited Mar. 16, 2005) [hereinafter Brief for Defendant-Appellant]. Additionally, Stewart is arguing that the district court erred in failing to permit her to respond "to those charges and prevented the jury from understanding what was—and was not—properly before it." *Id.*

8. *Id.* at 13.

9. *See* Constance L. Hays, *5 Months in Jail, and Stewart Vows, 'I'll Be Back'*, N.Y. TIMES, July 17, 2004, at A1.

10. United States v. Stewart, 433 F.3d 273 (2d Cir. 2006).

11. Brief for Defendant-Appellant, *supra* note 7, at 6.

12. *See* Kathleen F. Brickey, *Mostly Martha*, 44 WASHBURN L.J. 517 (2005).

13. *See* Transcript, *CNN Newsnight*, Aaron Brown (June 4, 2003), http://www-cgi.cnn.com/TRANSCRIPTS/0306/04/asb.00.html (last visited Mar. 16, 2005) (quoting James Comey, stating that "[t]his criminal case is about lying, lying to the FBI and lying to investors"); *see also Martha Stewart Indicted, to Step Down as CEO*, CTV.CA NEWS, http://www.ctv.ca/servlet/ArticleNews/story/CTVNews/20030605/martha_stewart_charges_030604/Entertainment?s_name= (last visited Mar. 16, 2005).

14. Superseding Indictment, *supra* note 1, at 35, http://news.findlaw.com/hdocs/docs/mstewart/usmspb10504sind.pdf.

15. *See, e.g.*, 26 U.S.C. § 7212 (2004) ("Attempts to interfere with administration of internal revenue laws").

16. 18 U.S.C. § 1504 (2004).

17. 18 U.S.C. § 1509 (2004).

18. 18 U.S.C. § 1511 (2004).

19. *Id.* § 1505 ("[o]bstruction of proceedings before departments, agencies, and committees"); *see also* United States v. Poindexter, 951 F.2d 369, 388 (D.C. Cir. 1991) (reversing § 1505 conviction).

20. 18 U.S.C. § 1518 (2004).

21. 18 U.S.C. § 1519 (2004).

22. 18 U.S.C. § 1520 (2004).

23. 18 U.S.C. § 1503 (2000) provides in part (a) of the statute:

> (a) Whoever corruptly, or by threats or force, or by any threatening letter or communication, endeavors to influence, intimidate, or impede any grand or petit juror, or officer in or of any court of the United States, or officer who may be serving at any examination or other proceeding before any United States magistrate judge or other committing magistrate, in the discharge of his duty, or injures any such grand or petit juror in his person or property on account of any verdict or indictment assented to by him, or on account of his being or having been such juror, or injures any such officer, magistrate judge, or other committing magistrate in his person or property on account of the performance of his official duties, or corruptly or by threats or force, or by any threatening letter or communication, influences, obstructs, or impedes, or endeavors to influence, obstruct, or impede, the due administration of justice, shall be punished as provided in subsection (b). If the offense under this section occurs in connection with a trial of a criminal case, and the act in violation of this section involves the threat of physical force or physical force, the maximum term of imprisonment which may be imposed for the offense shall be the higher of that otherwise provided by law or the maximum term that could have been imposed for any offense charged in such case.

Id.

24. The Judiciary Act of 1789, when it established the lower courts, gave these courts contempt powers. The Act of 1831 was designed to curtail the powers initially given the courts, as a result of what Congress considered to be an abuse of the contempt powers. Congress was perturbed with Judge James H. Peck's use of the contempt powers. When he was tried for impeachment, "[m]embers of Congress emphasized ... that the contempt power should be limited to those situations in which it was necessary for the preservation of judicial functions." United States v. Reed, 773 F.2d 477, 485 (2d Cir. 1985). Following that trial, the Act of March 2, 1831 was passed that limited contempt powers and divided the statute into two parts. Part one pertained to contempt, and part two was the predecessor to 18 U.S.C. § 1503. *Id.*

25. *See* Felix Frankfurter & James M. Landis, *Power of Congress over Procedure in Criminal Contempts in "Inferior" Federal Courts—A Study in Separation of Powers*, 37 HARV. L. REV. 1010, 1026–27 (1923).

26. *See* United States v. Essex, 407 F.2d 214, 217 (1969).

27. *See generally* ELLEN S. PODGOR & JEROLD H. ISRAEL, WHITE COLLAR CRIME IN A NUTSHELL 86 (3d ed. 2004).

28. 18 U.S.C. § 1512 (2000).

29. 18 U.S.C. § 1513 (2000).

30. *See id.* § 1512(h) (2000), 18 U.S.C. § 1513(d) (2000).

31. Sarah Roadcap, Note, *Obstruction of Justice*, 41 AM. CRIM. L. REV. 911, 915 (2004). There is disagreement among the circuits on what constitutes a pending proceeding. *Id.* at

916–18. Additionally, two circuits have claimed that there is no requirement for a pending proceeding. *Id.*

32. *See* United States v. Aguilar, 515 U.S. 593, 599 (1995) (requiring knowledge that the actions "are likely to affect the judicial proceeding").

33. *See, e.g.,* United States v. Howard, 569 F.2d 1331, 1333 (5th Cir. 1978) (obstructing justice by selling secret grand jury transcripts).

34. *See, e.g.,* United States v. Griffin, 589 F.2d 200, 204 (5th Cir. 1979) (finding that perjury by a witness can constitute obstruction of justice); *see also* Alicia M. Dixon, et al., Note, *Obstruction of Justice,* 34 AM. CRIM. L. REV. 815, 821 (1997).

35. *See* United States v. Atkin, 107 F.3d 1213 (6th Cir. 1997); United States v. Lahey, 55 F.3d 1289 (7th Cir. 1995); United States v. Silverman, 745 F.2d 1386 (11th Cir. 1984). *See generally Lawyer Convicted In Obstruction-of-Justice Trial,* CHICAGO DAILY LAW BULLETIN, June 12, 1997, at 2; James Jay Hogan & G. Richard Strafer, *The (Shrinking) Line Between Zealous Advocacy and Obstruction of Justice,* 1996 A.B.A. SEC. OF CRIMINAL JUSTICE AND CTR. FOR CONTINUING LEGAL EDUC. A-39.

36. *See, e.g.,* Cole v. United States, 329 F.2d 437 (9th Cir. 1964). In *Maness v. Meyers,* however, the Supreme Court found that a lawyer was not in contempt where in a civil proceeding the lawyer was alleged to have counseled "a witness in good faith to refuse to produce court-ordered materials on the ground that the materials may tend to incriminate the witness in another proceeding." 419 U.S. 449, 465 (1975). The Court held that the attorney "may not be penalized even though his advice caused the witness to disobey the court's order." *Id.*

37. *See, e.g.,* United States v. Cintolo, 818 F.2d 980 (1st Cir. 1987). Concerns of criminal defense attorneys are not limited to their exposure to obstruction of justice charges. *See generally* Paul G. Wolfteich, Note, *Making Criminal Defense a Crime Under 18 U.S.C. Section 1957,* 41 VAND. L. REV. 843 (1988).

38. *See* United States v. Brimberry, 744 F.2d 580, 583 (7th Cir. 1984) ("[T]he impossibility of accomplishing the goal of an obstruction of justice does not prevent a prosecution for the endeavor to accomplish the goal." (citation omitted)).

39. *See* Catrino v. United States, 176 F.2d 884, 887 (9th Cir. 1949) (endeavoring to have someone commit perjury can be sufficient to constitute obstruction of justice).

40. *See* United States v. Brand, 775 F.2d 1460, 1460 (11th Cir. 1985) (reversing convictions of obstruction of justice).

41. United States v. Thomas, 916 F.2d 647, 654 (11th Cir. 1990) (finding insufficient evidence that "the statements had a natural and probable effect of impeding justice"); *see also* United States v. Aguilar, 515 U.S. 593 (1995).

42. *See* United States v. Fassnacht, 332 F.3d 440, 448 (7th Cir. 2003) (finding that the conduct went beyond being a mere false statement).

43. The first part of the statute pertains to the Antitrust Civil Process Act. The second paragraph of the statute states:

> Whoever corruptly, or by threats or force, or by any threatening letter or communication influences, obstructs, or impedes or endeavors to influence, obstruct, or impede the due and proper administration of the law under which any pending proceeding is being had before any department or agency of the United States, or the due and proper exercise of the power of inquiry under which any inquiry or investigation is being had by either House, or any committee of either House or any joint committee of the Congress—

Shall be fined under this title or imprisoned not more than five years, or both.

18 U.S.C. § 1505 (2004).

44. United States v. Sprecher, 783 F. Supp. 133, 163 (S.D.N.Y. 1992) (holding premised on attorneys giving false testimony to a government agency).

45. *Id.*

46. *See supra* notes 27–30 and accompanying text.

47. Section 1505 also includes the language: "or the due and proper exercise of the power of inquiry under which any inquiry or investigation is being had by either House, or any committee of either House or any joint committee of the Congress." 18 U.S.C. § 1505.

48. Pub. L. No. 104-292, § 3(2), 110 Stat. 3459 (1996).

49. 18 U.S.C. § 1515 (2000).

50. Section 1515(b) provides: "[a]s used in [§] 1505, the term 'corruptly' means acting with an improper purpose, personally or by influencing another, including making a false or misleading statement, or withholding, concealing, altering, or destroying a document or other information." *Id.*

51. 951 F.2d 369 (D.C. Cir. 1991).

52. *Id.* at 379.

53. 18 U.S.C. § 1515(b).

54. Kungys v. United States, 485 U.S. 759, 770 (1988) (citations omitted).

55. In the Supreme Court decision of *Neder v. United States*, 527 U.S. 1 (1999), the Court referenced in a footnote the definition of materiality as used in the RESTATEMENT (SECOND) OF TORTS section 538 (1977), which provides that a matter is material if:

'(a) a reasonable man would attach importance to its existence or nonexistence in determining his choice of action in the transaction in question; or

(b) the maker of the representation knows or has reason to know that its recipient regards or is likely to regard the matter as important in determining his choice of action, although a reasonable man would not so regard it.'

Neder, 527 U.S. at 22 n.5.

56. *See, e.g.,* United States v. Waldemer, 50 F.3d 1379, 1382 (7th Cir. 1995) (holding that "[m]ateriality only calls for the lie to be a potential impediment, not an actual impediment, of the grand jury's inquiry"); United States v. Blandford, 33 F.3d 685, 705 (6th Cir. 1994) (rejecting defendant's claim that statements were not material); United States v. Johnson, 937 F.2d 392, 396 (8th Cir. 1991) (stating that actual reliance or success is not necessary).

57. *See, e.g.,* United States v. Pettigrew, 77 F.3d 1500, 1511 n.1 (5th Cir. 1996); United States v. Beuttenmuller, 29 F.3d 973, 982 (5th Cir. 1994) *overruled on other grounds* (finding that "[t]he concealment []must simply have the capacity to impair or pervert the functioning of a government agency" (quotation omitted)).

58. *See, e.g.,* United States v. Henningsen, 387 F.3d 585, 589 (7th Cir. 2004) (finding a sufficient scheme to defraud for purposes of mail fraud); United States v. Fernandez, 282 F.3d 500, 509 (7th Cir. 2002) (finding that the jury was adequately apprised that materiality was an element of the crime).

59. 18 U.S.C. § 1621 (2000).

60. 18 U.S.C. § 1623 (2000).

61. *See* United States v. Bednar, 728 F.2d 1043, 1047 (8th Cir. 1984) (holding that "the government has the burden of proving that the defendant's statements were material to is-

sues considered by the grand jury" (citations omitted)); United States v. Gremillion, 464 F.2d 901, 905 (5th Cir. 1972) ("[T]he Government has the burden of proving materiality" (citation omitted)).

62. 515 U.S. 506 (1995).

63. 18 U.S.C. § 1001 (2000).

64. *Gaudin*, 515 U.S. at 522–23.

65. *Id.* at 508–10.

66. *Id.* at 523. A concurring opinion of Justices Rehnquist, O'Connor, and Breyer noted that the government conceded that materiality is an element of the false statement statute. These Justices then state that "[c]urrently, there is a conflict among the Courts of Appeals over whether materiality is an element of the offense created by the second clause of § 1001." *Id.* at 524.

67. 519 U.S. 482 (1997).

68. *Id.* at 486 n.3.

69. *Id.* at 498–99.

70. *Id.* at 493. The Court also discussed precedent for the statutes that were consolidated by the enactment of § 1014. *Id.* at 494–95 (discussing the Court's holding in *Kay v. United States*, 303 U.S. 1 (1938)).

71. *Id.* at 505.

72. *Id.*

73. *Id.* at 505–09.

74. *Id.* at 509.

75. 527 U.S. 1 (1999).

76. 18 U.S.C. § 1341 (2004).

77. 18 U.S.C. § 1343 (2004).

78. 18 U.S.C. § 1344 (2000).

79. *Neder*, 527 U.S. at 4–5.

80. *Id.* at 25.

81. *Id.* at 20.

82. *Id.*

83. *Id.* at 21–22.

84. *Id.* at 22 (emphasis in original).

85. *Id.* at 25.

86. *Id.* at 24–25.

87. *Id.* at 25.

88. *See supra* notes 71–74 and accompanying text.

89. *Neder*, 527 U.S. at 29–30.

90. The dissenters "believe[d] that depriving a criminal defendant of the right to have the jury determine his guilt of the crime charged—which necessarily means his commission of *every element* of the crime charged—can never be harmless." *Id.* at 30.

91. *See* United States v. Mullins, 22 F.3d 1365, 1370 (6th Cir. 1994) (holding that in a § 1503 prosecution "the government need not prove, as an element of the crime, that the alternations made in response to a grand jury subpoena were relevant to the grand jury's investigation").

92. *See, e.g.*, United States v. Rankin, 1 F. Supp. 2d 445, 454 (E.D. Pa. 1998) (finding that materiality is not required for § 1503 and that "*Gaudin* is irrelevant").

93. *See* United States v. Sprecher, 783 F. Supp. 133, 163 (S.D.N.Y. 1992).

94. U.S. Sentencing Guidelines Manual §3C1.1 (2004). Although the guidelines are no longer mandatory, they are still to be used by courts in an advisory capacity. *See* United States v. Booker, 125 S. Ct. 738 (2005).

95. *See, e.g.,* United States v. White, 368 F.3d 911, 916 (7th Cir. 2004) (noting that if the perjury "could affect, to some reasonable probability, the outcome of the judicial process," it can be "a form of obstruction of justice"); United States v. Saunders, 359 F.3d 874 (7th Cir. 2004) (stating that if the perjury was "on an immaterial matter, even in court, there would be no obstruction of justice"); United States v. Anderson, 259 F.3d 853, 879 (7th Cir. 2001) (enhancing a sentence premised upon perjury under the obstruction guideline).

96. It states:

If (A) the defendant willfully obstructed or impeded, or attempted to obstruct or impede, the administration of justice during the course of the investigation, prosecution, or sentencing of the instant offense of conviction, and (B) the obstructive conduct related to (i) the defendant's offense of conviction and any relevant conduct; or (ii) a closely related offense, increase the offense level by 2 levels.

U.S. Sentencing Guidelines Manual §3C1.1 (2004).

97. *Id.*

98. *Id.* at cmt. n.4(d), (f)–(h) (2004).

99. *Id.* at cmt. n.4. Application notes f, g, and h all relate to false statement or perjurious forms of conduct. *Id.* at cmt. n.4(f)–(h). It can be argued, however, that note 4(d) requires a "material hindrance to the official investigation or prosecution of the instant offense or the sentencing of the offender." *Id.* at cmt. n.4(d).

100. 192 F.3d 708, 710 (7th Cir. 1999).

101. *Id.* at 710.

102. *Id.*

103. *See supra* notes 67–70 and accompanying text.

104. Neder v. United States, 527 U.S. 1, 21–22 (1999). Additionally, courts routinely insert a *mens rea* term into a statute when Congress omits such specific language in the statute. *See* United States v. Staples, 511 U.S. 600, 607 (1994) (finding that since the statute was not a public welfare offense, insertion of a *mens rea* term was appropriate).

105. *See* United States v. Wells, 519 U.S. 482, 498–99 (1997).

106. *See supra* note 13. In the case of Martha Stewart, materiality was included in the charge under the false statement statute, but omitted in the charge of obstruction of justice. For the obstruction count, the jury was instructed in part,

First, that before the defendant you are considering was interviewed in 2002, as set forth in the indictment, a proceeding was pending before the SEC; Second, that the defendant you are considering knew that a proceeding was pending before the SEC; and that the interviews were part of the proceedings; and

Third, that the defendant you are considering corruptly endeavored to influence, obstruct or impede the due and proper exercise of the power of inquiry or investigation of the SEC.

Instructions, United States v. Martha Stewart, Tr. 4867. The instructions included additional paragraphs on each of the above elements, but materiality was not used as a term in this portion of the instruction. *Id.*

107. *See* United States v. Lench, 806 F.2d 1443, 1445 (9th Cir. 1986) (stating that only an endeavor to conceal is necessary for § 1503).

108. *See* Daniel A. Shtob, Note, *Corruption of a Term: The Problematic Nature of 18 U.S.C. § 1512(c)*, 57 VAND. L. REV. 1429 1443 (2004) (stating that "'endeavor' as used in [§] 1503 signifies a standard lower than that of attempt and, while like attempt it does not require success").

109. *See* United States v. Ruggiero, 934 F.2d 440, 446 (2d Cir. 1991) (finding that § 1503 requires only an endeavor and not success).

110. 192 F.3d 708, 710 (1999).

111. *Id.* at 710.

112. *See* Neder v. United States, 527 U.S. 1 (1999); *supra* notes 75–90 and accompanying text.

113. *See* Jonathan D. Glater, *Corporate Conduct: The Strategy; On Wall Street Today, a Break from the Past*, N.Y. TIMES, May 4, 2004, at C1. (discussing coverup crimes).

114. *See* U.S. DEPT. OF JUSTICE, UNITED STATES ATTORNEYS' MANUAL § 9-110.200 (1997).

115. Ellen S. Podgor, *Department of Justice Guidelines: Balancing "Discretionary Justice,"* 13 CORNELL J.L & PUB. POL'Y 167, 169 (2004) (discussing the uses and abuses of Department of Justice guidelines).

CHAPTER 8

SHOULD MARTHA STEWART'S RULE 10b-5 CHARGE HAVE GONE TO THE JURY?*

Joan MacLeod Heminway

Martha Stewart's February 27, 2004 acquittal on a charge of securities fraud by a federal trial court judge[1] may well have been the brightest spot in her criminal trial. But was the court's acquittal of Stewart correct as a matter of law?[2] This chapter explores the answer to that question. Specifically, the chapter examines the legal basis for the court's opinion acquitting Stewart of the criminal securities fraud charge before handing the remainder of the case to the jury. This examination requires a specific application of the scienter element of securities fraud to the facts of the *Stewart* case in the context of the judicial review standards for granting a motion to acquit. The chapter concludes by making related observations about the *Stewart* case and other Rule 10b-5 cases like it that are based on the disclosure of personal, rather than corporate, facts.

The Government's Failed Case

The securities fraud charge brought against Stewart in Count Nine of her June 2003 indictment (as superseded in January 2004, the "Indictment"),[3] is based on alleged violations of Section 10(b) of the Securities Exchange Act of 1934, as amended (the "1934 Act"),[4] and Rule 10b-5 adopted by the Securi-

---

* This chapter is derived from *Martha Stewart Saved! Insider Violations of Rule 10b-5 for Misrepresented or Undisclosed Personal Facts or Transactions*, originally published at 65 MD. L. REV. 380 (2006), and is included here with the permission of the publisher, the Maryland Law Review.

ties and Exchange Commission (the "SEC") under Section 10(b) ("Rule 10b-5").[5] The Indictment avers that Stewart made four separate false statements to the public about the reasons why she sold 3,928 shares of stock of ImClone Systems Incorporated on December 27, 2001, and that these false statements deceived investors in the publicly traded stock of Martha Stewart Living Omnimedia, Inc., the corporation of which Stewart then was Chief Executive Officer.[6] Stewart's alleged misrepresentations include a June 6, 2002 statement made by Stewart, through a representative, to *The Wall Street Journal* (published on June 7, 2002),[7] two press releases (one issued by Stewart on June 12, 2002 and one issued by Stewart on June 18, 2002),[8] and a public reading by Stewart of the June 18th press release at a conference for securities analysts and investors.[9] Each statement offers the same explanation concerning Stewart's December 2001 stock trade, but the last three statements add facts to the basic story.

The government's securities fraud case against Stewart was founded on the three essential elements of a criminal claim under Rule 10b-5: (1) manipulative or deceptive conduct based on misstatements of material fact; (2) made in connection with a purchase or sale of securities; (3) with scienter.[10] The prosecution was required to prove each of these elements "beyond a reasonable doubt,"[11] a higher standard of proof than the "preponderance of the evidence" standard applicable in civil actions under Rule 10b-5.[12] The court granted Stewart's motion for acquittal based on the government's failure to present sufficient evidence of scienter in light of the applicable burden of proof. However, the opinion also summarizes the evidence as to the other two elements. Essentially, the court found that the government delivered at trial what it promised in the Indictment.

Manipulation or Deception

The court's opinion acquitting Stewart finds facts relating to each of the four allegedly false public statements underlying the government's securities fraud charges.

The June 6th Public Statement

The court indicates that the government proved the timing and content of the events relating to the June 7, 2002 *Wall Street Journal* article at trial.[13] Because Stewart's motion for acquittal did not focus on the truth of the statements she made to the *Journal*, the court did not summarize in its opinion the evidence supporting the government's contention that Stewart's June 6th representations were, in fact, false or misleading.[14] As to the government's support for the materiality of Stewart's June 6th statement, the court found the applicable facts to be as stated in the Indictment.[15] The court also found that evidence had been introduced at trial that substantiated the government's contention in the Indictment with respect to stock-price effects of the first public disclosure of Stewart's December 2001 ImClone stock trade.[16]

The June 12 Press Release

In finding the facts adduced at trial, the court's opinion granting Stewart's motion for acquittal quotes the June 12, 2002 press release, substantiating the government's allegations about its date and substance.[17] Again, the court did not summarize in its opinion the evidence supporting the government's contention that the June 12, 2002 statement was false or misleading, since this contention was not at issue in Stewart's motion for acquittal.[18] The court's findings of fact regarding the materiality of the June 7, 2002 statement also support the materiality of the June 12, 2002 statement.[19]

The June 18th Press Release and the June 19th Presentation

In its opinion acquitting Stewart, the trial court summarizes the facts about the June 18, 2002 statement by noting that "[a]t the close of business on June 18, 2002, Stewart issued a third statement that essentially repeated the June 12th statement, only adding that she was cooperating fully with the investigations."[20] Without addressing the truth or completeness of the June 18th press release,[21] the court also found that it had been read by Stewart at the June 19th conference, "a forum for the executives of media corporations to update the investment community about their financial health."[22] The opinion further states that the conference was "attended primarily by securities analysts and portfolio managers. Investors were also present."[23] Again, given the substantially similar nature of the June 18th and June 19th public statements to the June 12th and June 6th communications, the facts found in the trial court's opinion that support the materiality of the earlier statements also support the materiality of the facts conveyed in the June 18th press release and the June 19th republication of those same facts.[24]

"In Connection With" a Purchase or Sale of Securities

The court also found facts that show some linkage between the four public statements at issue in the securities fraud charge and purchases or sales of securities. Specifically, in granting Stewart's motion for acquittal on the Rule 10b-5 charge, the judge noted and evaluated evidence that reflected the public company status of MSLO.[25] The court's opinion also references evidence that would allow a reasonable jury to make an inference regarding the possible and actual impact that public statements and other publicly available information may have and have had on the public market for MSLO common stock.[26] The court does not, however, find that the evidence adduced by the government at trial supports a reasonable jury inference that Stewart actually intended to deceive public investors in MSLO in making her public statements.[27] In fact, the court notes evidence to the contrary in the text of its opinion.[28]

Scienter

The facts in the opinion supporting scienter are too numerous to set forth in full here, but they parallel, to a substantial extent, the statement of the government's case in the Indictment. The inferences that the court finds permissible on the basis of those facts include:

- "that Stewart had a significant financial stake in MSLO;"[29]
- "that Stewart was aware of the market price of her company's stock and of matters that could affect the price of that stock;"[30]
- "that Stewart was aware of the importance of her reputation to the continued health of MSLO;"[31]
- "that Stewart believed that the price of MSLO was falling in response to the negative publicity about the investigations" of Stewart in connection with the sale of her ImClone shares;[32] and
- that some MSLO executives had concerns about the effect of the negative publicity on the company's business that were not immediately tied to the falling stock price."[33]

Importantly, however, the court finds that the prosecution's case is fundamentally flawed in that "the Government had offered no evidence that Stewart evinced a concern for the price of MSLO stock at any time during the relevant period"[34] and that no reasonable inferences of intent can be drawn in this regard from the evidence adduced at trial.[35]

Saving Martha Stewart: A Good Thing?[36]

This part of the chapter examines the legal basis for the judge's decision to grant Stewart's motion for acquittal under Rule 29 of the Federal Rules of Criminal Procedure ("Rule 29").[37] This judicial decision is important for at least two reasons. First, by granting the motion to acquit, the court denied the jury the opportunity to find the facts and decide the case. The government cannot appeal Stewart's judgment of acquittal (because an appeal would subject Stewart to double jeopardy).[38] Accordingly, this action by the judge completely foreclosed criminal securities fraud liability on the part of Stewart for her alleged misrepresentations. Second, the court's opinion granting Stewart's acquittal has substantive import for, among others, practitioners (including transactional business lawyers, as well as litigators in the public and private spheres), judges, Congress, and the SEC. The following sections first summarize the law applicable to the court's opinion and then analyze the court's opinion in light of that law.

Law Applicable to a Judgment of Acquittal

A Rule 29 motion asks for acquittal of a criminal defendant because the government has failed to prove its case.[39] To decide a Rule 29 motion

> the evidence is to be viewed in the light most favorable to the prosecution and, in appraising its sufficiency, it is not necessary that the ... court be convinced beyond a reasonable doubt of the guilt of the defendant. The question is whether there is substantial evidence upon which a jury might justifiably find the defendant guilty beyond a reasonable doubt.[40]

"Another way of expressing the same rule is that the motion for judgment of acquittal must be granted when the evidence, viewed in the light most favorable to the government, is so scant that the jury could only speculate as to the defendant's guilt ... and is such that a reasonably-minded jury must have a reasonable doubt as to the defendant's guilt."[41] The court's role is to determine whether the prosecution's evidence, taken as a whole, could support a conviction by a "reasonable" jury.[42] A conviction requires proof of each element of the crime beyond a reasonable doubt.[43] The court must take pains not to appropriate the jury's task.[44] Rule 29 motions are rarely granted.[45]

The Correctness and Efficacy of the Judge's Acquittal of Stewart

In rendering its February 27, 2004 opinion acquitting Stewart of securities fraud, the court acknowledges that its role is to "determine whether the record evidence could reasonably support a finding of guilt beyond a reasonable doubt."[46] The standard that the court initially cites as applicable to her decision requires that she "determine whether upon the evidence giving full play to the right of the jury to determine credibility, weigh the evidence, and draw justifiable inferences of fact, a reasonable mind might fairly conclude guilt beyond a reasonable doubt."[47] Interestingly, this formulation of the applicable decisionmaking standard is relatively old and potentially more defendant-friendly than others,[48] although the court twice restates the applicable standard in a less slanted manner.[49] It is unclear from the opinion whether any particular articulation of the applicable decisionmaking standard most influenced the court's decision to acquit Stewart of securities fraud, but it is possible that her initial statement of the standard played a role in the outcome of the case.

In its opinion granting Stewart's motion for an acquittal, the *Stewart* court focuses its analysis on the scienter element of the government's case. The court finds that the facts adduced by the prosecution at trial fall short of proving beyond a reasonable doubt that Stewart acted with the scienter required under Rule 10b-5 and the willfulness required by Section 32(a) of the 1934 Act.[50] Specifically, the court concludes that a jury would have to speculate in order to find beyond a reasonable doubt that Stewart acted with the required state of mind—the intent to manipulate the price of MSLO's stock or deceive MSLO's investors.[51]

Two aspects of the court's opinion, taken together, raise questions about the correctness of its holding and undercut the efficacy of that holding. First (and most importantly), the court fails to adequately explain and support its view of the difference between a "justifiable inference"[52] (which a jury is permitted to make in finding guilt beyond a reasonable doubt) and speculation[53] (which a jury is not permitted to do in finding guilt beyond a reasonable doubt) in the context of proof of scienter or willfulness.[54] Moreover, in light of the weakness of its reasoning on the scienter element, the court should have been more inclusive in the matters addressed in its opinion. Specifically, the court's exclusive focus on scienter ignores alternative bases for an acquittal—other questionable elements of the government's case against Stewart—including most importantly whether Stewart's misrepresentations were made in connection with a purchase or sale of securities (a matter to which the court refers, albeit indirectly, in its opinion).[55] The collective impact of these attributes of the opinion is that the court shortcuts its reasoning in a manner that makes its decision appear somewhat goal-oriented, weakening its impact, if not its validity.

The Meaning of Scienter

Scienter, the state of mind requirement under Rule 10b-5 is somewhat ill-defined. Neither the statutory law nor the rule itself expressly requires that an actor have a particular state of mind when misrepresenting material facts in a deceptive or manipulative manner.[56] Accordingly, court interpretations have both established the scienter requirement and defined its content.

In general, scienter represents an intent to manipulate or deceive;[57] a defendant must be more than merely negligent in order to violate Rule 10b-5.[58] How much more, however, is still a matter of some debate. The Supreme Court has not yet ruled on whether recklessness may be sufficient, although it has alluded to the possibility that reckless behavior violates the rule.[59] Most federal courts generally acknowledge that recklessness is sufficient to meet the scienter requirement under Rule 10b-5.[60] Some courts require a high level of recklessness to ensure that the appropriate level of intent is satisfied.[61] In general, however, a successful claimant in a Rule 10b-5 action must establish that the defendant was aware of the "true state of affairs and appreciated the propensity of the misstatement or omission to mislead"[62] or acted with reckless disregard for the truth.[63]

Reasonable Inferences or Speculation?

In addressing the government's evidence of scienter, the court's opinion relies on a critical distinction—that between justifiable inferences from evidence adduced at trial and speculation. In its opinion, the court sets forth the facts that it believes the government has proven at trial and the reasonable inferences that the jury could make from those facts.[64] The court finds that the prosecution has not proven its case.[65] The court then states "that a reasonable juror could not, without resorting to speculation and surmise, find beyond a reasonable doubt that Stewart's purpose was to influence the market in MSLO securities."[66]

The court's reasoning in support of its opinion is conclusory. For example, in response to each of the government's arguments that an inference of scienter can be drawn from the context in which Stewart's statements were made, the court merely restates the proven facts and asserts that they do not constitute evidence of, or allow reasonable inferences as to, Stewart's intent.[67] The court does not describe the logical disconnect between the evidence adduced at trial, including permissible inferences drawn from that evidence, and the state of mind requisite to a criminal violation of Rule 10b-5. The court's approach is particularly disquieting as applied to Stewart's fourth misrepresentation—the reading of the June 18, 2002 press release at the June 19, 2002 conference attended by analysts and investors—which the court classifies as "a closer question."[68] Certainly in the case of this fourth misrepresentation (but also, to some extent, as to the other alleged misrepresentations) the facts adduced by the government at trial appear to be sufficient to establish beyond a reasonable doubt that Stewart could foresee the potential market impact of a misstatement.... [69] Under the circumstances, is it not possible that a jury would find that Stewart's actions in making false statements to the press, the public, and the analyst and investor communities were at least reckless?

Given the magnitude of the court's decision to grant Stewart an acquittal and the acknowledged closeness of the question as to whether the government may have proven its case against Stewart on the scienter element (at least with respect to the statements made at the June 19, 2002 conference), the court's reasoning is missing important definitional links, links that would help the court establish and clarify its view of the difference between justifiable, rational, or reasonable inferences and mere speculation, as each relate to this case. Admittedly, the distinction is a difficult one.[70] Fortunately, some guidance in this regard is provided by courts in other jurisdictions and contexts.

For example, in the civil context,[71] one federal district court roots the definition of a "reasonable inference" in logic and probability.

> The line between a reasonable inference that may permissibly be drawn by a jury from basic facts in evidence and an impermissible speculation is not drawn by judicial idiosyncracies [sp]. The line is drawn by the laws of logic. If there is an experience of logical probability that an ultimate fact will follow a stated narrative or historical fact, then the jury is given the opportunity to draw a conclusion because there is a reasonable probability that the conclusion flows from the proven facts.[72]

Another federal circuit court defines "reasonable" inferences as "inferences which may be drawn from the evidence without resort to speculation."[73] The same court notes that a civil case should be decided by the court, rather than a jury, "[w]hen the evidence is so one-sided as to leave no room for any reasonable difference of opinion as to how the case should be decided."[74] Of course, "[w]hen the record contains no proof beyond speculation to support the verdict, judgment as a matter of law is appropriate."[75] Yet, "[a]n inference is not unreasonable simply because it is based in part on conjecture, for an inference by definition is at least partially conjectural,"[76] but "an inference is unreasonable if it is at war with uncontradicted or unimpeached facts."[77] Although these judicial pronouncements regarding reasonable inferences were made in a civil law context and are not binding on the *Stewart* court, they are nevertheless instructive. Among other things, these defining statements indicate both that the evidence must be exceptionally weak in order for speculation to be necessary (and reasonable inference to be impossible) and that, by way of contrast, the meaning of the word "speculation" may be critical to a court's decision on a Rule 29 motion.

What, then, constitutes speculation? "Speculation" is (somewhat frustratingly) defined as "an act or instance of speculating."[78] Among other things, to "speculate" is "to take [something] to be true on the basis of insufficient evidence."[79] The concept of speculation often is tied to the related concepts of conjecturing,[80] guessing[81] or surmising[82] when it is found in decisional law under Rule 29 (including in the *Stewart* opinion).[83]

Based on these definitions and a review of the court's opinion, it is not clear that the court in the *Stewart* case properly understood the concept of a reasonable inference or was able to effectively separate inferences from speculation. Some of the court's trouble in this regard may well be attributable to its failure to clarify the contents of the scienter requirement on which the court decided the Rule 29 motion. Any lack of clarity on exactly what the government needed to prove, would make it easier for the court to find that the government's case was similarly unclear. Seemingly, however, the proven facts and permissible inferences noted by the court in its opinion constitute "substantial evidence"[84] of Stewart's criminal intent; certainly, one would not term them "scant."[85] The fact that the evidence is largely circumstantial is not a barrier to a jury determination.[86]

More particularly, one cannot say that, given the evidence adduced at trial, the government failed to prove, beyond a reasonable doubt, facts that, when taken in the light most favorable to the prosecution and combined with the inferences cited as permissible by the court, constitute the requisite state of mind for a criminal proceeding under Rule 10b-5. The adduced facts and permissible inferences[87] referenced by the court apparently would permit a reasonable juror to fairly conclude that the government proved its case on scienter beyond a reasonable doubt without the jury having to speculate, conjecture, guess, or surmise. Specifically, a reasonable juror could fairly find that Stewart's significant personal, financial interest in the price of MSLO's securities,[88] together with her knowledge of the market for MSLO securities,[89] her known effect on the pricing of MSLO's publicly traded securities,[90] her direction of inaccurate and misleading statements to investors (among others),[91] and her acknowledgement of the interest of those investors in the content of those statements[92] prove beyond a reasonable doubt that Stewart had the requisite level of intent to manipulate the market for MSLO's securities or deceive MSLO's investors.[93] The government's proof arguably establishes beyond a reasonable doubt that there is a reasonable probability that one or more of Stewart's alleged misstatements was made with the requisite intent.[94] Although it would be helpful if the jury also had before it evidence that Stewart was concerned about the market price of MSLO securities at the time she was making these statements, that evidence is not an essential component to the government's case.[95] The court should have left the securities fraud charge to the jury for decision.[96] The court's decision smacks of jury preemption.

Omission of an Analysis of the "In Connection With" Element

One also might question whether the court most effectively made its case by focusing its analysis exclusively on the scienter element. Presumably, the court's decision to focus on this element reflects its determination that scienter is the only—or at least the clearest—aspect of the case that the government did not prove beyond a reasonable doubt.[97]

Yet, interestingly, the same speculation that the court finds necessary to the government's case on scienter also provides an important, if not necessary, link between Stewart's public representations about the sale of her ImClone shares and the purchase and sale of MSLO's securities. In other words, if the government failed to prove beyond a reasonable doubt that Stewart "evinced a concern for the price of the MSLO stock at any time during the relevant period,"[98] that same failure makes it more difficult, if not impossible, for a reasonable juror to fairly conclude that Stewart's statements had the requisite connection with market transactions in MSLO's securities under Rule 10b-5.

The "in connection with" element of a Rule 10b-5 claim is the critical component of securities fraud that distinguishes it from other forms of manipulative, deceptive, and fraudulent conduct.[99] Although this element under Rule 10b-5 is intended to be read broadly,[100] the key federal court decisions illuminating the "in connection with" element do place certain (albeit sometimes contradictory) limits on the nature of the required nexus. The Supreme Court has said that the element is satisfied when the identified deception, manipulation, or fraud "coincides with" or "touches" a securities transaction;[101] the U.S. Court of Appeals for the Second Circuit looks for manipulative or deceptive conduct on which a reasonable investor would rely.[102]

Accordingly, absent factual proof or justifiable inference that Stewart was worried about the price of MSLO's publicly traded stock, the government may not have proven beyond a reasonable doubt to a rational juror that Stewart's misrepresentations about her private transaction in ImClone's securities "coincide" with[103] or "touch"[104] the public sales of MSLO's stock. Perhaps Stewart's misstatements are not manipulative or deceptive conduct on which a reasonable investor would rely.[105] Although Stewart's Rule 29 motion argued that any misrepresentation made by Stewart was not made in connection with the purchase or sale of MSLO's securities, there is no analysis of the "in connection with" element in the court's opinion.[106]

Judgments that the court makes in its opinion also could have been used by the court in attacking the government's case with respect to the "in connection with" requirement. Most importantly, in its reasoning on the scienter element, the court expressly acknowledges the weakness of any connection between Stewart's alleged misrepresentations and the public market for MSLO's securities. The court notes that Stewart's public statements "lack a direct connection to the supposed purpose of the alleged deception"[107] and "only circuitously relate to the purpose of deceiving investors in MSLO securities."[108] To the extent that the nexus between Stewart's public statements and any alleged manipulative or deceptive purpose or intent that she may have had in making them is tenuous, the connection between her statements and any trading in MSLO's securities necessarily would be similarly weak. Conversely, if Stewart had a manipulative or deceptive intent, she would have had to intend the necessary consequence of her actions[109]—namely, public trading in MSLO's securities resulting from her public statements. The court could have strengthened its decision or more clearly exposed its flaws by broadening the scope of inquiry to include a discussion of and decision on the "in connection with" element.

Observations on the *Stewart* Case and Other Cases Based on Misrepresented Personal Facts

The judge in the *Stewart* case termed the Rule 10b-5 charges "novel."[110] In light of that fact and given the relatively early and incomplete resolution of those charges, it seems appropriate to make some further general observations about the *Stewart* case and other cases that may, in the future, emanate from omissions or misrepresentations of personal information by corporate insiders.

Judicial Decision Making

Because the law under Rule 10b-5 is almost wholly judicial in nature, the exercise of judicial discretion may have important substantive effects. The court chose to decide Stewart's Rule 29 motion before putting case to the jury rather than waiting until after the jury returned a guilty verdict (at which time a Rule 29 motion still may be decided).[111] This is one of the relatively rare instances in which a federal trial judge in a criminal jury trial gets the opportunity to make significant law in a reported decision that is unappealable.[112] Notably, the acquittal opinion itself contributes to the decisional law relating to the scienter element of Rule 10b-5.[113] However, the court's failure to resolve latent issues relating to both scienter and the materiality and "in connection with" elements under Rule 10b-5 leaves a substantive void that the court could have helped fill. Judicial discretion should be exercised very carefully in this delicate procedural environment, especially in a cutting-edge case, like the *Stewart* case, in which the underlying substantive law is unclear.

Moreover, the timing of the court's decision may have caused the court to restrict the scope of its opinion. If the court had waited until after a guilty verdict to decide Stewart's Rule 29 motion, the court's opinion would have been appealable. [114] It is possible (although this *is* speculation) that, under those circumstances, where its decision is appealable, the court may have undertaken to write a more comprehensive opinion—one that addresses each element required to be proven by the government (or at least each element raised by Stewart in arguing the motion for acquittal).[115] The mere possibility of appellate review may incentivize a higher quality of judicial decision making, and actual appellate decisions should afford greater stability and certainty to the evolving decisional law under Rule 10b-5.[116] Accordingly, when a Rule 29 motion involves a complex and unsettled area of law (as it did in the *Stewart* case), there are important substantive reasons why a judge may want to wait to rule on the motion until after the jury has reached a guilty verdict.

Issues of Proof

The complexities involved in validly and adequately alleging violations of Rule 10b-5 for insider misrepresentations of personal facts translate into significant difficulties in proving out those allegations at trial. In particular, while direct, factual evidence may be available to satisfy some of the elements of a criminal or civil claim under Rule 10b-5 in this environment, circumstantial evidence typically constitutes all or substantially all of the evidence in satisfaction of the scienter element.[117] It would seem that, where the prosecution or a plaintiff is relying exclusively or primarily on circumstantial evidence to satisfy an element of its claim, sufficiency of evidence is much more likely to be an issue, making more probable a motion for acquittal or for a directed verdict. A Rule 29 motion challenging the sufficiency of circumstantial evidence is complicated for a court to decide, because of an increased likelihood of questions relating to whether inferences or speculation are necessary to finding the requisite facts.[118] Moreover, in a case where the nexus between the defendant's conduct and the securities market or investors is weak, circumstantial evidence and permissible inferences based on that evidence may impact more than just the scienter element of the claim. In particular, proof of the "in connection with" requirement is at risk. Given these evidentiary difficulties and the higher burden of proof applicable to criminal actions under Rule 10b-5, it is especially hard for a federal prosecutor to prove a case of this kind.[119] Criminal prosecution may not be appropriate under these circumstances.

Moreover, the standards-based decisional law sources for the elements of a Rule 10b-5 claim renders those elements somewhat amorphous and allows the federal courts to expand or contract the common understanding of one or more elements as new cases arise.[120] Accordingly, when a unique or rare type of Rule 10b-5 claim is brought, it is difficult for the government or plaintiffs to be certain that the facts adduced at trial are sufficient to satisfy the required elements. In addition, it is difficult for a defendant to know what evidence to present to refute the newfangled Rule 10b-5 claim brought against her. The ultimate determination of these issues will be based on multiple decisions by varied federal courts and may require Supreme Court intercession.

In this complex and ambiguous enforcement environment, the unique nature of the claims against Stewart had specific impacts on her motion for acquittal. For example, the *Stewart* court expressly contended with the uniqueness of the government's claim in addressing its request for an inference as to the scienter element of its case based on the falsity of Stewart's public statements. The court found that the prosecution was not entitled to that inference of scienter, expressly distinguishing this type of case from others under Rule 10b-5 in which an inference was permitted.

> In some securities fraud cases, the falsity of a defendant's statements may lend weight to an inference of intent to deceive. But in this case, the falsehoods lack a direct connection to the supposed purpose of the alleged deception. The falsehoods involve Stewart's personal trade in the securities of ImClone. Evidence of intent to defraud investors of a different company is not readily discernible from the content of the falsehoods.[121]

This area of the law under Rule 10b-5—determinations as to the circumstances in which an inference of scienter may be appropriate—is very unclear and is subject to further development in future actions.

Conclusion

Should an insider be found guilty or liable for violating Rule 10b-5 for lying to the public about personal transactions conducted in her individual capacity? This question remains unanswered by the court's opinion in the *Stewart* case. Perhaps, however, if the case had been permitted to go to the jury, we would have this and other answers.

Questions

1. Should federal law attempt to better define the difference between reasonable inference and speculation? Is this a useful distinction?
2. How do the scienter and "in connection with" elements of a Rule 10b-5 action overlap in the *Stewart* case? Which, if either, element appears to be easier to understand and prove?
3. Should we allow courts to grant motions for acquittal prior to the surrender of a criminal case to the jury? Why, or why not?

Notes

1. *See generally* United States v. Stewart, 305 F. Supp. 2d 368 (S.D.N.Y. 2004).

2. The result in the Stewart case, if not the court's reasoning, was promptly applauded by one law professor. Stephen Bainbridge, *I was right: Count 9 dismissed*, Feb. 27, 2004, *at* http://www.professorbainbridge.com/2004/02/i_was_ right_cou.html (Weblog post endorsing the judge's opinion acquitting Martha Stewart of securities fraud).

3. Superseding Indictment, United States v. Martha Stewart and Peter Bacanovic, S1 03 Cr. 717 (MGC) (S.D.N.Y. filed Jan. 7, 2004) *available at* http://news.findlaw.com/hdocs/ docs/mstewart/usmspb10504sind.pdf [hereinafter Indictment], ¶¶ 56–66.

4. 15 U.S.C. §78j(b) (2000). Section 10(b) of the 1934 Act broadly prohibits manipulation and deception in connection with the purchase or sale of securities and authorizes the SEC to adopt rules and regulations "necessary or appropriate in the public interest or for the protection of investors." *Id.*

5. 17 C.F.R. §240.10b-5 (2005). Rule 10b-5 proscribes the following in connection with the purchase or sale of a security: fraudulent devices, schemes, artifices; certain material misrepresentations and misleading omissions of material fact; and acts, practices, and courses of business that act or would act as a deceit.

6. 305 F. Supp. at 370. *See also supra* Chapter 5.

7. Indictment, *supra* note 2, at ¶61; 305 F. Supp. 2d at 373.

8. Indictment, *supra* note 2, at ¶¶63, 64; 305 F. Supp. 2d at 373–74.

9. Indictment, *supra* note 2, at ¶65; 305 F. Supp. 2d at 374. The court treats the four statements as three, since the last two statements are identical in content. *Id.* at 371 ("The count is based on three repetitive public statements").

10. MARC I. STEINBERG, SECURITIES REGULATION 524 (4th ed. 2004). *See also supra* Chapter 5.

11. Apprendi v. N.J., 530 U.S. 466, 476–477 (2000) (tracing the requirement to roots in constitutional due process and rights of the accused); United States v. Gaudin, 515 U.S. 506, 510 (1995) (same).

12. Herman & MacLean v. Huddleston, 459 U.S. 375, 387–90 (1983). *See also* Faulkner v. Los Angeles, 1990 U.S. App. LEXIS 19209, *2 n.1 (9th Cir. 1990) ("[T]he criminal 'beyond a reasonable doubt' measure of persuasion is higher than the civil 'preponderance of the evidence' measure."); Lane v. Sullivan, 900 F.2d 1247, 1252 (8th Cir. 1990) ("[T]he government's

burden has fallen off to only a preponderance in the civil proceeding from the much higher burden of beyond a reasonable doubt to which it was subject in the criminal proceeding.").

13. 305 F. Supp. 2d at 373.

14. For purposes of the motion, the court assumes that Stewart's public communications are false. *Id.* at 371 n.1.

15. *Id.* at 372. Chapter 10 of this volume provides a detailed analysis of the materiality element in the *Stewart* case.

16. *Id.* at 372–73.

17. *Id.* at 373–74.

18. *See supra* note 14. The court does, however, note the facts in the press release that the government alleges to be false. *Id.* at 374 n.2.

19. *See supra* note 15 and accompanying text.

20. 305 F. Supp. 2d at 374.

21. *See supra* notes 14 & 18 and accompanying text. The government's allegations as to the falsity of Stewart's various representations in the June 18, 2002 statement are, however, summarized in a footnote to the court's opinion. 305 F. Supp. at 374 n.3.

22. *Id.* at 374.

23. *Id.*

24. *See supra* note 15 and accompanying text.

25. *See, e.g.,* 305 F. Supp. 2d at 372 (noting that Stewart was the CEO of a public company and referencing the market price of MSLO's stock).

26. *Id.* at 372–73.

27. *Id.* at 370.

28. *Id.* at 375 n.4 (stating that a temporary rebound in MSLO's stock price is not evidence of Stewart's intent); *id.* at 377 (setting forth the court's interpretation of Stewart's statements at the June 19, 2002 conference).

29. *Id.* at 371–72.

30. *Id.* at 372.

31. *Id.* at 372.

32. *Id.* at 373.

33. *Id.* at 373.

34. *Id.* at 376.

35. *Id.* at 376–78.

36. The trademark for "Good Things" is registered in the name of MSLO. U.S. Patent & Trademark Office, Reg. No. 2947861, *available at* http://tess2.uspto.gov/ bin/showfield?f=doc&state=4nhf87.4.10. MSLO also has applied for a service mark for "Good Things." U.S. Patent & Trademark Office, Serial No. 78386149, *available at* http://tess2.uspto.gov/bin/showfield?f=doc&state=4nhf87.5.20. The trademark for "A Good Thing" was filed by another applicant and abandoned. U.S. Patent & Trademark Office, Serial No. 78080819, *available at* http://tess2.uspto.gov/bin/showfield?f=doc&state=4nhf87.2.33.

37. Motions for a judgment of acquittal are made under Rule 29, which provides:

> After the government closes its evidence or after the close of all the evidence, the court on the defendant's motion must enter a judgment of acquittal of any offense for which the evidence is insufficient to sustain a conviction. The court may on its own consider whether the evidence is insufficient to sustain a conviction.

If the court denies a motion for a judgment of acquittal at the close of the government's evidence, the defendant may offer evidence without having reserved the right to do so.

FED. R. CRIM. PROC. 29(a). The Rule goes on to note:

The court may reserve decision on the motion, proceed with the trial (where the motion is made before the close of all the evidence), submit the case to the jury, and decide the motion either before the jury returns a verdict or after it returns a verdict of guilty or is discharged without having returned a verdict. If the court reserves decision, it must decide the motion on the basis of the evidence at the time the ruling was reserved.

FED R. CRIM. PROC. 29(b).

38. *See* Fong Foo v. United States, 369 U.S. 141, 143 (1962).

Federal Rule of Criminal Procedure 29 enables the trial judge upon her own initiative or motion of the defense to direct a judgment of acquittal in a criminal trial at any time prior to the submission of the case to the jury. Once the judgment of acquittal is entered, the government's right of appeal is effectively blocked by the Double Jeopardy Clause of the U.S. Constitution, as the only remedy available to the Court of Appeals would be to order a retrial. No matter how irrational or capricious, the district judge's ruling terminating the prosecution cannot be appealed.

Richard Sauber & Michael Waldman, *Unlimited Power: Rule 29(A) and the Unreviewability of Directed Judgments of Acquittal*, 44 AM. U.L. REV. 433, 433–434 (1994) (footnote omitted). *See also* U.S. CONST. amend. V.

39. *See supra* note 37.

40. White v. United States, 279 F.2d 740, 748 (4th Cir.), *cert. denied*, 364 U.S. 850 (1960). *See also* United States v. O'Keefe, 825 F.2d 314, 319 (11th Cir. 1987); United States v Stirling, 571 F.2d 708 (2d Cir.), *cert. denied*, 439 U.S. 824 (1978); United States v. Robinson, 71 F. Supp. 9, 10 (D.D.C. 1947).

41. United States v. Fearn, 589 F.2d 1316, 1321 (7th Cir. 1978).

42. Although numerous statements of the Rule 29 standard exist, one trial court summarized:

In passing upon a motion for a judgment of acquittal, the trial judge must determine whether upon the evidence, giving full play to the right of the jury to determine credibility, weigh the evidence, and draw justifiable inferences of fact, a reasonable mind might fairly conclude guilt beyond a reasonable doubt. If he concludes that upon the evidence there must be such a doubt in a reasonable mind, he must grant the motion; or, to state it another way, if there is no evidence upon which a reasonable mind might fairly conclude guilt beyond reasonable doubt, the motion must be granted. But if a reasonable mind might fairly have a reasonable doubt or might fairly not have one, the case is for the jury.

United States v. Hufford, 103 F. Supp. 859, 860 (D. Pa. 1952). Recent Second Circuit opinions state the standard in a more succinct manner. *See* United States v. Chen, 378 F.3d 151, 158 (2d Cir. 2004) (citing the formulation of the standard in *Jackson v. Virginia*, 443 U.S. 307, 319 (1979)); United States v. Thorn, 317 F.3d 107, 132 (2d Cir. 2003) (same); United States v. Jackson, 335 F.3d 170, 180 (2d Cir. 2003) ("Under Rule 29, a district court will grant a motion to enter a judgment of acquittal on grounds of insufficient evidence if it concludes that no rational trier of fact could have found the defendant guilty beyond a reasonable doubt."); United States v. Reyes, 302 F.3d 48, 52 (2d Cir. 2002) ("a district court can enter a judgment of acquittal on the grounds of insufficient evidence only if, after viewing the evidence in the light most favorable to the prosecution and drawing all reasonable inferences in the government's favor, it concludes no rational trier of fact could have found the defendant guilty beyond a reasonable doubt.").

43. *See* United States v. Ubl, 472 F. Supp. 1236, 1237 (D. Ohio 1979) ("the trial judge must determine whether the Government has presented sufficient evidence from which reasonable jurors could conclude guilt beyond a reasonable doubt. This standard must be applied to each and every element of the offense charged"). *See also* Apprendi v. N.J., 530 U.S. 466, 476–477 (2000) (tracing the requirement to roots in constitutional due process and rights of the accused); United States v. Gaudin, 515 U.S. 506, 510 (1995) (same).

44. United States v. Guadagna, 183 F.3d 122, 129 (2d Cir. 1999) ("[T]he court must be careful to avoid usurping the role of the jury."); Curley v. United States, 160 F.2d 229, 233 (D.C. Cir. 1947) (stating that the determination of reasonable doubt "is the jury's function, provided the evidence is such as to permit a reasonable mind fairly to reach either of the two conclusions."). The *Curley* court explains the need for restraint in the context of the role of judge and jury in a criminal trial.

> If the judge were to direct acquittal whenever in his opinion the evidence failed to exclude every hypothesis but that of guilt, he would preempt the functions of the jury. Under such rule, the judge would have to be convinced of guilt beyond peradventure of doubt before the jury would be permitted to consider the case. That is not the place of the jury in criminal procedure. They are the judges of the facts and of guilt or innocence, not merely a device for checking upon the conclusions of the judge.

Id.

45. United States v. Stewart, 305 F. Supp. 2d 368, 370 (S.D.N.Y. 2004); Paul L. Hoffman, *The "Blank Stare Phenomenon": Proving Customary International Law in U.S. Courts*, 25 GA. J. INT'L & COMP. L. 181, 187 (1995/1996) ("Rule 29 motions are rarely granted even in cases where they should be, because most judges prefer to send the case to the jury rather than risk criticism for acquitting the defendant."); Amy Baron-Evans, *An Important but Modest Check on Prosecutorial Overreaching and Wrongful Conviction*, 48 B.B.J. 31, 32 (2004) ("Judges agonize over Rule 29 motions and deny them if the question is at all close.... In the rare cases in which the motion is granted, the rulings are not hidden, but are made in open court, often in published opinions, and appear on the docket.").

46. 305 F. Supp. 2d at 370 (quoting from *Jackson v. Virginia*, 443 U.S. 307, 319 (1979)).

47. *Id.* (citing to *United States v. Taylor*, 464 F.2d 240, 243 (2d Cir. 1972), quoting from *Curley v. United States,* 160 F.2d 229 (D.C. Cir. 1947)).

48. Recent articulations of the Rule 29 standard in the Second Circuit use fewer qualifying adjectives and adverbs. *See, e.g.,* United States v. Chen, 378 F.3d 151, 158 (2d Cir. 2004) (omitting the requirement that the trier of fact's findings of guilt beyond a reasonable doubt be fair); United States v. Thorn, 317 F.3d 107, 132 (2d Cir. 2003) (same); United States v. Jackson, 335 F.3d 170, 180 (2d Cir. 2003) (same); United States v. Reyes, 302 F.3d 48, 52 (2d Cir. 2002) (same). These recent versions of the Rule 29 standard may make it more difficult for a judge to acquit a defendant on a Rule 29 motion.

49. *See* 305 F. Supp. 2d at 370.

50. *Id.*

51. *Id.*

52. *See* United States v. Hufford, 103 F. Supp. 859, 860 (D. Pa. 1952) (noting that the the jury has the right to, among other things, draw justifiable inferences of fact).

53. *See* Daniels v. Twin Oaks Nursing Home, 692 F.2d 1321 (11th Cir. 1982) ("a jury will not be allowed to engage in a degree of speculation and conjecture that renders its finding a guess or mere possibility."); Curley v. United States, 160 F.2d 229, 232 (D.C. Cir. 1947) ("The jury may not be permitted to conjecture merely, or to conclude upon pure speculation").

54. *See* Galloway v. United States, 319 U.S. 372, 395 (1943) ("the essential requirement is that mere speculation be not allowed to do duty for probative facts, after making due allowance for all reasonably possible inferences favoring the party whose case is attacked."); Sunward Corp. v. Dun & Bradstreet, Inc., 811 F.2d 511, 521 (10th Cir. 1987) ("Although a jury is entitled to draw reasonable inferences from circumstantial evidence, reasonable inferences themselves must be more than speculation and conjecture.").

55. *See* 305 F. Supp. 2d at 378 ("[I]n this case, the falsehoods lack a direct connection to the supposed purpose of the alleged deception."). This author also has questions, as did Stewart, about whether Stewart's alleged misrepresentations are material under the tests set forth in *TSC Industries* and *Basic. See* chapter 10 of this volume. *See also* Stephen Bainbridge, *Was Martha Stewart's Denial Material? The Problem with Count 9*, Dec. 4, 2003, *at* http://www.professorbainbridge.com/ 2003/12/was_martha_stew.html (questioning the materiality of any misrepresentations made by Stewart). The court expressly declined to address both the materiality question and the "in connection with" requirement in its opinion. *See* 305 F. Supp. 2d at 378 n.5.

56. *See* 15 U.S.C. §78j(b) (2000) (Section 10(b) of the 1934 Act); 17 C.F.R. §240.10b-5 (2005) (Rule 10b-5).

57. Ernst & Ernst v. Hochfelder, 425 U.S. 185, 193 n.12 (1976); In re Merrill Lynch & Co., Inc. Research Reports Sec. Litig. 289 F. Supp. 2d 416, 427 (2003) ("[T]he requisite state of mind for actionable securities fraud under Rule 10b-5 is the intent to deceive, manipulate or defraud, not merely the intent to utter an untruth."); ALAN R. PALMITER, SECURITIES REGULATION 282 (2d ed. 2002).

58. 425 U.S. at 193.

59. *Id.* at 193 n.12.

60. *See, e.g.*, Rockies Fund, Inc. v. SEC, 428 F.3d 1088, 1093 (D.C. Cir. 2005); Nathenson v. Zonagen Inc., 267 F.3d 400, 408 (5th Cir. 2001); Hollinger v. Titan Capital Corp., 914 F.2d 1564, 1568 n.6 (9th Cir. 1990); Keirnan v. Homeland, Inc., 611 F.2d 785, 788 (9th Cir. 1980); Sunstrand Corp. v. Sun Chem. Corp., 553 F.2d 1033, 1045 (7th Cir. 1977); NAGY ET AL., SECURITIES LITIGATION AND ENFORCEMENT: CASES AND MATERIALS 110 (2003) ("[E]very federal court of appeals to confront the question has held recklessness sufficient for these purposes").

61. *Rockies Fund*, 428 F.3d at 1093 (D.C. Cir. 2005) ("Rule 10b-5 generally requires only 'extreme recklessness.'").

62. PALMITER, *supra* note 57, at 283. *See also* AUSA Life Ins. Co. v. Ernst & Young, 206 F.3d 202, 221 (2d Cir. 2000) (criticizing the district court's opinion on the basis that it "inappropriately makes the scienter issue one of 'what did the defendant want to happen' as opposed to 'what could the defendant reasonably foresee as a potential result of his ac-

tion.'"); SEC v. Falstaff Brewing Corp., 629 F.2d 62, 77 (D.C. Cir. 1980) (scienter exists when a defendant knows "the nature and consequences of his actions").

63. Advanta Corp. Sec. Litig., 180 F.3d 525, 535 (3d Cir. 1999).

64. *See supra* notes 29–35.

65. *See supra* notes 34 & 35 and accompanying text.

66. *Id.* at 376. By focusing on "purpose" in this statement, the *Stewart* court also may be criticized for ignoring (without explanation) decisional law on scienter that rejects this definition of scienter (preferring, instead, to focus on what the defendant reasonably could foresee as the consequence of her misstatement). *See* JAMES D. COX ET AL., SECURITIES REGULATION: CASES AND MATERIALS 28 (4th ed. 2005 Supplement); sources cited *supra* note 62. Chapter 9 of this volume also addresses this issue. Yet, the *Stewart* court is not the only court to define scienter by reference to the defendant's purpose. *See* In re Merrill Lynch & Co. Research Reports Sec. Litig., 289 F. Supp. 2d 416, 427 (S.D.N.Y. 2003).

67. The court twice indicates that the evidence would better substantiate scienter if it included proof that Stewart had a more active role in arranging for the dissemination of her statements. *See id.* at 376, 377. Yet in each case, Stewart chose to make her statements in forums that were easily accessible or targeted toward investors, including MSLO investors. The court even notes that Stewart verbally acknowledges the likely interest of the audience of analysts and investors in Stewart's statements about the sale of her ImClone shares. *Id.* at 377.

68. *Id.* Apparently, the more stringent burden of proof applicable to criminal actions played a key role in the judge's holding. *Id.* at 369–70. *See also* Cynthia A. Caillavet, Comment: *From Nike v. Kasky To Martha Stewart: First Amendment Protection For Corporate Speakers' Denials Of Public Criminal Allegations,* 94 J. CRIM. L. & CRIMINOLOGY 1033, 1040–41 (2004).

69. *See supra* notes 29–35 and accompanying text.

70. *See* Sunward Corp. v. Dun & Bradstreet, Inc., 811 F.2d 511, 521 (10th Cir. 1987) ("The line between 'reasonable inferences' and mere speculation is impossible to define with any precision.").

71. Although one generally would not want to apply language or reasoning from civil cases in the criminal context, they do serve a limited use here. In this regard, it is significant to note that "the power to direct an acquittal developed as a corollary to the directed verdict in civil cases." *See* Sauber & Waldman, *supra* note 38.

72. Tose v. First Pennsylvania Bank, N.A., 648 F.2d 879, 895 (3d Cir. 1981). *Accord* MERRIAM-WEBSTER'S COLLEGIATE DICTIONARY 640 (11th ed. 2004) (defining "inference" as, among other things, "the act of passing from one proposition, statement, or judgment considered as true to another whose truth is believed to follow from that of the former.").

73. Hauser v. Equifax, Inc., 602 F.2d 811, 814 (8th Cir. 1979). *Accord* United States v. Galbraith, 20 F.3d 1054, 1057 (10th Cir. 1994) ("An inference must be more than speculation and conjecture to be reasonable"). An alternative definition of "reasonable inferences" that was articulated more recently in the U.S. Court of Claims provides that "such inferences as are born of common experience or are the product of a decision maker's special expertise—are within the rightful province of the decider of fact to make." Snyder by Snyder v. Secretary of the HHS, 36 Fed. Cl. 461, 466 (Ct. Cl. 1996).

74. Admiral Theatre Corp. v. Douglas Theatre Co., 585 F.2d 877, 883 (8th Cir. 1978). *Accord* Sip-Top, Inc. v. Ekco Group, 86 F.3d 827, 830 (8th Cir. 1996) ("When the record contains no proof beyond speculation to support the verdict, judgment as a matter of law is appropriate.").

75. *Sip-Top,* 86 F.3d at 830.

76. Daniels v. Twin Oaks Nursing Home, 692 F.2d 1321, 1326 (11th Cir. 1982).

77. Helene Curtis Industries, Inc. v. Pruitt, 385 F.2d 841, 851 (5th Cir. 1967).

78. MERRIAM-WEBSTER'S COLLEGIATE DICTIONARY 1199 (11th ed. 2004).

79. *Id.*

80. *Id.* at 263 (defining the verb "conjecture" as "to arrive at or deduce by conjecture" and defining the noun "conjecture" as an "inference from defective or presumptive evidence" or "a conclusion deduced by surmise or guesswork").

81. *Id.* at 555 (defining the verb "guess" as "to form an opinion of from little or no evidence").

82. *Id.* at 1258 (defining the verb "surmise" as "to form a notion of from scanty evidence").

83. *See, e.g.,* United States v. Pinckney, 85 F.3d 4, 7 (2d Cir. 1996) ("a conviction cannot rest on mere speculation or conjecture."); Ford Motor Co. v. McDavid, 259 F.2d 261, 266 (4th Cir. 1958) ("it is the duty of the court to withdraw the case from the jury when the necessary inference is so tenuous that it rests merely upon speculation and conjecture."); United States v. Stewart, 305 F. Supp. 2d 368, 376 (S.D.N.Y. 2004) ("a reasonable juror could not, without resorting to speculation and surmise, find beyond a reasonable doubt that Stewart's purpose was to influence the market in MSLO securities."); United States v. Batka, 724 F. Supp. 350, 352 (E.D. Pa. 1989) ("There was no need for the jury to guess or speculate").

84. *See supra* note 40 and accompanying text.

85. *See supra* note 41 and accompanying text.

86. United States v. Fermin, 32 F.3d 674, 678 (2d Cir. 1994) ("a jury may always base its verdict on reasonable inferences from circumstantial evidence"). *See also* United States v. Serpico, 2001 U.S. Dist. LEXIS 9523 (D. Ill. 2001), *rev'd on other grounds*, 320 F.3d 691 (7th Cir. 2003) (citing *United States v. Pinckney,* 85 F.3d 4, 7 (2d Cir. 1996) in noting that "although 'a conviction may be based solely on reasonable inferences from circumstantial evidence, a conviction cannot rest on mere speculation or conjecture.'").

87. *See supra* notes 29–33 and accompanying text.

88. *See supra* note 29 and accompanying text.

89. *See supra* note 30 and accompanying text.

90. *See supra* note 31 and accompanying text.

91. United States v. Stewart, 305 F. Supp. 2d 368, 373, 376–77 (S.D.N.Y. 2004) (citing the facts as to the public release of each of Stewart's statements and the court's analysis of those facts). *See also supra* note 23 and accompanying text.

92. 305 F. Supp. 2d at 377.

93. This does not mean that Stewart actually would have been or should be convicted of securities fraud if the matter were brought before a jury for decision. That is neither the standard for decisions under Rule 29 nor the subject of this chapter.

94. *See supra* note 72 and accompanying text.

95. The court found that the government's evidence did, in fact, give rise to a permissible inference that, in general, executives at MSLO were concerned about the market price of MSLO's stock price during the period in which Stewart's public statements were made. 305 F. Supp. 2d at 373. The facts found by the court also include Stewart's status as an executive of MSLO. *See supra* note 25.

96. Substantiating this judgment is the fact that the court, in sifting through the evidence adduced at trial, appears to impermissibly weigh that evidence in ruling on Stewart's Rule 29 motion, substituting her judgment on the meaning and relative weight of the facts

proven at trial for that of the jury. *See, e.g., id.* at 377 (interpreting and weighing against each other certain statements made by Stewart at the April 19 conference). A case in another circuit calls this practice into question. United States v. Olbres, 61 F.3d 967, 973 (1st Cir. 1995).

97. There is a possibility that the court chose to rely on the scienter element for other reasons. For example, the court may have chosen to focus on scienter for strategic reasons related to legal, reputational, or other benefits associated with this approach. Certainly, the court was aware that, in deciding the Rule 29 motion before the jury had deliberated on the Rule 10b-5 charge, her decision would not be reviewable by a higher court. This timing choice also may have influenced, or been influenced by, the court's decision to focus on scienter. *See infra* note 114 and accompanying text.

98. *See* 305 F. Supp. 2d at 376.

99. *See* Chemical Bank v. Arthur Andersen & Co., 726 F.2d 930, 943 (2d Cir. 1984).

100. Sup't of Ins. v. Bankers Life and Cas. Co., 404 U.S. 6, 12 (1971) ("Section 10(b) must be read flexibly, not technically and restrictively."); SEC v. Softpoint, Inc., 958 F. Supp. 846, 862 (S.D.N.Y. 1997) ("courts have liberally construed the requirement that violative conduct must occur 'in connection with' the purchase or sale of a security.").

101. S.E.C. v. Zandford, 535 U.S. 813, 825 (2002) ("a fraudulent scheme in which the securities transactions and the breaches of fiduciary duty coincide" satisfies the "in connection with" requirement); *Sup't of Ins.*, 404 U.S. at 12–13 ("The crux of the present case is that Manhattan suffered an injury as a result of deceptive practices touching its sale of securities as an investor.").

102. S.E.C. v. Texas Gulf Sulphur Co., 401 F.2d 833, 860 (2d Cir. 1968) (en banc), *cert. denied*, 394 U.S. 976 (1969) ("Congress when it used the phrase 'in connection with the purchase or sale of any security' intended only that the device employed, whatever it might be, be of a sort that would cause reasonable investors to rely thereon, and, in connection therewith, so relying, cause them to purchase or sell a corporation's securities.").

103. *See supra* note 101 and accompanying text.

104. *See supra* note 101 and accompanying text.

105. *See supra* note 102 and accompanying text.

106. The court specifically notes that Stewart also raised Rule 29 arguments on the materiality of her public statements and the satisfaction of the "in connection with" element of a Rule 10b-5 action. United States v. Stewart, 305 F. Supp. 2d 368, 378 n.5 (S.D.N.Y. 2004). In an exercise of judicial restraint, the court expressly declined to address these issues because she deemed them "not necessary." *Id.*

107. 305 F. Supp. 2d at 378.

108. *Id.*

109. S.E.C. v. Falstaff Brewing Corp., 629 F.2d 62, 77 (D.C. Cir. 1980) (stating, with respect to scienter under Rule 10b-5, that "no area of the law not even the criminal law demands that a defendant have thought his actions were illegal. A knowledge of what one is doing and the consequences of those actions suffices.").

110. Memorandum Opinion, United States v. Martha Stewart and Peter Bacanovic, S1 03 Cr. 717 (MGC) (S.D.N.Y. dated Jan. 26, 2004) *available at* http://news.findlaw.com/ hdocs/docs/mstewart/usmspb12604opn.pdf (last visited July 6, 2005).

111. *See supra* note 37 (quoting from Rule 29).

112. *See supra* note 38 and accompanying text.

113. *See, e.g., supra* note 121 and accompanying text.

114. *See* Dawn M. Phillips, *When Rules are More Important than Justice*, 87 J. CRIM. L. & CRIMINOLOGY 1040, 1043 (1997) ("If a jury returns a guilty verdict, the government can appeal a trial court's order granting a motion for judgment of acquittal because a successful appeal by the government would not necessitate a retrial in violation of the Double Jeopardy Clause. Instead, the appeals court would remand the case for reinstatement of the jury verdict.").

115. Other factors may have influenced the court's decision on the substantive contents of her opinion. *See, e.g.*, Stephen M. Bainbridge & G. Mitu Gulati, *How Do Judges Maximize? (The Same Way Everybody Else Does—Boundedly): Rules of Thumb in Securities Fraud Opinions*, 51 EMORY L.J. 83, 100–11 (2002) (describing three features of judicial decisionmaking in the securities class action context that explain the use of heuristics in that decisionmaking, many of which would be applicable in other federal securities litigation contexts); Donald C. Langevoort, *Are Judges Motivated to Create "Good" Securities Fraud Doctrine?*, 51 EMORY L.J. 309, 313–18 (2002) (supplementing the Bainbridge & Gulati analysis with further observations about decision making in securities fraud cases).

116. *See* Sauber & Waldman, *supra* note 38, at 452–56 (making similar arguments in support of eliminating the power of trial judges to order pre-verdict judgments of acquittal).

117. *See* Herman & MacLean v. Huddleston, 459 U.S. 375, 390 n.30 (1983) (noting that proof of the requisite state of mind in a Rule 10b-5 action "is often a matter of inference from circumstantial evidence.").

118. *See* United States v. Ruiz, 105 F.3d 1492, 1499 (1st Cir. 1997) (describing the relationship among Rule 29, circumstantial evidence, and inferences). *Cf.* United States v. Mackay, 33 F.3d 489, 494 (5th Cir. 1994) ("Although the government may prove the existence of a conspiracy through circumstantial evidence, it 'must do more than pile inference upon inference upon which to base a conspiracy charge.'").

119. *See supra* notes 11–12; Caillavet, *supra* note 68, at 1040–41.

120. *See* Joan MacLeod Heminway, *Save Martha Stewart?: Observations About Equal Justice in U.S. Insider Trading Regulation*, 12 TEX. J. WOMEN & L. 247, 256–61 (2003) (describing an expansive pattern in insider trading litigation under Rule 10b-5); Donald C. Langevoort, *Rule 10b-5 as an Adaptive Organism*, 61 FORDHAM L. REV. S7 (1993) (a seminal work on Rule 10b-5's flexibility); Geraldine Szott Moohr, *Prosecutorial Power in an Adversarial System: Lessons from Current White Collar Cases*, 7 BUFF. CRIM. L. REV. 165, 179 (2004) (noting, in the context of a discussion of criminal litigation under Rule 10b-5, that a pattern of "prosecutors raising new interpretations and courts acceding to them—leads to an incremental, but inexorable, expansion of the laws.").

121. United States v. Stewart, 305 F. Supp. 2d 368, 378 (S.D.N.Y. 2004).

CHAPTER 9

REFLECTIONS ON SCIENTER[*]

Donald C. Langevoort

My interest is in shedding light on the scienter requirement under the law of fraud, particularly as applied under Rule 10b-5 under the Securities Exchange Act of 1934. Although it is clear that Rule 10b-5 has a scienter requirement,[1] its exact contours—indeed, what at heart the requirement really means—may still not be entirely certain.[2] To make the exercise more concrete, I will examine the Rule 10b-5 case against Martha Stewart. As most readers know, Stewart—the home products celebrity and then-CEO of her own publicly traded company, Martha Stewart Living Omnimedia (MSLO)—was tried and convicted in 2004 on federal charges involving the making of false statements to the government, arising out of an SEC and FBI investigation into her alleged insider trading in the shares of ImClone, a biotechnology company.[3] Prosecutors chose not to charge her for the insider trading itself (though the SEC did bring a parallel civil insider trading case against her[4]). The prosecutors did charge her with a Rule 10b-5 violation for lying publicly about the investigation, in a way that allegedly influenced the price of MSLO stock. Late in the trial, however, the court granted a judgment of acquittal on the securities fraud charge,[5] so that the case went to the jury only on the obstruction and false statement claims.

I think that the court was wrong on this as a matter of law, which I will explain. But my main point is that the underlying interpretive issue exposes how porous the definition of scienter is when applied in a difficult case. This is not to say that Stewart was innocent of a Rule 10b-5 violation—I think there is evidence to suggest that she did act with scienter as commonly understood. I

[*] This chapter is derived from *Reflections on Scienter (and the Securities Fraud Case Against Martha Stewart that Never Happened)*, originally published at 10 Lewis & Clark L. Rev. 1 (2006), Donald C. Langevoort © 2006. Reprinted with permission of the publisher, Lewis & Clark Law Review.

simply want to use the issues surrounding her case to emphasize the troubling distance between how the legal system applies state of mind rules and how social scientists might think about concepts such as awareness and motivation.

Martha Stewart's Alleged Criminal Securities Fraud Violation

The Story

As charged by government authorities, Martha Stewart's legal troubles began on December 27, 2001.[6] The day before, insiders at ImClone learned that the FDA would take adverse action with respect to its key anti-cancer drug under development, Erbitux. (The securities markets were anxiously awaiting a decision from the FDA; it was public knowledge that the FDA had until the last day of December to decide one way or the other). For reasons that themselves are hard to fathom given the unambiguous legal risk associated with such behavior, this news led ImClone's CEO, Sam Waksal, to try to sell his stock, and he succeeded in causing his daughter and father to sell out their holdings. Waksal's efforts to sell were channeled through his stockbroker at Merrill Lynch, Peter Bacanovic, who was also Stewart's broker.[7] Through his assistant, Bacanovic communicated to Stewart on the 27th that the price of ImClone was likely to be trading downward and that the Waksals were selling, which caused Stewart to direct that all of her ImClone stock be sold immediately. The price thereafter continued to fall, so that by selling when she did rather than at the bottom of the market, Stewart avoided a loss of approximately $45,000, an extraordinarily small amount compared to her total net worth.[8]

A federal investigation was commenced almost immediately, with Stewart readily identified as a seller with ties to Bacanovic, Waksal, and ImClone.[9] Stewart voluntarily appeared in early February and told investigators that she and Bacanovic had recently reviewed her portfolio and come to an understanding, among other things, that her ImClone stock should be sold should the price fall to $60 per share from the $70 or so that it was trading at in the late fall. Because the price fell below $60 on December 27, the sell order was triggered. She denied receiving any information about ImClone or the Waksals in the call that afternoon.

The government's ImClone investigation continued throughout the spring and led to a Congressional inquiry as well. Eventually, the press learned of Stewart's situation and she was asked to comment. Through her attorney, she told reporters the same story that she had told investigators, i.e., that she was

not guilty of any insider trading because she had received no inside information and that the sales were the result of the pre-arranged plan to sell at $60,
and these responses appeared in print on June 7. Essentially, this was repeated
in a more elaborate press release on June 12 and a meeting with securities analysts covering MSLO on June 19.

Largely based on cooperative testimony from the broker's assistant in return
for leniency, the investigators came to believe that Stewart's testimony and public statements were false—that there was no pre-existing sell order, and that
such a story had been fabricated (and an effort made to falsify documents) as
part of a cover-up devised by Stewart and Bacanovic once they learned of the
investigation. In the prosecutors' view this supported both the obstruction and
securities fraud charges, because the lies were directed to both the government
and the investing public (purchasers and sellers of MSLO shares). As noted,
the criminal indictment was silent with respect to the alleged insider trading.

The Dismissal of the Securities Fraud Claim

Stewart moved for of a judgment of acquittal pursuant to Rule 29 of the
Federal Rules of Criminal Procedure, which the court granted with respect to
the one securities fraud count late in the trial.[10] As the court framed the issue,
the question was whether a jury could find beyond a reasonable doubt—without mere speculation—that Stewart acted with scienter in making false statements to the investing public. The court did not address the question of
whether the "willfulness" standard application to criminal prosecutions under
Rule 10b-5 required a different state of mind showing than in a civil case. The
prosecution offered evidence that Stewart was the controlling shareholder of
MSLO and regularly concerned with the company's stock price (as a result of
publicity about the government's investigation, the price of MSLO stock
dropped by more than 30%). The inference was that Stewart had lied to coun-
teract the downward pressure on the stock.

The court ruled that a reasonable jury could not find beyond a reasonable
doubt that Stewart intended to deceive investors, even assuming the falsity of
her public statements. As the court saw it, the question was whether her "*purpose* was to influence the market in MSLO securities."[11] Essentially, the court
thought that there were too many other possible purposes for a jury to reach
that level of certainty:

> Here, the evidence and inferences are simply too weak to support a
> finding beyond a reasonable doubt of criminal intent. To compound
> that weak evidence with the reasonable inferences that Stewart pos-

sessed many other intents—to protest her innocence, to reassure her business partners, advertisers and the consumers of her products— would only invite the jury to speculate.[12]

The Law of Scienter

The court seems to have misunderstood the law. There has been a long-standing issue about whether purpose or motivation should be relevant to the scienter determination, and one can find occasional dicta that suggests that that purpose is relevant.[13] But the weight of authority is that the relevant question is not motive or purpose but *awareness*—did the defendant know or recklessly disregard that what she was saying was false?[14] The clearest statement of this, ironically, came in the only securities case cited by the court in its opinion (albeit on a different point of law), *AUSA Life Insurance Co. v. Ernst & Young*.[15] There, the Second Circuit admonished the trial court because it "inappropriately [made] the scienter issue one of 'what did the defendant want to happen' as opposed to 'what could the defendant reasonably foresee as a potential result of his action.'" That, of course, is exactly what the court did in *Stewart*, too. If one uses forseeability as the test, there were ample grounds for inferring that Stewart understood the likely impact of her lie on the MSLO market. Indeed, that was precisely how the prosecution had presented its evidence.

In fact, forseeability may not be the precise articulation either if what we are talking about is scienter. An appreciation of the falsity by the speaker is all that is necessary. The forseeability standard goes to something slightly different, subject-matter jurisdiction as embodied in the requirement that the fraud be "in connection with the purchase or sale of a security". Not all fraud is securities fraud, and the prevailing "in connection with" standard is whether the defendant's misrepresentation or omission was "reasonably calculated to influence the investing public."[16] Though the word "calculated" might connote purpose or motivation, courts have instead said—consistent with the scienter standard—that the test is whether the defendant appreciated the likely effect on investors, with forseeability being the best way to answer that question.[17] In this way, *AUSA* was conjoining the scienter and "in connection with" tests in a way that makes holistic sense in defining what constitutes *securities* fraud.

The awareness or appreciation standard—as opposed to motive or purpose—finds support in the way that the case law has evolved on a number of points. In dicta, the Supreme Court essentially endorsed it in *Basic Inc. v.*

Levinson when it rejected the idea that showing a "good business purpose" for a misrepresentation would insulate a defendant from liability.[18] It is also implicit in the now nearly universal recognition that recklessness suffices as the basis for scienter[19]—reckless disregard of the truth goes to the defendants' awareness or appreciation, not purpose.

Understanding why the court took such a wrong turn in rejecting the prosecution's securities fraud case against Stewart is hard; there is no legal analysis or citation of cases on this point. One possibility, which should be guarded against, is that the court was confused by the substantial body of law on *pleading* scienter under the heighted pleading standard of the Private Securities Litigation Reform Act.[20] There, there is a vast amount of case law about whether showing a strong enough motive will satisfy that burden, and the Second Circuit is one of the more receptive to motive-based analysis.[21] Because pleading cases are by far the most frequent context in which the issue is raised, it might be easy for a trial judge to think that the scienter requirement itself is about motive. However, the questions are entirely different. The pleading requirement is about whether plaintiffs get to go to discovery, where solid evidence about awareness or appreciation can be elicited through document production and depositions. Allegations of motive are made important because they help distinguish between strong and weak cases at that early stage, before the pressure to settle becomes overwhelming. But at the trial stage—after discovery has been allowed—the standard becomes the conventional one (although motive and opportunity may still be relevant evidence in arguing a circumstantial case of knowledge or recklessness).

Is it possible that the error was harmless? That would be so if there were some separate ground for making Stewart's purpose the controlling question. In a criminal case, violations of Rule 10b-5 must not only be with scienter but also "willful"—a stricter state of mind that arguably supports a motivation (specific intent) test. But here again, there is no compelling support in the case law. The Second Circuit has indicated that willfulness requires a realization on the part of the defendant that he was acting "wrongfully," which may (or may not) be something more than simply awareness of the falsity.[22] If we assume that Stewart knew that what she was saying was untrue, it is hard to find a lack of willfulness simply because her lie might have been directed more to the consuming public or company stakeholders than to investors.[23]

The judgment of acquittal seems to have been a legal error, then, substantially in Stewart's favor. If so, it was also a material error, because had the jury convicted her of securities fraud as well as making false statements, the likely criminal sentence would have been far greater than the five months she served. Especially after Sarbanes-Oxley, the likely sentence would have been crippling.[24]

A Cognitive Perspective on Defining Scienter

One contribution that the cognition research can offer is to help understand the nature and consequences of one approach or another to a legal standard like scienter. To me, the research strengthens the preference for an "awareness" standard rather than one based on motivation or purpose. Motivation is extraordinarily complex, and often unconscious. The conscious perception of one's own motive is often inaccurate—a rationalization designed to buffer anxiety or guilt, or maintain self-esteem. If securities fraud wants to reach harmful behavior, it should not let cognitive excuses (for example, a lie by Martha Stewart that she thought was necessary to protect company employees or customers who were so heavily invested in her brand) be relevant.

That said, we should realize that the preferable "awareness" standard is also on somewhat shaky cognitive ground. Although much of the judgment and decision-making literature deals with choice (especially risky choice) rather than perception, the two are inseparable—choices are largely defined by how the prevailing situation is perceived. And the psychology literature is filled with studies of how peoples' mental models of reality can diverge from reality objectively defined. There is a wonderfully metaphorical illustration of this created by University of Illinois researcher Daniel Simon, familiar to many who have been introduced to the behavioral research.[25] An audience is asked to watch a short video of a group of people moving about passing a basketball, some in black shirts, others in white. The audience is asked to pay close attention and count the number of time those dressed in one color catch the ball. This is not easy because of the rapid movements of the crowd in a confined space. When the viewing is over, the presenter asks the audience for the right number. Most come fairly close; many get it correct.

Then the presenter asks how many people noticed the man in the gorilla suit walking among the crowd in the video. Most did not.[26] Yet when the video is repeated the presence of the gorilla is clear and striking to everyone. The point is that perceptions are a product of prior expectations, especially when one is concentrating on something else. This is related to a phenomenon psychologists call cognitive conservatism, the tendency not to perceive a change in ones surroundings or situation because expectations are built around the situation as it had been.[27]

At the risk of oversimplification, my sense is that many (though certainly not all) actors caught up in financial scandals failed to notice the gorilla. Take a lawyer working for Enron, working excessively long hours in structured finance to put together a series of special purpose entities. The prevailing "schema" and task definition are narrow and focused; it becomes entirely possible that disconfirming information remains outside of attention until the problem is exposed in a vivid, salient fashion. If we ask whether the actor was actually aware of the fraud, the answer will often be no. This is so even if we shift to the recklessness component of scienter, which most all courts now define as "highly unreasonable omissions or misrepresentations that involve not merely simple or even excusable negligence but an extreme departure from the standards of ordinary care, [presenting] a danger of misleading buyers or sellers which is either known to the defendant or is so obvious that the defendant must have been aware of it."[28] This is a "subjective" standard of recklessness, essentially asking whether the defendant was aware that he or she didn't know whether what was being said was true (even though it might be). Once we start asking whether the risk was known or so obvious that the defendant must have been aware of it, we run into the same problem of biased perception.

Of course, as noted earlier, a defendant will only be found to lack awareness if the judge or jury so determines, and there are ample reasons to doubt whether either will be inclined to accept a claim of a schema-based defense. This is much the same as the hindsight bias problem: the jury will be told and shown that (metaphorically) the gorilla was in the room, and it may well then seem "so obvious that the defendant must have been aware of it."

Now let us return to Martha Stewart. If we assume that there was inside information passed on by Bacanovic's assistant and no pre-existing instruction to sell, it is not easy to make a case of cognitive blindness when she said otherwise to investigators and the public. (To be clear, I think the above discussion applies more easily to financial frauds that were characterized by a high degree of informational and normative ambiguity, as I have explored elsewhere.[29]) If asked to speculate, I would guess that Stewart suffered from an illusion of control typical of highly successful executives: the belief that bluffing and dissembling was something she had done well many times before and could get away with again, especially as against "mere" government functionaries and a manipulable public.

But I am not entirely sure of that. We do know from reports that she had met with Bacanovic a couple of weeks before and that selling ImClone had been discussed. (More on this meeting later.) Perhaps a figure of $60 was mentioned. Would it be possible that she was led to recall that meeting as coming to such an understanding, so that the ImClone stock was *supposed* to have been sold when the price dropped to that level? Cognitive research does show that motivation can bias recollections even with respect to fairly objective factual matters.

Of course, Stewart allegedly told investigators more than that—she made other misstatements about the phone call, and supposedly tried to alter documents—and these were the false statements upon which she actually was convicted.[30] With respect to these, awareness would be harder to deny. At this point, the more plausible account would be that if she had convinced herself that she was in fact not guilty of insider trading, she felt justified in misrepresenting certain facts that otherwise looked bad (for example, the fact that there was a phone call from the broker followed quickly by the sale, or that there was no good documentation of the instruction to sell). That is an all-too-human form of moral rationalization,[31] but as we saw above, nothing that undercuts a finding of scienter. As such, I suspect that her awareness in June would satisfy even a psychologically rigorous test for scienter.

Martha Stewart's Insider Trading

There was no trial with respect to allegations of insider trading by Martha Stewart because the prosecution chose not to charge her with such. Many observers viewed that as awkward, predicting that the jury would not be sympathetic to a claim of lying to investigators about conduct that the prosecutors decided wasn't unlawful. In hindsight, we know that the prosecution's strategy worked anyway.

The implicit message, however, was that there were flaws in the insider trading case that made it dangerous (or at least complicating) to take to the jury.[32] What were they? Much of the discussion has been with respect to the particular use of the misappropriation theory of liability that would be necessary to create liability. Though that may be partially so, I think that we also have to return to the scienter requirement.

The SEC's civil case against Stewart was fairly clear in its theory of liability. The material non-public information was the fact that the Waksals were selling, which allegedly was passed on in the telephone conversation just before Stewart unloaded her holdings of ImClone. Information that a controlling shareholder was secretly trying to sell off his own and family shares does seem to be the sort that a reasonable investor would likely consider important—the legal test for materiality.

This misappropriation theory of liability finds a violation of Rule 10b-5 when a person who is "entrusted" with confidential information secretly breaches his fiduciary duty by tipping or trading.[33] The SEC's claim (which presumably is the same as what prosecutors would have alleged had they brought the case) was that Bacanovic was the misappropriator, under a duty to Merrill Lynch and his customer to respect the confidentiality of any one customer's trading. Merrill indeed makes its official policy to that effect clear in training and compliance manuals. When he passed the information on to

Stewart, he violated that expectation. As to Stewart, the misappropriation theory makes her liable as a tippee if she knows or recklessly disregards that the information has been given to her in violation of the tipper's fiduciary duties.[34] The SEC emphasized that as a former stockbroker, Stewart would have been aware of the confidentiality rules.

Here we can see some legal arguments on Stewart's behalf. First, in contrast to what misappropriation is normally concerned with (fiduciary disloyalty), Bacanovic's action in taking care of a major client like Stewart was arguably in Merrill's best interest. As to Merrill, in other words, he was not "feigning loyalty" while acting disloyally – the essence of misappropriation. Moreover, it would not be surprising to learn that within the brokerage community this is an informal norm of "good for business" information sharing that departs from the formal confidentiality statement in company policy. As to duties Bacanovic owed to Waksal personally, one might wonder whether Waksal really had any expectation that his trading would be kept completely confidential and not shared with someone like Stewart, who was his close friend. After all, he was aggressively getting his father and daughter out of ImClone. None of these points is a clear winner for Stewart, but it is easy to see how the government's case becomes harder in light of them.

My sense, however, is that scienter is at least as interesting an issue, and raises another potential defense. This brings us back to Stewart's thought-process on and around December 27, and here we can draw on some background facts provided by behavioral finance scholar Meir Statman in a recent paper.[35] Stewart was not a very successful investor. She had a portfolio loaded with technology stocks (ImClone, in the biotech field, was one) and was badly hurt by the technology sector sell-off that occurred in 2000 and 2001. Her portfolio value (excluding MSLO) declined from $4,530,730 in June 2000 to $2,510,973 in December 2001.

What was most notable is how reluctant she was to sell her stocks, which may connect to a tendency often noted in the behavioral finance literature.[36] Stewart was regularly favored with IPO allocations, meaning that she was able to buy the stocks at a deep discount to likely near-term market values. Whether or not they "flip" immediately, many investors take their profit in the near-term. Stewart did not, holding the shares through expectedly dramatic price increases and then, later on, through the bursting of the tech stock bubble.[37] She thus managed to lose money even having started in such an extraordinarily favorable position.

Whose fault this was is not clear; Stewart apparently blamed Bacanovic and Merrill. In any event, Bacanovic met with Stewart in mid-December to urge her sell her "loss" stocks before the end of the year to offset against taxable income. They discussed each of the holdings, including ImClone, and

Stewart finally sold off all twenty-two of her loss stocks on December 21 and 24 for a combined loss of $1,037,874. Because ImClone was one of her few profitable stocks (and by far her most profitable), she held onto it.[38] Crucially, Stewart said that this selling "made her stomach turn,"[39] an interesting psychological point. In fact, the tax losses were quite valuable given Stewart's other income. However, having to finally admit defeat and take the losses—notwithstanding such potential for gain a year or two earlier—was devastating to Stewart's ego, and generated a good deal of anger and regret. So far as her investments were concerned, Stewart was in late December in an emotionally depressed state.

Then, on December 27, *just three days* after the stomach-turning sales were done, she got the phone call from Bacanovic's assistant indicating that her only remaining winner, ImClone, was also about to implode. One can at least appreciate what was no doubt a very emotional response—*not this one, too!* If she had a chance to avoid this loss by selling before the market adjusted, such risky behavior can at least be placed in context,[40] though it certainly wouldn't be a defense to insider trading.

What is legally a defense is the absence of scienter. Defining scienter with respect to insider trading has been controversial, with courts and the SEC disagreeing about whether it must be shown that the defendant "used" the inside information to profit (i.e., that he traded because of the information) or whether mere possession of the information is enough, without regard to motivation.[41] In 2000, the SEC sought to resolve the controversy via Rule 10b5-1, establishing an "awareness" standard that conforms closely to the prevailing standard in non-insider trading Rule 10b-5 cases, as we have seen.

This controversy largely assumed that the information was material and nonpublic, however, and focused solely on whether a causal link between that information and the trading is necessary. A more subtle scienter issue is what awareness the defendant must have as to either the materiality or the non-public nature of the information when there is some ambiguity. In particular, would a defendant lack scienter if he or she thought that the information was public, even though it wasn't? Although the case law on this is sparse, it would seem so.[42]

Now consider what Stewart learned from Bacanovic's assistant. Initially, there were two bits of information in the phone message—that the Waksals were selling and that Bacanovic expected the price to decline. She called the broker's assistant and learned one more fact—that the price had already fallen a good bit. My suspicion is that (especially in an angry and emotional state) she could easily construe this to mean that adverse information had already reached the market, and the big institutions were starting to bail out. She did not want to be left behind, again.

As to the Waksals' selling, I suspect that she construed this as the Waksals *and much of Wall Street.* In fact, it is hard to imagine (especially to a former stockbroker) that she would assume that she was being told that the Waksals were selling illegally—which would be the case if the information had not yet made it to the market. Illegal sales by senior executives do not usually occur in an unconcealed fashion through a reputable broker. Again, the more likely inference is that word about Erbitux had become public and that the Waksals were joining the crowd.

Whether this is a successful defense as a matter of law is a bit murky. As Rule 10b5-1 shows, the SEC prefers a simplified state of mind inquiry and could claim that even if the foregoing were true (1) Stewart still had one piece of information that the rest of the world did not, received from a private source in arguable breach of fiduciary duty;[43] (2) under these circumstances, she recklessly failed to ascertain the state of public knowledge before selling; and (3) that information does not become public until it is *fully* internalized by the market (i.e., trading by the smart money is not enough if the price is still adjusting).[44]

My point is not to argue the law on these questions,[45] but rather to point out that Stewart's actions may have fallen short of at least the spirit of the scienter requirement under Rule 10b-5, which requires conscious awareness. And even if she did act with scienter because the law (i.e., Rule 10b5-1) is construed to make scienter easier for the SEC or prosecutors to prove in the insider trading context, we see a consequence that might be somewhat troubling: people can be guilty of insider trading even under circumstances that evidence a very low level of moral culpability.[46] Perhaps that is a fair trade-off with respect to civil enforcement,[47] but the threat of criminal prosecution raises the stakes considerably. My impression that Stewart may have lacked a contemporaneous appreciation that this was illegal insider trading is supported by her own lack of any effort whatsoever to conceal the trading. Like the Waksals, she left the trading wide open for Merrill's internal compliance personnel and federal investigators to see. Either she made an emotional, angry decision without regard for the legal risks to avoid a tiny loss or she believed that what she did was justifiable. Probably it was a combination of the two.[48] In any event, it was very different from the kinds of behavior we generally think of as core insider trading abuses.[49]

Conclusion

Our clinical inquiry into the securities fraud cases against Martha Stewart that never happened considered only one dimension to an interesting event.

Others have looked at the case with a view toward other dimensions: ambiguities in the law of insider trading, for example, which permit factors such as envy, gender bias, or political bias to have an undue influence on prosecutorial decisions or trial outcomes,[50] or how celebrities are treated in the judicial system. I do not mean in this brief essay to have looked at the case from all angles.

Rather, my aim has been to stay close to the behavioral law and economics project, on which much of my research has focused. Legal standards that require some element of subjective intent, willfulness, or bad faith are usually imposed to describe highly culpable forms of behavior, thereby justifying harsh liability consequences. Securities fraud is certainly such, and recently the view has grown that those who commit securities fraud are bad actors deserving punishments that substantially exceed even those attaching to most violent crimes.

My sense is that culpability with respect to securities fraud is in fact very hard to parse out, running a broad range from the truly sociopathic (scams that prey on and devastate the finances of the unsuspecting elderly) to conduct that should have been better but reflected a good bit more myopia, rationalization and self-deception than any deliberate deceit. Used carefully, the tools of cognitive and social psychology under the rubric of behavioral law and economics can be of substantial help in parsing out how people (including, and perhaps especially, those who thrive in corporations or financial markets) perceive information and make judgments, which in turn will get us much closer to what those suspected of fraud were thinking, how much blame and punishment is deserved, and how the law might be reframed to encourage more thoughtful assessments of culpability.

Questions

1. Assuming that Martha Stewart was not telling the "whole truth" when she spoke publicly about the investigation to journalists and securities analysts, what do you think her motive was? How do you think the various audiences who read about her statements might have understood them?
2. One of the important facts regarding the alleged insider trading was that Stewart made no serious effort to conceal it at the time it occurred. This is some evidence that she did not have a contemporaneous appreciation that she was engaged in misconduct. To this line of argument, prosecutors simply responded that "smart people do stupid things" (see footnote 48). What do you think about both the defense and the retort?

3. If you were a juror in the *Stewart* case, how would you have reacted to the fact that she was only charged with obstruction-related acts, not the insider trading that was the subject of the government's investigation? Would it matter? Why?

Notes

1. Ernst & Ernst v. Hochfelder, 425 U.S. 185 (1976). *Hochfelder* was clear in its rejection of negligence as an appropriate state of mind standard: otherwise, it spoke only in dicta of scienter as "a mental state embracing intent to deceive, manipulate or defraud" and as action "other than in good faith." *Id.* at 193 n.12. *See generally* James D. Cox, Ernst & Ernst v. Hochfelder: *A Critique and Evaluation*, 28 Hastings L.J. 569 (1977).

2. *See* James D. Cox et al., Securities Regulation: Cases and Materials 648–51 (4th ed. 2004).

3. She was charged with other related crimes, including obstruction of justice and conspiracy.

4. SEC Litig. Rel. No. 18169, June 4, 2003 [hereinafter SEC Complaint]. Stewart and Bacanovic both subsequently settled with the SEC. *See* SEC Litig. Rel. No. 19794, Aug. 7, 2006, *available at* http://www.sec.gov/litigation/litreleases/2006/ lr19794.htm.

5. United States v. Stewart, 305 F. Supp. 2d 368 (S.D.N.Y. 2004). *See Jury Convicts Martha Stewart on Conspiracy, Obstruction Charges*, 36 Sec. Reg. & L. Rep. (BNA) 425 (March 8, 2004).

6. This account is taken from the criminal indictment, which I am assuming (in light of the conviction by the jury) basically to be true, and the SEC's civil complaint. *See* Superseding Indictment in United States v. Stewart and Bacanovic, S1 03 Cr. 717 (S.D.N.Y.); SEC Complaint, *supra* note 4. Obviously, the true facts may be different. For other commentaries on the securities fraud claim, see Dale Osterle, *Early Observations on the Prosecutions of the Business Scandals of 2002–03: On Sideshow Prosecutions, Spitzer's Clash with Donaldson Over Turf, the Choice of Civil or Criminal Actions, and the Tough Tactic of Coerced Cooperation*, 1 Ohio St. J. Crim. L. 443 (2004); Chapters 5 & 8 of this volume.

7. Importantly, Stewart and Waksal were also close friends; Waksal had once dated Stewart's daughter, and he and Stewart socialized frequently. For an interesting background on the Stewart case, including the trial, see Jeffrey Toobin, *A Bad Thing: Why Did Martha Stewart Lose?*, The New Yorker, March 22, 2004.

8. The irony is that the FDA eventually gave its approval to Erbitux, and by the time Stewart was being sentenced to prison, ImClone shares were trading at around $85 per share.

9. Merrill Lynch compliance officials set the investigation in motion.

10. Thereby making it non-appealable. The court had earlier refused to dismiss the securities charge, which had been argued by Stewart's lawyers largely on grounds that the June statements were immaterial as a matter of law.

11. 305 F. Supp. 2d at 376.

12. *Id.* at 378.

13. *See* State Teachers Retirement Board v. Fluor Corp., 654 F.2d 843, 850 (2d Cir. 1983). *Fluor* is an ambiguous precedent because the court was facing the problem of a company's affirmative duty to disclose, which it saw as presenting a separate problem.

14. *See* SEC v. Falstaff Brewing Co., 629 F.2d 62, 76 (D.C. Cir. 1980); 5C ARNOLD JA-
COBS, DISCLOSURE AND REMEDIES UNDER THE SECURITIES LAWS ¶ 12:75 (2001); 3B HAROLD
S. BLOOMENTHAL & SAMUEL WOLFF, SECURITIES AND FEDERAL CORPORATE LAW ¶ 13.20 (2d
ed. 2001) ("intent to deceive was actionable at common law irrespective of motive or purpose;" rule is the same under Rule 10b-5). One important consequence—quite relevant to
the Stewart question—is that one can be liable under 10b-5 even if the deception of investors was simply a consequence of a plan to deceive someone else (e.g., a defense contractor lying to the Defense Department). *See* Heit v. Weitzen, 402 F.2d 909 (2d Cir. 1968).

15. 206 F.3d 202 (2d Cir. 2000).

16. S.E.C. v. Texas Gulf Sulphur Co., 401 F.2d 833 (2d Cir. 1968) (en banc).

17. *See* Semerenko v. Cendant Corp., 216 F.3d 315 (3d Cir. 2000); *In re* Carter Wallace
Sec. Litig., 150 F.3d 153 (2d Cir. 1998); *In re* Ames Department Store Stock Litig., 991 F.2d
953 (2d Cir. 1993).

18. 485 U.S. 224, 239 n.17 (1988).

19. *See, e.g.,* Greebel v. FTP Software Inc., 194 F.3d 185 (1st Cir. 1999); COX ET AL.,
supra note 2, at 650.

20. This seems to have been the case in *AUSA. See* 206 F.3d at n.12.

21. *See, e.g.,* Novak v. Kosaks, 216 F.3d 300 (2d Cir. 2000).

22. *See* United States v. Dixon, 536 F.2d 1388 (2d Cir. 1976). Arguably, however, this
is too strict: some believe that willfulness only requires that the defendant simply know
the facts that underlie the offense. *See* William H. Widen, *Enron at the Margin*, 58 BUS.
LAW. 961 (2003); Norbert Beveridge, *Is Mens Rea Required for a Criminal Violation of the
Federal Securities Laws?*, 52 BUS. LAW. 35 (1996).

23. Had Stewart simply (but assume falsely) proclaimed her innocence without giving any
specific factual details, there is a good chance that this would be treated as the equivalent of
puffery (i.e., immaterial as a matter of law)—a general statement of the sort expected from a
defendant regardless of guilt, and thus not taken seriously by the reasonable investor. Indeed,
in its motion to dismiss, the Stewart defense argued that even the broader set of denials and
explanations by Stewart should be deemed immaterial. Having said more, the case for materiality is stronger and essentially factual, requiring a close look at market effect. One might
argue that Stewart *assumed* that the market would disregard even her factual statements as
puffery, but that is hardly self-evident and hardly a proper basis for a ruling as a matter of law.

24. Waksal was sentenced to seven years in prison, though the counts against him included tax evasion as well. *See* Leslie Eaton, *The Ghost of Waksal Past Hovers Over the Stewart Trial*, N.Y. TIMES, Feb. 17, 2004, at C-1.

25. The video can be found at http://viscog.beckman.uiuc.edu/djs_lab/ demos.html.

26. I certainly did not when I first viewed the video.

27. *See* Sara Kiesler & Lee Sproul, *Managerial Responses to Changing Environments: Perspectives on Problem Sensing from Social Cognition*, 27 ADMIN. SCI. Q. 548 (1982). For an
example with significant legal implications, see Dennis Gioia, *Pinto Fires and Personal
Ethics: A Script Analysis of Missed Opportunities*, 11 J. BUS. ETHICS 379 (1992).

28. Broad v. Rockwell Int'l Corp., 642 F.2d 929, 961–62 (5th Cir.), *cert. denied*, 454
U.S. 965 (1981).

29. *See* Donald C. Langevoort, *Technological Evolution and the Devolution of Corporate
Financial Reporting*, 46 WM. & MARY L. REV. 1 (2004).

30. The jury did not convict based on the $60 "understanding," which was significant
because of concerns that later surfaced that an expert witness for the prosecution com-

mitted perjury in his testimony. *See* United States v. Stewart, 323 F. Supp. 2d 606 (S.D.N.Y. 2004), *aff'd* 433 F.3d 273 (2d Cir. 2006).

31. Even more so if she thought that the investigation was unfair or politically motivated. *Cf.* Dale Miller, *Psychologically Naïve Assumptions About the Perils of Conflicts of Interest*, in Conflicts of Interest: Challenges and Solutions in Business, Law, Medicine and Public Policy 126, 28 (Don A. Moore et al. eds., 2005) ("Much unethical behavior is justified by the sense of fairness or entitlement").

32. *See* Michael Siegel & Christopher Slobogin, *Prosecuting Martha: Federal Prosecutorial Power and the Need for a Law of Counts*, 109 Penn. St. L. Rev. 1107 (2005).

33. United States v. O'Hagan, 521 U.S. 642 (1997).

34. There are interpretive questions about the precise scope of tipper-tippee liability under the misappropriation theory of liability, but they would not likely operate in Stewart's favor. *See* United States v. Falcone, 257 F.3d 226 (2d Cir. 2001).

35. Meir Statman, *Martha Stewart's Lessons in Behavioral Finance*, 7 J. Inv. Consulting 1 (2005).

36. *See* Hersh Shefrin & Meir Statman, *The Disposition to Sell Winners Too Early and Ride Losers Too Long: Theory and Evidence*, 40 J. Fin. 777 (1985). One magazine story suggests a different explanation: that Stewart often bought stocks in companies where she knew the CEO personally and felt that selling would be disloyal. *See* Toobin, *supra* note 7. Indeed, Stewart had a habit of holding onto winners *and* losers too long. *See* Statman, *supra* note 35, at 5.

37. For example, she bought 350 shares of Palm Inc. at $38 and watched the price go up to $95 on the first trading day. When she sold the shares, they were trading at $3.47.

38. She had bought ImClone at $16 and as of mid-December had a gain of some $186,000.

39. *See* Statman, *supra* note 35, at 4.

40. *See* Jessica Lerner & David Keltner, *Fear, Anger and Risk*, 81 J. Pers. & Soc. Psych. 146 (2001) (anger leads to riskier behavior). For a good review of the research on the role of emotions in securities trading—which generally suggests that more emotional traders perform more poorly than less emotional ones—see Andrew Lo et al., Fear and Greed in Financial Markets: A Clinical Study of Day-Traders (MIT working paper, March 22, 2005); *see also* Peter Huang, *Regulating Irrational Exuberance and Anxiety in the Securities Markets*, in The Law and Economics of Irrational Behavior 501 (Francesco Paresi & Vernon Smith, eds., 2005).

41. *See* Donna Nagy, *The Possession v. Use Debate in the Context of Securities Trading By Traditional Insiders: Why Silence Can Never be Golden*, 67 U. Cin. L. Rev. 1129 (1999).

42. For a discussion, see Donald C. Langevoort, Insider Trading: Regulation, Enforcement and Prevention § 5.5 (2004 ed.); *see also* Alan Horwich, *The Neglected Relationship Between Materiality and Recklessness Under Rule 10b-5*, 55 Bus. Law. 1023 (2000).

43. *See* United States v. Mylett, 97 F.3d 663 (2d Cir. 1996).

44. The SEC has fairly consistently held to the view that information is not public until it is generally available to the investing public. *See* Langevoort, *supra* note 42, § 5.4.

45. The case would have been more complicated as a criminal action because courts sometimes insist on a higher level of scienter in criminal insider trading cases as compared to civil. *See, e.g.,* United States v. Smith, 155 F.3d 1051 (9th Cir. 1998) (use rather than possession); United States v. Cassese, 290 F. Supp. 2d 443 (S.D.N.Y. 2003) (knowledge of tender offer in case brought under 14e-3).

46. *See* Carol Swanson, *Insider Trading Madness: Rule 10b5-1 and the Death of Scienter*, 52 U. Kan. L. Rev. 147 (2003).

47. The core remedy in a civil insider trading case is disgorgement; other remedies (e.g., an injunction or a civil penalty) are discretionary and vary with the perceived culpability of the conduct.

48. This issue was raised by Stewart's lawyers at her criminal trial. The prosecution responded by saying that white collar criminals often do stupid things. *See* Toobin, *supra* note 7.

49. To be sure, the SEC treats all insider trading enforcement actions as morality plays. *See* Donald C. Langevoort, *Rereading Cady Roberts: The Ideology and Practice of Insider Trading Regulation*, 99 COLUM. L. REV. 1319 (1999).

50. *See* Joan MacLeod Heminway, *Save Martha Stewart? Observations About Equal Justice in U.S. Insider Trading Regulation*, 12 TEX. J. WOMEN & L. 247 (2003); Daniel Richman & William Stuntz, *Al Capone's Revenge: An Essay on the Political Economy of Pretextual Prosecution*, 105 COLUM. L. REV. 583 (2005); Jeanne Schroeder, *Envy and Outsider Trading: The Case of Martha Stewart*, 26 CARDOZO L. REV. 2023 (2005). On the aspects of the case that emerged after the trial and conviction, see Kathleen Brickey, *Mostly Martha*, 44 WASHBURN L. REV. 517 (2005).

CHAPTER 10

MATERIAL MISSTATEMENTS?

Joan MacLeod Heminway

The jury in Martha Stewart's 2004 criminal trial found that public statements Stewart made relating to her sale of ImClone Systems, Inc. ("ImClone") stock on December 27, 2001 were untrue and, therefore, that Stewart was guilty of various crimes involving false statements and obstruction of justice.[1] Generally, misstatements are actionable under law only if they have a certain level of importance in a specified context. The law, inside and outside the criminal law context, often refers to this level of importance as "materiality."[2] For example, materiality is an element of proof for many federal perjury and other false statements crimes, including some of those brought against Stewart and her co-defendant stockbroker, Peter Bacanovic, in June 2003.[3]

In the same criminal trial, Stewart was acquitted by the judge of a federal securities fraud charge arising out of her asserted public misstatements—alleged misrepresentations surrounding the reasons for her disposition of ImClone stock on that fateful day in the last week of December 2001.[4] The government's indictment alleged that Stewart made these misstatements in an attempt to deceive the stockholders of Martha Stewart Living Omnimedia, Inc., a public corporation founded by Stewart to house various media and other commercial interests based on and surrounding Stewart's expertise in homemaking, entertaining, home décor, crafts, and other domestic arts ("MSLO").[5] Specifically, the government charged that Stewart's false public explanations regarding the sale of her ImClone stock violated Rule 10b-5,[6] the principal federal antifraud provision (adopted by the Securities and Exchange Commission ("SEC") under the Securities Exchange Act of 1934, as amended (the "1934 Act")[7]) governing misstatements of material fact in connection with a purchase or sale of securities.[8] Materiality is an element of proof in federal securities fraud charges brought under Rule 10b-5.[9] A defendant must misrepresent or omit to state a *material* fact in order to violate Rule 10b-5.[10] Accordingly, where federal securities law imposes a duty to disclose information, materiality defines the information that is required to be disclosed in accordance with that duty.[11]

The materiality, under Rule 10b-5, of Stewart's alleged misstatements was at issue in Stewart's criminal trial and in her motion for acquittal. However, the judge who acquitted Stewart of criminal securities fraud decided Stewart's motion on the basis of another element of the Rule 10b-5 charge—the "state of mind" or "scienter" element, making a materiality determination unnecessary. As a result, the court expressly declined to rule on the materiality of Stewart's misstatements in its judgment of acquittal.[12] Because the materiality question is both interesting and important as a matter of Rule 10b-5 jurisprudence, this chapter analyzes the materiality of the alleged misstatements that underlie Stewart's Rule 10b-5 charge. The analysis set forth in this chapter assumes, without definitively deciding the matter, that the public statements at issue in the government's indictment were false when made.

The Generalized Law Governing Materiality under Rule 10b-5

The concept of materiality, as it is used in criminal and civil actions brought under Rule 10b-5, is defined in decisional law.[13] In 1988, in *Basic Inc. v. Levinson*, the U.S. Supreme Court set forth two alternative formulations of a standard for materiality for use in Rule 10b-5 cases.[14] First, according to the Supreme Court, a fact is material if there is a "substantial likelihood" that the reasonable investor would find the fact important in making an investment decision.[15] The Court goes on to say that, an omitted fact is material if there is a "substantial likelihood that disclosure of the omitted fact would have been viewed by the reasonable investor as having significantly altered the 'total mix' of information made available."[16] The two formulations apparently are intended to be alternative means of determining materiality.[17]

In application, these two formulations of the Rule 10b-5 materiality standard are highly contextual.[18] Materiality determinations under the formulations are mixed questions of law and fact[19] that typically are difficult to decide on motions to dismiss or for summary judgment.[20] Materiality is evaluated based on the probable impact of disclosure on the objective "reasonable investor," not based on the definite impact of disclosure on any actual investor.[21] Consequently, our understanding of materiality in the Rule 10b-5 context is textured, evolving, and (therefore) incomplete.[22]

The Alleged Misstatements

In its criminal action against Stewart, the government asserted that Stewart made four material public misstatements that are actionable under Rule 10b-5. Each statement allegedly misrepresented the reason why Stewart sold her ImClone stock in December 2001.[23] These statements include:

- a June 6, 2002 representation made by Stewart's counsel, on Stewart's behalf, to *The Wall Street Journal* (published on June 7, 2002) that Stewart sold her ImClone shares because of a "stop loss" order that authorized and directed the sale of her shares "if the stock ever went below $60;"[24]
- a public announcement that Stewart caused to be prepared and issued on June 12, 2002 (a) revealing more detailed facts about the alleged $60 "stop loss" order relating to Stewart's ImClone shares and information regarding related communications between Stewart and her stockbroker and (b) representing that Stewart did not have nonpublic information about ImClone when she sold her ImClone shares;[25]
- a public statement prepared, approved, and caused to be issued by Stewart on June 18, 2002 (in contemplation of a public appearance to be made by her at a conference on the following day) that both repeats the information included in the June 12, 2002 public announcement and represents that she cooperated completely with the SEC and the U.S. Attorney's office;[26] and
- Stewart's reading of the June 18, 2002 public statement at the conference on June 19, 2002.[27]

The government's indictment and proof made out a case on materiality built on the fact that "STEWART's reputation, as well as the likelihood of any criminal or regulatory action against STEWART, were material to MSLO's shareholders because of the negative impact that any such action or damage to her reputation could have on the company which [sic] bears her name...."[28] The allegations and evidence of materiality included text from the MSLO initial public offering prospectus and stock trading information showing a drop in the price of MSLO's stock after the public announcement of Stewart's sale of her ImClone shares.[29]

Assessing Materiality

A thorough analysis of the materiality of any or all of Stewart's four alleged misstatements under Rule 10b-5 requires an assessment of both the importance of the misstated facts to the reasonable investor and the reasonable investor's view on the extent to which disclosure of omitted facts alters the total mix of information made available. If it is substantially likely that the reasonable investor either would (a) find the misstated or omitted facts concerning the reason for Stewart's 2001 ImClone stock trade important in making an investment decision in MSLO's stock or (b) view disclosure of the omitted facts relating to the reason for her trade as significantly altering the 'total mix' of information made available, then the misrepresented or omitted facts are material.

Analysis with a Focus on the Reasonable Investor

At the heart of materiality is the notion of the "reasonable investor." Who is the reasonable investor, and how do we determine the reasonable investor's assessments of the importance and total mix of information? These questions remain unanswered in a definitive manner by statutory and decisional law, regulatory interpretation and guidance, and empirical research and, accordingly, continue to be theorized by legal scholars.[30] What is apparent from the judicially constructed materiality standards, however, is the courts' desire to use an objective "litmus test" for determining information required to be disclosed to investors by those having a disclosure duty. Not every disclosure is required;[31] not every investor is protected.[32] Effectively, the reasonable investor is a proxy for the type of person intended to be protected by the proscriptions (and derivative disclosure prescriptions) of Rule 10b-5. In determining disclosure requirements under Section 5 of the Securities Act of 1933, as amended, the Supreme Court has described this type of person as one who cannot fend for himself.[33] Although this description has not been imported for judicial use in analyzing disclosure requirements under the 1934 Act, it nevertheless may be instructive in disclosure analyses under Rule 10b-5.

Given the *Basic* Court's articulation of the materiality standard under Rule 10b-5, it may be most productive to assess the materiality of Stewart's alleged misstatements by inquiring as to the reasons why an investor desiring to purchase or sell MSLO stock would find it important to know the reasons for Stewart's December 2001 sale of ImClone stock. Stated in the alternative, it may be useful to determine why that investor would view disclosure of the reasons for Stewart's ImClone stock trade as a significant alteration of the total mix of available information. More specifically, given the fact that Stewart's public statements about the reason for her ImClone stock trade apparently represent, if anything, unduly favorable disclosures (i.e., representations that would have a positive effect on the market for MSLO's publicly traded securities), the focus of our materiality analysis should be on why a putative purchaser of MSLO's securities in or about June 2002 would have found it important (or a significant alteration of the total mix of available information) to have complete and accurate information about Stewart's December 2001 ImClone stock trade. Having determined this, we then can assess whether that purchaser is a "reasonable investor"—the kind of investor intended to be protected by Rule 10b-5's antifraud regime.

Informational Context

Factual context is important in these analyses.[34] On June 7, 2002, when Stewart's first alleged misrepresentation was publicly released, certain information about MSLO already was publicly available to a purchaser of MSLO stock. That information included facts set forth in MSLO's periodic reports filed under the 1934 Act.[35] However, it also included the fact that Martha Stewart was being investigated by Congress for possible insider trading based on her December 2001 personal trading transaction in ImClone stock.[36] The four alleged misstatements at issue in the government's criminal action against Stewart in fact represent her responses to the public release of information relating to this investigation.[37] The materiality of Stewart's alleged misstatements must be evaluated in light of this then existing public information. Accordingly, our analysis seeks to determine the reason or reasons why an investor in the market at that time with that information would have found Stewart's public statements regarding the facts about her ImClone stock trade important in deciding to purchase MSLO stock. Said differently, we must identify the reason or reasons why a purchaser of MSLO stock in the market at that time would have been of the view that complete and accurate information about Stewart's December 2001 ImClone stock sale significantly altered the then-existing total mix of available information.

The Potential for Materiality

Materiality claims based on personal facts (noncorporate facts) are relatively rare in Rule 10b-5 actions.[38] At first blush, personal transactions may appear to be wholly outside the scope of factual matters that should give rise to claims of federal securities fraud. However, the materiality element of Rule 10b-5 does not, on its face, differentiate between corporate information and personal information. Although any actionable omission or misstatement must be made "in connection with" a purchase or sale of securities,[39] this requirement may be read broadly[40] to include omitted or misstated facts that are not related to the issuer of those securities. Accordingly, an omission or misstatement of personal information may be the subject of a securities fraud claim under Rule 10b-5, as long as it is material.[41]

It is not inconceivable that Stewart's public statements were important to a purchaser's assessment of the integrity of the management of MSLO (of which

Stewart then was a member).[42] Moreover, although Stewart's professional and personal integrity may not have been beyond reproach before her June 2002 public statements,[43] facts omitted from Stewart's representations may have been viewed by a purchaser as a significant alteration to the total mix of available information about Stewart as a key member of MSLO's management. Historically, management integrity has been a basis for both successful and unsuccessful claims of materiality, but materiality claims of this kind generally have not been favored by the courts.[44] Courts that have blessed management integrity as a basis for materiality generally rely on the presence of self-dealing motives in determining that misstatements or omissions are material for purposes of the federal securities laws.[45] Stewart's public statements did not apparently obscure any self-dealing involving MSLO or its stockholders,[46] although, as exculpatory statements, they may have been made in self-interest.[47] Stewart's alleged misstatements relate to a personal transaction in an unaffiliated company's stock, not a transaction undertaken by or on behalf of MSLO.[48] Accordingly, the relationship between Stewart's June 2002 public statements about her ImClone stock trade and her ability to effectively and honestly manage MSLO is somewhat attenuated.[49]

Stewart's public statements also may have been important to a purchaser's assessment of the operational and financial prospects for MSLO because of the importance of Stewart's reputation (and, perhaps, availability and attention) to those prospects.[50] This appears to be the key basis for materiality urged by the government in Stewart's case.[51] Yet, unlike other cases raising this type of materiality claim,[52] Stewart's case did not involve an omission to disclose information about a pending legal action. In June 2002, no legal action had been commenced against Stewart;[53] the investigation of Stewart only just had become public.[54] Moreover, at that time, the public already had information in its possession that cast doubt on Stewart's reputation and the legality of her ImClone stock trade.[55] Stewart's June 2002 public statements merely added her own, transparently self-serving, statement of the facts regarding her sale of ImClone stock to the existing mix of publicly available information.

How does one assess the importance, or significance to the total mix of available information, of the content of the four public statements for which Stewart was indicted under Rule 10b-5 in light of these two possible reasons for investor concern? In general, to the extent that Stewart's public statements were false (as we assume here), a purchaser of MSLO stock might be concerned that Stewart is unfit to manage MSLO or that her services would be unavailable to MSLO if she were found to have committed a criminal violation of Rule 10b-5. Falsity alone, however, cannot support a claim of materiality.[56] Equating falsity with materiality would conflate two separate elements of a Rule 10b-5 claim. There must be something more to materiality than mere untruth.

But what more? Professor Stephen Bainbridge shared his views in a December 2003 posting on his Weblog, ProfessorBainbridge.com.

> The ... question is whether the reasonable investor would factor Martha's explanation for the trade into the investor's calculus of whether Martha will get off, which in turn would have to then be factored into the investor's calculus of whether to buy ... MSO stock. In other words, they're either going to have to prove (1) a reasonable investor would have thought Martha was guilty of insider trading, would have changed his/her mind because of Martha's explanation for the trade, and therefore would have bought MSO stock or (2) a reasonable investor would have thought Martha was innocent of insider trading, would have had that belief confirmed by the explanation, and therefore would have bought MSO stock....

> ... My guess is most people either figure she didn't commit insider trading, in which case her allegedly false explanation for the trade is irrelevant, or (probably more likely) they figure she did do it but would give her a pass on the denial. Nobody would expect Martha to admit guilt.[57]

These observations are both compelling and telling. In neither posited case does the information provided by Stewart's public statements appear to be the dispositive factor in the purchaser's decision to purchase MSLO's publicly traded stock. In neither case is the investor relying on the completeness or truth of Stewart's assertions in making her assessment of the integrity of MSLO's management or the operational and financial prospects for MSLO as a predicate to her MSLO stock purchase. In other words, it is not substantially likely that a purchaser of MSLO stock in June 2002 would have found Stewart's public statements important to her investment decision or would have viewed disclosure of omitted facts in those statements as significantly altering the total mix of available information.

Whether an Investor Acting on These Facts is a "Reasonable Investor"

But what if an investor *did* purchase MSLO securities on the basis of Stewart's June 2002 public representations? Arguably, an investor who believed these statements and bought MSLO stock based on that belief (knowing that the government's investigation of Stewart's ImClone stock trade barely had begun and appreciating the human tendency to protest innocence in response to allegations of guilt) is not the kind of investor that Rule 10b-5 is intended to protect. None of Stewart's public statements, whether true or false, would have forestalled an ongoing investigation of Stewart's sale of ImClone stock or obviated the commencement of one or more civil or criminal actions against

Stewart relating to the ImClone trade. The facts contained in the four public assertions set forth in the government's Rule 10b-5 indictment, viewed in the light of public information then available, afford MSLO investors neither notable support for a positive assessment of management integrity at MSLO nor much assurance as to favorable operating and financial prospects of MSLO.[58] They are the generalized, optimistic, unsubstantiated assertions of a person who is the target of a governmental investigation of possible legal violations. As such, they may be seen as analogous to "mere puffery," which has been found immaterial as a matter of law.[59] Given the nature, timing, and source of the information in Stewart's June 2002 public statements, any investment decision made on the basis of the truth of those facts represents an informed assumption of risk by the investor. An investor purchasing MSLO securities on this basis in June 2002 should not be able to avail himself of the protection of the federal securities laws from the damages suffered by him as a result of the assumption of that calculated risk. That investor can fend for himself.

An Alternative View

However, it is important to note that materiality law and lore ask us to consider the effects of disclosure of omitted facts in cases that involve omitted facts. Although the *Stewart* case largely involves claims regarding misrepresented, rather than omitted, facts, the learning from fact-omission cases may be important in assessing the materiality of Stewart's public statements. Ultimately, in fact-omission cases, the relevant inquiry is whether it is substantially likely disclosure of the complete truth "would have assumed actual significance in the deliberations"[60] of the reasonable investor.

Assuming that the facts in Stewart's June 2002 public statements are, indeed, false, is it substantially likely that disclosure of the complete and accurate facts surrounding her ImClone stock trade would have assumed actual significance in the MSLO stock trading decisions of investors? No. Fully accurate disclosure of the facts surrounding Stewart's sale of ImClone stock (whatever they might be) would not have averted an ongoing investigation of, or prevented the commencement of one or more civil or criminal actions against Stewart relating to, that stock sale. The legality of that sale involves a complex analysis under the law of insider trading, and the legal theory eventually pursued against Stewart represents a questionable extension of existing Supreme Court decisional law.[61]

Moreover, a complete statement of accurate facts by Stewart relating to the ImClone stock trade, viewed in the light of other public information then available, would not have provided MSLO investors with significant new information about management integrity at MSLO or the operating and financial prospects of MSLO. We might expect those who assumed (in spite of their possession of the complete and accurate facts surrounding Stewart's ImClone stock trade) Stewart did not engage in insider trading to hesitate somewhat more in making a purchase decision but not necessarily be more likely to consider a sale transaction. Again, the accurate and complete facts would not necessarily constitute actionable conduct, and a legal action against Stewart based on them would not necessarily be successful.[62] For those who assumed Stewart did violate insider trading rules, the complete truth would merely confirm their assumption and therefore assume no significance in a purchase or sale decision.

Contingent or Speculative Facts?

Finally, it is possible to view the facts relating to Stewart's ImClone stock trade as speculative or contingent facts, since an investor's concerns about management integrity and business prospects are founded, to some extent, on the possible future civil or criminal liability of Stewart for that trade. In other words, an MSLO investor may be less interested in the facts surrounding Stewart's December 2001 sale of ImClone stock in their own right than whether the sale violated law.

The Supreme Court has fashioned a special test for use in gauging the materiality of speculative or contingent facts, in which the probability of the future event is balanced against the importance of that event to the subject company.[63] Although the Court expressly limited its application of this special test to merger negotiations,[64] a number of lower federal courts have applied the test in other situations involving current facts that may be predictive of future events.[65] In the *Stewart* case, the fit of this special test is less perfect than it is in other circumstances, since the future event at issue is the outcome of a legal action in which materiality is at issue (i.e., a potential legal action against Stewart for insider trading).

In applying the "probability vs. magnitude" test to an analysis of the materiality of the June 2002 facts relating to Stewart's ImClone stock sale, it is apparent that the probability of a lawsuit or legal violation based on those facts then would have been quite uncertain, and the magnitude of any lawsuit or legal violation to MSLO also would have been uncertain.[66] Many elements must be proven in order for those facts to constitute or provide evidence of legal violations.[67] Moreover, while Stewart's reputation and talents were important to MSLO, in June 2002, one could not have been certain of the nature and extent of the effects on MSLO of damage to Stewart's reputation or the loss of her talents for an unspecified period of time.[68] A balancing of the uncertain probability of a legal action against Stewart or Stewart's legal liability against the uncertain magnitude of that legal action or liability on MSLO does not indicate that the reasons for Stewart's sale of ImClone stock were material.

The Impact of Criminal Enforcement

Finally, it is important to assess materiality in the *Stewart* criminal action in light of the applicable burden of proof. As is true for essential elements of most other crimes, materiality in a criminal securities fraud prosecution must be proven by the government beyond a reasonable doubt.[69] Accordingly, to convict Stewart of a criminal violation of Rule 10b-5, the jury would have had to find beyond a reasonable doubt that any statements made by Stewart were both false and material. Given the limited importance of the facts relating to Stewart's ImClone stock sale and the limited effect that those facts would have had on the public information then available (in each case, as demonstrated in the analyses set forth in this chapter), a jury likely would have reasonable doubt as to the materiality of Stewart's alleged misrepresentations.

Conclusions

Because it decided the motion to acquit on different grounds, the court in the *Stewart* case did not have to determine the materiality of Stewart's alleged public misstatements made in June 2002. However, a materiality analysis of the facts in Stewart's public statements raises certain novel issues (based principally on the unusual nature of the disputed facts) and exposes for further thought some recurrent themes in materiality law and policy. Moreover, the *Stewart* case offers us the opportunity to outline and explore the use of a process for assessing materiality.

Where, as in the *Stewart* case, materiality is unclear, a two-staged analysis may be helpful. Specifically, it may be beneficial first to assess the ways in which the subject facts may be important to an investor (or, alternatively, significant to the total mix of available information) and then to reflect on whether an investor finding those facts important or significant on those bases should be afforded the protections of the federal securities laws (or whether he should be required to fend for himself). Alternative materiality analyses emanating from decisional law regarding factual omissions and contingent or speculative facts may be used to question, contradict, further substantiate, or reinforce the conclusion reached using the initial two-staged analysis. In Stewart's case, each of these analyses leads to the same conclusion: that the accurate and complete reasons for Stewart's December 2001 ImClone stock sale were not material facts at the time she issued her four public statements relating to that stock sale in June 2002.

Questions

1. Why is materiality an element of proof in securities fraud claims brought under Rule 10b-5? How does the judicial standard governing materiality help achieve this purpose?
2. In the criminal securities fraud action brought by the government against Martha Stewart for violating Rule 10b-5, does it matter whether any investor actually bought stock in MSLO as a result of Stewart's June 2002 public statements? If so, why? If not, why not?
3. If Stewart did make false public statements about her December 2001 sale of ImClone stock and these statements are determined to be immaterial in a criminal proceeding under Rule 10b-5, is that a good result for investors? If not, why not? If so, should we make that result more clear by fashioning a materiality rule that more precisely governs disclosures of this kind? How/by what rulemaking body would that rule be enunciated?

Notes

1. *See generally* United States v. Stewart, 433 F.3d 273 (2d Cir. 2006) (reviewing, on appeal, evidence from the Stewart trial and noting the jury verdict against Stewart on charges of "conspiracy, concealing material information from and making false statements to government officials, and obstructing an agency proceeding"); United States v. Stewart, 323 F. Supp. 2d 606 (S.D.N.Y. 2004) (summarizing the findings and verdicts in Stewart's earlier criminal trial in denying Stewart's motion for a new trial).

2. *See, e.g.,* BLACK'S LAW DICTIONARY 991 (7th ed. 1999) (defining "material" as "of such a nature that knowledge of the item would affect a person's decision-making process; significant; essential"); RESTATEMENT (SECOND) OF TORTS 538(2)(a) (1977) (a "matter is material if (a) a reasonable man would attach importance to its existence or nonexistence in determining his choice of action in the transaction in question; or (b) the maker of the representation knows or has reason to know that its recipient regards or is likely to regard the matter as important in determining his choice of action, although a reasonable man would not so regard it.); Renee M. Jones, *Rethinking Corporate Federalism in the Era of Corporate Reform*, 29 IOWA J. CORP. L. 625, 661 (2004) (equating materiality with impor-

tance); Jennifer O'Hare, *The Resurrection of the Dodo: The Unfortunate Re-emergence of the Puffery Defense in Private Securities Fraud Actions*, 59 Ohio St. L.J. 1697, 1702 (1998) (same); Jennifer O'Hare, *Good Faith and the Bespeaks Caution Doctrine: It's Not Just a State of Mind*, 58 U. Pitt. L. Rev. 619, 633 n.75 (1997) (same); Carl A. Pierce, *Client Misconduct in the 21st Century*, 35 U. Mem. L. Rev. 731, 802 (2005) ("Although there is no definition of 'material' in the Model Rules, one can infer ... that a material matter is an 'important' one.").

3. *See* Amy Messigian, *Perjury*, 42 Am. Crim. L. Rev. 755, 766–69 (2005); Ellen S. Podgor, *Arthur Andersen, LLP and Martha Stewart: Should Materiality be an Element of Obstruction of Justice?*, 44 Washburn L.J. 583, 594 (2005) ("[T]he perjury and false declarations statutes both explicitly recite materiality as a required element of proof, and courts have placed the burden on the government to prove this element beyond a reasonable doubt."). Interestingly, however, materiality need not be proven for some crimes involving obstruction of justice. *See* Podgor, *supra*, at 584 ("most courts have not included materiality as a required element for the crime of obstruction of justice").

4. *See* United States v. Stewart, 305 F. Supp. 2d 368 (S.D.N.Y. 2004).

5. Superseding Indictment, United States v. Martha Stewart and Peter Bacanovic, S1 03 Cr. 717 (MGC) (S.D.N.Y. filed Jan. 7, 2004) *available at* http://news.findlaw.com/hdocs/docs/mstewart/usmspb10504sind.pdf [hereinafter Indictment] ¶ 60 ("STEWART made these false and misleading statements with the intent to defraud and deceive purchasers and sellers of MSLO common stock and to maintain the value of her own MSLO stock by preventing a decline in the market price of MSLO's stock.").

6. 17 C.F.R. § 240.10b-5 (2006).

7. 15 U.S.C. § 78j(b) (2000).

8. Numerous scholars have noted the importance of Rule 10b-5 as an antifraud measure. *See, e.g.*, Lawrence A. Cunningham, *"Firm-Specific" Information and the Federal Securities Laws: A Doctrinal, Etymological, and Theoretical Critique*, 68 Tul. L. Rev. 1409, 1413 (1994); Renee M. Jones, *Dynamic Federalism: Competition, Cooperation and Securities Enforcement*, 11 Conn. Ins. L.J. 107, 127 (2004); Donald C. Langevoort, *Organized Illusions: A Behavioral Theory of Why Corporations Mislead Stock Market Investors (And Cause Other Social Harms)*, 146 U. Pa. L. Rev. 101, 105 (1997); Donald C. Langevoort & G. Mitu Gulati, *The Muddled Duty to Disclose Under Rule 10b-5*, 57 Vand. L. Rev. 1639, 1640 (2004); Mark J. Loewenstein, *The Supreme Court, Rule 10b-5 and the Federalization of Corporate Law*, 39 Ind. L. Rev. 17, 17 (2005); Paul G. Mahoney, *Technology, Property Rights in Information, and Securities Regulation*, 75 Wash. U. L. Q. 815, 818 (1997); Joel Seligman, *A Comment on Professor Grundfest's "Disimplying Private Rights of Action Under the Federal Securities Laws: The Commission's Authority,"* 108 Harv. L. Rev. 438, 457 (1994); Lawrence M. Solan, *Statutory Inflation and Institutional Choice*, 44 Wm and Mary L. Rev. 2209, 2238 (2003).

9. Basic Inc. v. Levinson, 485 U.S. 224, 226, 231 (1988); Anish Vashista et al., *Securities Fraud*, 42 Am. Crim. L. Rev. 877, 880–84 (2005).

10. *See Basic*, 485 U.S. at 231–41.

11. *See* TSC Indus. v. Northway, Inc., 426 U.S. 438, 448 (1976) ("Some information is of such dubious significance that insistence on its disclosure may accomplish more harm than good."). The Court has noted that mandating disclosure of less significant information may have negative effects on investors and the market. *Id.* at 448–49 ("[I]f the standard of materiality is unnecessarily low, not only may the corporation and its management be subjected to liability for insignificant omissions or misstatements, but also management's fear of exposing

itself to substantial liability may cause it simply to bury the shareholders in an avalanche of trivial information—a result that is hardly conducive to informed decisionmaking.").

12. *See* United States v. Stewart, 305 F. Supp. 2d 368, 378 n.5 (S.D.N.Y. 2004).

13. Marc I. Steinberg & Jason B. Myers, *Lurking in the Shadows: The Hidden Issues of the Securities and Exchange Commission's Regulation FD*, 27 J. Corp. L. 173, 187 (2002) (noting that "the SEC relies on case law to provide definitions" for the words "material" and "non-public"); C. Daniel Ewell, Note: *Rule 10b-5 and the Duty To Disclose Merger Negotiations in Corporate Statements*, 96 Yale L.J. 547, 560 (1987) ("the definition of materiality under 10b-5 is primarily a judicial creation.").

14. *See generally Basic*, 485 U.S. at 231–32 (adopting, in the Rule 10b-5 context, the alternative formulations of materiality from *TSC Indus. v. Northway, Inc., supra* note 11).

15. *Id.* at 231.

16. *Id.* at 231–32.

17. *See* Joan MacLeod Heminway, *Materiality Guidance in the Context of Insider Trading: A Call for Action*, 52 Am. U.L. Rev. 1131, 1138 n.22 (2003).

18. *See* In re Donald J. Trump Casino Sec. Litig., 7 F.3d 357, 369 (3d Cir. 1993) ("materiality is a relative concept, so that a court must appraise a misrepresentation or omission in the complete context in which the author conveys it."); Yvonne Ching Ling Lee, *The Elusive Concept Of "Materiality" Under U.S. Federal Securities Laws*, 40 Willamette L. Rev. 661, 673–675 (2004). To this point, courts have recognized equitable defenses to claims of materiality based on the context in which misstatements are made. *See, e.g.*, Eisenstadt v. Centel Corp., 113 F.3d 738, 746 (7th Cir. 1997) ("Where puffing is the order of the day, literal truth can be profoundly misleading, as senders and recipients of letters of recommendation well know. Mere sales puffery is not actionable under Rule 10b-5."); Trump Casino, 7 F.3d at 364 (relying on "what has been described as the 'bespeaks caution' doctrine, according to which a court may determine that the inclusion of sufficient cautionary statements in a prospectus renders misrepresentations and omissions contained therein nonactionable"). Moreover, Congress has enacted limited statutory safe harbors with respect to forward-looking statements, 15 U.S.C. §§77z-2 & 78u-5 (2000), and the SEC also has adopted a rule providing limited protection for forward-looking statements. 17 C.F.R. §230.175 (2006).

19. TSC Indus. v. Northway, Inc., 426 U.S. 438, 450 (1976) ("The issue of materiality may be characterized as a mixed question of law and fact, involving as it does the application of a legal standard to a particular set of facts.").

20. *Id. See generally* Tim Oliver Brandi, *The Strike Suit: A Common Problem of ohe Derivative Suit and the Shareholder Class Action*, 98 Dick. L. Rev. 355, 382 (1993) ("The courts have held … that summary judgment would usually be inappropriate for deciding questions like … materiality."); Edward A. Fallone, *Section 10(b) and the Vagaries of Federal Common Law: The Merits of Codifying the Private Cause of Action under a Structuralist Approach*, 1997 U. Ill. L. Rev. 71, 100 (1007) ("Under the definition of materiality adopted, it is difficult for a defendant to negate the element as a matter of law on a motion for summary judgment."). The court denied Stewart's motion to dismiss the Rule 10b-5 charge. Brief for Defendant-Appellant Martha Stewart, United States v. Martha Stewart and Peter Bacanovic, 04-3953(L)-cr (2d Cir. filed Oct. 20, 2004), at 16–17 *available at* http://law-professors.typepad.com/whitecollarcrime_blog/files/Brief.pdf.

21. *See* William O. Fisher, *Does The Efficient Market Theory Help Us Do Justice In A Time Of Madness?*, 54 Emory L.J. 843, 975 (2005) ("Materiality encompasses the notion that information be significant in the deliberations of a reasonable investor.").

22. *See* Steinberg & Myers, *supra* note 13, at 188 ("[T]he law surrounding the definition of materiality is an ever-changing one, often changing in subtle ways that make materiality determinations difficult.").

23. Indictment, *supra* note 5, at ¶ 60 ("STEWART made or caused to be made a series of false and misleading public statements during June 2002 regarding her sale of ImClone stock on December 27, 2001 that concealed and omitted that STEWART had been provided information regarding the sale and attempted sale of the Waksal Shares and that STEWART had sold her ImClone stock while in possession of that information.").

24. Indictment, *supra* note 5, at ¶ 61; United States v. Stewart, 305 F. Supp. 2d 368, 373 (S.D.N.Y. 2004).

25. Indictment, *supra* note 5, at ¶ 63; 305 F. Supp. 2d at 373–74.

26. Indictment, *supra* note 5, at ¶ 64; 305 F. Supp. 2d at 374.

27. Indictment, *supra* note 5, at ¶ 65; 305 F. Supp. 2d at 374.

28. Indictment, *supra* note 5, at ¶ 57. *See also* 305 F. Supp. 2d at 372 (indicating that evidence had been presented by the government at trial in support of the facts alleged in the Indictment).

29. Indictment, *supra* note 5, at ¶¶ 57, 58; 305 F. Supp. 2d at 372–3.

30. *See, e.g.,* William W. Bratton, *The Economic Structure of the Post-Contractual Corporation,* 87 Nw. U.L. Rev. 180, 204 (1992); Stephen J. Choi & A.C. Pritchard, *Behavioral Economics and the SEC,* 56 Stan. L. Rev. 1, 61–62 (2003); Peter H. Huang, *Moody Investing and the Supreme Court: Rethinking the Materiality of Information and the Reasonableness of Investors,* 13 S. Ct. Econ. Rev. 99, 109–12 (2005); Edmund W. Kitch, *The Theory and Practice of Securities Disclosure,* 61 Brooklyn L. Rev. 763, 825 (1995); Steven L. Schwarcz, *Temporal Perspectives: Resolving the Conflict Between Current and Future Investors,* 89 Minn. L. Rev. 1044 (2005).

31. In first enunciating the current materiality standard, the Supreme Court stated:

> Some information is of such dubious significance that insistence on its disclosure may accomplish more harm than good. The potential liability ... can be great indeed, and if the standard of materiality is unnecessarily low, not only may the corporation and its management be subjected to liability for insignificant omissions or misstatements, but also management's fear of exposing itself to substantial liability may cause it simply to bury the shareholders in an avalanche of trivial information....

TSC Indus. v. Northway, Inc., 426 U.S. 438, 448 (U.S. 1976).

32. *See generally* Mark Klock, *Two Possible Answers to the Enron Experience: Will It Be Regulation of Fortune Tellers or Rebirth of Secondary Liability?,* 28 Iowa J. Corp. L. 69, 87 (2002) ("The goal of federal securities regulation is not to protect investors from risk or eliminate all fraud, which would be impossible."); Andrew L. Merritt, *A Consistent Model of Loss Causation in Securities Fraud Litigation: Suiting the Remedy to the Wrong,* 66 Tex. L. Rev. 469, 508 (1988) ("Courts must be alert to protect investors' freedom to choose the risks they wish to encounter; correspondingly, they should be reluctant to allow plaintiffs who have willingly accepted certain risks to back out of their bargains when those risks actually come to pass."); Michael R. Powers, et al., *Market Bubbles and Wasteful Avoidance: Tax and Regulatory Constraints on Short Sales,* 57 Tax L. Rev. 233, 274 (2004) ("[T]he law should safeguard the integrity of the market, but should not necessarily protect each investor from placing foolish bets."); Brendan J. McCarthy, Note: *"In Connection with": The*

Need for Limitation to SEC Rule 10b-5 in Dissemination of Misleading Information Cases, 54 CASE W. RES. 1347, 1381 (2004) ("Although Congress intended to protect investors, it did not intend to protect all investor activities. It merely wished to reduce the risks of dealing in securities by providing a remedy when investors enter unfair transactions.") *Cf.* Norman Stein, *Three and Possibly Four Lessons about ERISA that We Should, but Probably Will Not, Learn from Enron*, 76 ST. JOHN's L. REV. 855, 861 (2002) ("There are certainly limits to how much the government can protect investors generally against the consequences of their own astigmatic judgments").

33. S.E.C. v. Ralston Purina Co., 346 U.S. 119, 125 (1953).

34. *See supra* note 18.

35. MSLO registered its common stock under Section 12 of the 1934 Act in October 1999, *see* Martha Stewart Living Omnimedia, Inc., Registration Statement on Form 8 A (filed Oct. 14, 1999), *available at* http://www.sec.gov/Archives/edgar/data/1091801/0000950123-99-009308.txt, at which time it became obligated to make periodic filings under Section 13 of the 1934 Act. A complete record of the public filings made by MSLO with the SEC can be found at http://www. sec.gov/cgi-bin/browse-edgar?company=martha+stewart+living&CIK=&filenum =&State=&SIC=&owner=exclude&action=getcompany.

36. Jennifer Waters, *Retail sector straddles a wobbly market*, CBS.MARKETWATCH.COM, June 7, 2002, *at* LexisNexis, News & Business file (noting "published reports" of Stewart's insider trading investigation); *supra* note 24.

37. *See supra* note 24.

38. *See* Henry Blodget, *The Charges Against Martha*, SLATE (Dec. 3, 2003), *at* http://www.slate.com/id/2091480/entry/2091866/ (noting that the judge in the *Stewart* case described the Rule 10b-5 securities fraud charge as "novel" and further observing that "[t]ypical securities fraud cases are based on false statements about a company's business, financial performance, or products. In this case, Stewart's statements were not about her company but about her personal sale of stock in *another* company.").

39. *See* U.S. v. Zandford, 535 U.S. 813 (2002); Sup't of Ins. v. Bankers Life & Cas. Co., 404 U.S. 6 (1971); S.E.C. v. Texas Gulf Sulphur Co., 401 F.2d 833 (2d Cir. 1968) (en banc), *cert. denied*, 394 U.S. 976 (1969).

40. *See Zandford*, 535 U.S. at 819 ("[T]he SEC has consistently adopted a broad reading of the phrase 'in connection with the purchase or sale of any security.'"); Anna Mae Maloney, Semerenko V. Cendant Corp.: *The Third Circuit Clarifies the Securities Exchange Commission's Rule 10b-5 in the Context of Public Misrepresentations*, 47 VILL. L. REV. 1171, 1172–1173 (2002) ("The majority of Rule 10b-5's jurisprudence construes the 'in connection with' requirement broadly, as to insure the protection of investors.").

41. For a more complete discussion of the "in connection with" requirement under Rule 10b-5, see Chapters 5 & 8 of this volume.

42. *See generally* Maldonado v. Flynn, 597 F.2d 789 (2d Cir. 1979); SEC v. Kalvex, Inc., 425 F. Supp. 310 (S.D.N.Y. 1975); *In re* Franchard Corporation, 42 S.E.C. 163 (1964). In June 2002, Stewart was the Chairman and Chief Executive Officer of MSLO. Indictment, *supra* note 5, at ¶ 1; Martha Stewart Living Omnimedia, Inc., Definitive Proxy Statement on Schedule 14A (filed March 31, 2003), *available at* http://www.sec.gov/Archives/edgar/data/1091801/000095012303003696/ y84919def14a.htm.

43. *See* CHRISTOPHER BYRON, MARTHA INC. 30–31 (2003) (indicating that Stewart exploited the talents and loyalty of others in order to achieve business success); Mike Straka, *Grrr! Martha Stewart: Oblivion of the Month*, FOXNEWS.COM, February 23, 2006, *at*

http://www.foxnews.com/story/0,2933,185746,00.html ("Stewart's integrity and public image has always been fodder for doubt and behind-the-scenes snickering").

44. *See generally* John M. Fedders, *Qualitative Materiality: The Birth, Struggles, and Demise of an Unworkable Standard*, 48 Cath. U.L. Rev. 41 (1998) (describing decisional law on this and other qualitative materiality claims).

45. *See id.* at 47-49.

46. For example, the government did not allege that Martha Stewart engaged in insider trading through purchases of MSLO's stock. The government did, however, attempt to circumstantially link Stewart's statements to maintenance of the market price of MSLO's stock, of which Martha Stewart then was the majority holder. Indictment, *supra* note 5, at ¶¶ 59 & 60.

47. If so, the appropriate cause of action may be a stockholder derivative suit alleging a breach of Stewart's fiduciary duty of loyalty as an officer and director of MSLO, although there would be significant questions about whether her statements were made on behalf of MSLO or in her capacity as an officer or director of MSLO.

48. *See* Blodget, *supra* note 38.

49. However, it is important to note that MSLO is required to disclose any nontrivial criminal proceeding in which Stewart is a defendant and any criminal conviction of Stewart, even if the violation relates to a personal transaction in the securities of an unaffiliated corporation. 17 C.F.R. § 229.401(f) (2006) (Regulation S-K Item 401(f)). No indictment was filed in the *Stewart* case until June 2003. *See* Indictment, *supra* note 5.

50. *See, e.g.,* GAF Corp. v. Heyman, 724 F.2d 727 (2d Cir. 1983) (finding immaterial, under Rule 14a-9, undisclosed allegations made in a private civil action brought against a corporate director by his sister); S.E.C. v. Electronics Warehouse, Inc., 689 F. Supp. 53, 66-68 (D. Conn. 1988) (successfully raising a materiality claim with respect to the undisclosed mail fraud indictment of a corporation's Chief Executive Officer in the corporation's public offering prospectus).

51. *See* Blodget, *supra* note 38 ("The prosecutors argue that, because Stewart's reputation is (or was) critical to the business of her company, reasonable investors would have viewed her explanation as having altered the 'total mix' of available information about the company's stock, and, therefore, because it was allegedly false, it would have defrauded them."); *supra* note 28 and accompanying text.

52. *See supra* note 50.

53. *See supra* note 49.

54. *See* Indictment, *supra* note 5, at ¶ 58; Alan Reynolds, *Martha's Mistrial: The Insider Trading Accusation Came from a Cowardly Press Leak from a Congressional Committee*, National Post's Financial Post & FP Investing (Canada), March 9, 2004, *available at* http://www.cato.org/research/articles/reynolds-040309.html.

55. *See supra* notes 36 & 43 and accompanying text.

56. Basic Inc. v. Levinson, 485 U.S. 224, 238 (1988) ("It is not enough that a statement is false or incomplete, if the misrepresented fact is otherwise insignificant.")

57. Stephen Bainbridge, *Was Martha Stewart's Denial Material? The Problem with Count 9*, ProfessorBainbridge.com (Dec. 4, 2003), *at* http://www.professorbainbridge.com/2003/12/was_martha_stew.html.

58. In a motion to dismiss the Rule 10b-5 charge, Stewart argued that her statements did not inject new information into the marketplace. *See* Memorandum of Law in Support of Martha Stewart's Omnibus Pre-Trial Motions at 7 (Oct. 6, 2003).

59. *See, e.g.,* Parnes v. Gateway 2000, Inc., 122 F.3d 539, 542 (8th Cir. 1997); Eisenstadt v. Centel Corp., 113 F.3d 738, 745-46 (7th Cir. 1997); In re Burlington Coat Factory Sec. Litig., 114 F.3d 1410, 1427 (3d Cir. 1997); Raab v. General Physics Corp., 4 F.3d 286, 289 (4th Cir. 1993); Howard v. Haddad, 962 F.2d 328, 331 (4th Cir. 1992); Picard Chem. Profit Sharing Plan v. Perrigo Co., 940 F. Supp. 1101, 1122 (D. Mich. 1996). *See generally* O'Hare, *supra* note 2, at 1697 (describing the history and uses of the "mere puffery" defense to materiality claims).

60. TSC Indus. v. Northway, Inc., 426 U.S. 438, 449 (1976) (made applicable to materiality analyses under Rule 10b-5 in *Basic Inc. v. Levinson*, 485 U.S. 224, 231 (1988)). *See also* Michael J. Kaufman, *No Foul, No Harm: The Real Measure Of Damages Under Rule 10b-5*, 39 CATH. U.L. REV. 29, 33 (1989) ("Resolving the question of materiality requires the determination of whether, under all of the circumstances, a strong probability exists that the information would have significantly altered the process by which the reasonable investor made the decision to purchase or sell the securities.").

61. For discussions of the insider trading claims brought against Stewart by the SEC in 2003, see Chapters 1 & 12 of this volume.

62. *See supra* note 61 and accompanying text.

63. Basic Inc. v. Levinson, 485 U.S. 224, 238-38 (1988).

64. *Id.* at 232 n.9 ("We do not address here any other kinds of contingent or speculative information, such as earnings forecasts or projections.").

65. *See, e.g.,* Lawton v. Nyman, 327 F.3d 30, 40-41 (1st Cir. 2003); United States SEC v. Fehn, 97 F.3d 1276, 1291 (9th Cir. 1996). *See also* John W. Bagby et al., *How Green Was My Balance Sheet?: Corporate Liability and Environmental Disclosure*, 14 VA. ENVTL. L.J. 225, 318-19 (1995) ("The speculative nature of the merger negotiations addressed in Basic is also a fundamental characteristic shared with environmental liabilities. This strongly suggests that the Basic probability/magnitude materiality formula should also apply to environmental disclosures."); Heminway, *supra* note 17, at 1212 n.114 (indicating that the *Basic* probability/magnitude test may be applicable to facts other than merger negotiations); Andrew K. Glenn, Note: *Disclosure of Executive Illnesses under Federal Securities Law and the Americans with Disabilities Act of 1990: Hobson's Choice or Business Necessity?*, 16 CARDOZO L. REV. 537, 593 n.111 (1994) ("Although the Court expressly disclaimed application of the probability-magnitude [sic] test in Basic to 'other kinds of contingent or speculative information,' the similarities between merger negotiations and illness disclosure make the analysis in Basic too pertinent to ignore.").

66. Although materiality is to be assessed at the time the disclosure allegedly was required to be made, a number of courts have engaged in determining materiality by hindsight. *See* Mitu Gulati et al., *Fraud by Hindsight*, 98 Nw. U.L. REV. 773, 809-11 (2004).

67. *See supra* note 61 and accompanying text.

68. With hindsight as 20/20 vision, we now can better evaluate the short-term and medium-range impacts on MSLO of the currently known facts regarding Stewart's ImClone stock sale, including the existence of a pending insider trading action and Stewart's five-month prison term and five months of home confinement (as part of two years of supervised release) based on her criminal convictions for conspiracy, obstruction of an agency proceeding, and making false statements. *See* Martha Stewart Living Omnimedia, Inc., Annual Report on Form 10-K (filed March 7, 2006), *available at* http://www.sec.gov/Archives/edgar/data/1091801/000095012306002702/y18218e10vk.htm; *infra* Chapter 11 of this volume (under the heading "Sentencing Issues" and the subheadings "Extraordinary Hardship" and "Applicability to Martha").

69. *See In re* Winship, 397 U.S. 358, 364 (1970) ("[W]e explicitly hold that the Due Process Clause protects the accused against conviction except upon proof beyond a reasonable doubt of every fact necessary to constitute the crime with which he is charged.").

PART III

LEGAL MATTERS OUTSIDE THE CRIMINAL ACTION

CHAPTER 11

THE AFTERMATH OF
THE CRIMINAL TRIAL[*]

Kathleen F. Brickey

December 2001 was remarkable from beginning to end. At 2:00 a.m. on Sunday, December 2, Enron electronically filed the largest bankruptcy in United States history. The filing occurred only days after Enron's board approved more than fifty-five million dollars in retention bonuses to keep five hundred key employees for just ninety days.[1] The following week, four thousand less fortunate Enron employees were summarily fired.

At 1:52 p.m. on Thursday, December 27, Martha Stewart sold all of her ImClone stock. The sale occurred shortly after she learned through a Merrill Lynch stockbroker that ImClone founder and CEO Sam Waksal was trying to sell all of the ImClone stock he held at Merrill Lynch. On Friday, the 28th, the FDA formally notified ImClone that the company's application for approval of its cancer drug, Erbitux, would not be accepted for filing. ImClone announced the FDA's rejection of the application after the market closed at the end of the day. On Monday, December 31, the first day of trading after the FDA's decision was publicly disclosed, the value of ImClone stock plunged eighteen percent.

One might have reasonably assumed that as a media event, the Enron bankruptcy filing would eclipse Stewart's sale of four thousand shares of stock. But history tells us otherwise. After a long legal tug of war and a media-genic six-week trial,[2] the Stewart jury returned a verdict after only twelve hours of deliberations. For Stewart and her stockbroker, Peter Bacanovic, the news was

---

[*] This chapter is adapted from an article entitled *Mostly Martha*, originally published at 44 WASHBURN L.J. 517 (2005), Kathleen F. Brickey © 2005.

somber. The jury found them guilty of lying about the sale of her stock. Although she entered the federal prison system on October 8 to serve a five-month term,[3] Stewart did not go quietly into the night.

This is a chronicle of the legal woes that sprang from Martha's decision to sell. But rather than dwelling on the trial itself, we will focus instead on a series of unexpected post-trial twists and turns that kept her case in the spotlight and provided new grounds for appeal.

We begin with consideration of the jury and the jury selection process. This part of the tale is ultimately about issues that swirled around Chappel Hartridge, a Bronx computer technician and outspoken juror who briefly enjoyed quasi-celebrity status after the trial. His post-trial interviews with the press and his answers during voir dire led to an unsuccessful motion for a new trial based on allegations of juror misconduct. The Hartridge controversy provides a case study that illustrates why the standard for granting a new trial for claimed juror misconduct is and should be rigorous.

We then move to post-trial allegations of government misconduct based on claims that the prosecution's expert witness lied on the stand. The first public accusations appeared in a perjury indictment sought by the same prosecutors who called the witness to testify. This unseemly turn of events led to a second unsuccessful motion for a new trial based on claimed government misconduct—i.e., that the prosecutors knew or should have known that their witness was lying. Stewart's claim of prosecutorial misconduct provides another case study that illustrates the difficulty of overturning a jury verdict based on a claim of witness perjury and explores why the perjured testimony of a government witness does not automatically entitle the defendant to a new trial.

We next turn to sentencing issues that arose after trial. Was a sentence of imprisonment warranted in Stewart's case, or would some alternative form of punishment have better served the ends of justice? If imprisonment was justified, what length term would be appropriate? Where on the spectrum of Federal Sentencing Guidelines did her case fall in view of the nature of her crimes? Was the business she founded so dependent on her guiding hand that the court should depart from the normal guideline range because a prolonged absence would impose undue hardship on the company and its employees?

These issues are all interesting in their own right. But since the misconduct claims are crucial to Stewart's appeal, let us begin with the jury that sat in judgment.

The Celebrity Juror

Recent high-profile trials have thrust jurors into the limelight. Few readers will forget Ruth Jordan—Tyco juror # 4—who reportedly gave the defense table an "O.K." sign on her way to the jury box during the trial of Tyco executives Dennis Kozlowski and Mark Swartz.[4] This courtroom incident, which came only days after the jury informed the judge that the atmosphere during deliberations had become "poisonous," generated enormous publicity. After several news organizations published her name, Jordan received an anonymous phone call and an angry letter that frightened her. Although she tried to carry on in her role as a juror, she privately admitted the threats had impaired her ability to continue deliberating. At that point, the judge had no choice but to declare a mistrial.[5]

Nothing quite so dramatic occurred in Martha Stewart's trial, but one of the jurors hearing her case became a controversial figure in his own right. The controversy, which began with his post-trial comments about the jury's verdict, later became more intense because of answers he gave on a questionnaire during the jury selection process. The juror was Chappel Hartridge, an outspoken and somewhat opinionated Bronx computer technician. He became an instant "celebrity juror" by speaking at length in widely-covered media interviews immediately after the trial. Although he wasn't the only juror who publicly talked about the case, he was one of the most vocal and, ultimately, most visible jury spokesmen.

So what did he say that generated such interest in his views? Here is a sampling of his comments on the verdict.

- "Maybe it's a victory for the little guy who loses money in the markets because of these types of transactions."[6]
- "It might give the average guy a little more confidence that people can invest money in the market and everything's going to be on the up and up."[7]
- "Investors may feel a little more comfortable now that they can invest in the market and not worry about these scams and that they'll lose their 401(k)."[8]
- "It's a message to the big wigs."[9]

His opinions, however, were not limited to the symbolic meaning of the verdict. He also expressed his sentiments about Martha Stewart herself.

- "She was a former stockbroker, so she should have known better."[10]
- "I expected a stronger reaction [at the verdict], and I didn't see anything."[11]
- "Maybe she thought she was above everything and didn't have to do things other people have to do."[12]

- "[Perhaps Stewart and Bacanovic felt that they were] special and didn't have to abide by the same rules as everybody else."[13]
- "[By not testifying, Stewart] seemed to say: 'I don't have anything to worry about. I fooled the jury. I don't have anything to prove.' "[14]

The defense team claimed both categories of statements showed that Hartridge was biased, that he failed to appreciate his role as a juror, and that he misunderstood the legal issues in the case. For contrary to what his public remarks implied, the trial had nothing to do with stock fraud or corporate greed. Instead, the charges against Stewart focused on allegations that she made false statements and obstructed justice. In light of what Hartridge's comments publicly revealed, did Stewart receive a fair trial? Had Hartridge fairly and conscientiously deliberated? Or had he used Martha Stewart to send inappropriate messages that reflected his own class bias? In the defense team's view, the inescapable conclusion was that Hartridge's statements reflected anger over the corporate fraud scandals and revealed biases that compromised Stewart's right to an impartial jury. But if Hartridge was truly biased, how did he come to sit on Martha's jury?

The Jury Selection Process

The barrage of publicity about Stewart's case raised concerns about finding an impartial jury pool. That in turn led to a jury selection process that was conducted in two stages. In the first phase of voir dire, several hundred potential jurors filed into the courthouse to fill out a questionnaire that had been jointly prepared by the prosecution and defense. When the questionnaires were completed, lawyers on both sides of the case reviewed the answers and made challenges for cause. After the challenges had been resolved, remaining members of the pool were questioned individually in Judge Cedarbaum's chambers until a panel was formed.[15]

Among other things, the questionnaires were designed to elicit information about prospective jurors' prior contacts with courts and law enforcement authorities. A post-trial investigation initiated by the defense team[16] led to claims that Hartridge had lied when he answered key questions about his past.[17] Specifically, the defense lawyers charged that Hartridge had falsely denied: (1) that he had ever been in court for anything but a minor traffic violation; (2) that he had ever been sued or accused of wrongdoing on a job; and (3) that neither he nor any member of his family had been criminally investigated or accused of committing a crime.

The lawyers maintained that Hartridge and his wife had each been sued multiple times and that several judgments had been entered against them;

that while Hartridge served as volunteer treasurer of the Kingsbridge Little League, he was accused of diverting league funds for personal use; that he had been arrested in 1997 for assaulting a woman with whom he lived at the time;[18] and that in 2000, his son had been convicted of attempted robbery.

But assuming the allegations were true, why would Hartridge lie about his run-ins with the law? In the defense lawyers' view, his motive was perfectly clear: he wanted to sit on Stewart's jury and feared that truthful answers would disqualify him from serving.[19]

Motion for New Trial Based on Juror Misconduct

Building on these claims, Stewart's lawyers filed a motion for a new trial based on alleged juror misconduct—perjury during voir dire—and used Hartridge's media statements to bolster their charge of bias and improper motive. Although the defense team did not argue that, standing alone, any one of the falsehoods would justify granting a new trial or an evidentiary hearing, they claimed that in the aggregate, these "unique" facts demonstrated a pattern of nondisclosure supporting an inference of bias.[20]

Voir dire is designed to promote a litigant's right to an impartial jury. Because questions posed during voir dire are designed to elicit possible biases a potential juror may have, the law places a premium on truthful answers.[21] Yet the hurdle for overturning a verdict is high because "a barrage of postverdict scrutiny of juror conduct" could undermine confidence in a system that relies both on "full and frank discussion" during jury deliberations and on the willingness of juries to return unpopular verdicts.[22] Thus, courts are reluctant to scrutinize juror conduct after a verdict has been returned.

The current standard of review requires a two-part showing. The defense must first show that the juror deliberately made a material misstatement during voir dire.[23] Neither a good faith but mistaken belief that the answer is true nor a deliberate but immaterial falsehood will suffice.[24] Thus, if Mr. Hartridge had a faulty recollection about past events, misunderstood the question, or lied about something that did not bear on his fitness to serve as a juror, the defense motion must fail.

If, on the other hand, the defense could prove that Hartridge had deliberately lied, it must then show that if he had told the truth, the court would have granted a challenge for cause based on his truthful answer.[25] Thus, unless Hartridge would have been disqualified from jury service if he had admitted that he had been sued, charged with assault, or accused of diverting little league funds, the defense could not satisfy the second prong of the test.

The Second Circuit has never overturned a verdict under this test on grounds that a juror withheld personal information during voir dire,[26] and it has only once remanded a case for consideration of possible juror nondisclosure.[27] Thus, the motion for a new trial based on juror misconduct faced significant legal hurdles.

Moreover, the factual basis for claiming misconduct and bias was weak. As Judge Cedarbaum observed, the allegations of juror misconduct were based on "little more than hearsay, speculation, and ... vague allegations."[28] In addition, the court found ambiguities in some of the questions to which the answers were said to be lies.[29]

In response to Question 45,[30] for example, Mr. Hartridge claimed that he had never been accused of a crime. The defense team asserted the answer was false because he had once been arrested and arraigned for assault.[31] But the complaining witness dropped the charges a few days after the arrest.[32] That fact is significant because New York law provides that dismissal of a criminal charge has specific legal consequences favorable to the defendant: (1) the arrest is deemed a nullity; (2) the defendant is restored, in the eyes of the law, to the status he had before the arrest (in this case, someone with no arrest record); and (3) unless specifically required by law, the defendant cannot be required to disclose information about the arrest.[33]

After the assault charge was dismissed, the record of Hartridge's arrest was sealed. In consequence, he could have reasonably believed the arrest need not be disclosed.[34] Thus, even if the answer to Question 45 was in fact false, the defense failed to show that Hartridge deliberately lied.

But assuming members of the defense team could prove his denial of the arrest was a deliberate lie, they would still have to show the arrest would disqualify him from serving on Stewart's jury. And therein lies the rub. The arrest was for assault—a crime totally unrelated to the cover-up crimes charged in Stewart's case. That being true, the arrest would not automatically bar Hartridge from serving on the jury.[35] Tellingly, the defense team cited no authority for the proposition that the mere fact of an arrest will support a challenge for cause. Indeed, the defense had strongly opposed the government's effort to strike a juror who failed to disclose that she had been the target of a securities fraud investigation.[36]

Question 43 delved into somewhat different aspects of the potential jurors' pasts. One part of the question asked whether the prospective juror or anyone close to him had been sued. Yet even if Hartridge had falsely denied that he and his wife had been sued or had judgments entered against them, what difference would that have made? It clearly would not support an inference of bias against a stranger to the suits and assuredly would not support a challenge for cause.[37]

Question 43 also asked whether Hartridge had ever been accused of wrongdoing on a job. Here the question was ultimately whether an average juror would think the word "job" includes doing volunteer work for the little league.[38] And what is the meaning of "accused" in this context? Hartridge was never formally charged with embezzling league funds, and the league board took no action against him.[39] At bottom, the allegations that he mishandled the funds were little more than hearsay and rumor gleaned from individuals who had no personal knowledge of the facts.[40]

Even though Stewart's motion for a new trial based on juror misconduct was doomed to fail in the end, the collateral question was whether Judge Cedarbaum at minimum should have held an evidentiary hearing. There are two problems with the defense request for a hearing on this point. First, the court is not required to allow post-verdict investigation of juror conduct unless "there is clear, strong, substantial and incontrovertible evidence that a specific, nonspeculative impropriety has occurred which could have prejudiced the trial."[41] Here, many of the allegations were speculative and based on rumor. But even with respect to allegations that were supported by substantial evidence—such as Hartridge's failure to disclose that he had been sued and that his son had been convicted of a crime—Judge Cedarbaum found that an evidentiary hearing would not help the defense because unrelated lawsuits against Hartridge and an unrelated conviction of his son did not give rise to an inference of bias that would support a challenge for cause.[42] Simply put, the answers had no bearing on his fitness to serve on the jury.

Thus, while disapproving Hartridge's apparent lack of candor, Judge Cedarbaum concluded "the law is clear that lack of candor, in the absence of evidence of bias, does not undermine the fairness of defendants' trial."[43]

The Expert Witness

Post-trial allegations of government misconduct arose from testimony provided by the prosecution's forensic expert. This part of the saga began with a worksheet prepared by Peter Bacanovic, a stockbroker at Merrill Lynch who handled Martha Stewart's accounts. The worksheet listed the values of all of the stocks she held in Merrill Lynch accounts as of the close of business on December 20—a week before the ImClone sale. Bacanovic had made handwritten notes—including planned stock transactions—in blue ball point pen on the worksheet. By the time the worksheet made its way into the SEC's hands, a critical notation—"@ 60"—appeared next to the ImClone listing.[44]

When Martha and Bacanovic were interviewed about the timing of the ImClone sale, they claimed that on December 20 they had agreed to sell the stock if its price dropped below sixty dollars a share. (And, indeed, on December 27, Bacanovic's Assistant sold Martha's four thousand shares at an average price of $58.53 per share.[45]) To corroborate their claim, they pointed to the "@ 60" notation on Bacanovic's worksheet.

The government contended there was no pre-sale agreement. Instead, the indictment charged that it was sometime *after* the stock was sold that Bacanovic altered the worksheet by adding the "@ 60" notation. The government's theory was simple and straight to the point: Martha and her stockbroker fabricated the "@ 60 agreement" as a cover story to provide a facially legitimate reason for the sale.

This part of the government's case hinged largely on its ability to prove that the ink used to write the "@ 60" notation did not match ink used to write the other notes on the worksheet, including a note written on the same line. Prosecutors hoped to use evidence that the inks did not match to support an inference that Bacanovic did not write the "@ 60" notation at the same time he wrote the other notes on the page.

Enter Larry Stewart, the Director of the Secret Service Laboratory ("the crime lab") and the government's expert witness on ink analysis. The substance of his testimony was as follows: his lab had tested the ink on the worksheet twice; the ink used to write the "@ 60" notation was different from the ink on the rest of the page; all of the writing on the worksheet except the "@ 60" notation was done with an inexpensive Paper Mate pen; the "@ 60" notation was written with a pen he could not identify; it was not feasible to "age test" the two inks to determine whether the "@ 60" notation was written later than the other notes on the page;[46] and it could not be reliably determined through a "batch to batch" analysis whether two different Paper Mate pens with different batches of the same ink were used to write the notes on the worksheet.[47]

The ink expert for the defense—Dr. Albert Lyter—testified that: the ink used to write the "@ 60" notation was different from the ink on the rest of the page; using a densitometer, it is possible to do a reliable "batch to batch" analysis to determine whether two different pens with the same type of ink—e.g., two different Paper Mate pens—were used to write the entries other than the "@ 60" notation; and multiple pens manufactured with different batches of the same type of ink were used to make the notations on the worksheet, other than the "@ 60" notation.[48]

Although the battle of the experts was uneventful at the time, two months after the trial another bizarre twist began to unfold. On Friday, May 14, the prosecutors received information suggesting that Larry Stewart had testified falsely during Martha's trial. After a week-long investigation, they wrote a letter to the court informing Judge Cedarbaum that they had probable cause to believe their expert had lied under oath and that they had charged him with two counts of perjury.[49]

The Perjury Charges

The indictment alleged that two series of answers Larry Stewart gave on the stand were false. Count one alleged that he lied about the nature and extent of his participation in testing the ink. He testified at trial that he was personally involved in testing and supervising the analysis of the ink on Peter Bacanovic's worksheet. Referring to co-worker Susan Fortunato, he stated that they had "worked the case together"[50] "side by side at the same time."[51] He described in elaborate detail how he took ink from the worksheet for examination and analysis[52] and the scientific techniques he used to analyze it.[53] The indictment charged that none of this was true. Instead, Susan Fortunato had performed all of the tests without any help from him.

Count two charged that he had lied about his knowledge of a book proposal prepared by two crime lab colleagues. This issue arose out of statements he made on cross-examination. When asked whether he was aware of the proposed book on ink analysis he replied, "Yes, I am familiar with this."[54] When asked about additional details of the book, including a chapter on "Instrumental methods for determining analytical features that do not tend to change with age," he said he had seen the chapter proposal.[55] The indictment charged that these were deliberate lies and that the aspiring authors had neither shown nor told him about their proposal.

Motion for New Trial Based on Perjured Testimony

Faced with the prospect that her conviction was based on perjured testimony, Martha Stewart's lawyers filed another motion for a new trial. But the prospect of winning a reversal on this ground was a long shot as well. First, the standard of review for a challenge based on false testimony is high. If the prosecution was unaware of the perjury, the defense must show the jury "probably would have acquitted" if the witness had told the truth.[56] Alternatively, if the prosecution knew or should have known about the perjury, the defense must show a "reasonable likelihood" that the perjured testimony could have influenced the jury.[57] Although the defense did not claim the government had actual knowledge of the perjury at the time of the trial,[58] it argued that the prosecutors should have known the testimony was false.

This argument was problematic in several significant respects. First, it was based on the improbable claim that Larry Stewart was a member of the prosecution team[59] because he was a government employee who assisted in the investigation and in the prosecution's preparation for trial.[60] If that hurdle could be overcome, his own knowledge that his testimony was perjured could be imputed to the prosecutors, thus lowering the burden of proof for the defense. Relieved of having to prove a probable acquittal but for the lies, the defense would only need to show a "reasonable likelihood that the false testimony could have affected the judgment of the jury"[61] and would make reversal of the conviction "virtually automatic."[62]

This reasoning proceeds from the faulty premise that Larry Stewart was an arm of the prosecution. But as Judge Cedarbaum found, he was not. He was an ordinary expert witness.[63] Although he assisted the prosecution in preparing for his own testimony and the cross-examination of his counterpart for the defense, he did not play an integral role in the initial investigation or assist in devising the trial strategy. Indeed, his role was limited to a single item of proof—whether the "@ 60" notation was written in a different ink than the other handwritten notes on the worksheet.

Simply put, his participation in the case was typical of the role expert witnesses customarily play. His status as a Secret Service employee did not make him a member of the prosecution team. Thus, if the government was neither actually nor constructively aware of the perjury during the trial, Martha and Bacanovic would not be entitled to a new trial unless the testimony was material and the court believed that "but for the perjured testimony, the defendant would most likely not have been convicted."[64]

Second, even if the government could be painted with knowledge that Larry Stewart's testimony was false, his conclusions about the ink used to make the "@ 60" notation were corroborated by substantial independent evidence. Dr. Lyter, the expert witness for the defense, agreed that the ink used to write "@ 60" was different from the ink Bacanovic used when he wrote the other notes on the page. Indeed, in his summation to the jury, Bacanovic's lawyer said: "We had a lot of expert testimony about this document. But our expert and their expert really agreed on almost everything about the main important points."[65]

Third, Larry Stewart was not charged with lying about the results of the ink analysis. The allegedly false testimony related solely to collateral points: whether he participated in performing the tests and whether he knew about the book proposal. Because those issues had little or no bearing on Martha Stewart's guilt, the defense argument that there was a "reasonable likelihood" that his false testimony influenced the jury was obviously weak.[66]

Fourth, substantial independent evidence unrelated to the "@ 60" allegations supported the jury's verdict. The principal witnesses were Bacanovic's Assistant, Doug Faneuil, who testified that Martha and Peter lied when they claimed to have spoken by phone about the price of ImClone stock on the day of the sale; Martha Stewart's Assistant, Ann Armstrong, who testified that Bacanovic's December 27 telephone message was about ImClone and that Martha altered the phone log; and witnesses[67] whose testimony supported the conclusion that Martha lied when she: (1) claimed she did not remember being told about Sam Waksal's intent to sell his stock; (2) claimed that she sold the stock because she did not want to deal with it on vacation; (3) claimed that she and Bacanovic discussed Martha Stewart Living Omnimedia, Inc. (MSLO) and Kmart during their (nonexistent) phone conversation on December 27; and (4) denied that she and Bacanovic discussed the SEC investigation into ImClone trading.[68]

That brings us to the last, and perhaps most important, point. The jury's verdict made it abundantly clear that Larry Stewart's testimony did not influence the outcome of the trial. The jury returned special verdicts on most counts in the indictment, and the verdict form provides strong evidence that the jury attached no weight to the claim that Martha and Peter concocted a false story about the "@ 60" agreement.[69] The special verdicts clearly identify the specific statements the jury found to be lies and, as seen in Tables 1 and 2,[70] the convictions obviously were not based on a finding that the defendants lied about the "@ 60" agreement.

Moreover, the jury found Bacanovic not guilty on count five (a false statements charge), in which the only allegation was that he altered the worksheet in January by adding the "@ 60" notation.[71] And while the jury convicted Martha and Bacanovic on other false statements and perjury charges, it rejected all of the specifications containing "@ 60" allegations as a factual basis for the verdicts.[72] Simply put, the jury convicted them of lying about matters other than the "@ 60" agreement, and the verdict would have been the same if Larry Stewart had never taken the stand.[73] Thus, the motion for a new trial based on perjured testimony rested on a very slender reed.

Larry Stewart's Perjury Trial

Larry Stewart's perjury trial lasted little more than a week. And in yet another ironic twist, during the second day of deliberations the jury acquitted him on both counts.[74] Post-verdict interviews with several jurors revealed that the government's case foundered in several respects. First, although Larry's testimony about performing the ink analysis and knowledge of the book proposal may have been untrue, some jurors believed he had not intended to lie.[75] As one juror said, "He put his foot in his mouth and he couldn't take it out because of his ego."[76] Other jurors did not find the principal government witness, laboratory co-worker Susan Fortunato, particularly effective[77] and thought she had "an ax to grind."[78] Still others believed that even if the two statements were false, the government failed to prove they were material.[79]

The *Brady* Claims

While the outcome of Larry Stewart's perjury trial had little to do with Martha's appeal, her lawyers argued that evidence introduced during Larry's trial proved the government had withheld exculpatory material from the defense, in violation of *Brady v. Maryland*.[80] The defense team raised the *Brady* issue in a nine-page letter they sent to the prosecutor and the court the day after Larry Stewart's acquittal.[81]

As might have been expected, the principal complaint centered on the ink testing controversy and Susan Fortunato, the lab employee who actually performed the tests. After testing the ink, Fortunato wrote a memo to the file summarizing the procedures she performed and describing her findings.[82] The defense letter made much ado about the testing of a small dash on the worksheet that appeared next to another stock Martha owned.[83] Although Fortunato tested the ink used in the "@ 60" notation against other written entries, she did not compare it with the dash. Nonetheless, her August 5, 2002 memo to the file stated that the "@ 60" ink was different from "all" of the other entries on the page[84]—a statement the defense said was false. At Larry Stewart's trial, Fortunato testified that she ran out of ink when she tested the dash and was thus unable to test it against the "@ 60" notation, but that she thought the ink used to write both entries was "probably the same."[85] At Martha Stewart's trial, Larry Stewart testified that the tests on the dash "were inconclusive."[86]

The letter contends that if the government had lived up to its *Brady* obligations and disclosed Fortunato's memo to the defense, the jury might well have concluded "that the government overreached in prosecuting Ms. Stewart"[87] and might have voted to acquit.[88] The letter also claims that the memo both proved Larry Stewart had lied on the stand and provided "powerful evidence that prosecutors should have known" something was amiss.[89]

This brings us back to where we began—the defense team's claim of government misconduct. To the extent that the *Brady* arguments were designed to establish the fact of perjury, they were more or less makeweight claims. Perjury by a prosecution witness does not automatically warrant upsetting the jury's verdict.[90] Moreover, for purposes of the motion for a new trial, Judge

Cedarbaum premised her ruling on an assumption that Larry Stewart perjured himself.[91] Judge Cedarbaum nonetheless concluded that the perjured testimony did not affect the integrity of the trial. After carefully examining the verdicts, she concluded that the acquittals on all of the specifications relating to the "@ 60" cover-up charge could only mean the jury gave no credence to this theory of the case. Thus, there was no reasonable probability that Larry Stewart's testimony affected the outcome of the trial.[92]

Moreover, the testimony of other witnesses provided "overwhelming" independent evidence to support the guilty verdicts.[93] Thus, Judge Cedarbaum ruled out the probability of an acquittal if the jury had known that Larry Stewart lied about his participation in testing the ink and his familiarity with the book proposal. And so we have come full circle.

Sentencing Issues

Although the federal system allocates sentencing decisions to judges rather than juries, the Federal Sentencing Guidelines severely constrain judicial discretion to tailor a sentence to fit the crime. The Guidelines designate a baseline sentence—expressed in a range of months—that sets the minimum and maximum sentence the defendant may be required to serve. The judge can set the length of the sentence imposed anywhere within the applicable guideline range.[94]

The Guidelines permit imposition of a sentence that is above or below the applicable range if the court finds "that there exists an aggravating or mitigating circumstance of a kind, or to a degree, not adequately taken into consideration by the Sentencing Commission in formulating the Guidelines that should result in a sentence different from that described."[95] Determinations about whether a *downward* departure is warranted are fact specific and must be based on highly unusual circumstances.

Under the Guidelines, considerations such as education and vocational skills, employment record, and civic, charitable, or public service are not ordinarily relevant to the question "whether a sentence should be outside the applicable guideline range," but such factors may be considered in truly "exceptional cases."[96]

This generally translates into a presumption against departures based on adverse effects that incarceration will have on a white collar offender's business.[97] Moreover, a Guidelines Policy Statement on departures expressly provides that departures based on specific offender characteristics should be reserved for the "extraordinary case"[98] and will thus be "extremely rare."[99] Nonetheless, Martha and her legal team sought leniency based on the good she has done throughout her life, the pain of her legal ordeal, and the best interests of her company.[100] It was against this backdrop that Judge Cedarbaum considered Martha's plea for leniency and determined what sentence to impose.

Extraordinary Hardship

Martha's legal team argued that incarcerating her would cause extraordinary hardship to her business and its employees.[101] The underlying theory was that Martha is essential to the company she founded. Without her guiding hand, the argument ran, MSLO would suffer a reversal of fortune, and valued employees would lose their jobs.[102]

Milikowsky and Somerstein

Martha's lawyers relied on two cases to support their request for a downward departure.[103] The first, *United States v. Milikowsky*,[104] was a 1995 Second Circuit decision upholding a departure granted to a business owner convicted of price fixing. Milikowsky was a principal in two businesses—a steel trading company and a steel pail manufacturing business.[105] The applicable guideline offense range for his crime was eight to fourteen months in prison. Because the offense level was relatively low, the Guidelines permitted imposition of a split sentence, part of which would be served in community confinement or home detention after the defendant served at least half of the minimum term in prison.

The trial court granted Milikowsky a downward departure that lowered the offense level to a point at which imprisonment was not required. The departure was based on the court's finding that incarcerating him would impose an extraordinary hardship on his employees and would have a severe financial impact on his businesses.[106]

The issue on appeal was whether Milikowsky's case involved "extraordinary circumstances."[107] Here, the court of appeals found there was persuasive evidence that Milikowsky was indispensable to both of his businesses. He was the only person with the "knowledge, skill, experience, and business contacts" to run the steel trading business on a daily basis.[108] He bought all of the steel, was the only person connected with the business who was capable of buying steel at competitive prices, and handled relations with the company's customers and suppliers. Moreover, his continued involvement in running the trading business from day to day was essential to the continued viability of the pail manufacturing business. Because he purchased all of the steel used in the manufacturing process, his ability to obtain competitively priced steel was crucial to the firm's continued viability.

In addition, both companies were in "extremely precarious financial condition" and were likely to fail if Milikowsky did not remain personally involved in their operations.[109] The companies were indebted to a steel conglomerate for twenty million dollars and could not obtain credit from other sources. The conglomerate would only extend credit if the businesses remained profitable, and if its credit were to be withdrawn, both companies would be bankrupt. Thus, the court found Milikowsky's circumstances were "extraordinary"[110] because without him, both businesses would probably fail and the livelihoods of several hundred employees would be lost.[111]

The second case was *United States v. Somerstein*,[112] a 1998 trial court decision from the Southern District of New York. The Somersteins, who operated a successful catering business on Long Island and a popular restaurant in Queens,[113] were convicted of defrauding a union benefit fund.[114]

The applicable guideline range for Mrs. Somerstein's crime was twelve to eighteen months in prison. She moved for a downward departure on the ground that incarceration would work an extraordinary hardship on her employees. Many supporters wrote letters attesting that her daily presence was indispensable to the continued survival of the catering business.[115] In granting a downward departure, the court found that Mrs. Somerstein was "an exceptional business woman, with a virtually unparalleled talent for catering affairs" and was the "public face" of the business.[116] It was "her unique talents, flair, dedication to detail, perfectionism, and responsiveness to customers' needs that [drew] the clients."[117]

The court observed that the catering operation was especially vulnerable because it had lost business during the eighteen months that criminal charges against the Somersteins were pending.[118] The general manager attributed the firm's survival during that time to the availability of both Somersteins to reassure clients and supervise daily operations.[119] Since Mr. Somerstein had already been sentenced to serve twenty-seven months in prison for his role in the fraud, there was no one else who could step in to run the show. Thus, her husband's unavailability made it even more essential to grant her a downward departure to prevent the firm from failing.[120] That being true, the judge bypassed a prison term and sentenced her to six months of home detention followed by three years on probation.[121]

Applicability to Martha

Martha's legal team argued that *Milikowski* and *Somerstein* supported granting her a downward departure.[122] To prevail under these precedents, she would have to show that she was indispensable to the company and that the business would likely fail if she were unable to remain at the helm.[123] But notwithstanding the exceptionally close identification between MSLO and Martha's name and face, her situation was starkly different from those of the business owners in *Milikowsky* and *Somerstein*.

To be sure, MSLO suffered a reversal of fortunes when Martha's legal woes began. The company lost money as magazine advertisers fled, television stations canceled her show, revenue from the sale of her merchandise went flat, and the company put her television show on "hiatus" until her legal problems were resolved.[124] Additionally, more than one hundred MSLO employees were laid off.[125] But from all appearances, MSLO was far from the brink of disaster. During Martha's five months in prison, news that Kmart would buy Sears sent the price of MSLO stock soaring because of the potential for both retail chains to market the Martha Stewart brand.[126] And once she began serving her term, advertisers began to return, some television stations resumed playing reruns of her show, and magazine sales improved.[127]

Beyond that, arguments for a downward departure based on extraordinary hardship were doomed to fail on the facts. First, Martha Stewart had played a significantly diminished role at MSLO after she was criminally charged. She stepped down as Chairman of the company when she was indicted, and she resigned from the board and relinquished her title as "creative director" upon conviction. Although she reportedly continued to work eighty-hour weeks at MSLO's Manhattan offices before she went to prison,[128] her leadership role clearly had changed. Yet the company survived with someone else at the helm. And if the SEC had prevailed in its lawsuit against her, she could be permanently barred from serving as a director of any public company—including her beloved MSLO—and the activities she can engage in as a corporate officer could be significantly curtailed.[129]

Equally important, the argument that MSLO was dependent on her continued leadership and close association with its products proved to be at odds with the post-conviction strategy the company had devised. To the chagrin of Martha's lawyers,[130] MSLO's new leadership said the company could get by without her and announced that it would accelerate plans to distance its products from such close identification with her.[131] In fact, in the year-end earnings call, CEO Sharon Patrick said: "We have evolved [MSLO] to the point our products don't have to be Martha."[132] So much for extraordinary hardship.

Alternative Sentence

In addition to arguing for a downward departure in the event that she was sentenced to prison, Martha's legal team also argued that imposition of any prison time was inappropriate. This approach relied on several interwoven themes.

Before her sentencing hearing, Martha wrote a letter to Judge Cedarbaum detailing her personal history from childhood to the present. The concluding paragraphs urged the judge to consider Martha's past good works, the painful experience of more than two years of government scrutiny, and Martha's desire to continue serving her community.[133]

Community service was a key consideration in her legal team's effort to fend off a prison term. Building on her record as the founder of an enormously successful company that was closely identified with her, Martha's lawyers characterized her as "unique" and "a role model for women who are entrepreneurial and career-oriented."[134] To capitalize on her skills and experience, the defense team asked the judge to impose a sentence of probation and allow Martha to work with economically disadvantaged women to help them improve their lives.[135]

Martha had worked out the details of the proposed alternative sentence with the Women's Venture Fund ("WVF"), a nonprofit organization in New York. The crux of her proposal was to teach low-income and minority women to become entrepreneurs, building on a curriculum she designed to teach them "the art and science of cleaning."[136] Although initially slow to warm to the idea, the WVF President later enthusiastically endorsed it.[137]

Of course, there were problematic aspects to this approach. It would effectively have allowed Martha to define her own sentence, based in part on relevant prior experience.[138] Martha, the entrepreneur, would continue doing what she knows and loves best. The implications for a system in which the majority of defendants are underprivileged and uneducated are obvious. Highly successful and skilled defendants would reap a special advantage, while the undereducated who have no place of privilege would be penalized because of their low socioeconomic status.

Needless to say, the government opposed the defense team's sentencing proposals. Prosecutors argued the proposals sought leniency "far beyond that which ordinary people" convicted of comparable crimes ordinarily receive under the Sentencing Guidelines, and observed that Guidelines sentences should adequately reflect the seriousness of the offense[139] and demonstrate the criminal justice system's "evenhandedness" in meting out punishment.[140]

The Sentence

Judge Cedarbaum rejected both defense bids. Finding *Milikowski* and *Somerstein* "entirely distinguishable" from this case,[141] she ruled there were no other mitigating factors that would justify a departure from the applicable Guidelines range.[142] For a first-time offender convicted of these crimes, the sentencing range was ten to sixteen months,[143] and Judge Cedarbaum sentenced Martha to serve five months in prison[144] followed by five months' home detention as a special condition of two years of supervised release.[145] She also imposed a $30,000 fine.[146]

Although Judge Cedarbaum agreed that, because the crimes were serious,[147] a sentence of imprisonment was justified and appropriate,[148] she imposed what she believed was the minimum possible term.[149] Her decision to sentence on the low end of the scale was influenced by Martha's status as a first-time offender, the hundreds of letters sent to the court by Martha's friends and fans,[150] and the belief that in this case the guilty verdict fulfilled the "public interest objective" of the criminal prosecution.[151]

Judge Cedarbaum granted a defense request to continue Martha's bail pending appeal, effectively staying the sentence until her conviction was affirmed. But two months later, before their appellate brief was filed, Martha and her legal team ended speculation that she might begin serving her sentence before the appeal. In a hand-delivered letter to Judge Cedarbaum, her lawyer asked the court to lift the stay of sentence and ask the Bureau of Prisons to quickly assign her to a prison camp so she could begin serving her term at the earliest possible time. In making this move, she sought "finality" and a chance to put this chapter in her life behind her and MSLO.[152]

At a hastily convened press conference the same day, Martha emphasized that she would vigorously pursue the appeal, which she anticipated would be a lengthy and indeterminate process.[153] But by immediately starting to serve her time, she signaled a date certain when she could return to play a stronger, more creative role in the company, thus minimizing uncertainty about MSLO's future. After being assigned to serve her sentence at a prison camp in Alderson, West Virginia (a.k.a., Camp Cupcake), she surrendered to the Bureau of Prisons on October 8.[154] By the time she was released the following March, Martha Stewart had become a billionaire.[155] "Prison, it turns out," may have been Martha's "best career move" in twenty-three years.[156]

Epilogue

Life is full of ironies. Martha Stewart sought "closure" and "finality" when she asked Judge Cedarbaum to send her to prison at the earliest possible date.[157] But despite her desire to "put this nightmare behind me,"[158] her odyssey from icon to ex-con and back is full of its own twists and turns.

Her continued pursuit of the appeal prolonged her legal saga as grist for the commentator's mill. And a week after she was released from Alderson, two of Sam Waksal's friends were charged with insider trading based on their sale of ImClone stock in December of 2001—allegedly on a tip from Waksal that bad news from the FDA was imminent.[159] The two pled not guilty and vowed to fight the charges. However long it takes to resolve the insider trading accusations against them, their case is likely to revive interest in Martha's contemporaneous ImClone sale, which in turn will be an inevitable reminder of her own prosecution and conviction. Nine months after her lawyers argued her appeal, moreover, the Second Circuit affirmed her conviction, ruling that none of the arguments provided a basis for disturbing the jury's verdict and ensuring her lifetime status as a convicted felon.[160]

But that was not the end of the line. There were yet-to-be resolved SEC charges stemming from the sale of her stock. The prolonged regulatory dispute was ultimately resolved in a settlement that required Martha to pay financial penalties totaling $195,000, barred her for five years from serving as a director of a public company, and imposed a five-year restriction on her role as an officer of MSLO.[161]

The counterweight to all of this may be that Martha emerged from prison as a wealthy celebrity whose star power seemed unscathed. With two new television shows in the works and new and expanding product lines bearing her name, there was hope that MSLO would enjoy a comeback of its own. But even though its stock price rose dramatically while Martha was serving her time, MSLO experienced a record sixty million dollar loss in 2004—far more than the company lost in 2003[162]—and the stock continued to fall after her new reality-based TV series received lukewarm ratings that led to early cancellation of the show.[163]

When will the uncertainty end, and how will things eventually turn out? That is difficult to say. But then, as Yogi Berra once observed, "It's tough to make predictions, especially about the future."[164]

APPENDIX A

UNITED STATES OF AMERICA v. MARTHA STEWART
AND PETER BACANOVIC
93 Cr. 717 (MCG)

JURY VERDICT FORM[165]

DEFENDANT MARTHA STEWART

COUNT ONE: Guilty __✓__ or Not Guilty ____
If and only if you find the defendant guilty on Count One, please check the
objects of the conspiracy which you found:

Obstruction of an Agency Proceeding	✓
False Statements	✓
Perjury	✓

COUNT THREE: Guilty __✓__ or Not Guilty ____
If and only if you find the defendant guilty on Count Three, please check each
of the specifications which you found:

Specification One	
Specification Two	✓
Specification Three	✓
Specification Four	✓
Specification Five	✓
Specification Six	✓
Specification Seven	✓

COUNT FOUR: Guilty __✓__ or Not Guilty ____
If and only if you find the defendant guilty on Count Four, please check each
of the specifications which you found:

Specification One	✓
Specification Two	
Specification Three	✓

COUNT EIGHT: Guilty __✓__ or Not Guilty ____

DEFENDANT PETER BACANOVIC

COUNT ONE: Guilty __✓__ or Not Guilty ____
If and only if you find the defendant guilty on Count One, please check the
objects of the conspiracy which you found:

Obstruction of an Agency Proceeding	__✓__
False Statements	__✓__
Perjury	__✓__

COUNT TWO: Guilty __✓__ or Not Guilty ____
If and only if you find the defendant guilty on Count Two, please check each
of the specifications which you found:

Specification One	_____
Specification Two	__✓__

COUNT FIVE: Guilty _____ or Not Guilty __✓__

COUNT SIX: Guilty __✓__ or Not Guilty ____
If and only if you find the defendant guilty on Count Six, please check each
of the specifications which you found:

Specification One	__✓__
Specification Two	_____
Specification Three	_____
Specification Four	_____
Specification Five	_____
Specification Six	_____
Specification Seven	_____

COUNT SEVEN: Guilty __✓__ or Not Guilty ____

Rosemary McMahon
FOREPERSON
Dated: _3/5_ , 2004

APPENDIX B

TABLE 1

JURY FINDINGS AGAINST MARTHA STEWART[166]

COUNT	SPECIFICATION	GUILTY	NOT GUILTY
ONE: Conspiracy[167] (18 U.S.C. §371)		✓	
	CRIMINAL OBJECT: Obstruction of Agency Proceeding	✓	
	CRIMINAL OBJECT: False Statements	✓	
	CRIMINAL OBJECT: Perjury	✓	
THREE: False Statements (18 U.S.C. §1001) (SEC, FBI, & US Atty (2/4/02))		✓	
	ONE: Prearrangement to sell ImClone @ 60		✓
	TWO: Spoke with Peter on 12/27/01	✓	
	THREE: Did not recall speaking with Peter's Assistant on 12/27/01	✓	
	FOUR: Spoke with Peter about MSLO stock & Kmart on 12/27/01	✓	
	FIVE: Sold ImClone on 12/27/01 to avoid being bothered on vacation	✓	

COUNT	SPECIFICATION	GUILTY	NOT GUILTY
	SIX: Did not know whether Peter's 12/27/01 phone message was in her Assistant's message log	✓	
	SEVEN: Spoke with Peter only once after 12/28/01 and only re: matters in public arena	✓	
FOUR: **False Statements** **(18 U.S.C. § 1001)** (SEC, FBI, & US Atty (4/10/02))		✓	
	ONE: Did not recall discussing Waksal with Peter on 12/27/01 or being told of Waksal's sale of Imclone	✓	
	TWO: Prearrangement with Peter to sell ImClone @ 60		✓
	THREE: Peter told her on 12/27/01 that ImClone was trading below $60 and told her to sell	✓	
EIGHT: **Obstruction of Justice** **(18 U.S.C. § 1505)** (Jan.–Apr. 2002)		✓	
	Lying to SEC re: ImClone sale[168]	✓	

APPENDIX C

TABLE 2

JURY FINDINGS AGAINST PETER BACANOVIC[169]

COUNT	SPECIFICATION	GUILTY	NOT GUILTY
ONE: Conspiracy[170] (18 U.S.C. § 371)		✓	
	CRIMINAL OBJECT: Obstruction of Agency Proceeding	✓	
	CRIMINAL OBJECT: False Statements	✓	
	CRIMINAL OBJECT: Perjury	✓	
TWO: **False Statements** (18 U.S.C. § 1001) (SEC (1/7/02))		✓	
	ONE: Prearrangement to sell ImClone @ 60		✓
	TWO: Told Martha on 12/27/01 that ImClone price had dropped below $60 and she told him to sell	✓	
FIVE: **False Statements** (18 U.S.C. § 1001) (SEC (Jan. 2002))			✓
	Altered worksheet by adding @ 60 and produced it to SEC[171]		✓

Count	Specification	Guilty	Not Guilty
Six: Perjury (18 U.S.C. § 1621)		✓	
	One: Did not tell Martha's Assistant ImClone price was dropping	✓	
	Two: Did not discuss ImClone with Martha after 12/28/01		✓
	Three: Agreed with Martha on 12/20/01 to sell ImClone @ 60		✓
	Four: Did not tell Martha that SEC was investigating ImClone sale		✓
	Five: Made @ 60 notation on worksheet on 12/20/01 per conversation with Martha that day		✓
	Six: Suggested the $60 sell price to Martha		✓
Seven: Obstruction of Justice (18 U.S.C. § 1505) (Jan.–Apr. 2002)		✓	
	Obstructing SEC proceeding[172]	✓	

Questions

1. In view of Chappel Hartridge's comments about Martha and the verdict and his apparent lack of candor on the juror questionnaire, is it clear that the factual basis for Martha's claim of misconduct and bias was weak? Why doesn't a juror's lack of candor during voir dire necessarily undermine the fairness of the trial?
2. If it was clear that the government's expert witness had perjured himself on the stand, why wouldn't Martha and Peter automatically be entitled to a new trial? Did the government's failure to fully vet the witness undermine the fairness of the trial? Would it make a difference if the government had known the expert was lying under oath?
3. How should the public evaluate Martha's sentence of five months at Camp Cupcake followed by five months of house arrest at her multimillion-dollar estate? Has she been punished enough? Too much? Would her proposal to teach the "art and science of cleaning" to economically disadvantaged women have been a more appropriate sentence?

Notes

1. Bethany McLean & Peter Elkind, The Smartest Guys in the Room: The Amazing Rise and Scandalous Fall of Enron 403–05 (2003).

2. The trial was colorful at times as well. For example, Douglas Faneuil, a Merrill Lynch stockbroker's assistant and one of the government's star witnesses, read from an e-mail he sent to a friend after Stewart treated him rudely on the phone. The source of her ire was apparently the "idiot" who was answering the Merrill Lynch phones. After asking Faneuil whether he knew what the telephone answerer sounded like, Martha "made the most ridiculous sound I've heard coming from an adult in quite some time, kind of like a lion roaring underwater." Constance L. Hays, Stewart Witness Sticks to Story On Intimidation, N.Y. Times, Feb. 6, 2004, at C1.

3. Chad Bray, Stewart's Sentence Expedited, Wall St. J., Sept. 22, 2004, at C7.

4. David Carr & Adam Liptak, In Tyco Trial, an Apparent Gesture Has Many Meanings: Publicity to Prompt Mistrial Motion, N.Y. Times, Mar. 28, 2004, at C1; Mark Maremont & Kara Scannell, Executives on Trial: Tyco Jury Resumes Deliberating: Defense Fails in Mistrial Bid Based on Media Coverage of Jury, but Incident Could Fuel Appeal, Wall St. J., Mar. 30, 2004, at C1. Jordan denied that she signaled "O.K." Mark Maremont & Kara Scannell, Tyco Juror Denied to Rest of the Panel That She Gave "OK," Wall St. J., Apr. 7, 2004, at C1; Andrew Ross Sorkin, No O.K. Sign and No Guilty Vote by Juror No. 4, N.Y. Times, Apr. 7, 2004, at A1.

5. Mark Maremont, Tyco Juror Maintains Her Stance, Wall St. J., Apr. 8, 2004, at B2; Sorkin, supra note 4.

6. Memorandum of Law in Support of Martha Stewart's Motion for New Trial Pursuant to Federal Rule of Criminal Procedure 33, United States v. Stewart (S.D.N.Y. Mar.

31, 2004) (S1-03-Cr-717 (MGC)), at 14 (on file with author) [hereinafter Stewart Mar. 31 Memorandum of Law].

7. *Id.*
8. *Id.*
9. *Id.*
10. *Id.*
11. *Id.*
12. *Id.*
13. *Id.* at 15.
14. *Id.*

15. The decision to question the jurors individually in chambers and without the press was made to ensure juror candor and preserve the defendants' right to a fair trial. As an alternative to allowing representatives of the press to be present during voir dire, Judge Cedarbaum released transcripts of each day's proceedings after redacting any "deeply personal information" the jurors had asked her to withhold. ABC, Inc. v. Stewart, 360 F.3d 90, 95 (2d Cir. 2004) (quoting *United States v. Stewart*, No. 03-CR-717 (MGC), 2004 U.S. Dist. LEXIS 426, at *3 (S.D.N.Y. Jan. 15, 2004)).

Not surprisingly, Judge Cedarbaum's decision was implemented over strong First Amendment objections from the press. Representatives of the press appealed to the Second Circuit, which held that it was inappropriate to exclude the public from the screening process. *Id.* at 100–06. Because the ruling came relatively late in the trial, it had no effect on jury selection procedures in Martha's case.

16. *See* Affidavit of Frank Senerchia, United States v. Stewart (S.D.N.Y. Mar. 31, 2004) (S1-03-Cr-717 (MGC)) (on file with author) [hereinafter Senerchia Affidavit] (affidavit of private investigator hired by Stewart's defense counsel to investigate whether Hartridge had lied).

17. Lying because of a desire to be empaneled on the jury does not, standing alone, disqualify a juror from serving. The substance of the lie must also support an inference of bias against the defendant. United States v. Greer, 285 F.3d 158, 173 (2d Cir. 2002). The withheld information must support a challenge for cause. McDonough Power Equip., Inc. v. Greenwood, 464 U.S. 548, 556 (1984); *see also* Dyer v. Calderon, 151 F.3d 970, 982 (9th Cir. 1998) (juror's failure to disclose that brother's murder was similar to murder defendant was accused of committing supported an inference of bias against defendant).

18. Although the defense team argued that Hartridge's assault on his then-girlfriend supported an inference of gender bias, the Government observed that Stewart did not challenge for cause another prospective juror who said he had been in court for domestic violence. Government's Memorandum of Law in Opposition to Martha Stewart's Motion for a New Trial Pursuant to Federal Rule of Criminal Procedure 33, United States v. Stewart (S.D.N.Y. Apr. 7, 2004) (S1-03-Cr-717 (MGC)), at 13 (on file with author) [hereinafter Government Apr. 7 Memorandum of Law].

19. Brief for Defendant-Appellant Martha Stewart, United States v. Stewart (2d Cir. Oct. 8, 2004) (04-3953(L)-CR), at 83–84 (on file with author); Stewart Mar. 31 Memorandum of Law, *supra* note 6, at 15; Notice of Motion (with Exhibits A–C) and Affirmation of Robert G. Morvillo, In the Matter of Chappell Hartridge (Notice filed in the Criminal Court of the City of New York), at 1 (N.Y. Crim. Ct. Mar. 31, 2004) on file with author [hereinafter Stewart Notice of Motion].

20. Reply Memorandum of Law in Further Support of Martha Stewart's Motion for New Trial Pursuant to Federal Rule of Criminal Procedure 33, United States v. Stewart (S.D.N.Y. Apr. 14, 2004) (S1-03-Cr-717 (MGC)), at 3–4 (on file with author).

21. McDonough Power Equip., Inc. v. Greenwood, 464 U.S. 548, 554 (1984).

22. Tanner v. United States, 483 U.S. 107, 120–21 (1987). *See also* McDonald v. Pless, 238 U.S. 264, 267–68 (1915) (If verdicts could be attacked by parties to the litigation, "all verdicts could be, and many would be, followed by an inquiry in the hope of discovering something which might invalidate the finding." This would lead to harassment of jurors by the losing party in an effort to dredge up sufficient evidence of misconduct to set aside the verdict. And this, in turn, could "make what was intended to be a private deliberation, the constant subject of public investigation, to the destruction of all frankness and freedom of discussion and conference.").

23. *McDonough*, 464 U.S. at 556.

24. United States v. Shaoul, 41 F.3d 811, 815 (2d Cir. 1994).

25. *See McDonough*, 464 U.S. at 556. *See also Shaoul*, 41 F.3d at 815; United States v. Moon, 718 F.2d 1210, 1234 (2d Cir. 1983).

26. United States v. Stewart, 317 F. Supp. 2d 432, 437 (S.D.N.Y. 2004) [hereinafter *Stewart I*].

27. *Id.* at 437–38 (citing United States v. Colombo, 869 F.2d 149 (2d Cir. 1989)).

28. *Id.* at 438.

29. Since the defense lawyers participated in drafting the questions, Judge Cedarbaum was not inclined to construe possible ambiguities in their favor. *Id.* ("The parties in this case had the opportunity to draft the questions exactly as they wanted them. They cannot now demand a new trial because a juror failed to place the broadest possible construction on those questions.")

30. Question 45: "Have you or has a family member or close friend ever been questioned by law enforcement, accused of, charged with, or convicted of any crime, or been the subject of a criminal investigation, other than a minor traffic violation?" Stewart Mar. 31 Memorandum of Law, *supra* note 6, at 2 n.4.

31. Question 45 did not ask specifically about arrests and arraignments, and Judge Cedarbaum thought it was unclear whether the question required disclosure of an arrest if the charges had been dropped. *Stewart I*, 317 F. Supp. 2d at 438.

32. In an affidavit prepared for the defense, she claimed that she dropped the charges because of pressure from Hartridge's family and because she "could not afford to miss any more time at work to pursue the matter." Stewart Notice of Motion, *supra* note 19, at Ex. B (Affidavit of Gail Outlaw). In a later interview with the New York Post, she said she did not press charges because she "just wanted to move on." Supplemental Affidavit of Robert G. Morvillo, United States v. Stewart, (S.D.N.Y. Apr. 14, 2004) (S1-03-Cr-717 (MGC)), at Ex. G, at ¶ 14 (on file with author) [hereinafter Morvillo Supplemental Affidavit].

33. N.Y. Crim. Pro. L. § 160.60 provides that after dismissal of the charges:

the arrest and prosecution shall be deemed a nullity and the accused shall be restored, in contemplation of law, to the status he occupied before the arrest and prosecution.... Except where specifically required or permitted by statute or upon specific authorization of a superior court, no such person shall be required to divulge information pertaining to the arrest or prosecution.

34. *Stewart I*, 317 F. Supp. 2d at 439. Indeed, the defense team filed a motion in state court to have the arrest record unsealed, but the court denied the motion on the ground that it was not in the interests of justice to do so. *Id.*

35. *Id.* The same reasoning would apply to Hartridge's failure to disclose his son's conviction for a totally unrelated crime. And, in Judge Cedarbaum's view, "[i]f anything, a prospective juror with a family member who had been convicted of a crime would more likely be considered biased in *favor* of criminal defendants." *Id.* at 442. *Cf.* United States v. Ross, 263 F.3d 844, 847 (8th Cir. 2001) (observing that inference of bias drawn from juror's prior arrest would be that juror "might well be biased in favor of defendants in general").

Defense counsel characterized the assault as a "gender-related incident" that supported an inference of gender bias. *Stewart I*, 317 F. Supp. 2d at 439. But this argument is premised on the assumption that he was guilty of assault (though he was neither tried nor convicted) and also implies that he maneuvered to get on the jury to convict *both* Bacanovic and Stewart because Stewart was a woman. *Id.*

36. *Id.* Nor did the defense team challenge for cause at least fourteen other prospective jurors who disclosed previous criminal charges or court appearances—including one member of the panel who had appeared in court for domestic violence, *see supra* note 18, and another who had been charged with obstruction of justice, an offense Martha was accused of committing. *See* Government Apr. 7 Memorandum of Law, *supra* note 18, at 12–14.

37. *Stewart I*, 317 F. Supp. 2d at 441.

38. *Id.*

39. *Id.* Indeed, one witness interviewed by Stewart's investigator said that his understanding was that the matter was never reported to law enforcement authorities. Senerchia Affidavit, *supra* note 16, at 2.

40. *Stewart I*, 317 F. Supp. 2d at 442.

A former league president claimed that when confronted with accusations of embezzlement, Hartridge admitted he took the money to support his cocaine habit. Morvillo Supplemental Affidavit, *supra* note 32, at ¶ 5 & Ex. B.

There were also uncorroborated allegations that Hartridge had been fired from his job at Citibank. One charge, made via an anonymous telephone call to defense counsel, was that Hartridge had been terminated for wrongdoing related to expense accounts. *Id.* at ¶ 3. Another source reported a rumor that Hartridge had been dismissed for illegal drug use. Senerchia Affidavit, *supra* note 16, at 4.

41. United States v. Moon, 718 F.2d 1210, 1234 (2d Cir. 1983).

42. *Stewart I*, 317 F. Supp. 2d at 443.

43. *Id.*

44. There was also a disputed dash—perhaps a stray mark—that played a role in the controversy over the worksheet. The dash was not fully tested during the forensic ink analysis. The reasons why the dash was not fully tested were also in dispute. *Compare* United States v. Stewart, 323 F. Supp. 2d 606, 613 (S.D.N.Y. 2004) [hereinafter *Stewart II*] (stating that Larry Stewart testified that the dash was not fully tested because the test might destroy so much of the sample that there would be too little left for the defense to examine) *with* Letter from Walter Dellinger, O'Melveny & Myers LLP, to David N. Kelley, United States Attorney, Southern District of New York Re: United States v. Martha Stewart (S.D.N.Y. Oct. 7, 2004) (03-Cr-717 (MJC)), at 2–3 (on file with author) [hereinafter Dellinger October 7 Letter] (quoting a memo indicating that the person who tested the ink had cautioned against testing the dash because of concern about "slight destruction of en-

tries," but that the FBI told her to test all of the entries and said it was "*Ok with the effect on the document*;" notwithstanding that directive, the ink on the dash was neither tested nor compared with the ink used to write the "@ 60" notation).

45. Superseding Indictment, United States v. Stewart (S.D.N.Y. Jan. 7, 2004) (03-CR-717 (MGC)), at 7–8, ¶17 (on file with author) [hereinafter Stewart Superseding Indictment].

46. Although ink can be age tested in some contexts, Larry Stewart testified that it was not feasible to age test the inks on the worksheet because multiple samples of the same ink must be written on the page over a longer period of time. *Stewart II*, 323 F. Supp. 2d at 613.

47. *Id.*

48. *Id.* at 613–14.

49. Letter from David N. Kelly, to The Honorable Miriam Goldman Cedarbaum, United States District Judge, Southern District of New York (May 21, 2004) (on file with author) [hereinafter Kelly Letter].

50. Sealed Complaint, United States v. [Larry F.] Stewart (Complaint filed in the United States District Court for the Southern District of New York) (S.D.N.Y. May 21, 2004), at 1–2 (on file with author) [hereinafter Larry Stewart Sealed Complaint] ("[she] and I worked the case together [and] I worked with her in creating these documents"); Indictment, United States v. Larry Stewart (S.D.N.Y. June 9, 2004) (04-CR-554), at 11 (on file with author) [hereinafter Larry Stewart Indictment] ("[Fortunato] and I worked on it … together").

51. Larry Stewart Sealed Complaint, *supra* note 50, at 5; Larry Stewart Indictment, *supra* note 50, at 11.

52. For example, he testified that:

> [I]f you look at the picture up there in Government Exhibit 479, on the left-hand side at the bottom, that little blue circle, that's where I first placed an ink. That is where I actually put it onto that plate…. I took a small amount of that AVEA ink and I turned it liquid again and I put it on this plate. I then did the same thing for the @60 ink. And that's the blue dot that is on the right side of the plate.

Larry Stewart Sealed Complaint, *supra* note 50, at 2–3; Larry Stewart Indictment, *supra* note 50, at 10.

53. "I performed a test to determine whether the @60 entry with the line underneath it and the remaining entries on the document were the same ink…. I did a technique called chromatography…." Larry Stewart Sealed Complaint, *supra* note 50, at 4.

54. *Id.* at 6.

55. *Id.* at 6–7.

56. United States v. Wallach, 935 F.2d 445, 446 (2d Cir. 1991).

57. United States v. Damblu, 134 F.3d 490, 493 (2d Cir. 1998).

Judge Cedarbaum's ruling on Martha's motion for a new trial was premised on an assumption that the allegations of perjury were true. *See Stewart II*, 323 F. Supp. 2d at 615 ("Although Lawrence has only been indicted, not convicted, it is assumed for the purpose of these motions that he did perjure himself."). In essence, Judge Cedarbaum's denial of the motion boiled down to a finding that even if Larry Stewart committed perjury, his perjured testimony did not prejudice Martha's case.

58. Memorandum of Law in Support of Martha Stewart's Motion for a New Trial Based Upon Government Misconduct, United States v. Stewart (S.D.N.Y. June 10, 2004) (S1-03CR-717 (MGC)), at 2 n.2 (on file with author) [hereinafter Stewart June 10 Memorandum of Law] .

59. *Id.* at 8–13.

60. *Id.* at 11–12.

61. United States v. Agurs, 427 U.S. 97, 103 (1976).

62. Stewart June 10 Memorandum of Law, *supra* note 58, at 13 (quoting *United States v. Wallach*, 935 F.2d 445, 456 (2d Cir. 1991)).

63. *Stewart II*, 323 F. Supp. 2d at 616.

64. *Id.* at 615 (quoting *United States v. Wallach*, 935 F.2d 445, 456 (2d Cir. 1988)).

65. *Id.* at 614 (citing Trial Transcript at 4657).

66. *Id.* at 615 (quoting *United States v. Damblu*, 134 F.3d 490, 493 (2d Cir. 1998)).

67. Other key witnesses at trial included Emily Perret (Sam Waksal's Assistant), and Mariana Pasternak (Martha Stewart's best friend). *Id.* at 612.

68. *Id.* at 621.

69. The jury verdict form is reproduced *supra* as Appendix A.

70. Tables 1 and 2, which I adapted from the jury verdict form and the superseding indictment, appear *supra* in Appendix B and Appendix C.

71. *See* Table 1, *supra* in Appendix B.

72. *See* Table 2, *supra* in Appendix C. There were no "@ 60" allegations in the obstruction of justice count. *See* Stewart Superseding Indictment, *supra* note 45, at 34–35.

Martha and Peter were both convicted on count one of the indictment, which charged them with conspiracy. Although the "@ 60" worksheet alteration was listed as one of six overt acts in furtherance of the conspiracy, the jury did not return a special verdict indicating which of the overt acts it found had occurred. But since the jury rejected all specifications relating to "@ 60" in the other counts of the indictment, "there can be no serious claim" that the conspiracy convictions were based on that overt act. Kelly Letter, *supra* note 49, at 4.

73. *Stewart II*, 323 F. Supp. 2d at 621.

74. If Larry Stewart had been convicted, that would have arguably shored up a key factual predicate for Martha's motion for a new trial, because the government would have proved beyond a reasonable doubt that its own witness had lied. But in reality this would have had little practical effect. For the limited purpose of ruling on the motion for a new trial, Judge Cedarbaum assumed he committed perjury. *See supra* note 57.

75. "He didn't walk into the courtroom intending to lie." Colin Moynihan, *Ink Expert in Stewart Trial Found Not Guilty of Perjury*, N.Y. TIMES, Oct. 6, 2004, at C5 (quoting a juror from Rockland County).

76. *Id.* (quoting a juror from Manhattan).

77. Although Fortunato sometimes looked the jury in the eye, at other times "[s]he lost all eye contact and she mumbled." *Id.* (quoting the same Manhattan juror).

78. *Id.*

79. Chad Bray, *Ink Expert in Stewart's Trial Is Found Not Guilty of Perjury*, WALL ST. J., Oct. 6, 2004, at C6.

80. 373 U.S. 83 (1963).

81. *See* Dellinger October 7 Letter, *supra* note 44, at 2–5.

82. The memo was dated January 26, 2004. *Id.* at 4.

83. *See supra* note 44.

84. Dellinger October 7 Letter, *supra* note 44, at 3.

85. *Id.* at 5.

86. *Id.* Query whether their statements are necessarily inconsistent.

87. *Id.* at 7.

88. *Id.* at 3.

89. *Id.*

90. *See supra* notes 56–57 and accompanying text.

91. *See supra* note 57.

92. *See supra* notes 69–73 and accompanying text.

93. *Stewart II*, 323 F. Supp. 2d at 621. *See supra* notes 67–68 and accompanying text.

94. 18 U.S.C. § 3553(b) (2000 & Supp. II 2001–2003). Judge Cedarbaum rejected a defense bid to declare the Sentencing Guidelines unconstitutional in light of *Blakely v. Washington*, 542 U.S. 296 (2004). *See* Affidavit of Robert G. Morvillo, United States v. Stewart, 2004 WL 1635576 (S.D.N.Y. July 8, 2004) (No. S1-03-717 (MGC)) (affidavit in support of defense motion for an order declaring the United States Sentencing Guidelines unconstitutional). Although *Blakely* did not specifically address the federal Guidelines, it held unconstitutional a similar Washington state sentencing regime because it permitted judicial factfinding on aggravating factors that would enhance the sentence imposed. *Blakely*, 542 U.S. at 303–04. Judge Cedarbaum denied the motion because the applicable Guidelines in Martha's case did not call for an enhancement. Constance L. Hays, *Stewart Loses in Attempt to Affect Sentencing*, N.Y. TIMES, July 16, 2004, at C4 (noting that Judge Cedarbaum made her ruling in a note written across the top of a copy of the defense motion). The Supreme Court has since declared the Guidelines' mandatory sentencing scheme unconstitutional. United States v. Booker, 543 U.S. 220 (2005).

95. 18 U.S.C. § 3553(b) (2000 & Supp. II 2001–2003).

96. U.S. SENTENCING GUIDELINES MANUAL § 5H1.1, Introductory Commentary at 386 (2003) [hereinafter SENTENCING GUIDELINES]. This guideline policy is echoed in a federal statute that directs the Sentencing Commission to assure that the Guidelines "reflect the general inappropriateness of considering the education, vocational skills, employment record, family ties and responsibilities, and community ties of the defendant." 28 U.S.C. § 994(e) (2000).

97. *See* United States v. Milikowsky, 65 F.3d 4, 7 (2d Cir. 1995) (citing cases from other circuits).

98. SENTENCING GUIDELINES, *supra* note 96, at § 5K2.0, cmt. at 393–94.

99. *Id.*, cmt. at 394.

100. *See generally* Sentence, United States v. Stewart (S.D.N.Y. July 16, 2004) (03-CR-717 (MGC)) (on file with author) [hereinafter Sentencing Hearing Transcript]; Letter from Martha Stewart, to The Honorable Miriam Goldman Cedarbaum (July 15, 2004) (on file with author) [hereinafter Stewart Letter].

101. *See generally* Darryl K. Brown, *Third-Party Interests in Criminal Law*, 80 TEX. L. REV. 1383 (2002).

102. *See infra* note 125 and accompanying text.

103. *See* Sentencing Hearing Transcript, *supra* note 100, at 6–7, 15.

104. 65 F.3d 4 (2d Cir. 1995).

105. He was also a principal in a firm that manufactured steel drums until the manufacturer's assets were sold to another firm.

106. The court sentenced him to two years on probation subject to the condition that he spend six months in home confinement, fined him $250,000, and required him to perform 150 hours of community service. *Milikowsky*, 65 F.3d at 5.

107. *Id.* at 8.

108. *Id.*

109. *Id.*

110. *Id.*

111. *Id.* at 8–9.

112. 20 F. Supp. 2d 454 (S.D.N.Y. 1998).

113. Mr. Somerstein was president and Mrs. Somerstein was vice-president of the catering business. *Id.* at 456.

114. They were required to contribute to the benefit fund pursuant to collective bargaining agreements with their union employees. *Id.* at 457. Mr. Somerstein was also convicted of embezzling from a private pension fund the catering service created for the benefit of its nonunion employees. *Id.*

115. A former manager of the catering business said of Mrs. Somerstein: "[She is] the backbone and creator of Somerstein Caterers. Without her, there will be no more Somerstein Caterers, no more beautiful parties, and most important, jobs for those now benefitting [by working there]. Somerstein Caterers will disappear from the face of the earth." *Id.* at 461.

116. *Id.*

117. *Id.*

118. Given the Somersteins' extensive personal involvement in running the catering operation, clients were understandably reluctant to book special events such as weddings, religious celebrations, and corporate parties until the future of the business was more certain. *Id.* at 461–62.

119. *Id.* at 461.

120. *Id.* at 462. The trial court also recognized a combination of three other circumstances that made this an extraordinary case: Mrs. Somerstein's many charitable activities and civic contributions, exceptional work habits, and experience as a survivor of the Holocaust. *Id.* at 463–64.

121. *Id.* at 464. The home detention component of the sentence allowed her to leave home only "for work, religious or medical reasons, or to care for her grandson." *Id.*

122. Sentencing Hearing Transcript, *supra* note 100, at 10.

123. The value of the company's stock declined steadily between the time the indictment was announced and the date of sentencing, Keith Naughton, *"I Will Be Back:" Martha Vows to Appeal Her Conviction; But Her Advertisers Wish She'd Just Apologize,* Newsweek, July 26, 2004, at 40 [hereinafter '*I Will Be Back*'], and the company posted third quarter losses of $15 million. Constance L. Hays, *Martha Stewart Living Replaces Chief Executive,* N.Y. Times, Nov. 12, 2004, at C3. Martha's lawyer argued that MSLO's very "ability to survive" hinged on the sentence Judge Cedarbaum imposed. Sentencing Hearing Transcript, *supra* note 100, at 6.

124. James Bandler, *Real Competition: Real Simple is Now a Real Rival to Martha Stewart Living,* Wall St. J., Dec. 28, 2004, at B1; '*I Will Be Back,*' *supra* note 123; Shira Ovide, *Selling Heats Up for Martha Stewart,* Wall St. J., Dec. 29, 2004, at C5; Kara Scannel & James Bandler, *Stewart Sentence Boosts Prospects of Her Company,* Wall St. J., July 19, 2004, at C1; *Sentencing Could Set in Motion Martha Stewart Brand Revival,* Wall St. J. Online, July 16, 2004 (on file with author).

125. Hays, *supra* note 123.

126. Keith Naughton, *Clean Start: The Sears-Kmart Marriage Had Wall Street Spinning; But Martha Stewart Could End Up the Biggest Winner; Let the Comeback Begin,* Newsweek, Nov. 29, 2004, at 40 [hereinafter *Clean Start*]. Indeed, notwithstanding that the defense team tried to enlist Judge Cedarbaum's sympathy at the sentencing hearing by claiming that Martha's assets had been "substantially depleted," Sentencing Hearing Transcript, *supra* note

100, at 6, the value of Martha's personal stock holdings in MSLO shot up to $563.4 million when Kmart acquired Sears. *Clean Start, supra*. And when Judge Cedarbaum asked her if she could designate the *one* residence where she would serve the home detention part of her sentence, she selected her $40 million, 153 acre estate in Bedford, New York. Sentencing Hearing Transcript, *supra* note 100, at 16; *'I Will Be Back,' supra* note 123.

127. *Clean Start, supra* note 126.

128. Patricia Sellers, *Stewart's Sentencing: Martha's Team Has a Secret Plan*, FORTUNE, Apr. 19, 2004, at 40.

129. Complaint, S.E.C. v. Stewart (S.D.N.Y. 2003) (03-CV-4070 (NRB)) (on file with author). The SEC has statutory authority to ask a court to bar a person who has violated any provision of the Securities Exchange Act of 1934 from serving as an officer or director of a public company, 15 U.S.C. §78u(d)(2) (2000 & Supp. II 2001–2003), and to issue such a bar in a cease and desist proceeding for violations of section 10b of the Act. 15 U.S.C. §78u-3(f) (2000 & Supp. II 2001–2003). At the sentencing hearing, Martha's lawyer erroneously linked these remedies to the outcome of her criminal appeal. *See* Sentencing Hearing Transcript, *supra* note 100, at 6 (stating that if her conviction is upheld, "she faces a lifetime bar" from serving as an officer and director of MSLO).

130. Sellers, *supra* note 128.

131. Kara Scannell, *Stewart Team to Base Its Plea for Leniency on Risk of Layoffs*, WALL ST. J., May 10, 2004, at A1. The plans included launching new products and programs with generic names like "Everyday Food" magazine and a television show called "Petkeeping with Marc Morrone." *Id.*

132. Sellers, *supra* note 128. MSLO reversed this strategy after a Sears-Kmart merger was announced and it became clear that the sympathy vote was still with Martha. Plans for new product lines with the Martha Stewart brand name and new television shows ensued. Brooks Barnes, *Martha Stewart's Return to TV: Is It a Good Thing?*, WALL ST. J., Dec. 9, 2004, at B1.

133. "I ask that in judging me you consider all the good that I have done, all the contributions I have made, and the intense suffering that has accompanied every single moment of the past two and a half years." Stewart Letter, *supra* note 100, at 4.

134. Sentencing Hearing Transcript, *supra* note 100, at 10.

135. *Id.* at 12.

136. Keith Naughton, *Martha Holds Out a Helping Hand: She's Reached Out to a Non-profit Group With an Offer to Teach Low-income Women How to be Entrepreneurs*, NEWSWEEK, June 7, 2004, at 44 (reporting a proposal to teach and mentor the women ten to twenty hours a week for one or two years). The idea reportedly came from her own difficult experience of finding suitable employees to clean her estates.

137. "Can you imagine if we had graduates of the Martha Stewart cleaning program bidding for contracts cleaning Hilton Hotels?" *Id.* (quoting WVF President Maria Otero).

138. As Professor John Coffee observed, "If you give it to Martha Stewart, then every white-collar defendant from Enron to WorldCom could ask for community service instead of jail." *Id.*

139. Although the defense argued that the offenses of conviction were not very serious, the government replied that the crimes had "serious implications" for the administration of justice because they were designed to impede legitimate investigations into her conduct. Sentencing Hearing Transcript, *supra* note 100, at 14–15.

140. *Id.* at 15.

141. *Id.*

142. *Id.* at 15–16. Judge Cedarbaum also ruled that no facts supported Martha's request for a two-level downward adjustment based on the claim that she played a minimal role in the crimes. *Id.* at 15.

143. SENTENCING GUIDELINES, *supra* note 96, at Ch. 5, Pt. A - Sentencing Table.

144. Sentencing Hearing Transcript, *supra* note 100, at 16. The judge refused a defense request to let Martha serve the sentence in a halfway house but agreed to recommend Martha's preference for the prison camp at which she would serve her term. *Id.* at 18–19. Although Martha's stated preference was to be assigned to the prison facility at either Danbury, Connecticut or Coleman, Florida, the Bureau of Prisons assigned her to a prison camp in Alderson, West Virginia. Barry Meier, *Martha Stewart Assigned to a Prison in West Virginia*, N.Y. TIMES, Sept. 30, 2004, at C1.

145. Sentencing Hearing Transcript, *supra* note 100, at 16. For a fuller description of how the sentence was calculated under the Sentencing Guidelines, *see* Brief for Appellee United States, United States v. Stewart (2d Cir. Nov. 24, 2004) (04-3953(L), 04-4081 (CON)), at 38–40 (on file with author) [hereinafter Brief for Appellee]. In a bizarre turn of events, her period of home detention was extended three weeks after she reportedly violated the terms of confinement by driving around her estate in an off-road vehicle and attending a yoga class off the premises. *Martha Stewart's House Arrest Is Extended*, N.Y. TIMES, Aug. 4, 2005, at C11.

Martha was allowed to select one residence where she would serve the home detention portion of her sentence, and she specified her home in Bedford, New York. Sentencing Hearing Transcript, *supra* note 100, at 16. To facilitate monitoring compliance with this part of the sentence, the conditions included a requirement that her home be equipped with a telephone that had no call forwarding, caller ID, modem, or call waiting and that was not a portable cordless phone, as well as a requirement that she wear an electronic monitoring bracelet. Brief for Appellee, *supra*, at 17.

Although the sentence allowed Martha to leave her home for employment, medical appointments, and other similar activities, the judge specified a maximum of forty-eight hours a week for activities away from home and required that there be one day a week during which she could not leave home. *Id.* at 16.

146. *Id.* Judge Cedarbaum ordered the fine to be paid immediately.

147. *Id.* at 17. The judge emphasized that lying to government agencies impedes the administration of justice regardless of whether the investigation uncovers other criminal conduct.

148. *Id.*

149. *Id.*

150. Judge Cedarbaum received more than fifteen hundred letters from Martha's supporters. *Id.* at 18.

151. *Id.* at 17–18.

152. Letter from Walter Dellinger, O'Melveny & Myers LLP, to Honorable Miriam Goldman Cedarbaum (Sept. 15, 2004) (on file with author); Transcript, Martha Stewart Press Conference (Sept. 15, 2004) [hereinafter Press Conference Transcript] (on file with author).

153. Staged in the clerestory of MSLO's downtown New York building, the press conference had all the hallmarks of an academy awards ceremony, an infomercial, and a soap opera. Flanked by the chairman of MSLO's board of directors and another member of the board, by the company's president and CEO, and by her team of appellate lawyers, Press Conference Transcript, *supra* note 152, at 2, Martha expressed pride and confidence in MSLO's board of directors and management team and thanked them "from the bot-

tom of my heart." *Id.* at 9–10. She also expressed immense gratitude for the support of family, friends, and colleagues, "and, of course, the millions of fans" who provided encouragement, "watched our shows, read our magazines and books, purchased our products and supported our brands." *Id.* at 10. Her relief that she was putting this behind her was tempered by sadness, *id.* at 6–8, but she was optimistic that better times were ahead, *id.* at 9 (stating her belief that MSLO's "best days are still ahead of it") and that she would be home in time for the spring planting season. *Id.* at 7.

154. Constance L. Hays, *As Stewart Enters Prison, Her Company Refurbishes*, N.Y. TIMES, Oct. 8, 2004, at C4.

155. Louisa Kroll & Lea Goldman, *Billion Dollar Babies*, FORBES, Mar. 28, 2005, at 125.

156. Keith Naughton, *Martha Breaks Out*, NEWSWEEK, Mar. 7, 2005, at 36 [hereinafter *Martha Breaks Out*]. *Cf. Martha Stewart: Going to Prison Was a Business Decision*, 19 CORP. CRIME REP. 1, 3 (Oct. 17, 2005) (appearing on an NPR radio show, she said "going to prison was a business decision that solved a problem").

157. Press Conference Transcript, *supra* note 152, at 4–5.

158. *Id.* at 4.

159. Sealed Complaint, United States v. Fuks, Complaint Filed in the United States District Court for the Southern District of New York (S.D.N.Y. Mar. 6, 2004) (on file with author); Jenny Anderson, *2 Are Charged Over Trading in ImClone: Friends Are Accused of Sales on Chief's Tip*, N.Y. TIMES, Mar. 10, 2005, at C1; Ianthe Jeanne Dugan, *Two More Are Arrested in ImClone Stock Case: Former Waksal Associates Face Insider-Trade Charges Brought by Justice Agency*, WALL ST. J., Mar. 10, 2005, at C4.

160. United States v. Stewart, 433 F.3d 273 (2d Cir. 2006) (also upholding Bacanovic's conviction but remanding the case for consideration of whether his sentence should be modified).

Martha's status as a convicted felon has had other unexpected consequences of its own. Thus, for example, after accepting an invitation to participate in a Pumpkin Regatta in Nova Scotia, she found that because she was a convicted felon who was then on probation, she could not enter Canada without a special visa. *Stewart Briefly Becomes Focus of a Canadian Political Quarrel*, N.Y. TIMES, Oct. 10, 2005, at C8.

161. Brooks Barnes, *Martha Stewart Settles With SEC On Civil Charges*, WALL ST. J., Aug. 8, 2006, at C3; Landon Thomas Jr., *Stewart Deal Resolves Stock Case*, N.Y. TIMES, Aug. 8, 2006, at C1; SEC Litig. Rel. No. 19794, Aug. 7, 2006, *available at* http://www.sec.gov/litigation/litreleases/2006/lr19794.htm. The settlement prohibited her from participating in activities involving financial reporting and disclosure, monitoring compliance with federal securities laws, internal controls, and other SEC-related functions.

162. *Martha Breaks Out, supra* note 156, at 39.

163. Julie Bosman, *Is the World Suffering From Too Much Martha?*, N.Y. TIMES, Sept. 23, 2005, at C1; Anne D'Innocenzio, *Will Fans, Investors Buy the New Martha Stewart?*, ST. LOUIS POST-DISPATCH, Oct. 5, 2005, at D5; *Martha's Show to End*, ST. LOUIS POST-DISPATCH, Nov. 11, 2005, at C3.

164. Michael Shermer, *Winner '04: Pick Your Crystal Ball*, LA TIMES, Nov. 1, 2004, at B11.

165. Reproduced from *Stewart II*, 323 F. Supp. 2d at 634–36.

166. Adapted from Jury Verdict Form, *supra* Appendix A, and Stewart Superseding Indictment, *supra* note 45, at 21–22, 25–28, 35.

167. There were no numbered specifications in Count One. Instead, Count One of the indictment alleged that the conspiracy had three criminal objectives: obstruction of justice (18 U.S.C. § 1505 (2000)), making false statements (18 U.S.C. § 1001 (2000)), and perjury (18

U.S.C. § 1621 (2000)). Stewart Superseding Indictment, *supra* note 45, at 21–22. The jury found Stewart and Bacanovic guilty of participating in a conspiracy that encompassed all three objectives. *See supra* Appendix A.

168. There were no numbered specifications in Count Eight. Instead, Count Eight incorporated by reference allegations contained in thirty-eight paragraphs of the indictment's background statement and charged that Martha obstructed the SEC proceeding "by providing and causing to be provided false and misleading information to the SEC relating to [her] sale of ImClone stock." Stewart Superseding Indictment, *supra* note 45, at 35.

169. Adapted from Jury Verdict Form, *supra* Appendix A, and Stewart Superseding Indictment, *supra* note 45, at 21–22, 25–28, 35.

170. There were no numbered specifications in Count One. Instead, Count One of the indictment alleged that the conspiracy had three criminal objectives: obstruction of justice (18 U.S.C. § 1505 (2000)), making false statements (18 U.S.C. § 1001 (2000)), and perjury (18 U.S.C. § 1621 (2000)). Stewart Superseding Indictment, *supra* note 45, at 21–22. The jury found Stewart and Bacanovic guilty of participating in a conspiracy that encompassed all three objectives. *See supra* Appendix A.

171. There were no numbered specifications in Count Five, but the only allegation in Count Five was that Bacanovic altered the worksheet by adding the "@ 60" notation and gave the altered document to the SEC. Stewart Superseding Indictment, *supra* note 45, at 29.

172. There were no numbered specifications in Count Seven. Instead, Count Seven incorporated by reference allegations contained in thirty-eight paragraphs of the indictment's background statement and charged that Bacanovic obstructed the SEC proceeding "by providing and causing to be provided false and misleading information and documents to the SEC relating to the sale of ImClone stock." *Id.* at 34–35.

CHAPTER 12

ENVY AND OUTSIDER TRADING[*]

Jeanne L. Schroeder

Corporate Irresponsibility

On March 5, 2004, Martha Stewart was convicted of four counts of obstruction of justice, lying to federal investigators, and conspiracy in connection with statements she made about her December 2001 sale of approximately 4,000 shares of ImClone Systems stock. The trial and its aftermath generated a media storm second only to that of O.J. Simpson. Although many if not most news accounts dutifully repeated the fact that Stewart was not even charged, let alone convicted, of insider trading, they frequently referred to the event as the "Martha Stewart insider trading case" in tones implying that she was morally, if not legally, guilty of that offense as well.[1]

In fact, it is far from clear whether Stewart's trades were unlawful and it is hard to identify any harm her acts directly caused anyone.[2] Indeed, the only clear harm to date has been to Stewart personally and the shareholders of Martha Stewart Living Omnimedia, the stock price of which has been buffeted by what might be false accusations against its eponymous founder. In early March 2003, Martha Stewart Living Omnimedia announced its first ever quarterly losses, which it attributed largely to adverse publicity.[3] As a result, the price of her own stock dropped so much that before her trial she reportedly suffered paper losses of approximately $200 million[4] and other losses aggregating about $400 million,[5] an amount that dwarfs any losses she allegedly tried to save by trading in ImClone stock. The price of Martha Stewart Omnimedia's stock dropped an additional 23 percent immediately upon the announcement of Stewart's conviction.[6]

---

[*] This chapter is derived from *Envy and Outsider Trading: The Case of Martha Stewart*, originally published at 26 CARDOZO L. REV. 2023 (2005). Reprinted with permission of the publisher, Cardozo Law Review © 2005.

To state what should be obvious, Stewart is not an insider of ImClone and is, therefore, incapable of engaging in classic insider trading. Nor could she have breached any duty of confidence and engaged in "outsider" trading under the more controversial "misappropriation theory." Moreover, to date, no facts have been made public that would support a claim that Stewart was a tippee of a classic insider. A prosecution of Stewart on insider trading charges would require a court to adopt a new interpretation of the law of both misappropriation and tipping far beyond existing precedents.[7] Consequently, the Department of Justice ("DOJ") was reduced, in effect, to arguing that it was illegal for her to lie about something that was not illegal and that her protestations of innocence constituted the fraud upon which she should be considered guilty![8] That is, rather than being accused of engaging in criminal insider trading, she was prosecuted for obstruction of justice and lying to the government in connection with its investigation of her trades. The SEC brought a civil action against Stewart, which has since been settled, on the grounds that she was a tippee of her broker who "stole" the fact that insiders were selling their stock—a novel theory beyond any other application of the misappropriation theory to date.

In other words, to securities lawyers, the public reaction to the Stewart affair appears wholly out of proportion, particularly when compared to the obvious corporate improprieties of 2001. What percentage of the American public can even identify such figures as Jeffrey Skilling, Andrew Fastow,[9] Dennis Kozlowski,[10] John Rigas,[11] or Scott Sullivan[12]—to name but a few potential inductees to the Corporate Hall of Shame? I would bet that few would even recognize the name of Sam Waksal, Stewart's friend and former chief of ImClone who was sentenced to more than seven years in prison time for his clear and admitted violation of the insider trading rules.

I suggest that the public reaction to the Stewart "scandal" may not be so much righteous outrage, but the ignominious sin of envy—the pain one feels in seeing another experience joy. Envy is the mirror image of *schadenfreude*[13]—the joy one feels in seeing another experience pain. In this chapter, I will use the Stewart episode as a jumping-off point for analyzing the two competing legal theories of unlawful securities trading on the basis of material non-public information: the so-called "classic" theory and the controversial "misappropriation" theory—more accurately termed "outsider trading"—adopted by the U.S. Supreme Court in the case of *United States v. O'Hagan*.[14] Although the misappropriation theory is widely criticized, I believe that no one, to date, has convincingly explained precisely why it seems so intuitively "wrong."

I posit that the distinction between the ethics of classic insider trading and misappropriation precisely reflects the distinction between the two often confused—but distinct—passions of jealousy and envy. Although the terms are often incorrectly used interchangeably, jealousy is the fear and anger one feels when contemplating the possibility that a rival either may take, or has taken, that which one believes rightfully belongs to one. Envy, in contrast, is the anger and pain one feels in observing the good fortune of another.

Similarly, classic insider trading reflects the fear of investors in a public company that rivals—specifically the company's management and other fiduciaries—might take what rightfully belongs to investors—non-public information concerning and obtained from that company. To be more precise, I posit that a prohibition on classic insider trading law should be seen as a rough corollary to the mandatory disclosure regime of the federal securities laws conceptualized as a congressional decision that certain information about public companies "belongs" to the investment public generally.

The misappropriation theory concerns the trading in securities based on information received from a source other than the issuer of the securities. It is based neither on the principles of federal securities law nor state corporate law, but derives from state trade secret law policy. This policy is, unfortunately, totally antithetical to securities law policy in that it reflects a state decision that the public, generally, has no right to certain information so long as it is kept secret. That is, federal securities law is about eliminating, or reducing, informational advantages with respect to one class of information, while state trade secret law is about protecting informational advantages with respect to another class of information.

The misappropriation theory, consequently, involves the resentment by the investment public that other persons have the good fortune to enjoy something to which the public has no right—non-public information obtained from third party sources who are the legally recognized owners of the information.

The ethical status of jealousy and envy are completely diverse. In jealousy, one wants to protect what one has, or believes one should have. In envy, one wants to destroy the possession of another. Jealousy is the assertion of one's own claim of possession. Envy is the wish to destroy the enjoyment of another whether or not it is rightful. Jealousy may not be an attractive emotion, but even God admits that He is jealous. Envy, however, is one of the seven deadly sins. Indeed, it is second only to pride in its potentially corruptive effect on the soul. As etymology reveals, envy—invidia—is the most invidious sin.

We need to remember, however, that sometimes even paranoiacs have real enemies. Perhaps it is also true that what first appears to be envy might, upon closer look, seem more like jealousy. That is, it might be the case that certain informational advantages that the law currently allocates to specific individuals should, for one policy reason or another, be allocated to the public. As Jerome Neu accurately says in his analysis of envy:

> That envy may be one reason for demanding equality does not mean that demands for equality are unjustified. There are other reasons, most importantly reasons of justice, for demanding (certain forms of) equality. But from another perspective the real issue is whether envy must form an inevitable obstacle to attempts to achieve justice and/or equality.[15]

In this chapter, I propose an internally consistent analysis of insider trading law based on any given allocation of property rights in non-public information. I am not, however, offering an apologia for the status quo. I believe the current case law is, and is doomed to remain, hopelessly inadequate because the Supreme Court's interpretation of the federal securities laws requires the government to force the square peg of insider trading into the round hole of actual fraud. This inevitably causes ambiguities that create the opportunity for prosecutorial abuse—as l'affaire Stewart illustrates. I believe that Congress should address the appropriate allocation of informational advantages based on the competing policies underlying the federal securities laws and trade secret law, among other ethical, legal, economic, and political considerations.

This chapter proceeds as follows. First, I analyze the distinction between envy and jealousy from theological, psychoanalytical, and philosophic perspectives. I will then explain the two rival theories of unlawful trading on the basis of material non-public information. Finally, I apply this analysis to insider trading law to explain that the misappropriation theory is incoherent and internally inconsistent because it attempts to piggy-back insider trading law on trade secret principles. The principles underlying these two different fields of law are logically antithetical.

The prohibition against insider trading implicitly reflects a congressional determination that investors in a public company have a beneficial interest in material non-public information about, and in the possession of, that company. It reflects a rare egalitarian moment within our generally individualistic, libertarian property regime. The public is, therefore, rightfully jealous if a traditional insider of a public company having privileged access to this type of information were to exploit it for her own advantage without sharing it with the public. In contrast, trade secret law is premised on the determination that the right to control and commercially exploit certain other categories of information resides exclusively in specific individuals and that the public generally has no such rights—it is fundamentally individualistic and monopolistic. For the government to assert that the investment public is defrauded when this information is used to trade in securities reflects envy.

Envy and Jealousy

Martha, Martha, Martha!

After I admired the silver chopsticks that had been set out, Stewart said, "You know, in China they say, 'The Thinner the chopsticks, the higher the social status.' Of course, I got the thinnest I could find." After a pause, she added, "that's why people hate me."[16]

The causes of the fracas about Martha Stewart are no doubt over-determined, involving among other things the misogyny of the public towards powerful women generally, Stewart's carefully developed, but annoyingly smug perfectionist public image specifically, as well as widespread public misunderstanding that all trading based on non-public information or secret tips is generally unlawful.[17] I argue that this fracas also illustrates that envy is a strong component of "outsider" trading law. Stewart's image inspires admiration, as well as ridicule and backbiting. As stated in an article on CNN.com concerning the effect of the insider trading allegations on Stewart's public image:

> The public has long had a love-hate relationship with Stewart. She is widely admired for her design and business acumen even as she's disparaged for her perfectionist impulses and sheer omnipresence.[18]

Indeed, the infuriating thing about Stewart is that, although she presents each of her suggested projects as eminently doable, it would be inconceivable to accomplish all of the projects suggested in even any one-hour show. That is, she inspires guilt because she presents her world as being both possible and impossible for anyone except her. As stated in a Washington Post article, Stewart's ostensible message is always "You can be just like me."[19] Her implicit message, however, is "Dream on!" I have to admit, that for all my feminist pretensions, she makes me green with envy.

Consequently, the press typically describe this successful entrepreneur, publisher, television personality, and former CEO of a New York Stock Exchange-listed corporation by such condescending terms as "homemaking," "domestic," or "lifestyle,"[20] "queen,"[21] "guru,"[22] or "diva."[23] But, how could she complain when this is precisely the image she has promoted?

The Passions Defined

It is my thesis that the confused analysis that treats misappropriation or "outsider trading" as equivalent to classic "insider trading" reflects the common conflation of envy and jealousy. Although the two passions overlap, they are analytically distinct. Most importantly, the ethical dimensions of the two are completely diverse. Since at least the sixth century when St. Gregory the Great added it to his list, envy has been considered one of the seven deadly sins[24] — not merely a wrongful act, but a disposition that corrupts the soul and serves as the occasion of additional sins.[25] Ethics suggests that we should, therefore, distinguish between the two. According to both theology and psychoanalytic theory, the difficulty in isolating envy from jealousy lies in the fact that envy, albeit radically evil, lies at the heart of human nature.

Envy as Deadly Sin

St. Augustine famously argued in his *Confessions* that the presence of envy in the heart of even the youngest children was evidence of the universality of Original Sin.[26] He called envy "the diabolical sin."[27] This concept builds on St. Paul's statement in the First Letter to the Corinthians that "Love envieth not."[28]

The *Catholic Catechism* identifies envy, along with avarice, as the concern of the tenth, and final Commandment—thou shalt not covet thy neighbor's property. According to the United States Conference of Catholic Bishops: "The tenth commandment concerns the intentions of the heart; ... it summarizes all the precepts of the Law."[29] The *Catechism* defines envy as:

> The sadness at the sight of another's goods and the immoderate desire to acquire them for oneself, even unjustly. When it wishes grave harm to a neighbor it is a mortal sin....

Envy represents a form of sadness and therefore a refusal of charity.[30]

Envy is both ethically and "historically" the second deadly sin, next only to pride.[31] According to a standard interpretation of the Bible, the first sin in the universe was Lucifer's pride that led him to lead the revolt of the rebel angels against God. The second sin was Lucifer's envy of Adam and Eve. Driven to destroy their happiness, Lucifer, in the form of the serpent, appealed to their pride—the first human sin—and seduced them into disobedience. That is, the serpent convinced Eve that if she ate of the Tree of the Knowledge of Good and Evil, she would become like God. This led, once again, to envy as the second human sin when Cain, infuriated by his envy at Abel's good fortune, killed his brother. Consequently, the Bible states that "by the envy of the Devil, death entered into the world, and who are of his portion make trial thereof."[32]

In the twentieth century, psychoanalysts Sigmund Freud and Jacques Lacan seized on this tradition to make envy central to psychoanalytic theory. Lacan's followers have argued that envy is not merely an individual sin, but the source of racism, anti-Semitism, terrorism, and the other horrors of contemporary life. Melanie Klein based a large part on her psychoanalytic theory on the concept of envy, which she describes as "the angry feeling that another person possesses and enjoys something desirable—the envious impulse being to take it away or to spoil it."[33] She contrasts it to its opposite, "gratitude."[34] She offers a psychoanalytic reason "why envy ranks among the seven 'deadly sins'" and "suggests that it is unconsciously felt to be the greatest sin of all, because it spoils and harms the good object which is the source of life."[35]

Envy is a particularly cancerous sin in that its goal is nothing but the destruction of the good. In Chaucer's words, "it is the worst of sins as it sets itself against all other virtues and goodness...."[36] As the Ulanovs explain:

> At first glance, envy seems to differ from other sins because they each point to a goal in itself not evil, except when indulged to excess. Gluttony is hunger gone wild, for example. Lust is sexual desire run rampant. Anger is self-assertion enraged. In contrast, envy presents itself as feeling demeaned by another's good fortune and wanting to belittle the other's good to protect oneself. Envy wants to make something alive into something dead.[37]

Jealousy and Theft of Property

Jealousy is the fear and anger one feels that a rival will steal away that which is rightfully hers. Envy is the rancor and bitterness one feels when observing the good fortune of another. As Mary Ashwin describes it:

> Envy comes from the Latin invidere: to look upon maliciously.... It is the feeling of mortification when we contemplate another's advantages; it is the need to spitefully criticize and denigrate; it is the fear that others are getting more than their fair share.[38]

She continues:

Jealousy is the affect in a triangular situation when a person fears that something that they believe belongs to them has been or is about to be taken away. Essentially the difference between envy and jealousy is that envy is between two objects; jealousy between three.[39]

Klein describes the distinction as follows:

Envy implies the subject's relation to one person only.... Jealousy is based on envy, but involves a relation to at least two people; it is mainly concerned with love that the subject feels is his due and has been taken away, or is in danger of being taken away, from him by his rival.[40]

In Neu's words:

Jealousy is typically over what one possesses and fears to lose, while envy may be over something one has never possessed and may never hope to possess. Going with this, the focus of envy is typically the other person, rather than the particular thing or quality one is envious over (a thing that may not in itself even be desirable to the envier, whatever its perceived value to the present possessor).[41]

In other words, the difference between jealousy and envy is that the former is triangular while the latter is bilateral. That is, the jealous party is concerned to protect or obtain the possession of an object of desire to the exclusion of a real or imagined rival.[42] The jealous is concerned with insuring her own jouissance—a technical psychoanalytic term that for our limited purposes can be somewhat inaccurately translated as "enjoyment." In contrast, the envious is concerned with preventing or destroying the jouissance of the other. The envious does not so much want to obtain, possess, or enjoy the object of desire for its own sake. Rather, the envious just wants to destroy the rival's excess enjoyment in her object by taking it away or destroying it.

The difference between jealousy and envy is illustrated in Freud's interpretation of the story of the judgment of Solomon. As is well known, it is recounted in the book of Kings that two prostitutes living together, perhaps in the same brothel,[43] gave birth to boys within days of each other. One of the women came to Solomon alleging that the child of the other woman died "because she lay on it."[44] The mother of the dead boy took its corpse and laid it by the side of the plaintiff while stealing the living child and placing it in the defendant's bed. "When I arose in the morning to nurse my child, behold, it was dead; but when I looked at it closely in the morning, behold, it was not the child I had borne."[45] Solomon, of course, ordered:

> "Divide the child in two, and give half to the one, and half to the other." Then the woman whose son was alive said to the king, because her heart yearned for her son, "Oh, my lord, give her the living child, and by no means slay it." But the other said, "It shall be neither mine nor yours; divide it." The king answered and said, "Give the living child to the first woman, and by no means slay it; she is its mother." And all Israel heard of the judgment which the king had rendered; and they stood in awe of the king, because they perceived that the wisdom of God was in him, to render justice.[46]

Solomon is extolled for his wisdom in identifying the true mother by her concern for the child. A supposedly more sophisticated version of this is that Solomon wisely identified, not necessarily the biological parent of the child, but the woman who would be a better parent.[47]

Freud correctly points out the fallaciousness of this interpretation.[48] The fact that the plaintiff tried to protect the innocent child proved neither that she was his mother nor that she was even benevolent. All it showed was that she was not psychotic.

Rather, Solomon's wisdom lay in his identification of which woman was more likely to harm the child in the future. Solomon was, in effect, testing the truth of the plaintiff's accusation. The only possible explanation for the behavior charged by the plaintiff was that the defendant was envious to the point of madness. A woman who would steal the child of another could not be driven by jealousy. She could not fear losing her own son—this had already happened—and no one else's child could be a substitute for the uniqueness of an individual who had been lost. Rather, bereft of the joys of motherhood, the defendant could not bear to see the plaintiff's joy. The defendant stole the living child not so that she would have him, but so that the plaintiff would not. Solomon understood that ordering the death of the living child would reveal the true jouissance of the defendant. And indeed, the defendant's enjoyment was in destruction—envy. In contrast, the jouissance of a "true" mother would be the love of her child. She might be expected to be jealous—frantic that that which by right belonged to her (her child) might be taken by a rival—but her love should overcome this jealousy if she thought that the alternative was losing her child through death.

Envy is always sinful. In contrast, jealousy can be either rightful or wrongful. For example, Yahweh correctly describes His passion as jealousy, not envy. By definition, God's passions are righteous. The all powerful, all confident Yahweh could not conceivably be envious of Baal and the other false gods. And yet, He can fear that His chosen, but weak, people might be seduced away by the idols. The history recounted by the Bible suggests that this fear was frequently justified.[49]

Jealousy can be wrong if it is unjustified or misplaced. An example of the former is the jealous spouse irrationally fears that his faithful spouse will betray him. The classic illustration of the distinction between wrongful jealousy and envy is the contrast between Othello and Iago—the envious Iago is evil, the jealous Othello merely tragic.[50] Many misogynist practices—such as purdah—are the institutionalization of unjustified jealousy.

When it is misplaced, the jealous party may have no rightful claim to the object to desire. The phenomenon of stalking is a frightening example of wrongful jealousy—the stalker fears the "loss" of the beloved who, in fact, never was his. Moreover, stalking is the point where wrongful jealousy threatens to pass over to envy, as when Othello strangles Desdemona.

Psychoanalysis

Envy plays a central role in the psychoanalytic tradition associated with Freud. Freud's theory of the role of penis envy in the feminine psyche is notorious. His followers take a more radical position. For example, without denying Freud's account of penis envy in the Oedipal stage of development, Klein argues that envy is an essential constitutional basis of all personality, masculine and feminine, that arises much earlier in the infant's development and derives from the child's empirical experience of the maternal breast (or substitute). It is "operative from the beginning of life."[51] Lacan takes Freud's analysis of envy to an even higher, philosophic level.

I find Freud and Klein's accounts of the origins unsatisfactory because they claim to be empirical and, therefore, deterministic. Lacan's account, in contrast, is theoretical and retrospective. That is, Freud seems to believe that children go through a stage in their lives when they literally wish to have sex with their mothers and kill their fathers. Girls literally are so impressed with the sight of a penis that they feel lacking the rest of their lives. Lacan, in contrast, states that "the Oedipus complex is Freud's dream. Like all dreams it needs to be interpreted."[52] Indeed, according to Lacan, even Oedipus did not have an Oedipal complex.[53]

Similarly, Klein's object psychology is based on the proposition that from the time of birth children literally form relationships based on the mother's breast. She quoted approvingly Freud's analogy of psychoanalysis to archeology:

> His [the psychoanalyst's] work of construction, or, if it is preferred,
> of reconstruction, resembles to a great extent an archaeologist's exca-

vation of some dwelling-place that has been destroyed and buried or of some ancient edifice. The two processes are in fact identical, except that the analyst works under better conditions and has more material at his command to assist him, since what he is dealing with is not something destroyed but something that is still alive—and perhaps for another reason as well. But just as the archaeologist builds up the walls of the building from the foundations that have remained standing, determines the number and position of the columns from depressions in the floor and reconstructs the mural decorations and paintings from the remains found in the debris, so does the analyst proceed when he draws his inferences from ... the behaviour of the subject of the analysis.[54]

The advantage to this approach is also its disadvantage—it arguably makes their theories falsifiable. If one studied infants and could show that they did not literally go through these stages, then the theories would be disproved.

Lacan, in contrast, works not only within the psychoanalytic tradition but also within the speculative philosophical tradition that is based on a study of human freedom.[55] Consequently, he seeks to eliminate any remaining biological determinism from Freud's theory. He seeks not to recover the child who once was, but to help the adult understand the person she is now. Lacan, following Hegel and Kant, posits that if the subject is essentially free, it is because subjectivity is nothing but a radical negativity. That is, the subject is subjected to no boundaries only because it has no positive characteristics. The Oedipal romance is, in a Lacanian reading, a sort of false-autobiography that we retroactively tell ourselves in order to explain, and give affirmative content to, our essential emptiness. Its very determinism is comforting not only because it seems to explain the modern subject's feeling of alienation, but also because it places the blame for her condition elsewhere. As I shall explain in the next part of this chapter, envy is one possible reaction that a subject can have when she is forced to confront her constituent negativity.

Lacan

The centrality of envy in Lacan's psychoanalytic theory can be seen in his repeated references to a passage in the Confessions of St. Augustine.[56] As noted, St. Augustine answered the critics of the doctrine of original sin who maintained a romantic belief in the innocence of children with the following anecdote. "I myself have seen and known even a baby envious; it could not speak, yet it turned pale and looked bitterly on its foster-brother."[57] Lacan explains how the passion identified by Augustine, which is sometimes translated as "jealousy," is more correctly understood as "envy."

Lacan points out that the word envy, the Latin "invidia" comes, in turn, from videre—to see.[58] It is the passion felt in seeing the enjoyment of the other.

> In order to understand what invidia is in its function as gaze it must not be confused with jealousy. What the small child, or whoever, envies is not at all necessarily what he might want—avoir envie, as one improperly puts it. Who can say that the child who looks at his younger brother still needs to be at the breast? Everyone knows that envy is usually aroused by the possession of goods which would be of no use to the person who is envious of them, and about the true nature of which he does not have the least idea.[59]

That is, Augustine's point is not that the child jealously fears the loss of the maternal breast. The bitter child has already been weaned and is well-fed. Rather, it is the very sight of his brother's enjoyment that fills him with envy. Consequently, he does not want to regain the breast, just to take it away from his hated little brother. This is sin.

Lacan agrees with Augustine that envy needs to be guarded against because it leads not only to personal and social evils, but also because it is constitutive of personality itself and, therefore, particularly invidious. A full account of Lacanian theory is far beyond the scope of this chapter. For our purposes suffice it to say that Lacan goes beyond Freud's theory of penis envy and Klein's theory of breast envy, with their lingering aura of crude biological determinism. Lacan posits that the very initiation of the subject into the symbolic realm of language, law and sexuality "splits" the subject leaving her with an insatiable feeling of lack.[60] Or, more accurately, as I have said elsewhere, the "subject is split" is not so much a description but a definition—subjectivity is nothing but an internal, constituent emptiness or splitting.[61]

To oversimplify, following Hegel, Lacan thought that subjectivity could only be created through intersubjective relationships with others—what he called the symbolic order of the big Other.[62] The subject is nothing but this hollow shell that gains content from the outside. Consequently, one's most intimate self lies external to oneself. Lacan coined the neologism "extimacy" to describe the uncanny sense of one's own self-alienation.[63] This constitutive lack appears even more negative when one realizes that the Other who gives the subject content also "does not exist."[64] That is, the intersubjective order of the symbolic has no pre-existing, objective, and permanent essence but consists merely of a contingent, intersubjective, and temporary appearance of specific, fleeting social relations among a community of split subjects.

Lacan will eventually combine his insight that the subject is split, and that the Other does not exist, to formulate his single most controversial slogan "Woman does not exist."[65] Although frequently dismissed as misogyny, Lacan's statement is more correctly interpreted as a statement of the human condition. To Lacan, true subjectivity is feminine in nature—the feminine is the part of personality that internalizes the fact of her own negativity.[66] The masculine is the part that denies the truth. Or, to paraphrase Lacanian philosopher Slavoj Žižek, a man is a woman who thinks she exists.[67]

The subject seeks an explanation of her sense of lack by formulating a retroactive account (an abduction or retroduction) of what must have happened. One way she does this is by identifying her lack of enjoyment (completion) with the excess enjoyment of someone else. She obsesses on the other's enjoyment and concludes that not only does the other enjoy, he does so excessively while she, in contrast, is lacking. She speculates that the reason why she lacks enjoyment and the other enjoys too much must be that the other has stolen her enjoyment. In Žižek's words:

> What we conceal by imputing to the Other the theft of enjoyment is the traumatic fact that we never possessed what was allegedly stolen from us: the lack ("castration") is originary, enjoyment constitutes itself as "stolen," or, to quote Hegel's precise formulation from his Science of Logic, it "only comes to be through being left behind."[68]

This is a false autobiography. Through this self-serving account, the subject tries to disguise her sinful envy as righteous jealousy—thereby shifting the blame from herself to the "thieving" other. This is both sinful and unjust.

Lacanians have extended and applied Lacan's theory of excess enjoyment to the political field. We associate the other who has excess enjoyment with other groups with which we are proximate. We concentrate on the difference in the way the other, with his strange customs, enjoys. For example, Jacques-Alain Miller, Lacan's son-in-law and editor, states:

> Now, what we are attempting to see is what makes the Other other, that is, what makes it particular, different, and in this dimension of alterity of the Other, we find war. Racism, for example, is precisely a question of the relation to an Other as such, conceived in its difference. And it does not seem to me that any of the generous and universal discourses on the theme of "we are all fellow beings" have had any effectiveness concerning this question. Why? Because racism calls into play a hatred that is directed precisely toward what grounds the Other's alterity, in other words, its jouissance. If no decision, no will,

no amount of reasoning is sufficient to wipe out racism, this is indeed because it is founded on the point of extimacy of the Other.

It is not simply a mater of an imaginary aggressivity that, itself, is directed at fellow beings. Racism is founded on what one imagines about the Other's jouissance; it is hatred of the particular way, of the Other's own way, of experiencing jouissance.... However, what is really at stake is that he takes his jouissance in a way different from ours. Thus the Other's proximity exacerbates racism: as soon as there is closeness, there is a confrontation of incompatible modes of jouissance. For it is simple to love one's neighbor when he is distant, but it is a different matter in proximity.

Racist stories are always about the way in which the Other obtains a plus-de-jouir: either he does not work or he does not work enough, or he is useless or a little too useful, but whatever the case may be, he is always endowed with a part of jouissance that he does not deserve. Thus true intolerance is the intolerance of the Other's jouissance.[69]

As Lacan says (in explanation of Augustine's anecdote):

Such is true envy—the envy that makes the subject pale before the image of a completeness closed upon itself, before the idea that the petit a, the separated a from which he is hanging, may be for another the possession that gives satisfaction.... [70]

Note that the theory of the relationship between the theory of excess enjoyment and racism lies precisely at the moment at which jealousy passes into envy—or, more accurately, when the guilty subject tries to disguise her sinful and deceitful envy as righteous jealousy. The subject pretends to be jealous—she tries to insist that the reason she is angry is because the Other has taken away that which is rightfully hers. But in her heart, she knows that her lack is constituent and is not caused by the absence of any specific thing. Consequently, what she really feels is envy. She is incensed at the supposed enjoyment of the Other in which she cannot participate.

All she can do, therefore, is try to destroy the other's enjoyment. Unfortunately, because the subject identifies the other's enjoyment with the other's alterity (i.e., whatever it is that distinguishes the other from the subject) destruction of the other's enjoyment requires the destruction of the other. Accordingly, in Lacan's late seminar, *Encore*, Lacan invents the neo-logism "jealouissance" for the envy of the excess enjoyment (jouissance) of the other first identified by Augustine.[71] Historically, as demonstrated in such examples of Lynch mobs, the Holocaust, the Serbian wars and, today, Islamacism and, perhaps, President Bush's invocation to the "Axis of Evil," this impulse becomes literal as political reality.

Law

Freud identified envy as the source of our sense of social justice. "If one cannot be the favourite oneself, at all events nobody else shall be the favourite."[72] But Freud thinks that humans are not naturally herd animals with benevolent social instincts.[73] Liberal legal theory, as well as Lacanian psychoanalysis, suggests that the matter is more complicated. Social justice requires that we distinguish righteous jealousy from destructive envy; we must not merely claim property rights for ourselves, we must respect the property of others. As I have already quoted: "That envy may be one reason for demanding equality does not mean that demands for equality are unjustified."[74]

Although I base my legal theory on the super-liberalism of Hegel, this is equally true of classic liberal theory associated with Locke. To Locke, property is a natural right that pre-exists society.[75] Under this interpretation, liberalism requires that we respect property rights. This means that appropriate jealousy—the protection of valid property rights[76]—is necessary even as envy—the desire to destroy the property rights of others—must be prohibited.

To Hegel, property and liberal society are self-constituting—property is created by liberal society, but liberal society logically requires property as its cornerstone.[77] This can be seen as a fundamental principle of Hegel's philosophy of right. To Hegel, the abstract individual posited by classical liberalism is too frail a creature to act as a subject, a creature capable of bearing rights and interacting in the symbolic order of society.[78] Related to this, he thinks that subjectivity could not exist in the state of nature posited by liberalism because one can only be a subject insofar as one is recognized as such by another subject.[79] Consequently, the person seeking subjectivity must first seek to give other persons the status and dignity of subjectivity; that is, subjectivity requires mutual recognition. For reasons that are beyond the scope of this chapter, Hegel argues that the most basic and primitive regime of mutual recognition is the private law of property and contract.[80] This means that subjectivity does not so much require that each individual claim and protect her own property rights. Rather, she must first grant and respect the property rights of others as a step in granting others the status of subjectivity.[81]

As already introduced,[82] Lacan, following Hegel, believes that even as the subject is alienated and envious, she is also essentially social; her subjectivity is created by, and only exists within, intersubjective relationships with other subjects in the symbolic order (the big Other). As Hegel argues, in the modern liberal constitutional state, this intersubjective order is sustained by a regime of property—the possession, enjoyment, and exchange of actual and imaginary objects of enjoyment.[83] Consequently, although the subject may on the one hand want to destroy the possession and enjoyment of the other, on the other hand, she requires the existence of a property regime that allocates objects among subjects. In this sense, jealousy is as important to her constitution as envy. Jealousy is necessary in that it helps maintain the intersubjective regime of property. Envy, in contrast, is self-contradictory in that it threatens to destroy the regime of property that is necessary for the subject's self-constitution.

This does not mean that society should necessarily respect any and all claims to property or that we should perpetuate the status quo of wealth and property distribution. The question is, how do we tell the difference between rightful and wrongful jealous claims to property, and between rightful jealous claims to property, and wrongful envious desires to destroy the property of others? Hegel argues that a property regime is a necessary and appropriate element of the modern liberal state, but he offers no advice as to what specific allocation of property is correct.[84] He leaves this, as he does with all policy decisions, to pragmatic reasoning and positive law.[85]

We can now return to the law of insider trading.

Insider Trading

Fraud

Disputes arise over the proper scope of prohibitions against securities trading on the basis of material non-public information because of the simple, albeit surprising, fact that the federal securities laws neither define, nor expressly prohibit, "insider trading."[86] Consequently, in the absence of congressional action, if the SEC, the DOJ, plaintiffs, and the courts believe that trading on the basis of material non-public information should be unlawful, they must imply appropriate rules from the general language and policy of the statutes, combined with case law developed under the very different legal regimes of state corporate and trade secrets law. Indeed, this is the single most disturbing aspect of insider trading law—it is essentially a common law federal crime. This jurisprudential objection is beyond the scope of the specific argument of this chapter, although it obviously informs it.

Both proponents and opponents of prohibitions on insider trading base their arguments on policies that they wished the law would follow, rather than on policies that the statute actually reflects. To oversimplify,[87] proponents of rules against insider trading tend to base their objections on the intuition that it is immoral, unfair, or, as expressed in the title of Kim Sheppele's classic article, *It's Just Not Right*.[88] Critics and opponents of prohibitions on insider trading tend to rely on an economic analysis of law that seeks to promote efficient securities markets.[89] The problem with both approaches is that neither of the two primary securities acts—the Securities Act of 1933 (the "1933 Act") and the Securities Exchange Act of 1934 (the "1934 Act")—contains any language expressly imposing either fairness or efficiency criteria with respect to the issuers of securities and their affiliates.[90] Consequently, while arguments made on fairness or efficiency grounds may be of great academic interest and would be relevant if Congress were considering a major overhaul of the regulatory regime, they are of less interest to the judge or lawyer who is trying to interpret the existing statutes. In contrast, in this chapter, I try to analyze insider trading within the statutory policy of mandatory disclosure of certain types of information by certain classes of legal actors.

The Acts require issuers and certain other persons to make disclosures and file forms with the SEC on certain occasions. The Acts frequently impose liability on issuers and certain others for material misstatements and certain material omissions.[91] The Acts also include general prohibitions against fraud[92] and manipulation.[93] Consequently, whether or not certain forms of trading on the basis of material non-public information should be prohibited because they are unfair, or permitted because they are efficient, the proponents of these positions must word their arguments within language that either mandates disclosure or prohibits fraud and manipulation. Indeed, most of the last thirty years of insider trading case law can arguably be characterized as an attempt by the Supreme Court to rein in the attempts by the SEC and the lower federal courts to ground insider trading jurisprudence in non-statutory fairness considerations.[94] This history is well known among securities lawyers and I shall only give an abbreviated account in this chapter.

Fairness

The catch-all anti-fraud provision of the federal securities laws is Section 10(b) of the 1934 Act, which makes it unlawful for a person to use the jurisdictional means "to use or employ, in connection with the purchase or sale of any security ... any manipulative or deceptive device or contrivance in contravention of such rules and the regulations as the Commission may prescribe...."[95] Rule 10b-5 promulgated under this section of the 1934 Act provides that:

> It shall be unlawful for any person, directly or indirectly, by the use of any means or instrumentality of interstate commerce, or of the mails or of any facility of any national securities exchange,
> (a) To employ any device, scheme, or artifice to defraud,
> (b) To make any untrue statement of a material fact or to omit to state a material fact necessary in order to make the statements made, in the light of the circumstances under which they were made, not misleading, or
> (c) To engage in any act, practice, or course of business which operates or would operate as a fraud or deceit upon any person, in connection with the purchase or sale of any security.[96]

Since the great retrenchment cases of *Ernst & Ernst v. Hochfelder*[97] and *Santa Fe Industries, Inc. v. Green*,[98] the Supreme Court has made it clear that 10(b)'s litany "manipulative or deceptive device or contrivance" indicates that Congress was codifying the traditional common law tort of deception, rather than proscribing negligent or unfair behavior or constructive fraud.[99] Although the language of Rule 10b-5 is broader than that of Section 10(b), under the basic principles of administrative rulemaking, the rule should not be read more expansively than the statute under which it is promulgated.[100] Consequently, Rule 10b-5 must also be limited to actual fraud.[101]

The Supreme Court applied this underlying principle to insider trading in the seminal case of *Chiarella v. United States*.[102] Because Section 10(b) only proscribes fraud the Court rejected the concept of "a general duty between all participants in market transactions to forego actions based on material, non-public information."[103] By doing so, the Court also implicitly rejected the SEC's holding in *In re Cady, Roberts & Co.*[104] and the Second Circuit's opinion in *S.E.C. v. Texas Gulf Sulphur*[105] implied that the rule against trading on non-public information applied universally because it was grounded in preventing unfairness.[106] In the Court's words, "not every instance of financial unfairness constitutes fraudulent activity."[107] In other words, even if all fraud is unfair, not all unfairness is fraudulent.

"Fraud" has many elements. In this chapter, I concentrate only on those that are most directly relevant to the issue at hand. First and foremost, fraud requires deception — misrepresentation, or nondisclosure, by the fraudster and reliance by the victim.[108] To put this in layperson's terms, deception is the allegation that "you intentionally lied to me and I relied on your lies to my detriment."[109]

Although the federal securities laws are designed to protect investors and maintain the integrity of the securities markets, even after the adoption of the much hyped Sarbanes-Oxley Act of 2002,[110] federal law applicable to issuers is generally not paternalistic in the same way that state law is. The federal securities laws generally applicable to issuers[111] have sometimes been termed "rotten egg" rules.[112] A substantive rule would prohibit the sale of rotten eggs (or, to put this in a corporate context, to enter into a transaction unfair to shareholders). In contrast, under the securities laws, "if the investor purchases the "rotten eggs' on an informed basis, [the federal securities law] provides no relief."[113] That is, issuers and insiders are allowed to treat investors unfairly, so long as they inform investors what they are in for. Consequently, under federal law, when a person speaks, she must not only speak truthfully, she must also speak completely—no lies, and no half-truths. This standard appears in the language of Rule 10b-5(b) quoted above that makes it unlawful "to make any untrue statement of a material fact or to omit a material fact necessary in order to make the statements made, in light of the circumstances under which they were made, not misleading."[114]

Silence

It is relatively simple to understand what this means as a practical matter when a person makes an affirmative public statement—it must be true and it must be complete. Virtually all alleged insider trading cases, however, involve complete silence, rather than incomplete statements; the trader trades without disclosing information in her possession. The analysis is much more difficult to apply, both practically and theoretically, in these cases. This is because Rule 10b-5 does not prohibit all omissions (silences) of material facts, but only omissions "necessary in order to make the statements made ... not misleading." Consequently, the rule against omissions applies only when either a person has spoken, but spoke incompletely, or if she has failed to speak when she has a duty to speak. To find that a person is guilty of unlawful insider trading under Rule 10b-5, therefore, we must first find that the trader had a duty to make a statement.

The securities acts impose statutory disclosure obligations on issuers and other actors in many circumstances. For example, under the 1934 Act, issuers must file with the SEC quarterly reports on Form 10-Q,[115] annual reports on Form 10-K,[116] periodic reports on Form 8-K[117] and proxy statements pursuant to Regulation 14A.[118] There is considerable, but highly confusing, case law as to whether and when issuers and other persons must update these mandatory reports.[119] Insider trading cases almost always fall within the ambiguous gap periods between mandatory statutory reports.

As *Chiarella* makes clear, the federal securities laws do not impose "a general duty between all participants in market transactions to forgo actions based on material, non-public information."[120] That is,

> silence in connection with the purchase or sale of securities may operate as a fraud actionable under 10(b).... But such liability is premised upon a duty to disclose arising from a relationship of trust and confidence between parties to a transaction.[121]

In other words, the mere possession of information giving a person an "unfair advantage over less informed buyers and sellers"[122] does not itself impose a duty to disclose or refrain from trading.[123] Examples of persons who may have a duty to speak given by the Supreme Court include traditional corporate insiders, agents, fiduciaries, and persons in whom sellers of securities have "placed their trust and confidence."[124] There is, according to the Court, no justification for imposing duties to speak on "a complete stranger who dealt with the sellers only through impersonal market transactions."[125]

If fraud requires deception, then this implies there must be some person or class of persons who is deceived. The deceived person(s) must have relied on the misrepresentation or omission to his detriment. As I shall discuss below,[126] one of the problems with the misappropriation theory as developed to date is that it threatens to disconnect these two interrelated aspects of the fraudster's deception—the person to whom the duty to speak runs is not necessarily the person who is deemed harmed by the omission. Ordinarily, one would assume that if securities fraud occurred by definition, there should be at least one person who could bring a private right of action under Rule 10b-5 for securities fraud. But, under the misappropriation theory, there can be no such plaintiff!

Informational Advantages

One major theme that runs throughout this chapter is that, even among those who intuit that insider trading is unfair, there is no clear consensus as to what is unfair about it, given certain basic premises of our capitalist economic system, generally, and American intellectual property law, specifically. Insider trading—the trading of securities on the basis of certain material non-public information—is the economic exploitation of an informational advantage by the possessor of the information, to the disadvantage of the rest of the public. Consequently, the regulation of insider trading can be seen as a limitation on informational advantages in the name of a more egalitarian distribution of information. But, neither American law generally, nor securities law specifically, has a policy of parity of access to information, as the Supreme Court expressly recognized in *Chiarella*.[127] As I discuss below,[128] informational advantages are frequently protected by our law as "trade secrets."[129] As Henry Manne states rather sharply, but accurately: "Lawyers especially, it would seem, should be very circumspect about characterizing the utilization of superior information as immoral. That is, after all, their stock in trade."[130] And indeed, Justice Ruth Bader Ginsburg will paradoxically attempt to ground her misappropriation theory, which reflects an egalitarian approach towards non-public information, on trade secret law, which grants monopolistic rights in non-public information to specific legal actors. My analysis leads to the conclusion both that Congress has been derelict in failing to reconcile these two different regimes of ownership of material non-public information and that the resulting confusion has encouraged the federal courts' inappropriate extension of insider trading law beyond the scope of the disclosure and anti-fraud policies of the securities laws.

How, then, do we reconcile these two competing approaches to the law of informational advantages? I suggest that it is precisely the contradictory approaches of securities and trade secret law that suggests the answer to their reconciliation. Courts should apply insider trading law only to that subset of information that our society has expressly or implicitly allocated to the public. The public can justifiably be jealous if a party tries to appropriate and exploit for his own personal benefit such information that is rightfully public. In contrast, insider trading prohibitions should not apply to that information that our society has allocated to specific economic actors under trade secret law, or otherwise. Any objection by the public to the owner's use of her non-public information is mere envy. The reason why the misappropriation theory of insider trading law as articulated by Justice Ginsburg in *O'Hagan* is so troublesome is precisely because it tries to base insider trading—the law of eliminating informational advantages—on trade secret law, the law of protecting informational advantages.

Of course, by positing my analysis in this form, I am arguably begging the essential policy question of what information should properly be allocated to the public and what should be allocated to specific individuals. This is intentional. Such policy decisions are not within the bailiwick of the federal courts or the SEC applying the federal securities laws, but of Congress and the legislatures and common law courts of the several states.

Classic Theory

Classic Insiders

The classic theory of insider trading holds that it is a fraud for a traditional corporate insider (such as an officer, director, senior employee, or control person of a corporation) to trade on equity securities issued by that corporation

on the basis of material non-public information obtained from the corporation. This rule is rather misleadingly known as the "disclose or refrain
rule"[131]—if a traditional insider is in possession of material non-public information, she must either refrain from trading in equity securities of that
corporation or she must make the information public before trading. This
name is misleading because the trader usually has no right, vis-à-vis the
source, to disclose the information. Consequently, as a practical matter, this
may more accurately be a "refrain rule."[132]

Fitting this prohibition within the law of fraud is a stretch—or, more accurately, a contortion. The underlying problem is that, rather than seeking implied duties to disclose from within the language and policy of the securities acts
themselves, the courts and the SEC have looked towards state corporate law. This
is problematic because, as mentioned, since at least *Santa Fe* and *Chiarella*, the
Supreme Court has held that the securities laws generally, and insider trading
law specifically, are designed only to require disclosure and to proscribe fraud.
State corporate law, in contrast, imposes fiduciary duties and proscribes substantive unfairness. It is not surprising, therefore, that a duty of disclosure based
on the latter will do an imperfect job in furthering the policies of the former.

In finding that insider trading constitutes fraud, courts have adopted a version of a common law rule of "special facts." Although the cases are far from
specific in explaining their reasoning, it seems to be roughly as follows: sometimes a fiduciary or other person in a confidential relationship has a duty to
make disclosures to her beneficiary. Consequently, a beneficiary is sometimes
entitled to rely on silence by the fiduciary as an implied negative representation. As Justice Powell stated in *United States v. Dirks*:[133]

> In an inside-trading case this fraud derives from the "inherent un-
> fairness involved where one takes advantage" of "information intended
> to be available only for a corporate purpose and not for the personal
> benefit of anyone." ... Thus, an insider will be liable under Rule 10b-
> 5 for inside trading only where he fails to disclose material non-pub-
> lic information before trading on it and thus makes "secret profits."[134]

Although rather confusingly worded in the language of fairness, the *Dirks*
opinion, in fact, reiterates the basic principal of *Chiarella* that federal securities laws do not impose duties on market participants generally merely because they are in possession of information. Consequently, the Supreme
Court exonerated the defendant (an alleged tippee) in this case precisely because he was not subject to the duty to disclose or abstain himself, and his
tipper, who did have such a duty, did not violate his duty. By invoking "fairness," Powell seems to be invoking state law which imposes fiduciary duties

of substantive fairness, but only on a limited class of people. Under state corporate law, traditional insiders of a corporation, such as officers and directors, have fiduciary duties to the corporation and to its equity security holders.[135]

A duty to speak is derived by analogy to the law applicable to trustees with respect to entrusted property. Under general principals of fiduciary duty law, a fiduciary may not deal on her own behalf in property of the beneficiary entrusted to her care. Non-public information generated by a corporation can be considered property of that corporation. Classic insiders can be analogized to trustees who hold this information as the corpus of a trust for the benefit of the corporation and its shareholders. Consequently, the classic insider's use of the information for her own individual purposes is a breach of the insider's duty of loyalty under corporate law analogous to a trustee's embezzlement of a corpus.[136] In Powell's language in *Chiarella*:

> Application of a duty to disclose prior to trading guarantees that corporate insiders, who have an obligation to place the shareholder's welfare before their own, will not benefit personally through fraudulent use of material, non-public information.[137]

Although I know of no case that specifically does so, this reasoning can also be analogized to the law of "corporate opportunity," which prohibits an officer or director of a corporation from exploiting a business opportunity that should belong to the corporation for his own personal advantage, at least not until he first offers the opportunity to the corporation.[138]

A literal-minded reading of the rule of fiduciary duty would suggest that it would prohibit only the purchase of equity securities by insiders on the basis of material non-public information but would not prohibit the sale. This is because state law duties run to the corporation's shareholders, not to the public generally. This simplistic statement does not, however, account for the practical realities of a publicly traded corporation in which the shareholders are not a stable class of identifiable individuals, but a constantly changing pool of investors who buy shares, hold them for a while, and sell them. Consequently, for the purposes of insider trading law, one needs to stretch the class of beneficiaries of the rule from the class of persons who happen to be shareholders on any specific day, to the pool of actual and potential future shareholders—i.e., the investment public generally. To put this another way, the moment an insider sells an equity security, the buyer who had been a stranger instantaneously becomes a beneficiary of the insider's fiduciary duty. Intuitively, it would seem strange to say that the insider has no fiduciary duties with respect to the transaction that creates the fiduciary relationship.

How does breach of fiduciary duty become fraud? Because a fiduciary has a duty not to use trust assets for her own benefit, whenever a person accepts the duties of a fiduciary, she is deemed to make an implied warranty of fidelity to her beneficiaries. Consequently, it is reasonable for the beneficiaries to rely on this implied warranty. This establishes the reliance factor of deception. Because of this justified reliance, the special facts rule imposes on the fiduciary a duty to disclose to the beneficiaries any attempt to breach the duty and invade the corpus.[139] In other words, when a classic insider trades without first disclosing material non-public information in her possession, she violates not only her duty of loyalty, but also her duty to speak. Violation of this duty, thereby, constitutes an "omission to state a material fact necessary ... in connection with the purchase or sale of any security" in violation of Rule 10b-5. This can be a fraud if the other elements of Section 10(b) and Rule 10b-5 are met.[140]

Once again, this is a stretch. The real wrong underlying this analysis is that the insider stole property (information) from the corporation (and its investors), not that he defrauded them. As Saikrishna Prakash has persuasively argued, if the true gravamen of the offense were fraud, the insider would be permitted to trade if he first disclosed his intention to the corporation's board of directors (or if the board or the shareholders grant him the right to trade).[141] Indeed, this is the rule in the analogous law of "corporate opportunity"—an insider may lawfully exploit an opportunity for his own benefit if he first obtains the permission of the disinterested board members or the shareholders after making full disclosure.[142] Moreover, as we shall see,[143] this is the approach that the Supreme Court will take towards disclosure under the misappropriation theory.

Nevertheless, the courts have not had the courage to follow the logic of the "special facts" rule to this logical conclusion and have, instead, required the classic insider to either disclose the non-public information in his possession—something he is usually prohibited from doing for other legal reasons—or refrain from trading. This anomaly would be avoided if, instead, the courts had grounded the insiders' duty to disclose within the policy of federal disclosure and anti-fraud policies, rather than state fiduciary and substantive fairness policies.

Temporary Insiders and Tippees

A more important problem with the traditional interpretation of the classic theory is that a very literal-minded approach to it would seem narrowly to limit the class of persons subject to its jurisdiction—i.e., corporate officers, directors, controlling shareholders, and perhaps senior employees. The courts have addressed this by recognizing two classes of remote traders who can be held liable under the classic theory: "temporary"[144] (or "constructive")[145] insiders and tippees. The former are persons who are not classic insiders who nevertheless take on a fiduciary or similar duty of confidence to the issuer either by professional status (such as that owed by outside counsel to an issuer or psychiatrist of a classic insider),[146] by express contract (such as when an independent contractor signs a confidentiality agreement),[147] or perhaps by implied contract, established by course of conduct (as when a classic insider regularly confides and discusses material non-public information with a family member for the purpose of obtaining business advice).[148] The latter are persons who, as the terminology suggests, are "tipped off" by an insider either because the insider-tipper hopes to receive a benefit from the tippee in return or because the tipper wants to benefit the tippee.[149]

I have found that students have a hard time telling the difference between tippees on the one hand and remote temporary insiders (and from misappropriators, whom I discuss in the next section) on the other. Actually, they are easily distinguished if one keeps in mind that the former is a reversed mirror-image of the latter. A remote temporary insider (like a misappropriator) is given information in a relationship of confidence for the source's own purposes under circumstances that prohibits the temporary insider from exploiting the information for her own purposes or from further disclosing the information to others. In contrast, a tippee is given non-public information with the expectation that the tippee shall trade on, or otherwise use, the information for her own purposes. In other words, when a remote temporary insider (or misappropriator) trades on the information, she is thwarting the will and violating the property rights of the source of the information. But when the tippee trades, she is fulfilling the intent of her tipper (albeit in violation of the tipper's duty to the source).

Under-, and Over-, Inclusiveness

The classic theory is troublesome to proponents of restrictions against trading on the basis of material non-public information in that it fails to cover behavior that seems equal in culpability. First, it is not at all clear that trading even by classic insiders in debt securities of an issuer is unlawful. This is because, under state law, the duties that an issuer (and, therefore, its insiders) owes to debt holders are contractual, rather than fiduciary, in nature.[150] Standard form debt contracts do not impose a general duty of disclosure and candor on the issuers of debt.[151] Consequently, the special circumstances doctrine that makes silence into a misrepresentation would not seem to apply. It is similarly not clear whether the managers of limited liability companies would be subject to insider trading prohibitions because it is not clear whether their duty to their members is contractual or fiduciary in nature. Second, the

Supreme Court assumed that the classic theory does not cover the facts of the *O'Hagan* case when an insider or temporary insider of a bidder in a tender offer used confidential information obtained by the bidder to trade on securities of the target. The bidder, and therefore its insiders, have no fiduciary duties to the target—indeed, their interests may be hostile.[152]

The critic of classic insider trading law may come to the opposite normative conclusion from the supporter. If these various cases are morally equivalent to insider trading, then whatever is intuitively "wrong" with insider trading cannot be fraud. Consequently, it is inappropriate for courts to find that even classic insider trading violates Section 10(b). If Congress believes that certain trading on the basis of certain categories of material non-public information is "wrong," then it should enact a statute prohibiting it. This is why the SEC has adopted Rule 14e-3 prohibiting trading on the basis of information received from bidders not as securities fraud, but as a prophylactic rule to prevent indirect violations of the substantive requirements applicable to tender offers.[153]

In contrast with both the traditional proponents of insider trading, and its traditional opponents, I argue that it is indeed coherent and appropriate to prohibit classic insider trading but not misappropriation on the grounds that only the former is consistent with the policy of the federal securities laws that allocates rights to certain information to the investment public.

Misappropriation Theory

Defined

In *O'Hagan v. United States*,[154] the Supreme Court adopted the alternate so-called misappropriation theory of outsider trading. The difference between the classic theory and the misappropriation theory is the identity of the original source of the information. Under the classic theory, the source must be the issuer of the security being traded. Under the misappropriation theory, it is sufficient that the trader misappropriates material non-public information in violation of a duty of confidence to any source of the information. That is, the source of the information need not be the issuer of the securities traded and the trader need have no duty running directly or indirectly back to the issuer, let alone indirectly to the investment public.[155]

O'Hagan was a partner in a law firm that had represented Grand Met in connection with a planned hostile tender offer for Pillsbury. Knowing that the price of a target's shares usually rises upon the announcement of a tender offer, he bought call options in Pillsbury before the announcement and reaped a profit of approximately $4.3 million when he exercised his options and sold

Pillsbury shares after the announcement. O'Hagan's actions clearly and un-ambiguously violated the prophylactic provisions of Rule 14e-3, prohibiting certain trading while in possession of material non-public information ob-tained from certain identified persons in connection with a tender offer. He also violated his ethical duties as an attorney to his firm's ex-client, Grand Met. However, he did not engage in classic insider trading under Rule 10b-5 for the obvious reason that the source of his information was not Pillsbury, the issuer of the traded securities. Moreover, because he had no previous relationship to Pillsbury, he owed no duties whatsoever to Pillsbury or its shareholders.

Although the misappropriation theory maintains the classic requirements that (i) silence cannot constitute fraud unless the silent party has a duty to speak imposed by a fiduciary or other confidential relationship and (ii) the recipient of the information must trade securities, it jettisons the requirement that the person who is defrauded and the person (or class of persons) with whom she trades must be one and the same. That is, under the misappropriation theory, it is not necessary that the duty of confidence (and related duty to speak) run to the issuer of the securities (and, thereby, to the shareholders of the issuer).[156] Consequently, the Court had to adopt an alternate interpretation as to how the fraud "is in connection with" the purchase and sale of securities.

In *O'Hagan*, both the majority and the otherwise vociferous dissent[157] as-sumed that the defendant had no duty of confidence to the investment pub-lic generally (an assumption I will question later). Indeed, Justice Ginsburg expressly stated that the misappropriation theory applies only if there is no such duty.[158] Moreover, they both accepted the proposition that a person who receives material non-public information in a relationship of confidentiality defrauds his source if he uses the information for his own use.

The reasoning is as follows: whenever one entrusts non-public information to a person in a confidential relationship for a specific purpose, the recipient of that information makes an express or implied representation and warranty to the source that he will not use that information for any other purpose.[159] The Supreme Court had already held in *United States v. Carpenter*[160] that confiden-tial information constitutes property for the purposes of the federal mail and wire fraud statute and that the use of the confidential information by the con-fidant for any other purpose can constitute a misappropriation of the property of the source.[161] The source has the right to rely on the confidant's contractual representations and warranties of loyalty. Consequently, if the recipient is in fact disloyal and intends to use the information for his own behalf, he has a duty to speak and warn the source that it should not rely on his loyalty. Accordingly, the use of the information in violation of the duty of confidence without prior disclosure constitutes fraud—specifically, it is analogous to embezzlement.

How does it constitute fraud "in connection with the purchase and sale of securities?" Justice Ginsburg asserts that O'Hagan "consummated" his fraud when he used the misappropriated information to trade in securities.[162] This aspect of Justice Ginsburg's opinion generated probably the most vociferous part of Justice Clarence Thomas's dissent. I will turn to the concept of "consummation" later.

Trade Secrets

The Supreme Court's holdings in *Carpenter* and *O'Hagan* that confidential information constituted property are highly controversial among intellectual property lawyers who have long debated whether trade secrets should be analyzed as property, contract, tort, or as a *sui generis* body of law.[163] By doing so, the Supreme Court transformed trade secret law into property law and virtually all contractual confidentiality breaches into fraudulent misappropriation of property.

These interesting issues are beyond the scope of this chapter. What concerns us is that the majority of the Supreme Court found that O'Hagan's misappropriation of confidential information constituted fraud in connection with the purchase or sale of securities within the meaning of Section 10(b) and Rule 10b-5. This was Justice Thomas's primary complaint, albeit on somewhat different reasoning from mine. The problem is that if, as Justice Ginsburg asserts, Grand Met, and not the public, was the owner of the information as a trade secret, then the investment public, by definition, has no property or other right in the information. Moreover, under trade secret law, the source of confidential information, and its confidants, has a right vis-à-vis the public, to commercially exploit the information to the detriment of the public. Consequently, for the public to complain that Grand Met (the source) or O'Hagan (its unfaithful confidant) was using this information is not jealousy, but envy—the pain at seeing others enjoying their good luck—and *O'Hagan* is wrongfully decided.

Anomalies

There are some obviously troubling anomalies about Ginsburg's formulation of the misappropriation theory. First, despite the fact that Justice Ginsburg states that such a misappropriation constitutes securities fraud, strangely enough, there are no identifiable victims of a securities fraud who could sue for damages. The source of the information may be the victim of fraud, but not of securities fraud. This is because the rule of *Blue Chip Stamps*[164] established that to be the victim of securities fraud, the plaintiff must show that it purchased or sold securities in reliance on the fraud. O'Hagan's source (Grand Met) did not do so, however. This does not mean that, absent the misappropriation theory, O'Hagan would be able to profit from his despicable behavior to his client. There are already many state and federal rules that vindicate the rights of the source—state trade secret and, perhaps, fraud law, state professional responsibility law, federal wire fraud law, and Rule 14e-3 promulgated under the 1934 Act specifically governing trading during tender offers. Consequently, the question at bar was not whether O'Hagan violated the law, or whether his source had legal redress, but whether the investment public was also harmed.

Under basic principles of Rule 10b-5 jurisprudence, however, even contemporaneous traders in the class of securities as the misappropriator are not deemed to be victims of securities fraud.[165] This is because the Court expressly stated that the misappropriator owed no duty to speak to these traders. Consequently, they cannot claim to have been defrauded by his silence.[166]

This anomaly is not of merely theoretical interest because it has practical implications for the application of the disclose-or-refrain rule. Indeed, in *O'Hagan* the Supreme Court took seriously the question of the substance of disclosure which courts had glossed over in their application of the classic theory.[167] That is, if the fraud consists in the confidant making an implied misrepresentation of his loyalty to the source, then the fraud can be avoided if the confidant discloses his intent to trade. But note, because the misappropriator's duty does not run to the investment public, no disclosure need be made to the investment public. In Justice Ginsburg's words:

> Similarly, full disclosure forecloses liability under the misappropriation theory: Because the deception essential to the misappropriation theory involves feigning fidelity to the source of information, if the fiduciary discloses to the source that he plans to trade on the non-public information, there is no "deceptive device" and thus no 10(b) violation.... [168]

In other words, Justice Ginsburg claims that the misappropriation theory is thus designed to "protect the integrity of the securities markets against abuses by 'outsiders' to a corporation who have access to confidential information that will affect the corporation's security price when revealed, but who owe no fiduciary or other duty to that corporation's shareholders."[169] In fact, however, the misappropriation theory does no such thing. Under the theory, misappropriators are perfectly free to trade on material non-public information to the detriment of the investment public so long as they do not "deceive" their sources (i.e., so long as they reveal their intent to trade to their sources).

This follows from the Supreme Court's grounding of the misappropriation theory in trade secret law. By definition, only the owner of the trade secret has the right to determine who may know or use the trade secret.[170]

Furthermore, the logic of *O'Hagan* implies that there are at least two other circumstances under which persons can trade on the same material non-public information without running afoul of Section 10(b). Justice Ginsburg does not discuss the first circumstance. The source would not violate Section 10(b) if it were to trade on behalf of the non-public information because the information belongs to the source and the source has no fiduciary duty to the issuer's shareholders. To state this more strongly, to say that the source owns this information is not merely to say that the source would not violate the law if it traded on the information, it is to say that it has the affirmative right to do so. In the specific facts of *O'Hagan*, such trading by Grand Met in Pillsbury stock may have been subject to the substantive and disclosure restrictions applicable to bidders in tender offers.[171] In other cases, the source would be under no limitations.

An example of permissible trading by a source is suggested by the facts of *Carpenter v. United States*.[172] The defendant, R. Foster Winans, was an employee of *The Wall Street Journal* who was one of the writers of the periodic *Heard on the Street* column that reports on market trends and rumors. Knowing that the market tended to react to information published in this column, Winans and his co-conspirators would, immediately before publication, trade on securities of issuers to be mentioned in the columns. The Supreme Court found that the content and timing of *The Wall Street Journal's* articles were confidential business information belonging to *The Wall Street Journal* and, therefore, property.[173] Because Winans had a duty of confidence to the newspaper pursuant to his employment agreement, by breaching this confidence, he had stolen property by fraud in violation of the federal mail fraud statute.[174] Although the Supreme Court split on whether this also constituted unlawful trading under 10(b), the reasoning anticipates its eventual adoption of the misappropriation theory in *O'Hagan*. Note, however, that in this case, although it might be a violation of journalistic ethics, *The Wall Street Journal* could have traded on the basis of the information in question without violating any federal law.[175]

Justice Ginsburg does recognize the second anomalous circumstance of lawful trading: the source could give the confidant permission to trade.

> The textual requirement of deception precludes 10(b) liability when a person trading on the basis of nonpublic information has disclosed his trading plans to, or obtained authorization from, the principal—even though such conduct may affect the securities markets in the same manner as the conduct reached by the misappropriation theory.[176]

Why a source might do so can be illustrated by looking at the facts of *O'Hagan*. O'Hagan was a partner in a law firm that represented Grand Met in a planned hostile tender offer for the stock of Pillsbury. O'Hagan used this information in violation of his attorney's duty of confidence to purchase call options on Pillsbury's stock making a profit of $4.3 million.[177] Lawyers are expensive and frequently negotiate premium fees over and above their hourly rate for complex transactions. Grand Met could, theoretically, have offered that, rather than paying a premium fee in cash, it would grant the firm the right to use the confidential information to trade in target securities. In this instant case, as Justice Ginsburg notes,[178] such an arrangement might violate the substantive and prophylactic provisions governing tender offers. But, according to Justice Ginsburg it would not constitute securities fraud under Section 10(b) and Rule 10b-5.

When Justice Thomas confronted Justice Ginsburg with this second anomaly (that confidants may freely trade with their source's permission),[179] Justice Ginsburg suggested half-heartedly—and tucked away in a footnote—that this is merely an unfortunate example of an under-inclusive law. "The fact that 10(b) is only a partial antidote to the problems it was designed to alleviate does not call into question its prohibition of conduct that falls within its textual proscription."[180]

This supposed defense, in fact, contradicts the entire basis of the misappropriation theory as articulated by Justice Ginsburg and implicitly reveals its intellectual bankruptcy. According to Justice Ginsburg, the confidant's use of non-public information constitutes a misappropriation (and, therefore, a fraud) because the source is the owner of the non-public information. Justice Ginsburg has also expressly recognized that O'Hagan owed no duty to the issuer or its shareholders,[181] implying that they have no property interest in the information. If, however, the source has a valid property interest in the information, then it should be entitled to use it however it sees fit. Indeed, trade secrets are nothing but a monopolistic power of the source to economically exploit its information for its own purposes, and to keep the information out of the hands of the public.

Consequently, the source should be entitled to buy securities of other issuers on the basis of the information. Moreover, the source should be able to transfer "its" property to whomever it wants and grant others the right to trade on this information.[182]

If, however, as Justice Ginsburg suggests, in an ideal world, the source would not be permitted to give others the permission to trade on the basis of the information, then she is suggesting that the source does not have a valid property interest in the information as a trade secret. But, if the source does not have a valid property interest in the information, then the confidant should be able to use the information without violating the source's rights or committing fraud. That is, the proposition that the confidant is committing securities fraud is parasitic on the proposition that it is not fraudulent for the source to trade on the information. Consequently, in order to find that trading on the basis of this type of non-public information constitutes securities fraud, it should first be necessary to find that the public, rather than the source, has rights in this information.

Securities Law and Trade Secret Policy

As discussed, the classic theory of insider trading holds that it is unlawful for traditional insiders of an issuer (i.e., officers, directors, employers, and other persons having a confidential relationship with the issuer) to trade in the equity securities of that issuer on the basis of material non-public information obtained from that issuer. The misappropriation theory of outsider trading holds that, in some cases, it is unlawful to trade in securities on the basis of material non-public information obtained in a relationship of confidence to the source of the information (who need not be the issuer of the securities traded). Although many proponents of the classic theory intuitively find the classic theory to be underinclusive in regulating objectionable behavior, others intuit that the misappropriation theory risks being objectionably overinclusive.

In this section, I argue that by combining an analysis of material non-public information in terms of property (or quasi-property) with a consideration of the disclosure regime established by Congress in the federal securities laws, one can bring some order into the seemingly chaotic law of insider trading. I argue that application of the distinction between envy and jealousy shows that the classic theory is, in fact, the correct analysis of insider trading as a violation of securities law policy and the misappropriation theory is an inappropriate extension of the doctrine of fraud. Classic theory addresses the righteous jealous fear of shareholders that rivals—classic insiders—will take away something that belongs to the shareholders—information that belongs to the issuer. The misappropriation theory, however, reflects the envy of the investment public of the good fortune of other traders who have informational advantages. Moreover, this judgment is implicit in Justice Ginsburg's internally contradictory language. Congress might decide to change the status quo and reallocate property rights in a broader category of non-public information to investors. There might also be other good reasons for Congress to adopt broad, prophylactic rules governing non-fraudulent trading on the basis of material non-public information. The misappropriation theory as articulated to date, however, represents judicial over-extension of the law of securities fraud.

Classic Theory: Information About the Issuer Belongs to the Public

As discussed, the classic theory of insider trading treats non-public information obtained from an issuer as property belonging indirectly to the shareholders of the issuer. Many academics who question the wisdom of an across-the-board prohibition of classic insider trading agree that non-public information should be analyzed as property, but challenge the assumption that this information belongs to the issuer's shareholders. This argument is based on the technical proposition that, under state law, shareholders are not recognized as the legal title holders of corporate property, but ignores the fact that the law often recognized beneficial and other equitable interests in property. Under basic principles of corporate law, the corporation and its shareholders are separate legal persons. Property owned by the corporation belongs to the corporation, and not its shareholders, even though the corporate officers and directors have a fiduciary duty to manage the corporation, and therefore, its property, for the benefit of the shareholder. This means that under corporate law, non-public information does not belong to the shareholders.[183] Critics argue from this that an issuer should be able to allocate its "property" in non-public information through private contracting in whatever way it deems fit so long as it follows its duties to its shareholders.

This argument is most closely identified with Henry Manne, one of the earliest and probably the most vociferous and consistent critic of rules against insider trading.[184] He specifically argues that, just as issuers may use other corporate assets to remunerate management, issuers should be able to grant corporate insiders the right to trade on inside information as part of their compensation package.[185] From this perspective, concerns about abusive insider trading are, in fact, no different than concerns about any other form of excessive executive compensation and conflicts of interest between management and shareholders. He believes that many of the traditional concerns expressed by the proponents of restrictions on insider trading can be addressed through full disclosure and, perhaps, prior approval by disinterested directors or the shareholders.[186] Indeed, this is the usual approach of the securities laws. Concerns about fairness should be left to state corporate law. For example, in order to keep such compensation plans within the protections of the business judgment rule, management should have them approved by a majority of disinterested directors (if any) or the public shareholders, after full disclosure.

It is often said that insider trading law is necessary because investors would flee the market if they thought the scales were tipped.[187] However, as Manne argues, no one has ever tested this empirical assumption.[188] One way to do so would be to allow corporate insiders to trade on non-public information so long as they disclosed their intent publicly and obtained consent from the issuer's board and/or shareholders.[189] If investors find such behavior objectionable, this should be reflected in the issuer's stock prices. If stock prices were negatively affected, one would expect corporations to react by imposing restrictions on trading. Alternately, if prices are not negatively affected, this would be strong evidence that investors do not care about such behavior.

The Classic Theory as a Corollary of Mandatory Disclosure

Needless to say, critics attack both the substantive and moral assumptions underlying Manne's arguments. I will not engage in this specific debate here because I believe it is beyond the limited point of this chapter. This debate relates to the question of what an ideal federal securities policy might be if we were starting from scratch from a state of nature before property rights in information have been allocated. I am interested, however, in analyzing the issue in the context of the given federal securities law regime and current securities practice.

I agree with Manne that the insider trading law is profitably analyzed as an issue of the allocation of beneficial interests in information conceived as a valuable asset, regardless of the location of legal title. However, I argue that the policy as to how beneficial interests should be allocated has already been decided by Congress. It is, therefore, not currently subject to reallocation either by regulation by the SEC, adjudication by the federal courts, or contract between issuers and their insiders.

Manne scoffs at the claims of supporters of insider trading regulation that certain information is the property of shareholders.[190] He is technically correct that under corporate law, legal title to corporate information resides in the corporate entity, and only indirectly to the shareholders who are separate legal persons. But the very example he uses to demonstrate that insider trading law is an aberration within American law,[191] in fact, illustrates the ambiguity of the concept of ownership in corporate law.

In *S.E.C. v. Texas Gulf Sulphur Co.*,[192] the Second Circuit found that classic insider trading by officers and directors violated Rule 10b-5, albeit on the now discredited fairness justification. In that case, the issuer, a mining company, learned that initial tests indicated that certain land contained a potentially rich mineral strike. Classic insiders purchased securities of the issuer before this information was made public. Manne proclaims:

> So notice the irony: TGS officials buying stock with knowledge of a
> new ore vein have somehow done something immoral, but the com-

pany itself buying surrounding land, utilizing precisely the same information, has merely performed in a business-like fashion.[193]

In other words, far from mandating parity of information, the usual rule of
American law is the protection of informational advantages.

This argument is supposed to support his contention that the argument that
insider information belongs to shareholders is empty, "not worthy of serious
attention" and fallacious.[194] To a corporate lawyer, however, this analogy is so
inapt that it comes close to being facetious. Manne's argument invokes the relative ownership rights in information of a corporation and a stranger. It does
not address the issue involved in insider trading—the relative property rights
in information among an issuer of registered securities, its insiders, and the issuer's investors, to whom the issuer and its insiders owe fiduciary duties. Manne
is suggesting that state real property and general fraud law would permit the issuer to buy neighboring land from a stranger without first disclosing its non-
public information to the stranger. Even if this is true, Manne is ignoring the
fact that it would almost certainly have been a violation of fiduciary duty under
corporate law for an insider of the issuer to purchase this land for her own benefit. The land would be deemed a "corporate opportunity" that belonged directly to the corporation for the indirect benefit of its shareholders.[195] Consequently, such a purchase by an insider would be a breach of the insider's duty
of loyalty. This is the more appropriate analogy to insider trading.

Manne's stronger argument is to analogize from the law of corporate opportunity to suggest a more appropriate rule for insider trading. An insider is permitted to take a corporate opportunity if he first offers it to the corporation and,
after full disclosure, the corporation declines to take it. That is, the modern rule
of corporate opportunity is not a complete ban, but is a matter of private contract between the board of directors and the opportunist coupled with a duty of
full disclosure that does not apply to contracts among strangers.[196] One might be
able to argue that, by analogy, insiders should be able to exploit non-public information belonging to the issuer if they obtain prior approval of the disinterested members of the board or the shareholders after full disclosure of their intent to do so. Even if one accepts this analogy, it is not clear what the appropriate
parallel law of insider trading would be. A board may not grant blanket approval
to insiders to take future corporate opportunities but must consider each opportunity on a case-by-case basis. Does this imply that an insider should seek
board approval each and every time she wishes to trade on insider information?

Manne also argues that property rights, generally, and ownership of information, specifically, are a matter of positive law and can be allocated however
society deems fit. In the absence of statutory allocation, this is left to the pri-

vate ordering of contract.[197] This may be true as a general rule of American law, but in arguing that it is true of classic insider information, Manne is, however, suppressing an important point he makes later in his argument.

As he admits, his critique "calls into doubt not simply the rule about insider trading, but the entire 'philosophy of full disclosure.'"[198] This is precisely correct: the classic theory of insider trading is inextricably linked to the existing mandatory disclosure regime. The one is the corollary of the other. Consequently, Manne may be correct that absent a statutory allocation of property rights in information, such allocation would be left to the private ordering of contract. However, Manne is wrong to suggest that Congress has not in fact already allocated a limited beneficial interest to the public in one class of information.[199]

It is my thesis that the mandatory disclosure regime of the federal securities laws should be analyzed as an implicit congressional allocation of an indirect or beneficial interest in information generated by and obtained from the issuers of registered securities to persons who trade in these securities. That is, a public corporation must either disclose the information to the public (i.e., give actual possession of the information to the investment public generally) or use it for corporate purposes (i.e., recognize its shareholders' right to enjoy the information indirectly through their investment in the corporation). Consequently, it is consistent with this policy that those who have special access to this information should not have incentives to keep the information non-public by allowing them to use it for themselves. That is, some form of classic insider trading prohibition is the corollary of a mandatory disclosure regime.[200]

As Manne understands, if one really believed, on efficiency or other grounds, that issuers should be able to adopt policies allowing classic insiders to trade on the basis of material non-public information, then, to be consistent, one should have the courage of one's convictions and also argue for a major revision, if not a complete abandonment, of the mandatory disclosure regime of the 1934 Act. Of course, many legal economists do challenge the wisdom or efficiency of the mandatory disclosure regime.[201] It is highly unlikely that Congress is about to radically amend the federal securities laws to eliminate or severely undermine this regime at this time.[202]

James Boyle has suggested that insider trading is a "puzzle"[203] because it is "a statutory island of egalitarianism at the very heart of capitalism."[204] In fact, the better metaphor would be that classic insider trading should be seen as only a prominent peninsula of a much larger egalitarian continent called mandatory disclosure.

Return to the Misappropriation Theory

As discussed above,[205] the majority of the Supreme Court in the *O'Hagan* opinion grounded its opinion on an analysis of trade secrets as a form of intellectual property belonging to the source of the information. The problem is that trade secret law's treatment of non-public information is diametrically opposed to the federal securities laws' treatment of such information. In the previous section, I argued that the federal securities acts in effect allocate beneficial rights in material non-public information generated by an issuer to the investment public generally (i.e., its existing and potential future shareholders). In contrast, trade secret law gives the generator of other types of non-public information the exclusive right to exploit this information for its own advantage so long as it keeps the information secret. Federal securities law generally, and insider trading law specifically, is designed to minimize the informational advantages of a certain class of persons vis-à-vis the public by granting rights in information to the public. It is egalitarian in spirit. In contrast, trade secret law is designed to maximize informational advantages of a certain class of persons vis-à-vis the public. It is individualistic, indeed monopolistic, in spirit. Consequently, any attempt to base an extension of insider liability based on trade secret law is doomed to contradiction. To do so conflates jealousy, the appropriate protection of one's rights, with envy, the inappropriate desire to deprive another of her rights.

The Uniform Trade Secrets Act defines a trade secret as follows:

> "Trade Secret" means information, including a formula, pattern, compilation, program, device, method, technique, or process that: (I) derives independent economic value, actual or potential, from not being generally known to, and not being readily ascertainable by proper means by, other persons who can obtain economic value from its disclosure or use, and (ii) is the subject of efforts that are reasonable under the circumstances to maintain its secrecy.[206]

The Restatement of Torts states that a "trade secret is any information that can be used in the operation of a business or other enterprise and that is sufficiently valuable and secret to afford an actual or potential economic advantage over others."[207] The differences between these two definitions are beyond the scope of this chapter.[208] What both definitions have in common is that trade secrets are non-public information that gives the source economically valuable information advantages over the public generally. Many commentators disagree with the Supreme Court's blanket assertion that trade secrets are a form of property rather than "a collection of other legal norms—contract, fraud and the like—united only by the fact that they are used to protect secret information."[209] Nevertheless, in any case a trade secret is a right of the claimant to exploit secret information and to prevent certain misappropriation of the secret by others.

Since at least Friedman, Landes, and Posner's classic article *Some Economics of Trade Secret Law*,[210] the predominant justification of trade secret law is that our society gives a limited monopolistic right to the source to exploit trade secrets as an incentive to create this information.[211] In order to make it financially attractive for the source to invest resources to create this information, we give the source a monopoly vis-à-vis the public to exploit this information commercially. The other competing, or complementary, rationale for trade secret law is business ethics—that is, to prevent certain "bad acts" in the sense of independent wrongs (i.e., such as theft, fraud, and breach of duty).[212] What both of these justifications have in common is the recognition that the source has the exclusive rights to commercially exploit secret information. The economic benefits of such exclusive rights can serve as the incentive desired under the first theory. Moreover, by definition, the appropriation of control over the information could not constitute a "bad act" under the second justification, unless one first presupposes that the source has valid and exclusive rights in the information that could be misappropriated.

Elsewhere I argue that from both a Hegelian jurisprudential perspective and as a practical matter, it is both coherent and analytically helpful to analyze exclusive trade secret rights as a limited form of property.[213] For the narrow purposes of this chapter, we do not need to reach the question of proper categorization. Whether we consider a trade secret right as property, contract, tort, or a *sui generis* combination of rights, it is a right of the source to keep the information secret from the public and the right to exploit that secrecy. It is a form of monopolistic informational advantage. The public by definition has no right to the information; in fact, a trade secret is nothing but the right to keep the information away from the public to the public's economic disadvantage.

This is why Justice Ginsburg's analysis of outsider trading in *O'Hagan* is so unsatisfactory. Her entire misappropriation theory is based on an analysis that the misappropriated information is a trade secret that belongs to the source. By definition, a trade secret does not belong to the public; under the basic logic of trade secret law, if information belonged to, or became known by, the public, it would not be a trade secret. Justice Ginsburg recognizes this when she states that the misappropriation theory only applies when the trader has no duty to the investment public. To say that the disloyal confidant's use of his source's information was wrongful vis-à-vis the source is to say that the source had a valid trade secret in the information. Putting these together, the public, by definition, has no entitlement to the information, and the use of the information does not, therefore, interfere with any rights of the investment public. Use of this information cannot, therefore, be securities fraud.

Justice Ginsburg implicitly realizes this contradiction when she opines that the fact that, under her theory, the confidant would not be engaging in securities fraud if he first obtained the consent of the source to trade as an unfortunate underinclusiveness of the statutory scheme. This is also equivalent to saying that, in an ideal world, Congress would have allocated the property rights in the source's material non-public information to the public. This means that the information should be allocated to the public, not the source. This is inconsistent with her grounding of the misappropriation theory in the infringement of the source's property rights in its information. That is, the first leg of the misappropriation theory (fraud on the source) depends on the judgment that the source's property rights in the information are legitimate, but the second leg (securities fraud) depends on the judgment that the source's property rights are illegitimate and that the property rights in the information should be allocated to the public.

Consequently, one can not consistently argue, as Justice Ginsburg does, that a misappropriator has stolen trade secrets from the source and that, ideally, the source would not have the right to grant the right to others to use the property.

A coherent insider/outsider trading policy would distinguish between information that "belongs" to the public and information belonging to the source. If the information belongs to the public, then no one but the public— not even the source—should be able to trade on the information without first making disclosure. If the information belongs to someone else, then the owner of the information should be able to exploit the information in whatever way it deems appropriate, including by securities trading. If a misappropriator trades on information, it should be deemed securities fraud only if the information belongs to the investment public. If, however, the information belongs to some other party, the law of trade secrets should apply.

A Brief Aside on Martha Stewart

The SEC's civil insider trading action against Stewart would have been based on a novel application of the misappropriation theory that would extend it even beyond Justice Ginsburg's stated justification. Presumably, the government first began investigating Stewart's trading in ImClone stock because she was a friend of Sam Waksal, ImClone's former chairman, who had admittedly engaged in illegal trading of ImClone stock in advance of the public announcement of bad news. Obviously, this raised the suspicion that Waksal had spoken to Stewart. If he had, Waksal would have been a classic tipper and Stewart might have been a tippee of a classic insider. Investigation, however, showed that this was not the case.

The only communication Stewart had with respect to ImClone stock on the date of her trade was indirectly with her broker Peter Bacanovic through his assistant Douglas Faneuil. At the trial, Faneuil testified that he told Stewart that Waksal was trying to sell his stock. Assuming the SEC's argument would have followed allegations made in the DOJ's indictment, it would have alleged that Bacanovic was a misappropriator because he violated Merrill Lynch's policy that forbids its brokers from piggy-backing on the investment strategy of its clients. That is, a Merrill Lynch broker is not supposed to tell his customers what his other customers are doing. If Stewart understood that Bacanovic was violating his duty then she might be a tippee of a misappropriator.

I would argue that, in fact, Bacanovic would not be a misappropriator under the rule of *O'Hagan*. In order to misappropriate information it is not enough that the defendant violate a fiduciary type duty of confidentiality, as Bacanovic might have done. The information disclosed must be the property of the person to whom the duty of confidentiality runs, otherwise the disclosure is not a misappropriation, merely a breach of contract. The SEC, therefore, would have had to maintain that Merrill Lynch was the proprietor of the fact that Waksal was trying to dump his stock.

Unlike the misappropriated information in *Carpenter* and *O'Hagan*, Merrill Lynch did not generate this information itself, nor was it the source. More importantly, as we have seen,[214] to be a trade secret, by definition, the claimant must derive actual or potential economic value from the fact that the information is not generally known. As I have discussed, this means that the claimant has the right to exploit the secret for its own economic benefit. To argue that the fact of Waksal's trading was the property of Merrill Lynch, therefore, the SEC, in effect, would have had to argue that Merrill Lynch was entitled to exploit this information—presumably by trading on this information on its own account! As this case was settled, we do not know whether the SEC could have persuaded a court to accept this theory.

Trade Secrets v. Securities Law Policies

Justice Ginsburg's intuition in *O'Hagan* that there is something anomalous in letting the source trade in information, does, however, raise a very different and valid concern: should our society grant trade secret protection to sources for the type of information involved in the misappropriation cases, or should society adopt a positive law granting the public generally a property right in this information (as it enjoys in information generated by issuers)? This question requires a balancing of the competing policies of federal securities law and state trade secret law.

Indeed, one criticism of *Carpenter* and *O'Hagan* from trade secret specialists is that the Supreme Court is overly solicitous towards the claimed property interests of the sources of information. The Court has assumed that the states have unequivocally granted property rights in certain information when the state law precedents are far more ambiguous. Arguably, *Carpenter* should better have been analyzed as a garden-variety breach of contract suit that did not invoke property, let alone fraud, at all. As others have asked before me, do we really want to reinterpret federal fraud law so broadly that we are criminalizing simple breaches of contract?[215]

The trade secret misappropriated by Winans in the *Carpenter* case was *The Wall Street Journal*'s publication schedule.[216] As discussed, the standard justification of trade secret law is that it incentivizes the creation of information through the grant of informational monopolies. It is intended to prevent potential competitors from using the information. Presumably, a newspaper needs a publication schedule as a practical matter and does not need further incentives to create one. Moreover, Winans and his conspirators were not attempting to compete with *The Wall Street Journal*; they did not intend to publish a rival newspaper and did not seek to sell the information to *The New York Times, Forbes*, or any other competitor. Consequently, when *The Wall Street Journal* exposed Winans' misdeeds on its front page and fired him, it was not because it was worried about competition. Presumably, it was concerned with its journalistic reputation—who would trust a newspaper that held itself out as a neutral reporter of business news if it was known that its writers were trading on information published in their articles? This may be an important ethical value, but it has nothing to do with the federal securities laws.

Similarly, there may be very good reasons why stock brokers should not reveal one customer's trading strategy to another customer or otherwise piggyback on that knowledge. This is presumably why Merrill Lynch prohibited its employees from doing so, and Merrill Lynch was justified for firing Bacanovic and Faneuil for violating the terms of their employment. These reasons might relate to the SEC's substantive regulation of registered broker-dealers under the 1934 Act. It is not clear, however, that these reasons invoke the anti-fraud concerns of Rule 10b-5.

Gaps and Anomalies Under the Current Statute

Under my analysis, a coherent insider trading law would be grounded on the statutory disclosure duties of the securities laws, conceptualized as an allocation of certain non-public information from the person having a disclosure duty to the investment public generally. It is a short-cut that allows us to avoid the circuitous route followed by the traditional special circumstances rule. That is, rather than relying on a multi-step process by which federal law would incorporate state law that imposes duties on an insider to a corporation, and on the corporation to its shareholders, and then expanding this to a duty of the corporation and its insiders to all potential shareholders (i.e., the investment public), my approach would recognize a federal duty imposed directly on the insiders of reporting companies and running directly to the investment public. That is, the insiders' duty not to trade would be reconceptualized as a duty related to the issuer's disclosure obligations. This analysis would probably leave the theories of temporary insiders and tippees largely intact.

Standing alone, however, this analysis may be correct as a matter of policy, but is probably insufficient as a matter of judicial jurisdiction and statutory interpretation. The catchall provision of Rule 10b-5 is limited to fraud, and the concept of fraudulent silence is dependent on a duty to speak. I have argued that as a matter of policy, an implied duty to speak for insiders is consistent with mandatory disclosure by issuers and others. Unfortunately, the statute does not contain an express duty to speak. Moreover the absence of an express duty to speak, by negative pregnant, should probably be read to imply that there is no such implied duty.

The federal securities laws do not currently mandate continuous disclosure. Rather, the statute expressly requires disclosures at specific times, such as at the end of the fiscal year and each fiscal quarter, and when parties take certain actions, such as making a public offering of securities, soliciting proxies, and making tender offers. The jurisprudence as to when parties have an implied duty to speak in the gap periods between these statutory disclosures is complex and confusing. A federal judge might justifiably be reluctant to adopt my theory and continue to rely on state law as the source of duties.

Consequently, a coherent insider trading law would probably require that Congress amend the 1934 Act. Ideally, Congress would specify when trading on the basis of material non-public information is unlawful. Alternately, Congress could change the language of Section 10(b) to make it more like the language of Rule 14e-3—authorizing the SEC not merely to define fraud (as it does now), but also promulgate prophylactic rules governing trading on the basis of non-public information.

Conclusion

Insider trading law should recognize the righteous jealousy of the investment public when insiders try to enjoy the public's information for their own benefit, but should not encourage the public's envy when others enjoy information that the law recognizes is rightfully theirs. Consequently, a coherent and ethical law of insider trading should begin with a consideration of the allocation of property rights in information. The misappropriation theory is both unethical and incoherent precisely because it tries to graft insider trading law upon trade secret law. The federal securities laws reflect a fundamental egalitarian moment in that they allocate certain types of material insider information to the public. Trade secret law, in contrast, is radically individualistic and libertarian in nature in that it grants exclusive monopolistic rights in non-public information. If Congress believes that trading on this type of information is somehow wrong, it needs to amend the law to supersede state trade secret law and re-allocate property rights in the information from the source to the public. This would not merely result in a law of insider trading that is consistent with the federal securities law policy, it would also remedy the current embarrassment that insider and outsider trading are *de facto* common law crimes.

Questions

1. Based on the facts presented at her trial, why do you think the Department of Justice chose not to prosecute Stewart for the unlawful insider trading under the classical theory? Could it have done so?
2. The author suggests that prosecuting Stewart under the misappropriation theory of insider trading would have required a new interpretation of that theory beyond existing precedents. What specifically would the Department of Justice have had to argue to present such a case?
3. The author believes that the misappropriation theory of insider trading does not further, or is inconsistent, with the purposes of the Securities Exchange Act of 1934. What do you think the purpose(s) of that Act is (are) or should be? What, if any, trading on the basis of material non-public information should be unlawful under the Act to achieve such purpose(s)? Why?
4. When trading on the basis of material non-public information in circumstances not involving tender offers is governed by judicial interpretation of the anti-fraud provisions of Sec. 10(b) of the Securities Exchange Act

of 1934, and of Rule 10b-5 thereunder. Should Congress adopt legislation defining unlawful trading? If so, what should be the definition? Should the SEC adopt broad prophylactic regulation prohibiting trading by certain persons based on certain non-public information similar to the Rule 14e-3 under the Securities Exchange Act prohibiting certain trading in the context of tender offers? Does it have the authority to do so?

Notes

1. The Securities and Exchange Commission ("SEC") brought a civil insider trading case against Stewart. Stewart eventually settled this case by agreeing to "pay $195,000 and accept a five-year ban on serving as a director of a public company." Brooks Barnes, *Moving the Market: Martha Stewart Settles with SEC on Civil Charges*, WALL ST. J., Aug. 8, 2006, at C.3.

2. One ground of Stewart's appeal from conviction is that because the judge improperly barred her counsel "from arguing that the ImClone trade was perfectly legal," the jurors may have been confused and "were left to make inferences about the propriety of the trade." Matthew Rose & Kara Scannell, *Lawyers for Stewart, Bacanovic Vow to Appeal, Defense Team Considers a Variety of Arguments for Another Court Battle*, WALL ST. J., Mar. 8, 2004, at C4; *see also* Constance L. Hays, *Appeal of Stewart Verdict Says Trial Was Full of Errors*, N.Y. TIMES, Oct. 22, 2004, at C3. Stewart ultimately lost this appeal. Michael Barbaro, *Court Rejects Appeal by Martha Stewart*, N.Y. TIMES, Jan. 7, 2006, at C2.

3. *See* Matthew Rose, *Martha Stewart Firm Has Loss as ImClone Inquiries Take Toll*, WALL ST. J., Mar. 5, 2003, at C11; *see also* Imclone 10-K *available at* http://www.sec.gov/Archives/edgar/data/765258/000104746904007817/a2130 910z10-k.htm.

4. *See* W. Michael Cox, *Markets Are Quick to Judge When Firms Fail to Behave*, INVESTOR'S BUS. DAILY, Nov. 21, 2002, at A17. Plaintiff lawyers filed breach of fiduciary duty law suits against Stewart on the theory that she should have known that her "illegal" activities would adversely affect the price of Martha Stewart Living Omnimedia stock and "insider trading" actions against other insiders of Martha Stewart Omnimedia on the grounds that, when they sold their stock, they must have known that insider trading allegations would eventually be raised against Stewart thereby depressing the price of the company's stock. At the time this chapter went to print, this litigation was still pending. *See infra* note 8.

5. *See* Jeffrey Toobin, *Lunch at Martha's; Problems With the Perfect Life*, NEW YORKER, Feb. 3, 2003, at 38.

6. *See* Gregory Zuckerman, *Martha: The Doyenne of Dilemmas: Fear is Media Buyers, Consumers will Shy Away From Company*, WALL ST. J., Mar. 8, 2004, at C1. Stewart's fortunes have been recovering. In what looks like a brilliant public relations move, she chose to serve her five-month prison term pending her appeal. After her release, she started a number of new television series. *See Martha Stewart to Star in New Apprentice*, J. NEWS, Jan. 3, 2005, at 9A. The stock price of Martha Stewart Living Omnimedia rebounded to a high of approximately $32 immediately prior to her release from prison in early March 2005 from a low of almost $8 following her sentencing. *See* Gregory Zuckerman & James Bandler, *Martha Stewart Living: No Bars*, WALL ST. J., Mar. 3, 2001, at C1. Although the company stock again fell almost 50%, many analysts think that the company is now posed for a turn-

around, particularly because investors are now beginning on concentrating more on the company itself, rather than on Stewart personally. Brooks Barnes, *Martha Might be Worth a Look*, WALL ST. J., Jan. 18, 2006, at C1, C6.

7. The DOJ's indictment did lay out alleged facts presumably designed to support an allegation that Peter Bacanovic, Stewart's friend, broker, and co-defendant, misappropriated the fact that Sam Waksal was trying to sell his ImClone stock from Bacanovic's employer, Merrill Lynch, in violation of a duty of confidentiality imposed by his employment agreement and that Stewart was Bacanovic's tippee. The indictment did not, however, expressly set forth these legal conclusions. This theory formed the heart of the SEC's civil action against Stewart. Stewart's lawyers unsuccessfully moved to have this section stricken from the indictment on the grounds that it is inflammatory and irrelevant given the fact that she has not been charged with insider trading. *See* Colleen Debaise, *Stewart Seeks Dismissal of Charges*, WALL ST. J., Oct. 7, 2003, at C12.

8. The charge that Stewart's statements concerning her ImClone stock constituted fraud upon the shareholders of Martha Stewart Living Omnimedia was eventually thrown out by the trial judge. Timothy E. Hoeffner & Risa B. Greene, *Prosecutors Too Bold*, NAT'L L.J., Apr. 12, 2004, at 43. However, similar accusations form the basis of a shareholders' suit against Martha Stewart Living Omnimedia. *See supra* note 4.

9. Skilling and Fastow are the former Chief Executive Officer and Chief Financial Officer, respectively, of Enron. Fastow pled guilty to multiple charges of securities fraud. Perhaps more well known by the public is the former Chairman of Enron, Kenneth Lay, because of the nickname "Kenny Boy" given him by President George W. Bush. At the time this chapter went to print, the trial of Lay and Skilling for securities fraud and related offenses was in its early stages. *See Judge Rejects Move to Dismiss Case Against Ex-Enron Officers*, N.Y. TIMES, Jan 10, 2006, at C1.

10. Kozlowski may have entered into the general public's collective consciousness because videos of the notorious toga party he threw for his wife on the island of Sardinia were played at his first trial, and were repeatedly aired on television news. Kozlowski was the former CEO of Tyco who was convicted in New York State for looting the company by causing the company to make and then forgive hundreds of millions of dollars of unapproved loans. Press reaction reflected more envy than jealousy. Story after story concentrated on Kozlowski's ostentatious life style, which included the purchase of a $6,000 shower screen and a $15,000 umbrella stand. From the perspective of both securities and corporate law, such extravagance per se is irrelevant. What is relevant is that he allegedly used corporate funds for this purpose without obtaining board approval or disclosing this remuneration to the public. Kozlowski is the subject of a *New Yorker* magazine article by James Stewart which states that Kozlowski, "more than any other executive who had prospered in the great bull market of the nineties, came to personify an epoch of corporate fraud, executive greed, and personal extravagance." James B. Stewart, *Spend! Spend! Spend!*, NEW YORKER, Feb. 17 & 24, 2003, at 132. New York's first attempt to convict Kozlowski ended in a mistrial. Based on their negative experience in the first trial, the prosecutors successfully retried Kozlowski by avoiding appeals to envy and directing the jury's attention to the elements of the alleged crimes. *See* Andrew Ross Sorkin, *Prosecutors Rewrite Script in New Trial of 2 at Tyco*, N.Y. TIMES, Jan. 27, 2005, at C1; Andrew Ross Sorkin, *Ex-Chief and Aide Guilty of Looting Millions at Tyco*, N.Y. TIMES, Sept. 20, 2005, at A5.

11. Rigas is the founder and former CEO of Adelphia who was convicted, along with one of his sons, of treating this public company as their personal bank account by embezzling hundreds of millions of dollars. *See* Barry Meier, *Corporate Conduct: The Overview;*

2 Guilty in Fraud at a Cable Giant, N.Y. TIMES, July 9, 2004, at A1. Although the first attempted prosecution of a second son ended in mistrial, he eventually pled guilty to falsifying records. *Son of Adelphia Founder Guilty of Falsifying Records*, N.Y. TIMES, Nov. 11, 2005, at C9.

12. Sullivan is the former WorldCom Chief Financial Officer who oversaw $11 billion in fraudulent accounting. The eventual discovery of this fraud led to the filing of the largest bankruptcy in U.S. history. Sullivan pled guilty to charges related to the accounting fraud and was a star witness in the successful federal prosecution of former CFO Bernard Ebbers. Ken Belson, *WorldCom Head is Given 25 Years for Huge Fraud*, N.Y. TIMES, Jul. 24, 2005, at A1.

13. "Schadenfreude (joy at another's suffering), [is] the inverse of envy (pain at another's success) ..." Jerome Neu, *Jealous Thoughts* in EXPLAINING EMOTIONS 425, 433 (Amelie Oksenberg Rorty ed., 1980).

14. 521 U.S. 642 (1997).

15. Neu, *supra* note 13, at 435.

16. Toobin, *supra* note 5, at 39.

17. As argued in a Wall Street Journal piece appearing the first trading day after the conviction:

> The culture demands scapegoats after periods of excess. So prosecutors—and a convinced jury—made an example of Martha Stewart.... The trial, of course, had nothing to do with individual investors losing money. Instead, it was about how Ms. Stewart and her brokers dealt with prosecutors, who were legitimately demanding honesty. Nevertheless, [a juror's] comments perfectly capture a general sense of outrage. Martha, by dint of her famous persona, seems to have been convicted, in part, of Trading While Rich.

Jesse Eisinger, *The Show Goes On: Show Trials are Easier than Lasting Reforms*, WALL ST. J., Mar. 8, 2004, at C1.

18. *Stewart Image Coming Under Attack*, CNN.COM, June 25, 2002, *at* http://www.cnn.com/2002/SHOWBIZ/News/06/25/martha.stewart (last visited Jan. 12, 2006) [hereinafter *Image Coming Under Attack*].

19. Paula Span, *Martha: In the Soup*, GOTRIAD.COM, Mar. 16, 2003, *at* http://www.go-triad.com/article/articleview/ 3361/1/20/ (last visited Mar. 24, 2005).

20. *Martha Stewart in Hot Water Over Possible Insider Trading*, BONGO NEWS, June 19, 2002, at http://www.bongo news.com/layout1.php?event=178.

21. *Image Coming Under Attack*, *supra* note 18.

22. *Judge in Trial Threat to Waksal*, FIN. TIMES, Jan. 7, 2003, at 27.

23. Cox, *supra* note 4, at A17.

24. See Mary Ashwin, *"... Against All Other Virtue and Goodness:" An Exploration of Envy in Relation to Concepts of Sin*, *available at* http://www.human-nature.com/free-associations/ashwin.html (last visited Jan. 12, 2006).

25. Neu holds out the hope that there can be admiring envy as well as malicious envy. "In the case of admiring envy, one wishes to raise oneself (to become like the other)." Neu, *supra* note 13, at 434. I do not believe that this form of admiration accurately fits within the category of envy. As even Neu admits, what he calls admiring envy "may have different instinctual sources and developmental paths" than malicious envy. *Id.*

26. *See infra* text at notes 57–60.

27. St. Augustine, *De catechizandis rudibus.*

28. I *Corinthians* 13.4 (American Standard Version).

29. UNITED STATES CONFERENCE OF CATHOLIC BISHOPS, CATECHISM OF THE CATHOLIC CHURCH *Article 10, The Tenth Commandment* P 2534, *available at* http://www.nccbuscc.org/catechism/text/pt3sect2chpt2art10.htm (last visited Mar. 6, 2005).

30. *Id.* PP 2539–40.

31. *See* Ashwin, *supra* note 24.

32. WISDOM OF SOLOMON 2:24 (American Standard Version).

33. MELANIE KLEIN, ENVY AND GRATITUDE AND OTHER WORKS 1946–1963, at 176, 181 (1984).

34. *Id.* at 186–88.

35. *Id.* at 189.

36. GEOFFREY CHAUCER, THE CANTERBURY TALES (*The Parson's Tale*), quoted in Ashwin, *supra* note 24.

37. ANA ULANOV & BARRY ULANOV, CINDERELLA AND HER SISTERS 91 (1993).

38. Ashwin, *supra* note 24.

39. *Id.*

40. KLEIN, *supra* note 33, at 181.

41. Neu, *supra* note 13, at 432–33.

42. Neu maintains that "jealousy is typically over people, while envy extends to things and qualities." *Id.* at 433. As a Hegelian, I find this analysis to be backwards, and argue that jealousy applies more appropriately to things. Indeed, when a person is the object of jealousy, this means precisely that the jealous treats the person who is the object of his desire as precisely that—an object. In other words, Neu believes that jealousy with respect to things is the treatment of objects as subjects, whereas I believe that jealousy with respect to people is the treatment of subjects as objects.

43. They "dwelled in the same house." 1 *Kings* 3:16.

44. *Id.* Today, we would probably assume that the unfortunate infant succumbed to Sudden Infant Death Syndrome. Traditionally however, it was assumed that the infant was smothered because his whorish mother rolled over him while in a drunken stupor or while entertaining a client. This was how this story was told to me in Sunday school.

45. *Id.* at 3:21.

46. *Id.* at 3:25–28.

47. In recent times, Ian Ayres and Eric Talley have suggested an egregiously incorrect interpretation of this story. *See* Ian Ayres & Eric Talley, *Solomonic Bargaining: Dividing a Legal Entitlement to Facilitate Coasean Trade*, 104 YALE L.J. 1027 (1995).

48. Sigmund Freud, *Group Psychology and the Analysis of the Ego*, in 18 THE STANDARD EDITION OF THE COMPLETE PSYCHOLOGICAL WORKS OF SIGMUND FREUD 67, 120–21 (James Strachey et al. eds., 1974); John Forrester, *Psychoanalysis and the History of the Passions: The Strange Destiny of Envy*, in FREUD AND THE PASSIONS 127, 128–29 (John O'Neill ed., 1996).

49. For example, Solomon, because of the love of his "many foreign woman ... seven hundred wives, princesses, and three hundred concubines ... turned away his heart after other gods; and his heart was not wholly true to the Lord his God...." 1 *Kings* 11:1–5.

50. Neu, *supra* note 13, at 432–33.

51. KLEIN, *supra* note 33, at 176.

52. JACQUES LACAN, SEMINAIRE LIVRE SVII: L'ENVERS DE LA PSYCHANALSE 159 (Jacques-Alain Miller ed., 1991).

53. *See* Jacques Lacan, The Seminar of Jacques Lacan Book VII: The Ethics of Psychoanalysis 1959–1960, at 304 (Dennis Porter trans. & Jacques-Alain Miller ed., 1992) (1988).

54. Klein, *supra* note 33, at 177–78 (quoting Sigmund Freud, Constructions in Analysis (1937)).

55. I explain this at length in Jeanne L. Schroeder, *The Stumbling Block: Freedom, Rationality and Legal Scholarship*, 44 Wm & Mary L. Rev. 263 (2002), and shall give only an abbreviated account of Lacan's theory in the immediately following section.

56. As discussed by Shuli Barzilai, "references to the anecdote appear in Lacan's writings from The Family Complexes (1938) to Encore (1973)." Shuli Barzilai, *Augustine in Contexts: Lacan's Repetition of a Scene From the Confessions*, 11 Lit & Theology 201 (1997).

57. "Vidi ego et expertus sum zelantem parvulum, non dum loquebatur, et intuebatur pallidus amaro aspectu *conlactaneum suum*." The Confessions of St. Augustine 11 (Edward B. Pusey trans. & Charles W. Eliot eds., 1909). In this passage, rather than using the more common "invidere," Augustine uses the relatively unusual word "zelantem" which some other translators have rendered as "jealousy." *See, e.g.*, Barzilai, *supra* note 56. As Lacan's analysis explains, the immediately following text explains that Augustine is referring to the passion that I am calling envy, not jealousy.

58. *See* Jacques Lacan, Four Fundamental Concepts of Psycho-Analysis 116 (Alan Sheridan trans. & Jacques-Alain Miller ed., 1981).

59. *Id.*

60. I explain this phenomenon at length elsewhere. *See, e.g.*, Jeanne Lorraine Schroeder, The Triumph of Venus: The Erotics of the Market (2003) [hereinafter Schroeder, Venus]; Jeanne Lorraine Schroeder, The Vestal and the Fasces: Hegel, Lacan, Property and the Feminine (1998) [hereinafter Schroeder, Vestal]; Jeanne L. Schroeder, *The Midas Touch: The Lethal Effect of Wealth Maximization*, 1999 Wis. L. Rev. 687, 731–35 [hereinafter Schroeder, *The Midas Touch*]; Jeanne L. Schroeder, *The End of the Market: A Psychoanalysis of Law and Economics*, 112 Harv. L. Rev. 483, 505–06 (1998) [hereinafter, Schroeder, *The End of the Market*]. The following text in the main body is an abbreviated version of these more complete discussions.

61. *See* Jeanne L. Schroeder, *The Four Discourses of Law: A Lacanian Analysis of Legal Practice and Scholarship*, 79 Tex. L. Rev. 15 (2000) [hereinafter Schroeder, *The Four Discourses*]; *see also* Bruce Fink, The Lacanian Subject: Between Language and Jouissance 45 (1995).

62. I explicate Hegel and Lacan's theory of the formation of subjectivity extensively in Schroeder, Vestal, *supra* note 60, at 1–106, and Jeanne L. Schroeder, *Pandora's Amphora: The Ambiguity of Gift*, 46 UCLA L. Rev. 815, 860–62 (1999) [hereinafter Schroeder, *Pandora's Amphora*].

63. In French, *extimité*. Jeanne L. Schroeder & David Gray Carlson, *Kenneth Starr: Diabolically Evil?* 88 Cal. L. Rev. 653, 659–60 n.31 (2000). *See generally* Jacques-Alain Miller, *Extimité* (Francoise Massardier-Kenney trans.), in Lacanian Theory of Discourse: Subject, Structure and Society 74 (March Bracher et al. eds., 1994).

64. Miller, *supra* note 63, at 81.

65. Jacques Lacan, The Seminar of Jacques Lacan Book XX: Encore, On Feminine Sexuality, the Limits of Love and Knowledge 1972–1973, at 72–74 (Bruce Fink trans. & Jacques-Alain Miller ed., 1998).

66. *See* Schroeder, Vestal, *supra* note 60, at 328–29.

67. *See* Slavoj Žižek, The Sublime Object of Ideology 75 (1989).

68. *See* Slavoj Žižek, Tarrying With the Negative: Kant, Hegel, and the Critique of Ideology 203–04 (1993)

69. Miller, *supra* note 63, at 79–80.

70. Lacan, *supra* note 58, at 116.

71. *See* Lacan, *supra* note 65, at 100.

72. Freud, *supra* note 48, at 119–20.

73. *See id.*

74. *See supra* text at note 15.

75. *See* John Locke, Two Treatises of Government (Peter Laslett ed., Cambridge Univ. Press 1988) (1690).

76. Neu maintains that "the notion of "possession' should not mislead us into thinking that what is at stake is property rights. What is at stake is the self, is an individual's identity." Neu, *supra* note 13, at 448. A Hegelian would agree with the second point, that jealousy concerns the establishment of identify (or what I call subjectivity) but disagree with the assertion that jealousy does not involve property. To a Hegelian, property is nothing but a moment in the creation of subjectivity.

77. *See* Schroeder, Vestal, *supra* note 60, at 24; Schroeder, *Pandora's Amphora, supra* note 62, at 861–64.

78. *See id.* at 862.

79. As Michel Rosenfeld says, according to Hegel "self-consciousness can only achieve satisfaction in another self-consciousness." Michel Rosenfeld, *Hegel and the Dialectics of Contract*, 10 Cardozo L. Rev. 1199, 1221 (1989).

80. *See, e.g.,* G.W.F. Hegel, Elements of the Philosophy of Right 70 (H.B. Nisbet trans. & Allen W. Wood ed., 1991).

> A person, in distinguishing himself from himself, relates himself to another person, and indeed it is only as owners of property that the two [persons] have existence ... for each other. Their identity in themselves acquires existence ... through the transference of the property of the one to the other by common will and with due respect of the rights of both—that is, by contract.

Id.

81. Consequently, Hegel believes that only the "most uncultured," "stubborn," and "emotionally limited" people "insist most strongly on their rights." *Id.* at 69. I explain this dialectic in Schroeder, Vestal, *supra* note 60, at 49–52, and Schroeder, *Pandora's Amphora, supra* note 62, at 873–82.

82. *See supra* text at notes 62–64.

83. This is the subject of the first section of the *Philosophy of Right*. I explain Hegel's argument in Schroeder, Vestal, *supra* note 60, at 15–52, and Schroeder, *Pandora's Amphora's, supra* note 62, at 864–70.

84. It is a common misperception that Hegel, like Locke, justified property on the basis of first appropriation. *See, e.g.,* Steven Munzer, A Theory of Property 69–70 (1990). As I argue elsewhere, this is a misreading of a single sentence in the beginning of Philosophy of Right taken out of context. If one reads further to his discussion of "wrong." Hegel expressly rejects the first-appropriation justification of specific property claims. Schroeder, Vestal, *supra* note 60, at 41 n.124; Jeanne L. Schroeder & David Gray Carlson, *The Appearance of Wrong and the Essence of Right: Metaphor and Metonymy in Law*, 24 Cardozo L. 2481 (2003); Jeanne L. Schroeder, *Unnatural Rights: Hegel on Personality and Intellectual*

Property, (2005) (unpublished manuscript, on file with the *Cardozo L. Rev.*) [hereinafter Schroeder, *Unnatural Rights*].

85. In Hegel's famous formulation from the introduction to Philosophy of Right, because his logic is retroactive in nature, philosophy always comes "too late" to give policy advice. HEGEL, *supra* note 80, at 23; *see* Schroeder, *The Stumbling Block, supra* note 55, at 323–25.

86. In 1984 and 1988, Congress amended the 1934 Act by adding provisions imposing civil liabilities on, and providing for a private right of action for persons trading contemporaneously with, "any person who has violated any provision of this chapter or the rules or regulations thereunder by purchasing or selling a security ... while in possession of material, non-public information in, or has violated any such provision by communicating such information." 15 U.S.C. 78t-1, 78u-1 (2000). Although this language reflects Congress's agreement that some forms of insider trading should be restricted, this legislation begs the question of exactly what forms should be restricted.

87. The chapter is not intended as a comprehensive treatment of the voluminous scholarship on insider trading, merely as an introduction to certain recurring themes. For two recent articles that survey the literature, see Kimberly D. Krawiec, *Fairness, Efficience, and Insider Trading: Deconstructing the Coin of the Realm in the Information Age*, 95 Nw. U. L. Rev. 443 (2001), and Saikrishna Prakash, *Our Dysfunctional Insider Trading Regime*, 99 COLUM. L. Rev. 1491 (1999). As many have pointed out before me, this is an area of law that has been characterized more by incoherence than any reasoned justification. *See, e.g.,* Stephen Bainbridge, *The Insider Trading Prohibition: A Legal and Economic Enigma*, 38 U. FLA. L. Rev. 35 (1986); James Boyle, *A Theory of Law and Information: Copyright, Spleens, Blackmail, and Insider Trading*, 80 CAL. L. Rev. 1413 (1992); James D. Cox, *Insider Trading and Contracting: A Critical Response to the 'Chicago School,'* 1986 DUKE L. J. 628 (1986); Jill E. Fisch, *Start Making Sense: An Analysis and Proposal for Insider Trading Regulation*, 26 GA. L. Rev. 179 (1991).

88. Kim Sheppele, *It's Just Not Right: The Ethics of Insider Trading*, 56 L. & CONTEMP. PROBS. 123 (1993); *see also* Alison Grey Anderson, *Fraud, Fiduciaries, and Insider Trading*, 10 HOFSTRA L. Rev. 341 (1982); Victor Brudney, *Insiders, Outsiders, and Informational Advantages Under the Federal Securities Laws*, 93 HARV. L. Rev. 322 (1979); Cox, *supra* note 87; Gary Lawson, *The Ethics of Insider Trading*, 11 HARV. J. L. & PUB. POL'Y 727 (1998); Roy A. Schotland, *Unsafe at Any Price: A Reply to Manne, Insider Trading and the Stock Market*, 53 VA. L. Rev. 1425 (1967); Alan Strudler, *Moral Complexity in the Law of Nondisclosure*, 45 UCLA L. Rev. 337 (1997); Alan Strudler & Eric W. Orts, *Moral Principle in the Law of Insider Trading*, 78 TEX. L. Rev. 375 (1999).

89. *See, e.g.,* JONATHAN R. MACEY, INSIDER TRADING: ECONOMIC POLITICS, AND POLICY (1991); HENRY G. MANNE, INSIDER TRADING AND THE STOCK MARKET (1966); Dennis W. Carlton & Daniel R. Fischel, *The Regulation of Insider Trading*, 35 STAN. L. Rev. 857 (1983); David D. Haddock & Jonathan R. Macey, *A Coasian Model of Insider Trading*, 80 Nw. U. L. Rev. 449 (1986); Edmund W. Kitch, *The Law and Economics of Rights in Valuable Information*, 9 J. LEGAL STUD. 683 (1980); Jonathan R. Macey, *From Fairness to Contract: The New Direction of the Rules Against Insider Trading*, 13 HOFSTRA L. Rev. 9 (1984) [hereinafter Macey, *Fairness*]; Henry G. Manne, *Insider Trading and the Law Professors*, 23 VAND. L. Rev. 547 (1970) [hereinafter Manne, *Insider Trading*].

90. Section 2 of the 1934 Act lists among the many reasons why regulation of the securities markets falls within the federal jurisdiction granted by the Commerce Clause of the U.S. Constitution the need "to insure the maintenance of fair and honest markets" and the fact that manipulation may "prevent the fair valuation of collateral for bank loans." 15

U.S.C. 78b (2000). None of the substantive provisions of that Act applicable to issuers or their control persons, however, contains any express fairness standard. This is in striking contrast to state corporate laws which, by statute or common law, impose substantive fiduciary duties of loyalty and due care on corporate insiders and frequently apply standards of fundamental fairness to corporate and insider behavior.

91. For example, Section 11 of the 1933 Act allows purchasers of securities sold pursuant to materially misleading registration statements to recover the purchase price from the issuer, its directors, the officers who signed the registration statements, and underwriters and professionals who expertised a portion of the registration statement (i.e., usually the issuer's auditor). The named defendants other than the issuer can raise the so-called "due-diligence" defense that they did not know and did not have reasonable grounds to believe (in some circumstances, after reasonable investigation) that the registration statement was misleading.

92. *See* 15 U.S.C. 77q, 78j (2000).

93. *See* 15 U.S.C. 78e.

94. This is eloquently expressed in the title of an article by Jonathan R. Macey that traces the development of insider trading law: *From Fairness to Contract: The New Direction of the Rules Against Insider Trading. See* Macey, *Fairness, supra* note 89. Indeed, since he was writing in 1984, after the *Chiarella* and *Dirks* opinions (discussed *infra* in text at notes 102–07, 120–24, 133–39), Macey's choice of title is perhaps better described as prescient of the next twenty years.

95. 15 U.S.C. 78j (b).

96. 17 C.F.R. §240.10b-5 (2004) .

97. 425 U.S. 185 (1976).

98. 430 U.S. 462 (1977).

99. The specific issue considered in *Ernst & Ernst* was whether or not mere negligent behavior could constitute a violation of Section 10(b) and Rule 10b-5. The Supreme Court found that the language of the statute "connotes intentional or willful conduct designed to deceive or defraud investors by controlling or artificially affecting the price of securities." *Ernst & Ernst*, 425 U.S. at 199. Consequently, a plaintiff in a private right of action must establish that the defendant acted with scienter. *Id.* at 201. *Santa Fe Industries* considered whether a plaintiff could maintain a Section 10(b) and Rule 10b-5 cause of action against management of an issuer on the grounds that the terms of a merger were unfair, and in breach of management's fiduciary duties without a showing that the defendants had made a misstatement or omission of a material fact. *Santa Fe Indus.*, 430 U.S. at 464–65.

100. "The rulemaking power granted to an administrative agency charged with the administration of a federal statute is not the power to make law...." As a consequence, the scope of Rule 10b-5 "cannot exceed the power granted by the Commission by Congress under 10(b)." *Id.* at 472–73.

101. *See id.*

102. 445 U.S. 222 (1980). The Supreme Court was overruling the Second Circuit which had sustained Chiarella's conviction on the ground that "anyone—corporate insider or not—who regularly receives material non-public information may not use that information to trade in securities without incurring an affirmative duty to disclose. And if he cannot disclose, he must abstain from buying or selling." United States v. Chiarella, 558 F.2d 1358, 1365 (2d Cir. 1978), *rev'd*, 445 U.S. 222 (1980).

103. *Chiarella*, 445 U.S. at 233.

104. 40 S.E.C. 907 (1961).

105. 401 F.2d 833 (2d Cir. 1968), *cert. denied sub nom.*, Coates v. SEC, 394 U.S. 976 (1969).

106. The Supreme Court has never expressly overruled *Cady, Roberts* and has, on occasion, stated that it accepts its basic principles including the principle of unfairness. *See, e.g.*, United States v. Dirks, 463 U.S. 646, 653 (1983). Despite this, the Supreme Court has consistently held that unfairness alone does not impose prohibitions on the trading of material non-public information. Rather fraud can only be established through the breach of a fiduciary-type duty.

107. *Chiarella*, 445 U.S. at 232.

108. Santa Fe Indus., Inc. v. Green, 430 U.S. 462, 476 (1977).

109. The Supreme Court has held that Section 10(b) also covers manipulation but reads the word "manipulation" as used in the statute as a "term of art" to refer to practices "that are intended to mislead investors by artificially affecting market activity." *Santa Fe Indus.*, 430 U.S. at 476. That is, the Court limits "manipulation," as defined by the statute, like "fraud," to a form of actual deception. Fraud, apparently, is deception through words, whereas manipulation also includes deception through deeds.

110. Sarbanes-Oxley Act of 2002, Pub. L. No. 107-204, 116 Stat. 745 (codified in scattered sections of 11, 15, 18, 28, and 29 U.S.C.).

111. The 1934 Act does contain paternalistic and substantive rules applicable to market professionals such as registered brokers and dealers. In addition, the rules applicable to parties (including issuers) engaged in tender offers do contain some substantive provisions, *see, e.g.*, 17 C.F.R. §§240.13e-4(f), 240.14d-7, & 240.14d-11 (2004), in addition to disclosure obligations. They also contain a catch-all prophylactic provision that allows the SEC to adopt rules designed to prevent fraud which is deemed broader than Section 10(b) and Rule 10b-5 (which only proscribe actual fraud). *See infra* text at note 155.

112. *See Panel Discussion, New Approaches to Disclosure in Registered Securities Offerings*, 28 Bus. Law. 505 (1975) (quoting panelist A.A. Sommer, Jr.).

113. Cheryl L. Wade, *The Integration of Securities Offerings: A Proposed Formulation that Fosters the Policies of Securities Regulation*, 25 Loy. U. Chi. L. J. 199, 202 n.11 (1994) (referring specifically to the Securities Act of 1933).

114. *See supra* text at note 111.

115. 17 C.F.R. §249.308a (2004).

116. *Id.* at §249.310.

117. *Id.* at §249.308.

118. *Id.* at §240.14a-1 et seq.

119. *See, e.g.*, James D. Cox et al., Securities Regulation: Cases and Materials 659–70 (4th ed. 2004).

120. 445 U.S. 222, 233 (1980).

121. *Id.* at 230.

122. *Id.* at 232.

123. *See id.* at 227.

124. *Id.* at 232.

125. *Id.* at 232–33.

126. *See infra* text at notes 164–82.

127. *See* 445 U.S. at 233.

128. *See infra* text at notes 163, 181–82, 205–13.

129. As Manne correctly points out, one of the most important early insider trading cases, *S.E.C. v. Texas Gulf Sulphur*, 258 F. Supp. 262 (S.D.N.Y. 1966), *rev'd*, 401 F.2d 833 (2d Cir. 1968), demonstrates the seemingly anomalous nature of insider trading law. In that case, the Second Circuit held that it would have been unlawful for the insiders of an issuer to trade on issuer stock on the basis of material information that the issuer had discovered a very valuable mineral strike. "So notice the irony: [issuer] officials buying stock with knowledge of a new ore vein have somehow done something immoral, but the company itself buying surrounding land, utilizing precisely the same information, has merely performed in a business-like fashion." Manne, *Insider Trading, supra* note 89, at 550–51.

Manne ridicules the government's position: "nor will it do, as one high official of the SEC tried, to distinguish these two cases on the not-so-obviously pertinent ground that 'after all, one case involved land and the other securities.'" *Id.* at 551. Manne is correct that this statement seems inane in that the SEC based its case on an intuition that exploitation of informational advantages is somehow immoral. I argue, however, if insider trading law is instead based on the allocation of property rights, then the SEC's distinction is both logically and legally defensible. By adopting the federal securities laws Congress has, in effect, granted a property-like right to certain information concerning securities, and only securities, to the investment public. It has allowed state law to govern the law of information concerning land. *See infra* text at notes 191–97.

130. Manne, *Insider Trading, supra* 89, at 551

131. John C. Coffee, Jr. & Joel Seligman, Securities Regulation: Cases and Materials 1071 (2003).

132. As I discuss below, things are a little more complex in the case of the most classic form of insiders—directors and executive officers of the issuer. This is because, while these persons may not have the right to disclose corporate information in their personal capacities, in their corporate capacities they may have considerable ability to cause the issuer to make the appropriate disclosure.

133. 463 U.S. 646 (1983).

134. *Id.* at 654 (citations omitted).

135. "Insiders ... have independent fiduciary duties to both the corporation and its shareholders." *Id.* at 655. Once again, this rule requires an additional tweak of the fiduciary duty traditionally imposed under state corporate law, as the Second Circuit noted in *United States v. Chestman*, 947 F.2d 551 (2d Cir. 1991) (en banc), *cert. denied*, 503 U.S. 1004 (1992).

> The insider's fiduciary duties [as applied in federal insider trading cases], it should be noted, run to a buyer (a shareholder-to-be) and to a seller (a pre-existing shareholder) of securities, even though the buyer technically does not have a fiduciary relationship with the insider prior to the trade.

Id. at 566 n.2. This is because, as the Supreme Court noted in *Chiarella*, although the insider does not technically have a fiduciary duty to the buyer immediately before the sale, the sale itself creates such a duty immediately upon its consummation. Consequently, "it would be a sorry distinction" to apply a lesser standard to the act that creates the fiduciary relationship. *Id.*

136. As we shall see, Justice Ginsburg makes this analogy to embezzlement in her analysis of outsider trading. *See infra* text at notes 159–62. My criticism of Ginsburg is that she extends this analogy beyond what I believe is the legitimate context of corporate insiders to all confidentiality agreements and trade secret law.

137. 445 U.S. at 230.

138. *See infra* text at notes 195–97.

139. *See infra* text at notes 160–62.

140. There are still problematic aspects of interpreting this as "fraud." Specifically, there is the difficulty of identifying who specifically is defrauded for the purposes of private causes of action. The insiders' duties to speak run not to any individual shareholder, but to past, present and future shareholders of the issuer as a class. They are all equally defrauded by the disloyal insider's silence. The problem is that, under the rule of *Blue Chip Stamps*, only individuals who actually purchase and sell securities in reliance on fraud can sue for securities fraud. Consequently, the shareholders who did not sell (or potential shareholders who did not buy) their shares are not deemed victims of securities fraud.

Limiting plaintiffs to person who actually trade securities raises its own set of problems. First, it is not possible, and may not be advisable, to limit plaintiffs to those individuals who actually purchased shares from, or sold shares to, the insider in the public markets. Under modern trading practices it is both practically and theoretically impossible to match trades executed over the public markets. Even if we could trace trades, it seems arbitrary to limit plaintiffs to those individuals who just happened to have traded with the insider, because the insider defrauded traders generally, not any individual specifically. Alternatively, we could allow everyone who traded contemporaneously with the insider to form a plaintiff class. This is consistent with the analysis that the insider defrauds the public generally. However, it has the problem that it would lead to unacceptably high damages. For example, assuming arguendo that Stewart did engage in unlawful insider trading, she avoided approximately $40,000 (or $10 per share) in losses by trading the day before the announcement of the FDA decision. Let's assume that other persons purchased an aggregate of 100,000 shares of ImClone stock on the same day that Stewart traded at a price that was inflated by $10 per share because of lack of disclosure. Should they be able to sue Stewart for an aggregate of $1 million? And then there is the unfortunate fact that for every shareholder who was hurt by buying at the inflated price, there was another shareholder who was helped by selling at the inflated price. That is, under this hypothetical, because Stewart only sold approximately 4,000 shares on December 27th, other shareholders sold the other 96,000 shares at the higher price. If Stewart had disclosed her non-public information prior to trading, these shareholders would have lost $10 per share. How is this prevention of loss to be factored into the damage award? Congress has partially addressed this by adopting 20A of the 1934 Act, which gives an express private right of action to any and all contemporaneous traders but limits the aggregate damages payable to all plaintiffs to the actual profits made (or losses avoided) by the insider minus any amount previously disgorged to the SEC. Section 20A does not by its terms preempt private rights of action under Section 10(b), so these questions of liability remain unanswered.

141. Prakash, *supra* note 87, at 1495–96. Unfortunately, Prakash tries to argue not merely that this should be recognized as the logical implication of the special facts law, but that it is already the law. This is incorrect in that there is no case that follows Prakash's analysis in the case of classic insider trading (i.e., where the source of the information is the issuer of the securities). As I discuss, Justice Ginsburg does adopt an analysis similar to Prakash's in the context of the misappropriation theory.

142. *See, e.g.*, AMERICAN LAW INSTITUTE, PRINCIPLES OF CORPORATE GOVERNANCE §5.05 (1994).

143. *See infra* text at notes 168–69.

144. S.E.C. v. Lund, 570 F. Supp. 1397 (C.D. Cal. 1983).

145. Coffee & Seligman, *supra* note 131, at 1106.

146. For example, in *Chestman*, looking to state law for guidance, found that duties of confidence can be imposed by virtue of status. Examples cited by the court include "attorney and client, executor and heir, guardian and ward, principal and agent, trustee, and trust beneficiary, and senior corporate official and shareholder." 947 F.2d 552, 568 (2d Cir. 1991) (en banc), *cert. denied* 503 U.S. 1004 (1992).

147. In order to become a temporary insider having duties of confidentiality, a person must have a pre-existing relationship with the shareholders of the issuers in which he traded, such as becoming "their agent ... a fiduciary ... [or] a person in whom [they] had placed their trust and confidence." Chiarella v. United States, 445 U.S. 222, 232–33 (1980). The Supreme Court has established in *Dirks* that mere access to information does not make a person into a temporary insider:

> The basis for recognizing this fiduciary duty is not simply that such persons acquired nonpublic corporate information, but rather that they have entered into a special confidential relationship in the conduct of the business of the enterprise and are given access to information solely for corporate purposes.

United States v. Dirks, 463 U.S. 646, 655 n.14 (1983). Basic principles of authority suggest that such duties can be established by contract.

148. For example, in *United States v. Reed*, 601 F. Supp. 685, 690 (S.D.N.Y. 1985), *rev'd on other grounds*, 773 F.2d 477 (2d Cir. 1985), it was shown that a father became a temporary insider because his son, a classic insider of an issuer, "frequently discussed business affairs" with him.

149. According to the Supreme Court in *Dirks*, "the test is whether the insider personally will benefit, directly, or indirectly, from his disclosure. Absent some personal gain, there has been no breach of duty to stockholders." 463 U.S. at 662. This element is met when the insider receives "a pecuniary gain or a reputational benefit that will translate into future earnings." *Id.* at 663. Tippee liability is prophylactic. It is designed to prevent the tipper from doing indirectly through the tippee what he is prohibited from doing directly (i.e., trading on securities on the basis of non-public material information received in a relationship of confidence). *Id.* at 659. Drawing on the basic principal that mere possession of information does not create duties, the Court rejected the SEC's proposition that a tippee "inherits" the insider's duties merely by receiving the information, even if the tippee knows that the tipper is an insider. *Id.* at 664. Rather, a tippee can only become subject to the duties of the disclose or refrain rule if she assumes these duties. This means that the tippee must know "the information was given to him in breach of a duty by a person having a special relationship to the issuer not to disclose the information." *Id.* at 661.

150. *See* Metro. Life Ins. Co. V. RJR Nabisco, Inc., 716 F. Supp. 1504, 1524–25 (S.D.N.Y. 1989).

151. *See, e.g., Revised Simplified Model Trust Indenture; Model Note Purchase Agreement, reprinted in* William Bratton, Corporate Finance: Cases and Materials a-1, a-35 (5th ed. 2003) (respectively).

152. I will challenge these assumptions later in this chapter and suggest that the securities laws might imply disclosure obligations in both of these cases. *See infra* text at note 183.

153. *See* 17 C.F.R. §240.14e-3 (2004).

154. 521 U.S. 642 (1997).

155. *Id.* at 652.

> The "misappropriation theory" holds that a person commits fraud "in connection with" a securities transaction, and thereby violates 10(b) and Rule 10b-5, when he misappropriates confidential information for securities trading purposes, in breach of a duty owed to the source of the information.... Under this theory, a fiduciary's undisclosed self-serving use of a principal's information to purchase or sell securities, in breach of a duty of loyalty and confidentiality, defrauds the principal of the exclusive use of that information.

Id.

156. "In lieu of premising liability on a fiduciary relationship between company insider and purchaser or seller of the company's stock, the misappropriation theory premises liability on a fiduciary-turned-trader's deception of those who entrusted him with access to confidential information." *Id.*

157. *See id.* at 679–701.

158. *See supra* note 156.

159. "An employee's undertaking not to reveal his employer's confidential information 'became a sham' when the employee provided the information to his co-conspirators in a scheme to obtain trading profits." United States v. O'Hagan, 521 U.S. 642, 654 (1997) (citing *Carpenter v. United States*, 484 U.S. 19 (1987)).

160. 484 U.S. 19 (1987).

161. "A company's confidential information, we recognized in Carpenter, qualifies as property to which the company has a right of exclusive use...." *O'Hagan*, 521 U.S. at 654.

162. *See id.* at 656.

> [The] element is satisfied because the fiduciary's fraud is consummated, not when the fiduciary gains the confidential information, but when, without disclosure to his principal, he uses the information to purchase or sell securities. The securities transaction and the breach of duty thus coincide.

Id.

163. *See, e.g.*, Roger G. Bone, *A New Look at Trade Secret Law: Doctrine in Search of Justification*, 86 CAL. L. REV. 241 (1998); Vincent Chiappetta, *Myth, Chameleon or Intellectual Property Olympian: A Normative Framework Supporting Trade Secret Law*, 8 GEO. MASON L. REV. 69 (1999); John C. Coffee, Jr., *Hush!: The Criminal Status of Confidential Information After* McNally *and* Carpenter *and the Enduring Problem of Overcriminilization*, 26 AM. CRIM. L. REV. 121 (1988); David D. Friedman et al., *Some Economics of Trade Secret Law*, 5 J. ECON. PERSP. 61 (1991); Geraldine Szott Moohr, *Federal Criminal Fraud and the Development of Intangible Property Rights in Information*, 2000 U. ILL. L. REV. 683 (2000); Pamela Samuelson, *Information as Property: Do* Ruckelhaus *and* Carpenter *Signal a Changing Direction in Intellectual Property Law?*, 38 CATH. U.L. REV. 365 (1989); Steven Wilf, *Trade Secrets, Property and Social Relations*, 34 CONN. L. REV. 787 (2002). Elsewhere I argue that, from an Hegelian perspective, trade secret protection can and should be coherently analyzed in terms of property. Similarly, in this chapter, I argue that it is useful to analyze non-public information in the context of insider trading in terms of the allocation of property or semi-property rights in such information. *See* Schroeder, *Unnatural Rights, supra* note 84.

164. Blue Chip Stamps v. Manor Drug Stores, 421 U.S. 723 (1975).

165. If the trading constitutes unlawful trading, then 20A of the 1934 Act, 15 U.S.C. §78t-1, gives contemporaneous traders a statutory cause of action to recover the trader's trading profits. This is not a fraud action as the plaintiff is not entitled to damages for her loss and has no right of recovery if the SEC has previously sought to recoup these ill-gotten gains. Moreover, as discussed *supra* note 140, the language of this section does not define what types of trade violate the Act.

166. Ginsburg realizes this in that she defines the misappropriation theory as applying only to persons "who owe no fiduciary or other duty to that corporation's shareholders." *O'Hagan*, 521 U.S. at 653. I will challenge this assumption later in this chapter.

167. *See supra* text at notes 142–44.

168. *O'Hagan*, 521 U.S. at 655

169. *Id.* at 653 (quoting from the government's brief).

170. *See infra* text at notes 182–85.

171. Once again, the tender offer rules impose both disclosure duties and substantive standards on the bidders in tender offers. Certain trading in target securities by a potential bidder may or not violate these rules.

172. 484 U.S. 19 (1987).

173. *See id.* at 23–26.

174. *See id.* at 27.

175. In *Carpenter*, "the conspirators agreed that the scheme would not affect the journalistic purity of the 'Heard' column, and the district Court did not find that the contents of any of the articles were altered to further the profit potential of petitioners' stock-trading scheme." *Id.* at 23. Accordingly, there were no facts to support an allegation that Winans was engaged in unlawful manipulation under 9(e) of the 1934 Act, 15 U.S.C. §78i(e). It seems likely to me, however, that the real concern of the DOJ in bringing the case was not so much insider trading, but the potential for manipulation.

176. *See* United States v. O'Hagan, 521 U.S. 642, 659 n.9 (1997) (emphasis added).

177. *See id.* at 648.

178. *See id.* at 657 n.8.

179. *See id.* at 689–90.

180. *Id.* at 659 n.9.

181. *See supra* text at notes 157–58.

182. I must once again emphasize that the Supreme Court's choice of *O'Hagan* to announce the misappropriation theory confuses the analysis because *O'Hagan* involves a tender offer. The substantive rules governing tender offers under Rule 14e-3 clearly limit the right of Grand Met and its disloyal confidant, O'Hagan, to freely trade on confidential information concerning the proposed tender offer. In my analysis, *O'Hagan* should not be considered a misappropriation case because it is consistent with the policy underlying the classic theory. That is, Congress and the SEC have allocated rights in information concerning tender offers to the investment public. Consequently, public resentment against O'Hagan's use of this information reflects jealousy, not envy. Unfortunately, as I discuss throughout this chapter, the fact that, under current statutory analysis, insider trading must be shoe-horned into the category of traditional fraud prevents a court from reaching this result. A consistent insider trading law would, therefore, probably require an amendment to the federal securities laws.

183. *See, e.g.,* Macey, *supra* note 89; Manne, *supra* note 89; *see also* Steven M. Bainbridge, *Insider Trading Regulation: The Path Dependent Choice Between Property Rights and*

Securities Fraud, 52 SMU L. Rev. 1589 (1999); Frank H. Easterbrook, *Insider Trading, Secret Agents, Evidentiary Privileges, and the Production of Information,* 1981 Sup. Ct. Rev. 309; Krawiec, *supra* note 87; Zohar Goshen & Gideon Parchomovsky, *On Insider Trading, Markets, and "Negative" Property Rights in Information,* 87 Va. L. Rev. 1229 (2001); Larry E. Ribstein, *Federalism and Insider Trading,* 6 Sup. Ct. Econ. Rev. 123 (1998).

184. Manne published his seminal book, *Insider Trading and the Stock Market,* back in 1966. He has continued his losing battle for the legalization of insider trading to this day. *See, e.g.,* Henry G. Manne, *The Case for Insider Trading,* Wall St. J., Mar. 17, 2003, at A14.

185. *See* Manne, *supra* note 89, at 565, 578–79, 582–83. In Frank Easterbrook's words:

> Insider trading should be permitted to the extent the firm that created the information desires (or tolerates) such trading. The firm extracts value through exploiting the knowledge itself or reducing the salary of those who exploit it. The firm's decision to allow insiders to profit through a given device is the same in principle as any ordinary compensation decision, or as any decision to license know-how in exchange for a payment. If the managers err in setting their compensation, redress lies in the market, which will reduce their future earnings.

Easterbrook, *supra* note 183, at 331.

186. Manne, *supra* note 89, at 581.

187. For example, Ginsburg partially defends her decision in *O'Hagan* on these policy grounds:

> The theory is also well-tuned to an animating purpose of the Exchange Act: to insure honest securities markets and thereby promote investor confidence.... Although informational disparity is inevitable in the securities markets, investors likely would hesitate to venture their capital in a market where trading based on misappropriated nonpublic information is unchecked by law. An investor's information disadvantage vis-à-vis a misappropriator with material, non-public information stems from contrivance, not luck; it is a disadvantage that cannot be overcome with research or skill.

United States v. O'Hagan, 521 U.S. 642, 658–59 (1997) (citations omitted). This concept of preventing informational advantages that cannot be overcome is most closely associated with Victor Brudney. *See* Brudney, *supra* note 88.

188. *See* Manne, *supra* note 89, at 555–57.

189. This would parallel the rule announced in *O'Hagan* that one can avoid liability as a misappropriator if one discloses one's intentions to trade to the source of the information. *See supra* text at notes 169–72. As discussed, Prakash has argued that this rule of permitted candid trading is already implicit under the classic theory. *See supra* note 141.

190. *See* Manne, *supra* note 89, at 549–50.

191. Boyle has called this an enigmatic "island of egalitarianism" in an otherwise individualistic ocean. *See infra* text at note 204.

192. 401 F.2d 833 (2d Cir. 1968) (en banc), *cert. denied,* 394 U.S. 976 (1969).

193. Manne, *supra* note 89, at 550–51.

194. *Id.* at 550.

195. The definition of "corporate opportunity" differs from state to state and case to case. However, the *Texas Gulf Sulfur* facts would seem to fall within all of the traditional

interest or expectancy, line of business, and fairness tests. Jeffrey D. Bauman et al., Corporations Law and Policy: Materials and Problems 788–91 (5th ed. 2003).

196. As discussed, Prakash goes so far as to suggest not merely that this should be the
rule, but that it is currently the rule. *See supra* note 141. This is empirically incorrect. No
court has so held.

197. *See id.*

198. Manne, *supra* note 89, at 569.

199. Manne is somewhat to be defended in that, writing in 1970, he does not make the
distinction between insider trading under the classic theory and outsider trading under the
misappropriation theory. (Consider, for example, that he includes in his definition of insider trading "any trading by any individual based on information which had not yet been
publicly disclosed or completely exploited by other traders." *Id.* at 562).

200. Manne claims that proponents of insider trading rules naively "assume that a rule
against insider trading is the equivalent of a full and timely disclosure rule perfectly enforced."
Id. at 552. I am not making the assumption that forbidding insider trading would encourage
disclosure. Rather, I am suggesting that it is a corollary to mandatory disclosure rules because
it removes one incentive to violate these rules.

201. *See, e.g.,* F.H. Easterbrook & Daniel R. Fischel, *Mandatory Disclosure and the Protection of Investors*, 70 Va. L. Rev. 669 (1984).

202. Indeed, the Sarbanes-Oxley Act, passed in the wake of the scandals of 2001, reflects a strengthening, not a dilution, of this regime.

203. Boyle, *supra* note 87.

204. *Id.* at 1491.

205. *See supra* text at notes 154–62.

206. Unif. Trade Secrets Act 1(4), 14 U.L.A. 537–51 (1980 & Supp. 1986).

207. Restatement 3d of Unfair Competition 39 (1995).

208. For a discussion of the differences, *see generally* Chiappetta, *supra* note 163, at 76–81.

209. The basis of trade secret law is so unclear that one analyst states bluntly that "there
is no such thing as a normatively autonomous body of trade secret law." Bone, *supra* note
163, at 245. Bone wishes to limit trade secret protection to rights "created by express contract or justified as contract default rules." *Id.* at 246.

210. *See supra* note 163.

211. "Our analysis of trade secret law is congruent with the basic economic explanation for patent protection—that it provides a means of internalizing the benefits of innovation." Friedman et al., *supra* note 163, at 64. Bone divides the efficiency rationale into
two forms. "The first argues that trade secret law enhances incentives to create. The second argues that it reduces the level of private investment in discovering and protecting secrets as well as the transaction costs associated with value-enhancing transfers." Bone, *supra*
note 163, at 262. I discuss the efficiency rationale elsewhere, *see* Schroeder, *Unnatural
Rights, supra* note 84, and shall not raise it further at this juncture.

212. Consequently, there are "two separate categories of trade secret misappropriation:
breach of duty and bad acts." Chiappetta, *supra* note 163, at 73. For example, the Uniform
Trade Secret Act, which has been adopted in over forty states, defines misappropriation of
trade secrets either as "(1) disclosure or use without consent when under a duty to maintain secrecy or limit use, or (2) an acquisition by improper means. 'Improper means' include 'theft, bribery, misrepresentation, breach [of duty] or inducement of a breach of duty
to maintain secrecy or espionage through electronic or other means.'" *Id.* at 78 (quoting

Unif. Trade Secrets Act 1(1), 1(2)(ii)(A)). In other words, the Uniform Trade Secret Act makes a clear distinction between mere breach of confidentiality and fraud—precisely the distinction the Supreme Court failed to perceive in *Carpenter* and *O'Hagan* when it found that mere misappropriation of confidential information constitutes fraud.

213. Schroeder, *Unnatural Rights, supra* note 84.

214. *See supra* text at notes 207–12.

215. *See supra* note 163 and accompanying text.

216. *See supra* text at note 173.

CHAPTER 13

MARTHA STEWART AND
DIRECTOR INDEPENDENCE*

Lisa M. Fairfax

This chapter uses the shareholder derivative action involving Martha Stewart to analyze the role, if any, social and personal ties should play in courts' evaluation of directors' independence. In that action, the Delaware Chancery Court appeared to give significant weight to personal and social ties between Martha Stewart and her fellow board members in its evaluation of the board's independence. However, the Delaware Supreme Court concluded that courts should rarely, if ever, use such ties to rebut directors' independence. First, this chapter demonstrates the importance of director independence to the ability of shareholders to litigate fiduciary actions. Second, this chapter explores the validity of the Delaware Supreme Court's conclusion by looking at various sources of evidence regarding the impact of social, personal, and professional ties on directors' ability to independently assess the actions of their fellow directors and officers. This exploration reveals that, while such ties should not be over-emphasized in the director independence inquiry, such ties can have a significant impact on directors' ability to objectively assess the actions of their colleagues. Thus, this chapter argues for the adoption of a more balanced approach to the consideration of social ties, and uses the facts of the Martha Stewart case to illustrate the manner in which courts can use that approach. As this chapter illuminates, the Martha Stewart case is important because the courts' pronouncements regarding the relevance of social connections among directors has far-reaching implications not only on the director independence

---

* This chapter relies in part on an article entitled *Sarbanes Oxley, Corporate Federalism, and the Declining Significance of Federal Reforms on State Director Independence Standards*, originally published at 31 OHIO N. U. L. REV. 381 (2005). Reprinted with permission of the publisher, Ohio Northern University Law Review © 2005.

inquiry, but ultimately on the ability of all shareholders to fully litigate their fiduciary duty actions.

Martha Stewart Derivative Action and Delaware's Demand Process

In 2002, shareholders of Martha Stewart Living Omnimedia, Inc. ("MSLO") brought a derivative suit against Martha Stewart. The shareholders claimed that Martha Stewart's sales of stock in ImClone Systems Incorporated ("ImClone") and subsequent statements regarding ImClone represented a breach of her fiduciary duty to MSLO because such activities negatively impacted MSLO and its financial viability.[1] Corporate directors and officers have a fiduciary duty to act in good faith and in a manner that they reasonably believe to be in the best interests of the corporation.[2] As a director, chair of the board and CEO of MSLO, Martha Stewart had an obligation to satisfy this duty.[3] Shareholders maintained that Martha Stewart's actions in relation to ImClone constituted a breach of that duty. As its founder and majority stockholder,[4] Martha Stewart's name and personal image were inextricably linked with the fate of MSLO and its products.[5] Thus, shareholders argued that by allegedly engaging in insider trading and seeking to cover it up, Martha Stewart damaged her personal and professional reputation, which in turn damaged the reputation and financial integrity of MSLO. As a result, her actions undermined the interest of MSLO and thus constituted a breach of her fiduciary duty of care.

MSLO responded to the shareholders' action by filing a motion to dismiss it for failure to make a demand. In order to hold a director or officer such as Martha Stewart liable for breaching her fiduciary duty, shareholders must bring a derivative action against that director or officer.[6] Under Delaware law, a shareholder cannot bring a derivative suit unless she has made a demand upon the corporation to take suitable action or has demonstrated that such a demand would be futile.[7] If a shareholder fails to make demand or fails to demonstrate that demand would be excused as futile, then the corporation can dismiss the suit, thereby preventing the shareholder from litigating her action on its merits.[8] In this case, MSLO shareholders did not make a demand upon the corporation and, thus, had the burden of proving demand was excused as futile. The purpose of demand is to provide the corporation with the opportunity to evaluate the merits of fiduciary actions.[9] Thus, courts only excuse demand when it appears that directors' evaluation of such actions would be tainted by bias.[10] Under *Aronson v. Lewis*, in order to demonstrate demand futility, shareholders must raise a reasonable doubt that (a) the directors in office at the time they filed their actions were independent and disinterested and (b) the transaction was otherwise the product of a valid business decision.[11] By satisfying *Aronson*, the shareholders' suit can move forward without demand. Consistent with Delaware law, MSLO shareholders had to overcome the demand process in order to avoid termination of their suit.

Success under *Aronson* does not automatically afford shareholders the opportunity to litigate their suits on the merits. Instead, the corporation has a second avenue for pre-suit dismissal of shareholders' actions. Under this avenue, the corporation can establish a special litigation committee of the board to assess the action and make a motion to dismiss. Under *Zapata Corp. v. Maldonado*,[12] courts will grant the committee's motion to dismiss only if the committee is independent and reached its decision in good faith following a reasonable investigation.[13] Because *Zapata* enables corporations a second opportunity to prevent shareholders from having their day in court, MSLO shareholders likely would have had to surmount two hurdles in order to fully litigate their fiduciary duty claims against Martha Stewart.

The Centrality of Director Independence to Shareholder Derivative Actions

Successful navigation of both hurdles often depends upon the directors' independence. This is because, under *Aronson*, demand will be excused as futile if shareholders raise a reasonable doubt that the directors upon whom they would have made a demand were disinterested or independent in the challenged transaction.[14] This means that if MSLO shareholders allege sufficient facts demonstrating that a majority of the MSLO directors holding their seats at the time shareholders filed their derivative suit lacked independence, then their suit moves forward. Independence also has significance under *Zapata*. Even if shareholders prevail under *Aronson*, the corporation has a second opportunity to seek dismissal by establishing a committee to make a motion to dismiss. While courts overwhelmingly defer to such committees,[15] courts will deny a committee's motion if the corporation fails to establish the independence of the directors sitting on the committee.[16] In this regard, director independence is a critical factor in both stages of a pre-suit motion to dismiss.

The fact that director independence represents a critical component of, and is even outcome-determinative to, fiduciary actions is no coincidence. Indeed, judges do not like to second-guess the business decisions of corporate directors and officers.[17] Judges do not consider themselves business people and, hence, do not believe that they are in the best position to resolve thorny business issues.[18] Moreover, business decisions often require some degree of innovation and risk-taking. Accordingly, courts like to give directors and officers the freedom to make such decisions without judicial, or even shareholder, second-guessing of their actions. For these reasons, courts are reluctant to hold directors and officers liable for their decisions. Instead, courts rely upon independent directors to ascertain the propriety of business actions and presume that those directors act in the best interests of the corporation.[19] On the one hand, courts believe that independent directors' expertise and authority within the corporate structure afford them the best opportunity to oversee the corporation's affairs and analyze the validity of the decisions made by corporate officers and directors. On the other hand, courts presume that directors' independence ensures that such oversight will be exercised free from bias and extraneous influences. Although empirical studies offer mixed support for this presumption,[20] courts view the independent director not only as an ideal check on corporate behavior, but also as the ideal person to whom courts should defer.[21] Hence, courts rely upon independent directors to assess the propriety of day-to-day business decisions as well as the propriety of shareholder fiduciary suits seeking to hold directors or officers liable for those decisions.

How do courts determine who qualifies as an independent director? Historically, courts defined independence without regard to the social or professional relationships directors shared with one another. In order to demonstrate independence, Delaware courts require a showing that a board member can make a decision free from personal financial interest or improper extraneous influences.[22] In other words, a director will be considered independent if she does not feel beholden to other directors because of personal or other relationships.[23] This definition leaves room for non-financial relationships to impact the director independence inquiry. Indeed, the Delaware Supreme Court has acknowledged that the social and professional ties among directors resulting from their membership on the same board may lead to feelings of empathy or a "structural bias" that cut against directors' independence.[24]

However, Delaware courts do not like to afford weight to these ties.[25] Thus, Delaware courts focus on financial considerations and have held repeatedly that allegations of close personal friendships among directors and corporate officers accused of wrong-doing were not enough to prove that such directors could not independently evaluate that wrong-doing.[26] For example, one court found that a fifteen-year personal relationship between a CEO and a director could not be used to raise a reasonable doubt as to the director's independence from the CEO.[27] Another court found a similar allegation of a life-long friendship to be insufficient to undermine a director's independence.[28] Delaware Supreme Court Chief Justice Norman Veasey asserted that courts should not presume that "friendship, golf companionship, and social relationships" jeopardize directors' independence.[29] His assertion is illustrative of Delaware courts' basic refusal to give any weight to such relationships in the director independence analysis.

Shareholders of MSLO prompted Delaware courts to re-examine this refusal by claiming that MSLO directors lacked independence because of personal and social ties between board members and Martha Stewart. Given the significance of director independence to the demand inquiry and fiduciary suits more generally, this reexamination has broad repercussions for all shareholders seeking to bring a fiduciary duty action against corporate directors or officers.

The Courts' Response on the Relevance of Social Ties to Director Independence

MSLO shareholders claimed that demand would be futile because close personal and social ties between Stewart and the other directors undermined such directors' independence, rendering those directors incapable of evaluating the merits of actions in which Stewart was a participant. Shareholders strongest allegations regarding social ties involved two directors: Arthur C. Martinez and Darla D. Moore.[30] Shareholders pointed out that a longtime personal friend and confidant of Stewart recruited Martinez to the MSLO board.[31] They also pinpointed a magazine article stating that Stewart considered Martinez to be an "old friend."[32] According to shareholders, these indicators of friendship undermined Martinez's independence. With regard to Moore, shareholders explained that in 1995 Moore attended a wedding reception hosted by Stewart's personal lawyer. Then, too, a 1996 *Fortune* magazine article described Moore and Stewart as close personal friends. Finally, Moore was nominated (presumably by Stewart) to serve on MSLO's board after the resignation of one of Stewart's longtime friends.[33] Shareholders insisted that this evidence of Stewart's personal relationship with Moore, like that of her personal relationship with Martinez, impeded Moore's ability to be deemed independent.

Amazingly, the Delaware Chancery Court took seriously the MSLO shareholders' allegations. Pointing to the wealth of prior case law on the irrelevance of social ties to the director independence assessment, the defendant directors argued that such relationships should have no bearing on the independence inquiry.[34] The court disagreed, insisting that some personal and professional friendships could raise a reasonable doubt as to a director's independence.[35]

The court further argued that such ties may be especially difficult to overcome when the allegations regarding directors' conduct raised serious questions of civil or criminal liability.[36] Hence, the court suggested that directors' social ties may be particularly relevant when their decision to allow the suit to move forward had a significant likelihood of exposing fellow directors or officers to personal liability. This appeared to be the case for MSLO directors. Indeed, at the time of opening arguments before the Delaware Chancery Court, the Department of Justice had indicted Martha Stewart on criminal charges, and the SEC had filed a civil action against her.[37] Moreover, in the two years prior to her suit, there had been a record number of corporate directors and officers either indicted or jailed for corporate misconduct, and for one of the first times in history, several outside directors had agreed to pay millions of dollars in order to settle a lawsuit against them alleging corporate wrongdoing. The corporate climate suggested that Martha Stewart faced a real threat of personal liability. Based on the court's reasoning, such a threat may have made the social relationships between Stewart and the directors more relevant to the director independence inquiry.

With these factors as context, the court considered the social ties between MSLO directors and Martha Stewart. With respect to Martinez, the court found the shareholders' allegations to be insufficient primarily because they appeared to rest on a single affirmation of friendship.[38] The court gave more weight to the allegations involving Moore. In the court's view, the allegations represented "quite a close call" as to the director's independence because they focused on a variety of incidences suggesting close ties between the two.[39] Ultimately, however, the court found the evidence presented by the shareholders to be insufficient to support the shareholders' claims regarding a strong personal friendship. In fact, the court berated the shareholders for resting their claim of demand futility on "precious little investigation beyond perusal of the morning newspaper."[40] The court further stated that the MSLO shareholders' failure to properly investigate directors' relationship with Stewart may have resulted in the dismissal of an otherwise meritorious claim.[41] In this sense, while the court found the shareholders' allegations to be insufficient, it nevertheless left the door open for the use of social ties in the director independence analysis if shareholders adequately researched those ties.

Other courts seemed willing to walk through that door. In *In re Oracle Derivative Litigation*, shareholders sued several officers and directors alleging that they had breached their fiduciary duty by selling their shares in the company based on inside information.[42] In response to the suit, the corporation established a special litigation committee of the board to investigate the directors' and officers' conduct. After an extensive investigation of the allegations in the suit,[43] the committee determined that the suit lacked merit and thus filed a motion to dismiss it.

The Delaware Chancery Court's decision on the motion turned on the extent to which social ties among directors undermined their independence. Relying on *Zapata*, the court assessed whether the corporation had proven the independence of the directors sitting on its committee. Like the defendants in the *Stewart* case, the defendants in *Oracle* argued that the court's independence analysis should focus solely on economic factors.[44] The defendants insisted that the committee members should be considered independent because they had no financial relationships with the defendant directors.[45] While the Delaware Chancery Court agreed that the committee members lacked any economic ties with defendant directors, it disagreed that such a fact ended the director independence inquiry.[46]

Instead, the court delved into the professional and social relationships that the committee members shared with the defendant directors.[47] The committee was comprised of two directors, Hector Garcia-Molina and Joseph Grundfest.[48] The court found it significant that both Garcia-Molina and Grundfest were tenured professors at Stanford and that three of the defendant directors had ties to Stanford. In particular, Grundfest, a tenured law professor at Stanford, had been taught by defendant Michael Boskin during the 1970's when Grundfest was a Stanford Ph.D. candidate.[49] According to the court, although they did not socialize, the two remained in contact over the years.[50] In addition, both Boskin and Grundfest were senior fellows and steering committee members at a Stanford research institute.[51]

The court described another defendant director, Donald Lucas, as a loyal alumnus who (through his foundation) donated millions of dollars to Stanford as well as $50,000 to Stanford Law School in appreciation for a speech given by Grundfest.[52] The court also pinpointed ties between the third director, Lawrence Ellison, the company's CEO, and Stanford, pursuant to which Ellison had made several donations to Stanford and had discussed the possibility of establishing a scholarship at Stanford in his name.[53] The court maintained that these ties were significant enough to hamper the committee's ability to impartially assess the defendant directors' conduct.[54] Thus, the court concluded that such ties rendered the committee members dependent.

Both the *Oracle* court and the *Stewart* court openly acknowledged that the decision to afford weight to non-economic relationships in the determination of director independence was in "tension" with the weight of Delaware law.[55] However, the *Oracle* court insisted that the failure to acknowledge such ties amounted to a failure to sufficiently account for human nature and the impact social settings play on human behavior in general and director interactions in particular.[56] Moreover, during this same time period, other Delaware courts focused on social and personal connections when evaluating director independence.[57] From this perspective, the *Stewart* case appeared to reflect a burgeoning trend among courts towards an inclusion of social ties in the director independence assessment.

The Delaware Supreme Court used its review of the *Stewart* case to effectively halt that trend.[58] Indeed, the court announced two general principles regarding the significance (or insignificance) of social ties to the director independence inquiry. First, the court dismissed the notion that claims of "structural bias" inherent in the social collegiality among directors could undermine a director's independence. In the court's view, such claims "presuppose that the professional and social relationships that naturally develop among members of a board impede independent decision making."[59] Judges should instead presume that directors' concern for their business reputation and personal integrity would outweigh "personal friendships."[60] Second, the court maintained that allegations of close business or social ties outside of the boardroom generally were inadequate to negate independence, even if those allegations revealed lifelong friendships.[61] Thus, whether personal collegial relationships arose before board membership or later as a result of that membership, generally those relationships should not hinder a director's independence.[62]

The court then applied these principles to the facts of the *Stewart* case with predictable results. The court easily dismissed shareholders' allegations regarding Martinez as relatively insignificant to the issue of director independence. According to the court, allegations that directors "moved in the same social circles," "developed business relationships," and "described each other as 'friends'" are insufficient to rebut the presumption of independence.[63] The Delaware Supreme Court similarly dismissed the allegations related to Moore. Disagreeing with the Chancery Court, the Delaware Supreme Court stated that Moore's social relationships with Stewart did not present a "close call" on the issue of her independence.[64] Instead, the allegations revealed a "bare social relationship" that does not create a reasonable doubt regarding a director's independence.[65] In this way, the Delaware Supreme Court used the *Stewart* case to emphasize its view that social ties warrant little weight in the director independence analysis.

In this spirit, the Delaware Supreme Court also limited the *Oracle* decision. The court did not overrule *Oracle* and its focus on social ties. However, the Supreme Court distinguished *Stewart* from *Oracle* by arguing that the burden of proof was different in the two cases, involving different presumptions regarding directors' independence.[66] According to the court, the independence inquiry in *Stewart* arose in the context of *Aronson*, pursuant to which shareholders had the burden of proving the director's lack of independence.[67] In that context, courts presume that directors are independent, and allegations of social affinities rarely can be used to rebut that presumption.[68] *Oracle*, however, arose in the context of a director independence inquiry under *Zapata* where the burden rested on the corporation. Satisfying this burden requires corporations to meet a "Caesar's wife-above reproach"[69] standard, and thus courts could consider all ties, including social and personal ones. With these distinctions, the Delaware Supreme Court limited consideration of such ties to the *Zapata* stage of shareholders' derivative actions.

This limitation could severely curtail the extent to which social and professional ties will play any role in fiduciary suits and the included director independence inquiry.[70] While such ties may prove relevant in the *Zapata* stage, getting to that stage is not guaranteed. Instead, shareholders' suits can be dismissed at the *Aronson* phase. As the Delaware Supreme Court emphasizes, shareholders not only carry the burden of proof in *Aronson*, but in *Aronson* directors have a presumption of independence. Thus, shareholders confront an uphill battle. The difficulty of that battle is reflected in the fact that courts dismiss a large number of suits at the *Aronson* stage.[71] From this perspective, *Aronson* represents a critical decisional moment for shareholder fiduciary duty actions. Therefore, the fact that social connections are not relevant at that moment may foreclose the relevance of those connections altogether. In fact, at the *Aronson* stage, shareholders do not get the benefit of discovery that is afforded to them under *Zapata*.[72] Accordingly, their burden to identify facts relevant to the independent inquiry may prove even more difficult. In this regard, the *Stewart* decision represents a clear limit on these connections in the director independence inquiry. Emphasizing this point, Chief Justice Veasey (author of the Delaware Supreme Court's *Stewart* decision) later wrote that the *Stewart* decision was Delaware's "answer" to the independence question.[73] The answer was no—absent extraordinary circumstances, social relations among directors cannot rebut the presumption of director independence.[74]

The Relevance of Social Ties to Director Independence

Is this answer the appropriate one? On the one hand, the Delaware Supreme Court correctly points out that it would be inappropriate to overemphasize social ties in the director independence inquiry not only because such ties may prove beneficial to board decision-making, but also because directors' concerns for other interests may outweigh the significance of those ties. On the other hand, in failing to sufficiently consider those ties, courts inevitably fail to acknowledge their impact on human behavior and director relationships. This impact is supported by empirical studies regarding group behavior and anecdotal evidence from recent corporate governance scandals. For this reason, this section concludes that the Delaware Supreme Court's answer on director independence was too restrictive. When courts do not allow social ties to play a more significant role in the director independence inquiry, such courts do not appropriately consider all of the factors that may undermine directors' ability to make objective assessments of corporate behavior.

Drawbacks of Over-Emphasizing Social Ties

First, directors' concerns for their professional reputations make it inappropriate to automatically presume that their social ties to other directors and officers will undermine their independence. Directors are prominent business people who presumably value their business reputations.[75] For example, MSLO director Martinez was the former chair and CEO of Sears Roebuck and the current chair of the Federal Reserve Bank of Chicago.[76] As a prominent business person, it seems reasonable that he would be interested in ensuring that his conduct on MSLO's board would not blemish his professional reputation. Additionally, while serving on MSLO's board, he also served on several other boards including the boards of Saks Fifth Avenue, Pepsico, Inc., and Liz Claiborne, Inc.[77] Certainly, he should be cognizant that his performance on MSLO's board could have repercussions for his role as director on these other boards. This means that Martinez would seek to act in a manner that enhances his reputation. In this regard, it seems appropriate to recognize that directors' desires to protect their professional reputations would influence their decisions on the board as much—if not more—than their desires to maintain close personal friendships.

Of course, it is unclear how this recognition cuts. It certainly appears true that directors would not want to take actions that undercut their professional reputation. However, the Delaware Supreme Court presumes that the board's failure to allow shareholders to bring suits against a director or officer might damage the directors' reputations.[78] Yet just the opposite may be true. Evidence suggests that some boards develop strong norms against criticizing fellow directors and officers.[79] In this same vein, if boardroom and corporate norms disfavor directors who allow shareholders' suits to move forward, then directors protect their reputation by terminating suits.[80] In this regard, the directors' decision to maintain close personal friendships may be consistent with their decision to impede the progress of shareholder lawsuits. From this perspective, arguments that discredit consideration of social ties based on directors' desire to protect their professional reputation may not carry as much weight as the court presumes.

Even if such arguments carry less weight, however, it would be inadvisable to automatically condemn all social ties among directors because those ties are important to the boards' effectiveness. Indeed, there are advantages to social ties in the boardroom that should not be overlooked. Board members need some degree of cohesion in order to effectively work together.[81] Developing this cohesion is the reason why board members host retreats and similar opportunities for social interactions among directors. Board members' effectiveness also depends on their ability to develop a positive working relationship with management and the CEO.[82] Thus, strong professional and social ties between directors and officers enhance the ability of directors to perform their monitoring and management functions. Because the cohesion stemming from these ties has a positive impact on boards, those ties cannot be automatically condemned.

Then too, over-emphasizing social ties may eviscerate courts ability to consider any director to be independent.[83] It is inevitable that board members will have social ties with one another. Indeed, entrée into the board often stems from the professional relationships people have with one another, and directors often come to the board with a familiarity and shared background.[84] Moreover, even if board members do not know each other prior to serving on the board, membership on the board fosters close personal and social ties. Sarbanes-Oxley and other reforms ensure that these ties will be closer than ever because such reforms impose increased responsibilities on boards and committees, ensuring that they work together for longer hours.[85] This practice necessarily deepens the social and professional bonds between board members. If these bonds jeopardize directors' independence, then it would be difficult for any board member to be viewed as truly independent. If courts considered all social ties to pose problems for director independence, then that characterization would be rendered meaningless. Given the critical role independence plays in our corporate governance regime, it certainly seems inadvisable to categorize all social ties as problematic.

Some Reasons to Credit Social Ties

Despite these drawbacks, however, there exists some strong evidence that social ties outside of the boardroom as well as the socialization process within the boardroom may compromise directors' independence.[86]

As a general matter, empirical and anecdotal evidence reveals that strong social ties, particularly those developed outside of the boardroom, may undermine directors' independence. Thus, reports evaluating recent corporate governance failures concluded that directors' close personal or social relationships undermined their ability to rigorously monitor corporate officers.[87] Such relationships proved just as detrimental as financial dependence.[88] Social science literature on group dynamics confirms this evidence. That literature reveals that groups with shared social and professional affiliations tend to be extremely cohesive, and such cohesion can hamper their ability to independently assess one another's conduct.[89] Applying this literature to corporate boards, several scholars note that the common business and professional ties among directors may impede undermine directors' ability to impartially assess management and their fellow directors.[90] Hence, the fact that directors have extensive social or professional ties outside of the board-room may undermine their independence.

Certain social interactions inside the boardroom also may undermine directors' independence. Thus, studies of boardroom behavior generally, and the behavior of boards embroiled in recent corporate governance scandals, indicate that directors who hold their seats for long periods of time develop strong social ties with one another and management that limit their impartiality.[91] Indeed, investigations of corporate boards at Enron and WorldCom revealed that several directors had served on those boards for years.[92] In fact, some Enron directors had served on the board for more than twenty years.[93] Commentators opined that such long tenures may have comprised directors' independence. Studies of board behavior confirm these opinions. Thus, in evaluating the effectiveness of independent directors, Professors Sanjai Bhagat and Bernard Black found that directors with long tenures on boards develop strong social relationships with officers and other directors that make it difficult for such directors to objectively evaluate others' conduct.[94]

Studies also demonstrate that some boards develop particular norms that limit directors' willingness to actively and vigorously monitor other directors' and officers' behavior.[95] The most common boardroom norm is one that that disfavors criticism of CEO and management.[96] This norm makes it difficult for directors to intervene in management decisions or otherwise vigorously question those decisions.[97] The norm also encourages acquiescence.[98] These observations of boardroom behavior confirm that social dynamics in the boardroom may stifle the ability of directors to critically assess managerial and director action.

Striking a Better Balance

Given the significance of director independence, it seems that courts should err on the side of considering any factor that may impede directors' ability to perform their obligations objectively. Empirical and anecdotal evidence suggests that social ties factor into a director's ability to be objective. While there are benefits to ensuring that courts do not give that factor too much weight, courts should do a better job of striking a balance by allowing courts to examine those ties in the first stage of a pre-suit motion to dismiss and by enunciating guidelines for carrying out that examination.

Like the independence inquiry more generally, that examination should be based on a case-by-case analysis of specific facts so that courts give more (but not undue) weight to social or professional relationships. Hence, this section suggest adopting an approach that relies upon the non-economic independence factors that, according to relevant studies, pose particular problems for a director's ability to make independent assessments. Such an approach should focus on three concerns. First, since evidence suggests that outside ties may impact directors' independence, courts should consider the duration and nature of the ties between directors outside of the boardroom when measuring a director's independence. Second, courts should consider the length of service on the board. Finally, courts should consider the nature of the decision-making process of the board in an effort to determine whether particular boardroom norms may have impeded directors' ability to behave independently. In assessing these norms, courts and shareholders should be mindful of the fact that some structural biases are inevitable within the boardroom. Shareholders would need to demonstrate boardroom norms particular to the corporation at issue in order to raise a doubt as to a director's independence. While it may be difficult to ascertain the existence of these norms, courts should provide shareholders the opportunity to raise them in the director independence inquiry. The above approach pinpoints those non-economic factors of particular concern to directors' impartiality—those worthy of consideration in the director independence inquiry.

Application to the *Stewart* Case

This part of the chapter will illustrate the application of this approach in relation to the facts presented in the *Stewart* case. As this analysis reveals, while the ultimate conclusion that the ties identified in the *Stewart* case were insufficient to hinder directors' independence may be the same, the approach allows courts to better assess those ties and, therefore, reach a more robust conclusion regarding directors' independence.

Outside Social Ties

Examining the outside connections between directors appears to be a relatively straightforward task. As the Delaware Chancery Court pointed out, MSLO shareholders presented very little evidence regarding the nature and extent of the ties between Stewart and other directors. Indeed, while shareholders pinpointed an article identifying Martinez as an "old" friend of Stewart, the article does not indicate the length of that friendship or its nature. In this regard, both courts correctly conclude that the magazine article is an adequate indication of the nature or duration of the social ties between Stewart and Martinez. The limited evidence suggests that Stewart and Moore had been friends at least six years prior to Moore's board service. Indeed, Moore was appointed to the MSLO board in 2001 and had attended a wedding hosted by Stewart's lawyer in which Stewart was present in 1995.[99] However, because the evidence does not indicate the nature of Moore and Stewart's friendship (and in fact could be construed to suggest that they may have been no more than casual acquaintances), the evidence does appear insufficient to undermine Moore's independence. Despite this conclusion, it would be inappropriate for a court not to consider that relationship when assessing the director's independence.

Length of Board Service

Studies indicate that a board member's tenure may impact her ability to objectively assess corporate officers' and directors' conduct. Thus, courts should consider board tenure when assessing directors' independence. In the case of MSLO directors, their tenure does not appear to be unduly long. Indeed, both Martinez and Moore had been appointed to the board in 2001, roughly one year before shareholders brought their suit.[100] Hence, while tenure may be an important factor, it appears irrelevant in this case.

Boardroom Norms

Countless studies suggest that boardroom culture may inhibit directors' abilities to monitor with appropriate rigor. In this vein, courts should seek to assess whether there are any factors suggesting that board members would defer to management or the CEO without critique. While this assessment may prove difficult, there may be some factors that the court can consider when seeking to ascertain the existence of some potentially problematic boardroom norms. For example, stock ownership may represent an important, but not determinative, consideration. This means that the court should find it relevant that Martha Stewart had voting control of 94.4% of the MSLO shares. Such control may indicate that Stewart had some greater level of influence and control over the board. Unlike other boards, however, there are no other factors to indicate that directors felt particularly compelled to acquiesce to Stewart's decisions.[101] Hence, the court should not, without more, presume the existence of influence and control in the case of the MSLO board.

Given the importance of the director independence inquiry, the conclusion that the social and professional ties at issue in the *Stewart* case were ineffective to render directors dependant is just as important as ensuring that courts reach that conclusion after full consideration of those ties.

Conclusion

Available research demonstrates that social ties can hinder directors' abilities to objectively assess officer conduct in the same manner that financial ties undercut directors' objectivity. Failing to account for these social ties, therefore, fails to capture all of those issues that impede directors' abilities to positively carry out their responsibility to independently monitor corporate behavior. While the Delaware Chancery Court was willing to give some weight to the social considerations, the Delaware Supreme Court was not. This chapter argues that the Delaware Supreme Court's approach is inadequate and, thus, proposes an alternative approach that would enable social and professional ties to play a bigger role in the director independence inquiry. In this regard, the *Stewart* case may have represented a missed opportunity to enunciate a more robust analysis of director independence that included an assessment of all relevant factors—economic and non-economic—that impact a director's ability to act independently.

Questions

1. In what ways is the independence of corporate directors important to the maintenance of a shareholder derivative suit for breach of fiduciary duty? Does this system of processing legal disputes against directors make sense? Why, or why not? How did the answers to these questions affect the shareholder derivative suit brought against Martha Stewart?

2. How may social ties among directors impact their independent judgment? Does it appear that any of these possible points of impact affected the judg-

ment exercised by directors of Martha Stewart Living Omnimedia, Inc.? Why are these difficult questions to answer?

3. What are the benefits and detriments of taking social ties into account in determining director independence? How does the author weigh and resolve these benefits and detriments? What other possible solutions exist? How does each of these solutions influence the desire and ability of a shareholder to bring a derivative claim against corporate directors for breach of fiduciary duty? How does each affect the corporation and its directors?

Notes

1. *See* Beam ex. rel Martha Stewart Living Omnimedia, Inc. v. Stewart, 833 A.2d 961 (Del. Ch. 2003). Monica A. Beam brought the suit derivatively on behalf of MSLO.

2. *See* MODEL BUS. CORP. ACT §8.30.

3. *See Beam,* 833 A.2d at 966. At the time the Delaware Chancery Court heard the *Stewart* case, Martha Stewart had been indicted and the Securities and Exchange Commission (the "SEC") had filed an action against her. *See id.* at 966 n.2. The shareholders' action also alleged other actions against MSLO directors and Martha Stewart.

4. At the time of the trial, Martha Stewart owned or beneficially held 100% of the Class B Common Stock of MSLO and enough of the Class A Common Stock that she controlled roughly 94.4% of the shareholder vote. *See id.* at 966.

5. *See id.* at 968 (noting prospectus' recognition of Martha Stewart's impact on MSLO's image and reputation).

6. *See* Aronson v. Lewis, 473 A.2d 805, 811 (Del. 1984) (noting that the derivative suit developed to "enable shareholders to sue in the corporation's name where those in control of the company refused to assert a claim belonging to it"). For further discussion of shareholder derivative suits and the demand process see, e.g., Daniel R. Fischel & Michael Bradley, *The Role of Liability Rules and the Derivative Suit in Corporate Law: A Theoretical and Empirical Analysis,* 71 CORNELL L. REV. 261, 286 (1986); Donald E. Schwartz, *In Praise of Derivative Suits: A Commentary on the Paper of Professors Fischel and Bradley,* 71 CORNELL L. REV. 322, 339–40 (1986); Carol B. Swanson, *Juggling Shareholder Rights and Strike Suits in Derivative Litigation: The ALI Drops the Ball,* 27 MINN. L. REV. 1339, 1349–50 (1993).

7. *See* Rales v. Blasband, 634 A.2d 927, 932 (Del. 1993); *Aronson,* 473 A.2d at 814.

8. *See id.; see also Beam,* 833 A.2d at 976–977.

9. *See* Swanson, *supra* note 6, at 1349–1350. *See also Aronson,* 473 A.2d at 811 (noting that the purpose of the demand requirement is to ensure that stockholders exhaust intra-corporate remedies).

10. *See Rales,* 634 A.2d at 935; *Aronson,* 473 A.2d at 814; McKee v. Rogers, 156 A. 191. 193 (Del. Ch. 1931) (demand is not necessary if directors are under an influence that sterilizes their discretion).

11. *See Aronson,* 473 A.2d at 814.

12. Zapata Corp. v. Maldonado, 430 A.2d 779, 788–89 (Del. 1981). *Zapata* involves a two-step analysis. The first focuses on the special litigation committee and requires the corporation to establish that such committee was independent, and conducted a good faith

investigation of the underlying claims. The second step requires the court to weigh in and determine, based on its own business judgment, if the committee's dismissal motion should be granted. *See id.*

13. *See id.*

14. *See Aronson*, 473 A.2d at 814.

15. *See* Swanson, *supra* note 6, at 1357.

16. *See Zapata*, 430 A.2d at 789.

17. *See, e.g.*, Paramount Communications v. QVC Networks, 637 A.2d 34, 42 (Del. 1994); *Aronson*, 473 A.2d at 812 (noting that judgment of directors will be respected by the courts).

18. *See Aronson*, 473 A.2d at 811–812; Dodge v. Ford Motor Co., 170 N.W. 668, 684 (Mich. 1919) (noting that "judges are not business experts").

19. *See Aronson*, 473 A.2d at 812. This presumption is known as the business judgment rule. *See id.*; *see also* Unocal Corp. v. Mesa Petroleum Co., 493 A.2d 946, 954 (Del. 1985).

20. *See* Sanjai Bhagat & Bernard Black, *The Uncertain Relationship Between Board Composition and Firm Performance*, 54 Bus. Law. 921, 931 (1999) (evaluating studies suggesting that independent directors do not perform better than other directors on a variety of task such as monitoring companies in financial distress or controlling fraudulent conduct); Lisa M. Fairfax, *Sarbanes-Oxley, Corporate Federalism, and the Declining Significance of Federal Reforms on State Director Independence Standards*, 31 Ohio N.U.L. Rev. 381, 406–408 (2005) (summarizing empirical work in this area); April Klein, *Firm Performance and Board Committee Structure*, 41 J. Law & Econ. 275, 283 (1998) (finding little evidence that committees comprised completely of independent directors enhance a company's performance); Laura Lin, *The Effectiveness of Outside Directors as Corporate Governance Mechanism: Theories and Evidence*, 90 Nw. U. L. Rev. 898, 922–25 (1996) (concluding that independent directors can make a difference for some tasks); Ira M. Millstein & Paul W. MacAvoy, *The Active Board of Directors and Performance of Large Publicly Traded Corporations*, 99 Colum. L. Rev. 1283, 1318 (1998) (finding a strong correlation between a corporation's performance and director independence).

21. *See* Bhagat & Black, *supra* note 20, at 921.

22. *See* Rales v. Blasband, 634 A.2d 927, 935 (Del. 1993); Beam ex. rel Martha Stewart Living Omnimedia, Inc. v. Stewart, 833 A.2d 961, 977 (Del. Ch. 2003).

23. *See Aronson*, 473 A.2d at 815.

24. *See id.* at 815 n.8 (noting that the "structural bias common to corporate boards throughout America, as well as the other unseen socialization processes" may cut against independence); *Zapata*, 430 A.2d at 787 (noting that the fact that directors must pass judgment on their fellow directors, and hence there may be a "there but for the grace of God go I" empathy that plays a rule in their decisions).

25. *See* Fairfax, *supra* note 20, at 397; Leo E. Strine, Jr., *Derivative Impact? Some Early Reflections on Corporate Law implications of Enron Debacle*, 57 Bus. Law. 1371, 1378 (2002).

26. *See* Kohls v. Duthie, 765 A.2d 1274, 1284 (Del. Ch. 2000) (personal friendships insufficient to challenge director's independence).

27. *See* Crescent/Mach I Partners, L.P. v. Turner, 846 A.2d 963, 980–81 (Del. Ch. 2000).

28. *See* Benerofe v. Cha, No. 14614, 1998 WL 83081, at *3 (Del. Ch. 1998).

29. *See* E. Norman Veasey, *The Defining Tension in Corporate Governance in America*, 52 Bus. Law. 393, 406 (1997). In the chief justice's opinion, courts should not rely on the "dubious presumption that the director would sell his or her soul for friendship." *See id.*

30. At the time of the suit, MSLO had five directors. Shareholders claimed that all five lacked independence for purposes of demand. With respect to directors Naomi O. Seligman

and Jeffrey W. Ubben, the Delaware Chancery court stated that the shareholders had made no particular allegations to raise a reasonable doubt about either directors' independence. *See* Beam ex. rel Martha Stewart Living Omnimedia, Inc. v. Stewart, 833 A.2d 961, 980–981 (Del. Ch. 2003). By contrast, the court quickly concluded that the sole inside director, Sharon L. Patrick, who was the president, chief operating officer of MSLO and received $980,000 in salary in 2001, lacked independence because of her financial dependence on MSLO. *See id.* at 977–78.

31. *See id.* at 967.
32. *See id.* at 979–80.
33. *See id.* at 980.
34. *See id.* at 979.
35. *See id.*
36. *See id.*
37. *See id.* at 966.
38. *See id.* at 979–980.
39. *See id.*
40. *See id.* at 982.
41. *See id.*
42. *See In re* Oracle Corp. Derivative Litig. Consol., 824 A.2d 917, 920, 923 (Del. Ch. 2003).
43. *See id.* at 925–928 (discussing the corporation's investigation process and noting that the corporation hired counsel and financial experts to assist in the investigation).
44. *See id.* at 936.
45. *See id.* at 929–930 & 936.
46. *See id.* at 930.
47. *See id.* at 938–39.
48. *See id.* at 923–924.
49. *See id.* at 931.
50. *See id.*
51. *See id.*
52. *See id.* at 931–932.
53. *See id.* at 932–933.
54. *See id.* at 942–43.
55. *See* Beam ex. rel Martha Stewart Living Omnimedia, Inc. v. Stewart, 833 A.2d 961, 979 n.60 (Del. Ch. 2003); *Oracle*, 824 A.2d at 939 n.55. *See also* Fairfax, *supra* note 20, at 401–402 (noting acknowledgements by both courts and pinpointing reforms as causing this shift in focus).
56. According to the *Oracle* court,

> Delaware law should not be based on a reductionist view of human nature that simplifies human motivations on the lines of the least sophisticated notions of the law and economics movement. Nor should our law ignore the social nature of humans. To be direct, corporate directors are generally the sort of people deeply enmeshed in social institutions. Such institutions have norms, expectations that, explicitly and implicitly, influence and channel the behavior of those who participate in their operation ... In being appropriately sensitive to this factor, our law cannot assume—absent some proof of that point—that corporate directors are, as a general matter,

persons of unusual social bravery, who operate heedless to the inhibitions that social norms generate for ordinary folk.

Id. at 938.

57. *See* Telxon Corp. v. Meyerson, 802 A.2d 257, 265 (Del. 2002) (focusing on personal friendship between chairman and other directors); Biondi ex. rel. HealthSouth Corp. v. Scrushy, 820 A.2d 1148, 1165 (Del. Ch. 2003) (focusing on lengthy social and professional ties).

58. *See* Beam ex. rel. Martha Stewart Living Omnimedia, Inc. v. Stewart, 845 A.2d 1040, 1044 (Del. 2004).

59. *See id.* at 1050–51.

60. *See id.* at 1052 n.32.

61. *See id.* at 1051–52.

62. *See id.* at 1051.

63. *See id.*

64. *See id.* at 1053–54.

65. *See id.* at 1054.

66. *See id.* at 1055.

67. *See id.* at 1054.

68. *See id.*

69. *See id.*

70. *See* Fairfax, *supra* note 20, at 405.

71. *See* Swanson, *supra* note 6.

72. *See* Zapata Corp. v. Maldonado, 430 A.2d 779, 788 (Del. 1981).

73. *See* E. Norman Veasey, *Musings from the Center of the Corporate Universe,* 7 Del. L. Rev. 163, 173 (2004).

74. *See id.*

75. *See* Irwin Borowski, *Corporate Accountability: The Role of the Independent Director,* 9 J. Corp. L. 455, 461 (1984) (noting that independent directors get most of the benefits of their directorship from being a director).

76. *See* Beam ex. rel Martha Stewart Living Omnimedia, Inc. v. Stewart, 833 A.2d 961, 967 (Del. Ch. 2003).

77. *See id.*

78. *See* Beam ex. rel. Martha Stewart Living Omnimedia, Inc. v. Stewart, 845 A.2d 1040, 1052 n.32 (Del. 2004) (explaining that directors' concern for professional reputation would outweigh allegiance to personal friendships).

79. *See infra* note 96; *see also* Fairfax, *supra* note 20, at 410–411.

80. *See* Fairfax, *supra* note 20, at 412–413.

81. *See* Strine, *supra* note 25, at 1378.

82. *See* Richard C. Breeden , Restoring Trust: Report to the Honorable Jed S. Rakoff on Corporate Governance for the Future of MCI 795 (August 2003), *available at* http://www.concernedshareholders.com/CCS_MCI_BreedenReport.pdf (noting that "positive chemistry" among the CEO and board members is very important to a successful company).

83. The remainder of this paragraph is reprinted, with permission of the *Ohio North-ern University Law Review,* from Fairfax, *supra* note 20, at 413.

84. *See* Aronson v. Lewis, 473 A.2d 805, 812 (Del. 1984).

85. *See* KORN/FERRY INTERNATIONAL, 31ST ANNUAL BOARD OF DIRECTORS STUDY 2004 14–15 & 25–26 (noting increased meetings and time commitment caused by Sarbanes-Oxley).

86. *See* Fairfax, *supra* note 20, at 408–412.

87. *See* BREEDEN, *supra* note 82, at 817 (noting that "close or extended personal ties between directors and the CEO can lead to just as much trouble for shareholders as lack of financial independence.")

88. *See id.*

89. *See* Marleen A. O'Connor, *The Enron Board: The Perils of Groupthink*, 71 U. CIN. L. REV. 1233 (2003) (describing literature on group dynamics and phenomenon of "group-think").

90. *See id.*

91. *See, e.g.,* BREEDEN, *supra* note 82, at 805; Bhagat and Black, *supra* note 20, at 953.

92. In assessing the problems at Enron, Delaware Vice Chancellor Strine pointed out that the lengthy service of some directors may have fostered strong feelings of kinship and collegiality that hindered such directors' ability to assess fellow directors' actions. *See* Strine, *supra* note 25, at 1391; *see also* BREEDEN, *supra* note 82, at 805 (noting that directors at WorldCom who served for long periods together may have been unable to aggressively carry out their responsibilities).

93. *See* O'Connor, *supra* note 89, at 1246 (noting that many Enron directors served on the board for more than 20 years); Troy A. Paredes, *Enron: The Board, Corporate Governance and Some Thoughts on the Role of Congress,* in NANCY B. RAPOPORT & BALA G. DHARAN, ENRON: CORPORATE FIASCOS AND THEIR IMPLICATIONS 511 (2004) (same).

94. *Cf.* Bhagat & Black, *supra* note 20, at 953 (directors on board for long time may be less energetic).

95. *See* JAY W. LORSCH, PAWNS OR POTENTATES: THE REALITY OF AMERICA'S CORPORATE BOARDS 1–2 (1989).

96. *See id.* at 91–93.

97. *See* Lin, *supra* note 20, at 915 (noting that boardroom culture can be characterized by politeness that too often discourages dissent against directors and management).

98. *See* Bhagat & Black, *supra* note 20, at 921; John C. Coffee, Jr. & Donald E. Schwartz, *The Survival of the Derivative Suit: An Evaluation and a Proposal for Legislative Reform,* 81 COLUM. L. REV. 261, 283–84 (1981); Charles M. Elson, *Director Compensation and the Management-Captured Board—The History of A Symptom and Cure,* 50 SMU L. REV. 127, 161 (1996) (noting the difficulties directors experience with challenging the actions of fellow friends); Ronald J. Gilson & Reinier Kraakman, *Reinventing the Outside Director: An Agenda for Institutional Investors,* 43 STAN. L. REV. 863, 875 (1991) (noting that even financially independent directors have social ties that limit their ability to effectively monitor management).

99. *See* Beam ex. rel Martha Stewart Living Omnimedia, Inc. v. Stewart, 833 A.2d 961, 967 (Del. Ch. 2003).

100. *See Beam,* 833 A.2d at 967.

101. *See* O'Connor, *supra* note 89, at 1263–64 (discussing boardroom norms at Enron).

About the Authors

Kathleen F. Brickey – Kathleen Brickey is the James Carr Professor of Criminal Jurisprudence at Washington University in St. Louis. Professor Brickey received both her A.B. degree and her J.D. degree with honors from the University of Kentucky. Her three-volume treatise, *Corporate Criminal Liability*, and her casebook, *Corporate and White Collar Crime*, are leading works in the field. She is a member of the American Law Institute and the Society for the Reform of Criminal Law and has served as chair of the Association of American Law Schools Criminal Justice Section and as a consultant to the United States Sentencing Commission. Her recent publications include: a new edition of her casebook, *Corporate and White Collar Crime* (4th ed. 2006) (Aspen Publishers); "White Collar Crime," in *The Oxford Companion to American Law* (Oxford University Press 2002); *In Enron's Wake: Corporate Executives on Trial*, 96 J. Crim. L. & Criminology 397 (2006); *Enron's Legacy*, 8 Buff. Crim. L. Rev. 221 (2004); *From Enron to Worldcom and Beyond: Life and Crime After Sarbanes-Oxley*, 81 Wash. U. L. Q. 357 (2003); and *Andersen's Fall From Grace*, 81 Wash. U. L. Q. 917 (2003).

Lisa M. Fairfax – Lisa Fairfax is Professor of Law and Director of the Business Law Program at the University of Maryland School of Law, where she teaches Business Associations, Securities Regulation, Unincorporated Business Entities, and Contracts II. In 2003, Professor Fairfax was voted "Teacher of the Year," by the University of Maryland Law students. In 2002, Professor Fairfax was voted "Professor of the Year," by Maryland's Black Law Students Association. Professor Fairfax is an honors graduate of both Harvard College and Harvard Law School and serves on the Executive Committee of the Securities Regulation Section of the Association of American Law Schools. Her recent published works include: *Spare the Rod, Spoil the Director? Revitalizing Directors' Fiduciary Duty through Legal Liability*, 42 Hous. L. Rev. 393 (2005); *Some Reflections on the Diversity of Corporate Boards: Women, People of Color, and the Unique Issues Associated with Women of Color*, 79 St. John's L. Rev. 1105 (2005); *Achieving the Double Bottom Line: A Framework for Cor-*

porations Seeking to Deliver Profits and Public Services, 9 STAN. J.L. BUS. & FIN. 199 (2004); and *The Thin Line Between Love and Hate: Why Affinity-Based Securities and Investment Fraud Constitutes a Hate Crime*, 36 U.C. DAVIS L. REV. 1073 (2003).

Stuart P. Green – Stuart Green is the L. B. Porterie Professor of Law at Louisiana State University, where he teaches courses in Criminal Law, Criminal Procedure, White Collar Crime, Punishment and Sentencing, and Legal Ethics. Professor Green serves as Director of LSU's Pugh Institute for Justice and as a member of Louisiana's Task Force on Indigent Defense. He previously served as Chair of the Association of American Law School's Sections on Criminal Justice and on Comparative Law. During the 2002–03 academic year, he was a Fulbright Distinguished Scholar at the University of Glasgow School of Law. Professor Green is a 1988 graduate of the Yale Law School and clerked for Judge Pamela Ann Rymer of the U.S. Ninth Circuit Court of Appeals and U.S. District Court, in Los Angeles. He is the author of *Lying, Cheating, and Stealing: A Moral Theory of White Collar Crime*, and co-editor, with Professor R.A. Duff, of *Defining Crimes: Essays on the Special Part of the Criminal Law*. His current project is a book tentatively titled *Property, Crime, and Morals: Theft Law in the Information Age*.

Joan MacLeod Heminway – Joan Heminway is a tenured Associate Professor of Law at The University of Tennessee College of Law. Professor Heminway received the Chancellor's Award for Teaching Excellence in 2006, and the College of Law's 2005 Marilyn V. Yarbrough Faculty Award for Writing Excellence and 2004 Harold C. Warner Outstanding Teacher Award. Her stock merger module for the College of Law's Representing Enterprises course was recognized by UT's Innovative Technology Center in its September 2002 Best Practices@UT Showcase. Professor Heminway received her J.D. degree in 1985 from New York University School of Law (where she was an editor of the *Moot Court Casebook*) and her A.B. degree in International Relations and History in 1982 from Brown University, *magna cum laude*. Professor Heminway's recent publications have appeared in the *Albany Journal of Science and Technology, American University Law Review, University of Cincinnati Law Review, Fordham Journal of Corporate & Financial Law, Maryland Law Review, Southern California Review of Law and Women's Studies, Texas Journal of Women and the Law*, and *Transactions: The Tennessee Journal of Business Law*. She has coauthored (with several Tennessee practitioners) a series of annotated merger and acquisition agreements that have been published in the Spring 2003, 2004, 2005, and 2006 issues of *Transactions: The Tennessee Journal of Business Law* (http://www.law.utk.edu/centers/entrep/claytontransactions.htm).

Donald C. Langevoort – Donald Langevoort is the Thomas Aquinas Reynolds Professor of Law at the Georgetown University Law Center, where he teaches Contracts, Securities Regulation, various seminars on corporate and securities issues, and Corporations. Prior to joining the Georgetown Law Center faculty in 1999, Professor Langevoort was the Lee S. and Charles A. Speir Professor at Vanderbilt University School of Law, where he joined the faculty in 1981. Professor Langevoort is the co-author, with Professors James Cox and Robert Hillman, of *Securities Regulation: Cases and Materials* (Aspen Publishers), and the author of a treatise entitled *Insider Trading: Regulation, Enforcement and Prevention* (West Group). He has also written many law review articles, a number of which seek to incorporate insights from social psychology and behavioral economics into the study of corporate and securities law and legal ethics. Professor Langevoort received his B.A. degree from the University of Virginia and his J.D. degree from Harvard University.

Geraldine Szott Moohr – Gerry Moohr is Alumnae Law Center Professor of Law at the University of Houston Law Center, where she has taught since 1995. After graduating from the University of Illinois and earning her M.S. from Bucknell University, Professor Moohr obtained her law degree from The American University, where she was first in her class and editor-in-chief of the *American University Law Review*. Following graduation, she clerked for the Honorable James M. Sprouse of the United States Court of Appeals for the Fourth Circuit. Her areas of expertise include white collar crime, federal criminal law, federal fraud offenses, employment law, employment discrimination, and sexual harassment. Her many publications include articles in the *American University Law Review*, *Boston University Law Review*, *Buffalo Criminal Law Review*, *Florida Law Review*, *North Carolina Law Review*, *University of Illinois Law Review*, *Washington & Lee Law Review*, and *Washington University Law Quarterly*.

Ellen S. Podgor – Ellen Podgor currently is the Associate Dean of Faculty Development and Distance Education at Stetson University College of Law, a position she has held since July 1, 2006. Prior to that time, she was Professor of Law at Georgia State University College of Law. Professor Podgor teaches in the areas of international criminal law, white collar crime, criminal law and procedure, and professional responsibility. She is the co-author of books on criminal law, white collar crime, and international criminal law and has authored articles on computer crime, international criminal law, lawyer's ethics, criminal discovery, prosecutorial discretion, corporate criminality, and other white collar crime topics. Her recent works have appeared in, among other publications, the *American Criminal Law Review*, *American University Law Re-*

view, Cardozo Law Review, Cornell Journal of Law and Public Policy, Fordham Law Review, Georgetown Journal of Legal Ethics, Georgia Journal of International and Comparative Law, Notre Dame Journal of Law, Ethics & Public Policy, U.C. Davis Law Review, and *The Wayne Law Review.* In addition to her law degree, Professor Podgor earned an M.B.A. from the University of Chicago and an L.L.M. from Temple University. She is member of the Board of Directors of the National Association of Criminal Defense Lawyers, a member of the International Society for the Reform of Criminal Law and the American Law Institute, and an honorary member of the American Board of Criminal Lawyers.

Jeanne L. Schroeder – Jeanne Schroeder is Professor of Law at the Benjamin N. Cardozo School of Law. Her scholarly interests range from commercial law doctrine to feminist jurisprudential theory. Her current work is on recent amendments to Article 8 of the Uniform Commercial Code and in developing a feminist theory of law and economics incorporating the political philosophy of G.W.F. Hegel and the psychoanalytic theories of Jacques Lacan. Her first book on this subject, *The Vestal and the Fasces: Hegel, Lacan, Property, and the Feminine,* was published in 1998, and her second, *The Triumph of Venus: The Erotics of the Market,* was published in 2004. Professor Schroeder received her B.A. in 1975 from Williams College and her J.D. in 1978 from Stanford University. Her recent works have been published in *The American Bankruptcy Law Journal, California Law Review, Cardozo Law Review, The George Washington Law Review, Oregon Law Review, Texas Law Review, William & Mary Law Review,* and *Yale Journal of Law & the Humanities.*

Michael L. Seigel – Michael Seigel is Professor of Law at the University of Florida Levin College of Law, where he teaches Evidence, Professional Responsibility, Criminal Law, and White Collar Crime. He served as Associate Dean for Academic Affairs of the College from 2000–2002 and has visited at the University of British Columbia, Stetson University, and the University of San Diego. Professor Seigel also has held many federal prosecutorial posts, including: Special Assistant U.S. Attorney, Eastern District of Pennsylvania (2000–01); First Assistant United States Attorney, Middle District of Florida (Tampa, 1995–99); Assistant U.S. Attorney, U.S. Attorney's Office, Organized Crime Strike Force (Philadelphia, PA., 1990); and Special Attorney, U.S. Department of Justice, Organized Crime and Racketeering Section, Philadelphia Strike Force (1985–89). His publication credits include a newly released mystery novel, *Improbable Events: Murder at Ellenton Hall* (2005), and scholarly works in, among other publications, the *American Journal of Criminal Law,*

Boston University Law Review, *Hofstra Law Review*, and *Northwestern University Law Review*. Professor Seigel received his J.D. from Harvard Law School, *magna cum laude*, and his A.B. from Princeton University, *magna cum laude*.

Christopher Slobogin – Christopher Slobogin is Stephen C. O'Connell Chair, Professor of Law and Associate Director of the Center on Children and the Law at the University of Florida Levin College of Law. He served as Associate Dean for Faculty Development (1996–99 and 2001–03) and was an Alumni Research Scholar (1994–98) and Teacher of Year (1986–87) and also serves as an Affiliate Professor of Psychiatry at the University of Florida. Professor Slobogin has received the TIP Award for Teaching (1996–97) and the Professorial Excellence Award (1998–99) at the College of Law, and he also has been a Fulbright Scholar at Kiev University (Ukraine). He is a frequent faculty visitor, having spent teaching time at Hastings College of Law, Monash University (Melbourne, Australia), University of Frankfurt, University of Nebraska, University of Southern California, and University of Virginia. He has published several books on criminal law topics (both academic press and educational texts) and articles in (among other publications) the *Duke Law Journal*, *George Washington Law Review*, *Illinois Law Review*, *Minnesota Law Review*, *Northwestern University Law Review*, *U.C.L.A. Law Review*, *University of Pennsylvania Law Review*, *Vanderbilt Law Review*, *Virginia Law Review*, *Washington & Lee Law Review*, and *William & Mary Law Review*. Professor Slobogin earned his LL.M. and J.D. at the University of Virginia and his A.B. at Princeton University.

Index